Canadian Dictionary for English Learners

Canadian Dictionary for English Learners

edited by
Daniel Liebman

Don Mills, Ontario · Reading, Massachusetts · Menlo Park, California
Wokingham, England · Amsterdam · Sydney · Singapore · Tokyo
Madrid · Bogota · Santiago · San Juan

We wish to thank the teachers of English as a second language who assisted in the development of this dictionary, especially Marjorie Fraser, who gave us a better understanding of the learner's point of view.

We also wish to thank Dr. Bernard Brunner, Stella Harmen, and Gerda Morrow for their tireless efforts in verifying pronunciations, and Dalton London, who identified those entries that may present special difficulties for the francophone English learner.

Design: Paul Kaufhold
Illustration: Peter Grau, Bernard Martin, Suzanne Thyer
Editorial: Bruce Bartlett, Grace Delottinville, Jon Kaplan, Zoë C. Rolko
Consultants: Dr. Bernard Brunner, Stella Harmen, Dr. Dalton London, Gerda Morrow

Canadian Cataloguing in Publication Data
Liebman, Daniel
Canadian dictionary for English learners

ISBN 0-201-05392-6

1. English language–Canada. 2. English language–Dictionaries, Juvenile. 3. English language–Text-books for second language learners. I. Title.

PE1628.5.L54 1987 j423 C87-093298-5

Printed and bound in Canada.

ISBN 0-201-05392-6

B C D E F G —DEY— 92 91 90 89 88 87

Table of Contents

How to Use this Dictionary

entry word
Each main entry is printed in large, boldface type. The special symbol indicates entries that may require special attention on the part of francophone learners.

definition
Clear, basic definitions form the essential part of each entry.

special note
From time to time, a note points out a possible difficulty.

example
Sample phrases or sentences are provided to show typical usage or to clarify definitions.

pronunciation
All major entries contain a pronunciation guide, divided into syllables, that also shows primary and secondary stress.

part of speech
Abbreviations are used to identify the selected parts of speech entered. These abbreviations are found in the List of Abbreviations on page 357.

definition number
Where more than one definition is provided, each one is numbered.

Doberman pinscher → donation 84

for a living? Would you do the dishes please? **2.** to be acceptable: *That amount will do; you've chopped enough wood today.*
doing. did (did). **done** (dun). he **does** (duz).
do away with to stop; to put an end to: *to do away with an old-fashioned law.*
do up to tie, wrap, or fasten: *Do up your coat before you go outside.*
How do you do? a greeting that means 'how are you?'
Note: **do** is sometimes used with another verb: *I do want to go there.* It is also used to ask a question: *Do you want to go?*

Doberman pinscher (dob′ ər mən pin′ shər) a large black or brown dog with a long head and a shiny coat.

dock (dok) *n.* a place by the water where a ship can load, unload, or be repaired. *v.* **1.** to bring a boat to such a place. **2.** to take away a portion of: *The company docked Jill's pay because she always left work early.*

doctor (dok′ tər) *n.* **1.** a person who has a licence to practise medicine. **2.** a person who has the highest degree possible from a university: *a doctor of philosophy.*

document (dok′ yů mənt) *n.* a written or printed paper, such as a passport or map, that gives information and may be used to prove a fact.

documentary (dok′ yů ment′ ə rē) *n.* a film or television program that deals with real events: *We watched a documentary about the Calgary Stampede.* *pl.* **documentaries.**

dodge (doj) *v.* to keep away from something by moving to one side quickly. **dodging. dodged.**

doe (dō) *n.* a female rabbit, deer, or antelope.

does see **do.**

doesn't (duznt) short for **does not.**

dog (dog) *n.* an animal that has four legs, makes a barking noise, and is kept as a pet.

doghouse (dog′ haůs′) *n.* a small, outdoor house for a dog.

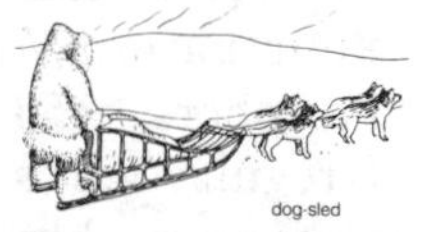

dog-sled

dog-sled (dog′ sled′) *n.* a sleigh pulled by dogs.

doll (dol) *n.* a toy that looks like a person.

dollar (dol′ ər) *n.* the unit of money used in Canada, the United States, and some other countries. One hundred cents make one dollar ($1.00).

dolly (dol′ ē) *n.* a small platform with wheels, used to move heavy objects: *Don't carry the stove yourselves; move it on a dolly.* *pl.* **dollies.**

dome (dōm) *n.* a roof shaped like a half a ball.

domestic (də mes′ tik) *adj.* **1.** having to do with home: *Domestic jobs include cooking and sewing.* **2.** tame; not wild: *The cow is a domestic animal.* **3.** made in a person's own country: *domestic cheese.*

dominoes (dom′ i nōz′) *n.pl.* a game played with black, oblong tiles that have dots on one side.

donate (dō′ nāt, dō nāt′) *v.* to make a gift: *We donated time and money to the children's hospital.* **donating. donated.**

donation (dō nā′ shən) *n.* a gift; a contribution: *a large donation to a charity.*

familiar speech
Informal uses are identified.

guide words
These words identify the *first* and the *last* entries that begin on each page.

plural form
Where the plural of a noun is not formed by simply adding "s", or where there may be some difficulty, the plural form is provided.

irregular form
In the case of spelling irregularities, these entries allow you to refer to a main entry.

inflected forms
Inflected forms are supplied wherever a verb does not follow a regular pattern.

short form
The main entry to search for is given.

comparative/superlative forms
Where the comparative and superlative forms of an adjective do not follow the pattern of adding *-er* or *-est*, these forms are shown in examples.

idioms
These sub-entries show idiomatic uses, sometimes informal, of an entry word. Each idiom is defined, often with examples.

85 **done → draft, draught**

done see **do.**

donkey (dong′ kē) *n.* an ass; an animal that has long ears and looks like a small horse. *pl.* **donkeys.**

don't (dōnt) short for **do not.**

donut see **doughnut.**

door (dôr) *n.* **1.** a movable section of wood or metal, used to open or close the entrance of a building, room, etc.: *the door of a closet; the door of a house.* **2.** a doorway.

doorway (dôr′ wā′) *n.* an opening that leads into or out of a building or room, often closed by a door. *pl.* **doorways.**

dope (dōp) *n.* *(informal)* **1.** a narcotic drug. **2.** a very unintelligent person.

dose (dōs) *n.* the amount of medicine to be taken at one time.

dot (dot) *n.* *a small spot.* *v.* to make such a spot. **dotting. dotted.**

⊖**double** (dubl) *adj.* twice as much: *Frank took a double serving of ice cream.* *v.* **1.** to grow to twice the size; to multiply by two: *What number do you get when you double three?* **2.** to fold or bend: *Marla doubled over the sheet of paper and tore it in half.* **doubling. doubled.**
double back to go back over the same route again: *Marc doubled back to the office, looking for the lost letter.*
double-cross to promise to do one thing, but do another.
double park to park illegally beside another parked car.
double up **1.** to fold over. **2.** to bend the upper part of the body towards the legs: *I doubled up when the football hit me in the stomach.*

⊖**doubt** (daůt) *n.* an unsure feeling about something: *I have my doubts about driving in this weather.* *v.* to be suspicious of; not to be sure: *I doubt that he is telling the truth.*

dough (dō) *n.* a stiff mixture of flour, yeast, and water, baked to make bread, cake, or cookies.

doughnuts

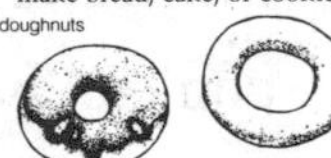

doughnut, donut (dō′ nut′) *n.* a small, round piece of fried cake, usually with a hole in the centre.

dove (duv) *n.* a kind of pigeon.

dove see **dive.**

down (daůn) *n.* **1.** the very soft feathers of a bird. **2.** in Canadian football, one of three chances that a team has to move the ball forward. *prep.* **1.** from a higher to a lower place: *They walked down the hill.* **2.** along: *The car drove down the street.* *adv.* **1.** on or to a lower place: *Please sit down.* **2.** as part of a payment for: *to pay a hundred dollars down for a chesterfield.*

downpour (daůn′ pôr′) *n.* a heavy rain.

downstairs (daůn′ sterz′) *adv.* down to a lower floor.

downtown (daůn′ taůn′) *adv.* to the main part of a city: *We go downtown to shop.*

doze (dōz) *v.* to sleep for a short time; to nap: *Jane dozed in the chair.* **dozing. dozed.**

dozen (duz′ ən) *adj.* twelve: *a dozen eggs.*

Dr. short for **doctor**; always used with a name: *Dr. Dixon.*

drab (drab) *adj.* dull; colourless: *a drab day, a drabber day; the drabbest day of all.*

draft, draught (draft) *n.* **1.** a current of air, often in an enclosed area: *He felt a draft from under the door.* **2.** a sketch or plan of something:

Pronunciation Key

a	apple, cat	**p**	pan, cap
ā	ape, cake	**r**	ring, car
ȧ	arm, car	**s**	sun, chess, cent
aů	owl, brow	**sh**	shoe, dish, nation
b	bat, cab	**t**	toe, mat
ch	chocolate, watch	**th**	birthday, earth
d	dog, head	**<u>th</u>**	that, mother
e	elbow, head	**u**	umbrella, judge
ē	eagle, feet	**ů**	cookie, bull
f	foot, photograph	**ū**	boot, two, true
g	goat, log	**ûr**	earth, fur
h	hat, behind, who	**v**	van, oven
i	bit, tip	**w**	wind, woman
ī	tie, try, buy, eye	**y**	year, young
j	jaw, gem	**yū**	you, view
k	cat, seek, tuque	**z**	zoo, rose
l	lip, ball	**zh**	treasure, rouge
m	man, dome		
n	nose, pan	**ə**	father, above, upon
ng	ring, singer	**ks**	extra, box
o	off, top	**gz**	exam
ō	oats, toe, blow, go	**hw**	whisker
ȯ	door, corn	**kw**	quick
ȯi	oil, boy		

PRIMARY (HEAVY) STRESS: ˈ

SECONDARY (LIGHT) STRESS: ˌ

A

a (ā, ə) *article* one; any; each: *a glass of water; a day of the week; once a month.*

abandon (ə ban′ dən) *v.* to leave someone or something, and never return: *The sailors abandoned the sinking ship.*

abbreviate (ə brē′ vi āt′) *v.* to make a word or a group of words shorter, so that the short form replaces the whole thing: *To abbreviate British Columbia, we write B.C.* **abbreviating. abbreviated.**

abbreviation (ə brē′ vi ā′ shən) *n.* a short form of a word or group of words: *Jr. is the abbreviation for junior. MP is the abbreviation for Member of Parliament.*

abdomen (ab′ də mən, ab′ dō′ mən) *n.* the belly; the part of the body that contains the stomach and other organs.

⊖**ability** (ə bil′ i tē) *n.* the power, knowledge, or skill to do something: *A fish has the ability to swim. pl.* **abilities.**

able (ā′ bl) *adj.* having the power, knowledge, or skill to do something: *A bird is able to fly. an able student; an abler student; the ablest student of all.*

aboard (ə bȯrd′) *adv.* on or into a ship, plane, bus, or train.

abort (ə bȯrt′) *v.* **1.** to end a pregnancy before the fetus is able to live on its own. **2.** to stop an action or plan before it is completed.

abortion (ə bȯr′ shən) *n.* the act of aborting something, such as an embryo.

about (ə bau̇t′) *prep.* **1.** close to; approximately: *It was about two o'clock.* **2.** having to do with: *Ann's book is about games.* *adv.* everywhere: *The children were running about.* **about to** just going to; ready to begin: *I was about to go out when Renata came in.*

above (ə buv′) *prep.* higher than; over: *The picture hangs above the table.*

abroad (ə brȯd′) *adv.* overseas; in or to another country: *My father lived abroad before he came to Canada.*

absence (ab′ səns) *n.* being away: *Jack's absence meant that Pat would have to work late.*

absent (ab′ sənt) *adj.* not there: *Maria was absent from school.*

absent-minded (ab′ sənt mīn′ dəd) *adj.* not aware of what is happening, usually because something else is occupying a person's attention; forgetful: *The absent-minded man forgot to hang up the telephone.*

⊖**absolutely** (ab′ sə lūt′ lē, ab′ sə lūt′ lē) *adv.* completely; entirely: *I am absolutely sure that his answer is wrong.*

⊖**absorb** (ab zȯrb′, ab sȯrb′) *v.* **1.** to soak up a liquid: *Sponges absorb water.* **2.** to take in; to understand: *He tried to absorb all the new formulas in chemistry class.* **3.** to occupy the full attention or time of: *Don't disturb Ann. She is absorbed in the television program.*

abuse (ə byūs′) *n.* unkind treatment of someone or bad use of something: *The machine took much abuse from the new operator.*

⊖**abuse** (ə byūz′) *v.* to treat someone or something badly: *Children must learn not to abuse their pets.* **abusing. abused.**

academic (ak′ ə dem′ ik) *adj.* having to do with school, studying, or education: *an academic term; an academic award.*

Acadia (ə kā′ di ə) *n.* the area of North America first inhabited by French settlers. Acadia included what is now New Brunswick and Prince Edward Island, and parts of Nova Scotia.

Acadian (ə kā′ di ən) *n.* a person who settled in Acadia, or a descendant of such a person.

accelerate (ak sel′ ə rāt′) *v.* to increase the speed of something: *to accelerate an automobile.* **accelerating. accelerated.**

accelerator (ak sel′ ə rā′ tər) *n.* a pedal on a machine that controls the speed of its engine.

accent (ak′ sent) *n.* a special way of speaking: *My employer has a Spanish accent because she grew up in Madrid.* *v.* when speaking, to say part of a word in a stronger way; to stress or emphasize: *When you say 'Canada', you accent 'Can'.*

accept (ak sept′) *v.* to take something that is offered: *to accept a gift.*
Note: Do not confuse **accept** and **except**; **except** means 'other than'.

access (ak′ ses) *n.* the permission or chance to enter a place or use something: *We have access to the factory on the weekend. Let your sister have access to your tools.* *pl.* **accesses.**

accident (ak′ si dənt) *n.* something that happens, usually through lack of attention, that may cause harm or damage: *a traffic accident.*
by accident not on purpose: *He found the purse by accident when he was walking along the street.*

accidental (ak′ si den′ təl) *adj.* not planned; not on purpose; unexpected: *an accidental fall.*

ə**accommodate** (ə kom′ ə dāt′) *v.* to hold; to have space for: *The hotel can accommodate fifty people.* **accommodating. accommodated.**

accompany (ə kom′ pa ni′) *v.* **1.** to go with: *I accompanied my friend to the movie.* **2.** to play a musical instrument while someone performs: *The pianist accompanied the singer.* **accompanying. accompanied.**

accomplish (ə kom′ plish) *v.* to do or to finish: *We accomplished all our work by four o'clock.* **accomplishing. accomplished.** he **accomplishes.**

according to (ə kȯrd′ ing tu) from what someone says: *According to the weather report, Thursday will be a sunny day.*

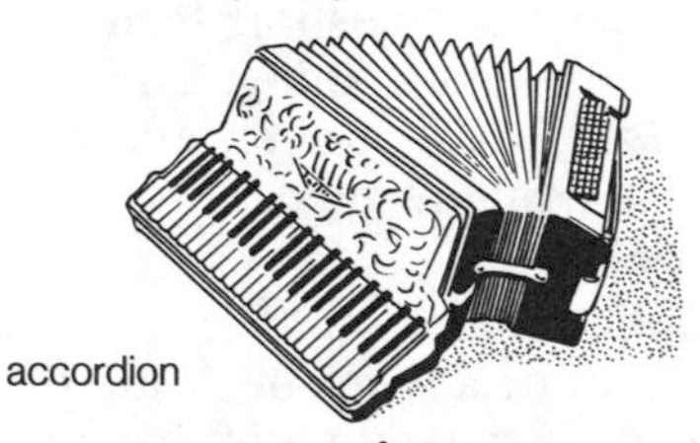
accordion

accordion (ə kȯr′ dē ən) *n.* a musical instrument with keys at each end and a bellows in the middle to push air past metal reeds.

account (ə kau̇nt′) *n.* **1.** a record of money spent, owed, or saved: *a bank account.* **2.** a telling of events: *Jean gave a full account of her trip.*
account for to explain: *How do you account for your absence?*
on account of because of: *There was no school on account of the snowstorm.*

accountant (ə kau̇nt′ ənt) *n.* a person whose job is to keep a record of money paid out and money taken in.

accurate (ak′ yər ət) *adj.* always correct; very exact: *My watch is accurate.*

accuse (ə kyüz′) *v.* to blame someone; to say someone is guilty: *He accused the man of taking his wallet.* **accusing. accused.**

accustomed to (ə kus′ təmd tu) used to; familiar with: *He can't get accustomed to going to bed so late.*

ace (ās) *n.* a playing card with only one spot in the middle.

ache (āk) *n.* a long-lasting pain: *headache; toothache; earache.* *v.* to have a pain: *I ache all over!* **aching. ached.**

⊖**achieve** (ə chēv′) *v.* to reach a goal: *To achieve his goal of playing on the team, Walter practised every day.* **achieving. achieved.**

acid (as′ id) *n.* a liquid that can eat away metals.

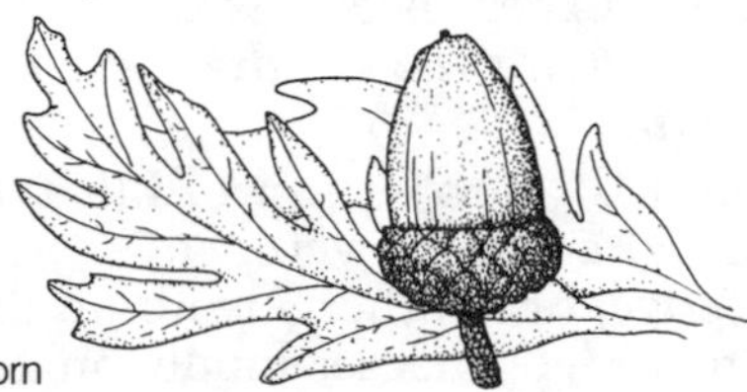
acorn

acorn (ā′ kȯrn) *n.* the nut-like fruit of the oak tree.

acquire (ə kwīr′) *v.* to get; to obtain: *Lee has just acquired some new books.* **acquiring. acquired.**

acre (ā′ kər) *n.* an area of land equal to about 4000 m^2.

acrobat (ak′ rə bat′) *n.* a person who does skilful leaps, jumps, and balancing stunts, often on a trapeze or tightrope.

across (ə kros′) *prep.* to the other side of: *They swam across the river.* *adv.* on the other side: *They were safely across.*

act (akt) *n.* **1.** something that is done; a deed: *an act of bravery.* **2.** a part of a play: *The play is in three acts.* **3.** a law made by Parliament. *v.* **1.** to do something: *That boy needs help. Act now!* **2.** to pretend: *Margaret and René acted as if they were ill.* **3.** to take part in a play.

action (ak′ shən) *n.* **1.** something that is done; a deed. **2.** movement: *the action of a clock.*

active (ak′ tiv) *adj.* lively; full of motion: *Andrea is an active girl, always doing things.*

activity (ak tiv′ i tē) *n.* movement, action, or something that a person does: *Baseball is my favourite outdoor activity.* *pl.* **activities.**

actor (ak′ tər) *n.* a boy or man who performs in the movies, on TV, or on stage.

actress (ak′ tris, ak′ trəs) *n.* a girl or woman who performs in the movies, on TV, or on stage. *pl.* **actresses.**

⊖**actual** (ak′ chū əl) *adj.* real; not imaginary: *I thought it cost $12.95, but the actual price was $10.95.*

ad (ad) *n.* short for **advertisement.**

Adam's apple (ad′ əmz apl′) the lump in the front of the neck that moves up and down when a person swallows.

adapt (ə dapt′) *v.* to change attitudes or behaviour in order to adjust to a place or situation: *When we moved to the farm, we had to adapt to working early in the morning.*

add (ad) *v.* **1.** to put one thing together with another: *to add milk to tea.* **2.** to find the total of two or more numbers: *3 added to 4 equals 7.*

addict (ad′ ikt) *n.* a person who has a habit that he or she cannot control: *a drug addict.*

⊖**addition** (ə dish′ ən) *n.* **1.** the adding of one thing to another. **2.** adding numbers.
in addition and also; as well as: *I have two dogs in addition to this one.*

additional (ə dish′ ən əl) *adj.* more or extra: *Do you have additional time to help me finish the job?*

address (ə dres′, ad′ res) *n.* **1.** the house, street, and town where a person lives. **2.** a speech: *The visitor gave the students a short address.* *pl.* **addresses.**

address (ə dres′) *v.* **1.** to write on a letter or package where it is to go.

2. to give a speech to a group of people. **addressing. addressed.** she **addresses.**

adequate (ad′ i kwət) *adj.* as much as a person needs; as much as is necessary: *We have adequate time to drive to the Maritimes on our vacation.*

adjective (aj′ ək tiv) *n.* a word that tells more about somebody or something. In the examples 'a red rose', 'an iron gate', and 'a good man', the adjectives are *red, iron,* and *good.*

adjust (ə just′) *v.* to change something to make it work better or be more comfortable: *Brian adjusts the TV to get a good picture.*

admiration (ad′ mi rā′ shən) *n.* a feeling that something or someone is excellent: *I have great admiration for that talented singer.*

admire (ad mīr′) *v.* **1.** to think of something or someone with wonder or respect: *I admire the doctor because she is smart and kind.* **2.** to look at something with pleasure. **admiring. admired.**

admission (ad mish′ ən) *n.* **1.** going in; entry: *Admission to the movies is free today.* **2.** a confession: *Her look was an admission of guilt.*

admit (ad mit′) *v.* **1.** to let in: *This ticket admits two people.* **2.** to confess: *She had to admit that she was wrong.* **admitting. admitted.**

adolescent (ad′ ə les′ ənt) *n.* a person who is growing from a child to an adult.

adopt (ə dopt′) *v.* **1.** to bring up someone else's child as one's own. **2.** to accept and use: *to adopt an idea; to adopt a plan.*

adorable (ə dȯr′ əbl) *adj.* cute and lovable.

adore (ə dȯr′) *v.* to love very much. **adoring. adored.**

adult (a′ dult, ə dult′) *n.* **1.** a person who is fully grown. **2.** a plant, animal, or insect that is fully grown.

advance (əd vans′) *v.* to move forward: *The people advanced towards the building.* **advancing. advanced.**

⊖**advantage** (əd van′ tij) *n.* something that puts a person ahead of others: *Our football players had the advantage of being bigger than the others.*

adventure (əd ven′ chər) *n.* an exciting experience: *It was an adventure for the children to go camping.*

adverb (ad′ vûrb) *n.* a word that tells more about a verb, an adjective, or another adverb. In the sentence 'He sneezes loudly on a very cold day,' the adverbs are *loudly* and *very.*

⊖**advertise** (ad′ vər tīz′) *v.* to announce something (usually for sale) in the newspaper, on the radio, or on TV. **advertising. advertised.**

⊖**advertisement** (ad vûr′ tis mənt, ad′ vər tiz′ mənt) *n.* an announcement of something to be sold: *The newspaper advertisement says that milk is on sale.*

⊖**advice** (ad vīs′) *n.* helpful suggestions: *Father gave Choy advice on choosing new shoes.*

⊖**advise** (ad vīz′) *v.* to offer helpful suggestions: *She advised him not to go into the park alone at night.* **advising. advised.**

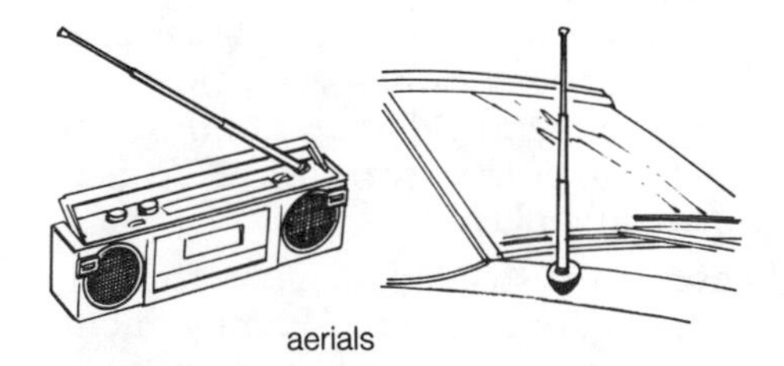
aerials

aerial (er′ i əl) *n.* a wire or set of wires used for receiving or sending radio or television signals.

ə**affair** (ə fer′) *n.* an action or occasion: *The party was a happy affair.*

affect (ə fekt′) *v.* to cause a change: *Louise's illness will affect her holiday plans.*
Note: Do not confuse **affect** and **effect**; **effect** means 'the result of a change'.

affection (ə fek′ shən) *n.* fondness; liking someone or something very much: *I have great affection for my grandparents.*

ə**affectionate** (ə fek′ shən ət) *adj.* showing a gentle kind of love: *an affectionate puppy.*

afford (ə fôrd′) *v.* to have enough money or time for something: *I cannot afford to buy a new coat. I cannot afford the time to go to the store.*

afraid (ə frād′) *adj.* **1.** frightened; full of fear: *After listening to his grandfather's ghost story, the boy was afraid of the dark.* **2.** sorry: *I'm afraid that the train has left without us.*

African (af′ ri kən) *n.* a person born in Africa, or a citizen of a country in Africa. *adj.* having to do with the continent of Africa.

after (af′ tər) *prep.* later than; behind: *after dinner; after me.*
after all despite what happened before: *Although they argue often, they remain good friends after all.*

afternoon (af′ tər nün′) *n.* the time between twelve noon and evening.

afterwards (af′ tər wərdz) *adv.* later.

again (ə gen′, ə gān′) *adv.* once more; one more time.

against (ə genst′, ə gānst′) *prep.* **1.** facing: *to walk against the wind.* **2.** touching: *Mario leaned against the fence.* **3.** opposed to; having the opposite opinion: *Are you for or against closing the school?*

age (āj) *n.* **1.** how many years a thing has lasted or a person has lived: *Val's age is five years.* **2.** a time in history: *Many dinosaurs died during the Ice Age.* *v.* to grow old. **aging. aged.**

agency (ā′ jən sē) *n.* a company that acts for a person or another company: *a travel agency; an employment agency.* *pl.* **agencies.**

agent (a′ jənt) *n.* **1.** a person who works for a company or another person: *The travel agent arranged our trip to Montreal.* **2.** anything that produces change.

aggressive (ə gres′ iv) *adj.* **1.** quick to attack or start an argument: *an aggressive country.* **2.** very bold or forceful: *an aggressive hockey player.*

ago (ə gō′) *adj.* gone by; in the past: *ten years ago.*
long ago many years past.

ə**agree** (ə grē′) *v.* **1.** to be willing; to say yes: *Ruth agreed to play baseball.* **2.** to share the same ideas, opinions, beliefs, etc.: *We agree with his plan to build a new arena.* **agreeing. agreed.**

ə**agreement** (ə grē′ mənt) *n.* an understanding with others; a sharing of the same ideas, opinions, beliefs, etc.: *We reached an agreement on who would take out the garbage and who would wash the dishes.*

agriculture (ag′ ri kul′ chər) *n.* farming.

ahead (ə hed′) *adv.* forward; in front: *The leader went ahead.*

aid (ād) *n.* help; assistance. *v.* to help: *He aided her in her search for new furniture.*

aim (ām) *n.* **1.** the pointing of a gun or other weapon at a target. **2.** a goal: *Joe's aim is to join the team.* *v.* **1.** to point a gun or other weapon at something. **2.** to have a goal: *Jill and Bob aim to be the best dancers.*

air (er) *n.* the mixture of gases that fills the space around the earth: *The air in large cities is often polluted.*

air conditioner (er′ kən dish′ ən ər) a machine that cools and cleans the air in a room, building, etc.

aircraft (er′ kraft′) *n.* any flying machine. *pl.* **aircraft.**

airline (er′ līn′) *n.* a company that operates aircraft.

airmail (er′ māl′) *n.* mail carried by aircraft.

airplane (er′ plān′) *n.* a motor-driven aircraft.

airport (er′ pȯrt′) *n.* a place where airplanes land and take off.

airtight (er′ tīt′) *adj.* closed so tightly that air cannot escape or enter: *He kept the salad fresh in an airtight container.*

⊖**aisle** (īl) *n.* a long, narrow passage, usually between rows of seats: *She walked down the aisle, looking for her seat.*

fire alarm

alarm clock

alarm (ə lȧrm′) *n.* **1.** a warning of danger. **2.** a bell, as on an alarm clock.

Alberta (al bûr′ tə) *n.* the province between British Columbia on the west and Saskatchewan on the east; its capital is Edmonton. Short form: **Alta.** A person living in or born in Alberta is an **Albertan.**

album (al′ bəm) *n.* **1.** a book to hold a collection: *a stamp album; a photograph album.* **2.** a cardboard case for holding a phonograph record, or the record itself.

alcohol (al′ kə hol′) *n.* **1.** the intoxicating liquid in beer, wine, and liquor: *Wine contains more alcohol than beer.* **2.** any intoxicating liquor.

alcoholic (al′ kə hol′ ik) *adj.* made with alcohol: *They served their guests both alcoholic drinks and juice.*

ale (āl) *n.* a strong, light-coloured beer.

alert (ə lûrt′) *adj.* ready to act quickly: *The guard stayed alert all night.*

alike (ə līk′) *adj.* nearly the same: *The sisters are alike in many ways.*

alive (ə līv′) *adj.* **1.** living; not dead. **2.** lively.

all (ȯl) *adj.* **1.** every one: *All the runners finished the race.* **2.** the entire amount of: *They used all the flour to bake the cake.*

allergic (ə lûr′ jik) *adj.* having an allergy or caused by an allergy: *Because Ben is allergic to cats, he sneezes when they are around.*

allergy (al′ ər jē) *n.* sensitivity to certain foods, plants, animals, pollens, etc., that some but not all people have: *Rashes, hay fever, or sneezing may be caused by an allergy.* *pl.* **allergies.**

alley (al′ ē) *n.* a narrow lane between two buildings. *pl.* **alleys.**

allow (ə lau̇′) *v.* to let; to give permission: *We must allow him to go.*

allowance (ə lau̇′ əns) *n.* a regular amount of money: *Carol gets a weekly allowance from her parents.*

all right (ȯl′ rīt′) **1.** very well; agreed: *All right, I'll go.* **2.** in good health: *I'm all right, thanks.* **3.** correct: *This is all right. You get 100%.*

ally (al′ ī) *n.* a country or person who helps another in a war or struggle. *pl.* **allies.**

almond (ȧʹ mənd) *n.* a nut from a tree that grows in warm places.

almost (ȯlʹ mōst) *adv.* nearly: *We're almost there!*

alone (ə lōnʹ) *adv.* with nobody else; with nothing else: *He prefers to study alone because he is easily distracted.*

along (ə longʹ) *prep.* following the direction or path of: *along the road; along the beach.* *adv.* **1.** on; forward: *Move along!* **2.** with another; together with: *My brother went along with me to the movies.* **all along** always; from the beginning: *We knew all along that our lost dog would come home.* **get along 1.** to agree; to be in harmony: *The two roommates get along well.* **2.** to manage or survive successfully: *I can get along on only five hours of sleep a night.*

alongside (ə long′ sīdʹ) *prep.* by the side of; beside.

aloud (ə laůd) *adv.* loudly, so that all can hear: *Claudia read the story aloud to the class.*

alphabet (alʹ fə bet′) *n.* the letters of a language; A,B,C, etc.: *There are 26 letters in the English alphabet.*

already (ȯl redʹ ē) *adv.* before this time; by now: *Charles was already there when we arrived.*

also (ȯlʹ sō) *adv.* too; as well: *Should I also bring my brother?*

altar (ȯlʹ tər) *n.* a table, usually in the front of a church, used for a religious ceremony.

alter (ȯlʹ tər) *v.* to change: *Jan has to alter her plans.*

⊖**alteration** (ȯl′ tər āʹ shən) *n.* a change: *The tailor is making alterations to my new suit.*

alternate (ȯlʹ tər nət) *n.* a substitute: *There are five alternates on the team.* *adj.* every other: *We visit our grandparents on alternate weekends.*

alternate (ȯlʹ tər nāt′) *v.* to take turns; to follow one after the other: *Rose and Robert alternate in walking the dog.* **alternating. alternated.**

although (ȯl t͟h͟ōʹ) *conj.* but; even if: *I will go out although I do not like the rain.*

altitude (alʹ ti tyūd′, alʹ ti tūd′) *n.* the height of something above a standard point, usually sea level.

altogether (ȯlʹ tə ge͟t͟h′ ər) *adv.* completely; entirely.

aluminum (ə lūʹ mi nəm) *n.* a light, silver-coloured metal used to make kitchen utensils, vehicles, and building materials.

always (ȯlʹ wāz) *adv.* forever; every time: *I will always try to be early.*

a.m. the time from midnight to noon: *I woke up at seven a.m.*

am (am) *v.* a form of the verb (to) **be**; used only with 'I': *I am going to sleep.*

⊖**amateur** (amʹ ə chər, amʹ ə tər) *n.* a person who does something only for pleasure, not for money: *Amateurs compete in the Olympics.*

amaze (ə māzʹ) *v.* to surprise very much: *The magician amazed us with his tricks.* **amazing. amazed.**

ambassador (am basʹ ə dər) *n.* the person who has the authority to represent his or her country in a foreign land.

amber (amʹ bər) *n.* a deep golden-yellow colour: *Traffic lights are red, green, and amber.* *adj.* having this colour.

ambition (am bishʹ ən) *n.* **1.** a strong wish to reach a goal: *an ambition to win a gold medal at the Olympics.* **2.** something that a person strongly wishes to achieve; a goal: *My ambition is to become a teacher.*

ambitious (am bish′ əs) *adj.* having a great wish to do or get something: *Because Dan is ambitious to be promoted, he works extra hours at the factory.*

ambulance (am′ byu ləns) *n.* a van for carrying ill or injured people to a hospital.

amen (ā′ men′, ȧ′ men′) *n.* a word at the end of a prayer, meaning 'So be it'.

American (ə mer′ i kən) *adj.* **1.** belonging to or coming from the United States. **2.** belonging to or coming from North, Central, or South America.

ammunition (am′ yu nish′ ən) *n.* **1.** bullets, shells, or rockets that can be fired from a gun. **2.** *(informal)* information or other material used in an argument or debate.

among (ə mung′) *prep.* **1.** surrounded by: *Kim walked among the trees.* **2.** with each of: *Share the sandwiches among you.*

amount (ə maůnt′) *n.* **1.** quantity: *a large amount of sugar.* **2.** total of money: *What is the amount of our bill?* *v.* to add up to: *The bill amounts to $3.50.*

ampere (am′ pir) *n.* a unit of measurement for an electric current.

amphibian (am fib′ i ən) *n.* an animal that is able to live both on land and in water: *Toads and frogs are amphibians.*

amuse (ə myūz′) *v.* to make someone laugh or smile; to entertain. **amusing. amused.**

amusement (ə myūz′ mənt) *n.* **1.** entertainment. **2.** enjoyment: *We showed our amusement by laughing at the clown's tricks.*

an (an, ən) *article* one; any; each. 'An' is used in place of 'a' when the next word begins with the vowel sound *a, e, i,* o, or *u: an apple, an egg, an iceberg, an orange, an hour, an uncle.*

analyse, analyze (an′ ə līz′) *v.* to look at closely; to study carefully: *The reporter analysed the election results in order to write his article.* **analyzing. analyzed.**

ancestor (an′ ses tər) *n.* a relative who lived a long time ago.

anchor (ang′ kər) *n.* a heavy metal object, usually with hooks, dropped into the water to keep a boat from drifting. *v.* to hold a boat with an anchor.

anchovy (an′ chō vē, an′ chə vē) *n.* a small, salt-water fish used for food. *pl.* **anchovies.**

⊖**ancient** (ān′ shənt) *adj.* very old; living or existing long ago: *an ancient tree; an ancient city.*

and (and, ənd) *conj.* as well as; plus: *Jack and Sue are friends; one and one are two.*

angel (ān′ jəl) *n.* a messenger or servant of God; a protecting spirit.

angle (angl) *n.* **1.** the shape formed when two straight lines or sides meet. **2.** the space between two straight lines or sides that meet.

anglophone (ang′ glə fōn′) *n.* in Canada, a person who uses English as his or her main language.

angry (ang′ grē) *adj.* bad-tempered; in a rage: *an angry bear; an angrier bear; the angriest bear of all.*

animal (an′ i məl) *n.* anything living that is not a plant.

ankle (angkl) *n.* the joint between the foot and leg: *He twisted his ankle when he ran down the stairs.*

⊖**anniversary** (an′ i vûrs′ ə rē) *n.* a day that is remembered each year because of something important that happened on it: *a wedding anniversary.* *pl.* **anniversaries.**

announce (ə nauns′) *v.* to let everyone know something: *The principal announced a holiday.* **announcing. announced.**

announcement (ə nauns′ mənt) *n.* something that is announced or made known to people: *We read the announcement about the meeting.*

announcer (ə nauns′ ər) *n.* a person who makes announcements or reads the news, usually on radio or TV.

annoy (ə nȯi′) *v.* to trouble or irritate someone.

annual (an′ yū əl) *adj.* happening once each year: *The annual party takes place each May fifteenth.*

anorak (an′ ə rak′) *n.* a weatherproof outer jacket with a hood; a parka: *Anoraks were originally made by Inuit.*

another (ə nuth′ ər) *adj.* **1.** one more: *Take another piece of cake.* **2.** different: *Choose another dress.*

answer (an′ sər) *n.* **1.** a reply to a question. **2.** a reply to a letter. *v.* to reply to a question or a letter.

ant

ant (ant) *n.* a small insect that lives in the ground with many others of its kind.

Antarctic (ant ärk′ tik) *n.* the south polar region that includes Antarctica and the waters inside the Antarctic Circle.

antarctic (ant ärk′ tik) *adj.* of or about the Antarctic.

Antarctica (ant ärk′ ti kə) *n.* the ice-covered continent that surrounds the South Pole.

Antarctic Circle (ant ärk′ tik sûrkl′) an imaginary circle around the earth that is the limit of the south polar zone.

antelope (an′ tə lōp′) *n.* a swift, four-legged animal that looks like a deer.

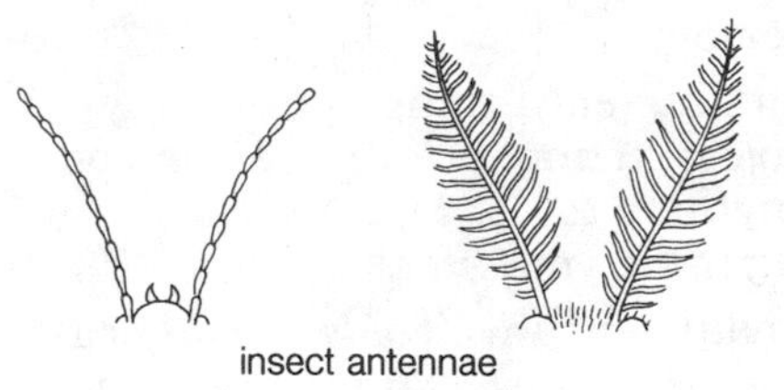
insect antennae

antenna (an ten′ ə) *n.* **1.** one of two feelers on the head of a crab, lobster, or insect. *pl.* **antennae** (an ten′ ē, an ten′ ī). **2.** an aerial; a system of metal rods and wires used to send or receive signals for television or radio. *pl.* **antennas.**

anthem (an′ thəm) *n.* a song about loyalty, praise, or devotion: *The national anthem of our country is 'O Canada'.*

anti- (an′ ti) a prefix meaning 'against': **antifreeze** is put into the radiator of a car to stop the water from freezing.

anticipate (an tis′ i pāt′) *v.* to expect: *We anticipate receiving a diploma at the end of the course.* **anticipating. anticipated.**

⊖**antique** (an tēk′) *n.* something made long ago, such as a piece of furniture or a tool: *This chair is an antique.* *adj.* from a long time ago: *This antique chest was carved in Nova Scotia one hundred years ago.*

antlers (ant′ lərz) *n.pl.* the horns of a deer, elk, moose, etc.

anxious (angk′ shəs) *adj.* **1.** worried; fearful: *When his daughter didn't come home on time, he became very anxious.* **2.** wanting very much for something to happen: *Mark was anxious to be on the baseball team.*

any (en′ ē) *adj.* **1.** one of several: *Can you visit us any day this week?* **2.** some: *Have you any money?*

anybody (en′ i bud′ ē, en′ i bod′ ē) *pron.* any person.

anyone (en′ i wun′) *pron.* any person.

anything (en′ i thing′) *pron.* any object, action, or event: *Have you anything to do? I will accept anything you offer.*

anyway (en′ i wā′) *adv.* in any case; still: *If it rains, can we have the picnic anyway?*

anywhere (en′ i wer′, en′ i hwer′) *adv.* in any place; to any place: *Is there anywhere you would like to go?*

apart (ə pärt′) *adv.* **1.** separate; alone: *Leslie stood apart from the others.* **2.** in pieces: *Mother took the machine apart.*

apartment (ə pärt′ mənt) *n.* a group of rooms to live in, which are part of a larger building: *Our apartment is on the third floor.*

ape (gorilla)

ape (āp) *n.* a kind of monkey with no tail.

apiece (ə pēs′) *adv.* each; for, to, or from each one: *The books cost three dollars apiece.*

apologetic (ə pol′ ə jet′ ik) *adj.* full of regret; feeling sorry: *The store sent an apologetic letter because they had made an error.*

apologize (ə pol′ ə jīz′) *v.* to say that you are sorry for something. **apologizing. apologized.**

apology (ə pol′ ə jē) *n.* a statement that a person is sorry for doing something. *pl.* **apologies.**

apostrophe (ə pos′ trə fē) *n.* a punctuation mark that shows that a letter or letters have been left out. Apostrophes are used in words such as *I'm* (meaning *I am*) and *can't* (meaning *cannot*). **2.** a punctuation mark that shows ownership, possession, or relationship: *This book is Anna's. My father's sister lives in Portugal.*

apparent (ə par′ ənt, ə per′ ənt) *adj.* easy to see; plainly understood; evident: *It is apparent from your smile that you like your teacher.*

appeal (ə pēl′) *v.* **1.** to interest greatly: *Hockey appeals to Stanley and Rita.* **2.** to ask for help: *Henry appealed to his sister when he couldn't lift the heavy box by himself.*

appear (ə pir′) *v.* **1.** to come into view or sight: *Marion appeared from around the corner.* **2.** to seem: *Norman appears to be tired.*

appearance (ə pir′ əns) *n.* **1.** coming into view: *The appearance of the police made the robbers run.* **2.** how someone or something looks: *The appearance of the building made us feel that it was not safe.*

appendix (ə pen′ diks) *n.* **1.** a small growth in the lower part of the abdomen that is attached to the large intestine. The appendix has no function. **2.** extra material at the end of a book: *The atlas contained an appendix listing the capital cities of the world.* *pl.* **appendixes**, or **appendices** (ə pen′ di sēz).

appetite (ap′ ə tīt′) *n.* **1.** enjoyment of or desire for something, especially food: *Billy has a good appetite, and can eat at any time.* **2.** a strong desire: *an appetite for work.*

applaud (ə plȯd′) *v.* to cheer; to clap hands to show that you enjoyed something: *Everyone applauded at the end of the play.*

applause (ə plȯz′) *n.* cheering; clapping hands.

apple (apl) *n.* a roundish fruit that is red, green, or yellow in colour.

appliance (ap lī′ əns) *n.* a machine or other device, often using electricity, used to do something: *This store sells household appliances like refrigerators and washing machines.*

⊖**application** (ap′ li kā′ shən) *n.* **1.** a request, usually for a job: *The company received ten applications for the job of computer operator.* **2.** a written form to be filled in with information by a person applying for a job. **3.** the act of putting something onto something else: *The dark wall needs a second application of white paint.* **4.** use or practical purpose: *People use computers for many different applications.*

⊖**apply** (ə plī′) *v.* **1.** to ask; to make a request: *Al applied for the job of coach.* **2.** to put on: *Apply the bandage.* **3.** to put into use: *Dina applied the brakes to stop the car. The clerk applied the new sales tax to the groceries we bought.* **applying. applied.** he **applies.**

appoint (ə pȯint′) *v.* to select or choose someone for a task or job: *The mayor appointed a new assistant.*

⊖**appointment** (ə pȯint′ mənt) *n.* **1.** the choosing of someone. **2.** an agreement to meet someone at a certain place and time: *I have a doctor's appointment tomorrow morning.*

appreciate (ə prē′ shi āt′) *v.* to be thankful for something: *We appreciate the gift.* **appreciating. appreciated.**

apprentice (ə pren′ tis) *n.* a person who is learning a skill or a profession from an experienced worker.

approach (ə prōch′) *v.* to move towards: *The cat approached the mouse very carefully.* **approaching. approached.** he **approaches.**

approval (ə prü′ vəl) *n.* agreement; permission: *Don joined the club with his parents' approval.*

approve (ə prüv′) *v.* to agree to; to give permission: *Mother and Dad approve of Karen's plans.* **approving. approved.**

approximately (ə prok′ si mət lē) *adv.* almost; about; around: *There are approximately fifty people in this room.*

apricot (ā′ pri kot′, ap′ ri kot′) *n.* a soft fruit, pale orange in colour and smaller than a peach.

April (ā′ pril, ā′ prəl) *n.* the fourth month of the year.

apron (ā′ prən) *n.* a piece of clothing, worn on the front and tied at the waist, to keep clothes clean when working.

aquarium (ə kwer′ i əm) *n.* a glass container, filled with water, holding fish and other animals and plants.

Arabian (ə rā′ bi ən) *adj.* having to do with Arabs or with Arabia, an area in the Near East.

arbitration (ȧr′ bi trā′ shən) *n.* the settling of a dispute or disagreement by a neutral person.

⊖**arch** (ȧrch) *n.* **1.** the curved top of a doorway, tunnel, or bridge. **2.** the part of the foot between the heel and toe. *pl.* **arches.**

archery (ȧr′ chər ē) *n.* the use of bows and arrows.

architect (ȧr′ ki tekt′) *n.* a person who designs and draws plans for buildings.

Arctic (ärk′ tik) *n.* the region around the North Pole and north of the Arctic Circle.

arctic (ärk′ tik) *adj.* of or about the Arctic: *an arctic wind.*

arctic char (ärk′ tik chär′) a fish found in northern waters and used for food.

Arctic Circle (ärk′ tik sûrkl′) an imaginary circle around the earth that is the limit of the north polar zone.

Arctic Ocean (ärk′ tik ō′ shən) the ocean inside the Arctic Circle.

are (är) *v.* a form of the verb (to) **be**; used with 'you', 'we', and 'they': *You are a doctor. We are students of English. They are going to sleep.*

area (er′ i ə) *n.* **1.** the size or amount of a surface. **2.** a space, section, or region: *the area around the city. pl.* **areas.**

area code (er′ i ə kōd′) a three-digit number, added before a telephone number, that a person dials when making a telephone call to a place that is far away.

arena (ə rē′ nə) *n.* a large space for games or shows, with raised seats all around. *pl.* **arenas.**

aren't (ärnt) short for **are not.**

⊖**argue** (är′ gyū) *v.* to disagree with someone; to have a different point of view: *Jane argued with her brother over who should clean the room.* **arguing. argued.**

⊖**argument** (är′ gyə mənt) *n.* **1.** a disagreement with someone, in which each person tells his or her opinions. **2.** a reason for or against something: *My old bicycle will be expensive to fix. That is a good argument for buying a new one.*

arise (ə rīz′) *v.* to occur or take place: *Call me if any problems arise.* **arising. arose** (ə rōz′). I have **arisen** (ə riz′ ən).

arithmetic (ə rith′ mə tik′) *n.* working with numbers: *Adding, subtracting, multiplying, and dividing are the main parts of arithmetic.*

⊖**arm** (ärm) *n.* **1.** the part of the body from the shoulder to the hand. **2.** anything like an arm in appearance or use: *the arms of a chair. v.* to supply a person, country, etc. with weapons.

armchair (ärm′ cher′) *n.* a chair with an arm on each side of the seat.

arms of Canada

arms (ärmz) *n. pl.* **1.** weapons. **2.** symbols in an emblem or badge that identify a family, organization, or country.

army (är′ mē) *n.* **1.** a great number of soldiers. **2.** a very large number: *an army of insects. pl.* **armies.**

aroma (ə rō′ mə) *n.* a pleasant smell: *the aroma of freshly baked bread. pl.* **aromas.**

around (ə raůnd′) *adv.* **1.** in a circle: *The wheel spun around.* **2.** in the opposite direction: *She turned around to see the house.* **3.** from place to place: *We walked around until we found the hospital.* **4.** nearby: *Stay around until I return. prep.* about; near: *We arrived at the theatre around noon.*

⊖**arrange** (ə rānj′) *v.* **1.** to put in order: *to arrange books on a shelf.* **2.** to make plans: *to arrange to meet a friend.* **arranging. arranged.**

arrangement (ə rānj′ mənt) *n.* **1.** a number of things put in order: *an arrangement of flowers.* **2.** a plan; something agreed to: *We made arrangements to meet at the bus station.*

arrest (ə rest′) *v.* to hold someone and keep him or her as a prisoner: *The police arrested the robber.* **under arrest** being kept prisoner.

arrival (ə rīv′ əl) *n.* coming to a place at the end of a trip: *They waited for the plane's arrival at the airport.*

⊖**arrive** (ə rīv′) *v.* **1.** to reach a place after a trip: *We arrived in Toronto after a five-hour drive.* **2.** to come to: *After a long time, he arrived at a decision.* **arriving. arrived.**

arrow (ar′ ō, er′ ō) *n.* a pointed stick with feathers at one end, shot from a bow.

art (ärt) *n.* **1.** painting, sculpture, or drawing. **2.** the making of beautiful things. **3.** any skill or craft: *the art of weaving; the art of baking.*

arthritis (är thrī′ tis) *n.* a disease that causes pain in the fingers, knees, and other joints of the body, making them difficult to move.

article (är′ tikl) *n.* **1.** a single thing; an object. **2.** a piece of writing in a newspaper or magazine: *We read an article on fishing.* **3.** a part of speech. The words *a, an,* and *the* are called articles.

artificial (är′ ti fish′ əl) *adj.* not real or natural; imitation: *artificial flowers.*

artist (är′ tist) *n.* someone who paints pictures or makes or does other beautiful things: *Dancers, painters, singers, and actors are all artists.*

artistic (är tis′ tik) *adj.* **1.** fond of art and beautiful things. **2.** good at art.

as (az, əz) *adv.* **1.** for example; for instance: *Some dogs, such as spaniels, have long hair.* **2.** the same: *I am as old as Judy.* *conj.* **1.** while: *As they were talking, the snow stopped.* **2.** in the way that: *We did just as we were asked.*

ash (ash) *n.* **1.** the powder left after a fire. **2.** a kind of tree. *pl.* **ashes.**

ashamed (ə shāmd′) *adj.* feeling sorry for or upset about something wrong or silly that has been done: *He was ashamed of his foolish mistake. I am ashamed that I hit my brother.*

ashore (ə shór′) *adv.* to or on the shore: *The ship was driven ashore by the storm.*

Asian (ā′ zhən) *n.* a person born in Asia, or a citizen of a country in Asia. *adj.* having to do with the continent of Asia.

aside (ə sīd′) *adv.* to or on one side: *Kay stepped aside to avoid the crowd.*

ask (ask) *v.* to question; to search for an answer: *We were lost and had to ask the way.*

asleep (ə slēp′) *adv., adj.* not awake; sleeping: *She fell asleep while reading. He was asleep when the telephone rang.*

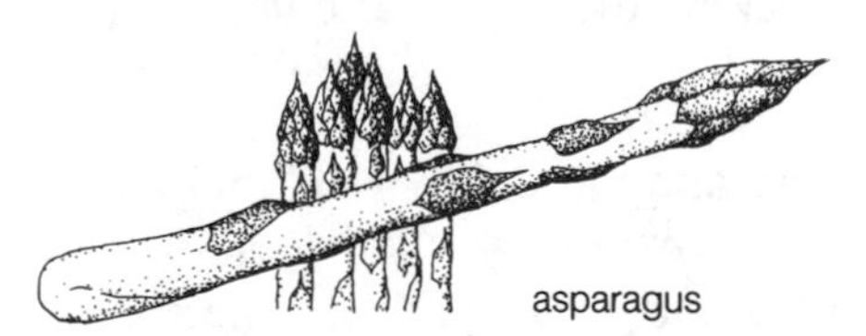

asparagus

asparagus (əs par′ ə gəs) *n.* a vegetable, green in colour and sold in bunches.

asphalt (as′ fólt) *n.* a sticky, black substance that is mixed with gravel or sand and used to pave roads.

aspirin (as′ pi rin, as′ pə rin) *n.* a medicine used to lower fever and lessen pain caused by headaches, colds, etc.

ass (as) *n.* **1.** a donkey. **2.** *(informal)* a silly, foolish person. *pl.* **asses.**

assemble (ə sembl′) *v.* **1.** to come together: *A crowd assembled near the accident.* **2.** to put together: *to assemble a model ship.* **assembling. assembled.**

assembly (ə sem′ blē) *n.* a meeting: *We saw a movie at the school assembly. pl.* **assemblies.**

asset (as′ et) *n.* **1.** something useful; an advantage: *My experience with horses was an asset when I applied for a job on the ranch.* **2.** an item that is owned and can be sold for cash: *The company's assets of property and machinery are worth a million dollars.*

⊖**assign** (ə sīn′) *v.* **1.** to give something, such as a job or task: *The teacher assigned us two pages of homework.* **2.** to fix; to set: *to assign a limit to the number of people in a restaurant.*

assignment (ə sīn′ mənt) *n.* something that is given, fixed, or assigned: *The English assignment is not difficult.*

⊖**assist** (ə sist′) *n.* **1.** help given: *With an assist from my family, I was able to buy a new car.* **2.** in hockey, the help that one player gives to another who scores a goal. *v.* to give help.

⊖**assistance** (ə sis′ təns) *n.* help: *I fell down and needed assistance.*

⊖**assistant** (ə sis′ tənt) *n.* a person who helps another: *Sarah is an assistant to the swimming teacher.*

association (ə sō′ si ā′ shən) *n.* a group of people who share a common interest or purpose: *My sister is a member of the builders' association.*

assortment (ə sort′ mənt) *n.* a mixture of different kinds: *an assortment of sandwiches.*

assume (ə syūm′, ə sūm′) *v.* **1.** to believe or accept something without knowing if it is real or true: *We assume that all the cousins will come to dinner.* **2.** to take on or upon: *Mario assumed the role of foreman at the factory.* **assuming. assumed.**

astonish (əs ton′ ish) *v.* to surprise very much; to amaze: *I was astonished to see Ted at work. I thought he had the flu.* **astonishing. astonished.** it **astonishes.**

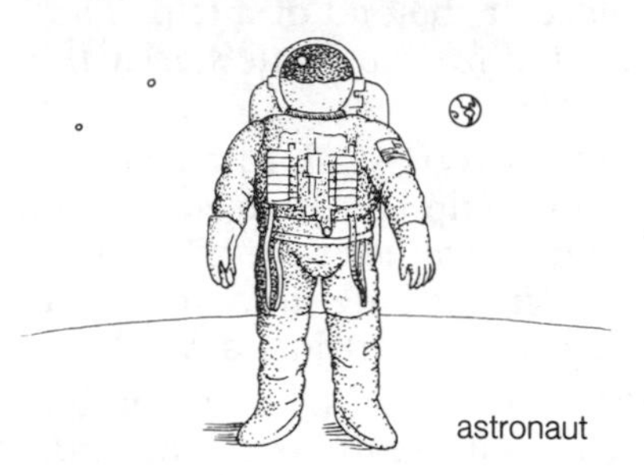

astronaut

astronaut (as′ trə nȯt′) *n.* a traveller in a spaceship.

astronomer (əs tron′ ə mər) *n.* someone who studies astronomy.

astronomy (əs tron′ ə mē) *n.* the study of the stars, planets, sun, moon, etc.

at (at) *prep.* **1.** by; on; near; in: *Fran is at her aunt's house.* **2.** in the direction of: *Bill pointed his finger at Tim.* **3.** for: *I bought two hats at a dollar each.* **4.** around the time of: *Wendy wakes up at nine on Saturdays.*

ate see **eat.**

athlete (ath′ lēt) *n.* a person who is active in sports.

athletic (ath let′ ik) *adj.* **1.** active in sports. **2.** physically fit.

Atlantic (at lan′ tik) *adj.* having to do with the Atlantic Ocean: *Atlantic salmon.*

Atlantic Ocean (at lan′ tik ō′ shən) the ocean extending from North America and South America to Europe and Africa.

Atlantic Provinces (at lan′ tik prov′ in səs) New Brunswick, Newfoundland, Nova Scotia, and Prince Edward Island.

atlas (at′ ləs) *n.* a book containing many maps of the different countries of the world. *pl.* **atlases.**

atmosphere (at′ mə sfir′) *n.* the air around the earth.

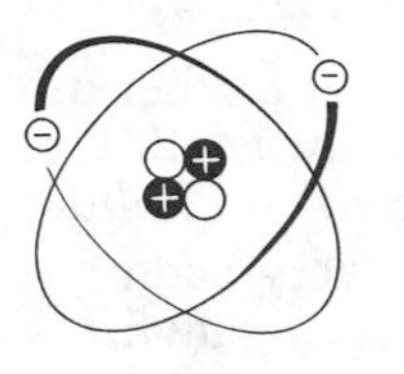
atom

atom (at′ əm) *n.* **1.** the smallest part of an element that can take part in a chemical reaction. **2.** a very small part of anything.

attach (ə tach′) *v.* to join together: *The farmer attached the horse to the plough.* **attaching. attached.** she **attaches.**
attached to being very fond of: *Laura is attached to her grandmother.*

attachment (ə tach′ mənt) *n.* a part or device that can be fastened to something else: *The attachments for the sewing machine help you make special stitches.*

attack (ə tak′) *n.* **1.** a fight or battle. **2.** forceful criticism. **3.** a quick and unexpected illness: *a heart attack.* *v.* to start to fight, battle, or criticize forcefully.

attempt (ə tempt′) *n.* an effort; a try: *After many attempts, I was able to thread the needle.* *v.* to try to do something: *We attempted to fix the car.*

⊖**attend** (ə tend′) *v.* to be present at: *He attends elementary school. We attended the meeting at one o'clock.*

attendance (ə ten′ dəns) *n.* **1.** the number of persons present: *There was a large attendance at the soccer game.* **2.** being present: *Your attendance at the meeting is important.*

attention (ə ten′ shən) *n.* care; thought: *Give attention to your work.*

attic (at′ ik) *n.* a room just under the roof of a house.

attitude (at′ i tyūd′, at′ i tūd′) *n.* the way a person thinks, acts, or feels: *a cheerful attitude.*

attorney (ə tûr′ nē) *n.* a lawyer. *pl.* **attorneys.**

attract (ə trakt′) *v.* to pull to itself: *A magnet attracts iron nails.*

attraction (ə trak′ shən) *n.* something that is liked and brings people to it: *The circus was a great attraction.*

⊖**attractive** (ə trak′ tiv) *adj.* pleasant; likable; lovely: *Christine's dress is very attractive.*

auction (ȯk′ shən) *n.* a sale at which each thing is sold to the person who will give the most money for it.

⊖**audience** (ȯd′ i əns) *n.* a crowd of people listening to or watching a performance or meeting.

audio (ȯd′ i ō) *adj.* having to do with sound: *Stereos, radios, and tape recorders are all audio equipment.*

auditorium (ȯd′ i tȯr′ i əm) *n.* a large room for an audience.

August (ȯ′ gəst) *n.* the eighth month of the year.

aunt (ant) *n.* **1.** a sister of a person's father or mother. **2.** the wife of a person's uncle.

Australian (ȯ strāl′ yən) *n.* a person born in or a citizen of Australia. *adj.* having to do with the continent of Australia.

authentic (ȯ then′ tik) *adj.* real; not imitation; genuine: *Is this an authentic diamond, or is it glass?*

author (ȯ′ thər) *n.* a writer of books.

authority (ə thȯr′ i tē) *n.* **1.** the power or ability to command or make decisions: *The mayor has the authority to govern the city.* **2.** a person or group having the power to command or give orders. **3.** an expert: *Nicholas is an authority on coins and stamps.* *pl.* **authorities.**

authorize (ȯ′ thə rīz′) *v.* to give permission or the power to do something: *The principal authorized the librarian to buy new books.* **authorizing. authorized.**

autograph (ȯ′ tə graf′) *n.* a person's name written by himself or herself.

automatic (ȯ′ tə mat′ ik) *adj.* working by itself: *I wish we had an automatic dishasher—I'm tired of doing the dishes by hand.*

automobile (ȯ′ tə mə bēl′) *n.* a motor car.

autumn (ȯ′ təm) *n.* the season after summer, also called **fall**.

avalanche (av′ ə lanch′) *n.* a large fall of snow and rocks down the side of a mountain.

avenue (av′ ə nyü′, av′ ə nü′) *n.* a road or street, often a wide one.

average (av′ ər ij) *n.* the amount found by adding several numbers and then dividing the total by the number of amounts added: *The average of 5, 6, and 10 is 7.* *adj.* ordinary; typical: *George is of average weight for his age.* *v.* to find or have the numerical average of: *to average a column of figures.* **averaging. averaged.**

aviation (ā′ vi ā′ shən) *n.* making or flying aircraft.

aviator (ā′ vi ā′ tər) *n.* a pilot of an aircraft.

avocado (av′ ə kȧ′ dō) *n.* a pear-shaped fruit that has dark green skin, greenish-yellow flesh, and a large seed. *pl.* **avocados.**

avoid (ə vȯid′) *v.* to keep clear of; to keep away from: *When I'm on a diet, I avoid all desserts.*

await (ə wāt′) *v.* to wait or stay for.

awake (ə wāk′) *adj.* not sleeping.

award (ə wȯrd′) *n.* a prize, honour, or reward given for winning or for doing something well. *v.* to give such a prize, honour, or reward.

aware (ə wer′) *adj.* knowing; alert to: *Thelma was aware of the fire before she saw the flames.*

away (ə wā′) *adv.* **1.** further off: *The man walked away.* **2.** absent: *We have been away on holiday.*

awful (ȯ′ fəl) *adj.* very bad or severe: *We are having awful weather!*

awfully (ȯ′ fə lē) *adv.* very; terribly: *You are awfully brave!*

awhile (ə wīl′, ə hwīl′) *adv.* for a short period of time: *Could you stay awhile and have dinner with us?*

awkward (ȯk′ wərd) *adj.* clumsy; not graceful: *He is very awkward, always falling over things.*

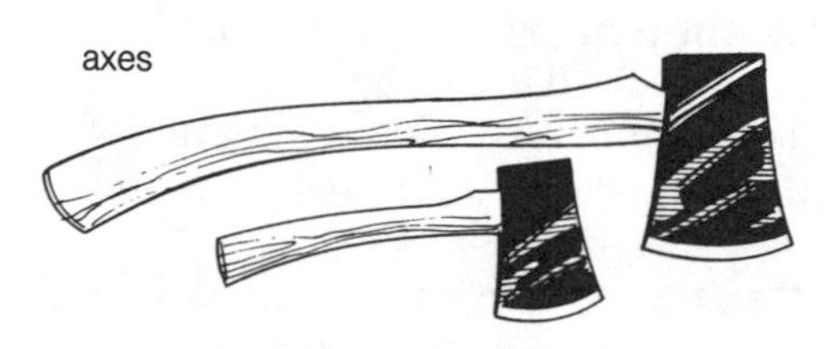

⊖**axe** (aks) *n.* a tool, used for cutting wood, with a heavy metal blade on the end of a handle.

axis (ak′ sis) *n.* a line, not always a real one, around which an object turns: *The earth turns on its axis.* *pl.* **axes.**

axle (aksl) *n.* the shaft on which a wheel or pair of wheels turns.

B

baby (bā′ bē) *n.* an infant; a very young child. *pl.* **babies.**

baby bonus see **Family Allowance.**

babysitter (bā′ bi sit′ ər) *n.* a person who takes care of young children when the parents are away.

⊖**bachelor** (bach′ ə lər) *n.* a man who has never married.

back (bak) *n.* **1.** the part of a person's body that is opposite to the front part. **2.** the part of anything that is behind the front part: *the back of the house.* *adj.* opposite to or behind the front: *the back seat.* *adv.* in return: *Jean gave the ticket back.* *v.* **1.** to move backwards: *She backed up the truck to the loading area.* **2.** to support, help, or agree with someone: *We backed the decision of our Member of Parliament.*
back and forth first in one direction and then in the opposite direction: *I walked back and forth across the room.*
back up to support: *The scientist backed up the statement with evidence.*

backbone (bak′ bōn′) *n.* the spine; a line of small bones down the back of the body.

background (bak′ graund′) *n.* **1.** the section of a picture that appears to be in the distance. **2.** a person's previous experience: *Because of Jim's background in cooking for his family, he was appointed cook for the camping trip.*

backpack (bak′ pak′) *n.* a leather or canvas bag that holds clothing and equipment; it is carried on a person's back.

backside (bak′ sīd′) *n.* *(informal)* the buttocks; the part of the body on which a person sits.

backwards, backward (bak′ wərdz, bak′ wərd) *adv.* in the direction opposite to the front: *Jeff tried walking backwards.*

backyard (bak′ yȧrd′) *n.* a yard behind a house.

bacon (bā′ kən) *n.* the meat taken from the back and sides of a pig: *Many people eat bacon and eggs for breakfast.*

bacteria (bak tir′ ē ə) *n.pl.* very tiny living things: *Some bacteria cause disease.*

bad (bad) *adj.* **1.** not good or right: *The first song is bad. The second one is worse. The third song is the worst of all.* **2.** rotten; spoiled: *These plums have gone bad.*

badge (baj) *n.* a symbol worn on clothes, showing that a person belongs to a special group.

badger (baj′ ər) *n.* an animal with coarse fur, short legs, and long claws; it lives underground.

badly (bad′ lē) *adv.* **1.** wrongly; not well: *badly.* **2.** very much: *The house is badly in need of repairs.*

badminton

badminton (bad′ min tən) *n.* a game played by using a racket to hit a small object back and forth across a high net.

⊖**bag** (bag) *n.* a sack, often made of paper, cloth, leather, or soft plastic: *a handbag; a shopping bag.*

bagel (bā′ gəl) *n.* a hard bread roll, shaped like a ring.

baggage (bag′ ij) *n.* cases and bags that hold what a person needs when taking a trip.

baggy (bag′ ē) *adj.* hanging loosely or slackly: *baggy pants; baggier pants; the baggiest pants of all.*

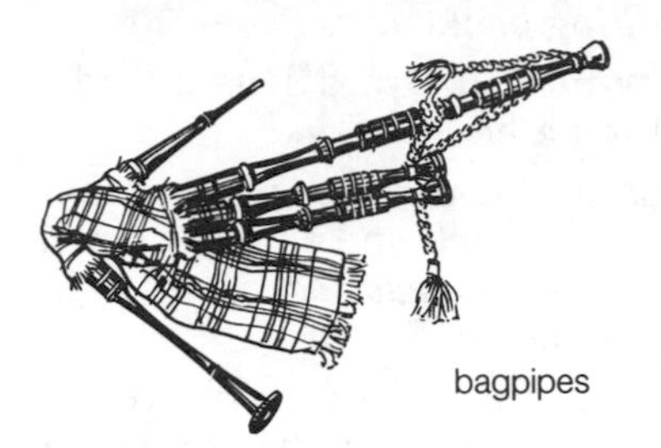
bagpipes

bagpipes (bag′ pīps′) *n.pl.* a musical instrument with a bag and pipes. Air is blown into the bag and then forced through the pipes by squeezing the bag.

⊖**bail** (bāl) *n.* money paid to a court of law to keep someone out of jail until his or her trial: *The prisoner's bail was set at $3000.00.* *v.* to scoop water out of a boat.

bait (bāt) *n.* something, usually food, used to tempt a fish to a hook or an animal into a trap.

bake (bāk) *v.* to cook in an oven. **baking. baked.**

baker (bāk′ ər) *n.* someone who bakes bread and cakes.

bakery (bāk′ ər ē) *n.* a place where bread and cakes are baked or sold. *pl.* **bakeries.**

⊖**balance** (bal′ əns) *n.* **1.** steadiness: *Keith kept his balance when walking along the painted line.* **2.** an instrument for weighing things, used by chemists and others. **3.** the remainder; the part left: *a bank account balance.* *v.* to keep steady, as when walking on a tightrope. **balancing. balanced.**

balcony (bal′ kə nē) *n.* **1.** a platform built outside the upper floors of a building. **2.** an upstairs floor of a theatre. *pl.* **balconies.**

bald (bȯld) *adj.* having no hair on the head.

bale (bāl) *n.* a bundle of things securely wrapped with rope or wire for storage or shipping: *There were hundreds of bales of hay on the farm.*

ball (bȯl) *n.* **1.** something round, like a sphere: *a ball of wool; a tennis ball.* **2.** a big party with dancing.

ballerina (bal′ ə rē′ nə) *n.* a female ballet dancer. *pl.* **ballerinas.**

ballet (ba lā′, bal′ ā) *n.* a story or play told in the form of graceful dancing.

⊖**balloon** (bə lūn′) *n.* an airtight bag filled with air or light gas.

⊖**ballot** (bal′ ət) *n.* a piece of paper or other thing used to record a person's vote: *They counted the votes on the ballots to find out who won the election.*

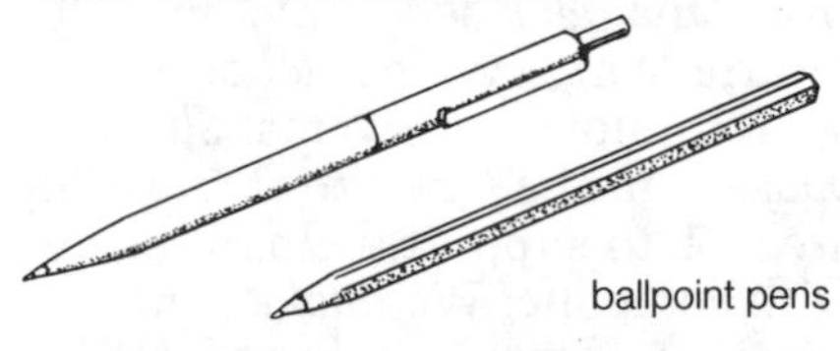
ballpoint pens

ballpoint pen (bal′ point pen′) a tool, used for writing, that has a small metal ball at one end and a cartridge containing semisolid ink.

bamboo (bam bū′) *n.* a tall, woody grass that grows in hot climates.

banana (bə nan′ ə) *n.* a long, curved fruit with thick, yellow skin and yellow flesh.

band (band) *n.* **1.** a narrow strip used for holding things together: *an elastic band.* **2.** a group of people playing music. **3.** in Canada, registered Indians living on land set apart by the federal government.

bandage (ban′ dij) *n.* a narrow strip of cloth or other material used to cover wounds or bind injuries. *v.* to cover a wound or injury with strips of cloth or other material. **bandaging. bandaged.**

bandit (ban′ dit) *n.* a robber.

bang (bang) *n.* a loud noise. *v.* to make such a noise.

banister (ban′ i stər) *n.* the rail and posts of a staircase.

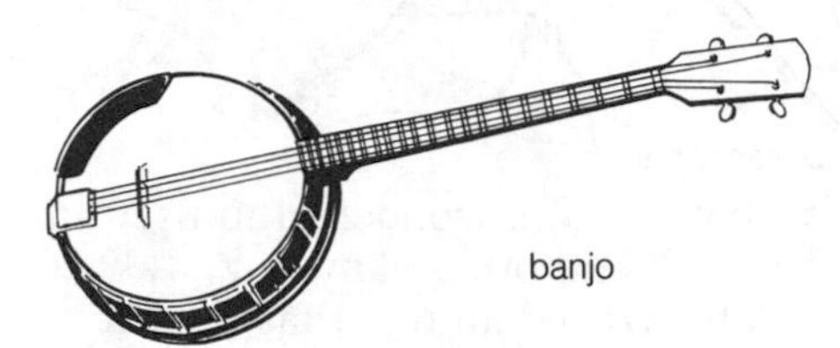
banjo

banjo (ban′ jō) *n.* a musical instrument of the guitar family. It has a long neck, a round body, and several strings. *pl.* **banjos.**

⊖**bank** (bangk) *n.* **1.** a place where money is kept safe. **2.** a pile of earth or snow. **3.** the side of a river. **4.** a shallow place under water: *The Grand Banks off Canada's east coast are famous for fishing.*

banner (ban′ ər) *n.* a flag or similar piece of cloth: *The football fans waved their team's banner in the air.*

banquet (bang′ kwit) *n.* a large feast or dinner party.

bantam (ban′ təm) *n.* a small farm fowl.

baptism (bap′ tizm) *n.* a religious ceremony in which a person is sprinkled or covered with water, showing that he or she is cleansed of sin and is now a member of that religion.

baptize (bap′ tīz) *v.* to perform the baptism ceremony. **baptizing. baptized.**

⊖**bar** (bȧr) *n.* **1.** a long, narrow piece of wood, metal, etc., usually used to block movement: *the bars of a cage.* **2.** a piece of solid material, usually rectangular: *a bar of chocolate; a bar of soap.* **3.** a place where alcoholic drinks are sold or drunk at a counter. *v.* **1.** to block or hinder: *to bar the way.* **2.** to forbid or prohibit: *Talking is barred in the library.* **barring. barred.**

barbecue (bȧr′ bə kyū′) *n.* **1.** an open fireplace for outdoor cooking. **2.** a meal cooked outdoors. *v.* to cook over an open fireplace. **barbecuing. barbecued.**

barbed wire (bȧrbd′ wīr′) wire with sharp spikes, used for fences.

barber (bȧr′ bər) *n.* a person who cuts hair, usually for men and boys.

bare (ber) *adj.* **1.** plain: *the bare truth.* **2.** empty; containing nothing: *a bare room.* **3.** naked; without clothes.

barely (ber′ lē) *adv.* hardly: *I have barely enough time to do all my work.*

bargain (bȧr′ gən) *n.* **1.** something that is bought cheaply. **2.** an agreement that everyone will do something. *v.* **1.** to try to get something at a cheaper cost by suggesting that the salesperson lower the price. **2.** to try to agree on the terms of a contract or an agreement: *The employees bargained for better working conditions.*

barge (bȧrj) *n.* a flat-bottomed boat, usually used to carry freight.

bark (bȧrk) *n.* **1.** the outside skin or cover of a tree trunk or branch. **2.** the sharp cry of a dog or wolf. *v.* to make this sound.

barley (bȧr′ lē) *n.* a grain, grown like wheat, that is used for food.

barn (bȧrn) *n.* a farm building used for storing crops or sheltering animals.

barnyard (bȧrn′ yȧrd′) *n.* the farmyard next to a barn.

barometer (bə rom′ ə tər′) *n.* an instrument that measures the pressure of the air and can show changes in the weather.

barrel (bar′ əl, ber′ əl) *n.* **1.** a wooden tub. **2.** the tube of a gun.

barrier (bar′ i ər, ber′ i ər) *n.* a wall, fence, or anything else that stops forward movement.

⊖**base** (bās) *n.* **1.** the part that something stands on; the lowest section. **2.** in baseball and other games, a place to start, finish, or rest. *v.* (followed by **on**) to use as the basis or support for: *Her opinions were based on the book she read.* **basing. based.**

baseball (bās′ bȯl′) *n.* **1.** a team game played with bat and ball on a field with four bases. **2.** the ball used in this game.

basement (bās′ mənt) *n.* the lowest floor of a building, usually below the ground.

bashful (bash′ fəl) *adj.* shy; timid.

BASIC (bā′ sik) *n.* a language, or set of codes, used to control a computer: *This program is written in Basic. adj.* using this language: *a Basic program.*

basic (bā′ sik) *n., adj.* forming a base; forming the main or most important sections: *Tires and an engine are some of the basic parts of a car.*

basin (bā′ sən) *n.* a round bowl, usually for holding liquids.

basis (bā′ sis) *n.* the main or most important part of something: *The basis of this pudding is milk. pl.* **bases** (bā′ sēz).

⊖**basket** (bas′ kət) *n.* a container usually made of woven straw or twigs.

basketball (bas′ kət bȯl′) *n.* **1.** a team game played with a large ball on a court with two raised hoops. **2.** the ball used in this game.

bass (bas) *n.* a fish that can be eaten. *pl.* **bass.**

⊖**bass** (bās) *n.* a musical instrument with strings that make deep tones. *pl.* **basses.**

baste (bāst) *v.* **1.** in cooking, to pour melted fat or other liquids over: *You baste a turkey to keep it juicy.* **2.** in sewing, to make long, loose stitches. **basting. basted.**

bat (bat) *n.* **1.** a wooden club used in baseball and other games. **2.** a small, winged animal that flies at night. *v.* to use a bat in baseball. **batting. batted.**

batch (bach) *n.* a number of things of the same kind: *a batch of cookies. pl.* **batches.**

bath (bath) *n.* the washing of the whole body.

bathe (bāth) *v.* to take a bath. **bathing. bathed.**

bathing suit (ba′ thing sūt′) clothing worn for swimming.

bathrobe (bath′ rōb′) *n.* a loose piece of outer clothing, often worn before or after taking a bath.

bathroom (bath′ rūm′) *n.* a room with sink, toilet, and bathtub or shower.

bathtub (bath′ tub′) *n.* a large container in which to wash the body.

batter (bat′ ər) *n.* **1.** a mixture of eggs, flour, and milk, beaten together and cooked: *pancake batter.* **2.** a person who hits a ball with a bat.

⊖**battery** (bat′ ər ē) *n.* a container that produces electricity: *a car battery. pl.* **batteries.**

battle (batl) *n.* **1.** a fight between two armies. **2.** a hard struggle: *a battle against a storm at sea; a battle against a disease. v.* to have such a fight or struggle. **battling. battled.**

bawl (bȯl) *v.* to shout or cry loudly.

bay (bā) *n.* **1.** a part of an ocean or a lake partly enclosed by a big curve of land. **2.** the deep howl of a dog. *pl.* **bays.**

be (bē) *v.* to stay; to happen; to exist; to belong to a group. See the following words, all forms of the verb 'to be': **am, is, are, was, were, being, been.**
Note: **be** and its different forms are sometimes used along with other verbs.

beach (bēch) *n.* the flat shore of an ocean, lake, etc., either sandy or covered with pebbles. *pl.* **beaches.**

bead (bēd) *n.* **1.** a small piece of glass, metal, etc., in a necklace. **2.** any small, round thing, especially a drop of liquid: *a bead of rain on the window.*

beak (bēk) *n.* the hard, pointed part of a bird's mouth.

beam (bēm) *n.* **1.** a long piece of wood or metal. **2.** a small ray of light: *a sunbeam. v.* **1.** to shine. **2.** to smile broadly: *Dad beamed when I won the race.*

bean (bēn) *n.* **1.** a seed from a pod. Some beans can be eaten as a vegetable: *pork and beans.* **2.** the pod and beans together: *green beans.*

bear (ber) *n.* a very heavy, furry animal with a short tail: *a brown bear; a polar bear. v.* **1.** to carry or support: *The mule can bear heavy loads.* **2.** to put up with: *I cannot bear the pain.* **3.** to produce: *This tree bears many plums.* **bearing. bore** (bōr). I have **borne** (bȯrn).

beard (bird) *n.* the hair on a man's face except his eyebrows.

beast (bēst) *n.* a four-footed animal.

beat (bēt) *n.* **1.** a stroke made again and again: *the beat of the drums.* **2.** the rhythm in music. *v.* **1.** to keep on hitting: *We beat the dirt out of the rug.* **2.** to defeat or do better than another person or group: *We beat the other team by three goals.* **3.** to mix quickly: *to beat eggs.* **beating. beat.** I have **beaten.**

beautiful (byūt′ i fəl) *adj.* having beauty; lovely; very pretty.

beauty (byūt′ ē) *n.* **1.** great loveliness; a quality that gives much pleasure: *There is beauty in her flower garden.* **2.** a lovely person or thing: *That cat is a beauty! pl.* **beauties.**

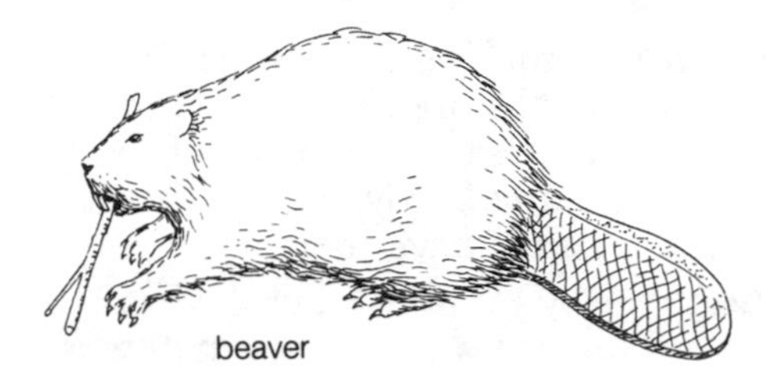
beaver

beaver (bē′ vər) *n.* a furry animal that is part of the rat family, with a broad tail and webbed feet. Beavers live on water as well as on land.

because (bi kȯz′) *conj.* for this reason: *Karen came back because it was raining hard.*

become (bi kum′) *v.* to come or grow to be: *Barbara wants to become a doctor.* **becoming. became** (bē kām′). I have **become.**

bed (bed) *n.* **1.** a piece of furniture to sleep or rest on. **2.** ground where flowers or vegetables are grown: *a bed of lettuce.* **3.** the bottom of an ocean, river, etc. **4.** a foundation layer: *The flagpole was fixed in a bed of cement.*

bedroom (bed′ rūm′) *n.* a room to sleep or rest in.

bee (bē) *n.* a flying insect that lives in groups and makes honey and wax.

beech (bēch) *n.* a tree with smooth, grey bark. *pl.* **beeches.**

⊖**beef** (bēf) *n.* meat from cattle.

beehive (bē′ hīv′) *n.* a hive or house where bees live.

been (bin, bēn) *v.* a form of the verb (to) **be**. 'Been' is always used with 'have', 'had', 'has', or 'having': *I have been shopping.*

beer (bir) *n.* an alcoholic drink made from malt and hops.

beet (bēt) *n.* a vegetable with a round, dark red root that can be eaten.

beetle (bētl) *n.* an insect with hard, shiny front wings that protect its thin back wings when they are not in use.

before (bi fôr′) *prep.* **1.** in front of: *Ted stood before the shop window.* **2.** earlier than: *I was here before school started.* *adv.* at some time in the past: *I have seen you before.*

beg (beg) *v.* **1.** to ask humbly for food or money: *The poor man was begging in the street.* **2.** to ask humbly for a favour: *I beg you to forgive me.* **begging. begged.**

beggar (beg′ ər) *n.* a poor person who lives by begging for food or money.

begin (bi gin′) *v.* to start. **beginning. began** (bi gan′). I have **begun** (bi gun′).

beginner (bi gin′ ər) *n.* someone who is just starting to learn something.

behave (bi hāv′) *v.* **1.** to act. **2.** to act in a good or proper way: *Behave as a thoughtful host when your cousins visit.* **behaving. behaved.**

behaviour, behavior (bi hāv′ yər) *n.* the way someone behaves or acts.

behind (bi hīnd′) *n.* *(informal)* the buttocks. *prep.* **1.** at the back of; to the rear of: *Stand behind me.* **2.** after; later than: *The bus was behind schedule because of the storm.* *adv.* **1.** not on time: *I am behind in my work.* **2.** at the back or rear: *The team came from behind to win the game.*

beige (bāzh) *n.* a light-brown colour. *adj.* having this colour.

being (bē′ ing) *n.* a living creature: *There is not a single being living on the moon.* *v.* a form of the verb (to) **be**: *He is being silly.*

belief (bi lēf′) *n.* something believed in; a strong view or attitude toward something: *It is my belief that tennis is a very good game.* *pl.* **beliefs.**

believable (bi lē′ vəbl) *adj.* able to be believed; easy to be believed: *Your story is believable because something like it happened to me.*

believe (bi lēv′) *v.* to think that something is true; to feel sure about something: *Donald believes that he can win the race.* **believing. believed.**

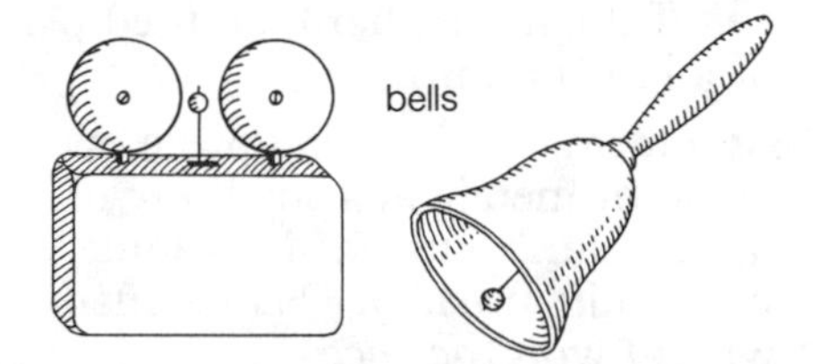

⊖**bell** (bel) *n.* an object shaped like an upside-down cup, which gives a ringing sound when it is struck.

bellow (bel′ ō) *v.* to shout or roar.

bellows (bel′ ōz) *n. pl.* an instrument used for blowing a stream of air into a fire to make it burn, or into the reeds of an organ or an accordion to produce sounds.

belly (bel′ ē) *n.* the lower part of the front of the body; the stomach. *pl.* **bellies.**

belong (bi long′) *v.* **1.** to be owned or possessed by: *That book belongs to Billy.* **2.** to be a member of: *Marg belongs to the music club.*

below (bi lō′) *prep.* under; beneath; lower than: *My apartment is one floor below yours.* *adv.* in or to a lower place: *From the roof, we saw the children playing below in the garden.*

belt (belt) *n.* **1.** a strap worn around the waist, usually made of leather or plastic. **2.** an area with distinct features: *a snow belt.*

bench (bench) *n.* **1.** a long seat, usually made of wood, stone, or metal: *Three of us sat on the bench in the park.* **2.** a work table: *a carpenter's bench. pl.* **benches.**

bend (bend) *n.* a curve: *a bend in the road. v.* **1.** to curve something: *to bend a wire.* **2.** to lean over: *to bend over your desk.* **bending. bent** (bent).

beneath (bi nēth′) *prep.* under; below; lower than: *beneath the tree.*

⊖**benefit** (ben′ ə fit) *n.* something that is helpful; an advantage: *A warm coat is a great benefit on a cold day. v.* to be of help to; to improve: *Sleep will benefit the exhausted traveller. The apprentice benefited from the older worker's advice.*

berry (ber′ ē) *n.* a small, juicy fruit: *a raspberry; a blackberry. pl.* **berries.**

beside (bi sīd′) *prep.* near; by the side of, next to: *The house is beside the river.*

besides (bi sīdz′) *prep.* other than; but; except: *Nobody came to the party besides my relatives. adv.* also; moreover: *The coat is pretty, and besides, it is warm.*

best (best) *adj.* the very finest: *This team is good, that team is better, and the third team is the best of all.*

bet (bet) *n.* a promise to give something to someone if he or she is right and you are wrong: *We made a bet on who would win the Stanley Cup. v.* to gamble that something will happen; to predict. **betting. bet.**

better (bet′ ər) *adj.* finer; worth more: *This ring is good; that one is better; the gold ring is the best of the three.*

between (bi twēn′) *prep.* **1.** one or the other: *Choose between the two pictures.* **2.** with another person: *Share the cake between you. adv.* in the middle of two people or things: *There is a distance of two metres between the chairs.*

beverage (bev′ ər ij) *n.* a liquid for drinking: *Milk, tea, water, and coffee are all beverages.*

beware (bi wer′) *v.* to be cautious or wary; to watch out for: *Beware of the bull!*

beyond (bi yond′) *prep.* **1.** farther than: *We went to the grocery store, which is beyond the school.* **2.** not within the ability or understanding of: *To walk into town from the farm is beyond my power; it is too far.*

⊖**bias** (bī′ əs) *n.* prejudice; a strong opinion for or against a person or thing. *pl.* **biases.**

bib (bib) *n.* a little cloth tied around a person's neck to stop food from falling on his or her clothes: *a baby's bib.*

Bible (bībl) *n.* **1.** the book of the sacred writings of the Christian and Jewish religions. **2. bible**, any book thought to contain complete information about a subject.

bicycle

bicycle (bī′ sikl) *n.* a two-wheeled vehicle; the rider uses his or her feet to turn pedals to make the bicycle move.

bid (bid) *n.* an offer of money for something, usually at an auction. *v.* to make an offer of money, usually at an auction: *I bid one dollar for that lamp.* **bidding. bid.**

big (big) *adj.* large: *a big cat; a bigger cat; the biggest cat on the street.*

bike (bīk) *n.* short for **bicycle.**

bilingual (bī ling′ gwəl) *adj.* **1.** able to speak two languages: *a bilingual secretary.* **2.** written in two languages: *a bilingual sign.* **3.** in Canada, able to speak and write the two official languages, English and French; written in English and French.

bill (bil) *n.* **1.** a printed notice of money that a person owes and has an obligation to pay: *Gino paid the gas bill.* **2.** a bird's beak; the hard part of a bird's mouth. **3.** a piece of paper money. *v.* to give or send a printed notice of money that is owed: *The store billed Nadia for the dress that she bought.*

ə**billiards** (bil′ yərdz) *n.pl.* a game played with hard balls on a green, cloth-covered table. The balls are hit with a long wooden stick called a **cue.**

billion (bil′ yən) *n., adj.* a thousand million (1 000 000 000).

bin (bin) *n.* a large box or other container: *a garbage bin; a bread bin; a grain bin.*

bind (bīnd) *v.* to tie or fasten together; to tie up; to wrap. **binding. bound** (baůnd).

ə**binoculars** (bi nok′ yu lərz) *n.pl.* two very small telescopes fastened side by side, used for looking at distant objects with both eyes.

biography (bī og′ rə fē) *n.* a written history of a person's life. *pl.* **biographies.**

biology (bī ol′ ə jē) *n.* the science of plant and animal life: *In biology, we study how living things grow and develop.*

birch (bûrch) *n.* a tree with smooth bark, often white, which peels off like paper. *pl.* **birches.**

bird (bûrd) *n.* a feathered animal that lays eggs, has wings and two legs, and is usually able to fly.

birth (bûrth) *n.* being born; coming into life or existence: *the birth of a baby; the birth of an idea.*

birth certificate (bûrth′ sûr tif′ i kit′) an official paper or card that shows the place and date of a person's birth and other information.

birthday (bûrth′ dā′) *n.* the day of the year on which someone or something was born. *pl.* **birthdays.**

biscuit (bis′ kit) *n.* a cracker; a thin, crisp cookie.

bison

bison (bī′ sən, bī′ zən) *n.* a North American wild animal related to cattle; a buffalo. *pl.* **bison.**

bit (bit) *n.* **1.** a small piece or amount: *a bit of cheese; a bit of time.* **2.** the metal part of a horse's bridle, held in its mouth. **3.** the removable part of a drill that makes holes. *v.* see **bite.**

bite (bīt) *v.* to take hold of, or cut off, with the teeth: *He bit off a piece of chocoloate.* **biting. bit** (bit). I have **bitten** (bit′ ən).

bitter (bit′ ər) *adj.* **1.** not sweet; having a sharp taste: *This medicine is bitter.* **2.** very cold: *a bitter wind.* **3.** angry and resentful: *We felt bitter about the large increase in our rent.*

black (blak) *n.* the darkest colour, opposite to white. *adj.* having this colour.

black-fly (blak′ flī′) *n.* a small, biting insect. *pl.* **black-flies.**

blacksmith (blak′ smith′) *n.* a person who makes things with iron, such as shoes for horses.

blade (blād) *n.* **1.** the flat, cutting part of a knife or sword. **2.** a long, thin leaf: *a blade of grass.*

⊖**blame** (blām) *n.* responsibility for something that is bad or wrong: *Fred took the blame for the damage.* *v.* to find fault with; to consider responsible for a mistake: *Yoko blamed her sister for making them late for the movie.* **blaming. blamed.**

blank (blangk) *n.* an empty space, usually to be filled in: *Put your name and address in the blanks on this insurance form.* *adj.* empty; not written on: *a blank page in the book.*

⊖**blanket** (blang′ kət) *n.* a heavy bed-cover.

blast (blast) *n.* **1.** a rush of air: *a blast of wind.* **2.** an explosion; a blowing up: *We heard a blast coming from the factory.* **3.** a loud sound: *a blast of trumpets.* *v.* to blow up, usually with explosives.

blast-off (blast′ of′) *n.* the sending off of rockets and missiles.

blaze (blāz) *n.* **1.** a bright fire throwing out flames. **2.** a brightly shining light. *v.* to burn or shine intensely. **blazing. blazed.**

bleach (blēch) *n.* something that makes an object white by taking out its colour: *laundry bleach.* *pl.* **bleaches.** *v.* to make clean or white: *We bleached the dirt out of the clothes.* **bleaching. bleached.** it **bleaches.**

bleachers (blēch′ ərz) *n.pl.* rows of seats placed one above another at outdoor games such as baseball or tennis: *The bleachers at the baseball game were full of people.*

bleat (blēt) *v.* to make a noise like a goat or sheep.

bleed (blēd) *v.* to lose blood. **bleeding. bled** (bled).

blend (blend) *v.* to mix with each other: *He blended the paints to make the right colour.*

⊖**bless** (bles) *v.* **1.** to wish health or happiness: *Bless you all!* **2.** to make sacred or holy. **3.** to ask God's aid or kindness towards: *Bless this happy marriage.* **blessing. blessed.** she **blesses.**

blessing (bles′ ing) *n.* **1.** a good wish. **2.** something that produces happiness: *This rain is a blessing to the farmers.* **3.** a prayer: *She said a blessing before the meal.*

blew see **blow.**

blind (blīnd) *adj.* unable to see; not having sight.

blink (blingk) *v.* to drop and raise the eyelids quickly: *She blinked in the bright light.*

blister (blis′ tər) *n.* a watery swelling under the skin: *The new shoes caused blisters on his feet.*

blizzard (bliz′ ərd) *n.* a heavy snowstorm with strong winds.

block (blok) *n.* **1.** a solid piece: *a block of ice.* **2.** an area of a town or city bounded by successive, intersecting streets: *Let us walk around the block.* **3.** any side of a block in a town or city: *The two children lived on the same block.* *v.* to get in the way of; to stop: *The stalled car is blocking traffic.*

⊖**blond** (blond) *adj.* having fair hair and a light skin.

blood (blud) *n.* the red liquid pumped through the body by the heart.

bloom (blūm) *n.* a flower; a blossom. *v.* to open up into a flower.

blossom (blos′ əm) *n.* a flower, usually of a fruit tree: *The apple tree is in blossom.* *v.* to open up into a flower.

blot (blot) *n.* a stain: *an ink blot.*

⊖**blouse** (blaủs, blaủz) *n.* a loose kind of shirt worn by women and girls.

blow (blō) *n.* **1.** a hard knock: *a blow with your fist.* **2.** a sudden, unhappy event: *Father's accident was a blow to us all.* *v.* **1.** to move along: *The wind blows.* **2.** to puff at: *to blow a match out.* **3.** to play a musical instrument using air from the lungs: *to blow a trumpet.* **4.** *(informal)* to melt an electrical fuse: *Don't use too many appliances at once—you might blow a fuse!* **blowing. blew** (blü). I have **blown** (blōn).
blow up **1.** to destroy with an explosion: *The car is on fire and may blow up.* **2.** to make a photograph larger. **3.** to add air to a tire, balloon, etc. **4.** to show strong anger: *Mother blew up when I arrived late for the wedding.*

blowtorch (blō′ tȯrch′) *n.* a small torch that sends out a hot flame. A blowtorch is often used to melt metal. *pl.* **blowtorches.**

blubber (blub′ ər) *n.* the fat of whales and some other sea animals. It is used for making oil.

⊖**blue** (blü) *n.* the colour of a clear, cloudless sky during the day. *adj.* **1.** having this colour. **2.** sad; not happy: *I'm blue because my best friend is sick. a bluer shirt; the bluest shirt of all.*

blueberry (blü′ ber′ ē) *n.* a small, round, blue berry. *pl.* **blueberries.**

bluebird (blü′ bûrd′) *n.* a small North American bird that has blue feathers on its back.

bluejay (blü′ jā′) *n.* a North American bird with bright blue feathers. *pl.* **bluejays.**

blueprint (blü′ print′) *n.* a construction plan for a building or a machine, usually showing white lines on blue paper.

blues (blüz) *n.pl.* **1.** sad feelings: *Rene has the blues because he didn't win the contest.* **2.** a type of slow, sad music.

blunt (blunt) *adj.* **1.** not sharp; having a dull edge: *a blunt knife.* **2.** frank and insensitive in speaking or writing: *Mr. Graham was blunt and told his cousin that she was a fool.*

blur (blûr) *v.* to make something hazy and not easy to see: *Mist blurred the view.* **blurring. blurred.**

blush (blush) *v.* to go red in the face because of shyness, excitement, or shame. **blushing. blushed.** he **blushes.**

boar (bȯr) *n.* a male pig.

dartboard

diving board

board (bȯrd) *n.* **1.** a long, thin piece of wood: *a floor board.* **2.** a flat piece of wood used for a certain reason: *a dart board; a diving board.* *v.* **1.** to enter a ship, train, or bus. **2.** to live somewhere, paying for food and a room: *They boarded at a house near school.*

boarder (bȯr′ dər) *n.* a person who pays for meals and a room at another person's home.

boarding house (bȯrd′ ing haůs′) a house where meals and rooms are provided in exchange for payment.

boast (bōst) *v.* to brag; to praise your own qualities, abilities, possessions, or deeds too much: *She boasted about being elected president.*

boastful (bōst′ fəl) *adj.* always boasting: *The boastful child told everyone how smart he was in arithmetic.*

boat (bōt) *n.* a small open ship, such as a rowboat.
in the same boat sharing similar circumstances, problems, etc.:

We're in the same boat; neither of us can operate this machine.
miss the boat to fail to take advantage of a good chance: *I missed the boat by not studying when I had free time; now I'm too busy to do it.*
rock the boat to disturb the usual state or condition: *Don't rock the boat by suggesting a change in our work hours.*

bob (bob) *n.* **1.** a small hanging object, such as the weight at the end of a pendulum. **2.** a cork or other floating object tied to a fishing line above the hook. *v.* to move up and down quickly and often: *The buoy bobbed up and down in the rough water.* **bobbing. bobbed.**

bobby pin (bob′ i pin′) a bent piece of strong wire, used to keep a girl's or a woman's hair in place.

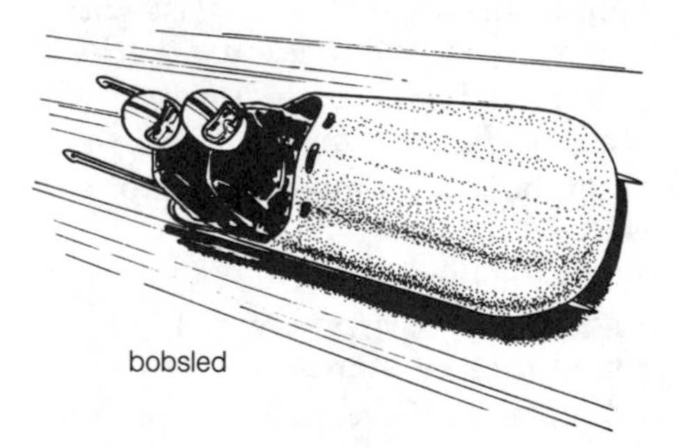
bobsled

bobsled (bob′ sled′) *n.* a long sled with two sets of runners, for sliding down snowy hills.

body (bud′ ē, bod′ ē) *n.* **1.** the whole of a person, other animal, or thing. **2.** the main part of an animal or thing; the trunk: *Bend your body from the hips.* **3.** a group of people, things, or ideas: *a body of soldiers.* **4.** a mass or grouping of matter: *Lake Winnipeg is a large body of water. The stars are heavenly bodies. pl.* **bodies.**

bog (bog) *n.* soft, wet ground; a marsh.

bog down (bog′ daun′) *v.* to get or become stuck: *I got bogged down in the work and didn't get home until late.* **bogging down. bogged down.**

boil (boil) *n.* a small, painful swelling on the skin. *v.* **1.** to heat a liquid until it bubbles and starts to make steam. **2.** to cook something in boiling water: *to boil potatoes.*

bold (bōld) *adj.* **1.** daring; having much courage: *a bold hunter.* **2.** bright or very clearly marked: *bold colours; bold lines.*

bologna (bə lō′ nē, bə lō′ nə) *n.* a large sausage, usually made of ground-up, smoked pork and beef.

bolt (bōlt) *n.* **1.** a sliding bar used to fasten a door or gate. **2.** a thick metal pin, like a screw without a point. **3.** a flash of lightning. **4.** a sudden run: *The prisoner made a bolt for the woods. v.* **1.** to close or fasten with a bolt. **2.** to make a sudden run: *The frightened squirrel bolted for its nest.*

⊖**bomb** (bom) *n.* a container filled with something that can explode, usually used as a weapon. *v.* to fight and attack with a bomb.

bombard (bom bärd′) *v.* **1.** to attack with shells or bombs. **2.** to overwhelm: *to bombard with work.*

⊖**bond** (bond) *n.* **1.** anything that binds, ties, or fastens: *This glue is a good bond.* **2.** a feeling that brings people close together: *There is a bond of friendship between Joe and Marie.* **3.** a certificate that promises to pay back money that has been borrowed: *a Canada Savings Bond.*

bone (bōn) *n.* one of the hard, white pieces that make up a skeleton.

bonus (bō′ nəs) *n.* something extra that is given: *In addition to his salary, George received a bonus of ten dollars. pl.* **bonuses.**

bony (bō′ nē) *adj.* made of bone; like a bone: *a bony tail; a bonier tail; the boniest tail of all.*

book (bu̇k) *n.* sheets of paper bound together for reading or for writing in: *a library book; a notebook.* *v.* to reserve space: *to book a hotel room; to book seats for next Thursday's hockey game.*

bookcase (bu̇k′ kās′) *n.* a piece of furniture with shelves for books.

bookkeeper (bu̇k′ kē′ pər) *n.* a person who keeps a record of money spent and money earned, usually for a business.

booklet (bu̇k′ lət) *n.* a small book, sometimes having a paper cover.

boom (būm) *n.* a deep, rumbling sound. *v.* to make such a sound.

boost (būst) *n.* *(informal)* a push from behind or a lift from below: *Please give me a boost so that I can climb the tree.* *v.* **1.** to give such a push or lift. **2.** to make larger; to raise: *The stores boosted the price of beef.*

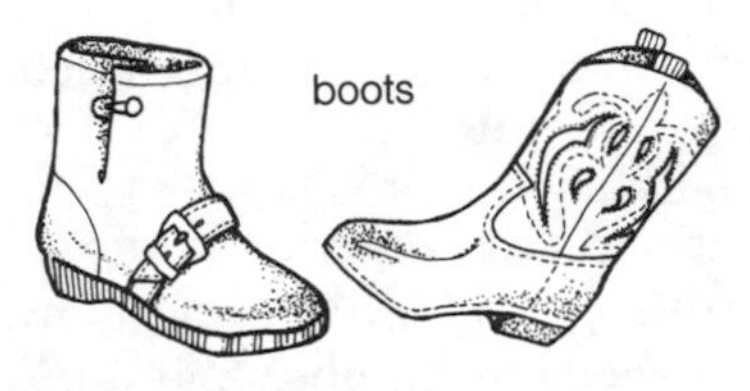

boot (būt) *n.* a leather, rubber, or plastic cover for the foot and ankle.

booth (būth) *n.* a place at a fair or market where things are shown or sold. *pl.* **booths** (būt͟hz).

border (bȯr′ dər) *n.* **1.** an outside edge: *a flower border around a lawn.* **2.** a boundary where two countries, provinces, states, etc., meet.

bore (bȯr) *n.* a person who makes someone tired, or no longer interested, by talking too much about dull things. *v.* **1.** see **bear.** **2.** to drill a hole. **3.** to make someone tired by dull talk. **boring. bored.**

born (bȯrn) *adj.* **1.** brought into life: *The baby was born last night.* **2.** natural: *Lois is a born leader.*

borne see **bear.**

borrow (bor′ ō, bōr′ ō) *v.* to take something for a while, promising to give it back later: *Val borrowed a pen from me.*

borscht (bȯrsht) *n.* a vegetable soup that usually contains beets and is served either hot or cold.

bosom (bu̇z′ əm, būz′ əm) *n.* **1.** the chest of a man or a woman. **2.** the breasts of a woman.

boss (bos) *n.* *(informal)* a leader; someone in charge. *pl.* **bosses.**

both (bōth) *adj., pron.* the two: *Both girls went fishing. They both caught trout.*

bother (bot͟h′ ər) *v.* to cause trouble; to annoy: *Flies bothered the people sitting in the park.*

bottle (botl) *n.* a container for liquids, usually made of glass with a narrow neck: *a medicine bottle.*

bottom (bot′ əm) *n.* the lowest section: *the bottom of the hill.*

bough (bau̇) *n.* a main branch of a tree.

bought see **buy.**

boulder (bōl′ dər) *n.* a very large, round rock or stone.

boulevard (bu̇l′ ə vȧrd′) *n.* a street, often a wide one.

bounce (bau̇ns) *v.* to throw or toss something so that it will come back: *She bounced the ball up and down in the driveway.* **bouncing. bounced.**

bound (bau̇nd) *n.* **1.** a leap: *The rabbit raced away in great bounds.* **2.** a limit; a boundary. *v.* **1.** to be the boundary of: *That fence bounds the east side of the ranch.* **2.** see **bind.**

out of bounds **1.** outside the area where people are allowed to go. **2.** outside the limits, as of a playing area: *The ball rolled out of bounds.*

boundary (baůn′ dər ē) *n.* anything marking a limit; a dividing line: *The river was the boundary between the two cities.* *pl.* **boundaries.**

bouquet (bō kā′, bū kā′) *n.* a bunch of picked flowers.

⊖**boutique** (bū tēk′) *n.* a small shop, often selling just one kind of item.

bow (baů) *n.* **1.** the front part of a ship. **2.** a bending forward of the body or head, to show respect. *v.* to bend forward to show respect: *The actors bowed to the audience at the end of the play.*

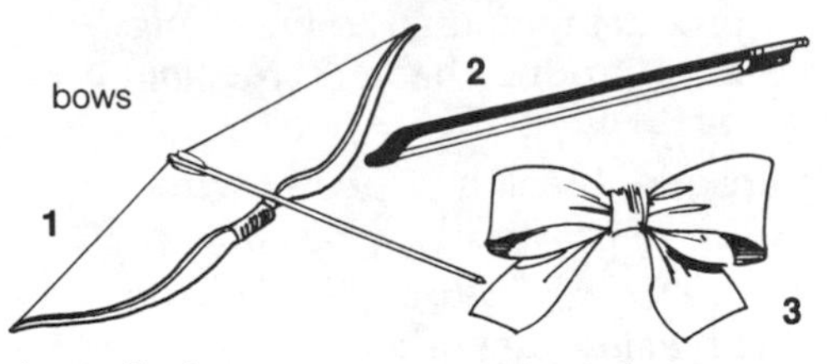

bow (bō) *n.* **1.** a weapon used to shoot arrows. **2.** a stick strung with horsehair, for playing a stringed instrument such as a violin. **3.** a ribbon tied in loops.

bowels (baů′ əlz) *n.pl.* the intestines; the tubes in the body that carry waste matter from the stomach.

bowl (bōl) *n.* a basin; a deep, round dish: *He served the cereal in a large bowl.* *v.* to play the sport of bowling.

bowling (bōl′ ing) *n.* a sport in which a ball is rolled at an object or a group of objects.

box (boks) *n.* a container with stiff sides and, usually, a cover: *a matchbox; a box of cookies.* *pl.* **boxes.** *v.* to fight, with gloves, another person for sport. **boxing. boxed.** he **boxes.**

boxer (bok′ sər) *n.* **1.** someone who fights for sport, using padded gloves. **2.** a kind of tall, brown dog.

boy (bȯi) *n.* a male child. *pl.* **boys.**

boycott (bȯi′ kot′) *n.* a refusal to buy, to use, or to participate: *the boycott of the 1980 Olympic Games by the United States.* *v.* to carry out such a refusal: *We boycotted the imported lettuce because it was too expensive.*

Boy Scouts (bȯi′ skaůts′) an organization for boys that teaches fitness, outdoor skills, and good character.

brace (brās) *n.* **1.** anything used as a support, to keep things in place: *The dentist put braces on my teeth so that they wouldn't grow crooked.* **2.** the part of a hand-powered drill that holds and turns the bit.

bracelet (brās′ lət) *n.* a piece of jewellery worn on the wrist.

brag (brag) *v.* to boast; to praise or talk highly about yourself. **bragging. bragged.**

braid (brād) *n.* a band formed by weaving together strands of hair, ribbon, rope, etc. *v.* to weave together such strands.

brain (brān) *n.* the grey mass that is inside the head of people and other animals: *The brain lets us think, feel, learn, move, and remember.*

brake (brāk) *n.* a piece of machinery, or a system of levers, for slowing or stopping a vehicle such as a bicycle, car, or train: *When the car would not stop, she realized the brakes were not working.*

bran (bran) *n.* the outer covering of wheat and other grains: *The bran is separated from the flour by sifting.*

⊖**branch** (branch) *n.* **1.** an arm of a tree growing out from the trunk; a bough. **2.** one of a group of stores or offices, but not the major one: *a branch of the bank.* *pl.* **branches.**

brand (brand) *n.* a certain make of product: *What is your favourite brand of orange juice?* *v.* to mark by burning the skin with hot metal: *The farmer branded the cattle.*

brand-new (brand′ nū′) *adj.* absolutely new; never used before: *Your running shoes are so white they must be brand-new!*

brass (bras) *n.* **1.** a yellow metal, made by melting copper and zinc together. **2.** certain musical instruments, such as the trumpet or trombone, made of metal.

⊖**brave** (brāv) *adj.* fearless; not afraid of pain or danger: *a brave deed; a braver deed; the bravest deed of all.*

bravery (brā′ vər ē) *n.* courage; fearlessness.

brawl (bròl) *n.* a noisy quarrel that turns into a fight.

bread (bred) *n.* a food made by shaping a mixture of flour, yeast, and water into a loaf and then baking it.

break (brāk) *v.* **1.** to split; to smash into pieces: *Don't break the cup!* **2.** to disobey: *Don't break the rules!* **3.** not to carry out: *Don't break a promise!* **breaking. broke** (brōk). I have **broken** (brō′ kən).
break down to stop working and need repairs: *The printing press broke down, so we can't publish the newspaper.*
break into to enter by force: *The burglars broke into our house.*
break up 1. to come to an end: *The meeting broke up at ten o'clock.* **2.** to bring a relationship to an end: *He broke up with his girl friend.*

breakable (brāk′ əbl) *adj.* easily broken; able to be broken: *Because the pottery dish is very thin, it is quite breakable.*

breakers (brā′ kərz) *n.pl.* large ocean waves that break into white foam.

breakfast (brek′ fəst) *n.* the first meal of the day, usually eaten in the morning.

breast (brest) *n.* **1.** the chest. **2.** the part of the body of a female mammal that can produce milk to feed her young.

breath (breth) *n.* air taken into and pushed out of the lungs.
out of breath puffing and panting after running or doing exercises.

breathe (brē<u>th</u>) *v.* to take air into and push it out of the lungs. **breathing. breathed.**

breed (brēd) *n.* a particular kind of animal: *Jerseys are a breed of cow, good for milking.* *v.* **1.** to raise animals for the purpose of producing young: *to breed pigs.* **2.** to produce babies. **breeding. bred** (bred).

breeze (brēz) *n.* a gentle wind.

breezy (brē′ zē) *adj.* windy: *a breezy day; a breezier day; the breeziest day of all.*

brew (brū) *v.* to make a drink by soaking and boiling: *To brew tea, add boiling water to the leaves.*

bribe (brīb) *n.* money or a gift offered to persuade someone to do something dishonest. *v.* to make such an offer. **bribing. bribed.**

brick (brik) *n.* a block of baked clay, used in building: *a brick house; a brick fireplace.*

bridal (brīd′ əl) *adj.* belonging to a bride: *the bridal gown.*

⊖**bride** (brīd) *n.* a woman on her wedding day.

bridegroom (brīd′ grūm′) *n.* a man on his wedding day.

bridesmaid (brīdz′ mād′) *n.* an unmarried woman who helps the bride at a wedding.

⊖**bridge** (brij) *n.* **1.** a road built over a river or valley so that people and vehicles may cross it. **2.** the bony top part of the nose. **3.** an attachment for false teeth. **4.** a card game played by two pairs of players.

bridle (brīdl) *n.* the part of a harness fitting over a horse's head.

brief (brēf) *adj.* short, usually in time: *a brief speech.*

bright (brīt) *adj.* **1.** shining; giving out much light: *a bright fire.* **2.** smart; intelligent: *Jean is a bright boy.* **3.** cheerful: *Her bright smile makes me feel happy.*

brighten (brī′ tən) *v.* to make or become bright or cheerful: *Frank's face brightened when he heard the good news.*

brilliant (bril′ yənt) *adj.* **1.** shining very brightly: *a brilliant diamond.* **2.** very smart: *a brilliant student.*

brim (brim) *n.* **1.** the edge of a cup or bowl: *The glass was full to the brim.* **2.** the edge of a hat.

bring (bring) *v.* **1.** to take along with; to carry with: *Pam brought her lunch when she went to work.* **2.** to take or carry to a person or place: *Please bring me a glass of water.* **bringing. brought** (brōt).
bring about to cause to occur: *The violent rainstorm brought about the flood.*
bring out to create or make for the use of others: *Car companies bring out new models every year.*
bring up **1.** to take care of during childhood: *They brought up a big family.* **2.** to vomit.

brink (bringk) *n.* the edge of the top of a high place: *We stood on the brink of the cliff.*

brisk (brisk) *adj.* quick; rapid: *We went for a brisk walk.*

bristle (brisl) *n.* a stiff, short hair: *the bristles of a toothbrush.*

British (brit′ ish) *adj.* having to do with Great Britain (England, Scotland, and Wales).

British Columbia (brit′ ish kə lum′ bi ə) the province with the Pacific Ocean on the west and Alberta on the east; its capital is Victoria. Short form: **B.C.** A person living in or born in British Columbia is a **British Columbian.**

brittle (britl) *adj.* easily snapped or broken: *Glass, china, and ice are all brittle.*

broad (brȯd) *adj.* very wide.
broad daylight full daylight.

broadcast (brȯd′ kast′) *v.* to spread news, especially by radio or television: *The news was broadcast at ten o'clock.* **broadcasting. broadcast.**

broccoli (brok′ ə lē) *n.* a large, dark green vegetable with flower heads that can be eaten.

brochure (brō shůr′) *n.* a thin book or pamphlet with information about a certain subject: *The travel brochure described places to visit in the city.*

broil (brȯil) *v.* to cook something at a very high temperature, either over or under the heat.

broke (brōke) *adj.* *(informal)* having no money: *I'm broke. Can you lend me a dollar?* *v.* see **break.**

bronco (brong′ kō) *n.* a western pony, often partly wild. *pl.* **broncos.**

bronze (bronz) *n.* a metal made by melting copper and tin together.

⊖**brooch** (brōch) *n.* a piece of jewellery fastened to clothing by a pin. *pl.* **brooches.**

brood (brūd) *n.* **1.** a group of birds that all hatched together. **2.** young animals that have the same parents. *v.* to worry about something in a quiet, moody way: *Don't brood over your lost ring. We'll find it.*

brook (brůk) *n.* a small stream of water.

broom (brūm) *n.* a long-handled brush used for sweeping.

broth (broth) *n.* **1.** a thin, watery soup. **2.** the liquid in which meat, vegetables, or other food has been cooked.

brother (bruth′ ər) *n.* a man or boy who has the same parents as another person.

brought see **bring.**

brow (braů) *n.* the forehead; the part of the face above the eyes.

brown (braůn) *n.* the colour of chocolate or the earth. *adj.* having this colour.

Brownie (braůn′ ē) *n.* a junior Girl Guide.

brownie (braůn′ ē) *n.* a small chocolate cake.

bruise (brūz) *n.* a mark on the skin, caused by a fall or from being hit.

brunch (brunch) *n.* a meal eaten in place of breakfast and lunch, often including foods from both meals. *pl.* **brunches.**

brush (brush) *n.* a cluster of hairs fastened to a handle for cleaning, grooming, or painting: *a clothes brush; a paint brush. pl.* **brushes.** *v.* **1.** to clean, groom, or paint with a brush: *Brush your teeth.* **2.** to touch lightly: *Lee brushed my shoulder as he walked by.* **brushing. brushed.** she **brushes.**

Brussels sprouts (brus′ əl spraůts′) very small, green, cabbage-like vegetables.

bubble (bubl) *n.* a thin balloon of liquid filled with air: *a soap bubble.*

buck (buk) *n.* **1.** a male deer, goat, rabbit, or antelope. **2.** *(informal)* a dollar.

bucket (buk′ ət) *n.* a large pail with a handle, used for holding liquids.

buckle (bukl) *n.* a clasp on a belt or shoe. *v.* to close or fasten with a buckle. **buckling. buckled.**

bud (bud) *n.* a young growth on a plant stem that will grow into a leaf, flower, or branch.

buddy (bud′ ē) *n.* *(informal)* a very close friend. *pl.* **buddies.**

budge (buj) *v.* to move slightly or a little bit: *The television program was so interesting that Yves would not budge from his chair.* **budging. budged.**

budget (buj′ ət) *n.* a plan for spending or earning money in a period of time: *Our budget for the trip is two hundred dollars. The prime minister announced the country's budget for next year.* *v.* to make a plan for spending or earning money.

budgie (buj′ ē) *n.* a small bird, with colourful markings, usually kept in a cage.

buffalo (buf′ ə lō′) *n.* a large, wild, North American animal related to cattle. *pl.* **buffalo.**

⊖**buffet** (bu fā′) *n.* **1.** a meal at which guests serve themselves from large plates on a table and then sit in groups. **2.** a cabinet, usually in a dining room, for holding tablecloths, glasses, etc.

bug (bug) *n.* **1.** any insect: *Bees, flies, and ants are all bugs.* **2.** *(informal)* a germ causing a disease: *a flu bug.*

buggy (bug′ ē) *n.* a light carriage with one seat. *pl.* **buggies.**

build (bild) *v.* to make or construct something by joining different parts together. **building. built** (bilt).

builder (bil′ dər) *n.* a person who builds things, especially houses.

building (bil′ ding) *n.* something built, usually with four walls and a roof, to hold people or things.

⊖**bulb** (bulb) *n.* **1.** an underground bud that looks like an onion: *Tulips, lilies, daffodils, and onions all grow from bulbs.* **2.** a rounded, bulb-shaped object: *a light bulb.*

bulge (bulj) *v.* to swell out or curve outwards: *The apple made her pocket bulge.* **bulging. bulged.**

bulk (bulk) *n.* **1.** the main part: *Lee did the bulk of the work when we moved.* **2.** largeness in size or mass: *the bulk of a farm tractor.* **in bulk** loose; not in a package: *We bought the candy in bulk.*

bulky (bul′ kē) *adj.* large and sometimes a little hard to handle: *a bulky sweater; a bulkier one; the bulkiest sweater on the rack.*

bull (bủl) *n.* the male of cattle.

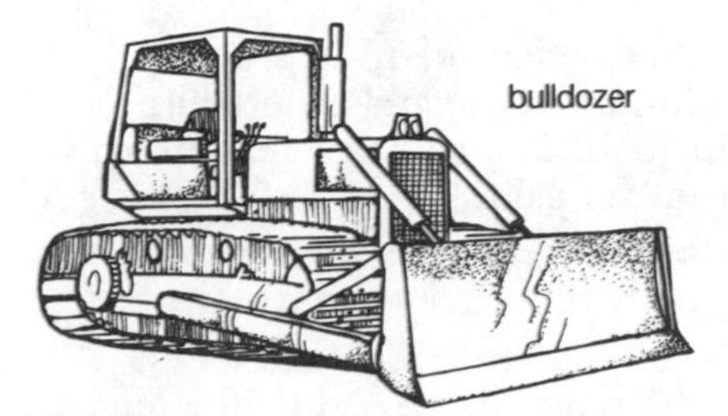

bulldozer (bủl′ dōz′ ər) *n.* a powerful tractor that moves soil and rocks.

bullet (bủl′ ət) *n.* a piece of metal fired from a rifle or revolver.

⊖**bulletin** (bủl′ ə tin) *n.* a brief announcement of recent, important information: *TV programs are sometimes interrupted by news bulletins.*

bulletin board (bủl′ ə tin bȯrd′) a board hung on a wall and used to display pictures, notes, etc.

bully (bủl ē) *n.* someone who frightens and hurts a smaller or weaker person. *pl.* **bullies.**

bum (bum) *n.* **1.** *(informal)* a tramp; a person who has no permanent home or job and travels about. **2.** *(informal)* the buttocks.

bump (bump) *n.* **1.** a sudden knock or jolt: *The plane landed with a bump.* **2.** a swelling or lump that may come from a sudden blow: *Bob got a bump on his head where the hockey puck hit him.* *v.* to knock into or against something: *The tall woman bumped her head when she stood up.*

bumper (bum′ pər) *n.* a metal or rubber bar at the front or back of a car.

bumpy (bum′ pē) *adj.* causing or full of bumps: *a bumpy ride on a bumpy road; a bumpier ride; the bumpiest ride of all.*

bun (bun) *n.* a sweet roll; a round type of bread.

bunch (bunch) *n.* a group of things of the same kind, kept together: *a bunch of bananas.* *pl.* **bunches.**

bundle (bundl) *n.* a number of objects that are tied or wrapped together: *a bundle of rags.* *v.* to tie or wrap things together. **bundling. bundled.**

bungalow (bung′ gə lō′) *n.* a house that has all rooms on the ground floor.

bunk (bungk) *n.* a narrow bed or beds set against a wall, usually one above the other.

buoy (bȯi, bū′ ē) *n.* a floating object, used to guide swimmers or ships away from danger.

burden (bûr′ dən) *n.* **1.** a heavy load, often one carried by an animal. **2.** a duty that is difficult to perform: *It is a burden for Anna to work, to go to school, and to take care of her family.*

⊖**bureau** (byūr′ ō) *n.* **1.** a piece of furniture with drawers; a dresser. **2.** a business office or agency: *an employment bureau; a travel bureau.*

burglar (bûr′ glər) *n.* someone who breaks into a house to steal.

burglary (bûr′ glər ē) *n.* breaking in and stealing. *pl.* **burglaries.**

burial (ber′ i əl) *n.* putting a dead body in a grave, tomb, the sea, etc., often as part of a funeral.

buried, buries see **bury.**

burn (bûrn) *n.* **1.** an injury to the skin caused by fire or heat. **2.** any mark on cloth, wood, etc., caused by fire or heat. *v.* to be or to set on fire.

burr (bûr) *n.* a prickly part of some plants: *The burrs stuck to Phil's coat as he walked through the woods.*

burst (bûrst) *v.* **1.** to blow up: *The balloon burst with a loud bang.* **2.** to break: *The water pipe burst because of the cold weather.* **3.** to enter or leave suddenly: *Paul burst into the room.* **bursting. burst.**

bury (ber′ ē) *v.* **1.** to cover up and hide: *The squirrel buried the nuts under some leaves.* **2.** to place a dead body in the ground or the sea. **burying. buried.** he **buries.**

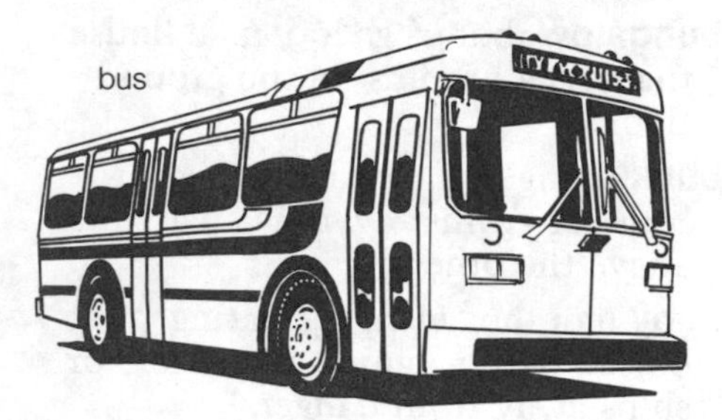
bus

bus (bus) *n.* a large motor vehicle with seats for passengers. *pl.* **buses.**

bush (bu̇sh) *n.* **1.** a shrub; a small tree with many branches. **2.** the forest: *The lumberjack went into the bush to cut trees. pl.* **bushes.**
beat around the bush to talk about something in a general way in order to avoid the main point.

bushy (bu̇sh′ ē) *adj.* looking like a bush; thick like a bush: *a bushy tail; a bushier tail; the bushiest tail of all.*

busily (biz′ i lē) *adv.* in a busy way.

business (biz′ nəs) *n.* **1.** an occupation; a person's work: *Mr. and Mrs. Shin have a printing business.* **2.** something that a person looks after and attends to: *It is my business to take care of the dog. pl.* **businesses.**

busy (biz′ ē) *adj.* **1.** hard at work; having a lot to do: *Shirley was busy; Andy was busier; Sheila was the busiest of all.* **2.** full of motion and activity: *a busy street.* **3.** referring to a telephone line that is in use: *I tried to telephone home, but the line was busy.*

but (but, bət) *conj.* **1.** though: *I will go, but I do not want to.* **2.** except: *Everyone but Simone saw the movie.*

butcher (bu̇ch′ ər) *n.* **1.** a person who kills cattle and other animals for food. **2.** a person who cuts up meat for sale.

butler (but′ lər) *n.* a male servant, usually the head servant.

butt (but) *n.* the thick end of something, or the end that is left: *a cigarette butt.*
butt in to interrupt; to take part in someone else's conversation or activities without being asked.

butter (but′ ər) *n.* a yellowish fat, separated from milk or cream by churning. *v.* to spread butter on something, such as a slice of bread.

butterfly (Monarch)

butterfly (but′ ər flī′) *n.* an insect with large, brightly coloured wings. *pl.* **butterflies.**

buttermilk (but′ ər milk′) *n.* the sour liquid and solids left after butter has been made from cream or milk.

butterscotch (but′ ər skoch′) *n.* a candy made from butter and brown sugar.

buttocks (but′ əks) *n.pl.* the two round, fleshy parts of the body that a person sits upon.

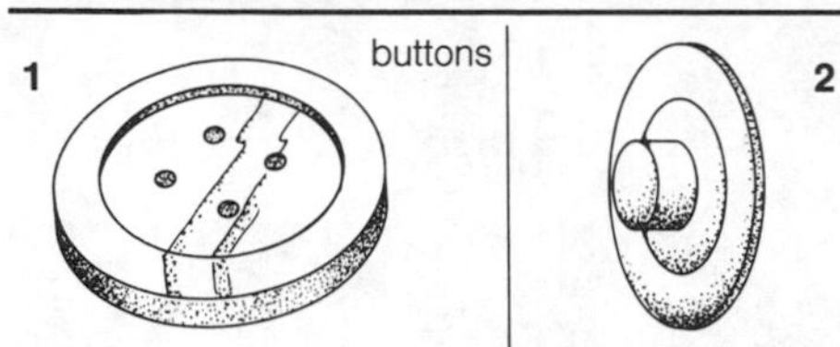

button (but′ ən) *n.* **1.** a flat piece of metal, plastic, bone, etc., stitched to a person's clothes, to hold parts of them together. **2.** a round knob that is pressed or turned to make a machine work: *David pushed the button to start the press.* *v.* to close with buttons.

buy (bī) *v.* to get something by exchanging money for it. **buying. bought** (bȯt). she **buys.**

buzz (buz) *n.* the humming sound made by a fly or bee. *pl.* **buzzes.** *v.* to make such a sound.

buzzer (buz′ ər) *n.* an electrical button that makes a buzzing noise.

by (bī) *prep.* **1.** at the side of: *He stood by the door.* **2.** because of someone's action or efforts: *It was painted by me.* **3.** earlier than: *Finish it by Tuesday.* **4.** with the use of: *We travelled by train.* *adv.* past: *She walked by on her way to the store.*

'bye see **good-bye.**

bylaw (bī′ lȯ′) *n.* a rule made by a town, city, club, etc.

by-pass (bī′ pas′) *n.* a road going around a city or town. *pl.* **by-passes.**

C

cab (kab) *n.* **1.** a car and driver that can be hired, usually for short trips: *a taxicab* **2.** the part of a truck or van where the driver sits.

cabbage (kab′ ij) *n.* a large, round vegetable with thick green leaves.

⊖**cabin** (kab′ in) *n.* **1.** a wooden hut. **2.** a small room in a ship.

⊖**cabinet** (kab′ i nit) *n.* **1.** a piece of furniture with drawers. **2.** a group of ministers, almost always Members of Parliament, who help the prime minister to govern.

cable (kābl) *n.* **1.** a strong steel rope: *The ship was tied to the dock with a cable.* **2.** a bundle of wires used to carry electric power or telephone messages.

cable television (kābl′ tel′ ə vizh′ ən) a system in which television programs are carried over wires. Cable television offers programs on special channels to people who pay for this service.

caboose (kə būs′) *n.* a railway car at the back of a freight train, where the crew works.

cackle (kakl) *n.* the screeching noise made by a hen, or a noise like it: *the witch's cackle.* *v.* to make such a sound. **cackling. cackled.**

cactus (kak′ təs) *n.* a very prickly type of plant that grows in the desert. *pl.* **cacti,** or **cactuses.**

⊖**cadet** (kə det′) *n.* a person in training to be an officer.

⊖**café** (ka fā′) *n.* **1.** any small restaurant. **2.** a coffee shop; a place that serves only beverages and snacks.

cafeteria (kaf′ ə tir′ i ə) *n.* a place to eat where people serve themselves. *pl.* **cafeterias.**

caffeine (kaf ēn′) *n.* a stimulating drug found in coffee.

cage (kāj) *n.* a box with wires or metal bars, used to hold a bird or animal.

⊖**cake** (kāk) *n.* **1.** a baked mixture of flour, butter, eggs, sugar, and other things **2.** a flat lump: *a cake of soap; a cake of mud.*

calculate (kal′ kyə lāt′) *v.* to work with numbers (add, subtract, multiply or divide) to obtain a result; to compute: *Gary calculated the number of days to his birthday.* **calculating. calculated.**

calculation (kal′ kyə lā shən) *n.* the act, process, or result of calculating.

calculator

⊖**calculator** (kal′ kyə lā′ tər) *n.* a machine that can add, subtract, multiply, divide, etc.

calendar (kal′ ən dər) *n.* a list of the days, weeks, and months of the year.

calf (kaf) *n.* **1.** the young of a cow, elephant, whale, and some other animals. **2.** the back of a person's leg, below the knee. *pl.* **calves** (kavz).

call (ċol) *n.* **1.** a shout: *a call for help.* **2.** an attempt to reach someone by telephone: *We made a call to our family in Europe.* *v.* **1.** to shout. **2.** to name: *We called our dog 'Tiger'.* **3.** to telephone: *The house is on fire. Call the fire department!*

calm (kȧm) *adj.* **1.** quiet; without wind: *a calm day.* **2.** not excited: *A calm police officer directed heavy traffic.*

came see **come.**

camel (kam′ əl) *n.* a desert animal with one or two humps on its back.

⊖**camera** (kam′ ə rə) *n.* a machine used for taking photographs or making movies. *pl.* **cameras.**

camouflage (kam′ ə flȧzh′) *n.* something that makes a person, creature, or thing seem to be part of its surroundings. *v.* to disguise something so that it blends in with the surroundings: *The squirrel camouflaged its nest by covering the entrance with branches and leaves.* **camouflaging. camouflaged.**

⊖**camp** (kamp) *n.* a number of tents, cabins, or campers grouped together. *v.* to stay and sleep out of doors.

⊖**campaign** (kam pān′) *n.* several actions organized for a certain purpose, such as an election. *v.* to organize or work on a campaign: *We helped Mr. Wong campaign for mayor.*

camper (kam′ pər) *n.* **1.** a person who stays at a camp for recreation. **2.** a vehicle, also equipped as a dwelling, used by people for camping.

campfire (kamp′ fīr′) *n.* an outdoor fire.

campus (kam′ pəs) *n.* the buildings and land that make up a school, college, or university. *pl.* **campuses.**

⊖**can** (kan) *n.* a metal container: *a can of beans.* *v.* **1.** to seal food or drink in cans or jars. **canning. canned.** **2.** a verb placed before another verb to mean 'be able to': *She can skate very well. I could finish the job if I had more time.* **could** (ku̇d).

Canada goose (kan′ ə də gūs′) a large, wild, North American goose.

Canadian (kə nā′ di ən) *n.* a person who is a citizen of Canada. *adj.* having to do with Canada.

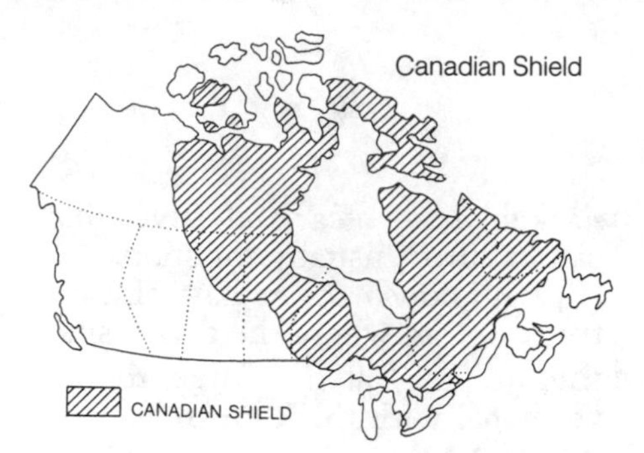

Canadian Shield (kə nā′ di ən shēld′) a large area rich in minerals, surrounding Hudson Bay. The Canadian Shield covers almost half of Canada's land area.

⊖**canal** (kə nal′) *n.* a waterway that has been dug across land: *Boats and barges travel through canals.*

canary (kə ner′ ē) *n.* a yellow songbird, usually kept in a cage. *pl.* **canaries.**

⊖**cancel** (kan′ səl) *v.* **1.** to stop something that has been arranged: *They cancelled the concert planned for next month.* **2.** to cross out so as to make invalid: *to cancel a postage stamp on an envelope; a cancelled cheque.* **cancelling. cancelled.**

cancer (kan′ sər) *n.* a disease that usually causes a harmful growth in the body.

candidate (kan′ di dāt′) *n.* a person who seeks or is nominated for an elected office, a job, or an award: *Three candidates want to be our Member of Parliament.*

candle (kandl) *n.* a stick of wax with a wick in it, burned to give light.

candy (kan′ dē) *n.* something sweet to eat, usually made with sugar and flavouring. *pl.* **candies.**

⊖**cane** (kān) *n.* **1.** the hard, springy stem of a bamboo or sugar plant. **2.** a stick that is used to help a person walk.

cannot (kan′ ot, ka not′) *v.* to be unable to: *We cannot see through the fog.*

canoe

canoe (kə nū′) *n.* a very light, narrow boat, moved with a paddle.

can't (kant) short for **cannot.**

cantaloupe (kan′ tə lōp′) *n.* a melon that has sweet, juicy, orange-coloured flesh.

Canuck (kan uk′) *n.* *(informal)* a Canadian.

canvas (kan′ vəs) *n.* a strong cloth used for shoes, tents, and sails.

canyon (kan′ yən) *n.* a steep valley.

⊖**cap** (kap) *n.* **1.** a soft hat with a peak. **2.** a lid for a bottle. *v.* to cover with a cap: *to cap a bottle.* **capping. capped.**

capable (kā′ pəbl) *adj.* able to do something well: *Franco is a very capable writer.*

capacity (kə pas′ ə tē) *n.* **1.** the amount of space in a room, cup , bowl, etc.: *What is the seating capacity of the auditorium?* **2.** ability: *She has the capacity to become a doctor. pl.* **capacities.**

⊖**cape** (kāp) *n.* **1.** an overcoat that has no sleeves and fastens around the neck. **2.** a piece of land sticking out into a body of water such as a lake or an ocean.

capital (kap′ ə təl) *n.* **1.** a city where the government meets: *Ottawa is Canada's capital. Victoria is British Columbia's capital.* **2.** any letter of the alphabet written in its large form: *A, B, and C are capitals.* **3.** money or property owned by a business or individual, especially when used to produce more wealth: *My son has enough capital to open his own store.*

capsize (kap′ sīz) *v.* to overturn: *The canoe capsized in the rough water.* **capsizing. capsized.**

⊖**capsule** (kap′ səl) *n.* **1.** a small container: *a medicine capsule.* **2.** the front part of a rocket, usually used to carry people, equipment, etc.

captain (kap′ tən) *n.* a person who leads a team or group: *the captain of a hockey team; the captain of a ship.*

capture (kap′ chər) *v.* to take by force and hold: *to capture a runaway steer.* **capturing. captured.**

⊖**car** (kȧr) *n.* a vehicle on wheels, usually an automobile.

caramel (kar′ ə məl, kȧr′ məl) *n.* a candy made from sugar, cream, and butter.

carbon paper (kȧr′ bən pā′ pər) paper with a dark coating on one side, used to make copies by transferring the coating to another surface under the pressure of writing or typewriter keys.

carburetor (kȧr′ bə rā′ tər) *n.* the part of an engine where air and gasoline are combined in an explosive mixture to power the engine: *the carburetor of an automobile.*

⊖**card** (kȧrd) *n.* **1.** a piece of stiff paper, often with a printed message: *a birthday card.* **2.** one of a set of pieces of stiff paper, marked with figures and numbers, used in games such as bridge or poker. **3. cards** any of several games, such as poker or bridge, played with a deck of cards.

cardboard (kȧrd′ bȯrd′) *n.* a thick kind of stiff paper, used for making boxes.

cardinal (kȧr′ də nəl) *n.* **1.** a high-ranking member of the Roman Catholic clergy, next in line to the pope. **2.** a bright red songbird.

care (ker) *n.* **1.** worry; trouble: *Steve sang happily, without a care in the world.* **2.** close, serious attention: *Work with care when you use that sharp knife.* *v.* to feel concerned about: *I do not care what he says.* **caring. cared.**
care for 1. to look after; to be concerned with: *Jane cared for my cat while I was away.* **2.** to like or enjoy: *I like to drink milk, but I don't care for tea.*
take care to be cautious or careful: *Take care that you don't burn your hand on the radiator.*
take care of to look after: *to take care of a sick friend.*

career (kə rēr′) *n.* long-term work; a profession: *a career in teaching.*

careful (ker′ fəl) *adj.* cautious; taking care: *Always be careful when using matches.*

careless (ker′ ləs) *adj.* not taking care; not cautious.

caretaker (ker′ tāk′ ər) *n.* someone who looks after a building; a janitor.

⊖**cargo** (kȧr′ gō) *n.* freight; goods carried by ship, truck, plane or train. *pl.* **cargoes.**

Caribbean (kə rib′ ē ən, kar′ ə bē′ ən) *adj.* having to do with the Caribbean Sea or the Caribbean islands: *Jamaica, Barbados, and Trinidad are some Caribbean countries.*

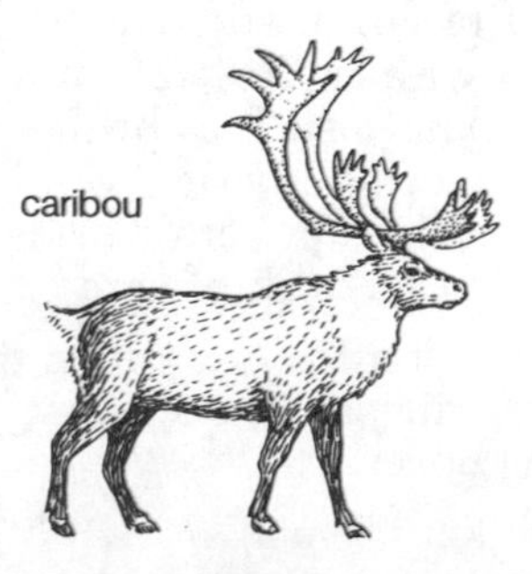
caribou

caribou (kar′ ə bū′) *n.* a North American reindeer. *pl.* **caribou.**

carnation (kȧr nā′ shən) *n.* a sweet-smelling garden flower, often white, yellow, pink, or red.

⊖**carnival** (kȧr′ nə vəl) *n.* an event with games, rides, food, etc.

carol (kar′ əl) *n.* a song of joy, such as a Christmas carol.

carpenter (kȧr′ pən tər) *n.* a person who makes and repairs wooden furniture and the wooden parts of buildings.

carpentry (kȧr′ pən trē) *n.* the work that a carpenter does.

⊖**carpet** (kȧr′ pət) *n.* a thick fabric covering for floors and stairs.

carriage (kar′ ij) *n.* **1.** a vehicle pulled by one or several horses. **2.** a small wagon for a baby, pushed by someone. **3.** a movable part of a machine that holds another part: *the carriage of a typewriter.*

carrot (kar′ ət) *n.* a plant with a long, orange root that is eaten as a vegetable.

carry (kar′ ē) *v.* **1.** to take something from one place to another. **2.** to stock in a store for sale: *The grocery store carries a large selection of vegetables.* **carrying. carried.** she **carries.**
carry away to be moved emotionally: *I was so carried away by the sad song that I cried.*
carry on to continue doing something: *Though her brother tried to interrupt, Lina carried on with her story.*
carry out to do; to make happen: *Please carry out my wishes.*

⊖**cart** (kȧrt) *n.* a wagon used to carry things: *a shopping cart.* *v.* to haul or carry with effort.

⊖**carton** (kȧr′ tən) *n.* a cardboard box.

cartoon (kȧr tūn′) *n.* **1.** a funny drawing. **2.** a short, funny movie made with drawings.

cartridge (kȧr′ trij) *n.* **1.** a case in a gun that holds the gunpowder and bullet. **2.** a small case: *a film* *cartridge; a tape cartridge; a stereo cartridge.*

carve (kȧrv) *v.* **1.** to cut wood or stone into a shape. **2.** to cut meat into slices. **carving. carved.**

⊖**case** (kās) *n.* **1.** a box or container in which to keep things: *a pencil case, a jewel case.* **2.** an example: *The traffic accident was a case of careless driving.* **3.** a condition: *He has a case of chicken pox.* **4.** the facts about a matter presented in a court of law: *The lawyer presented her client's case to the judge.*
in any case whatever happens: *Rain or shine, I'll go in any case.*
in case if it should happen: *Take your coat in case it rains.*

⊖**cash** (kash) *n.* money in the form of coins or bank notes: *The teller in the bank handles lots of cash.* *v.* to get money from a bank or other place: *Marlene cashed her cheque at the bank.* **cashing. cashed.** she **cashes.**

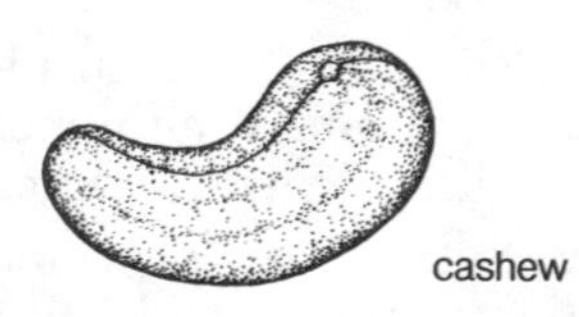
cashew

cashew (kash′ ū) *n.* a sweet, curved nut.

cashier (kash ēr′) *n.* a person in charge of money, usually in a bank or store.

cash register (kash′ rej′ is tər) a machine used in a store to hold money and to add up the number and cost of things that are sold.

⊖**casserole** (kas′ ə rōl′) *n.* **1.** a covered dish in which food is baked and served. **2.** the food prepared in such a dish.

cassette (kə set′) *n.* a cartridge for photographic film or magnetic tape.

cast (kast) *n.* **1.** a plaster support, used to protect broken bones while they are mending. **2.** the actors in a play, program, or movie. **3.** something made by pouring a soft material into a mould and letting it harden: *A cast of a horse and rider stood in the centre of the park.* **4.** the mould used in such a process. *v.* **1.** to throw: *Fred cast his fishing line into the river.* **2.** to choose actors for a play, program, or movie. **3.** to shape by placing a soft material in a mould and letting it harden: *to cast a metal engine part.* **casting. cast.**
cast a ballot to vote in an election.

castle (kasl) *n.* a palace.

casual (kazh′ ů əl) *adj.* **1.** for everyday use: *casual clothes.* **2.** happening without much planning: *a casual visit.*

cat (kat) *n.* **1.** a small, furry animal, with short ears, long whiskers, and claws, kept as a pet. **2.** a member of the cat family: *Lions, tigers, and leopards are large, wild cats.*

catalogue, catalog (kat′ ə log′) *n.* a list of things: *a catalogue of books in a library; a department store catalogue.*

catastrophe (kə tas′ trə fē′) *n.* a sudden and terrible disaster, such as an airplane crash or a violent earthquake.

catch (kach) *v.* **1.** to seize something and hold it: *to catch a ball.* **2.** to wait for and enter: *to catch a bus.* **3.** to become ill with: *to catch a cold.* **catching. caught** (kȯt). he **catches.**
catch fire to begin to burn.
catch on to understand: *Did you catch on to the way the machine works?*
catch up to come from behind and be even with: *She caught up to the runner.*

catcher (kach′ ər) *n.* in baseball, the player who stands behind home plate.

catching (kach′ ing) *adj.* contagious; able to be passed from one person to another: *Be careful; her illness is catching.*

category (kat′ ə gȯr′ ē) *n.* a group of things that share a certain quality: *Roses, daisies, and tulips are part of the flower category.* *pl.* **categories.**

cater (kā′ tər) *v.* to provide food, drink, and other services for a party: *The restaurant catered my brother's wedding.*

caterpillar (kat′ ər pil′ ər) *n.* the worm-like larva of a butterfly or moth.

cathedral (kə thē′ drəl) *n.* the main church of a large district.

catsup see **ketchup.**

cattle

cattle (katl) *n.* bulls, cows, and steers.

caught see **catch.**

cauliflower (kȯl′ i flaů′ er) *n.* a vegetable that has a head of small, hard, white flowers that are edible.

caulk (kȯk) *v.* to fill up a crack or joint so that it will not leak: *Bob caulked the spaces around the window frame so that heat wouldn't escape from the room.*

cause (kȯz) *n.* **1.** a person or thing that makes something happen: *Careless smoking was the cause of the fire.* **2.** a worthy organization or subject to which people devote themselves, often by giving time or money: *the cause of world peace.* *v.* to start something happening: *The boys caused a fire by playing with matches.* **causing. caused.**

⊖**caution** (kȯ′ shən) *n.* **1.** care or attention in doing something: *Handle this box of eggs with caution.* **2.** a warning. *v.* to warn of danger: *The guard cautioned us not to touch the animals in the cage.*

cautious (kȯ′ shəs) *adj.* careful; watching for danger: *a cautious driver.*

⊖**cave** (kāv) *n.* a large hole in a cliff or hillside.
cave in to collapse; to fall in or down: *The cabin caved in when the avalanche struck it.*

cavern (kav′ ərn) n. a large cave.

cavity (kav′ i tē) *n.* a hollow place: *a cavity in a tooth.* *pl.* **cavities.**

cease (sēs) *v.* to stop; to come to an end: *The audience ceased talking when the orchestra began to play.* **ceasing. ceased.**

cedar (sē′ dər) *n.* an evergreen tree with spreading branches and fragrant wood.

ceiling (sē′ ling) *n.* **1.** the inside top surface of a room. **2.** an upper limit: *a ceiling on wage increases.*

⊖**celebrate** (sel′ i brāt′) *v.* to mark or honour an occasion by doing something special: *to celebrate a birthday.* **celebrating. celebrated.**

celebration (sel′ i brā′ shən) *n.* a happy event in honour of someone or something.

celery (sel′ ə rē) *n.* a vegetable with long, green, leafy stems.

cell (sel) *n.* **1.** a small unit of life: *All animals and plants are made of cells.* **2.** a small room in a prison. **3.** the part of a battery where energy is produced.

cellar (sel′ ər) *n.* a room below the surface of the ground, often used for storing things.

cello (chel′ ō) *n.* a musical instrument with strings; it is larger than a violin and is held between the knees. *pl.* **cellos.**

Celsius (sel′ sē əs) *adj.* a scale on which to measure temperature; °C is the symbol. Water boils at one hundred degrees Celsius and freezes at zero degrees Celsius.

⊖**cement** (sə ment′) *n.* **1.** a grey powder made with clay and other ingredients. Cement is mixed with water and used for building sidewalks, holding bricks together, etc. **3.** any soft material that becomes hard and is used to make things stick together: *plastic cement.*

cemetery (sem′ ə ter′ ē) *n.* a place where the dead are buried. *pl.* **cemeteries.**

census (sen′ səs) *n.* an official counting of the population in a country or other area. *pl.* **censuses.**

⊖**cent** (sent) *n.* a Canadian or American coin, one-hundredth of a dollar.

centimetre (sen′ tə mi′ tər) *n.* a measure of length; **cm** is the symbol. 100 cm is equal to 1 m.

⊖**central** (sen′ trəl) *adj.* **1.** at or near the centre: *I work in the central part of the city.* **2.** most important: *Pierre works in the central office of the insurance company.*

centre, center (sen′ tər) *n.* **1.** the middle point. **2.** a place or person around which attention or activity is concentrated: *a centre of industry.* **3.** in some sports, the person who has the middle position of the playing area. *v.* to put in the middle. **centring. centred.**

century (sen′ chə rē) *n.* one hundred years. *pl.* **centuries.**

ceramics (sə ram′ iks) *n. pl.* **1.** the art or process of making pots, tiles, dishes, etc. out of clay and then hardening them by baking. **2.** articles made by this.

cereal (sēr′ i əl) *n.* **1.** corn, rice, wheat, and other grains used for food. **2.** a breakfast food made from any of these grains.

ceremony (ser′ ə mō′ nē) *n.* a formal occasion that can be either happy or sad: *a wedding ceremony; a funeral ceremony; a graduation ceremony. pl.* **ceremonies.**

certain (sûr′ tən) *adj.* **1.** sure; free from doubt: *Are you certain he will be there?* **2.** special; particular: *I am looking for a certain kind of dog, one that is friendly.*

certainly (sûr′ tən lē) *adv.* without doubt; surely: *I will certainly be there.*

certificate (sûr tif′ i kət) *n.* a signed document stating that something is true: *a birth certificate.*

⊖**chain** (chān) *n.* a number of rings or links joined together in length. *v.* to fasten with a chain: *The dog was chained to the tree.*

⊖**chair** (cher) *n.* a seat with a back, for one person.

chairperson (cher′ pûr′ sən) *n.* a person who is the leader of a committee or a meeting.

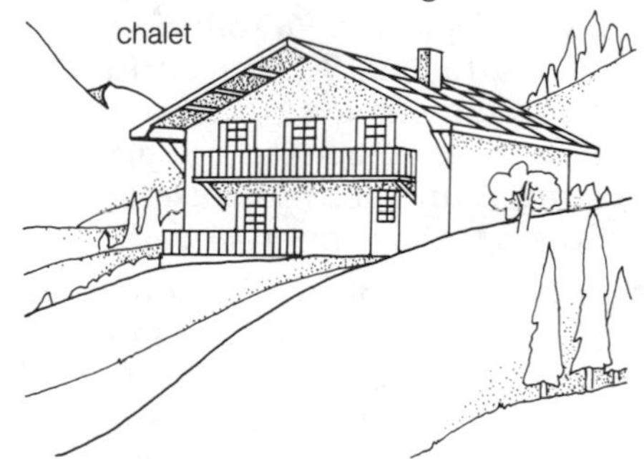

chalet (shal ā′) *n.* a cabin with wide, overhanging eaves, often built in snowy areas: *a ski chalet.*

chalk (chȯk) *n.* **1.** a soft white stone, seen in some cliffs. **2.** a marking stick made from this stone, used for writing on chalkboards.

chalkboard (chȯk′ bȯrd) *n.* a smooth surface used for drawing or writing on with chalk.

challenge (chal′ ənj) *n.* a task or goal that requires a special skill or effort: *It is a challenge for me to try to swim across the lake.* *v.* to dare someone to compete in a contest or game: *Pete challenged Esther to a game of checkers.* **challenging. challenged.**

champion (cham′ pi ən) *n.* the winner of a contest or game: *The tennis champion received a gold cup.*

chance (chans) *n.* **1.** an opportunity: *He has a good chance of getting that job.* **2.** the possibility of something happening: *There is a chance that I will join you.*
by chance with luck: *It was only by chance that Kate found her lost wallet.*

⊖**change** (chānj) *n.* **1.** difference: *There is no change in the weather; it is still hot.* **2.** money that is returned when the amount given is more than the amount owed: *Al bought the fifty-cent container of milk with a dollar bill and received fifty cents change.* **3.** loose coins. *v.* **1.** to become or make different: *The supervisor changed the hours of our work shift.* **2.** to exchange; to replace: *I changed my shoes because it was snowing.* **changing. changed.**

channel (chan′ əl) *n.* **1.** a long, narrow stretch of water joining two larger bodies of water: *The English Channel joins the North Sea and the Atlantic Ocean.* **2.** a course or route through which something may be moved. **3.** a frequency range given to a TV or radio station.

chap (chap) *n.* *(informal)* a man or boy: *He is a nice chap.* *v.* for skin to be rough and cracked: *My lips become chapped in the cold weather.* **chapping. chapped.**

chapel (chap′ əl) *n.* a small church or part of a large church.

chapter (chap′ tər) *n.* **1.** a section of a book, usually given a number. **2.** the local branch of an organization.

character (kar′ ik tər, kar′ ak ter) *n.* **1.** the nature of a person; what he or she is like: *Tim has a good character; he is honest and helpful.* **2.** a person in a book, movie, play, etc.

charcoal (chȧr′ kōl′) *n.* a black substance, made of partly burned wood, used in artists' pencils and as a fuel, filter, or absorbent.

⊖**charge** (chȧrj) *n.* **1.** money to be paid: *There is no charge to visit the museum.* **2.** an amount of electric current. **3.** an attack, as by soldiers. **4.** an explosive put into a gun or other weapon. **5.** a formal accusation, as by the police: *a charge of theft.* *v.* **1.** to put a price on something: *The store charged two dollars for the ice cream.* **2.** to buy items with a credit card: *Will you pay cash or will you charge the groceries?* **3.** to fill with electricity: *to charge a battery.* **4.** to attack or rush at: *The hockey team charged their opponents.* **5.** to blame or accuse formally: *The officer charged him with careless driving.* **charging. charged.**
in charge of taking care of: *Robert is in charge of the baby while Mother is out.*

charge account (chȧrj′ ə kaůnt′) a system that allows customers to buy things now and pay for them later.

charity (char′ i tē) *n.* **1.** help and kindness shown to people, such as giving money to the poor. **2.** an organization created for this purpose. *pl.* **charities.**

Charlottetown (shȧr′ lət taůn′) *n.* the capital city of Prince Edward Island.

charm (chȧrm) *n.* **1.** a magic spell. **2.** an object that is supposed to bring good fortune: *a lucky charm.* **3.** a pleasant manner: *a child of great charm.* *v.* **1.** to put under a magic spell. **2.** to delight someone: *Pam's laugh always charms her friends.*

charred (chȧrd) *adj.* scorched; blackened with fire: *charred wood.*

chart (chȧrt) *n.* a large piece of paper, such as a map, with information on it.

charter (chȧr′ tər) *n.* an official paper that lists certain rights, responsibilities, and privileges. *v.* to lease or hire a bus, plane, boat, etc., for a special purpose: *The school chartered a bus for the trip to the zoo.*

⊖**chase** (chās) n. a running or riding after: *a car chase through the city.* *v.* to run after or ride after: *The dog chased the fire engine.* **chasing. chased.**

⊖**chat** (chat) *n.* a friendly, informal talk between people. *v.* to talk in an easy, friendly way. **chatting. chatted.**

chatter (chat′ ər) *n.* constant and sometimes silly talk. *v.* to talk in such a way.

⊖**chauffeur** (shō fər′, shō′ fer) *n.* a person paid to drive a car.

cheap (chēp) *adj.* not costing much.

cheat (chēt) *n.* someone who swindles others or is dishonest. *v.* to swindle someone; to be dishonest.

⊖**check** (chek) *n.* **1.** a mark to show that something is correct: ✓. **2.** a review to make sure that something is correct. **3.** a restaurant bill. **4.** someone or something that holds back action. **5.** a pattern of small squares. *v.* **1.** to examine carefully to make sure everything is correct: *She checked the car before leaving on the trip.* **2.** to stop someone or something; to hold back. **3.** to leave for safekeeping: *Check your coat at the door.*
check in to register at a hospital, hotel, or motel.
check on to try to find out more about: *Check on whether dinner will be late tonight.*
check out **1.** to pay for and leave a room in a hospital, hotel, or motel. **2.** to add up and pay for purchases, especially in a grocery store. **3.** to investigate: *Alice checked out the new clothes in the store.*

checkers (chek′ ərz) *n. pl.* a game played with red and black pieces on a board of sixty-four squares.

checkup (chek′ up) *n.* a thorough examination: *a checkup by a doctor; a car's checkup by a mechanic.*

cheek (chēk) *n.* the side of a person's face below each eye.

cheer (chēr) *n.* a shout of joy or encouragement: *The crowd gave a cheer for the baseball team.* *v.* to shout joy or encouragement: *They cheered when the team scored a goal.*
cheer up to make someone feel happier: *I was feeling lonely, but your visit cheered me up.*

cheerful (chēr′ fəl) *adj.* happy; bright: *Mrs. Lopez is cheerful because her sister is visiting from Mexico.*

cheese (chēz) *n.* a solid or creamy food made from milk solids: *a ham and cheese sandwich.*

⊖**chef** (shef) *n.* a cook, usually the head cook in a restaurant.

chemical (kem′ i kəl) *n.* a substance used in chemistry.

chemist (kem′ ist) *n.* a person who studies chemicals and uses them to make substances, such as dyes and medicines.

chemistry (kem′ is trē) *n.* the science of the structure and other qualities of any substance:

Chemistry shows us how substances can be mixed to make new substances.

cheque (chek) *n.* a written order to a bank to pay money to someone from the writer's account.

cherry (cher′ ē) *n.* a small, round, red fruit with a hard pit inside. *pl.* **cherries.**

chess

chess (ches) *n.* a game played with black and white pieces on a board of sixty-four squares.

chest (chest) *n.* **1.** a large, strong box. **2.** the top front part of the body, around the ribs.

chesterfield (ches′ tər fēld′) *n.* a long couch with a back and arms.

chestnut (ches′ nut) *n.* **1.** the brown nut of the chestnut tree. **2.** a reddish-brown colour. *adj.* having this colour.

chew (chū) *v.* to use the teeth to crush or grind food.

chick (chik) *n.* a very young bird, especially a young chicken.

chicken (chik′ ən) *n.* a hen or rooster.

chicken pox (chik′ ən poks′) *n.* a contagious disease. A person with chicken pox develops a rash and fever.

chief (chēf) *n.* the leader of a group. *adj.* main; most important: *His chief job was to replace the broken window.*

child (chīld) *n.* **1.** a young boy or girl. **2.** a son or a daugher: *The Li family has four children.* *pl.* **children.**

chili (chil′ ē) *n.* **1.** a dried seed from red pepper, used to make foods hot and spicy. **2.** a stew made with meat, tomato sauce, beans, and hot spices. *pl.* **chilies.**

chill (chil) *n.* a cold feeling, with shivering. *v.* to make cold.

chilly (chil′ ē) *adj.* uncomfortably cold: *a chilly day; a chillier day; the chilliest day of the week.*

chime (chīm) *n.* a kind of bell. *v.* for bells to ring, or for a clock to ring the hour. **chiming. chimed.**

⊖**chimney** (chim′ nē) *n.* a long, hollow structure that lets smoke escape from a fireplace or furnace. *pl.* **chimneys.**

chimpanzee (chim′ pan zē′, chim pan′ zē) *n.* a kind of African ape. It lives in trees and is smaller than a gorilla.

chin (chin) *n.* the part of the face below the mouth.

china (chī′ nə) *n.* fine, delicate dishes made from clay.

Chinese (chī nēz′) *n.* the language spoken in China. *adj.* belonging to or coming from China.

chinook (shi nůk′) *n.* a warm winter wind that blows across parts of western Canada.

chip (chip) *n.* **1.** a small piece that is broken or cut off: *When the carpenter finished building the chair, she swept up the wood chips.* **2. chips** *(informal)* potato chips or French fries. *v.* to break off a small piece: *I chipped the plate when I dropped it.* **chipping. chipped.**

chipmunk

chipmunk (chip′ mungk) *n.* a small animal, like a squirrel, only striped.

chirp (chûrp) *n.* the short squeak of some birds and insects: *the chirp of sparrows. v.* to make such a noise.

chisel (chiz′ əl) *n.* a tool with an edge used for cutting and shaping wood or stone. *v.* to use such a tool. **chiselling. chiselled.**

chocolate (chok′ ə lət, chok′ lət) *n.* a food made from cacao seeds and used in candy, cake, and drinks.

choice (chȯis) *n.* **1.** the selecting of something: *It is hard to make a choice because I like everything.* **2.** the thing chosen: *Vanilla ice cream is my choice.*

choir (kwīr) *n.* a group of trained singers, especially one that sings in a church.

choke (chōk) *n.* a device that reduces the flow of air to the carburetor of a gasoline engine. *v.* **1.** to have trouble breathing properly: *Carl choked when a piece of apple stuck in his throat.* **2.** to block or check: *Weeds choked the vegetables in the garden. Sara choked back her anger.* **choking. choked.**
choke up to be so full of emotion that speech is difficult: *I was choked up when I heard of his death.*

choose (chūz) *v.* to select or decide: *I choose this piece of cake.* **choosing. chose** (chōz). I have **chosen** (chōz′ ən).

chop (chop) *n.* a small piece of meat joined to a bone: *a pork chop. v.* to cut with sharp blows: *to chop down a tree.* **chopping. chopped.**

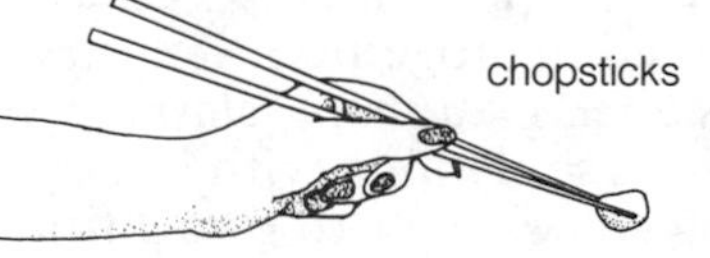

chopsticks (chop′ stiks′) *n.* two long, narrow sticks, held between the thumb and fingers and used for eating.

chore (chȯr) *n.* a task: *Drying the dishes is one of my daily chores.*

chorus (kȯr′ əs) *n.* **1.** a group of people singing together. **2.** the part of a song that is repeated. *pl.* **choruses.**

chose see **choose.**

christening (kris′ ən ing) *n.* the ceremony of baptizing a baby.

Christmas (kris′ məs) *n.* the yearly festival held on December 25, to honour the birth of Jesus Christ. *pl.* **Christmases.**

chrome (krōm) *n.* short for **chromium**, a hard, shiny metal that does not rust: *Many automobiles have chrome on their bumpers.*

chubby (chub′ ē) *adj.* plump; a little overweight: *a chubby baby; a chubbier baby; the chubbiest baby of all.*

chuckle (chukl) *n.* a quiet laugh. *v.* to laugh quietly. **chuckling. chuckled.**

chum (chum) *n.* *(informal)* a close friend; a pal.

chunk (chungk) *n.* a thick piece: *a chunk of meat for the dog.*

church (chûrch) *n.* a building where people meet for religious worship. *pl.* **churches.**

churn (chûrn) *n.* a container in which cream is shaken or beaten to make butter. *v.* **1.** to shake or beat cream into butter. **2.** to move with a beating motion.

⊖**chute** (shūt) *n.* a narrow passage through which objects may pass: *a garbage chute.*

cider (sī′ dər) *n.* the juice of apples, used as a drink or to make vinegar.

cigar (si gär′) *n.* rolled tobacco leaves, used for smoking.

cigarette (sig′ ə ret′, sig′ ə ret′) *n.* shredded tobacco rolled in a paper tube, used for smoking.

⊖**cinders** (sin′ dərz) *n.pl.* partly burned pieces of wood or coal left after a fire.

cinema (sin′ ə mə) *n.* a theatre that shows motion pictures. *pl.* **cinemas.**

cinnamon (sin′ ə mən) *n.* a spice used to flavour cakes and other food.

circle (sûrkl) *n.* a perfectly round ring. *v.* **1.** to move around in a circle: *The airplane circled above the airport before landing.* **2.** to draw a circle around: *to circle an answer on an exam.* **circling. circled.**

circuit (sûr′ kət) *n.* **1.** a moving around: *the moon's circuit of the earth.* **2.** the complete path of an electric current.

circular (sûr′ kyə lər) *n.* a letter, advertisement, or notice sent to a number of people: *We received a circular about the sale at the store.* *adj.* in the shape of a circle.

circulate (sûr′ kyə lāt′) *v.* to move around: *to circulate blood through the body; to circulate news in the office.* **circulating. circulated.**

circumference (sər kum′ fə rəns) *n.* **1.** the boundary line of a circle. **2.** the distance around an object: *the circumference of a tree.*

circumstances (sûr′ kəm stans′ əz) *n. pl.* the facts connected to an event, such as the time or the place: *What were the circumstances of the accident?*

circus (sûr′ kəs) *n.* a travelling show with clowns, acrobats, animals, etc. *pl.* **circuses.**

citizen (sit′ i zən) *n.* a member of a nation, by birth or by choice.

citizenship (sit′ i zən ship′) *n.* the status of being a citizen, including certain rights and responsibilities.

citrus fruit (sit′ rəs frūt′) lemons, limes, oranges, grapefruit, and tangerines.

city (sit′ ē) *n.* a very large town; a place where many people live and work. *pl.* **cities.**

city hall (sit′ ē hȯl′) the building where the government of a city meets.

civil servant (siv′ əl sûr vənt) a person who works in a government department: *Letter carriers are civil servants.*

claim (clām) *n.* **1.** a demand for something as a right: *We filed a claim with the insurance company for the cost of the car repairs.* **2.** a statement that something is true. *v.* **1.** to say that a person has a right to something, that it belongs to him or her: *Rita claimed the glove that I found.* **2.** to state that something is true.

clams

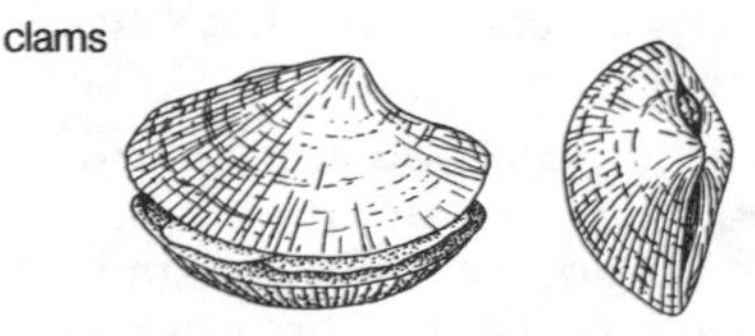

clam (klam) *n.* a shellfish that lives in sand.

clamp (klamp) *n.* a piece of metal or plastic equipment that holds parts together firmly. *v.* to fasten with this or a similar piece of equipment.

clap (klap) *n.* **1.** a slapping together of the hands. **2.** a quick and unexpected noise: *a clap of thunder.* *v.* **1.** to slap the hands together. **2.** to slap lightly and in a friendly way: *to clap someone on the shoulder.* **clapping. clapped.**

clarinet (klar′ ə net′) *n.* a musical wind instrument, shaped like a tube.

clasp (klasp) *n.* a hook, used to hold something together: *Her purse was fastened by a metal clasp.* *v.* **1.** to fasten something with a clasp. **2.** to hug someone or to give a firm handshake.

class (klas) *n.* **1.** a group of students who are taught together. **2.** a number of persons, animals, or things that are alike in one or more ways: *People and apes belong to the class called 'mammals'.* *pl.* **classes.**

classroom (klas′ rūm′) *n.* a room in which school classes are held.

clatter (klat′ ər) *n.* a sharp, rattling sound: *the clatter of dishes.* *v.* to make such a sound.

claw (klȯ) *n.* the hooked nail of a bird and some other animals. *v.* to tear at something with claws: *The tiger clawed at the meat.*

clay (klā) *n.* a smooth, sticky kind of earth, which can be moulded when wet and then hardened: *Bricks and pottery are made of clay.*

clean (klēn) *adj.* **1.** free from dirt; neat and tidy: *a clean room.* **2.** thorough; complete: *Our team had a clean victory in the game; we won by over twenty points.* *adv.* completely; thoroughly: *I threw the ball clean across the field.* *v.* to free from dirt: *Please clean the floor; your shoes are covered with mud.*
clean out to remove the contents; to empty: *The cat cleaned out its dish of milk.*
clean up to tidy; to remove a mess: *Who will clean up after lunch?*

cleaner (klēn′ ər) *n.* **1.** a substance that removes dirt: *He sprayed oven cleaner into the stove.* **2.** a person who cleans certain things: *She took her stained dress to the cleaners.*

cleanser (klenz′ ər) *n.* a substance that can clean: *a bathtub cleanser.*

clear (klēr) *adj.* **1.** bright and cloudless: *a clear sky.* **2.** easily seen, heard, or understood: *We heard every word because she has a clear voice.* **3.** easily seen through: *clear glass.* *v.* **1.** to become bright and cloudless: *After the storm, the sky cleared.* **2.** to clean up: *At the end of the day, Al cleared his desk.*
clear out to leave or go away.
clear up **1.** to make or become better: *The sky cleared up after the storm.* **2.** to explain: *Yvon cleared up the question of his absence.*

cleaver (klē′ vər) *n.* a tool with a heavy blade and a short handle, used for chopping meat.

clergy (klûr′ jē) *n.pl.* people trained to teach religion and lead religious services.

clerical (kler′ i kəl) *adj.* having to do with clerks: *Filing is a clerical job.*

⊖**clerk** (klûrk) *n.* **1.** a salesperson in a store. **2.** an office worker who looks after files and does other jobs.

clever (klev′ ər) *adj.* quick at learning; able to do things well.

click (klik) *n.* a sharp, little sound: *the click of a camera.* *v.* to make such a sound.

client (klī′ ənt) *n.* a customer; a person who receives service from a professional person.

cliff (klif) *n.* a high, steep rock face, especially where land meets sea.

climate (klī′ mət) *n.* the kind of weather that a place usually has.

climb (klīm) *v.* **1.** to move upwards: *to climb the stairs, to climb a hill.* **2.** to rise steeply: *The airplane climbed in the sky.*

cling (kling) *v.* to hold fast to: *The little raccoon clung to its mother.* **clinging. clinged** or **clung** (klung).

clinic (klin′ ik) *n.* a place where a person can see a dentist or doctor for treatment and not have to stay overnight.

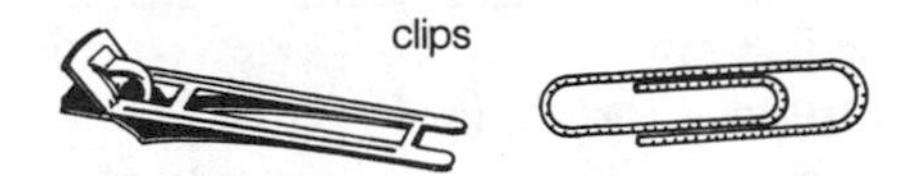

clip (klip) *n.* a fastener: *a hair clip; a paper clip.* *v.* to trim with scissors or shears: *to clip a hedge.* **clipping. clipped.**

clipper (klip′ ər) *n.* **1.** a tool used for cutting: *a hair clipper.* **2.** a large, fast sailing ship, once used for carrying goods across the ocean.

cloak (klōk) *n.* a cape; a coat without sleeves.

clock (klok) *n.* a machine that tells the time. *v.* to measure the speed at which something happens: *to clock a runner's sprint.*

clockwise (klok′ wīz′) *adj., adv.* the direction in which a clock's hands move: *Turn the wheel clockwise.*

clog (klog) *v.* to choke or block: *Grease clogged the pipe, and water would not go down the sink.* **clogging. clogged.**

close (klōz) *v.* **1.** to shut: *Close the door, please!* **2.** to come to an end: *The meeting will close at 10 p.m.* **closing. closed.**
close in to approach; to surround: *We closed in on the runaway bull.*

close (klōs) *adj.* **1.** having strong ties of loyalty and affection: *Robert and I are close friends; Anne and I are closer; Joe is my closest friend.* **2.** almost equal: *The game was close, but our team won by one point.* *adv.* near; not far from: *The bird flew close to the trees.*

closely (klōs′ lē) *adv.* carefully: *Muriel examined the photograph closely.*

closet (kloz′ ət) *n.* a small room for storing things such as towels, clothes, or sheets.

cloth (kloth) *n.* fabric woven from thread such as cotton, wool, silk, nylon, or linen: *a dish cloth.*

clothes (klōz, klō<u>th</u>z) *n.* garments; items that people wear, such as dresses, coats, ties, jackets, shirts, or jeans.

clothing (klō<u>th</u>′ ing) *n.* clothes.

cloud (klaůd) *n.* **1.** a white or grey mass floating in the sky, made up of tiny water drops. **2.** anything like a cloud: *a cloud of smoke.* *v.* to cover over; to make hazy.

cloudy (klaůd′ ē) *adj.* **1.** filled with clouds: *a cloudy sky; a cloudier sky; the cloudiest sky of all.* **2.** not transparent; not very clear: *cloudy water; a cloudy TV picture.*

clover (klō′ vər) *n.* a meadow plant with leaves in three or sometimes four parts.

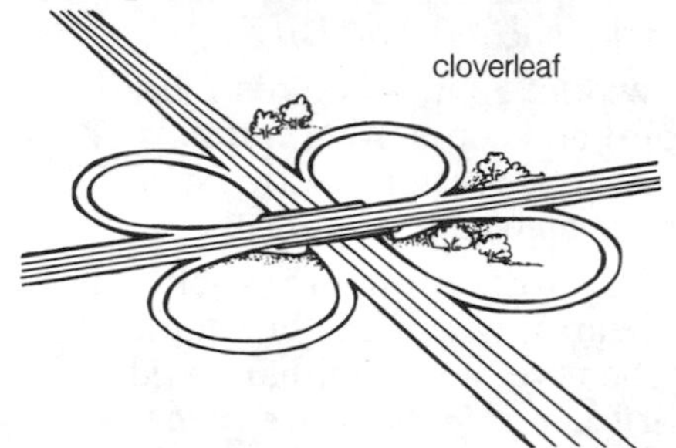

cloverleaf (klō′ vər lēf′) *n.* a road crossing that is in the shape of a four-leaf clover. A cloverleaf is built so that vehicles may move from one highway to another without having to cross in front of other traffic. *pl.* **cloverleaves** (klō′ vər lēvz′).

clown (klaůn) *n.* a circus performer who makes everyone laugh with jokes and tricks. *v.* to act like a clown.

⊖**club** (klub) *n.* **1.** a thick stick used as a weapon. **2.** a stick with a special head for hitting a ball: *a golf club.* **3.** a group of people who meet to enjoy some interest together: *a hiking club.* **4.** a playing card with one or more ♣ marks on it. *v.* to hit with a club. **clubbing. clubbed.**

cluck (kluk) *v.* to make a noise like a hen.

clue (klū) *n.* some small thing that helps in solving a mystery or answering a riddle or puzzle.

clump (klump) *n.* a number of flowers, trees, or other plants growing together.

clumsy (klum′ zē) *adj.* awkward in moving about; not always good at holding or carrying things. *You are* *clumsy, but I am clumsier. He is the clumsiest of all.*

clung see **cling.**

cluster (klus′ tər) *n.* a bunch; a group: *a cluster of grapes.*

clutch (kluch) *n.* a device in a car and other machines that makes it possible to connect or disconnect the parts that supply or carry power. *pl.* **clutches.** *v.* **1.** to grab. **2.** to hang on to: *The baby clutched his mother's hand.* **clutching. clutched.** he **clutches.**

clutter (klu′ tər) *n.* a collection of things left lying about in an untidy way: *There is so much clutter on the table that I can't find my keys. v.* to fill or cover with such a collection of things.

coach (kōch) *n.* **1.** a large, closed, four-wheeled carriage pulled by horses. **2.** a railway car. **3.** someone who trains a sports team. *pl.* **coaches.** *v.* to train someone for a sport, or to prepare someone for a test. **coaching. coached.** she **coaches.**

coal (kōl) *n.* a hard, black mineral used as fuel.

coarse (kȯrs) *adj.* **1.** rough: *coarse sandpaper; coarse wool.* **2.** not fine; composed of large particles: *coarse sand.* **3.** crude, unrefined, inferior: *a coarse person; a coarser person; the coarsest person of all.*

coast (kōst) *n.* the seashore. *v.* to travel along in an easy manner: *The boat coasted on the waves. The sled coasted down the hill.*

coat (kōt) *n.* **1.** a warm outer garment with sleeves and either buttons or a zipper down the front. **2.** the natural outer covering of an animal: *Our dog has a shiny coat.* **3.** a covering: *a coat of paint on a wall. v.* to cover with a layer of paint, varnish, etc.

coax (kōks) *v.* to persuade gently, using kind words: *We had to coax the puppy to come to us.* **coaxing. coaxed.** he **coaxes.**

cob (kob) *n.* the hard, middle part of an ear of corn.

cobbler (kob′ lər) *n.* **1.** someone who mends boots and shoes. **2.** a pastry made with fruit.

cobra (kō′ brə) *n.* a poisonous snake of Asia and Africa. *pl.* **cobras.**

cobweb (kob′ web′) *n.* a spider's net, used for catching insects.

cock (kok) *n.* a male chicken; a rooster.

cocker spaniel (kok′ ər span′ yəl) a small dog with long hair and drooping ears.

cockpit (kok′ pit′) *n.* the place in an aircraft where the pilot sits.

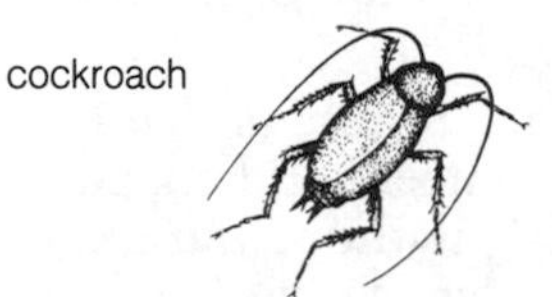

cockroach (kok′ rōch′) *n.* an insect pest, sometimes found near food. *pl.* **cockroaches.**

⊖**cocoa** (kō′ kō) *n.* **1.** a brown powder made from the seeds of the cacao tree. **2.** a hot chocolate drink made from this powder.

coconut (ko′ kə nut′) *n.* the large nut of the coco palm tree, which grows in hot climates.

cocoon (kə kün′) *n.* the silky case spun for protection by some young insects: *The caterpillar spins a cocoon before it changes into a moth or a butterfly.*

cod (kod) *n.* a fish that is found in the northern Atlantic Ocean and used for food. *pl.* **cod.**

C.O.D. short for **cash on delivery**, which means that a person pays for an item when it arrives.

⊖**code** (kōd) *n.* **1.** signs or secret words used to make a secret message. **2.** a set of rules: *The* *traffic code explains the rules for drivers to follow.*

coffee (ko′ fē) *n.* a drink made from the roasted seeds of the coffee plant.

coffin (kof′ in) *n.* the box in which a dead person is buried.

cog (kog) *n.* one of the teeth on the edge of a gear or other wheel.

coil (kȯil) *n.* a wire or rope wound around and around in a spiral. *v.* to wind around in a spiral.

⊖**coin** (kȯin) *n.* a piece of metal money. v. to invent; to make up: *to coin a new word.*

coincidence (kō in′ si dəns) *n.* two or more things happening by chance at the same time: *By coincidence, my two favourite books were written in the same year.*

cold (kōld) *n.* an illness that causes a person to sneeze and cough. *adj.* **1.** being without warmth; not hot: *a cold day; a cold hand.* **2.** not friendly or sympathetic: *a cold greeting.*

coleslaw (kōl′ slȯ′) *n.* a salad made from chopped cabbage.

collapse (kə laps′) *v.* to fall down suddenly; to break down: *The old barn collapsed in the storm.* **collapsing. collapsed.**

⊖**collar** (kol′ ər) *n.* **1.** the part of a shirt, blouse, or coat that fits around the neck. **2.** something worn around the neck: *a dog collar.*

collateral (kə lat′ ər əl) *n.* something valuable belonging to a person who borrows money, which the lender can sell if the person does not pay back the money: *She borrowed ten thousand dollars to start a business, using her house as collateral.*

colleague (kol′ ēg) *n.* someone with whom a person works: *He went to lunch with some of his office colleagues.*

collect (kə lekt′) *v.* **1.** to gather together: *Eric collects stamps as a hobby. A crowd collected around the accident.* **2.** to take in, often as payment: *The government collects taxes.*

collection (kə lek′ shən) *n.* a number of things collected: *a coin collection.*

collector (kə lek′ tər) *n.* a person who collects things for his or her own use or for someone else: *a stamp collector; a tax collector.*

⊖**college** (kol′ ij) *n.* **1.** a school that a person can go to after completing high school: *a community college; a business college.* **2.** a building that is part of a university.

collegiate (kə lē′ jət) *n.* in Canada, a secondary school or high school that offers an academic education. *adj.* in Canada, having to do with an academic high school.

collide (kə līd′) *v.* to bump hard into something: *There was a loud noise as the two cars collided.* **colliding. collided.**

collie

collie (kol′ ē) *n.* a large, shaggy dog with a long pointed nose.

collision (kə lizh′ ən) *n.* a large crash when one thing knocks hard into another.

⊖**colon** (kō′ lən) *n.* **1.** a punctuation mark(:). **2.** a part of the large intestine in the body.

colonel (kûr′ nəl) *n.* an officer in the Canadian Armed Forces. The colonel's rank is just below that of general.

⊖**colony** (kol′ ə nē) *n.* **1.** a group of people settling in a new land. **2.** the settlement made by such a group. **3.** a country or area ruled by another distant country. **4.** a group of people of similar interests or background who live together as a community: *an artists' colony.* **5.** a group of animals or plants of the same kind, living together: *an ant colony. pl.* **colonies.**

colour, color (kul′ ər) *n.* red, blue, and yellow, or any combination of these. *v.* to give colour to, or change the colour of, something.

colourful, colorful (kul′ ər fəl) *adj.* full of colour; bright.

colt (kōlt) *n.* a young male horse.

column (kol′ əm) *n.* **1.** a pillar that helps to support a building. **2.** a list of numbers, one below the other: *to add up a column of figures.* **3.** a long, narrow area of print on a page: *There are two columns of print on each page of the dictionary.*

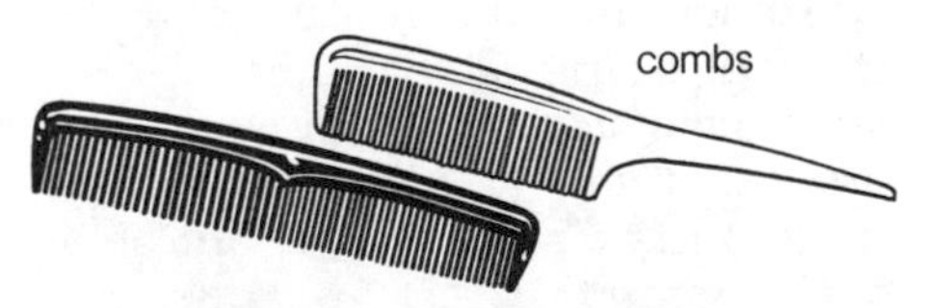
combs

comb (kōm) *n.* a thin piece of plastic, metal, or other material with teeth, used to arrange the hair. *v.* **1.** to arrange the hair with a comb. **2.** to search everywhere: *We combed the house for the lost ring.*

combat (kom′ bat) *n.* battle or fight.

combat (kəm bat′, kom′ bat) *v.* to fight or struggle against. **combatting. combatted.**

combination (kom′ bə nā′ shən) *n.* **1.** a mixture: *She made the salad using a combination of lettuce and tomatoes.* **2.** the series of numbers that opens some kinds of locks: *the combination to a bicycle lock.*

combine

combine (kom′ bīn) *n.* a machine that is driven over a field, cutting grain and removing the seeds.

combine (kəm bīn′) *v.* to join together; to mix: *To make the soup, he combined water, meat, and vegetables.* **combining. combined.**

combustible (kəm bus′ təbl) *adj.* able to catch fire and burn: *Dry wood is very combustible.*

combustion (kəm bus′ chən) *n.* the process of burning: *the combustion of gasoline in an automobile.*

come (kum) *v.* **1.** to move near; to approach: *I can hear the train coming.* **2.** to arrive: *On which day will they come?* **coming. came** (kām). I have **come.**

come about to occur; to happen: *The accident came about because I was careless.*

come across to find or meet by accident: *Deborah came across the book that she lost last week.*

come down to become sick: *to come down with a cold.*

come out to end; to result: *Did the photographs you took come out well?*

come out with to tell frankly: *She came out with the real reason that she was late.*

come to to add up to: *The restaurant bill comes to ten dollars.*

come true to become real; to be fulfilled: *My wish came true. Our dream came true.*

come up to come into being; to arise: *The subject of her health came up in conversation.*
come up with to think of; to provide: *to come up with an answer.*

⊖**comedian** (kə mē′ di ən) *n.* a performer who tells jokes or who does amusing things in a comedy.

⊖**comedy** (kom′ ə dē) *n.* a funny play, movie, or program. *pl.* **comedies.**

comet (kom′ ət) *n.* a star-like body in the sky, with a long, glowing tail.

comfort (kum′ fərt) *n.* a relaxed feeling: *Uncle Dennis sat in the armchair in great comfort.* *v.* to help someone by kind actions and words: *The nurse tried to comfort the crying child.*

⊖**comfortable** (kum′ fər təbl) *adj.* **1.** at ease; relaxed; content: *That extra pillow will make you feel comfortable. I feel comfortable when I am with my family.* **2.** providing a relaxed feeling: *a comfortable bed; a comfortable sweater.*

comic (kom′ ik) *n.* **1.** a comedian. **2.** short for **comic book**, a thin book of cartoon stories, usually read by young people. *adj.* funny: *a comic actor.*

comical (kom′ i kəl) *adj.* funny; amusing; entertaining.

⊖**comics** (kom′ iks) *n.pl.* the cartoon stories found in many newspapers.

comma (kom′ ə) *n.* a punctuation mark (,). *pl.* **commas.**

⊖**command** (kə mand′) *n.* **1.** an order: *The command was, 'Walk the dog!'* **2.** responsibility over; control of: *The captain has command of the ship.* *v.* **1.** to order someone to do something. **2.** to have control of: *The captain commands his ship.*

commander (kə man′ dər) *n.* a leader; a chief officer.

commence (kə mens′) *v.* to begin: *Her new job commences next week.* **commencing. commenced.**

comment (kom′ ent) *n.* an opinion or other remark, either spoken or written down. *v.* to make such a remark: *Tim commented that this winter seems colder than last winter.*

commerce (kom′ ərs) *n.* the buying and selling of many goods, as between two countries.

⊖**commercial** (kə mûr′ shəl) *n.* an advertisement on radio or television. *adj.* having to do with commerce.

⊖**commission** (kə mish′ ən) *n.* **1.** a group of people who are authorized to do certain work: *to appoint a commission to study the need for more downtown parking.* **2.** the part of the selling price of something that is earned by the person or agency who sold it: *Julia received a commission for every house she sold.* *v.* to authorize to do something: *to commission a study of traffic safety.*
out of commission not in working order; not able to be used: *Because it has a flat tire, the car is out of commission.*

commit (kə mit′) *v.* **1.** to do something, usually something wrong: *to commit a crime.* **2.** to promise to do something: *She committed herself to speaking at the meeting.* **3.** to place someone or something under the care of another; to entrust: *The child was committed to the care of his grandparents.* **committing. committed.**

commitment (kə mit′ mənt) *n.* a promise: *I have made a commitment to finish the job by Friday.*

committee (kə mit′ ē) *n.* a small group of people who meet to make rules and plan programs: *The* *football committee meets on Monday.*

common (kom′ ən) *adj.* happening or found often or everywhere; not rare: *Daisies are common flowers.* **common sense** good judgement in everyday matters; practical knowledge gotten from experience: *It is common sense to look both ways before crossing the street.* **in common** belonging to everyone; shared: *Our family has many hobbies in common.*

Commons (kom′ ənz) *n.* short for **House of Commons.**

Commonwealth (kom′ ən welth′) *n.* short for **Commonwealth of Nations**, the association of nations and colonies that are or were ruled by Great Britain. Many Commonwealth countries, including Canada, are now independent.

commotion (kə mō′ shən) *n.* a noisy disturbance.

communicable (kə myū′ ni kəbl) *adj.* able to be given to others: *Measles is a communicable disease.*

communicate (kə myu′ ni kāt′) *v.* to provide information to others by talking, writing, etc. **communicating. communicated.**

communication (kə myū′ ni kā′ shən) *n.* providing information to others by talking, writing, etc.

community (kə myū′ ni tē) *n.* a group of people living in a neighbourhood. *pl.* **communities.**

community college (kə myū′ ni tē kol′ ij) a school where a person may go after high school, usually to study a certain program such as computer studies or fashion design.

commute (kə myūt′) *v.* to travel a long distance to and from work by train, bus, or car: *Every morning, thousands of people commute to downtown Toronto from the suburbs.* **commuting. commuted.**

compact (kom′ pakt) *adj.* closely and firmly put together: *The emergency tool kit is light and compact.*

compact (kəm pakt′) *v.* to squeeze something and make it smaller: *The machine compacted the old car into a cube of metal.*

companion (kəm pan′ yən) *n.* a friend who goes somewhere or shares time with a person.

companionship (kəm pan′ yən ship′) *n.* friendship.

company (kum′ pə nē) *n.* **1.** guests: *We had company at our house yesterday.* **2.** a business firm: *I work for Smith and Company.* *pl.* **companies.** **3.** companionship: *I enjoy your company when I go shopping.*

compare (kəm per′) *v.* to look at things and see their similarities and differences: *Compare these cars carefully before buying one.* **comparing. compared.**

comparison (kəm per′ i sən) *n.* the comparing of things.

compartment (kəm pårt′ mənt) *n.* a separate section of something: *the compartments in a jewellery box.*

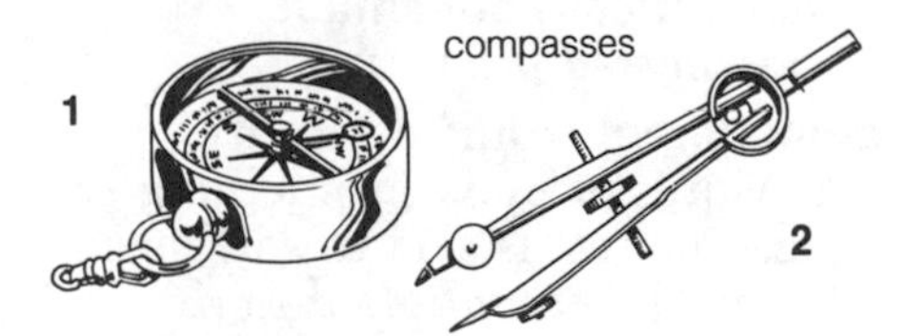

compass (kum′ pəs) *n.* **1.** an instrument that shows directions. The needle of a compass points to the north. **2.** an instrument used for drawing circles or measuring distances on a drawing. *pl.* **compasses.**

compensation (kom′ pən sā′ shən) *n.* something that is given to pay for work done or for loss or injury: *Jan received compensation from his employer when he was injured at work.*

compete (kəm pēt′) *v.* to try to win a race, game, or other contest: *The skater will compete in the Olympics.* **competing. competed.**

competition (kom′ pə tish′ ən) *n.* a race, game, or other contest that several people or teams try to win: *a competition for a job.*

competitor (kəm pet′ i tər) *n.* someone who takes part in a competition.

complain (kəm plān′) *v.* to tell someone that something is wrong, or that you are not pleased; to find fault: *She complained that the milk was sour.*

⊖**complaint** (kəm plānt′) *n.* the finding of a fault: *Helen had a complaint about the slow service in the restaurant.*

⊖**complete** (kəm plēt′) *adj.* whole; with everything there: *Marc gave Gord his complete train set.* *v.* to finish: *Complete your homework before you go out.* **completing. completed.**

complexion (kəm plek′ shən) *n.* the appearance of the skin on the face: *a smooth, dark complexion.*

complicated (kom′ pli kāt′ əd) *adj.* difficult; not simple: *a complicated problem.*

compliment (kom′ pli mənt) *n.* words of praise; something pleasant that is said to someone: *We paid a compliment to the singer.*

compose (kəm pōz′) *v.* to create or put something together: *to compose a song; to compose a story or poem.* **composing. composed.**

composer (kəm pō′ zər) *n.* someone who writes music.

composition (kom′ pə zish′ ən) *n.* **1.** the way something is done or formed together: *the composition of a farm's soil.* **2.** a piece of writing or music.

⊖**compromise** (kom′ prə mīz) *v.* to settle an argument by having each side give up some of its demands: *My sister and I compromised by sharing the housework.* **compromising. compromised.**

compute (kəm pyūt′) *v.* to figure out; to calculate: *Please compute this sum.* **computing. computed.**

computer

computer (kəm pyū′ tər) *n.* an electronic machine that stores information and can do calculations at a very fast speed.

conceal (kən sēl′) *v.* to hide; to keep secret: *to conceal a gift; to conceal information.*

conceited (kən sē′ təd) *adj.* having too high an opinion of yourself: *That conceited singer thinks that he has the best voice in the world.*

concentrate (kon′ sən trāt′) *v.* **1.** to give careful attention to one thing only: *Concentrate on your work.* **2.** to be together in one place: *Many factories are concentrated near the river.* **3.** to make stronger by reducing the amount of liquid: *Always add water to concentrated orange juice.* **concentrating. concentrated.**

concentration (kon′ sən trā′ shən) *n.* careful attention to something: *Accidents are often caused by lack of concentration.*

concern (kən sûrn′) *n.* something that is of interest or importance: *Getting good grades is my main concern.* *v.* **1.** to be about; to have to do with: *The news today concerns the fire downtown.* **2.** to be important to: *The new law concerns anyone who drives.*

concert (kon′ sûrt) *n.* a performance of music by a number of players.

conclude (kən klüd′) *v.* to finish; to end. **concluding. concluded.**

conclusion (kən klü′ zhən) *n.* **1.** an ending: *She signed her name at the conclusion of the letter.* **2.** an opinion or decision: *After a week of illness, he came to the conclusion that he should see a doctor.*

concrete (kon′ krēt) *n.* a kind of stone used in building, made from cement, water, and sand or gravel.

condemn (kən dem′) *v.* **1.** to criticize in a strong way. **2.** to sentence someone: *to condemn a thief to two years in jail.* **3.** to say that something is not safe for use: *The health inspector condemned the very old building.*

condense (kən dens′) *v.* to make shorter: *to condense a ten-page report into two pages.* **condensing. condensed.**

condition (kən dish′ ən) *n.* the state something is in: *This pony is in poor condition.*
on condition as part of an agreement: *She received more money on condition that she work an extra day.*

condominium (kon′ də min′ i əm) *n.* **1.** an apartment building in which each apartment is owned by the people who live in it or rent it to others. **2.** an apartment in such a building.

conduct (kon′ dukt) *n.* behaviour: *Neil's conduct is always excellent.*

conduct (kən dukt′) *v.* **1.** to lead: *The guide conducted the people through the museum.* **2.** to direct a chorus or an orchestra.

⊖**conductor** (kən duk′ tər) *n.* **1.** someone who directs an orchestra or a chorus. **2.** the person in charge of a train or streetcar. **3.** something that passes along electricity, heat, or sound: *Copper is a good conductor of electricity.*

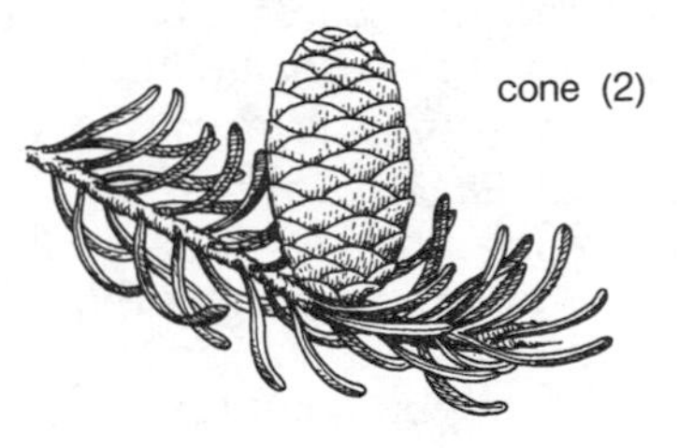
cone (2)

cone (kōn) *n.* **1.** anything shaped with a flat, circular base at one end and a point at the other: *an ice cream cone.* **2.** the woody fruit of an evergreen tree.

confederation (kən fed′ ə rā′ shən) *n.* **1.** a group of provinces, states, organizations, or other units joined for some purpose.
2. Confederation, the ten provinces of Canada.

⊖**conference** (kon′ fər əns) *n.* a meeting of people to talk about a certain subject: *Rosa attended a conference about new uses for computers in medicine.*

confess (kən fes′) *v.* to admit; to tell of having done something wrong: *Pat confessed that he had taken the bicycle.* **confessing. confessed.** he **confesses.**

confession (kən fesh′ ən) *n.* the admitting of a person's own guilt or mistakes.

⊖**confidence** (kon′ fi dəns) *n.* complete trust or belief: *I have confidence that they will be home in an hour.*

confident (kon′ fi dənt) *adj.* sure of a person's abilities; believing completely: *Dennis felt confident that he would enjoy the party.*

confirm (kən fûrm′) *v.* to make sure: *I will confirm that the train will leave at noon.*

conflict (kon′ flikt) *n.* a fight or struggle: *Many people were hurt in the conflict between the two armies.*

conflict (kən flikt′) *v.* to disagree with another fact or idea: *Her account of the accident conflicted with that of the other witness.*

ɵ**confuse** (kən fyūz′) *v.* **1.** to mix up someone: *Edgar confused me because he spoke so quickly.* **2.** to mistake one thing for another: *Sue confused the two houses and went to the wrong one.* **confusing. confused.**

confusion (kən fyū′ zhən) *n.* a mix-up; disorder: *I lost my hat in the confusion after the soccer game.*

congratulate (kən grat′ yə lāt′) *v.* to express happiness to someone because something good has happened to him or her: *I congratulated Peter when he won the race.* **congratulating. congratulated.**

congratulations (kən grat′ yə lā′ shənz) *n.pl.* good wishes said to someone because something good has happened to him or her.

ɵ**congregation** (kong′ gri gā′ shən) *n.* a gathering of people.

conjunction (kən jungk′ shən) *n.* a joining word. In 'ham and cheese', the word 'and' is the conjunction.

connect (kə nekt′) *v.* to join or fasten one thing to another.

connection (kə nek′ shən) *n.* **1.** the joining together of two parts: *Electrical connections allow current to flow.* **2.** relationship; involvement: *She no longer has any connection with that company.*

conquer (kong′ kər) *v.* to defeat someone or something: *to conquer an army; to conquer a disease.*

conquest (kong′ kwest) *n.* the winning, usually of a battle.

conscience (kon′ shəns) *n.* a feeling that something is right or wrong.

conscientious (kon′ shi en′ shəs) *adj.* careful and paying attention to details: *She is a conscientious worker in the office.*

conscious (kon′ shəs) *adj.* awake and aware of everything around.

ɵ**consent** (kən sent′) *v.* to agree to something; to give permission.

consequence (kon′ si kwens′) *n.* a result: *She tried to walk on the slippery ledge, and as a consequence she fell off.*

Conservative (kən sûr′ və tiv′) *n.* in Canada, a member of the Progressive Conservative Party.

conservative (kən sûr′ və tiv′) *adj.* not liking things to change; doing things the way that they have been done before: *He is a conservative dresser, wearing clothes that are not unusual.*

ɵ**conserve** (kən sûrv′) *v.* to save, such as from loss or from being used up: *To conserve energy, we turn down the heat at night.* **conserving. conserved.**

consider (kən sid′ ər) *v.* to think about; to turn over in the mind: *Consider all the choices before giving your answer.*

considerable (kən sid′ ər əbl) *adj.* rather large: *A considerable number of people came to the wedding.*

considerate (kən sid′ ər ət) *adj.* kind; thoughtful about others: *Bill is considerate; he's always ready to help people.*

consist of (kən sist′ əv) *v.* to be made up of: *The book consists of 120 pages.*

consonant (kon′ sə nənt) *n.* any letter of the alphabet that is not one of the five vowels (a, e, i, o, u). There are twenty-one consonants in the English alphabet.

constable (kon′ stəbl) *n.* a police officer.

constant (kon′ stənt) *adj.* **1.** always happening: *the constant ticking of a clock.* **2.** always present: *My dog is my constant companion.*

constituency (kən stit′ yū ən sē) *n.* in Canada, the people of an area that is represented in Ottawa by one Member of Parliament, and in provincial capitals by one Member of the Legislative Assembly. *pl.* **constituencies.**

constitution (kon′ sti tyū′ shən) *n.* the set of principles used to govern a country or organization: *A country's laws are based on its constitution.*

construct (kən strukt′) *v.* to build; to put together: *to construct a tower.*

construction (kən struk′ shən) *n.* **1.** something that is built or put together: *That sculpture is a large construction.* **2.** the building of something: *The construction of the house took longer than we expected.*

consult (kən sult′) *v.* **1.** to ask the advice of someone: *to consult a doctor about your health.* **2.** to seek information from: *to consult a dictionary for the spelling of a word.*

consumer (kən syu′ mər, kən sū′ mər) *n.* a person who buys and uses clothes, food, or other products.

contact (kon′ takt) *v.* to get in touch with: *Contact the newspaper if you want more information.*

contact lens (kon′ takt lenz′) a small piece of plastic worn in the eye to improve eyesight: *She used to wear glasses, but now she wears contact lenses.* *pl.* **contact lenses.**

contagious (kən tā′ jəs) *adj.* able to be spread from one person to another, such as an illness: *I stayed home because my cold was highly contagious.*

contain (kən tān′) *v.* to hold; to have as contents: *This box contains nuts and bolts.*

container (kən tān′ ər) *n.* a box, jar, barrel, etc. used to hold something.

⊖**content** (kən tent′) *adj.* pleased; satisfied with what you have: *Gail was content with her work, but Mary wanted another job.*

contents (kon′ tents) *n.pl.* the things that are found in a book or a container. *Towels and sheets were the only contents of the closet.*

contest (kon′ test) *n.* a race or game that people try to win.

contestant (kən tes′ tənt) *n.* someone who takes part in a contest: *a contestant on a quiz show.*

continent (kon′ ti nənt) *n.* a very large mass of land. Europe, Asia, Africa, North America, South America, Australia, and Antarctica are the seven continents of the world.

continual (kən tin′ yū əl) *adj.* often happening; frequent: *There was continual laughter during the movie.*

continue (kən tin′ yū) *v.* **1.** to keep on doing something: *It continued raining all day.* **2.** to start again after stopping: *After a break for lunch, the team continued cycling.* **continuing. continued.**

continuous (kən tin′ yū əs) *adj.* happening without stopping: *the continuous roar of traffic.*

contract (kon′ trakt) *n.* an agreement, often formal and in writing: *Miguel signed a contract to play for the soccer team.*

contract (kən trakt′) *v.* to become smaller; to shrink: *The pupils of your eyes contract in a bright light.*

contraction (kən trak′ shən) *n.* a shortened form of two words: *'Isn't' is the contraction of 'is not'.*

contradict (kon′ trə dikt′) *v.* to say something that goes against what another person has said: *Whenever I say something, you say the opposite. Why do you contradict me?*

contrast (kon′ trast) *n.* an obvious difference between two things: *The black square is in contrast to the white paper on which it is drawn.*

contrast (kən trast′) *v.* **1.** to be noticeably different: *The flat beaches of Nova Scotia contrast with the tall mountains of Alberta.* **2.** to show how two things are different by comparing them: *to contrast the heat of summer with the cold of winter.*

contribute (kən trib′ yūt) *v.* to give money, time, or help: *Sharon contributed ten dollars for the hospital's new building.* **contributing. contributed.**

contribution (kon′ tri byū′ shən) *n.* something paid or put into a fund.

control (kən trōl′) *n.* **controls**, the devices used to guide or operate a machine: *Deborah used the controls to run the crane.* *v.* to be in charge of; to direct: *He can control the wild horse. We controlled the heat in our apartment last winter.* **controlling. controlled.**

convene (kən vēn′) *v.* to gather for a meeting: *Parliament will convene after the holidays.* **convening. convened.**

convenience (kən vēn′ yəns) *n.* something that makes things easier: *Buses are a great convenience for getting downtown.*

convenient (kən vēn′ yənt) *adj.* handy; saving trouble: *That store is a convenient place to shop; it's so close to home.*

convention (kən ven′ shan) *n.* a large meeting arranged for a certain purpose: *At their convention, the doctors talked about heart disease.*

conversation (kon′ vər sā′ shən) *n.* a chat; a friendly talk among people.

convert (kon′ vûrt) *n.* someone who has changed his or her beliefs: *He is a recent convert to our religion.*

convert (kən vûrt′) *v.* to change into something else: *When we went to England, we converted our dollars into pounds. He converted part of the basement into a bedroom.*

convict (kon′ vikt) *n.* someone who has been sent to prison.

convict (kən vikt′) *v.* to find someone guilty: *He was convicted of the crime.*

convince (kən vins′) *v.* to persuade someone: *Carol convinced me that she was right.* **convincing. convinced.**

cook (kůk) *n.* a person who prepares food. *v.* to prepare food by heating it.

cookie (kůk′ ē) *n.* a small, sweet biscuit.

cool (kūl) *adj.* **1.** slightly cold: *the evening air was cool.* **2.** calm; not excited: *When he entered the cage, the lion tamer was very cool and relaxed.* *v.* to become or make cool.

coop (kūp) *n.* a pen or cage for small animals such as rabbits or chickens.

co-operate (kō op′ ər āt′) *v.* to work together; to help: *If we co-operate, we might finish the project by tonight.* **co-operating. co-operated.**

co-operation (kō op′ ər ā′ shən) *n.* help; the act of working together to achieve some goal: *The mayor has given us her co-operation by making a donation to our charity.*

co-operative (kōp′ ər ə tiv) *n.* a business organization, such as a grocery store, owned and run by its members.

co-ordinate (kō ȯr′ di nāt′) *v.* to work or allow to work well together: *Cheryl co-ordinated the* *volunteers who worked as ushers at the show.* **co-ordinating. co-ordinated.**

cope (kōp) *v.* to struggle with sucessfully: *Can you cope with the extra work that you have to do at your new job?* **coping. coped.**

copper (kop′ ər) *n.* a reddish-brown metal.

⊖**copy** (kop′ ē) *n.* **1.** anything made to look like something else. **2.** one of a number of printed papers or books: *a copy of today's newspaper.* *pl.* **copies.** *v.* to make or do a similar thing: *Matthew copies famous pictures.* **copying. copied.** she **copies.**

coral (kȯr′ əl) *n.* a hard, pink or white substance made up of the skeletons of small ocean creatures.

cord (kȯrd) *n.* **1.** a thick string or something resembling a thick string: *a cord to tie up a dog; the spinal cord of the human body.* **2.** a covered wire used to connect a machine such as a toaster to an electrical socket.

corduroy (kȯr′ də roi′) *n.* a strong, velvety material that has ridges.

core (kȯr) *n.* the centre of something: *the core of an apple.* *v.* to remove the core of something. **coring. cored.**

cork (kȯrk) *n.* a stopper for a bottle, made from the bark of a cork tree.

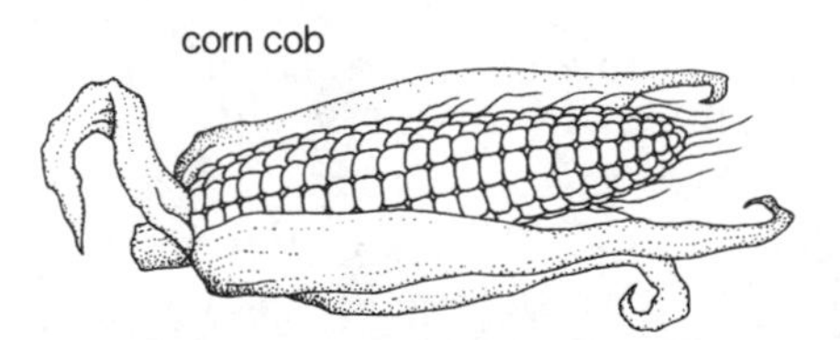

⊖**corn** (kȯrn) *n.* **1.** a grain with yellow kernels: *an ear of corn.* **2.** a hard lump that some people have on a toe.

corner (kȯr′ nər) *n.* a place where two walls, lines, roads, etc., meet. *v.* to force into a corner; to force into a difficult or dangerous position: *After many attempts, they cornered the wild animal.*

coronation (kȯr′ ə nā′ shən) *n.* the crowning of a king or queen.

corporal (kȯr′ pər əl) *n.* a soldier higher in rank than a private, lower in rank than a sergeant.

corporation (kȯr′ pə rā′ shən) *n.* a large business organization, such as a bank or an insurance company, that has a charter giving it certain rights and privileges.

⊖**corpse** (kȯrps) *n.* a dead body.

corral (kə ral′) *n.* a closed-in area for horses, cattle, and other farm animals.

correct (kə rekt′) *adj.* without an error. *v.* to put right: *Correct your mistakes.*

correction (kə rek′ shən) *n.* something that has been made right: *The store made a correction when the manager saw that the price was wrong.*

correspond (kȯr′ ə spond′) *v.* to write letters to each other: *My cousin and I have been corresponding for two years.*

correspondence (kȯr′ ə spon′ dəns) *n.* letters: *The magazine received a great deal of correspondence from its readers.*

corridor (kȯr′ i dər) *n.* a long hall in a building.

corrode (kə rōd′) *v.* to wear away gradually: *Rust is corroding the body of our car.* **corroding. corroded.**

cosmetics (koz met′ iks) *n.pl.* lipstick, powders, colours, and other items used to make the face and the hair more beautiful.

cost (kost) *n.* the price of anything: *What is the cost of this toy?* *v.* to sell for: *It costs two dollars.* **costing. cost.**

costly (kost′ lē) *adj.* costing a great deal: *a costly hobby; a costlier one; the costliest one of all.*

⊖**costume** (kos′ tyūm, kos′ tūm) *n.* **1.** clothes worn by an actor or actress in a play, motion picture, or TV program. **2.** a style of dress: *a display of national costumes.*

cosy, cozy (kō′ zē) *adj.* warm and snug; comfortable: *a cosy corner; a cosier one; the cosiest one in the house.*

cot (kȯt) *n.* a small bed, sometimes for a baby.

cottage (kot′ ij) *n.* a small house, usually in the country.

cottage cheese (kot′ ij chēz′) a soft, white, lumpy cheese.

cotton (kot′ ən) *n.* **1.** the soft, white fibres of the cotton plant. **2.** thread or cloth woven from these fibres.

couch (kaủch) *n.* a sofa or long seat for three or four people. *pl.* **couches.**

cough (kȯf) *n.* the sharp sound made when a person clears air from the lungs. *v.* to make such a sound.

could see **can.**

couldn't (kủd′ ənt) short for **could not.**

coulee (kū′ lē) *n.* a dry river bed.

council (kaủn′ səl) *n.* a group of people called together to discuss something or to make laws and govern: *the town council.*

councillor (kaủn′ sə lər) *n.* a member of a council: *Mr. Williams was elected councillor from his district of the town.*

counsel (kaủn′ səl) *n.* **1.** advice; helpful suggestions: *My counsel is that you look for a job that pays better.* **2.** a lawyer: *counsel for the defence; counsel for the prosecution.* *v.* to give advice; to offer helpful suggestions: *She counselled her son to be honest.* **counselling. counselled.**

counsellor (kaủn′ sə lər) *n.* a person who gives advice: *The school counsellor thought my sister should go to university.*

count (kaủnt) *n.* **1.** in some countries, a male member of a noble family. **2.** the total amount or number: *A count of the votes showed that Jean had won.* *v.* **1.** to add numbers: *Count the votes in the election.* **2.** to say numbers in order: *to count from one to ten.* **3.** to include in a count; to consider: *Let's not count weekends as part of our vacation days.*
count in to include: *Count me in for the trip.*
count on to rely or depend on: *We are counting on Willa to play on the team.*
count out to omit; to leave out: *Count me out if you're going to the concert.*

countdown (kaủnt′ daủn′) *n.* the time just before the firing of a missile or rocket, counting backward from a certain time to zero.

counter (kaủnt′ ər) *n.* a long table in a kitchen, shop, bank, etc.: *The toaster is on the kitchen counter.*

counter-clockwise (kaủnt′ ər klok′ wīz′) *adj., adv.* in the direction opposite to the way a clock's hands move.

country (kun′ trē) *n.* **1.** land away from towns: *We had a lovely time at a farm in the country.* **2.** a nation: *Canada is the second largest country in the world.* *pl.* **countries.**

county (kaủn′ tē) *n.* a government district, found in some countries, provinces, and states. *pl.* **counties.**

couple (kupl) *n.* two; a pair: *I caught a couple of fish. Mr. and Mrs. Klein are a happy couple.* *v.* to connect; to join together. **coupling. coupled.**

⊖**coupon** (kyū′ pon, kū′ pon) *n.* a ticket that can be exchanged for something else: *With the coupon, I saved ten cents on gas.*

courage (ku′ rij) *n.* bravery.

courageous (kə rā′ jəs) *adj.* brave; without fear.

⊖**course** (kôrs) *n.* **1.** the direction that something takes when it is moving: *the course of the river.* **2.** a series of lessons: *Donald took a course in first aid.* **3.** a part of a meal: *The main course was salmon.* **4.** an area for a sport or game: *a golf course.*
of course naturally; yes; certainly.

⊖**court** (kôrt) *n.* **1.** a place where some game is played: *a tennis court.* **2.** a place where law cases are heard. **3.** a royal palace. *v.* to try to win the love or approval of.

courteous (kûr′ ti əs) *adj.* polite; well-mannered.

courtesy (kûr′ tə sē) *n.* politeness; good manners.

cousin (kuz′ ən) *n.* the son or daughter of a person's aunt or uncle.

cove (kōv) *n.* a small bay.

cover (kuv′ ər) *n.* something put on top of another thing, usually to protect or hide it. *v.* **1.** to spread one thing over another: *We covered the firewood with a waterproof sheet.* **2.** to include; to deal with: *the cost of the trip covers meals as well as transportation.* **3.** to travel or go over: *We covered twenty kilometres on our bicycle trip.*
cover up to conceal something, often something wrong: *to cover up an accident by not reporting it.*

covering (kuv′ ə ring) *n.* something that covers: *a covering of snow on the ground.*

cow (kau̇) *n.* a full-grown female of cattle or other large animals such as the moose or elephant.

coward (kau̇′ ərd) *n.* someone who runs away from trouble or danger.

cowboy (kau̇′ boi′) *n.* a man who looks after cattle or who rides in a rodeo or stampede. *pl.* **cowboys.**

cowgirl (kau̇′ gûrl′) *n.* a woman who looks after cattle or who rides in a rodeo or stampede.

coyote (kī ō′ tē, kī′ ōt) *n.* a wild prairie animal that looks like a small wolf.

cozy see **cosy.**

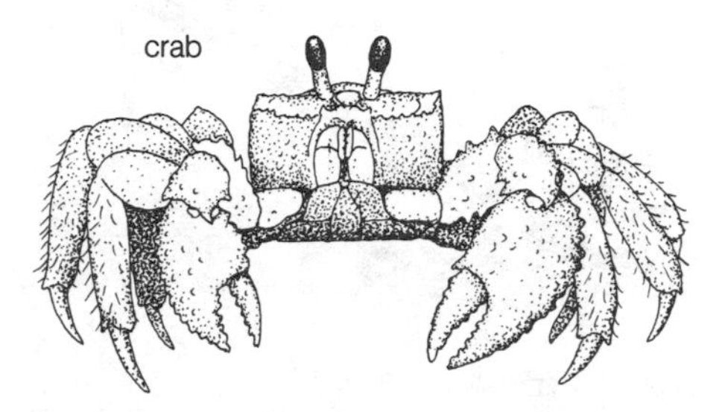

crab (krab) *n.* a shellfish with a round body, several legs, and claws.

crack (krak) *n.* **1.** a split or narrow opening: *a crack in a cup.* **2.** a sharp sound: *the crack of a whip.* **3.** a hard blow. *v.* **1.** to split: *to crack a vase.* **2.** to break open: *to crack a nut.* **3.** to make a sharp sound: *to crack a whip.*
crack a joke to say something funny or tell a joke.
crack up to crash something, often a vehicle: *Louis cracked up the car when he drove into the wall.*

cracker (krak′ ər) *n.* a thin biscuit.

crackle (krakl) *n.* a cracking noise: *the crackle of a fire.* *v.* to make such a sound: *The wood crackled on the fire.* **crackling. crackled.**

cradle (krādl) *n.* a baby's bed, often built so that the baby can be rocked to sleep.

craft (kraft) *n.* **1.** the art of making things with the hands: *Knitting, weaving, and pottery are crafts.* **2.** an airplane, boat, or ship.

crafty (kraf′ tē) *adj.* sly; cunning: *a crafty fox; a craftier fox; the craftiest fox of all.*

cram (kram) *v.* to stuff: *the monkey crammed the food into its mouth.* **cramming. crammed.**

cramp (kramp) *n.* a pain from a strained muscle, often in the leg or arm.

cranberry (kran′ ber′ ē) *n.* a sour, dark-red berry that grows in marshes. *pl.* **cranberries.**

crane

crane (krān) *n.* **1.** a large machine with a long arm for lifting and moving heavy weights. **2.** a wading bird with a long beak and long legs. *v.* to stretch the neck to see better. **craning. craned.**

crank (krank) *n.* a handle turned to start or move heavy things: *She turned the crank to lower the bucket into the well.* *v.* to turn a handle to make a machine work: *Mick cranked the old car.*

crash (krash) *n.* **1.** the noise of something being smashed. **2.** falling, breaking, or colliding noisily: *a car crash.* *v.* to fall, break, or collide with great noise. **crashing. crashed.** it **crashes.**

crate (krāt) *n.* a large wooden case for holding goods: *a crate of oranges.*

crater (krāt′ ər) *n.* **1.** the opening in a volcano. **2.** a hole shaped like a bowl.

craving (krā′ ving) *n.* a great desire for something, often food: *He had a craving for chocolate.*

crawl (kröl) *n.* **1.** a very slow pace. **2.** an overarm stroke in swimming. *v.* to move on hands and knees, or along the ground.

⊖**crayon** (krā′ on) *n.* a coloured stick of chalk or wax used for drawing pictures.

crazy (krā′ zē) *adj.* **1.** mad; silly: *a crazy idea; a crazier idea; the craziest idea of all.* **2.** *(informal)* very enthusiastic or eager: *I'm crazy about soccer.*

creak (krēk) *n.* a small squeaking noise: *the creak of an old door.* *v.* to make such a noise.

cream (krēm) *n.* **1.** the fatty part of milk, from which butter and other foods are made. **2.** a soft foam or lotion put on the skin: *shaving cream.*

crease (krēs) *n.* a mark made when cloth or paper is folded and pressed. *v.* to make such a fold. **creasing. creased.**

create (krē āt′) *v.* to make something new: *The scientist created a new chemical substance.* **creating. created.**

creation (krē ā′ shən) *n.* **1.** the making of something new: *A fashion designer's job is the creation of new styles of clothing.* **2.** something that has been made: *That cake is a magnificent creation.*

creative (krē ā′ tiv) *adj.* able to think of and make new things: *a creative poet; a creative fashion designer.*

creature (krē′ chər) *n.* a living animal.

credit (kred′ it) *n.* **1.** honour or praise for something done: *It was Angela's idea, so give her credit for it.* **2.** time allowed for the payment of goods: *To buy something on credit means to pay for it at a later time.* *v.* to apply to someone's account as a deposit: *The department store credited Brigitte's account with fifty dollars when she returned the dress.*
give credit for to say that someone has done something well: *Give*

your mother credit for sewing skills; the dress that she made is beautiful.

credit card (kred′ it kȧrd′) a plastic card that allows a person to buy something without paying for it immediately.

creditor (kred′ i tər) *n.* a person who is owed a debt: *Dad became my creditor when he lent me money to open my store.*

creek (krēk) *n.* a small stream.

creep (krēp) *v.* to move slowly and quietly, sometimes on the toes: *The cat creeps on its paws.* **creeping. crept** (krept).

cremate (krēm āt′, krēm′ āt) *v.* to burn a dead body until only ashes are left. **cremating. cremated.**

cremation (krēm āsh′ ən) *n.* **1.** the act of cremating. **2.** a kind of funeral.

crest (krest) *n.* **1.** the highest point: *the crest of a hill.* **2.** a bunch of feathers on the head of a bird.

crew (krū) *n.* the people who work on a ship, plane, train, etc.

crib (krib) *n.* **1.** a baby's bed. **2.** a box that holds food for horses and cattle to eat from.

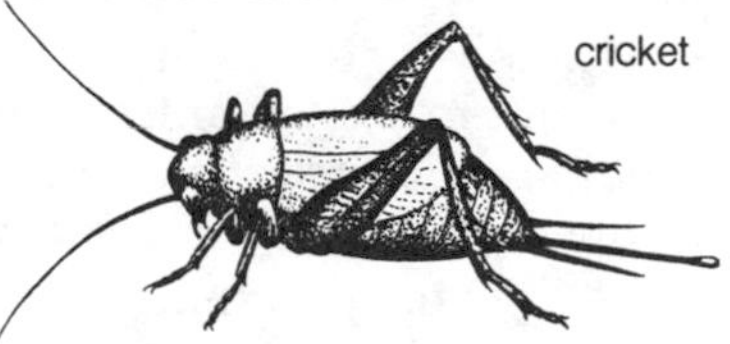
cricket

cricket (krik′ ət) *n.* **1.** a black or brown insect that looks like a grasshopper. **2.** a popular English game played with a ball and bats on a grass field.

cried, cries see **cry.**

crime (krīm) *n.* the breaking of the law in a serious way.

criminal (krim′ i nəl) *n.* someone guilty of a crime.

crimson (krim′ zən) *n.* a deep purplish-red colour. *adj.* having this colour.

crippled (kripld) *adj.* **1.** being unable to walk or to move a part of the body in the proper way, because of an injury or disease. **2.** damaged or made weak: *The crippled airplane had a broken engine.*

crisis (krī′ səs) *n.* **1.** a dangerous situation: *The explosion in the plant was a crisis for the workers.* **2.** an important and deciding point in an illness, war, or other serious situation: *The patient reached a crisis and then began to get better.* *pl.* **crises.**

crisp (krisp) *adj.* **1.** fresh and firm, but easily broken into pieces: *a slice of crisp toast.* **2.** clear and fresh, cool: *a crisp day in spring.*

crisscross (kris′ krȯs′) *v.* to mark with lines that cross each other. **crisscrossing. crisscrossed.** it **crisscrosses.**

critical (krit′ i kəl) *adj.* **1.** often finding something wrong or disapproving of things. **2.** serious or dangerous: *a critical stage in an experiment.*

criticism (krit′ i sizm′) *n.* **1.** the act of saying what is good or bad about someone or something. **2.** disapproving remarks about someone or something: *He receives criticism from almost everyone who reads his stories.*

criticize (krit′ i sīz′) *v.* to examine someone or something, saying what is good and what can be improved: *Gina criticized her friend's new hairstyle.* **criticizing. criticized.**

croak (krōk) *n.* a deep and husky sound, like the noise that a frog makes. *v.* to make such a noise.

⊖**crochet** (krō shā′) *n.* a form of needlework, in which threads are looped into other loops with a hook. *v.* to do this work. **crocheting** (krō shā′ ing). **crocheted** (krō shād′).

crocus (krō′ kəs) *n.* a small spring flower that grows from a bulb. *pl.* **crocuses.**

crook (kru̇k) *n. (informal)* a swindler; a thief.

crooked (kru̇k′ əd) *adj.* **1.** bent; not straight: *a crooked line.* **2.** *(informal)* against the law; dishonest.

crop (krop) *n.* plants grown for good: *Wheat is the main crop of the Prairies.* *v.* to bite or cut the top of: *to crop a field with a scythe.* **cropping. cropped.**

cross (krȯs) *n.* **1.** a mark shaped like + or ×. **2.** the badge or emblem of Christianity. *pl.* **crosses.** *v.* **1.** to go from one side to another: *to cross the road.* **2.** to draw a line through: *to cross a name off a list.* **3.** to place one thing across another: *Don't cross your legs when you sit at the table.* **4.** to intersect: *Main Street crosses Front Street near the river.* **crossing. crossed.** he **crosses.** **cross a person's mind** to occur as a thought: *It didn't cross my mind that you'd be late.*

crossing (krȯ′ sing) *n.* **1.** a place where a person can travel from one side of a street, river, etc. to the other. **2.** a place where train tracks cross a road.

crosswalk (krȯs′ wȯk′) *n.* in some towns and cities, a special path where traffic must yield to pedestrians as they cross the street.

crouch (krau̇ch) *v.* to bend low: *Lise crouched to get under the rail.* **crouching. crouched.** she **crouches.**

crow (krō) *n.* a large, black bird. *v.* to make a noise like a rooster.

crowbar (krō′ bȧr′) *n.* a heavy metal bar with one flattened end, used as a lever.

crowd (krau̇d) *n.* a great number of people together in one place. *v.* **1.** to come together quickly, often in a tight space: *The people crowded into the store.* **2.** to shove or push: *Don't crowd the person ahead of you.*

crown (krau̇n) *n.* the head covering of gold and jewels worn by a king or queen.

Crown (krau̇n) *adj.* In Canada, representing the authority of the Monarch: *a Crown corporation.*

cruel (krū′ əl) *adj.* very unkind; causing pain: *a cruel animal trainer; a cruel wind.*

cruelty (krū′ əl tē) *n.* the causing of pain or suffering. *pl.* **cruelties.**

cruise (krūz) *n.* a pleasure trip on a ship. *v.* for a ship, car, or plane to travel for a while at a steady speed. **cruising. cruised.**

cruiser (krū′ zər) *n.* a police car.

crumb (krum) *n.* a tiny bit of bread, cake, cookie, etc.

crumble (krumbl) *v.* to break into small pieces or parts. **crumbling. crumbled.**

crumple (krumpl) *v.* to crush something and make wrinkles in it: *Ruth crumpled the paper bag and threw it away.* **crumpling. crumpled.**

crush (krush) *v.* to squeeze hard: *to crush lemons to make lemon juice.* **crushing. crushed.** he **crushes.**

crust (krust) *n.* a hard outer covering: *a pie crust; a crust of bread.*

crutch (kruch) *n.* a thick stick with a padded end to fit under the arm, used for support by lame or injured people. *pl.* **crutches.**

⊖**cry** (krī) *n.* a loud call; a loud shout. *pl.* **cries** *v.* **1.** to shout loudly: *Ed cried for help when he fell down.* **2.** to shed tears of sadness or joy. **crying. cried.** he **cries.**

crystal (kris′ təl) *n.* **1.** a hard mineral that looks like ice. **2.** a piece of glass cut to look like this mineral.

cub (kub) *n.* a young fox, bear, wolf, lion, tiger, etc.

Cub (kub) *n.* a junior Boy Scout.

cube (kyūb) *n.* a solid object with six square faces or sides, all equal: *a sugar cube.*

cucumber (kyū′ cum bər) *n.* a long, thin vegetable used in salads. It has light green flesh and a thin, dark green skin.

cud (kud) *n.* food that comes back into the mouth from the stomach of cows and other animals, to be chewed again.

cuddle (kudl) *v.* to hug someone in a loving way: **cuddling. cuddled.**

cue (kyū) *n.* **1.** the stick used to hit the balls in the game of billiards. **2.** a hint to begin doing or saying something.

cuff (kuf) *n.* **1.** the turned-over end of a pant leg. **2.** the end of a sleeve near the wrist.

culprit (kul′ prit) *n.* someone who has done something wrong.

cultivate (kul′ ti vāt′) *v.* to prepare and work on land in order to raise crops. **cultivating. cultivated.**

ə**cultivator** (kul′ ti vā′ tər) *n.* a machine or tool that loosens the soil and removes weeds around growing plants.

cultural (kul′ chər əl) *adj.* having to do with culture.

culture (kul′ chər) *n.* the art, beliefs, and customs of a group of people: *This book is about the culture of the ancient Greeks.*

cunning (kun′ ing) *adj.* sly; clever at fooling people.

cup (kup) *n.* **1.** a small container with a handle, used for drinking. **2.** a trophy shaped like a cup or vase, presented to a winning team.

cupboard (kub′ ərd) *n.* a closet with shelves for clothes, books, dishes, or other things: *a kitchen cupboard.*

cupful (kup′ fụl) *n.* as much as a cup will hold. *pl.* **cupfuls.**

curb (kûrb) *n.* the concrete edge at each side of a street. *v.* to hold back; to control: *Curb your appetite.*

curdle (kûrdl) *v.* to go sour: *Milk curdles if it is left in a warm place.* **curdling. curdled.**

cure (kyūr) *n.* something used to help make a sick person healthy again: *My grandmother's cure for a cold is to eat chicken soup.* *v.* **1.** to heal; to make well: *The medicine cured Linda's sore throat.* **2.** to preserve meat or skins by drying. **curing. cured.**

curiosity (kyū ri o′ si tē) *n.* a desire to learn or know.

curious (kyū′ ri əs) *adj.* **1.** wanting to know: *Sharon was curious about what I had in my desk.* **2.** unusual; interesting: *We found some curious shells on the beach.*

curl (kûrl) *n.* a twisted lock of hair. *v.* **1.** to twist something, such as hair. **2.** to play the game of curling. **curl up** to sit or lie down with the legs tucked up comfortably: *to curl up in a chair after a hard day's work.*

curlers (kûr′ lərz) *n.pl.* metal or plastic rollers around which hair is wound to make curls.

curling (kûr′ ling) *n.* a game played on ice in which heavy stones are slid towards a target.

curly (kûr′ lē) *adj.* in curls; not straight: *Bob's hair is curly. Glen's hair is curlier. Eileen's hair is curliest of all.*

currant (ku′ rənt) *n.* **1.** a small, dried grape. **2.** a small, round, sour berry: *a redcurrant; a blackcurrant.*

currency (ku′ rən sē) *n.* the money of a country: *The yen is the Japanese unit of currency.* *pl.* **currencies.**

current (ku′ rənt) *n.* **1.** a stream of air or water flowing quickly: *Wind is a current of air.* **2.** a flow of electricity along a wire or cable. *adj.* happening at the present time: *Joan reads the newspaper every day because she is interested in current events.*

curriculum (kə rik′ yə ləm) *n.* the subjects studied at school or in a particular program. *pl.* **curricula,** or **curriculums.**

curry (ku′ rē) *n.* a dish of food prepared with **curry powder**, a yellowish mixture of spices. *pl.* **curries.**

curse (kûrs) *n.* an evil wish: *The children read a story about a witch's curse.* *v.* **1.** to swear; to use bad language. **2.** to wish evil on someone. **cursing. cursed.**

curtain (kûr′ tən) *n.* a hanging cloth in front of a window or a theatre stage, used to keep out light or to hide something.

curve (kûrv) *n.* a smooth bend: *a curve in the road.*

cushion (ku̇sh′ ən) *n.* a soft pillow for a chair or chesterfield.

custard (kus′ tərd) *n.* a pudding made of milk, eggs, and sugar.

custodian (kəs tō′ di ən) *n.* a person in charge of the care of someone or something: *Our school custodian cleans the building at night.*

custom (kus′ təm) *n.* a habit; a certain way of doing things: *It is John's custom to eat very little at breakfast.*

customer (kus′ tə mər) *n.* someone who buys; a person who shops.

customs (kus′ təmz) *n. pl.* **1.** taxes on goods brought in from another country. **2.** government offices at a border between countries: *When we went to Washington, we had to go through customs.*

cut (kut) *n.* **1.** an opening made by a sharp object: *I got that cut on my foot from a nail that I stepped on.* **2.** a reduction; a lowering in amount: *My new job is interesting, but I took a cut in pay.* *v.* **1.** to slash or divide with a knife, scissors, or other sharp object. **2.** to divide a price; to reduce: *to cut the price of shoes in half.* **3.** to cross or pass through: *She cut through the yard instead of going around the block.* **cutting. cut.**
cut down to make fall by cutting: *to cut down a bush.*
cut in to move in quickly: *The other car suddenly cut in front of ours.*
cut it out to stop doing it.
cut off to turn or shut off: *Our electricity was cut off when we didn't pay the bill.*
cut up to cut into small pieces or bits: *Father cut up the meat for the baby to eat.*

cute (kyūt) *adj.* lovable or pretty: *a cute baby; a cuter baby; the cutest baby of all.*

cutlery (kut′ lə rē) *n.* knives, forks, spoons, etc.; the tools used for eating and serving food.

cycle (sīkl) *n.* the repeating of things, always in the same order: *the cycle of the seasons.* *v.* to ride on a bicycle or motorcycle: *We cycled through the park.* **cycling. cycled.**

cyclist (sī′ klist) *n.* someone riding a bicycle or motorcycle.

cyclone (sī′ klōn′) *n.* a heavy storm, with winds moving in a spiral towards the centre.

cylinder (sil′ ən dər) *n.* **1.** a hollow or solid object that is shaped like a tube. **2.** a piece of metal in this shape, used in gasoline and other engines.

cymbals (sim′ bəlz) *n.pl.* brass plates used by a drummer to make a clashing sound.

D

dab (dab) *n.* a small amount of a moist substance: *I put a dab of butter on the peas.* *v.* to touch lightly: *I dabbed some lotion on the sunburn.* **dabbing. dabbed.**

dad (dad) *n.* *(informal)* father.

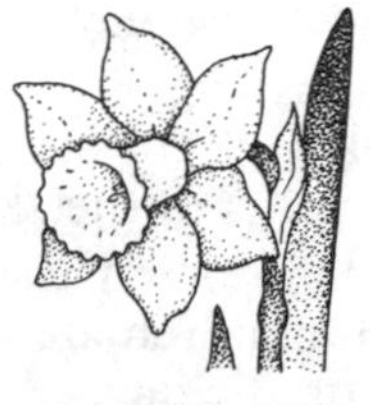

daffodil

daffodil (daf′ ə dil′) *n.* a tall plant with yellow or white flowers.

dagger (dag′ ər) *n.* a small knife with a short, pointed blade.

daily (dā′ lē) *adv.* every day: *The newspaper comes out daily.* *adj.* coming out or happening every day: *a daily newspaper.*

dainty (dān′ tē) *adj.* pretty and delicate: *dainty flowers; daintier flowers; the daintiest flowers in the garden.*

dairy (der′ ē) *n.* a place where milk and cream are made into cheese and butter. *pl.* **dairies.**

daisy (dā′ zē) *n.* a small plant with white flowers with a yellow centre. *pl.* **daisies.**

⊖**dam** (dam) *n.* a wall built to hold back the water of a river, stream, creek, etc.

⊖**damage** (dam′ ij) *n.* **1.** breaking, injury, or harm: *The accident caused great damage to the bike.* **2. damages**, money paid to make up for some injury or harm: *Eva asked for a thousand dollars in damages from the man who hit her car.* *v.* to break, injure, or harm. **damaging. damaged.**

damp (damp) *adj.* moist; slightly wet.

dance (dans) *n.* **1.** movement in time with music. **2.** a party where people dance. *v.* to move the feet and body in time with music. **dancing. danced.**

dandelion

dandelion (dan′ di lī′ ən) *n.* a weed with a bright yellow flower and leaves.

dandruff (dan′ drəf) *n.* small white pieces of dead skin that fall from the scalp.

danger (dān′ jər) *n.* risk; the chance of harm or death: *The storm can bring danger to the sailors.*

dangerous (dān′ jə rəs) *adj.* not safe: *Skating on thin ice is dangerous.*

dangle (dangl) *v.* to hang or swing loosely: *The keys dangled from the chain.* **dangling. dangled.**

dare (der) *v.* **1.** to risk; to take a chance: *Ed dared to walk up to the bull.* **2.** to challenge someone: *She dared her sister to eat one more piece of cake.* **daring. dared.**

dark (dȧrk) *adj.* **1.** without light: *a dark room.* **2.** deep in colour: *a dark coat.*
in the dark without information or knowledge: *I'm in the dark about when we leave for the restaurant.*

darling (dȧr′ ling) *n.* someone very dear to a person.

darn (dȧrn) *v.* to fix a hole in cloth: *Please darn my socks.*

dart (dȧrt) *n.* **1.** a small arrow thrown by hand at a board. **2.** a seam in a piece of clothing that makes the clothing fit better. *v.* to move quickly: *When the rabbit saw me, it darted away.*

dash (dash) *n.* **1.** a rush or quick movement. **2.** a small line (-) used in writing. **3.** a tiny amount that is added: *a dash of pepper.* *pl.* **dashes.** *v.* to move forward quickly: *Jean dashed by me as he ran for the door.* **dashing. dashed.** she **dashes.**

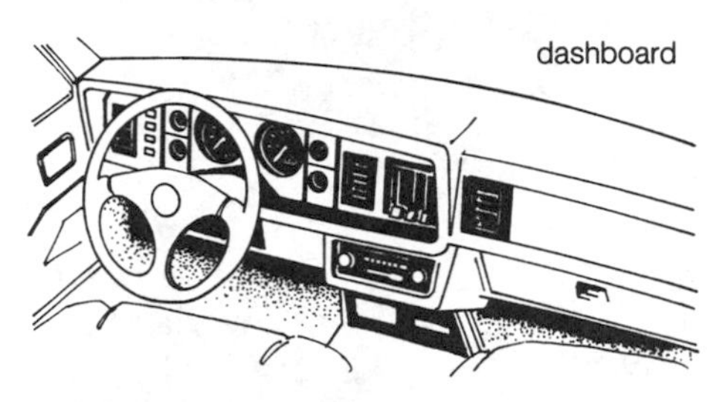

dashboard (dash′ bȯrd′) *n.* the panel in a car that holds the instruments.

data (dā′ tə, da′ tə) *n.pl.* facts; pieces of information; statistics. *sing.* **datum.**

data processing (dā′ tə pros′ e sing) the use of a computer to handle large amounts of data.

⊖**date** (dāt) *n.* **1.** the day, month, and year of some event: *What is today's date?* **2.** an arrangement to go with someone to a certain place at a certain time: *We have a date to go to the movies tomorrow.* **3.** the person with whom another person has made this arrangement. **4.** the brown, sticky fruit of a palm tree. *v.* to go out with a member of the opposite sex. **dating. dated.**
date from to belong to a certain time: *This chair dates from the last century.*
out-of-date old fashioned.
to date until the present time: *No one has applied for the job to date.*
up-to-date in fashion; very new.

daughter (dȯ′ tər) *n.* a female child: *My grandmother has one daughter. My mother has two daughters.*

daughter-in-law (dȯ′ tər in lȯ′) *n.* the wife of a person's son. *pl.* **daughters-in-law.**

dawn (dȯn) *n.* sunrise; daybreak.

day (dā) *n.* **1.** the time between sunrise and sunset. **2.** a period of twenty-four hours, from one midnight to the next. **3.** the time that a person works: *Doug works an eight-hour day at the factory.* **4.** a specific period of time: *the present day; the days of the dinosaurs.* *pl.* **days.**
call it a day to stop doing something: *Let's call it a day; you look tired.*

daybreak (dā′ brāk′) *n.* the time when sunlight appears in the sky.

day-care centre (dā′ ker sen′ tər) a place where small children are looked after during the day.

daydream (dā′ drēm′) *n.* a wishing or imaginary happening that comes to mind while a person is awake.

daylight (dā′ līt′) *n.* **1.** sunlight. **2.** dawn.

daylight-saving time (dā′ līt sā′ ving tīm′) one hour later than standard time: *When we switch to daylight-saving time in the spring, we have an extra hour of sunlight at the end of the day.*

daytime (dā′ tīm′) *n.* the time between sunrise and sunset.

daze (dāz) *v.* to confuse; to stun: *Jim was so dazed when he fell that he didn't know where he was.* **dazing. dazed.**

dazzle (dazl) *v.* **1.** to blind or confuse someone by shining a bright light in his or her eyes. **2.** to amaze with skill, magnificence, etc.: *The gymnast dazzled the crowd with her act.* **dazzling. dazzled.**

dead (ded) *adj.* **1.** not alive: *a dead person.* **2.** without power: *a dead battery.* **3.** complete: *dead silence.*

dead end (ded′ end′) a street closed at one end.

deadline (ded′ līn′) *n.* a time by which something must be finished: *a deadline for applying for a job.*

deadly (ded′ lē) *adj.* **1.** causing death: *a deadly poison; a deadlier one; the deadliest poison of all.* **2.** full of hatred: *deadly enemies.*

deaf (def) *adj.* not able to hear.

deal (dēl) *n.* **1.** an amount: *a great deal of laughter.* **2.** *(informal)* a bargain: *We got a deal when we bought the carpet.* **3.** *(informal)* an arrangement: *I made a deal with Anne. She'll fix the door and I'll shovel the snow.* *v.* **1.** in a card game, to give cards to the players. **2.** to be about: *This book deals with ancient history.* **3.** to behave or act in a certain way: *Alma dealt unfairly with her brother by not paying him the money that he had earned.* **4.** to carry out business by buying or selling: *My store deals in office supplies.* **dealing. dealt** (delt).

dealer (dē′ lər) *n.* **1.** a trader who buys and sells something. **2.** in a card game, the person who gives out the cards to the other players.

dealt see **deal.**

dear (dēr) *n.* a lovable person. *adj.* **1.** lovable; kindly. **2.** a greeting at the beginning of a letter: *Dear Rita.* **3.** expensive. *interj.* an exclamation of surprise, disappointment, etc.: *Oh dear! I broke the vase.*

death (deth) *n.* the end of life. **put to death** to kill.

debate (di bāt′) *n.* a discussion between two people or two groups of people who believe different things: *the debate over the prime minister's plans.* *v.* to discuss the reasons for or against something: *The Members of Parliament debated the subject for two hours.* **debating. debated.**

debt (det) *n.* something that one person owes to another: *He is in debt to his father, but he hopes to pay back the money by July.*

debtor (de′ tər) *n.* a person who owes something to another person.

decade (dek′ ād) *n.* a period of ten years: *The time from 1980 to 1990 is one decade.*

decaffeinated (di kaf′ i nāt′ əd) *adj.* with the caffeine removed: *I drink only decaffeinated coffee.*

decay (di kā′) *n.* rot, or the beginning of a rotting condition: *the decay in the tree.* *v.* to rot and waste away.

deceased (di sēst′) *n.* a particular dead person: *The deceased left his property to his favourite nephew.* *adj.* dead: *Three of my grandparents are deceased.*

⊖**deceive** (di sēv′) *v.* to make someone accept as true something that is not true: *Fran deceived her sister by pretending to be asleep.* **deceiving. deceived.**

December (di sem′ bər) *n.* the twelfth month of the year.

decent (dē′ sənt) *adj.* well-mannered; respectable; considerate; honest: *a decent neighbour.*

decide (di sīd′) *v.* to make up your mind: *It took me a long time to decide what I wanted to buy.* **deciding. decided.**

decimal (des′ i məl) *adj.* based on the number 10: *The metric system is a decimal system.*

decision (di sizh′ ən) *n.* something that has been or will be decided: *Whose decision was it to start work so early?*

deck (dek) *n.* **1.** a floor on a ship. **2.** a set of cards.

declaration (dek′ lə rā′ shən) *n.* an announcement; a public statement.

declare (di kler′) *v.* to announce; to say something in public: *The government declared a spring election.* **declaring. declared.**

decline (di klīn′) *v.* **1.** to refuse in a polite way: *to decline an invitation to a party.* **2.** to become less; to decrease: *Her interest declined as the speaker kept repeating the same ideas.* **declining. declined.**

decorate (dek′ ə rāt′) *v.* **1.** to make something look more attractive, especially a house or the walls of a room. **2.** to pin a medal or ribbon on someone as an honour. **decorating. decorated.**

decoration (dek′ ə rā′ shən) *n.* **1.** something used to decorate: *party decorations.* **2.** a badge, medal, or ribbon awarded as an honour.

decrease (di krēs′) *v.* to grow smaller; to become less: *In winter, the daylight decreases. In summer, it increases.* **decreasing. decreased.**

dedicate (ded′ i kāt′) *v.* to set aside for a special use or purpose: *to dedicate a statue to a dead hero.* **dedicating. dedicated.**

deduct (di dukt′) *v.* to take away something from a total: *He had income tax deducted from his weekly pay.*

deed (dēd) *n.* **1.** an action; the doing of something: *a brave deed.* **2.** an official paper that shows a person owns a piece of property: *a deed to a house.*

deep (dēp) *adj.* **1.** going a long way down from the top: *a deep river; deep feelings.* **2.** low: *a deep voice.*

deeply (dēp′ lē) *adv.* very much: *I was deeply sorry to hear about your accident.*

deer (dēr) *n.* a wild animal with hoofs that runs quickly; the male deer has antlers. *pl.* **deer.**

defeat (di fēt′) *n.* the loss of a game or battle. *v.* to beat someone in a game or battle.

defect (dē′ fekt) *n.* a weakness; a fault; something that is wrong: *He returned the lamp because there was a defect in the wiring.*

defect (di fekt′) *v.* to leave a group, political party, country, etc., in order to go to one that has different ideas or beliefs.

defence, defense (di fens′) *n.* **1.** protection: *The wall around the fort was built as a defence.* **2.** a team or the players protecting a goal. **3.** a defendant and the defendant's lawyer.

defend (di fend′) *v.* to protect; to guard from attack.

defendant (di fen′ dənt) *n.* in a court of law, the person who is accused of having done something wrong.

define (di fīn′) *v.* to make clear the meaning of something: *A dictionary defines words.* **defining. defined.**

definite (def′ i nət) *adj.* clear; firm; sure: *Janet made a definite promise to be home early.*

definitely (def′ i nət′ lē) *adj.* certainly; for sure: *I am definitely going to the movies tonight.*

definition (def′ i nish′ ən) *n.* the meaning of a word: *Some words have more than one definition.*

defrost (di frôst′) *v.* to thaw; to remove ice from: *to defrost a frozen steak; to defrost a refrigerator.*

defy (di fī′) *v.* **1.** to refuse to obey: *He defied all the rules.* **2.** to dare: *I defy you to prove that the job can't be done.* **defying. defied.** she **defies.**

⊖**degree** (di grē′) *n.* **1.** a unit of measurement: *The temperature today is 20 degrees Celsius (20°C).* **2.** a title given to a university or college student when he or she graduates.

dehydrated (dē hīd′ rāt′ əd) *adj.* with all water removed: *dehydrated milk; dehydrated potatoes.*

delay (di lā′) *n.* a wait; a putting off: *There is a delay in the game because of the rain. pl.* **delays.** *v.* **1.** to put off till a later time: *The test was delayed for a week.* **2.** to slow down or make late: *We were delayed because we stopped to eat lunch.*

deliberate (di lib′ ə rət) *adj.* done on purpose: *The teacher made a deliberate mistake on the chalkboard. The class had to find what it was.*

deliberate (di lib′ ə rāt′) *v.* to think seriously about something: *The jury deliberated for a long time before they reached a decision.* **deliberating. deliberated.**

delicate (del′ i kət) *adj.* weak; tender; sensitive: *Delicate plants will die in the frost.*

delicatessen (del′ i kə tes′ ən) *n.* a store that sells prepared foods such as cold meats and salads.

delicious (di lish′ əs) *adj.* very good to smell or taste: *a delicious pie.*

delight (di līt′) *n.* a great pleasure: *Charles welcomed his friend with delight. v.* to please a great deal.

delightful (di līt′ fəl) *adj.* very pleasing or entertaining: *We read a delightful story.*

deliver (di liv′ ər) *v.* to hand over something to someone: *to deliver newspapers.*

delivery (di liv′ ə rē) *n.* the handing over of something: *The milk delivery is at seven o'clock. pl.* **deliveries.**

delta (del′ tə) *n.* a triangle of earth and sand formed at the mouth of some rivers. *pl.* **deltas.**

deluxe (di luks′) *adj.* very fancy and expensive: *a deluxe hotel room.*

demand (di mand′) *v.* **1.** to ask firmly for something, as if it is a right: *I demand a reason for your bad behaviour!* **2.** to need or require: *Lee's work at the factory demands good eyesight.*

democracy (di mok′ rə sē′) *n.* a country or group that elects its leaders. *pl.* **democracies.**

democratic (dem′ ə krat′ ik) *adj.* believing in and practising democracy: *We chose our class president the democratic way: we held an election.*

demolish (di mol′ ish) *v.* to pull down or destroy: *The explosion demolished the warehouse.* **demolishing. demolished.** it **demolishes.**

demon (dē′ mən) *n.* an evil spirit.

demonstrate (dem′ ən strāt′) *v.* **1.** to show how something is done, using examples: *The salesman demonstrated how to use the new lawn mower.* **2.** to show openly: *Hugging is one way to demonstrate affection.* **3.** to join a parade or meeting in order to complain or make demands about something: *The workers demonstrated for safer working conditions.* **demonstrating. demonstrated.**

den (den) *n.* **1.** a cave where a wild animal lives. **2.** a small room, often used for reading.

denim (den′ im) *n.* a heavy blue cloth.

denominator (di nom′ ə nā′ tər) *n.* in a fraction, the number below the line: *In the fraction ¾, the 4 is the denominator.*

dense (dens) *adj.* **1.** tightly packed: *a dense crowd of people.* **2.** very thick: *a dense cloud of smoke; a denser cloud; the densest cloud of all.*

⊖**dent** (dent) *n.* a small hollow made by pressure: *If you drop the hammer, you'll make a dent in the wood.* *v.* to make such a hollow.

dental (den′ təl) *adj.* having to do with teeth: *Jim went to the dental clinic to have his teeth examined.*

dentist (den′ tist) *n.* a doctor who takes care of people's teeth.

dentures (den′ chərz) *n.pl.* false teeth.

deny (di nī′) *v.* **1.** to say that something is not true: *Do you admit saying that? No. I deny it.* **2.** to refuse to give: *The bank manager denied my request for the loan.* **denying. denied.** he **denies.**

deodorant (dē ōd′ ə rənt) *n.* a preparation that prevents or takes away unpleasant odours.

⊖**depart** (di pårt′) *v.* to go away; to leave: *The train departs from Platform 1.*

⊖**department** (di pårt′ mənt) *n.* an important part or section of a store, office, government, etc.: *the furniture department of the store; the fire department.*

department store (di pårt′ ment stör′) a large store that sells many different types of things.

depend on (di pend′ on′) *v.* **1.** to trust; to rely on: *I depend on you to help me with my work.* **2.** to decide because of something else: *I don't know if I will buy the coat. It depends on the price.*

dependable (di pend′ əbl) *adj.* reliable; to be trusted: *a dependable person.*

dependant (di pen′ dənt) *n.* a person who relies on someone else for food, clothing, and a home: *She listed the names of her three dependants on the income tax form.*

deport (di pōrt′) *v.* to send out of the country; to send back to the country of origin.

deposit (di poz′ it) *n.* **1.** something stored in a safe place: *a deposit of money in the bank.* **2.** an amount of money given as part of a payment for something, with a promise to pay the rest at a later time. **3.** an amount of some mineral in the ground or in rock: *a deposit of iron ore.* *v.* **1.** to put something down: *Father deposited the luggage on the rack.* **2.** to put into a bank or other safe place: *Cindy deposited some money in her bank account.*

depot (dē′ pō) *n.* **1.** a bus or train station. **2.** a warehouse.

depreciate (di prē′ shi āt′) *v.* to become less valuable: *Every year, the value of my car depreciates.* **depreciating. depreciated.**

depressed (di prest′) *adj.* very sad: *Charlie was depressed because his dog had died.*

depression (di presh′ ən) *n.* **1.** a period of slow economic activity and high unemployment. **2.** a period during which a person feels particularly unhappy.

depth (depth) *n.* how deep something is; the distance from top to bottom: *The swimming pool has a depth of three metres at one end.*

⊖**Deputy** (dep′ yə tē) *n.* in Quebec, a person who belongs to the National Assembly.

⊖**deputy** (dep′ yə tē) *n.* someone who can take the place of the person he or she works for: *the sheriff's deputy.* *pl.* **deputies.**

⊖**descend** (di send′) *v.* **1.** to go down: *the plane descends onto the runway.* **2.** to climb down: *The climbers descended the mountain.*

descendant (di sen′ dənt) *n.* someone who has a certain ancestor or group of ancestors: *a descendant of Chinese settlers.*

describe (di skrīb′) *v.* to tell or write all about something or someone: *We described our* *summer holidays.* **describing. described.**

description (di skrip′ shən) *n.* a picture in words; a statement about some event, place, or person: *His description of the book made me want to read it.*

ə**desert** (dez′ ərt) *n.* dry land on which very few plants grow: *A desert is usually sandy or stony.*

desert (di zûrt′) *v.* to leave behind; to leave or run away from someone or something that should not be left: *None of his friends deserted him when he needed help.*

ə**deserve** (di zûrv′) *v.* to have earned a reward or a punishment: *You deserve to win the prize.* **deserving. deserved.**

design (di zīn′) *n.* **1.** a drawing or outline that is used as a guide: *The builder showed us the design of the new house.* **2.** a pattern: *The wallpaper has a design of flowers.* *v.* to draw or plan out: *to design a house.*

desire (di zīr′) *n.* a great wish: *Do you have a desire to travel?* *v.* to want very much; to wish for. **desiring. desired.**

desk (desk) *n.* a writing table, often used in an office or classroom.

despair (di sper′) *n.* a feeling of being without hope: *The lost child was in despair.* *v.* to give up hope: *They despaired of ever seeing their friends again.*

desperate (des′ pə rət) *adj.* made reckless by despair: *The house was on fire, and the desperate man was ready to jump out of the window.*

despise (di spīz′) *v.* to hate very much. **despising. despised.**

despite (di spīt′) *prep.* although there is; in spite of: *Despite the bad weather, we played soccer.*

dessert (di zûrt′) *n.* fruit, cake, pudding, pie, etc., served at the end of a meal.

destination (des′ ti nā′ shən) *n.* the place a person or thing is travelling to: *The train reached its destination on time. My destination is Quebec City.*

destroy (di strȯi′) *v.* to ruin completely: *The fire destroyed the warehouse.*

destruction (di struk′ shən) *n.* ruin; the smashing or breaking down of anything.

detach (di tach′) *v.* to separate; to disconnect: *Carl detached the key from the chain.* **detaching. detached.** it **detaches.**

detail (dē′ tāl) *n.* a small part of something: *Karen told us every detail of her trip.* *v.* to discuss fully, part by part: *Ron detailed the work we had to do by tonight.* **in detail** section by section: *Tell us about your plans in detail.*

detect (di tekt′) *v.* to discover; to notice something that is hard to see: *Betty detected a small hole in the pipe.*

detective (di tek′ tiv) *n.* someone who tries to solve a crime.

detergent (di tûr′ jənt) *n.* a liquid or powder used for cleaning dishes or clothes.

determine (di tûr′ mən) *v.* **1.** to decide with a firm intention: *Olga determined to finish the book before the weekend.* **2.** to find out: *The mayor formed a committee to determine the need for more downtown parking.* **determining. determined.**

detest (di test′) *v.* to hate very much: *Many people detest spiders.*

detour (dē′ tūr) *n.* a roundabout route, replacing the regular way for a time: *We took a detour in our drive because the bridge was being repaired.*

develop (di vel′ əp) *v.* **1.** to grow: *Exercise will develop your muscles.* **2.** to change from one form to another: *We had the pictures developed.* **developing. developed.**

development (di vel′ əp mənt′) *n.* **1.** the process of growing into something bigger or different. **2.** a group of buildings put up by the same company: *a housing development.*

device (di vīs′) *n.* any tool, instrument, or machine used for a certain purpose: *A toaster is a device that toasts bread.*

devil (de′ vəl) *n.* **1.** an evil spirit. **2.** a very wicked person.

devote (di vōt′) *v.* **1.** to give time or attention to a job or project: *Carlos devotes a few hours each week to his hobby.* **2.** to be loyal or faithful: *Our dog is devoted to my mother.* **devoting. devoted.**

devour (di vaůr′) *v.* to eat greedily: *The hungry cat devoured its food.*

dew (dyū, dū) *n.* drops of water that form on cool surfaces: *Dew appears at night as the air cools down.*

diagnosis (dī′ əg nō′ sis) *n.* a careful examination made by a doctor to discover what illness a person has. *pl.* **diagnoses.**

diagonal (dī ag′ ə nəl) *n.* a slanting line, going from one corner of a square or rectangle to the opposite corner.

diagram (dī′ ə gram′) *n.* a drawing or plan that shows how something works or is made.

dial (dī′ əl) *n.* the face of a clock, compass, speedometer, phone, or something similar. *v.* to make a phone call by moving the dial or pressing the buttons. **dialling. dialled.**

dialect (dī′ ə lekt) *n.* a form of a language that is spoken in an area of a country: *There are many dialects that can be heard in England.*

dial tone (dī′ əl tōn′) the regular hum on a telephone which shows that a person can make a call on that telephone.

diameter (dī am′ ə tər) *n.* the length of a straight line that joins two points of a circle and passes through its centre.

diamond (dī′ mənd, dī′ ə mənd) *n.* **1.** a precious, clear stone, the hardest substance known. **2.** a shape like this: ◆. **3.** the part of a baseball field which is inside the lines that connect the bases. **4.** a playing card with one or more diamond shapes on it.

diaper (dī′ pər, dī′ ə per) *n.* a piece of cloth or paper, folded and used as underpants for a baby.

diarrhea (dī′ ə rē′ ə) *n.* an illness of the intestines, in which the bowels move often, uncontrollably, and in a liquid form.

diary (dī′ ə rē) *n.* a small notebook in which to write down what a person does each day. *pl.* **diaries.**

dice

dice (dīs) *n.pl.* small cubes with a different number of spots marked on each side, used in certain games. *sing.* **die.** *v.* to cut into small pieces or cubes. **dicing. diced.**

dictation (dik tā′ shən) *n.* the saying or reading of words to another person, who writes them down.

dictionary (dik′ shən er′ ē) *n.* a book that lists words in alphabetical order and tells what each word means. *pl.* **dictionaries.**

did see **do.**

didn't (didnt) short for **did not.**

die (dī) *n.* **1.** see **dice.** **2.** a tool used to cut out or shape a design on an object: *Canada's mint uses a die to stamp the Monarch's picture on coins.* *v.* **1.** to stop living; to lose all life. **2.** to finish or come to an end: *The sound of the bell died away.* **dying. died.** he **dies.**

diesel engine (dē′ zəl en′ jən) an engine that burns fuel oil.

diet (dī′ ət) *n.* **1.** the regular food and drink of a person or animal: *What is the diet of a lion?* **2.** special food eaten by a person who is ill, or is trying to lose or gain weight. *v.* to eat only certain foods in order to lose or gain weight.

⊖**differ** (dif′ ər) *v.* to disagree: *Mr. and Mrs. Brown differed over when to take their vacation.*

difference (dif′ rəns, dif′ ə rəns) *n.* **1.** the way in which one thing is unlike another: *What is the difference between a pen and a pencil?* **2.** the amount left after one number is subtracted from another.

different (dif′ rənt, dif′ ə rənt) *adj.* unlike; not the same: *My brother is different from me; he likes to read and I do not.*

difficult (dif′ i kult′) *adj.* **1.** not easy to do; hard to understand: *The test was difficult, because it had so many words that I didn't know.*

difficulty (dif′ i kul′ tē) *n.* something hard to do or understand: *We had difficulty finding your house at night.* *pl.* **difficulties.**

dig (dig) *v.* **1.** to turn over the earth with a shovel, hands, claws, etc. **2.** to get or make by digging: *to dig a tunnel; to dig potatoes.* **digging. dug** (dug).

digest (dī jest′) *v.* **1.** to change food in the stomach, so that the body can use it. **2.** to think over for a while and understand: *It will take a long time to digest all the information.*

digestion (dī jes′ chən) *n.* the changing of food so that it can pass into the body from the stomach and intestines.

digit (dij′ it) *n.* **1.** any of the numbers 0, 1, 2, 3, 4, 5, 6, 7, 8, 9. **2.** one finger or toe.

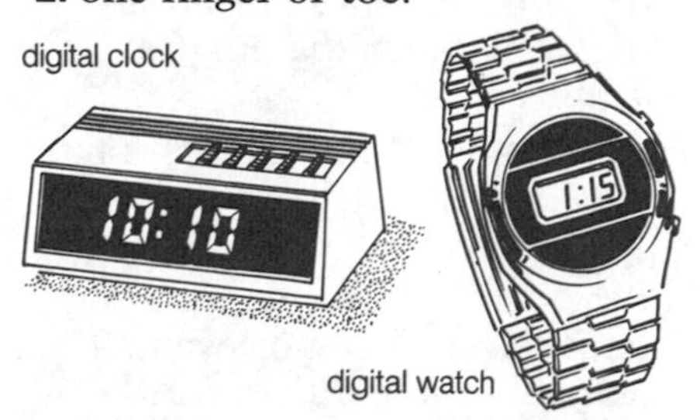

digital (dij′ it′ əl) *adj.* **1.** processing data in a numerical manner: *a digital computer.* **2.** giving information by numbers: *a digital watch; a digital clock.*

dignified (dig′ ni fīd′) *adj.* looking important, noble, serious, and proud: *a dignified princess.*

dike (dīk) *n.* a ditch or wall, built to protect an area against floods.

dill (dil) *n.* a plant whose leaves and seeds are used to flavour pickles and other foods.

dilute (di lūt′, dī lūt′) *v.* to make something weaker by adding liquid to it: *You dilute orange juice with water. You dilute oil paint with turpentine.* **diluting. diluted.**

dim (dim) *adj.* not bright or clear: *a dim light; a dimmer light; the dimmest light in the house.*

dime (dīm) *n.* a coin of Canada or the United States, worth ten cents.

dimensions (di men′ shənz) *n.pl.* the measurement of the length, width, and thickness of an object: *What are the dimensions of the closet?*

dimple (dimpl) *n.* a little hollow in the flesh, usually in the cheek or chin.

dine (dīn) *v.* **1.** to eat the main meal of the day. **2.** to eat any meal. **dining. dined.**

⊖**diner** (dī′ nər) *n.* **1.** a person who is eating. **2.** a small eating place, usually on a main road.

dinghy (ding′ ē, ding′ gē) *n.* a small boat. *pl.* **dinghies.**

dingy (din′ jē) *adj.* dull; looking grey or dirty: *dingy curtains; dingier curtains; the dingiest curtains of all.*

dining room (dī′ ning rūm′) a room where meals may be eaten.

dinner (din′ ər) *n.* **1.** the main meal of the day. **2.** a formal meal honouring a person or event: *The company gave a dinner for the retiring foreman.*

dinosaur (dī′ nə sȯr′) *n.* a huge reptile that lived millions of years ago.

dip (dip) *n.* **1.** a thick sauce for dipping crackers, slices of raw vegetables, etc. **2.** a plunge into and out of something: *a dip in the pool.* *v.* **1.** to put one thing into a liquid for a short time: *to dip your hand into warm water.* **2.** to slope down: *The road dipped into the valley.* **dipping. dipped.**

diploma (di plō′ mə) *n.* an official piece of paper given to a student when he or she graduates. *pl.* **diplomas.**

diplomat (dip′ lə mat′) *n.* **1.** a person who represents his or her nation in other countries. **2.** any person who is skilled in dealing with people, often in difficult matters: *Carol is a diplomat. She calmed her brothers just as they were about to fight.*

dipper

dipper (dip′ ər) *n.* a cup, often with a long handle, used to lift liquids: *Raoul used the dipper to take more sauce out of the pot.*

direct (di rekt′, dī rekt′) *adj.* straight: *What is the most direct way to school?* *v.* **1.** to show the way: *Can you direct me to the station?* **2.** to be in charge of; to manage: *Mr. Aquino will direct the new business.*

direction (di rek′ shən, dī rek′ shən) *n.* the point towards which something faces or moves: *The ship sailed in a westerly direction.*

directions (di rek′ shənz, dī rek′ shənz) *n.pl.* words that tell a person how to do something or how to get to a certain place: *Follow the directions when you clean the machine.*

directly (di rekt′ lē, dī rekt′ lē) *adv.* **1.** at once: *I'll be with you directly.* **2.** straight; with no stops: *Doris went directly to the library.*

director (di rek′ tər, dī rek′ tər) *n.* a person who manages something: *the director of a business, an orchestra, a play, a movie, or a TV show.*

directory (di rek′ tə rē, dī rek′ tə rē) *n.* a list of names, addresses and other facts: *a telephone directory.* *pl.* **directories.**

dirt (dûrt) *n.* **1.** filth; mud; dust. **2.** soil or earth: *Weeds grew in the dirt at the edge of the road.*

dirty (dûr′ tē) *adj.* not clean: *a dirty dog; a dirtier dog; the dirtiest dog of all.*

dis- a prefix meaning 'not': **disagree** means not to agree; a **disadvantage** means not an advantage; **dislike** means not to like; **disobey** means not to obey.

disability (dis′ ə bil′ i tē) *n.* a handicap; a lack of power or strength: *She did not let her disability keep her from getting a good job.* *pl.* **disabilities.**

disable (dis ābl′) *v.* to take away power or strength for a temporary or permanent period: *His injury* *disabled him for two weeks.* **disabling. disabled.**

disagree (dis′ ə grē′) *v.* **1.** not to agree about something: *We disagreed over which car was the safest.* **2.** to have a harmful or uncomfortable effect: *Curry disagrees with me when I eat it.* **disagreeing. disagreed.**

disappear (dis′ ə pēr′) *v.* to go out of sight: *The clerk disappeared behind the counter.*

disappearance (dis′ ə pēr′ əns) *n.* going out of sight; the act of disappearing: *What happened to the keys? Nobody could explain their disappearance.*

disappoint (dis′ ə point′) *v.* to make unhappy at not getting what is hoped for: *I was disappointed because the team played badly.*

disappointment (dis′ ə point′ mənt) *n.* the feeling of sadness that a person has when he or she doesn't get what is hoped for: *The hockey game was a disappointment. No goals were scored.*

disarmament (dis ȧrm′ ə mənt) *n.* the reduction of armed forces and their weapons: *The two enemy nations met to discuss a treaty of disarmament.*

disaster (di zas′ tər) *n.* a great misfortune, accident, or tragedy: *Plane crashes, floods, and fires are all disasters.*

disastrous (di zas′ trəs) *adj.* causing great misfortune and ruin: *a disastrous earthquake.*

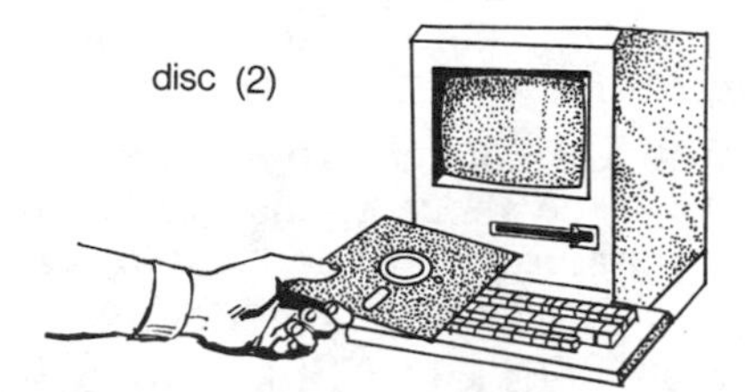
disc (2)

disc, disk (disk) *n.* **1.** a flat, circular plate, or anything like it. **2.** a thin, flat device used for storing computer programs or data.

discard (dis kȧrd′) *v.* to throw aside as worthless or unwanted: *He discarded the broken record.*

⊖**discharge** (dis chȧrj′) *v.* to let go; to unload; to dismiss: *The hospital discharged the mother and her new baby.* **discharging. discharged.**

disciple (di sīpl′) *n.* a person who follows and learns from a leader.

discipline (di′ si plin) *n.* **1.** order or control: *Children who misbehave have very little discipline.* **2.** punishment imposed for this purpose.

discolour, discolor (dis kul′ ər) *v.* to stain or change the colour of: *The sunlight has discoloured the curtains.*

disconnect (dis′ kə nekt′) *v.* to unfasten; to unplug: *Please disconnect the radio before fixing it.*

discothèque (dis′ kō tek′) *n.* a night club where people dance to music.

discount (dis′ kaůnt) *n.* an amount taken off a usual price: *During the sale there was a discount on the price of cameras.*

discourage (dis kûr′ ij) *v.* **1.** to try to stop someone from doing something: *We discouraged him from driving in the storm.* **2.** to take away the hopes of: *Carla's accident did not discourage her from diving again.* **discouraging. discouraged.**

discover (dis kuv′ ər) *v.* to find out; to see for the very first time.

discovery (dis kuv′ ə rē) *n.* the finding of something new: *the discovery of a new star in the sky. pl.* **discoveries.**

discretion (dis kresh′ ən) *n.* **1.** care in action and speech; cautious judgment: *Use discretion when you talk with Lynn; she gossips about* *everything.* **2.** the power to act according to your own judgment: *It's up to Bill's discretion to choose his new assistant.*

discrimination (dis krim′ i nā′ shən) *n.* prejudice; the unfair treatment of different people or things.

discuss (dis kus′) *v.* to talk about something with other people: *The family discussed plans for the summer holiday.* **discussing. discussed.** she **discusses.**

discussion (dis kush′ ən) *n.* a talk with other people about some matter.

disease (di zēz′) *n.* illness; sickness.

disgrace (dis grās′) *n.* a person or thing that brings shame: *The dirty, old train station is a disgrace to our town.*

disguise (dis gīz′) *n.* a change of clothing or appearance so that people will not recognize someone or something. *v.* to change the appearance so that people will not recognize a person or thing. **disguising. disguised.**

disgust (dis gust′) *n.* great dislike that may make a person feel sick: *I look upon cruel people with disgust.* *v.* to cause such a great dislike: *The bad smell disgusted me.*

dish (dish) *n.* **1.** a plate; something to hold or serve food in. **2.** a kind of food: *Stew is a meat dish.* *pl.* **dishes.** *v.* to put into a dish or dishes: *Who will dish out the dessert?* **dishing. dished.** he **dishes.**

ə**dishonest** (dis on′ əst) *adj.* not honest.

disinfect (dis′ in fekt′) *v.* to kill germs that may cause disease: *to disinfect a wound with alcohol.* **disinfecting. disinfected.**

disintegrate (dis in′ tə grāt′) *v.* to break apart into small pieces: *the miners disintegrated the rock by using dynamite.* **disintegrating. disintegrated.**

disk see **disc.**

dislike (dis līk′) *v.* not to like. **disliking. disliked.**

ə**dislocate** (dis′ lə kāt′) *v.* to make a bone in a joint shift out of place: *Susan dislocated her shoulder when she tried to lift the heavy chair.* **dislocating. dislocated.**

dismiss (dis mis′) *v.* to send away: *The teacher dismissed the class after the test.* **dismissing. dismissed.** he **dismisses.**

disobedient (dis′ ō bē′ di ənt) *adj.* not obedient; not doing what a person is told.

disobey (dis′ ō bā′) *v.* not to do what a person is told.

dispense (dis pens′) *v.* to distribute; to give to others: *The machine in the store dispenses coffee.* **dispensing. dispensed.**

ə**displace** (dis plās′) *v.* **1.** to take the position or role of: *Sharon has displaced Jesse as the top salesperson.* **2.** to move from a usual position: *The fire displaced our family; we had to move.* **displacing. displaced.**

display (dis plā′) *n.* a show; an exhibition: *a fireworks display; a display in a store window.* *pl.* **displays.** *v.* to show or exhibit something.

dispose (dis pōz′) *v.* to get rid of: *Please dispose of the garbage.* **disposing. disposed.**

disposition (dis′ pə zish′ ən) *n.* a person's usual way of feeling, thinking, or acting: *a happy disposition; a quarrelsome disposition.*

ə**dispute** (dis pūt′) *n.* an argument. *v.* to argue about; to disagree with: *I disputed some of the facts in his story.* **disputing. disputed.**

disqualify (dis kwol′ i fī) *v.* to make unable to do something: *The team was disqualified because they had* *broken an important rule.* **disqualifying. disqualified.** she **disqualifies.**

dissatisfied (dis sat′ is fīd) *adj.* not happy or pleased: *The dissatisfied shopper never came back to the store.*

dissolve (di zolv′) *v.* to mix something with water or other liquid until it disappears: *to dissolve sugar in a cup of tea.* **dissolving. dissolved.**

distance (dis′ tәns) *n.* **1.** the amount of space between two places: *What is the distance from your house to your office?* **2.** a place far away: *Can you see the tower in the distance?*

distant (dis′ tәnt) *adj.* **1.** a long way off: *a distant star in the sky.* **2.** not friendly: *She's been distant ever since we quarrelled.*

distinct (dis tingkt′) *adj.* **1.** heard or seen clearly: *The words of the singer are very distinct.* **2.** separate; different: *We heard two distinct sounds.*

distinguish (dis ting′ gwish) *v.* **1.** to see a difference: *to distinguish between one shade of brown and another.* **2.** to make famous by some action: *Liv distinguished herself in the race by winning first place.* **distinguishing. distinguished.** she **distinguishes.**

⊖**distract** (dis trakt′) *v.* to take someone's mind away from something: *Music distracts me when I'm reading.*

distress (dis tres′) *n.* great worry or anxiety: *Leon was in distress when his wife was ill.*

distribute (dis trib′ yūt) *v.* to hand out; to give to each: *He distributes the paycheques every Friday.* **distributing. distributed.**

district (dis′ trikt) *n.* a part of a town, county, or country: *a school district.*

disturb (dis tûrb′) *v.* to upset; to interfere; to trouble: *Please do not disturb me. I am reading.*

ditch (dich) *n.* a narrow, long hole cut in the ground: *This ditch drains water away. pl.* **ditches.**

dive (dīv) *n.* a downward plunge, usually into water. *v.* to make such a plunge. **diving. dived** or **dove** (dōv). he has **dived.**

diver

diver (dī′ vәr) *n.* **1.** someone who swims under water, usually in a diving suit. **2.** someone who dives for sport.

divide (di vīd′) *v.* **1.** to separate into parts or groups. *The tall bookcase divides the room.* **2.** in arithmetic, to separate into equal parts: *Eight divided by 2 equals 4.* **dividing. divided.**

dividend (div′ i dend′) *n.* money that is part of the profits of a business, shared by the owners of the business.

division (di vizh′ әn) *n.* a dividing; seeing how many times one number goes into another.

divorce (di vȯrs′) *n.* the legal ending of a marriage. *v.* to end a marriage legally. **divorcing. divorced.**

dizzy (diz′ ē) *adj.* feeling that you are turning quickly and about to fall; not steady; feeling confused: *I was dizzy after the roller coaster ride; she was dizzier; he was the dizziest.*

do (dū) *v.* **1.** to make; to work; to start something: *What do you do*

for a living? Would you do the dishes please? **2.** to be acceptable: *That amount will do; you've chopped enough wood today.* **doing. did** (did). **done** (dun). he **does** (duz).
do away with to stop; to put an end to: *to do away with an old-fashioned law.*
do up to tie, wrap, or fasten: *Do up your coat before you go outside.*
How do you do? a greeting that means 'how are you?'
Note: **do** is sometimes used with another verb: *I do want to go there.* It is also used to ask a question: *Do you want to go?*

Doberman pinscher (dob′ ər mən pin′ shər) a large black or brown dog with a long head and a shiny coat.

dock (dok) *n.* a place by the water where a ship can load, unload, or be repaired. *v.* **1.** to bring a boat to such a place. **2.** to take away a portion of: *The company docked Jill's pay because she always left work early.*

doctor (dok′ tər) *n.* **1.** a person who has a licence to practise medicine. **2.** a person who has the highest degree possible from a university: *a doctor of philosophy.*

document (dok′ yū mənt) *n.* a written or printed paper, such as a passport or map, that gives information and may be used to prove a fact.

documentary (dok′ yū ment′ ə rē) *n.* a film or television program that deals with real events: *We watched a documentary about the Calgary Stampede.* *pl.* **documentaries.**

dodge (doj) *v.* to keep away from something by moving to one side quickly. **dodging. dodged.**

doe (dō) *n.* a female rabbit, deer, or antelope.

does see **do.**

doesn't (duznt) short for **does not.**

dog (dog) *n.* an animal that has four legs, makes a barking noise, and is kept as a pet.

doghouse (dog′ haůs′) *n.* a small, outdoor house for a dog.

dog-sled

dog-sled (dog′ sled′) *n.* a sleigh pulled by dogs.

doll (dol) *n.* a toy that looks like a person.

dollar (dol′ ər) *n.* the unit of money used in Canada, the United States, and some other countries. One hundred cents make one dollar ($1.00).

dolly (dol′ ē) *n.* a small platform with wheels, used to move heavy objects: *Don't carry the stove yourselves; move it on a dolly.* *pl.* **dollies.**

dome (dōm) *n.* a roof shaped like a half a ball.

domestic (də mes′ tik) *adj.* **1.** having to do with home: *Domestic jobs include cooking and sewing.* **2.** tame; not wild: *The cow is a domestic animal.* **3.** made in a person's own country: *domestic cheese.*

dominoes (dom′ i nōz′) *n.pl.* a game played with black, oblong tiles that have dots on one side.

donate (dō′ nāt, dō nāt′) *v.* to make a gift: *We donated time and money to the children's hospital.* **donating. donated.**

donation (dō nā′ shən) *n.* a gift; a contribution: *a large donation to a charity.*

done see **do.**

donkey (dong′ kē) *n.* an ass; an animal that has long ears and looks like a small horse. *pl.* **donkeys.**

don't (dōnt) short for **do not.**

donut see **doughnut.**

door (dȯr) *n.* **1.** a movable section of wood or metal, used to open or close the entrance of a building, room, etc.: *the door of a closet; the door of a house.* **2.** a doorway.

doorway (dȯr′ wā′) *n.* an opening that leads into or out of a building or room, often closed by a door. *pl.* **doorways.**

dope (dōp) *n. (informal)* **1.** a narcotic drug. **2.** a very unintelligent person.

dose (dōs) *n.* the amount of medicine to be taken at one time.

dot (dot) *n. a small spot. v.* to make such a spot. **dotting. dotted.**

⊖**double** (dubl) *adj.* twice as much: *Frank took a double serving of ice cream. v.* **1.** to grow to twice the size; to multiply by two: *What number do you get when you double three?* **2.** to fold or bend: *Marla doubled over the sheet of paper and tore it in half.* **doubling. doubled.**
double back to go back over the same route again: *Marc doubled back to the office, looking for the lost letter.*
double-cross to promise to do one thing, but do another.
double park to park illegally beside another parked car.
double up **1.** to fold over. **2.** to bend the upper part of the body towards the legs: *I doubled up when the football hit me in the stomach.*

⊖**doubt** (daůt) *n.* an unsure feeling about something: *I have my doubts about driving in this weather. v.* to be suspicious of; not to be sure: *I doubt that he is telling the truth.*

dough (dō) *n.* a stiff mixture of flour, yeast, and water, baked to make bread, cake, or cookies.

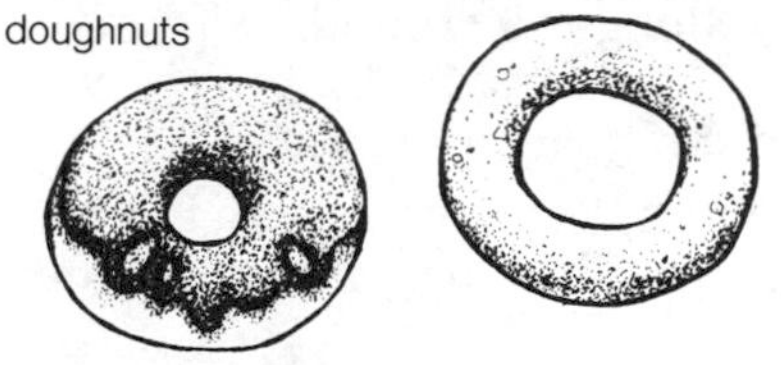
doughnuts

doughnut, donut (dō′ nut′) *n.* a small, round piece of fried cake, usually with a hole in the centre.

dove (duv) *n.* a kind of pigeon.

dove see **dive.**

down (daůn) *n.* **1.** the very soft feathers of a bird. **2.** in Canadian football, one of three chances that a team has to move the ball forward. *prep.* **1.** from a higher to a lower place: *They walked down the hill.* **2.** along: *The car drove down the street. adv.* **1.** on or to a lower place: *Please sit down.* **2.** as part of a payment for: *to pay a hundred dollars down for a chesterfield.*

downpour (daůn′ pȯr′) *n.* a heavy rain.

downstairs (daůn′ sterz′) *adv.* down to a lower floor.

downtown (daůn′ taůn′) *adv.* to the main part of a city: *We go downtown to shop.*

doze (dōz) *v.* to sleep for a short time; to nap: *Jane dozed in the chair.* **dozing. dozed.**

dozen (duz′ ən) *adj.* twelve: *a dozen eggs.*

Dr. short for **doctor**; always used with a name: *Dr. Dixon.*

drab (drab) *adj.* dull; colourless: *a drab day, a drabber day; the drabbest day of all.*

draft, draught (draft) *n.* **1.** a current of air, often in an enclosed area: *He felt a draft from under the door.* **2.** a sketch or plan of something:

The architect showed us the draft of our new house. **3.** a request from one bank to another, asking for a payment to be made.

drag (drag) *v.* **1.** to pull something heavy along the ground. **2.** to move slowly: *The time is dragging. I'm bored.* **dragging. dragged.**

dragon (drag′ ən) *n.* an imaginary monster with wings; it breathes out fire.

dragonfly (drag′ ən flī′) *n.* a large insect that has long legs and two pairs of wings. *pl.* **dragonflies.**

drain (drān) *n.* a ditch, pipe, tube, etc., that carries away unwanted liquid. *v.* **1.** to empty unwanted liquid. **2.** to tire or exhaust: *I feel drained after all that work.*

drama (drȧ′ mə, dram′ ə) *n.* **1.** a play that is not a comedy. **2.** any play meant to be seen in a theatre. *pl.* **dramas.**

dramatic (drə mat′ ik) *adj.* **1.** having to do with the theatre. **2.** exciting: *a dramatic rescue.*

drank see **drink.**

drapes, draperies (drāps, drāp′ ə rēz) *n.pl.* large, heavy curtains that hang over windows.

draught see **draft.**

draw (drȯ) *n.* **1.** a tie; the result of a game in which neither side wins. **2.** a lottery; the picking of tickets, for a prize. *v.* **1.** to make a picture on paper with pencil or crayon. **2.** to pull or take out: *to draw entries for a prize; to draw a cork from a bottle.* **3.** to pull along. *The horse drew the wagon.* **4.** to move together: *It is too bright. Please draw the curtains.* **drawing. drew** (drū). I have **drawn** (drȯn).
draw out to make longer: *She drew out the story for half an hour.*
draw up 1. to prepare or arrange in proper form: *to draw up a will or a contract.* **2.** to come to a stop: *The train drew up to the station.*

drawback (drȯ′ bak′) *n.* something that makes a situation less pleasing: *The one drawback of my leaving now is that I'll miss your birthday party.*

drawbridge (drȯ′ brij′) *n.* a bridge that can be lifted, lowered, or moved to the side.

drawers

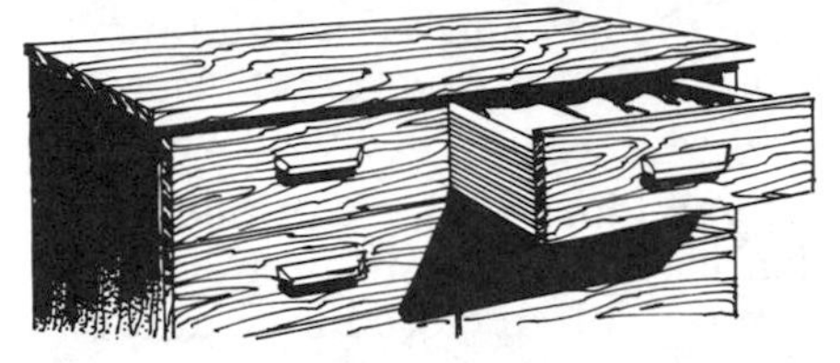

drawer (drȯr) *n.* a sliding box in a cabinet, desk, or other piece of furniture: *The spoons go in the top drawer.*

drawing (drȯ′ ing) *n.* a picture made with pencil, ink, or crayon.

dread (dred) *v.* to dislike a lot; to be afraid of: *to dread the dark.*

dreadful (dred′ fəl) *adj.* **1.** awful; frightening: *a dreadful accident.* **2.** very bad: *a dreadful party.*

dream (drēm) *n.* **1.** a picture that comes into a person's mind while asleep. **2.** a hope; a goal: *Her dream is to become a famous artist.* *v.* **1.** to imagine things are happening, while you are asleep. **2.** to hope; to have a goal. **3.** to suppose or imagine: *I didn't dream that you'd forget the party.* **dreaming. dreamed** or **dreamt** (dremt).

dreary (drēr′ ē) *adj.* dull; uninteresting: *a dreary day; a drearier one; the dreariest day of the week.*

drench (drench) *v.* to wet completely: *Get out of the rain before you're drenched!* **drenching. drenched.** it **drenches.**

⊖**dress** (dres) *n.* a piece of clothing worn by women and girls, which covers the body both above and below the waist. *pl.* **dresses.** *v.* **1.** to put on clothes. **2.** to prepare or arrange: *to dress a turkey.* **3.** to put on bandages, medicine, etc.: *to dress a wound.* **dressing. dressed.** she **dresses.**

ə**dresser** (dres′ ər) *n.* a piece of bedroom furniture with drawers for clothes.

dressing (dres′ ing) *n.* **1.** a bandage on a cut or wound. **2.** a sauce: *salad dressing.* **3.** a mixture of bread, vegetables, and herbs, often used to stuff a turkey.

drew see **draw.**

dribble (dribl) *v.* **1.** to drip water. **2.** in basketball and soccer, to run and tap or kick the ball in front of you. **dribbling. dribbled.**

dried see **dry.**

drier see **dryer** and **dry.**

dries see **dry.**

drift (drift) *n.* sand, snow, etc., blown into a pile by water or wind. *v.* **1.** to be heaped into a pile: *The snow is drifting on the road.* **2.** to be carried along by water or wind; *We drifted along in the boat.*

electric drill

drill (dril) *n.* **1.** a tool used for making holes: *an electric drill.* **2.** exercises being done over and over again: *a spelling drill; a marching drill.* *v.* **1.** to make a hole with a special tool. **2.** to teach or train people by having them do something over and over again.

drink (dringk) *n.* **1.** a beverage; any liquid that is swallowed: *a cold drink.* **2.** a serving of beer, wine, whisky, or another alcoholic beverage. *v.* **1.** to swallow some liquid, such as water. **2.** to swallow an alcoholic beverage. **drinking. drank** (drangk). I have **drunk** (drungk).

drip (drip) *n.* something falling in drops. *v.* to fall in drops: *Water drips from a leaking tap.* **dripping. dripped.**

drip-dry (drip′ drī′) *adj.* needing little or no ironing: *a drip-dry shirt.*

drive (drīv) *n.* **1.** a wide path leading to a house. **2.** a ride in a car. **3.** a special attempt to accomplish something: *The hospital held a drive to raise money for a new building.* *v.* **1.** to steer and control a vehicle: *to drive a train.* **2.** to use force or skill to push or move along: *She drove the nail into the wood. Can you drive away the insects?* **driving. drove** (drōv). I have **driven** (drivən).
drive at to mean; to have as a purpose: *What are you driving at by that remark?*

drive-in (drīv′ in′) *n.* a place where people can watch a movie, eat food, etc., while sitting in a car.

driveway (drīv′ wā′) *n.* a private road that leads from the street to a house or garage. *pl.* **driveways.**

drizzle (drizl) *n.* a fall of light rain. *v.* to rain lightly. **drizzling. drizzled.**

droop (drūp) *v.* to hang down with no strength; to sag: *The dog's ears are drooping.*

drop (drop) *n.* **1.** a tiny bit of liquid: *a drop of rain.* **2.** something shaped like this: *She took a cough drop for her sore throat.* **3.** a fall: *a great drop from the top of a tower.* **4.** the distance between one thing and something else that is below it: *There is a drop of eight metres from the roof of the house to the ground.* *v.* **1.** to fall or let fall: *The eyeglasses broke when Ted dropped them.* **2.** to let out of a car, cab, boat, etc.: *The rowboat dropped the passengers at the dock.* **dropping. dropped.**

drop by, drop in, drop over to come for an informal visit: *Drop by if you see my car in front of the house.*
drop off **1.** to decrease: *Sales of new cars have dropped off recently.* **2.** to bring and leave: *When you go to the post office, please drop off my package.*

drought (draüt) *n.* a long period of very dry weather.

drove see **drive.**

drown (draün) *v.* to die under water by being unable to breathe.
drown out to cover a sound with another that is louder: *The crowd's shouts drowned out our conversation.*

drowsy (draü′ zē) *adj.* very tired; ready to fall asleep: *a drowsy child; a drowsier child; the drowsiest child in the room.*

drug (drug) *n.* **1.** a medicine; a chemical substance that causes a change in the body and is used to treat illness. **2.** a habit-forming chemical substance, often illegal.

⊖**drugstore** (drug′ stör′) *n.* a store where medicines and other things (candy, soap, tissues, etc.) are sold.

drum (drum) *n.* **1.** a large, round, musical instrument that makes sounds when beaten with sticks. **2.** a large metal container for liquids: *an oil drum.* *v.* to beat a drum. **drumming. drummed.**

drumstick (drum′ stik′) *n.* **1.** a stick for beating a drum. **2.** the lower part of a cooked chicken or turkey leg.

drunk (drungk) *adj.* having had too much beer, wine, whisky, etc. *v.* see **drink.**

dry (drī) *adj.* not wet or damp: *a dry plant; a drier one; the driest one in the garden.* *v.* to make dry; to get rid of wetness: *Please dry the clothes after you wash them.* **drying. dried.** it **dries.**

dry cleaning (drī′ klēn′ ing) a process of cleaning clothes, curtains, and other items without using water.

dryer, drier (drī′ ər) *n.* **1.** a machine for drying clothes. **2.** a small machine for drying hair.

duck (duk) *n.* **1.** a bird with a flat bill and webbed feet that help it to swim. *v.* to dip the body or head quickly: *Marlene ducked under the low doorway as she entered the room.*

due (dyū, dū) *adj.* expected or owed: *The train is due now. The rent is due tomorrow.*
adv. directly; straight: *If you walk due north, you'll arrive at our house.*
due to because of: *The train is late due to fog.*

duel (dyū′ əl, dū′ əl) *n.* a fight between two people with swords or pistols. *v.* to take part in such a fight. **duelling. duelled.**

dues (dyūz, dūz) *n.pl.* a fee paid by a person to be a member of an organization: *union dues.*

duet (dyū et′, dū et′) *n.* a piece of music for two players or singers.

dug see **dig.**

dugout (dug′ aüt′) *n.* **1.** a shelter, hollowed out in the ground. **2.** an area at the side of a baseball field, used by team members waiting to bat. **3.** a type of canoe or boat made by hollowing out a log.

dull (dul) *adj.* not clear or bright: *a dull day.* **2.** not sharp: *a dull knife.* **3.** not interesting: *a dull talk.*

dumb (dum) *adj.* **1.** not able to talk. **2.** *(informal)* stupid.

dummy (dum′ ē) *n.* **1.** a model of a person, seen in a store window. **2.** *(informal)* a very unintelligent person; a dope. *pl.* **dummies.**

dump (dump) *n.* a place where piles of garbage are thrown. *v.* to drop or toss, often carelessly: *He dumped his money on the table. Dump the soil that is in the wheelbarrow near the garden.*

dumpling (dump′ ling) *n.* a ball of dough, boiled and served in some soups and stews.

dune (dyūn, dūn) *n.* a hill of sand.

dung (dung) *n.* manure; the solid waste matter of cows, horses, and other animals.

duplex (dyū′ pleks, dū′ pleks) *n.* **1.** a building that has two apartments. **2.** an apartment in this building. *pl.* **duplexes.**

duplicate (dyū′ pli kət, dū′ pli kət) *n.* a copy that is exactly like the original: *a duplicate of the photograph.*

duplicate (dyū′ pli kāt′, dū′ pli kāt′) *v.* to make an exact copy: *Can you duplicate this key?* **duplicating. duplicated.**

during (dyûr′ ing, dûr′ ing) *prep.* in the time of: *We played football during the morning.*

dusk (dusk) *n.* the time just before it gets dark in the evening.

dust (dust) *n.* fine powdered dirt which floats in the air. *v.* **1.** to clean with a cloth or brush: *Wanda and Karl dusted the furniture.* **2.** to cover with a dust or powder of some kind: *to dust crops in order to kill insects; to dust a cake with sugar.*

dusty (dus′ tē) *adj.* needing cleaning or dusting: *a dusty table; a dustier one; the dustiest table of all.*

Dutch (duch) *n.* the language spoken in the Netherlands. *adj.* belonging to or coming from the Netherlands.

duty (dyū′ tē, dū′ tē) *n.* **1.** something that a person has to do: *It is our duty to follow the law. One of her duties is to shovel the snow.* **2.** a tax on goods brought into or taken out of the country. *pl.* **duties.**

dwarf (dwȯrf) *n.* any living thing that is much smaller than the usual size. *pl.* **dwarfs** or **dwarves.**

dwell (dwel) *v.* to live in some place: *Fish dwell in the water.* **dwelling. dwelled** or **dwelt.**

dwelling (dwel′ ing) *n.* a place where people live.

dye (dī) *n.* a liquid or powder used to colour materials. *v.* to colour with such a liquid or powder. **dyeing. dyed.**

dying (dī′ ing) *adj.* *(informal)* extremely eager or excited: *I'm dying to go to the soccer game!* *v.* see **die.**

dynamite (dī′ nə mīt′) *n.* a powerful explosive used for breaking up rock. *v.* to use this explosive. **dynamiting. dynamited.**

E

each (ēch) *pron.* every single one: *Each of them knows how to drive.* *adj.* every: *Each child has a hamburger.*
each other each one to the other: *Because the two cousins had birthdays on the same day, they gave presents to each other.*

eager (ē′ gər) *adj.* wanting very much to have or to do something: *Julius was eager to join the hockey team.*

eagle (ēgl) *n.* a large and powerful bird that hunts small animals.

ear (ēr) *n.* **1.** the part of the body that allows people and animals to hear. **2.** the part of certain plants, such as corn or wheat, on which the grain is found.

early (ûr′ lē) *adj.* **1.** happening at the start of a period of time: *Ravi and his sister arrived in the early afternoon.* **2.** happening before the usual time: *We had an early winter this year; it began snowing in October.* *adv.* before the usual time or start: *Work begins at nine, and Tom is always early; Louise arrives earlier; Sam arrives earliest of all.*

earn (ûrn) *v.* to get payment for working: *The children earn money for raking the leaves.*

earnings (ûr′ ningz) *n.pl.* payment for work.

earphones

earphone (ēr′ fōn′) *n.* the part of a telephone, telegraph, radio, etc., that is held to the ear.

earring (ēr′ ring) *n.* a small ring or jewel worn on the ear.

earth (ûrth) *n.* **1.** the world. **2.** ground; soil.

earthquake (ûrth′ kwāk′) *n.* a shaking of the earth's surface, caused by rocks moving underground, sometimes causing great damage.

ease (ēz) *n.* comfort; rest: *He sat at ease in his armchair.* *v.* **1.** to make less difficult or uncomfortable: *Will it ease your work if I help? The aspirin will ease the pain.* **2.** to move or shift, using great care: *I eased the truck into the parking space.* **easing. eased.**
ease up to become looser or lighter: *Ease up on the gas pedal. My headache eased up after I took the aspirin.*

easel (ē′ zəl) *n.* a stand on which to rest a picture.

easily (ēz′ ə lē) *adv.* **1.** without trouble: *I can do the magic trick easily.* **2.** without doubt or question: *She is easily the most qualified person for the job.*

east (ēst) *n.* the direction of sunrise, opposite to west.

eastern (ēst′ ərn) *adj.* in the direction of the east: *Ottawa is in eastern Ontario.*

easy (ēz′ ē) *adj.* **1.** not difficult; not hard to do: *an easy puzzle; an easier one; the easiest one of all.* **2.** without trouble or discomfort: *an easy and restful vacation.*

eat (ēt) *v.* **1.** to take food through the mouth and swallow it. **2.** to have a meal: *When will we eat?* **eating. ate** (āt). I have **eaten.**
eat away to wear away; to corrode: *Acid can eat away at metal.*
eat out to eat in a restaurant, not at home.

eaves (ēvz) *n.pl.* the lower edge of a roof.

eavesdrop (ēvz′ drop′) *v.* to listen secretly: *Don't eavesdrop! This is a private conversation!*

echo (ek′ ō) *n.* a sound that bounces back from something like a hill or the wall of a cave. *pl.* **echoes.**

eclipse (ē klips′) *n.* the darkening of the sun or moon: *When the moon passes between the sun and the earth, we have an eclipse of the sun.*

⊖**economical** (ek′ ə nom′ i kəl, ē′ kə nom′ i kəl) *adj.* using money, goods, or time carefully: *Ann tries to be economical with her weekly paycheque. My car is economical; it doesn't cost too much money to operate.*

economy (i kon′ ə mē, ē kon′ ə mē) *n.* **1.** the trading of goods and spending of money by a country, province, city, company, etc.: *Wheat, oil, and fish are all important to Canada's economy.* **2.** the careful use of money, goods, or time: *We practise economy by buying clothes when they are on sale.* *pl.* **economies.**

edge (ej) *n.* **1.** a rim or border: *the edge of the woods.* **2.** the sharp side of a blade: *the edge of a knife.* *v.* to move slowly and with care: *Ivan edged towards the door so he wouldn't wake up the baby.* **edging. edged.**
on edge nervous; easily upset or excited: *She was on edge until she heard that she had gotten the job.*

edible (ed′ ibl) *adj.* safe to eat or able to be eaten.: *The flowers on the cake are not edible.*

⊖**edition** (ə dish′ ən) *n.* one of the copies of a newspaper, magazine, etc., printed at the same time: *The Canadian edition of a book; the afternoon edition of a newspaper.*

⊖**editor** (ed′ i tər) *n.* a person who checks the writing of other people and prepares this material for printing.

editorial (ed′ i tȯr′ i əl) *n.* a comment, either printed or broadcast, about a specific topic: *I read an editorial in this morning's newspaper about the next election.*

Edmonton (ed′ mən tən) *n.* the capital city of Alberta.

⊖**educate** (ej′ u̇ kāt′, ej′ ə kāt′) *v.* to teach or train people; to help people learn. **educating. educated.**

education (ej′ u̇ kā′ shən, ej′ ə kā′ shən) *n.* **1.** the helping of people to learn, usually in schools. **2.** the knowledge that a person has acquired. *Her education is in chemistry.*

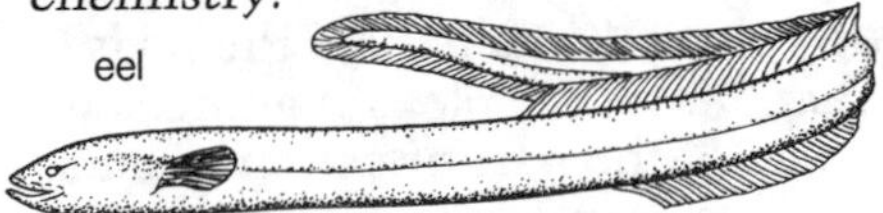
eel

eel (ēl) *n.* a long, thin fish that is shaped like a snake.

⊖**effect** (ə fekt′) *n.* the result of a change: *The medicine had a good effect on Arthur.*
Note: Do not confuse **effect** and **affect**; **affect** means 'to cause a change'.
in effect in use; happening at a certain time: *The new law is in effect as of yesterday.*
take effect to begin to be effective; to have a result: *The medicine won't take effect for several hours.*

⊖**effective** (ə fek′ tiv) *adj.* having the effect or producing the result that was wished for: *This medicine is effective. I am feeling much better.*

efficient (ə fish′ ənt) *adj.* able to get a job done well and without wasting time, effort, money, etc.: *She is an efficient worker. An electric drill is an efficient tool.*

effort (ef′ ərt) *n.* using strength or energy to do something: *The farmer made a great effort to lift the heavy stone.*

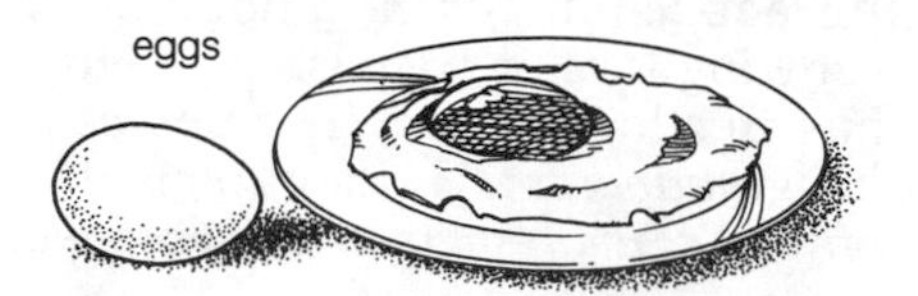

egg (eg) *n.* **1.** a roundish object with a thin shell, out of which young animals are hatched: *Eggs are laid by birds, fish and reptiles.* **2.** the contents of an egg, usually a hen's egg, eaten as food.

eggplant (eg′ plant′) *n.* a roundish vegetable that has a shiny, dark purple skin.

eh (e, ā) *interj. (informal)* isn't that right? *That was a good game, eh?*

eight (āt) *n., adj.* one more than seven (8).

eighteen (ā′ tēn′) *n., adj.* ten more than eight (18).

eighth (ātth) *adj.* following seventh (8th).

eighty (ā′ tē) *n., adj.* ten times eight (80). *pl.* **eighties.**

either (ē′ thər, ī′ thər) *adj.* **1.** one or the other of two: *Here are two cups. Take either one.* **2.** each; both: *There are houses on either side of the street.* *conj.* a word used to show choice: *Either I'll go to your house or you'll come to mine.* *adv.* also: *I didn't eat, and you didn't either.*

elaborate (i lab′ ə rət) *adj.* having many details; not simple: *an elaborate pattern on a dress.*

elaborate (i lab′ ə rāt) *v.* to add facts and details to a story or project. **elaborating. elaborated.**

elastic (i las′ tik) *n.* a rubber band or other material that stretches when pulled. *adj.* stretchy; able to go back to its own shape after being squeezed or pulled.

elbow (el′ bō) *n.* the joint between the lower arm and the upper arm.

elder (el′ dər) *adj.* older.

elderly (el′ dər lē) *adj.* old: *Our group helps elderly people go shopping.*

elect (i lekt′) *v.* to select by voting.

election (i lek′ shen) *n.* choosing by vote: *an election for mayor.*

electric (i lek′ trik) *adj.* having to do with electricity; *an electric lamp.*

electrical (i lek′ tri kəl′) *adj.* having to do with electricity: *an electrical engineer.*

electrician (i lek′ trish′ ən) *n.* a person who builds, puts in, or fixes electrical equipment.

electricity (i lek′ tris′ i tē) *n.* a powerful form of energy that can produce light and heat.

electronic (i lek′ tron′ ik) *adj.* having to do with the minute quantities of electricity that allow certain machines or devices to function: *an electronic calculator; an electronic watch.*

elegant (el′ ə gənt) *adj.* very beautiful; very rich and fine in appearance: *an elegant old hotel.*

element (el′ ə mənt) *n.* **1.** one of more than a hundred chemical substances from which all other things are made. **2.** a basic part of anything.

elementary school (el′ ə ment′ ə rē skūl′) a school that begins with kindergarten or grade one and goes to grade six, seven, or eight.

elephant (el′ ə fənt) *n.* a huge, grey land animal that lives in Asia and Africa. An elephant has thick skin, tusks, a trunk and large ears.

elevator (el′ ə vā′ tər) *n.* **1.** a machine that carries people or things up and down. **2.** a building used for storing grain: *a grain elevator.*

eleven (ə lev′ ən) *n., adj.* one more than ten (11).

eligible (el′ ij′ ibl) *adj.* having the right qualifications for a job, a position, an award, etc.: *You are not eligible for that job until you pass the examination.*

eliminate (ə lim′ i nāt′) *v.* to remove or to leave out: *When you tell the story, eliminate the facts that are not important.* **eliminating. eliminated.**

elk (elk) *n.* a large deer of North America: *The male elk has broad antlers. pl.* **elk**, or **elks.**

elm (elm) *n.* a tall shade tree.

else (els) *adj.* other: *I thought I saw Mary but it was somebody else.* *adv.* differently: *How else can you do it?*
or else or suffer for not doing something: *Be back by six o'clock, or else you'll miss dinner. Stop making that noise—or else!*

elsewhere (els′ wer′, els′ hwer′) *adv.* to or in some other place: *It's muddy here. Let's go elsewhere.*

⊖**embarrass** (em bar′ əs) *v.* to make someone feel shy or ashamed, often because of incorrect or silly behaviour: *He embarrassed his family by shouting in front of the guests.*

embassy (em′ bə sē) *n.* the home and offices of an ambassador: *Many embassies are located in Ottawa. pl.* **embassies.**

emblem (em′ bləm) *n.* a badge or sign that identifies a country, school, organization, etc.: *The maple leaf is an emblem of Canada.*

embrace (em brās′) *n.* a hug, showing love or friendship. *v.* to hug in a loving way: *He embraced his grandparents as they stepped off the plane.* **embracing. embraced.**

embroider (em bròid′ ər) *v.* to sew designs on cloth, using coloured thread.

embroidery (em bròid′ ə rē) *n.* designs sewn on cloth.

embryo (em′ bri ō′) *n.* the earliest stage of any living thing before birth. *pl.* **embryos.**

emerald (em′ ə rəld) *n.* a bright green jewel.

emerge (i mûrj′) *v.* to appear; to come into sight: *The swimmer emerged from under the water.* **emerging. emerged.**

emergency (i mûr′ jən sē) *n.* a sudden situation that must be looked after at once: *A house on fire is an emergency.* *pl.* **emergencies.**

emigrant (em′ i grənt) *n.* a person who leaves one country to live in another.

emigrate (em′ i grāt′) *v.* to leave one country to live in another. **emigrating. emigrated.**

⊖**emit** (ē mit′) *v.* to give off: *The car emitted smoke as it travelled down the street.* **emitting. emitted.**

emotion (i mō′ shən) *n.* a strong, sudden feeling such as love, fear, anger, happiness, sadness.

emperor (em′ pər ər) *n.* a man who is the head of an empire.

emphasize (em′ fə sīz′) *v.* to show the importance of a sound, word, fact, idea, etc.: *When you say 'Canada', you emphasize 'Can'. The doctor emphasized the need to get enough sleep.* **emphasizing. emphasized.**

empire (em′ pīr) *n.* a group of countries under one ruler.

⊖**employ** (em plȯi′) *v.* to hire someone to work: *Stores employ more people before Christmas.*

employee (em plȯi′ ē) *n.* someone who is hired to work and receives wages.

employer (em plȯi′ ər) *n.* someone who pays others to work for him or her.

employment (em plȯi′ mənt) *n.* work; a job: *My sister is looking for summer employment.*

empress (em′ prəs) *n.* **1.** a woman who rules over an empire. **2.** the wife of an emperor. *pl.* **empresses.**

empty (emp′ tē) *adj.* holding nothing: *an empty box. v.* to unload; to make bare: *If you empty your pockets, you may find a dime.* **emptying. emptied.** she **empties.**

enable (in ābl′) *v.* to allow to happen; to make able: *The loan from the bank enabled Franca to buy a new car.* **enabling. enabled.**

enamel (ə nam′ əl) *n.* **1.** a paint that dries into a shiny, hard surface. **2.** a hard, glass-like substance used as a coating for metal, pottery, etc.

enclose (in klōz′) *v.* **1.** to shut in on all sides: *The fence encloses the yard.* **2.** to put in a wrapping or envelope: *The money is enclosed with my letter.* **enclosing. enclosed.**

encourage (in kûr′ ij) *v.* to give someone hope and courage to do something: *His teacher encouraged him to be a writer.* **encouraging. encouraged.**

encouragement (in kûr′ ij mənt) *n.* something given or said to someone to help him or her try harder.

encyclopedia (in sī′ klə pē′ di ə) *n.* a large book, or set of books, with facts and information on many things. *pl.* **encyclopedias.**

end (end) *n.* the last part; the finish: *the end of the story. v.* to finish: *The story ends on the next page.*
end to end with the end of one thing next to the end of another: *Put the tables end to end.*
end up to become; to finish: *She'll end up a doctor if she studies hard.*
in the end at last; at the finish: *We discussed visiting different cities, but in the end we went to Saskatoon.*

endorse (in dȯrs′) *v.* **1.** to sign your name on the back of a cheque so that the bank will cash it or deposit it. **2.** to support something; to approve: *We endorsed the plan to repair the road.* **endorsing. endorsed.**

⊖**endure** (in dyūr′, in dūr′) *v.* to last or continue; to put up with: *The pyramids in Egypt have endured for thousands of years. Glen endured many months of hard work before he was promoted.* **enduring. endured.**

enemy (en′ ə mē) *n.* **1.** a person or a country that is on the other side in a quarrel or a war. **2.** anything that is harmful or dangerous: *The beetles were an enemy of the farmer's potato crop. pl.* **enemies.**

energetic (en′ ər jet′ ik) *adj.* full of energy or force: *After the rest, the swimmers felt energetic again.*

energy (en′ ər jē) *n.* liveliness, force, and power: *The boxer fought with all his energy. pl.* **energies.**

engaged (in gājd′) *adj.* **1.** promised to marriage: *They are engaged, and will be married in June.* **2.** busy; involved with: *Mr. Gomez is engaged; please phone him later. Joan is engaged in finding a business partner.*

engagement (in gāj′ mənt) *n.* **1.** a promise of marriage. **2.** an appointment; a meeting with another person at a certain time.

engine (en′ jin) *n.* **1.** any machine that produces power to make things work. **2.** a locomotive: *The engine pulled the train up the hill.*

engineer (en′ ji nēr′) *n.* **1.** a person who works with engines and machinery. **2.** the driver of a locomotive.

engineering (en′ ji nēr′ ing) *n.* the development and use of machines for practical purposes such as building dams or bridges, mining, or drilling for oil.

English (ing′ glish) *n.* the language spoken in England, Canada, the United States, and other countries. *adj.* belonging to or coming from England.

enjoy (in jȯi′) *v.* to be pleased by something: *The boys and girls enjoyed the circus.*

enjoyable (in jȯi′ əbl) *adj.* giving pleasure: *an enjoyable picnic.*

enjoyment (in jȯi′ mənt) *n.* pleasure; happiness: *Books bring enjoyment to many people.*

enlarge (in lȧrj′) *v.* to make or grow bigger: *to enlarge a photograph; to enlarge a hospital by adding another building.* **enlarging. enlarged.**

enormous (i nȯr′ məs) *adj.* extremely large; huge.

enough (i nuf′) *adj.* as much or as many as are needed or wanted: *I have enough money to buy the shirt.*

enquire see **inquire.**

enrol, enroll (in rōl′) *v.* to become a member of a school, class, group, etc.: *Alice enrolled in law school.* **enrolling. enrolled.**

ensure (in shûr′) *v.* to make certain or safe: *Leaving early will ensure that we will get to the movie on time.* **ensuring. ensured.**

enter (en′ tər) *v.* **1.** to go in: *They entered the house.* **2.** to join: *I will enter the contest.*

⊖**entertain** (en′ tər tān′) *v.* **1.** to amuse: *The clowns entertained the children.* **2.** to have guests: *They entertained ten people at the birthday dinner.*

entertainment (en′ tər tān′ mənt) *n.* something that entertains or interests people, such as a movie or play.

enthusiastic (in thyū′ zī as′ tik) *adj.* being very interested in something and showing your excitement for it: *The enthusiastic crowd at the ball game cheered the winning team.*

entire (in tīr′, en tīr′) *adj.* complete; the whole of anything: *The entire crew was saved from the explosion.*

entrance (en′ trəns) *n.* a way in; a doorway: *the entrance to the theatre.*

entry (en′ trē) *n.* **1.** a going in; a way in: *The entry to the house is by the side door.* **2.** someone or something who enters a contest. **3.** a small section that is listed in a book, diary, etc.: *The next entry in this dictionary is* **envelope.** *pl.* **entries.**

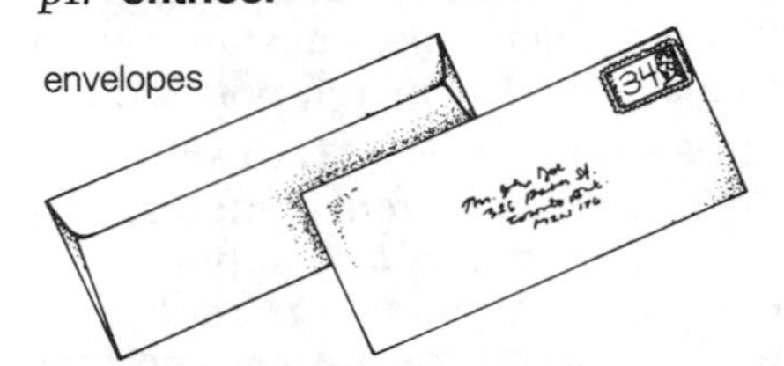
envelopes

envelope (en′ və lōp′, on′ və lōp′) *n.* a folded and sealed paper cover for a letter.

envious (en′ vi əs) *adj.* feeling full of jealousy: *He's so envious! He wants everything I own.*

environment (en vī′ rən mənt) *n.* the things that surround and affect people, animals and plants: *I cannot study in a noisy environment. Our city is working for a cleaner environment.*

⊖**envy** (en′ vē) *v.* to feel jealous: *He envies his sister because she has a new car.* **envying. envied.** she **envies.**

epidemic (ep′ i dem′ ik) *n.* a very quick spreading of a disease from one person to another: *an epidemic of the flu.*

equal (ē′ kwəl) *adj.* of the same number or value as something else: *The big cat and the little pup are equal in size.* *v.* in arithmetic, to be the same as; the symbol is =. **equalling. equalled.**

equation (i kwā′ zhən) *n.* in mathematics or chemistry, a statement that two things are equal: *3 + 2 = 5 is an equation.*

equator (i kwā′ tər) *n.* an imaginary circle around the middle of the world. The equator is halfway between the North and South Poles.

equip (i kwip′) *v.* to provide with everything necessary: *to equip a hockey team with uniforms, sticks, and pucks.* **equipping. equipped.**

equipment (i kwip′ mənt) *n.* items that a person needs in order to do certain jobs, play certain sports, etc.: *skiing equipment.*

erase (i rās′) *v.* to rub out: *Please erase the writing on the board.* **erasing. erased.**

eraser

eraser (i rās′ ər) *n.* something used for rubbing out marks or writing: *a pencil eraser; a chalkboard eraser.*

erect (i rekt′) *adj.* straight up: *The people in the parade walked erect.* *v.* to set up or build: *A statue was erected to honour our first prime minister, Sir John A. Macdonald.*

erode (i rōd′) *v.* to wear away slowly: *Rust will erode some kinds of metal.* **eroding. eroded.**

erosion (i rō′ zhən) *n.* the act of eroding: *erosion of the soil.*

errand (er′ ənd) *n.* a small trip made to collect or deliver a message or package.

error (er′ ər) *n.* a mistake.
in error by mistake: *Mrs. Lim knocked on the wrong door in error.*

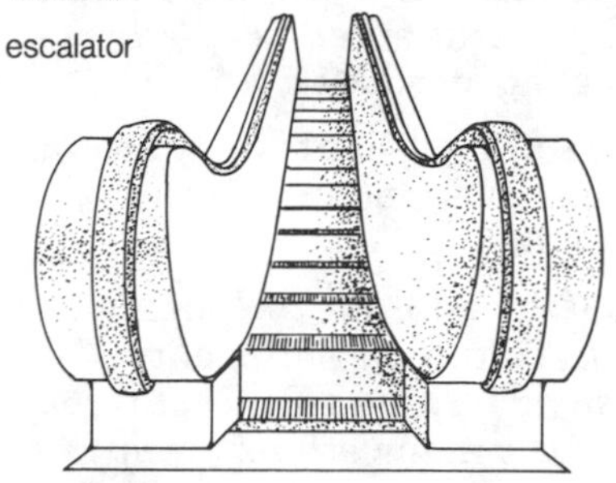
escalator

escalator (es′ kə lā′ tər) *n.* a stairway that moves.

escape (əs kāp′) *n.* getting free: *a lucky escape from danger.* *v.* to get away: *to escape from a boring speech.* **escaping. escaped.**

Eskimo (es′ ki mō′) *n.* a people living in the Arctic, or one of these people. *pl.* **Eskimo** or **Eskimos.** *Note:* **Inuit** is the name these people use for themselves.

especially (əs pesh′ ə lē) *adv.* most of all: *I like dogs, especially poodles.*

⊖**essay** (es′ ā) *n.* a short piece of writing in which the author explains his or her ideas and opinions about one subject. *pl.* **essays.**

essential (i sen′ shəl) *adj.* really necessary: *To play the piano well, it is essential to practise.*

establish (əs tab′ lish) *v.* to start something that should last a long time: *Mr. Kelly established a new restaurant in our neighbourhood. We established our friendship many years ago.* **establishing. established.** he **establishes.**

estate (əs tāt′) *n.* the things that someone owns: *In her will, Rita left her estate to her brothers.*

estimate (es′ tə mət) *n.* a guess about the size, amount, or price of something: *My estimate is that the tree is five metres tall.*

estimate (es′ tə māt′) *v.* to guess the size, amount, or price of something: *Juana estimates that there are a hundred people here.* **estimating. estimated.**

etc. (et set′ ə rə) short for **et cetera**, which means 'and other things', 'and so on'.

ethnic (eth′ nik) *adj.* belonging to a certain culture or nationality: *Italians, Poles, and Pakistanis are a few of the many ethnic groups in Canada.*

European (yū′ rə pi′ ən) *n.* a person born in or living in Europe. *adj.* having to do with the continent of Europe.

evaporate (i vap′ ə rāt′) *v.* to change from solid or liquid into vapour or gas when heated. **evaporating. evaporated.**

eve (ēv) *n.* **1.** evening. **2.** the day or evening before a special event: *New Year's eve.*

even (ē′ vən) *adj.* **1.** smooth; level: *an even piece of wood.* **2.** equal: *At the end of the game, the score was even.* **3.** able to be divided by two. *adv.* **1.** still; yet: *You play the piano well. If you practise, you'll play even better.* **2.** actually: *The pot is warm, even hot, from sitting in the sun.* **3.** though it is not expected: *Even my dog likes to watch television.*
break even neither to make money nor to lose money: *Mr. Jackson said that his store broke even last year.*
get even to have revenge; to do something unkind to a person because you think that he or she has done something unkind to you.

evening (ēv′ ning) *n.* the time between day and night.

event (i vent′) *n.* **1.** some special happening: *The prime minister's visit is an important event.* **2.** one of the items in a sports program: *The short race was the third event.*
in any event whatever happens: *In any event, we will go to the movies.*
in the event of, in the event that in case of; if it should happen that: *In the event of a snowstorm, the factory will be closed.*

⊖**eventually** (i ven′ chū ə lē) *adv.* finally; at last: *Eventually, he found a pair of shoes that he liked.*

ever (ev′ ər) *adv.* at any time: *If you're ever in town, come and see me.*

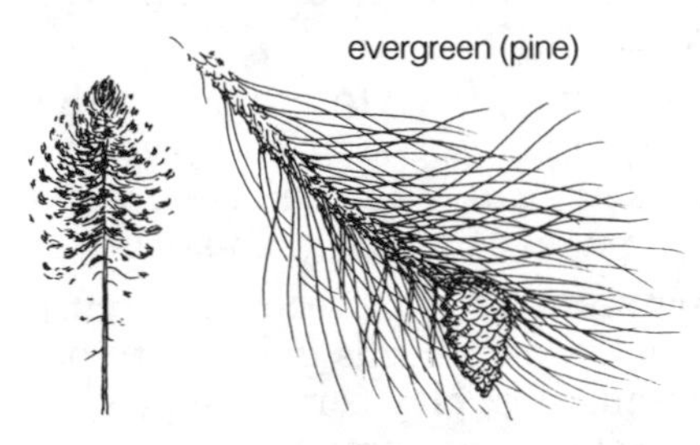
evergreen (pine)

evergreen (ev′ ər grēn′) *n.* a tree or other plant that is always green and whose leaves look like needles: *The pine tree is an evergreen.*

every (ev′ rē) *adj.* each: *I pass the house every day.*
every now and then occasionally; sometimes: *She writes to her cousin every now and then.*
every other each second; skipping every other one: *Andrew is paid every other week.*

everybody (ev′ rē bud′ ē, ev′ rē bod′ ē) *pron.* each person; all the people: *Is everybody away?*

everyday (ev′ rē dā′) *adj.* **1.** for ordinary days rather than special occasions: *an everyday dress.* **2.** daily.

everyone (ev′ rē wun′) *pron.* everybody: *Everyone is going home.*

everything (ev′ rē thing′) *pron.* each thing; all the things: *Everything is ready for the party.*

everywhere (ev′ rē wer′, ev′ rē hwer′) *adv.* in every place: *We looked everywhere for my lost key.*

evict (ə vikt′) *v.* to require that a tenant leave a building, apartment, etc.: *They were evicted from the hotel because they were too noisy.*

⊖**evidence** (ev′ i dəns) *n.* information that proves something: *The lawyer presented her evidence to the judge.*

evident (ev′ i dənt) *adj.* clear; easily seen or realized.

evil (ē′ vəl, ē′ vil) *adj.* wicked; very bad: *an evil person; an evil deed.*

ewe (yū) *n.* a female sheep.

exact (ig zakt′) *adj.* just right; correct: *The exact time is two minutes past one.*

exactly (ig zakt′ lē) *adv.* without even a small mistake: *The clock is exactly right.*

exaggerate (ig zaj′ ə rāt′) *v.* to say something is bigger, better, more important, etc., than it really is: *He says he can drive home in ten minutes, but I know he is exaggerating.* **exaggerating. exaggerated.**

exam (eg zam′) short for **examination.**

examination (ig zam′ i nā′ shən) *n.* **1.** a careful check: *She went to the doctor for a physical examination.* **2.** a test of what a person knows: *a history examination.*

examine (ig zam′ in) *v.* **1.** to look at closely. **2.** to test someone's knowledge of some subject. **examining. examined.**

example (ig zampl′) *n.* **1.** a model to be copied: *They set a good example for their children.* **2.** something to use as a sample: *Give me an example of a large city.*

excavate (iks′ kə vāt′) *v.* to dig out from the earth: *Old bones were excavated from the ground.* **excavating. excavated.**

exceed (ek sēd′) *v.* to be larger, more, or greater than: *to exceed the speed limit.*

excellent (ek′ sə lənt) *adj.* extremely good.

except (ek sept′) *prep.* other than; leaving out: *Everyone except Joe lives on a farm.*
Note: Do not confuse **except** and **accept**; **accept** means 'to take something that is offered'.

exception (ek sep′ shən) *n.* someone or something not included; someone or something different: *With one exception, all the meetings are in the morning.*

excess (ik′ ses, ek′ ses) *n.* the part that is too much or more than is needed: *Dina used the excess batter to make a second cake.* *pl.* **excesses.**

exchange (iks chānj′, eks chānj′) *n.* a place where people trade, buy, or sell various things: *a stock exchange.* *v.* to give one thing in return for another: *Alan exchanged an Australian stamp for a Canadian one.* **exchanging. exchanged.**
exchange rate the value of one currency expressed in another: *What is the exchange rate between the Canadian and American dollar?*
exchange student a student who attends a school or university in another country.

excite (ik sīt′) *v.* to cause strong feelings or emotions: *They are excited about the new car.* **exciting. excited.**

⊖**excitement** (ik sīt′ mənt) *n.* fuss; activity; strong feelings: *There was a lot of excitement when we saw our picture in the newspaper.*

exclaim (iks klām′) *v.* to shout out with excitement.

exclamation (eks′ klə mā′ shən) *n.* an excited shout.

exclamation mark (eks′ klə mā′ shən märk) a mark (!) put at the end of a sentence to show anger, excitement, or surprise: *Hurray! We have won!*

exclude (ik sklūd′) *v.* **1.** to keep out: *Children under 14 are excluded from certain movies.* **2.** not to count: *When counting workdays, you must exclude Sundays and holidays.* **excluding. excluded.**

exclusive (ik sklūs′ iv′) *adj.* **1.** special; not available to everyone: *an exclusive club; an exclusive interview.* **2.** *(informal)* expensive: *an exclusive hotel; an exclusive store.*

excuse (ik skyūs′) *n.* a reason that a person gives for something: *an excuse for being late.*

excuse (ik skyūz′) *v.* **1.** to forgive: *Please excuse me for leaving early. I'm in a hurry today.* **2.** to be allowed not to do some job or duty: *You are excused from working because you are ill.* **excusing. excused.**

⊖**execute** (ek′ si kyūt′) *v.* to put someone to death by law. **executing. executed.**

⊖**executive** (ig zek′ yə tiv) *n.* a person or group that acts as a manager: *Rachel is an executive in her company; she hires all the new employees.*

exempt (ig zempt′) *adj.* not required to do or give something: *I am exempt from working in the field because of my broken arm.*

exercise (ek′ sər sīz′) *n.* **1.** something that gives practice: *a spelling exercise.* **2.** an activity for training the body or mind: *Jogging is my favourite exercise.* *v.* to train the body or mind. **exercising. exercised.**

exhale (eks hāl′) *v.* to breathe out: *She sucked in air, then slowly exhaled.* **exhaling. exhaled.**

exhaust (ig zȯst′) *n.* used steam or gas that escapes from an engine. *v.* to tire out: *The long climb exhausted us.*

exhibit (ig zib′ it) *n.* a public display of things such as paintings, old cars, or costumes. *v.* to show or display something.

exhibition (ek′ si bish′ ən) *n.* **1.** a show; a display: *an exhibition of pictures in an art gallery.* **2.** a large fair: *the Canadian National Exhibition.*

exile (eg′ zīl, ek′ sīl) *v.* to send someone away from his or her home or country, sometimes as a punishment. **exiling. exiled.**

exist (ig zist′) *v.* to live; to be: *Rabbits exist on wild plants. Do people exist on other planets?*

exit (eg′ zit, ek′ sit) *n.* a way out: *The exit from the hall was marked with a sign.*

expand (ik spand′) *v.* to grow bigger: *Many objects expand in the heat and contract in the cold.*

expect (ik spekt′) *v.* to think something will happen; to suppose: *I expect to see my brother tomorrow.*

⊖**expedition** (ek′ spə dish′ ən) *n.* a journey for some special purpose: *a hiking expedition.*

expel (ik spel′) *v.* to force out; to send someone away officially: *He was expelled from the club because he refused to pay his dues.* **expelling. expelled.**

expense (ik spens′) *n.* a cost: *What were your expenses on the trip?*

expensive (ik spen′ siv) *adj.* costing a lot: *an expensive piece of jewellery.*

⊖**experience** (ik spēr′ i əns) *n.* knowledge gained by having done things: *Our family has* *experience as farmers. He told us about his experiences as a miner.* *v.* to feel; to have happen; to live through: *I did not experience snow until I came to Canada.* **experiencing. experienced.**

experienced (ik spēr′ i ənst) *adj.* good at something because of practice: *Mrs. Thomas is an experienced carpenter.*

experiment (ik sper′ i ment) *n.* a test to find what will happen: *a science experiment.*

experiment (ik sper′ i ment′) *v.* to test in order to find something: *The baker was experimenting with different flavourings.*

expert (ek′ spûrt) *n.* someone who knows a great deal about a subject: *an expert in sewing.*

expire (ik spīr′) *v.* to end; to no longer be useful, valid, etc.: *I must apply for a new driver's licence—my old one has expired.* **expiring. expired.**

explain (ik splān′) *v.* to describe the meaning or cause of something: *The coach explained the rules carefully.*

explanation (ek′ splə nā′ shən) *n.* a reason: *I asked why my foot hurt. The doctor gave me a long explanation.*

explode (ik splōd′) *v.* to burst into pieces; to blow up. **exploding. exploded.**

explore (ik splȯr′) *v.* **1.** to look around; to look at carefully: *to explore an old lighthouse.* **2.** to travel to discover new lands. **exploring. explored.**

explosion (ik splō′ zhən) *n.* a bursting into pieces; a blowing up.

explosive (ik splō′ siv) *n.* something that can explode: *Gunpowder is an explosive.*

export (ek′ spȯrt) *n.* a product sold to or in another country.

export (ik spȯrt′, ek′ spȯrt) *v.* to send something out of the country: *Canada exports wheat to many countries.*

expose (ik spōz′) *v.* **1.** to show; to leave unprotected: *Don't expose your hands in the cold weather.* **2.** to let light reach and affect photographic film: *You exposed the film when you opened the camera.* **exposing. exposed.**

express (ik spres′) *n.* a fast elevator, bus, or train that makes only a few stops. *v.* to tell or show through words, action, or a look on the face: *My smile expressed the way I was feeling. We expressed our sorrow on her loss.* **expressing. expressed.** she **expresses.**

expression (ik spresh′ ən) *n.* **1.** a look on the face: *a worried expression; a happy expression.* **2.** a word or series of words that are often used together to express a thought: *'Look before you leap' is a common expression.*

expressway (ik spres′ wā′) *n.* a divided highway, built for fast travelling. *pl.* **expressways.**

extend (ik stend′) *v.* **1.** to make longer: *The class will be extended by ten minutes.* **2.** to stretch; to go on: *the land extends for many kilometres.*

exterior (ek′ stēr′ i ər) *n.* the outside of anything: *The exterior of the car was clean and shiny. The interior was dirty.*

extinguish (ik sting′ gwish) *v.* to put out a flame or fire. **extinguishing. extinguished.** he **extinguishes.**

extra (ek′ stra) *adj.* more than usual: *Mother was given an extra day's holiday.*

extract (ek′ strakt) *n.* something that is taken out or removed: *Peppermint extract, used as a flavouring, comes from peppermint leaves.*

extract (ik strakt′) *v.* to pull or take out: *to extract a tooth.*

extraordinary (ik strôr′ di ner′ ē) *adj.* unusual; special; worth attention.

extreme (ik strēm′) *adj.* **1.** the greatest: *Take extreme care.* **2.** the farthest: *Len stood on the extreme edge of the cliff.*

extremely (ik strēm′ lē) *adv.* very much so: *an extremely playful dog.*

eye (ī) *n.* the part of the body that allows a person or animal to see.
catch a person's eye to attract a person's interest and attention: *The sign caught my eye as I went by the store.*
keep an eye on to take care of: *Keep an eye on my apartment while I'm away, please.*
see eye to eye to agree completely: *The committee members don't see eye to eye on where to build the new road.*

eyebrow (ī′ brou′) *n.* the small ridge of hair over each eye.

eyeglasses

eyeglasses (ī′ glas′ əz) *n.pl.* a pair of glass or plastic lenses that help a person to see better.

eyelash (ī′ lash′) *n.* one of the hairs on the edge of the eyelid.
pl. **eyelashes.**

eyelid (ī′ lid′) *n.* the movable cover of skin over each eye.

eyesight (ī′ sīt′) *n.* the power to see.

eyewitness (ī′ wit′ nes) *n.* a person who sees, or has seen, something happen: *She was an eyewitness to the bank robbery.*
pl. **eyewitnesses.**

F

fable (fābl) *n.* a short story that is meant to teach a lesson.

⊖**fabric** (fab′ rik) *n.* cloth.

⊖**fabulous** (fab′ yū ləs, fab′ yə ləs) *adj.* **1.** excellent: *We had a fabulous time.* **2.** amazing; almost unbelievable: *a fabulous adventure story.*

⊖**face** (fās) *n.* **1.** the front of the head. **2.** the front of a clock, building, playing card, etc. *v.* to look towards; to have the front towards: *Our house faces a school.* **facing. faced.**
face up to to admit and accept; to meet confidently: *to face up to a crime; to face up to a hard job.*

face-off

face-off (fās′ of′) *n.* the putting of the hockey puck into play.

facial (fā′ shəl) *adj.* having to do with the face.

⊖**facilities** (fə sil′ i tēz) *n.pl.* something that makes actions possible or easier: *The city's transportation facilities make it easy to travel.*

fact (fakt) *n.* something that is true or real.

factory (fak′ tə rē) *n.* a building in which things are made in large amounts, most often with the help of machines. *pl.* **factories.**

fade (fād) *v.* **1.** to lose colour in sunlight or by washing: *The curtains have faded from a dark blue to a pale blue.* **2.** to become weak or dim: *The light fades towards evening.* **fading. faded.**

⊖**fail** (fāl) *v.* **1.** not to be able to do something that is attempted: *to fail a test.* **2.** not to work as expected: *The player's chess strategy failed.*

failure (fāl′ yər) *n.* **1.** an unsuccessful try: *He took more lessons after his failure to get a driver's licence.* **2.** a person or thing that fails: *Take out the candles. We have a power failure.*

faint (fānt) *adj.* not strong or clear: *a faint call from across a field; a faint stain on a carpet.* *v.* to feel dizzy and ill; to pass out: *Some people faint when they see blood.*

fair (fer) *n.* a market or a show of farm animals and homemade goods. *adj.* **1.** light in colour: *She has fair hair.* **2.** less than good: *His work is only fair.* **3.** honest: *The person was given a fair trial.* **4.** not raining or cloudy: *fair weather.*

fairly (fer′ lē) *adv.* somewhat; rather: *He's a fairly good ballplayer. He's not the best, but he's not the worst, either.*

fairy (fer′ ē) *n.* an imaginary little creature with magical powers. *pl.* **fairies.**

fairy tale (fer′ ē tāl′) a story of fairies or other magical creatures.

faith (fāth) *n.* strong belief; trust: *I have faith that we will see each other again.*

faithful (fāth′ fəl) *adj.* loyal; to be trusted: *Joanne is a faithful friend, ready to help if I need her.*

fake (fāk) *adj.* copied; not real; made to look like something better: *fake money; fake jewels.*

falcon (fol′ kən) *n.* a kind of hawk that is sometimes trained for hunting.

fall (fòl) *n.* **1.** the season after summer, also called 'autumn'. **2.** coming down from a higher position: *a bad fall.* **3. falls** waterfalls: *Niagara Falls.* *v.* **1.** to drop; *The egg fell off the table. It fell on the floor.* **2.** to become lower in price, value, etc. *The price of the house has fallen since last year.* **3.** to happen: *Kristine's birthday falls on Tuesday this year.* **falling. fell** (fel). I have **fallen** (fòlən).
fall asleep to go to sleep: *Nina fell asleep in the chair.*
fall back on to rely on for support or help: *David fell back on his savings when his business did not succeed.*
fall behind to be unable to reach or stay at a certain level: *Production in the factory fell behind when the machinery broke.*
fall in love to start to feel a great affection for someone: *I fell in love the first time I saw her.*
fall off to become less: *My interest in studying has fallen off since I started playing on the soccer team.*
fall through to fail to be successful: *Ahmad's weekend plans fell through when his mother became ill.*

false (fòls) *adj.* **1.** not true: *a false story.* **2.** not real: *false teeth.*

fame (fām) *n.* glory; honour; being well-known: *Over the years, she gained fame as a scientist.*

familiar (fə mil′ yər) *adj.* well-known: *Birds are a familiar sight in these woods. Your face is familiar to me.*
familiar with to know about: *Doctors are familiar with most common diseases.*

family (fam′ i lē, fam′ lē) *n.* **1.** a parent or parents and their children. **2.** close relatives. *pl.* **families.**

Family Allowance (fam′ i lē ə laù′ əns) In Canada, money that is given every month by the government to parents for each child who is under eighteen.

family name (fam′ i lē nām′) a last name; a name shared with other members in a family.

famine (fam′ in) *n.* a great shortage of food in a district or in a country.

⊖**famous** (fā′ məs) *adj.* extremely well-known: *a famous actor.*

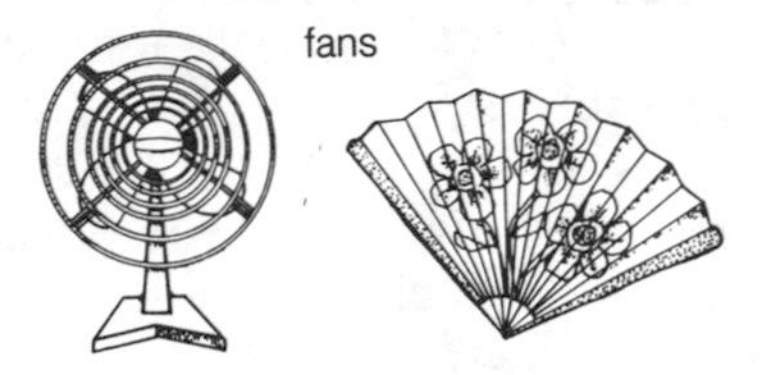

fan (fan) *n.* **1.** something to make a cooling breeze: *an electric fan; a paper fan.* **2.** someone who very much likes a sports team, a singer, an actor, etc. *v.* to cool with a fan. **fanning. fanned.**

fancy (fan′ sē) *adj.* not plain; covered with decorations: *a fancy blouse; a fancier one; the fanciest one in the store.*

fang (fang) *n.* **1.** a long, sharp tooth of a dog or wolf. **2.** a snake's tooth, which is hollow and sometimes contains poison.

fantastic (fan tas′ tik) *adj.* amazing; almost unbelievable; wonderful: *a fantastic meal.*

far (får) *adv.* **1.** a long way off. *I live far from the store; you live farther; he lives farthest of us all.* **2.** much: *It would be far better if you could come today instead of tomorrow.* *adj.* not near: *the far end of the road.*
by far certainly; without question or doubt: *Iris is by far the best pitcher on the team.*
so far until now: *I have not missed any school so far this year.*

fare (fer) *n.* the price of a trip on a bus, ship, taxi, train, or plane.

farewell (fer′ wel′) *n.* a good-bye; a parting wish: *We said our farewells, then drove away.*

farm (fárm) *n.* a piece of land that is used to grow crops and raise animals. *v.* to look after or work on a farm.

farmer (fárm′ ər) *n.* a person who looks after or works on a farm.

far-sighted (fár′ sīt′ əd) *adj.* able to see things that are far away, but not things that are close.

farther (fár′ t͟hər) *adv.* at or to a greater distance: *He lives farther from school than I do.*

farthest (fár′ t͟həst) *adv.* at or to the greatest distance: *Of all the students, Jenny lives the farthest from school.*

fascinate (fas′ i nāt′) *v.* to hold someone's attention; to be of great interest: *These pictures fascinate me. I can't stop looking at them.* **fascinating. fascinated.**

fashion (fash′ ən) *n.* a style that is popular at the present time: *Bright colours are now in fashion.* *v.* to make or form: *to fashion a shelf out of wooden boxes.*

fast (fast) *n.* a time or act of going without food. *adj.* **1.** quick; speedy; *a fast car.* **2.** later than the correct time: *The kitchen clock is thirty minutes fast.* *adv.* quickly: *Shari can run fast.* *v.* to go without food for a time.
fast asleep totally asleep: *Noreen is fast asleep in her bed.*

fasten (fas′ ən) *v.* to tie, join, or close: *Please fasten the string around the box.*

ɵ**fat** (fat) *n.* **1.** the greasy part of meat and other substances. **2.** the substance under the skin which keeps people and animals warm. *adj.* plump; big and round: *a fat cat; a fatter cat; the fattest cat on the street.*

ɵ**fatal** (fā′ təl) *adj.* causing death: *a fatal accident.*

fate (fāt) *n.* the future; the final outcome; what will happen eventually: *My father is a doctor; my fate is to become one also.*

father (fát͟h′ ər) *n.* **1.** a man who is a parent. **2.** a Roman Catholic or Anglican priest.

father-in-law (fát͟h′ ər in ló′) *n.* the father of a person's wife or husband. *pl.* **fathers-in-law.**

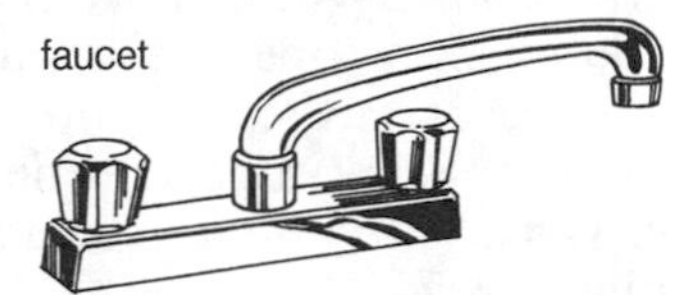

faucet (fó′ sət) *n.* a device used for turning water or other liquid on or off.

fault (fólt) *n.* an error; something wrong: *The accident was the fault of the truck driver. I was at fault when I forgot to lock the kitchen door.*
find fault with to criticize; to complain about: *Why do you always find fault with the way I wash the dishes?*

favour, favor (fā vər) *n.* a kindness: *Will you do me a favour? Please walk my dog.*
in favour of in support of; in agreement with: *Everyone in favour of a shorter work week, raise your hands.*
in someone's favour to someone's advantage: *You should apply for that job; it's in your favour that you have experience with computers.*

favourite, favorite (fāv′ ə rit) *adj.* most liked: *This is my favourite hat.*

fawn (fón) *n.* a young deer.

fear (fēr) *n.* a feeling that something dangerous may happen: *a fear of flying in an airplane.* *v.* to feel afraid of: *There is no reason to fear the dog.*

fearful (fēr′ fəl) *adj.* full of fear.

feast (fēst) *n.* a very large meal.

feat (fēt) *n.* an action that requires courage or skill: *To walk on a tightrope is a great feat.*

feather (feth′ ər) *n.* one of the many light, fluffy growths that cover a bird's body.

feature (fē′ chər) *n.* **1.** a part or quality of something: *A main feature of our new house is the large kitchen.* **2.** one of the main parts of the face; the eyes, nose, mouth, etc. **3.** an important news story: *What is the main feature in the magazine?*

February (feb′ rü er′ ē) *n.* the second month of the year.

fed see **feed.**
fed up with not interested in any more: *Find me something else to do. I'm fed up with reading!*

federal (fed′ ə rəl) *adj.* having to do with the government of a country, not of a province or city: *Members of Parliament are elected in a federal election.*

fee (fē) *n.* a charge: *the doctor's fee.*

feeble (fēbl) *adj.* very weak; not strong: *a feeble person; a feebler person; the feeblest one of all.*

feed (fēd) *n.* food for animals: *We gave the hens some chicken feed.* *v.* to give food to: *Please feed the baby.* **feeding. fed** (fed).

feel (fēl) *v.* **1.** to touch: *Simon felt the key in his pocket.* **2.** to be in a mood: *Ruth feels happy because it's her birthday.* **3.** to have an opinion: *I feel this is what we should do.* **feeling. felt** (felt).
feel like to want: *I feel like a rest. I feel like a steak.*

feeling (fēl′ ing) *n.* **1.** the sense of touch: *By feeling, we can tell what is hard and what is soft.* **2.** a mood that a person is in: *a happy feeling.*

feelings (fēl′ ingz) *n.pl.* a way someone feels about himself or herself, about someone else, or about something.

feet plural of **foot.**

fell (fel) *v.* **1.** see **fall.** **2.** to cut down: *to fell a tree.*

fellow (fel′ ō) *n.* a friendly name for a man or boy: *He's a good fellow.*

felt (felt) *n.* a thick kind of cloth. *v.* see **feel.**

female (fē′ māl) *n.* **1.** a girl or a woman. **2.** an animal that is, will be, or can be a mother: *A cow is a female. A bull is a male.*

feminine (fem′ i nin) *adj.* having to do with girls or women: *'She' is a feminine pronoun. 'He' is a masculine pronoun.*

fence (fens) *n.* a railing or wall put around an area such as a garden or field. *v.* to fight with swords. **fencing. fenced.**

fender (fen′ dər) *n.* the metal part that protects a car or bicycle wheel.

fern (fûrn) *n.* a plant with long, feathery leaves.

ferry (fer′ ē) *n.* a boat that carries people and goods across a body of water. *pl.* **ferries.**

fertilizer (fûr′ ti līz′ ər) *n.* a substance added to soil, to make it better for growing crops.

festival (fes′ ti vəl) *n.* a holiday or time of celebration, often with music, art, drama, or food.

fetch (fech) *v.* to go after something and bring it back: *Please fetch my scarf.* **fetching. fetched.** he **fetches.**

fetus (fē′ təs) *n.* in a mammal, the later stages of an embryo. *pl.* **fetuses.**

fever (fē′ vər) *n.* **1.** a body temperature that is higher than usual. **2.** the common name for illnesses that make a person hot and restless.

few (fyū) *adj.* small in number: *I read a few pages and then fell asleep.*

fiancé (fē′ än sā′) *n.* a man who is engaged to marry a woman.

fiancée (fē′ än sā′) *n.* a woman who is engaged to marry a man.

fib (fib) *n.* a small, unimportant lie.

fibre, fiber (fī′ bər) *n.* a thread or something like thread: *Our muscles are made of fibres.*

⊖**fiction** (fik′ shən) *n.* a story or book about things that did not really happen.

fiddle (fidl) *n.* a violin. *v.* to play the fiddle. **fiddling. fiddled.**

fiddlehead (fidl′ hed′) *n.* the small, curled leaves of some ferns, eaten as a vegetable.

field (fēld) *n.* **1.** a piece of land used for crops or for pasture. **2.** land where sports are played. **3.** land that contains some natural product: *an oil field.*

fierce (fērs) *adj.* angry and wild: *a fierce lion; a fiercer one; the fiercest lion of all.*

fifteen (fif tēn′) *n., adj.* ten more than five (15).

fifth (fifth) *adj.* following fourth (5th).

fifty (fif′ tē) *n., adj.* ten times five (50). *pl.* **fifties.**

fig (fig) *n.* a soft, sweet fruit, full of seeds, that grows in warm climates.

fight (fīt) *n.* a struggle; a quarrel; a battle. *v.* to struggle or battle against someone or something. **fighting. fought** (fòt).

⊖**figure** (fig′ yər) *n.* **1.** a number symbol: *2, 9, and 74 are figures.* **2.** the shape of something: *I saw the figure of a man in the distance.* *v. (informal)* **1.** to calculate; to count. **2.** to expect; to believe. **figuring. figured.**
figure out to understand: *I can't figure out your writing. I can't figure out why she did that.*

filament (fil′ ə mənt) *n.* a very thin thread, or something like a very thin thread: *The filament in a light bulb glows to give off light.*

filbert (fil′ bərt) *n.* the small, round, brown nut from the hazel tree.

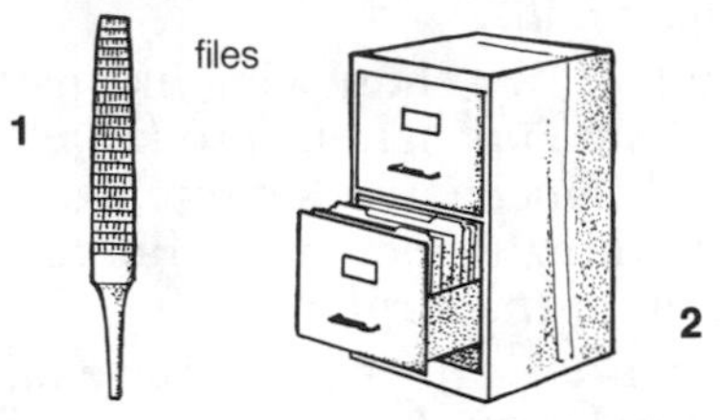

⊖**file** (fīl) *n.* **1.** a tool with a rough side, used for smoothing wood or metal. **2.** a box or container that contains important papers, kept in order. **3.** a line of people, one behind another.
on file recorded in a file.

fill (fil) *v.* **1.** to put into a container until there is no more room: *to fill a pail with water.* **2.** to give what is asked for: *to fill a prescription.*
fill in, fill out to write information in the empty spaces: *Please fill in the forms.*

⊖**fillet, filet** (fil lā′) *n.* a piece of fish or meat with the bones removed.

filling (fil′ ing) *n.* a substance used to fill something: *The dentist put a filling in my tooth.*

filly (fil′ ē) *n.* a young female horse. *pl.* **fillies.**

film (film) *n.* **1.** a thin layer: *a film of dust on a shelf.* **2.** a roll of thin material that is put into a camera and used to take photographs. **3.** a movie.

filmstrip (film′ strip′) *n.* a roll of film, usually with pictures, to be projected onto a screen.

filter (fil′ tər) *n.* a device through which liquid, smoke, air, etc., is passed, in order to strain out solid or impure substances.

filthy (fil′ thē) *adj.* very dirty: *filthy hands; filthier hands; the filthiest hands of all.*

⊖**fin** (fin) *n.* **1.** a short wing-like part of a fish: *Fins help fish to keep their balance when swimming.* **2.** anything shaped like a fin: *the tail fin of the airplane.*

final (fīn′ əl) *adj.* the last; the end: *the final part of a story.*

finally (fīn′ əl ē) *adv.* at last: *He finally arrived when everyone else was going home!*

finals (fīn′ əlz) *n.pl.* the last and most important game or test in a series: *the finals in a tennis tournament.*

finance (fī′ nans, fi nans′) *n.* the control of money, usually in large amounts. *v.* to supply money for something: *The bank helped them finance their house.* **financing. financed.**

finch (finch) *n.* a small songbird: *The canary and sparrow are types of finches. pl.* **finches.**

find (fīnd) *v.* to discover; to locate: *Ken found a penny on the street.* **finding. found** (faủnd).
find out to come to know something new: *I just found out who won the prize.*

fine (fīn) *n.* money paid as a punishment for breaking a rule: *a fine on a library book.*
adj. **1.** sunny and dry: *a fine summer day; a finer one; the finest day of all.* **2.** thin and small: *a fine point on the pencil.* **3.** very good; very well: *a fine job. I was ill yesterday, but now I'm fine.*

finger (fing′ gər) *n.* one of the five long parts on the hand.

fingernail (fing′ gər nāl′) *n.* the thin, hard layer at the end of each finger and the thumb.

fingerprint (fing′ gər print′) *n.* a mark made by a finger.

finish (fin′ ish) *n.* **1.** the end; the last part: *the finish of a race.* **2.** the kind of surface of an object, such as a piece of furniture: *That cabinet has an enamel finish to make it shine. pl.* **finishes.** *v.* to complete: *Please finish your breakfast.* **finishing. finished.** he **finishes.**

fir tree

fir (fûr) *n.* a tall evergreen tree that has needle-like leaves.

fire (fīr) *n.* the heat, flames, and light from something burning. *v.* **1.** to shoot a gun or rifle. **2.** to dismiss; to send away from a job: *She fired the waiter for breaking too many dishes.* **firing. fired.**

firearm (fīr′ ärm′) *n.* a small gun.

firecracker (fīr′ krak′ ər) *n.* a small cardboard tube filled with gunpowder.

fire engine

fire engine (fīr′ en′ jən) a truck that has equipment for fighting fires.

fire escape (fīr′ əs kāp′) a ladder or stairway used to leave a burning building.

fire extinguisher (fīr′ ik sting′ gwish ər) a container filled with chemicals that will put out a fire.

firefighter (fīr′ fīt′ ər) *n.* a person trained to put out fires.

firefly (fīr′ flī′) *n.* a small insect that gives off flashes of light. *pl.* **fireflies.**

fireplace (fīr′ plās′) *n.* an open place built to hold a fire: *A fireplace is found under the chimney.*

fireproof (fīr′ prūf′) *adj.* made so something should not burn, or not burn easily: *The firefighter's clothing is fireproof.*

fireworks (fīr′ wûrks′) *n.pl.* firecrackers, rockets, etc. that make a loud noise or give off a colourful display.

⊖**firm** (fûrm) *n.* a business: *Mother works for an engineering firm.* *adj.* **1.** solid, steady: *That's not a firm chair; don't sit in it.* **2.** not easily changed: *My decision is firm; you can't go to the movies.*

first (fûrst) *adj.* chief: *first prize.* *adv.* **1.** before all the others: *Mark came first in the race.* **2.** for the first time: *Carmen first saw the house when she came on a visit.* **at first** in the beginning: *At first, I did not like the book.*

first aid (fûrst′ ād′) treatment given to a sick or injured person while he or she is waiting for the doctor to arrive.

first-class (fûrst′ klas′) *adj.* of the best or most expensive kind: *first-class work; a first-class plane ticket.*

fish (fish) *n.* an animal that breathes through gills and lives only in water. *pl.* **fish** or **fishes.** *v.* to try to catch fish.

fishery (fish′ ə rē) *n.* **1.** the business of catching fish. **2.** the location of such a business. *pl.* **fisheries.**

fist (fist) *n.* a tightly closed hand.

fit (fit) *n.* a sudden attack: *a fit of laughter.* *adj.* in good condition; healthy: *Exercising keeps you fit. a fit person; a fitter one; the fittest one of all.* *v.* **1.** to be of the right size: *The bolt fits into this hole.* **2.** to attach or put in: *Can you fit two more people in your car?* **fitting. fit** or **fitted.**

five (fīv) *n., adj.* one more than four (5).

fix (fiks) *v.* to repair: *I'll fix the broken bike.* **2.** to fasten: *Bill fixed the flag onto the pole.* **3.** to prepare or arrange: *Will you help me fix dinner tonight? Fix your hair before the guests arrive.* **fixing. fixed.** she **fixes.**

fixture (fiks′ chər) *n.* something that is attached to stay in one place: *a lighting fixture on the ceiling.*

flabby (flab′ ē) *adj.* hanging loose; soft: *flabby skin; flabbier skin; the flabbiest skin of all.*

flag of Canada

flag (flag) *n.* a piece of cloth with an emblem or decoration on it: *Each country has its own flag.*

flake (flāk) *n.* a small, thin chip or piece: *a snowflake.*

flame (flām) *n.* the glowing, moving part of a fire. *v.* to burst into a blaze. **flaming. flamed.**

flammable (flam′ əbl) *adj.* able to burn easily: *Some types of gas are very flammable.*

flannel (flan′ əl) *n.* a soft cloth made of fine wool.

flap (flap) *n.* a piece of paper or other material that is attached on one side only: *the flap of the envelope.* *v.* to move up and down or sideways: *A bird flaps its wings.* **flapping. flapped.**

flare (fler) *n.* a very bright blaze of light, which may be used as a signal. *v.* to blaze up suddenly: *The fireworks flared in the darkness.* **flaring. flared.**

flash (flash) *n.* **1.** a sudden light: *a flash of lightning.* **2.** a sudden and short feeling: *a flash of anger.* *pl.* **flashes.** *v.* to shine suddenly: *The car flashed its headlights.* **flashing. flashed.** it **flashes.**
in a flash quickly; in a short time: *I'll be home in a flash.*

flash bulb (flash′ bulb′) a bulb that is attached to a camera, used for taking pictures indoors or at night.

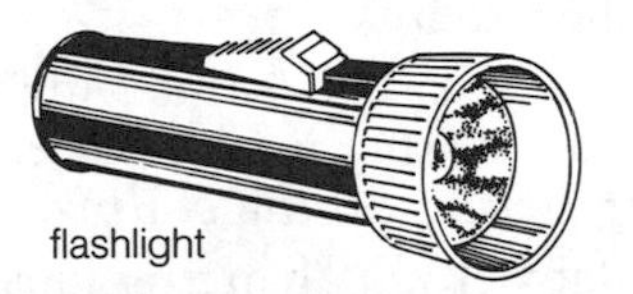
flashlight

flashlight (flash′ līt′) *n.* a small light, powered by batteries, that is used to see one's way in the dark.

flat (flat) *n.* rooms; a place to live: *We live in a flat above our store.* *adj.* **1.** level; smooth; without bumps: *a flat road; a flatter road; the flattest road of all.* **2.** with little or no air: *a flat tire.* **3.** set and not changeable: *to pay a flat fee for electricity.*

flatten (flat′ ən) *v.* to make or become flat.

flatter (flat′ ər) *v.* to say nice things to someone, often not sincerely: *I don't believe her kind words. She flatters everyone.*

flavour, flavor (flā′ vər) *n.* the taste of something, making it different from another food or drink: *The drink has an orange flavour.*

flaw (flȯ) *n.* a small mistake or sign of damage: *The towels are on sale because they have flaws in them.*

flax (flaks) *n.* **1.** a thin plant with small leaves and blue flowers. **2.** the fibres from this plant, which are spun into linen thread.

flea (flē) *n.* a small, hopping insect without wings. *pl.* **fleas.**

flee (flē) *v.* to go quickly away from trouble or danger: *Catch the thief before he flees!* **fleeing. fled** (fled).

fleece (flēs) *n.* the natural covering of wool on a sheep.

fleet (flēt) *n.* a number of ships, planes, or cars grouped together.

⊖**flesh** (flesh) *n.* **1.** the soft part of the body that covers the bones. **2.** the soft part of a fruit or vegetable; not the skin, core, or stem.

flew see **fly.**

flexible (flek′ səbl) *adj.* able to be bent easily without breaking: *a flexible rubber hose; a flexible work schedule.*

flick (flik) *v.* to brush lightly with a whip, finger, etc.: *She flicked the dirt off her jacket.*

flicker (flik′ ər) *v.* to shine with a blinking light: *The candle's flame flickers just before it goes out.*

flies see **fly.**

flight (flīt) *n.* **1.** the movement of birds, insects, or airplanes through the air. **2.** an airplane trip. **3.** a set of stairs.

flinch (flinch) *v.* to draw back from something threatening: *I flinched when he raised his hand suddenly.* **flinching. flinched.** he **flinches.**

fling (fling) *v.* to throw hard; to hurl: *How far can you fling the stone?* **flinging. flung** (flung).

flint (flint) *n.* a very hard kind of stone that makes a spark when rubbed against steel.

flip (flip) *v.* to turn over quickly: *Flip a coin.* **flipping. flipped.**

⊖**flipper** (flip′ ər) *n.* **1.** the flat limb of some animals, such as a seal, walrus, whale, or turtle. **2.** a piece of rubber, shaped like a seal's flipper, worn on a swimmer's foot to help the person move faster in the water.

float (flōt) *n.* **1.** something that stays on top of water. **2.** a long platform with wheels that is used in parades to exhibit something: *The parade has a float with Santa Claus riding on it.* *v.* **1.** to rest on water. *Can* *you float on your back?* **2.** to move slowly in the air: *The bird's feather floated down to the ground.*

flock (flok) *n.* a group of animals: *a flock of geese; a flock of sheep.*

flood (flud) *n.* **1.** a great overflow of water. **2.** the sudden appearance of a large amount: *A flood of letters came on her birthday. v.* to become covered or filled with water: *Our house was flooded in March.*

floor (flȯr) *n.* **1.** the bottom of a room, on which people walk. **2.** a storey in a building: *Our apartment is on the tenth floor of the building.*

flop (flop) *n. (informal)* a failure: *The movie was a flop and closed in three days. v.* to drop down heavily: *I was so tired at the end of the week, I flopped into an armchair.* **flopping. flopped.**

florist (flȯr′ ist) *n.* a person whose job is to sell flowers.

flour (flaůr) *n.* the fine powder made by grinding grain and used to make bread, cake, muffins, etc. *v.* to cover with flour: *Flour the chicken legs before you cook them.*

flow (flō) *v.* to move along smoothly: *The river flowed past our home.*

flower (flaůr) *n.* the blossom of a plant.

flown see **fly.**

flu (flū) short for **influenza**, a sickness that is like a bad cold.

flue (flu) *n.* a passage for smoke in a chimney.

fluffy (fluf′ ē) *adj.* **1.** covered with soft hair or fur: *a fluffy rabbit; a fluffier one; the fluffiest one of all.* **2.** soft and light: *Beat the eggs until they are fluffy.*

fluid (flū′ id) *n.* a liquid or gas; a substance that can flow: *Ink, water, and milk are fluids.*

flung see **fling.**

flurry (flu′ rē, flû′ rē) *n.* **1.** a sudden, small amount of snow. **2.** sudden, hurried excitement or confusion: *a flurry of activity. pl.* **flurries.**

flush (flush) *adj.* exactly even with; flat against: *The chair is flush against the wall. v.* **1.** to go red in the face; to blush. **2.** to wash out with water: *to flush the toilet.* **flushing. flushed.** he **flushes.**

flute (flūt) *n.* a pipe-like musical wind instrument, made of wood or metal. A flute has a series of finger holes, and is played by blowing across a hole in the side.

flutter (flut′ ər) *v.* **1.** to wave back and forth in the breeze: *The flags flutter in the wind.* **2.** for an insect to flap its wings lightly.

fly (flī) *n.* **1.** one of several kinds of small insects with two wings: *a black-fly; a housefly.* **2.** an opening in the front of pants, usually having a zipper. *pl.* **flies.** *v.* **1.** to move through the air on wings. **2.** to travel by airplane. **3.** to make something stay up in the air: *Jo flies a kite.* **flying. flew** (flū). it **flies.** it has **flown** (flōn).

foal (fōl) *n.* a young horse or donkey.

foam (fōm) *n.* many small white bubbles: *the foam on an ocean wave.*

foam rubber (fōm′ rub′ ər) a light rubber, used for pillows, cushions, etc.

focus (fō′ kəs) *n.* a point where rays of light come together. **2.** a centre of interest or attraction: *The new painting is a focus of interest in the museum. pl.* **focusses**, or **foci.**

v. to adjust a camera, microscope, etc. in order to get a clear picture. **focussing. focussed.**

fodder (fod′ ər) *n.* the food eaten by farm animals.

foe (fō) *n.* an enemy.

fog (fog) *n.* a thick cloud of mist that comes close to the ground.

foggy (fog′ ē) *adj.* filled with fog: *a foggy day; a foggier day; the foggiest day of the year.*

foil (fȯil) *n.* a thin, silvery sheet of metal: *aluminum foil.*

fold (fōld) *n.* a crease caused by doubling something over. *v.* **1.** to double something over: *to fold clean sheets.* **2.** to bend close to the body: *Anna folded her legs under her.*

folder (fōld′ ər) *n.* a piece of light cardboard, folded to hold papers.

folks (fōk) *n.pl. (informal)* parents or any group of people: *How are your folks? Our neighbours are nice folks.*

follow (fol′ ō) *v.* **1.** to go after or come after: *The dog follows her everywhere. The salad follows the soup at dinner.* **2.** to move or go along: *If you follow the river, you'll come to the town.* **3.** to do according to: *Follow the directions in the cookbook on how to bake a cake.* **4.** to understand: *I don't follow what you are saying.*
follow through to do completely: *Follow through on your cleaning; sweep the porch as well as the house.*
follow up to try to increase a result by doing something more: *Jeff followed up on his job interview by calling the next day to see if he'd been hired.*

fond of (fond′ ov) liking very much: *Jill is fond of dogs.*

food (fūd) *n.* what people, animals, and plants eat to keep alive.

fool (fūl) *n.* a silly person. *v.* to trick someone: *He fooled me by saying the lake was warm. It was cold!*

foolish (fūl′ ish) *adj.* silly; not wise.

foot (fu̇t) *n.* **1.** the part of each leg on which a person or animal stands. **2.** the bottom part: *the foot of a tower.* **3.** a measure of length, equal to about 30 cm. *pl.* **feet.**

football

⊖**football** (fu̇t′ bȯl′) *n.* **1.** a large leather ball, used in football and other kicking games. **2.** a game in which the football is kicked, passed, or carried to the goal.

foothills (fu̇t′ hilz′) *n.pl.* the low hills that are found at the bottom of a mountain.

footprint (fu̇t′ print′) *n.* the mark of a foot on soft ground or on a clean floor.

footstep (fu̇t′ step′) *n.* the distance covered or the sound heard when someone takes a step.
follow in a person's footsteps to do the same thing that another person has done: *Mitsu followed in her mother's footsteps and became a lawyer.*

for (fȯr) *prep.* **1.** in return: *I'll give you a dollar for a hat.* **2.** because of: *She was rewarded for her good deed.* **3.** as far as; as long as: *We hiked for ten kilometres.* **4.** with a purpose: *The tub is for water.*

forbid (fȯr bid′) *v.* to tell someone he or she is not to do something: *I forbid you to go there alone!* **forbidding. forbade** (fȯr bad′). I have **forbidden.**

force (fôrs) *n.* **1.** power; strength *the force of the wind.* **2.** a group of people working together: *a police force.* **3. forces**, the army, navy, and other military groups. *v.* **1.** to make someone do something against his or her wishes: *He tried to force his brother to tell the secret.* **2.** to do something using power and energy: *The firefighters forced open the door.* **forcing. forced.**
in force in use: *That rule is in force until next year.*

fore- a prefix meaning 'in front of' or 'before': **forehead** means the front part of the head; to **forecast** the weather means to say in advance what it will be like.

forecast (fôr′ kast′) *v.* to say in advance what is likely to happen: *to forecast the result of a ball game.* **forecasting. forecast.**

forefinger (fôr′ fing′ gər) *n.* the finger nearest the thumb; it is also called the 'index finger'.

forehead (fôr′ hed′) *n.* the part of a person's face above the eyes.

foreign (fôr′ ən) *adj.* belonging to a country other than a person's own.

foreman (fôr′ mən) *n.* a worker in charge of a group of workers. *pl.* **foremen.**

forest (fôr′ əst) *n.* a large area of land thickly covered with trees.

forest ranger (fôr′ əst rānj′ ər) a person whose job is to guard a part of the forest.

forestry (fôr′ əs trē) *n.* the planting and taking care of trees and forests.

forever (fôr ev′ ər) *adj.* always: *Bob is forever laughing.*

⊖**forge** (fôrj) *n.* a place where metal is made very hot and then hammered into shape: *a blacksmith's forge.* *v.* to copy someone's handwriting for a dishonest reason. **forging. forged.**

forget (fôr get′) *v.* not to remember: *She forgot her brother's birthday.* **forgetting. forgot** (fôr gôt′). I have **forgotten** (fôr gôt′ ən).

forgetful (fôr get′ fəl) *adj.* always or often forgetting something.

forgive (fôr giv′) *v.* to pardon; to no longer be angry at someone who did something wrong. **forgiving. forgave** (fôr gāv′). I have **forgiven** (fôr giv′ ən).

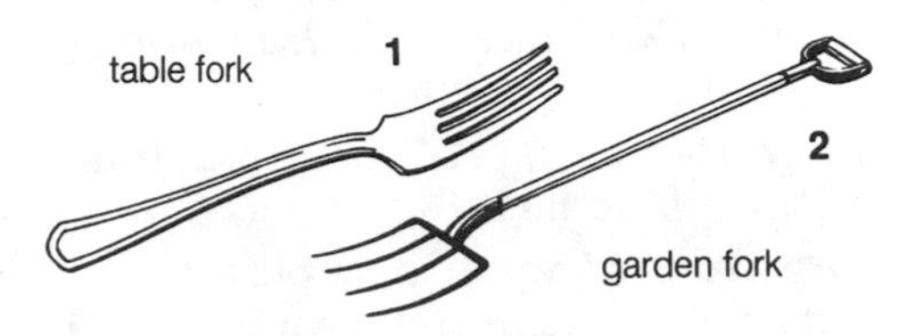

fork (fôrk) *n.* **1.** a handle with sharp points, used to lift food. **2.** a big garden tool with prongs, used to lift earth or roots. **3.** a place where a road or river divides.

form (fôrm) *n.* **1.** a shape, kind, or condition: *This cup has an unusual form. When water freezes, it takes the form of ice.* **2.** a sheet of paper with printed questions and spaces for the answers. *v.* to make into a shape, a condition, etc. *He formed the clay into a ball. The workers formed a union.*

⊖**formal** (fôr′ məl) *adj.* **1.** following certain rules; not familiar: *It was a formal party. All the guests were wearing their fanciest clothes.* **2.** official; done the proper way: *to sign a formal agreement to rent an apartment.*

former (fôr′ mər) *adj.* **1.** being or happening at an earlier time: *The Member of Parliament is a former teacher.* **2.** the first of two things named: *I walk or drive to work, usually the former.*

formula (fôr′ myə lə) *n.* **1.** in math or science, a set of letters, numbers, or symbols that explain something. **2.** a set way of doing something to get a certain result: *Eating well and getting enough sleep is the formula for good health.* **3.** a mixture used for feeding babies. *pl.* **formulas**, or **formulae** (fôr′ myə lī).

⊖**fort** (fôrt) *n.* a strong building made for defence against attack.

fortunate (fôr′ chən ət) *adj.* lucky.

fortune (fôr′ chən) *n.* **1.** wealth; a large amount of money: *Jim's father was left a fortune by his uncle.* **2.** chance; luck: *Jean won the prize by good fortune.*

forty (fôr′ tē) *n., adj.* ten times four (40). *pl.* **forties.**

forward (fôr′ wərd) *n.* a player on the front line in some games. *adj.* in front: *the forward position. adv.* ahead: *The scouts marched forward. v.* to send ahead to someplace else. *to forward a letter to a new address.*

fossil (fos′ əl) *n.* the hardened remains of an ancient plant or animal.

foster parents (fôs′ tər par′ ənts) parents who care for a child as their own, even though they are not related to him or her.

fought see **fight.**

foul (faůl) *adj.* **1.** horrible; awful; dirty: *foul weather; a foul smell.* **2.** not allowed by the rules of a game: *She hit a foul ball.*

found see **find.**

foundation (faůn dā′ shən) *n.* a base or support for something: *the foundation of a house; the foundation of a scientific experiment.*

foundry (faůn′ drē) *n.* a place where metal is melted and shaped into different forms. *pl.* **foundries.**

fountain (faůn′ tən) *n.* a spray of water shooting upwards and falling back into a pool or other container.

four (fôr) *n., adj.* one more than three (4).

Four-H Club an organization that instructs young people in farming methods. The aim of the Four-H Club is to improve head, heart, hands, and health.

fourteen (fôr tēn′) *n., adj.* ten more than four (14).

fourth (fôrth) *adj.* following third (4th).

fowl (faůl) *n.* a bird, especially a chicken.

red fox

fox (foks) *n.* a wild animal that has a bushy tail, pointed ears, is often red, and looks like a dog. *pl.* **foxes.**

fraction (frak′ shən) *n.* a part of a whole amount: *One-half (½) and one-quarter (¼) are fractions.*

fracture (frak′ chər) *n.* a breaking: *a fracture in a bone. v.* to break; to cause a fracture. **fracturing. fractured.**

fragile (fraj′ īl, fraj′ əl) *adj.* delicate: easy to break: *This glass vase is fragile.*

fragrance (frā′ grəns) *n.* a sweet, pleasant smell.

fragrant (frā′ grənt) *adj.* sweet-smelling: *a fragrant rose.*

frail (frāl) *adj.* weak; delicate in health: *a frail old cat.*

frame (frām) *n.* a border of wood or metal around something: *a picture frame; a window frame. v.* to put a border around. **framing. framed.**

framework (frām′ wûrk′) *n.* a structure that gives form or support to something: *the wooden framework of a tent.*

francophone (frangk′ ə fōn′) *n.* in Canada, a person whose native language is French.

frank (frangk) *adj.* saying what you really think: *She is always frank. Today she said the cake was dry.*

frankfurter (frangk′ fər tər) *n.* a hot dog; a sausage, often served in a bun.

frantic (fran′ tik) *adj.* almost mad with excitement or worry: *Jill was frantic when she lost her wallet.*

fraud (frȯd) *n.* a tricking in order to cheat someone: *It is fraud to sell new furniture as antiques.*

freak (frēk) *adj.* unnatural; extraordinary: *a freak snowstorm in May.*

freckles (freklz) *n.pl.* light brown spots on the skin.

Fredericton (fred′ rik tən) *n.* the capital city of New Brunswick.

free (frē) *adj.* **1.** loose; not tied: *The dog was free to run.* **2.** not forced to act in a certain way: *A free citizen; a freer citizen; the freest citizen of all.* **2.** costing nothing: *a free show.* *v.* to let go: *He freed the bird from its cage.* **freeing. freed.**

freedom (frē′ dəm) *n.* the state of being free.

freeze (frēz) *v.* **1.** to become very cold. **2.** to turn into ice. **3.** to stop moving completely: *I froze when I saw the car hit the tree.* **4.** to make something numb with drugs: *The dentist froze part of Lynn's mouth before pulling her tooth.* **freezing. froze** (frōz). it has **frozen** (frōz′ ən).

freight (frāt) *n.* cargo; the things carried by a truck, train, ship, etc.

freighter (frāt′ ər) *n.* a cargo ship.

French (french) *n.* the language spoken in France, Canada, and other countries. *adj.* belonging to or coming from France.

French fries (french′ frīz′) potatoes that have been cut into strips, then fried in oil or fat.

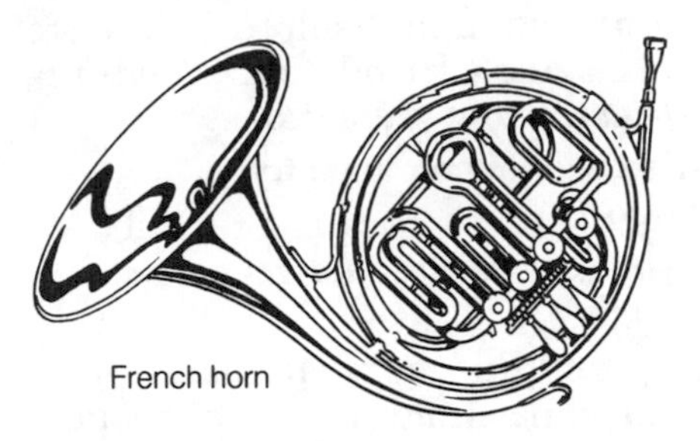
French horn

French horn (french′ hȯrn′) a large musical instrument, made of brass. A French horn has a long, rolled-up tube and a very wide, bell-shaped 'mouth'.

frequency (frē′ kwən sē) *n.* the rate at which something happens: *the frequency that a bus stops here.* *pl.* **frequencies.**

frequent (frē′ kwənt) *adj.* happening or appearing often: *Pat is a frequent visitor. We see him about three times a week.*

fresh (fresh) *adj.* **1.** not stale; just made: *fresh cake.* **2.** not in a can or frozen: *fresh fruit.* **3.** cool; clean: *fresh air.* **4.** not salty: *fresh water.* **5.** *(informal)* rude; not polite: *a fresh answer to a question.*

friction (frik′ shən) *n.* **1.** the rubbing of one thing against another. **2.** the force that tries to stop one thing from rubbing smoothly against another. **3.** a disagreement or struggle between people, caused by different opinions: *friction between countries.*

Friday (frī′ dā, frī′ dē) *n.* the sixth day of the week. *pl.* **Fridays.**

fridge (frij) *n.* *(informal)* a refrigerator.

fried (frīd) *adj.* cooked in hot fat: *fried eggs.* *v.* see **fry.**

friend (frend) *n.* someone whom a person knows well and likes.

friendly (frend′ lē) *adj.* like a friend; nice: *a friendly person; a friendlier one; the friendliest one I have ever met.*

friendship (frend′ ship) *n.* the state of having a friend: *Our friendship began many years ago.*

fries see **French fries; fry.**

fright (frīt) *n.* a scare; a fearful shock: *The thunder gave us a fright.*

frighten (frīt′ ən) *v.* to make someone afraid: *The story about ghosts frightened the young child.*

frill (fril) *n.* lace or cloth on the edges of material.

fringe (frinj) *n.* loose threads or cords hanging from the edge of cloth.

fringe benefit (frinj′ ben′ ə fit) something valuable that a worker may receive besides his or her salary: *A car, free meals, and medical insurance are some fringe benefits of my job.*

frog

frog (frog) *n.* a small jumping animal that lives in and out of water.

from (frum, from) *prep.* **1.** out or off of: *I took it from the box. I stood up from the chair.* **2.** between: *I played from four to five o'clock.* **3.** beginning at: *Read from the first line.* **4.** because of: *The plant died from the frost.*

⊖**front** (frunt) *n.* the forward part; not the back: *the front of a train.*
in front of before a person or place: *We waited for Martin in front of his house.*

frost (frost) *n.* powdered ice that appears on a surface on a cold day. *v.* to cover with icing.

frostbite (frost′ bīt′) *n.* the freezing of a part of the body.

frosting (frost′ ing) *n.* icing.

frown (fraun) *n.* a wrinkling together of the eyebrows. *v.* to wrinkle the forehead, showing that a person may be angry or thinking hard.
frown on to disapprove of: *The company frowns on people leaving work early.*

froze, frozen see **freeze.**

fruit (frūt) *n.* a juicy food from a tree, bush, or vine: *Grapes, apples, and oranges are some fruits.*

frustrated (frus′ trāt əd) *adj.* disappointed, unhappy because of not being able to do something, go somewhere, etc.: *The frustrated student could not finish the exam.*

fry (frī) *v.* to cook in oil or fat. **frying. fried** (frīd). she **fries.**

frying pan (frī′ ing pan′) a pan used for frying eggs and other food.

fudge (fuj) *n.* a soft, creamy candy made of sugar, butter, nuts, and other ingredients.

fuel (fyū′ əl) *n.* anything that is burned to give heat or energy: *Coal, oil, and wood are fuels.*

fulfil, fulfill (fu̇l fil′) *v.* to do or satisfy: *to fulfil the requirements of a job; to fulfil a request.* **fulfilling. fulfilled.**

full (fu̇l) *adj.* **1.** filled completely; having no more room: *The hall is full of people. I'm full—I can't eat any more!* **2.** complete; whole: *Come to a full stop at the red light.*
full of having much of: *He was full of happiness when her letter came.*

full moon (fu̇l′ mūn′) the moon when it appears perfectly round.

full-time (fu̇l′ tīm′) *adv.* the complete amount of time: *Last year I worked in the mornings. Now I work full-time—all day long.*

fumble (fumbl) *v.* **1.** to handle something in a clumsy way: *to* *fumble the ball.* **2.** to feel about: *to fumble for a key in your pocket.* **fumbling. fumbled.**

fumes (fyūmz) *n.pl.* unpleasant gases or smoke from something burning.

fun (fun) *n.* enjoyment; amusement: *I had fun skiing.*
make fun of to laugh at: *Don't make fun of me; I'm doing the best I can.*

function (fungk′ shən) *n.* **1.** the purpose for which a thing has been made: *The function of gloves is to keep hands warm.* **2.** an important meeting, party, or ceremony: *a function to honour the skiing champions.* *v.* to work; to run; to serve a purpose: *My body does not function well without regular sleep.*

fund (fund) *n.* **1.** money put away for a special purpose: *a fund to help our Olympic team.* **2. funds,** money available for use.

funeral (fyūn′ ə rəl) *n.* a burial or cremation service for a dead person.

fungus (fung′ gəs) *n.* a kind of plant that has no leaves, flowers, or green colour. *pl.* **fungi** (fung′ gī), or **funguses.**

funnel (fun′ əl) *n.* an object that has a thin tube at one end and a wide cone at the other; it is used for pouring liquid into a small opening.

funny (fun′ ē) *adj.* **1.** amusing; making someone laugh: *My story was funny; your story is funnier; his story is the funniest one that I have ever heard.* **2.** strange; unusual; odd: *That's funny. It's sunny but I was sure it was raining.*

fur (fûr) *n.* the soft, hairy coat of some animals.

furious (fyůr′ i əs) *adj.* very, very angry.

furnace (fûr′ nəs) *n.* **1.** a machine that heats houses and other buildings. **2.** a very hot fire, used to heat water for a large boiler, or to melt metals.

furnish (fûr′ nish) *v.* **1.** to supply a room with furniture. **2.** to supply: *to furnish an excuse for being late.* **furnishing. furnished.** he **furnishes.**

furniture (fûr′ ni chər) *n.* the things needed in a room, such as a chair, table, dresser, bed, and lamp.

furry (fûr′ ē) *adj.* made of fur or covered with fur: *a furry cat; a furrier one; the furriest cat of all.*

further (fûr′ t͟hər) *adj.* more: *Do you need further help?*

fuse (fyūz) *n.* **1.** a piece of thin wire, set in a small container, which will break or melt if the electric current is too strong: *The light went out. Did somebody blow a fuse?* **2.** string or other material that burns slowly, attached to something that will explode.

fuss (fus) *n.* bother; excitement: *My dog makes a fuss when I come home.*

fussy (fus′ ē) *adj.* very interested in details; very difficult to please: *Dentists are fussy; accountants are fussier; editors are the fussiest people of all.*

future (fyū′ chər) *n.* what is still to happen; the time that lies ahead: *Val wants to go to England in the future.*

fuzz (fuz) *n.* fine hair or fibres on something: *the fuzz on a tennis ball.*

fuzzy (fuz′ ē) *adj.* blurred; not easy to see: *a fuzzy picture; a fuzzier picture; the fuzziest picture.*

G

gag (gag) *v.* **1.** to put a cloth around someone's mouth so that the person can't call for help. **2.** to choke on a piece of food. **gagging. gagged.**

gain (gān) *v.* to get; to increase; to add to what is there: *He gained two kilograms last year.*

galaxy (gal′ ək sē) *n.* a large group of stars. *pl.* **galaxies.**

gale (gāl) *n.* a very strong wind.

gallery (gal′ ə rē) *n.* a building used for showing sculpture and paintings: *an art gallery. pl.* **galleries.**

gallon (gal′ ən) *n.* a measure of liquids, equal to about 4.5 L.

gallop (gal′ əp) *v.* for a horse to run at full speed.

galoshes

galoshes (gə losh′ əz) *n.pl.* high overshoes, worn in the snow or slush.

gamble (gambl) *v.* **1.** to play a game for money. **2.** to take a risk that is not really necessary: *The sailors gambled their lives. They crossed the ocean in a tiny boat.* **gambling. gambled.**

game (gām) *n.* **1.** a contest or sport in which the players follow certain rules. **2.** wild birds or animals that are hunted.

gang (gang) *n.* a group of people going around together: *a gang of robbers.*

gangster (gang′ stər) *n.* someone who belongs to a gang of criminals.

gap (gap) *n.* an opening or space: *a gap in a fence.*

garage (gə rȧzh′, gə rȧj′) *n.* a building where cars, trucks, or buses are kept or repaired.

garbage (gȧr′ bəj) *n.* waste, usually from the kitchen.

garden (gȧr′ dən) *n.* a piece of ground used for growing flowers, vegetables, or fruit.

gardener (gȧrd′ nər, gȧr′ dən ər) n. a person who looks after a garden.

garlic (gȧr′ lik) *n.* a strong-smelling plant bulb, used in cooking.

garment (gȧr′ mənt) *n.* any piece of clothing.

gas (gas) *n.* **1.** an invisible air-like substance, some types of which burn: *Gas is used for heating and cooking. pl.* **gases. 2.** short for **gasoline**, a liquid fuel used by cars, buses, and other vehicles.

gash (gash) *n.* a long, deep cut: *The doctor treated him for a gash over his eye. pl.* **gashes.**

gasp (gasp) *v.* to open the mouth and breathe in suddenly and deeply: *The swimmer gasped for air after swimming across the lake.*

gate (gāt) *n.* a hinged door in a fence or wall.

gather (ga<u>th</u>′ ər) *v.* **1.** to collect: *to gather flowers.* **2.** to come together: *A crowd gathered around the movie actor.* **3.** to come to a conclusion; to have an opinion about something: *Since you have your coat on, I gather that you are leaving.*

gauge (gāj) *n.* a device for measuring; a meter: *The gauge showed that the water pressure was too high. v.* to measure; to guess at a measure: *She gauged the distance at thirty metres.* **gauging. gauged.**

gauze (gȯz) *n.* very thin cloth: *Gauze is often used for bandages.*

gave see **give.**

gaze (gāz) *n.* a steady look. *v.* to look long and steadily: *She gazed at the sky.* **gazing. gazed.**

gear (gēr) *n.* **1.** a wheel with teeth around the edge; these teeth fit into the teeth of other wheels. **2.** items used or needed for a certain purpose: *fishing gear, camping gear.*
in gear attached to and run by a motor or another gear.
out of gear not attached to a motor or another gear.

gearshift (gēr′ shift′) *n.* the part of a vehicle that connects the motor to the gears.

geese plural of **goose.**

gem (jem) *n.* a jewel or valuable stone: *Rubies, emeralds, and diamonds are gems.*

⊖**gender** (jen′ dər) *n.* the sex of a person or animal: *It is hard to be sure of a hamster's gender, since males and females look very similar.*

general (jen′ ə rəl) *n.* an army commander. *adj.* **1.** usual; ordinary: *Walking is the general way that I get to school.* **2.** for all or most: *The Prime Minister called for a general election in June.* **3.** not detailed: *I have a general idea how to get to Edith's house.*
in general usually: *In general, I take my vacation during the summer.*

generally (jen′ ə rəl ē) *adv.* not always, but usually: *They are generally a happy family.*

generation (jen′ ə rā′ shən) *n.* **1.** people born in the same period of time: *the teen-age generation.* **2.** one step in the history of a family: *My parents are the generation just before my sisters and me.*

generator (jen′ ə rā′ tər) *n.* a machine that makes a form of energy, such as electricity.

generous (jen′ ə rəs) *adj.* kind and unselfish in sharing things with others.

genius (jēn′ yəs) *adj.* a person who is very, very smart. *pl.* **geniuses.**

⊖**gentle** (jentl) *adj.* **1.** quiet: *a gentle voice.* **2.** mild; not rough: *a gentle breeze.*

gentleman (jentl′ mən) *n.* a man who is kind, helpful, and polite. *pl.* **gentlemen.**

⊖**gently** (jent′ lē) *adv.* mildly; quietly.

genuine (jen′ yū in) *adj.* real; not fake or a copy: *genuine gold.*

geography (jē og′ rə fē) *n.* the study of the world and the people who live in different places: *We learned about Canada's natural resources when we studied geography.*

geology (jē ol′ ə jē) *n.* the study of rocks and the earth's surface.

geometry (jē om′ ə trē) *n.* the mathematics of lines, shapes, angles, etc.

gerbil (jûr′ bəl) *n.* a small pet that looks like a mouse.

⊖**germ** (jûrm) *n.* a tiny living thing that can cause illness and disease.

German (jûr′ mən) *n.* the language spoken in Germany and other countries. *adj.* belonging to or coming from Germany.

German measles (jûr′ mən mē′ zəlz) a contagious disease that causes a rash.

German shepherd

German shepherd (jûr mən shep′ ərd) a large dog, brown or grey and black in colour.

get (get) *v.* **1.** to receive; to go for: *to get some food to eat.* **2.** to become; to cause to happen: *to get cold; to get ready.* **3.** to arrive: *I got to work late. The bus got in early.* **getting. got** (got). I have **gotten** (got′ ən).
get along with to be friendly with: *Ron and Ella get along with each other very well.*
get around **1.** to go from one place to another: *It's hard for me to get around without a car.* **2.** to become known by many people: *The news of Jeff's engagement got around the office quickly.*
get at to mean: *What are you getting at with that remark?*
get away to leave; to escape.
get away with to do something wrong without being punished: *He's always late, but he comes in so quietly that he gets away with it.*
get by to manage well; to be successful.
get even to pay someone back for a wrong.
get lost **1.** to be unable to find your way: *A good taxi driver never gets lost.* **2.** to leave; to go away.
get off to move out of or down from: *Sara got off the tractor to eat lunch.*
get on **1.** to move into or up on: *to get on a motorcycle.* **2.** to be friendly: *My sister and I don't get on since our fight.*
get out to leave: *to get out of a room.*
get over to recover from a sickness or from sadness: *It took him a long time to get over the death of his aunt.*
get together to have a meeting.
get up **1.** to wake up. **2.** to stand up.

ghost (gōst) *n.* the spirit of a dead person or animal.

giant (jī′ ənt) *n.* any living thing that is much bigger than the usual size. *adj.* larger than usual: *This is a giant potato. It's enough for three people!*

gift (gift) *n.* **1.** something given to a person; a present. **2.** a talent: *The singer has a special gift.*

gigantic (jī gan′ tik) *adj.* enormous in size.

giggle (gigl) *v.* to laugh in a silly way. **giggling. giggled.**

gills (gilz) *n.pl.* two openings in the head of a fish, used for breathing.

ginger (jin′ jər) *n.* the root of a plant that is sometimes ground into a powder and used as a spice for cooking.

gingerbread (jin′ jər bred′) *n.* a brown cookie or cake, flavoured with ginger.

giraffe (ji raf′) *n.* a tall African animal with a very long neck and spotted skin.

girl (gûrl) *n.* a female child.

Girl Guides (gûrl′ gīdz′) an organization for girls that develops character, fitness, and certain skills.

give (giv) *v.* **1.** to hand over something to someone: *Please give me the book.* **2.** to cause: *Don't give them trouble.* **3.** to say: *He gave a cry of pain.* **giving. gave** (gāv). I have **given** (giv′ ən).
give away **1.** to let someone find out a secret: *Although he promised not to tell the answer, he gave it away to his friend.* **2.** to give

someone something that is not wanted: *She gave away her books when she moved.*

give back to return: *Please give me back the dollar you borrowed.*

give in to surrender; to yield: *Finally I gave in to Miriam's demand for more money.*

give off to send out: *A skunk gives off a bad odour if it is disturbed.*

give out **1.** to hand to different people: *The store is giving out free samples of its new ice cream.* **2.** to use up or tire completely: *Our money gave out on the trip. Dana gave out near the end of the ten-kilometre run.*

given name (giv′ ən nām′) a first name; a name that comes before a family name.

glacier (glā′ shər, glas′ yər) *n.* a huge river of ice that moves very slowly down a mountainside or along a valley.

glad (glad) *adj.* pleased; happy: *My sister is glad that I got a new job; my parents are gladder; I am gladdest of all.*

glamorous (glam′ ə rəs) *adj.* very attractive and interesting: *He could not help staring as the glamorous movie star entered the room.*

glance (glans) *n.* a fast look. *v.* to take a fast look: *I glanced at the library book before I borrowed it.* **glancing. glanced.**

glare (gler) *n.* a strong light: *the glare of the sun.* *v.* to stare at someone in an angry way: *She glared at the man who was talking in the theatre.* **glaring. glared.**

⊖**glass** (glas) *n.* **1.** a hard substance that breaks easily and can be seen through, used in making windows, eyeglasses, etc. **2.** a glass container used for drinking. **3.** the amount that a drinking glass can contain: *a glass of juice.* *pl.* **glasses.**

glasses (glas′ əz) *n.pl.* short for **eyeglasses.**

gleam (glēm) *n.* a flash of light: *a gleam of sunshine through the clouds.* *v.* to shine: *The furniture gleamed after he polished it.*

glide (glīd) *v.* to slide smoothly: *The skaters glided over the ice.* **gliding. glided.**

glider (glīd′ ər) *n.* a light aircraft with no motor.

glimpse (glimps) *n.* a fast look; a glance: *I caught a glimpse of Arlene as she drove by.*

glisten (glis′ ən) *v.* to shine; to sparkle: *The lake glistened in the sun.*

glitter (glit′ ər) *v.* to sparkle; to flash: *Diamonds glitter in the light.*

globe (glōb) *n.* **1.** a ball, or anything in the shape of a ball. **2.** the earth; the world.

gloomy (glū′ mē) *adj.* **1.** dark; dim: *a gloomy cave.* **2.** sad; not cheerful: *a gloomy person; a gloomier person; the gloomiest person in the room.*

glorious (glȯr′ i əs) *adj.* splendid; beautiful: *a glorious day.*

gloss (glos) *n.* a shiny look or finish: *Tanya gave the car a gloss when she waxed it.*

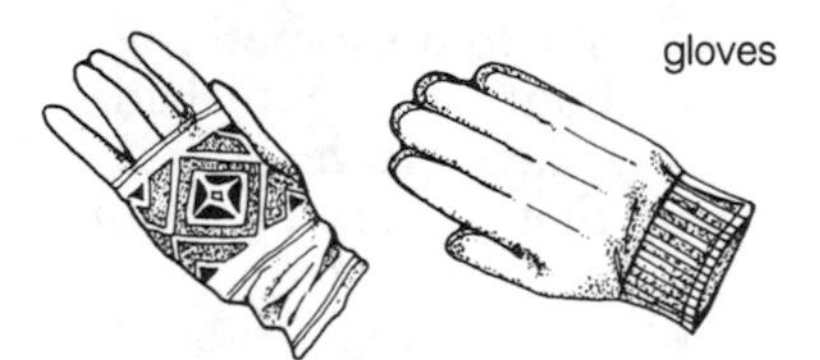

glove (gluv) *n.* a covering for the hand, usually with separate parts for each finger.

glow (glō) *n.* a shine, often from something hot: *a glow from the campfire.* *v.* to give out light and warmth, without flames: *The hot coals glowed in the barbecue.*

glue (glū) *n.* a sticky liquid or paste used to hold things together. *v.* to put glue on something. **gluing. glued.**

gnat (nat) *n.* a very small fly that can sting.

gnaw (nȯ) *v.* to chew away at: *The dog gnaws on a bone.*

go (gō) *v.* **1.** to move; to move away: *Do you want to go to the movies? Let's go home.* **2.** to be moving or working: *The clock is going.* **3.** to pass: *The time is going very quickly.* **4.** to reach: *Those stairs go to the basement.* **5.** to belong: *The knives go in that drawer.* **6.** to make a sound: *The clock goes 'tick'.* **going** (gō′ ing). **went** (went). he **goes** (gōz). he has **gone** (gon).
go ahead to continue doing something: *Go ahead with your work; I won't bother you.*
go along to agree: *Sheila went along with the plans for the party.*
go bad to become rotten; to spoil: *Throw away these tomatoes—they have gone bad.*
go by to pass: *My time at work goes by slowly.*
go into to begin a profession: *Richard went into law after he finished university.*
go off **1.** to ring: *The fire alarm went off last night.* **2.** to stop operating: *The television will go off if I turn this switch.*
go on **1.** to continue: *I can't go on working such long hours.* **2.** to start operating: *The gas went on when Albert pulled the knob on the stove.* **3.** to occur; to happen: *What's going on in the kitchen?*
go out **1.** to stop burning or shining: *A fire or a light can go out.* **2.** to date; to be very social: *Elise has been going out with Miguel for a year.*
go over to study or look at carefully: *to go over an income-tax form.*
go through **1.** to finish; to use up: *Sara went through a box of tissues when she had a cold.* **2.** to look through or search carefully: *Go through your desk and see if you have another pencil.*
go with to belong or be suitable for: *Those shoes don't go with your dress.*

goal (gōl) *n.* **1.** a person's aim or purpose: *Their goal is to own a restaurant.* **2.** a place where players must put the puck or ball in games such as hockey or football in order to score. **3.** a score in a game of hockey and in some ball games.

goalie, goaltender (gōl′ ē, gōl′ tend′ ər) *n.* a player who defends the goal in hockey, lacrosse, soccer, and other games.

goat (gōt) *n.* a farm animal with horns and long hair, usually raised for meat or milk.

God (god) *n.* in some religions, the creator and controller of everything.

god (god) *n.* a being thought by some people to have great power over their lives: *My older brother was a god to me when I was young.*

goddess (god′ əs) *n.* a female being thought by some people to have great power over their lives. *pl.* **goddesses.**

godfather (god′ fȧth′ ər) *n.* a male adult, other than a baby's parent, who makes vows for that baby when it is baptized.

godmother (god′ muth′ ər) *n.* a female adult, other than a baby's parents, who makes vows for that baby when it is baptized.

goes see **go.**

goggles (goglz) *n.pl.* large glasses worn to protect the eyes from dust, strong wind, bright lights, etc.

going see **go.**

gold (gōld) *n.* **1.** a very valuable yellow metal. **2.** a yellowish colour. *adj.* having this colour.

golden (gōld′ ən) *adj.* made of gold or looking like gold.

goldfish (gōld′ fish′) *n.* a small fish, often red or orange in colour, that is kept as a pet. *pl.* **goldfish**, or **goldfishes.**

golf (golf) *n.* an outdoor game in which players use clubs to hit a small ball into a series of holes.

gone see **go.**

good (gu̇d) *adj.* right; satisfactory; kind; well-behaved: *Your work is good. His is better. Hers is best of all.*

for good forever: *Marie is leaving this city for good.*

good afternoon, good day, good evening, good morning, good night wishes or greetings said to a person at different times of the day. 'Good afternoon', for example, means 'I hope that you have a good afternoon'.

good and very much; extremely: *We got good and wet in the rain.*

good for valid or used for a certain time or under certain conditions: *The warranty for the toaster is good for only three months. That ticket is good for weekday admission to the fair.*

make good **1.** to be a success: *She made good in her new job.* **2.** to keep; to satisfy: *Dan will make good his promise to visit his mother.*

no good worthless; without merit: *It's no good arguing with me; my mind is made up. Don't listen to him; his opinion is no good.*

goodbye, good-bye (gu̇d′ bī′) *n.* a word said when someone is leaving; a farewell.

good-looking (gu̇d′ lu̇k′ ing) *adj.* attractive; nice to look at: *a good-looking person; a better-looking person; the best-looking person of all.*

goodness (gu̇d′ nəs) *n.* the act or state of being good.

goods (gu̇dz) *n.pl.* belongings; possessions; things a person owns that can be moved or sold: *We packed our goods in large boxes. The store sold its paper goods at half price.*

goose (gūs) *n.* a large, long-necked water bird with a flat bill and webbed feet. *pl.* **geese** (gēs).

gorgeous (gȯr′ jəs) *adj.* magnificent; beautiful: *a gorgeous day; a gorgeous picture.*

gorilla (gə ril′ ə) *n.* the largest and strongest ape. *pl.* **gorillas.**

gossip (gos′ ip) *n.* talk about other people that is not always true, and is sometimes unkind. *v.* to talk about others in such a way.

got, gotten see **get.**

goulash (gū′ lȧsh) *n.* a stew made from meat and vegetables.

govern (guv′ ərn) *v.* to rule.

government (guv′ ərn mənt) *n.* **1.** the act of governing. **2.** the people who govern a country, seeing that laws are followed and making new laws.

governor (guv′ ər nər, guv′ nər) *n.* **1.** someone who governs. **2.** in the United States, the elected head of a state. **3.** a device that controls an engine's speed.

Governor General (guv′ ər nər jen′ ə rəl) *n.* the representative of the queen (or king) of the United Kingdom in Canada or in some other countries of the Commonwealth. *pl.* **Governors General.**

gown (gaůn) *n.* a long dress or robe.

grab (grab) *v.* to snatch; to take hold of something suddenly: *The baby grabbed his toy.* **grabbing. grabbed.**

grace (grās) *n.* a short prayer said before a meal.

graceful (grās′ fəl) *adj.* charming; beautiful and smooth in movement: *a graceful skater.*

gracious (grā′ shəs) *adj.* having courtesy and consideration: *The gracious dinner guest helped wash the dishes.*

grade (grād) *n.* **1.** a year or division in a school curriculum: *He is in Grade 9.* **2.** a letter or number that tells how well a person has done in school work; a mark: *Helena got a grade of C on her history test.* **3.** a step or stage in quality, size, value, etc.: *This is a better grade of apples than we had before.* **4.** the level of a road or railway track. *v.* **1.** to make level and smooth: *to grade land for a new road.* **2.** to mark; to assign a grade: *Teachers have to grade many school tests.* **grading. graded.**

gradual (graj′ ū əl) *adj.* gentle; slow: *There has been a gradual improvement in the weather.*

graduate (graj′ ū ət) *n.* a person who has successfully finished a school or university program.

⊖**graduate** (graj′ ū āt′) *v.* to be successful in completing a school or university program and receive a diploma: *My cousin graduated from university two years ago.* **graduating. graduated.**

⊖**graduation** (graj′ ū ā′ shən) *n.* **1.** the successful completion of a school or university program. **2.** the ceremony that takes place then: *We went to my sister's graduation.*

grain (grān) *n.* **1.** the seed of corn, wheat, oats, and other cereal plants. **2.** a speck: *grains of dust.* **3.** the markings on wood, stone, etc.: *That block of marble has a grain in it.*

grain elevator (grān′ el′ ə vā′ tər) a building in which grain is stored.

gram (gram) *n.* a measure of mass; g is the symbol. 1000 g = 1 kg.

grammar (gram′ ər) *n.* the study of how a language works, seen in the forms of words and how the words are arranged in sentences. Good grammar is based on a series of rules.

granary (gran′ ə re, grān′ ə rē) *n.* a place where grain is stored. *pl.* **granaries.**

⊖**grand** (grand) *adj.* **1.** great in size: *A grand piano is a larger piano than an upright one.* **2.** magnificent; splendid: *a grand display of flowers.* **3.** complete: *the grand total of a person's income for three years.*

grandchild (grand′ chīld′, gran′ chīld′) *n.* a child of a son or daughter; a **granddaughter** or **grandson**. *pl.* **grandchildren.**

grandfather (grand′ fäth′ ər, gran′ fäth′ ər) *n.* a person's mother's father or father's father.

grandmother (grand′ muth′ ər, gran′ muth′ ər) *n.* a person's mother's mother or father's mother.

grandparent (grand′ par′ ənt, gran′ par′ ənt) *n.* a grandfather or grandmother.

grandstand (grand′ stand′) *n.* the main seating place on a sports field.

granite (gran′ it) *n.* a very hard, grey rock, used in building.

grant (grant) *v.* **1.** to give; to allow: *He granted me an extra day's holiday.* **2.** to admit as true: *I grant that you've worked hard, but so have I.*
take for granted to expect to happen, without asking: *We take it for granted that dinner will be ready at six o'clock every day.*

⊖**grape** (grāp) *n.* a juicy fruit that grows in clusters on a vine; it is red, purple, or green in colour.

grapefruit (grāp′ frūt′) *n.* a citrus fruit that looks like a large orange; it has a yellowish skin and is yellowish or pink inside.

graph (graf) *n.* a chart, usually made of lines and dots, that shows changes in weather, mass, height, etc.: *a graph that shows how business has grown in Saskatoon during the last hundred years.*

grasp (grasp) *v.* to take hold of something tightly: *He grasped my hand when he started to fall.* **2.** to understand: *I don't grasp the instructions. Can you explain them another way?*

grass (gras) *n.* the green plant making up a lawn or meadow. *pl.* **grasses.**

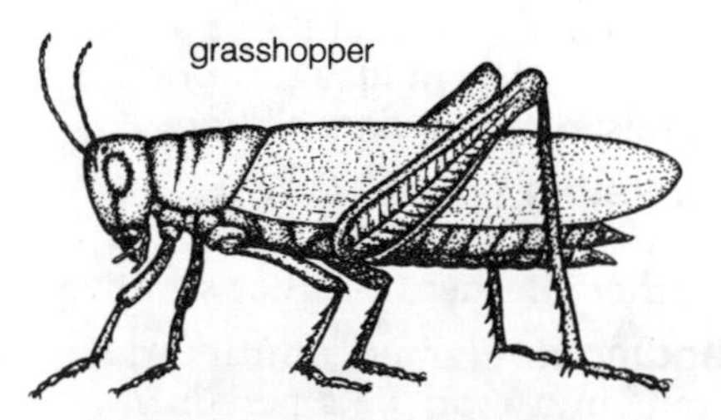

grasshopper (gras′ hop′ ər) *n.* a jumping insect with long back legs.

grate (grāt) *n.* the part of a fireplace that holds burning coal or wood. *v.* to rub into little pieces: *The cook grated some cheese.* **grating. grated.**

grateful (grāt′ fəl) *adj.* thankful: *I am grateful that you were so kind when I was ill.*

gratitude (grat′ i tyud′, grat′ i tūd′) *n.* a feeling of being thankful for something kind that has been done by another.

⊖**grave** (grāv) *n.* a hole in the earth in which someone is buried. *adj.* serious: *Her grave look showed me that something was wrong. a grave injury; a graver one; the gravest one of all.*

gravel (grav′ əl) *n.* small pebbles and stones, used on the surface of some roads.

graveyard (grāv′ yȧrd′) *n.* a place for burying the dead.

gravity (grav′ i tē) *n.* a natural force that pulls objects towards the centre of the earth. Gravity makes objects have mass and causes things to fall when they are dropped.

gravy (grā′ vē) *n.* the juice of cooked meat, sometimes mixed with other ingredients. *pl.* **gravies.**

gray see **grey.**

graze (grāz) *v.* **1.** to eat grass, as cows do. **2.** to touch or rub against something while passing it: *One car grazed the other when they passed on the narrow road.* **3.** to scrape the skin lightly. **grazing. grazed.**

grease (grēs) *n.* **1.** soft, oily fat of an animal. **2.** a thick oil used to keep the parts of some engines running smoothly. *v.* to put grease on something: *to grease a pan.* **greasing. greased.**

greasy (grē′ sē) *adj.* containing much grease: *a greasy piece of chicken; a greasier one; the greasiest piece of all.*

great (grāt) *adj.* **1.** large: *That clock costs a great deal of money. That job takes a great amount of time.* **2.** important: *The automobile is a great invention.* **3.** famous; well known: *a great artist.*

great-grandchild (grāt′ grand′ chīld′, grāt′ gran′ chīld′) *n.* a great-granddaughter or great-grandson; the child of a grandchild.

great-grandparent (grāt′ grand′ par′ ənt, grāt′ gran′ par′ ənt) *n.* a great-grandfather or great-grandmother; the parent of a grandparent.

Great Lakes (grāt′ lāks′) the group of five large, connected lakes in central North America. They are Lake Erie, Lake Huron, Lake Michigan, Lake Ontario, and Lake Superior.

greedy (grē′ dē) *adj.* wanting more than your share; always wanting more: *a greedy cat; a greedier cat; the greediest cat of all.*

Greek (grēk) *n.* the language spoken in Greece. *adj.* belonging to or coming from Greece.

green (grēn) *n.* **1.** the colour of grass. **2. greens**, the green stems and leaves of plants, eaten as food: *Our greens at dinner were lettuce and celery.* *adj.* **1.** having the colour of grass. **2.** not ripe: *This fruit is still green; let it ripen before you eat it.*

greenhouse (grēn′ haůs′) *n.* a building where plants are grown. It is kept warm and bright all year.

greet (grēt) *v.* to welcome: *The family greeted us at the door.*

greeting (grēt′ ing) *n.* a welcome; a message of welcome or good wishes: *A birthday greeting arrived in the mail.*

grew see **grow.**

grey, gray (grā) *n.* a colour made by mixing black and white together: *Grey is the colour of dark clouds.* *pl.* **greys, grays.** *adj.* having this colour.

grid (grid) *n.* **1.** a frame of metal, plastic, or wooden bars across each other. **2.** numbered squares on a map that help the reader find the position of a place.

griddle (gridl) *n.* a flat pan for cooking pancakes and other food.

⊖**grief** (grēf) *n.* sadness, sorrow: *He was filled with grief at his friend's death.*

grill (gril) *n.* a frame of metal bars used to cook food, especially meat. *v.* to cook by placing near a fire; to broil: *to grill steaks on a barbecue.*

grim (grim) *adj.* stern; looking unfriendly or unhappy: *a grim look; a grimmer look; the grimmest look of all. Don't look so grim. The weather will improve soon.*

grime (grīm) *n.* dirt that is difficult to remove.

grin (grin) *n.* a wide smile. *v.* to smile broadly. **grinning. grinned.**

grind (grīnd) *v.* **1.** to crush into powder or very small pieces: *Please grind the coffee beans.* **2.** to rub together: *to grind your teeth.* **grinding. ground** (graůnd).

grip (grip) *v.* to hold tightly. *She gripped the coins in her hand.* **gripping. gripped.**

grit (grit) *n.* a small bit of stone or sand. *v.* to hold or grind the teeth together. **gritting. gritted.**

grizzly bear (griz′ lē ber′) *n.* a large, fierce bear, greyish or brownish in colour.

groan (grōn) *n.* a deep sigh of disappointment or pain. *v.* to make such a sound.

grocer (grō′ sər) *n.* a person who sells food and other goods for household use.

⊖**groceries** (grōs′ ə rēz) *n.pl.* food and other goods sold at a grocery store.

grocery store (grōs′ ə rē stòr′) a store that sells food and other goods for the house.

groom (grūm) *n.* **1.** a man on his wedding day. **2.** a person who looks after horses. *v.* to make neat and tidy: *to groom a dog.*

groove (grūv) *n.* a narrow slot cut into plastic, wood, or metal: *a groove in a record.*

⊖**gross** (grōs) *n.* a group of twelve dozen; 144. *pl.* **gross.** *adj.* **1.** very bad or rude: *gross conduct.* **2.** very big: *He had become gross, and it was time to diet.* **3.** total; complete: *My gross income, before taxes are deducted, is twenty thousand dollars.*

ground (graůnd) *n.* **1.** the earth that is walked on. **2.** an area used for a special purpose: *a fairground.* *v.* **1.** see **grind. 2.** to cause to remain on or come to the ground: *to ground an airplane.* **3.** to connect an electric wire to the ground so that it will not be dangerous.

groundhog

groundhog (graůnd′ hog′) *n.* a North American animal that digs burrows or holes; it is also called a **woodchuck**.

grounds (graůndz) *n.pl.* **1.** the property surrounding and belonging to a building. **2.** reasons: *What are the grounds for your complaint?* **3.** the small, solid pieces that are found at the bottom of some liquids: *coffee grounds.*

group (grūp) *n.* a number of people or things that are together: *a group of friends; a group of books.* *v.* to form into groups: *She grouped the towels according to colour.*

grow (grō) *v.* **1.** to increase in size: *You have grown since last year.* **2.** to plant and develop crops: *We grow tomatoes.* **3.** to develop or happen gradually: *It is growing warmer every day. He has grown a beard.* **growing. grew** (grū). I have **grown** (grōn).
grow out of to become bigger than: *Sally grew out of her dress by the end of the year.*
grow up to become older; to become an adult: *Zoltan's children have grown up since I last saw them.*

growl (graůl) *v.* to make a low noise from deep in the throat. *The lion growled in its cage.*

grown-up (grōn′ up′) *n.* an adult.

growth (grōth) *n.* **1.** an increase in size; development: *the growth of an acorn into an oak tree.* **2.** a lump in or on the body, sometimes caused by disease.

grudge (gruj) *n.* a feeling of dislike, often over a long time: *Irma bears a grudge against me because I broke our promise.*

grumble (grumbl) *v.* to complain; to find fault: *Vince grumbled because he had to get up early on Saturday.* **grumbling. grumbled.**

grumpy (grum′ pē) *adj.* miserable; unhappy: *I am grumpy when I get up; my sister is grumpier; my father is grumpiest of all.*

grunt (grunt) *n.* the kind of sound that a pig makes. *v.* to make such a sound: *She grunted as she lifted the heavy chair.*

guarantee (gar′ ən tē′) *n.* a promise; an agreement that if something goes wrong, it will be fixed without charge: *The store gave us a two-year guarantee on the stove.* *v.* to make such a promise: *The store guranteed the stereo for a year.* **guaranteeing. guranteed.**

guard (gȧrd) *n.* a person or thing that protects and looks after someone or something: *a bank guard; a guard on a sports helmet.* *v.* to watch and protect; to defend: *A goalie guards the goal in a hockey game.*
guard against to stop from happening by being careful: *You can guard against cold weather by dressing warmly.*

ə**guardian** (gȧr′ di ən) *n.* a person who, by law, looks after someone or something: *Her aunt became her guardian after her parents died.*

guerilla (gə ril′ ə) *n.* a member of an unofficial military group that fights for a political cause. *pl.* **guerillas.** *adj.* of or by guerillas: *a guerilla war.*

guess (ges) *n.* a feeling or opinion about something without enough information to know for certain: *My guess is that it will rain tomorrow.* *pl.* **guesses.** *v.* **1.** to say what you think is true, without knowing for certain: *Jean-Paul guessed my age.* **2.** to suppose; to think: *I guess we can go now; the movie is over.* **guessing. guessed.** she **guesses.**

guest (gest) *n.* **1.** a visitor who is invited somewhere: *We had guests at our house for dinner.* **2.** a person who stays at a hotel or motel.

Guide (gīd) *n.* a person who is a member of the Girl Guides.

guide (gīd) *n.* **1.** a person who shows the way: *The guide took us to the fishing area.* **2.** a book that gives instructions or other information: *a guide to Canada's parks.* *v.* to lead; to show the way. **guiding. guided.**

guilt (gilt) *n.* a bad feeling that a person has from knowing that he or she has done something wrong: *Thinking of the crime only increased his guilt.*

guilty (gil′ tē) *adj.* having done wrong or taken part in a crime: *a guilty person; a guiltier person; the guiltiest one of all. The prisoner was found guilty of stealing.*

guinea pig (gin′ ē pig′) *n.* a small animal about the size of a rat. A guinea pig is kept as a pet and is also used in scientific experiments.

guitar (gi tȧr′) *n.* a musical instrument with strings that are plucked.

gulf (gulf) *n.* a very large bay that goes far inland: *the Gulf of St. Lawrence.*

gull (gul) *n.* a bird with long wings, seen near bodies of water, and often grey and white in colour. Also called a **sea gull.**

gulp (gulp) *v.* **1.** to swallow quickly: *He gulped down his milk and then* *went out.* **2.** to gasp; to swallow air quickly: *Maria gulped when the teacher asked her for the answer.*

ə**gum** (gum) *n.* **1.** a sticky liquid from plants and trees. **2.** chewing gum. **3. gums** the red flesh around the teeth.

gun (gun) *n.* **1.** a weapon with a metal tube from which shells or bullets are fired. **2.** something like a gun in its shape or use: *a steam gun for removing wallpaper; a glue gun.*

gunpowder (gun′ pau̇′ dər) *n.* black, explosive powder used in fireworks and bullets.

gush (gush) *v.* to blurt out suddenly: *The water gushed out of the pipe.* **gushing. gushed.** it **gushes.**

gust (gust) *n.* a sudden, strong wind.

gut (gut) *n.* the lower part of the intestine. *v.* **1.** to destroy the inside of a building, as by fire. **2.** to remove the insides of: *to gut a fish.* **gutting. gutted.**

ə**gutter** (gut′ ər) *n.* **1.** a channel or ditch for carrying off waste water. **2.** a long, narrow, open container on the edge of a roof, used to carry off rain water.

guy (gī) *n. (informal)* a man; a fellow: *a friendly guy. pl.* **guys.**

gym (jim) *n.* a gymnasium.

gymnasium (jim nā′ zi əm) *n.* a large room for physical exercise and sports.

gymnastics (jim nas′ tiks) *n.pl.* exercises that help to develop the muscles of the body, as well as co-ordination and balance.

H

⊖**habit** (hab′ it) *n.* something that a person does the same way all the time: *Lee has a habit of waking up very early. I have good habits and bad habits.*

hack (hak) *v.* to chop or cut with strong blows: *The butcher hacked several steaks from the large piece of beef.*

had see **have.**

had better should; must: *I had better leave now or I'll be late.*

haddock (had′ ək) *n.* an ocean fish that can be eaten. Haddock is related to cod, but it is not as big. *pl.* **haddock.**

hadn't (hadnt) short for **had not.**

hail (hāl) *n.* frozen rain.

hair (her) *n.* **1.** one of the fine threads that grow on the skin. **2.** the covering of a person's head, or of an animal's body.

haircut (her′ kut′) *n.* the cutting and trimming of hair.

hairpin (her′ pin′) *n.* a U-shaped pin made of wire or plastic, used to keep a person's hair in place.

hairstyle (her′ stīl′) *n.* the way in which a person's hair is cut and worn.

hairstylist (her′ stīl′ ist) *n.* a person who takes care of or cuts people's hair.

hairy (her′ ē) *adj.* covered with hair: *a hairy ape; a hairier ape; the hairiest ape in the cage.*

half (haf) *n.* one of two equal parts that make up a whole. *pl.* **halves** (havz). *adv.* partly: *I was only half ready to go when you arrived.*

half-time (haf′ tīm′) *n.* a rest period in the middle of certain games, such as football and soccer.

halfway (haf′ wā′) *adv.* half the way: *We are halfway home.*

halibut (hal′ i bət) *n.* an ocean fish that can be eaten. Halibut is a large flatfish. *pl.* **halibut.**

Halifax (hal′ i faks′) *n.* the capital city of the province of Nova Scotia.

hall (hȯl) *n.* **1.** the entrance space behind the door of a building. **2.** a corridor that separates the rooms in a building or to which such rooms open: *Marta lives down the hall from me.* **3.** a large room for meetings, concerts, parties, etc. **4.** a building for public business: *city hall; town hall.*

Halloween, Hallowe'en (hal′ ə wēn′, hal′ o ēn′) *n.* the evening of October 31, when children put on funny clothes and knock on doors, asking for coins, candy, etc.

hallway (hȯl′ wā′) *n.* a hall or passage in a building. *pl.* **hallways.**

halo (hā′ lō) *n.* **1.** a ring of light around the sun, moon, or a star. **2.** a ring of light around the head, shown in some pictures of angels or holy people. *pl.* **halos.**

halve (hav) *v.* **1.** to separate into two parts that are equal: *Arthur halved the apple so that the two children could each get a piece.* **2.** to make smaller by half. **halving. halved.**

ham (ham) *n.* **1.** cooked meat from a pig. **2.** *(informal)* an amateur radio operator. **3.** *(informal)* a person, usually an actor, who exaggerates his or her speech or feelings.

hamburger

hamburger (ham′ bûr′ gər) *n.* **1.** a patty of ground beef or other meat, fried or broiled and served in a bun: *I'll have ketchup and onions on my hamburger, please.*

2. ground beef: *We bought a kilogram of hamburger at the supermarket.*

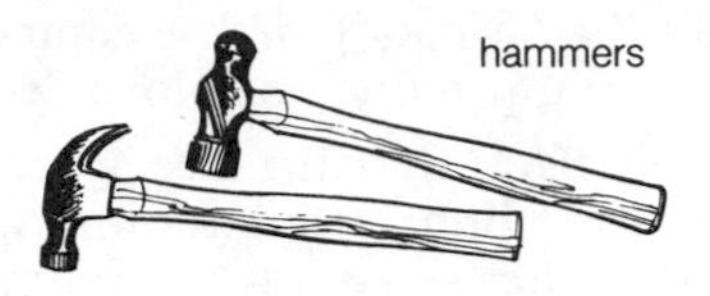

hammer (ham′ ər) *n.* a tool used for driving in nails, shaping metal, or breaking up stone.

hamper (ham′ pər) *n.* a large container, often a basket with a cover: *a clothes hamper; a picnic hamper.*

hamster (ham′ stər) *n.* a small pet that looks like a rat with a short, hairy tail.

hand (hand) *n.* **1.** the end of the arm, used to hold things: **2.** a pointer on a clock. **3.** a deal of cards: *I won the card game because I had the best hand.* **4.** *(informal)* a member of a ship's crew or other group: *All hands on deck!* **5.** a share or part in doing something: *We all had a hand in building the new garage.* **6.** help; assistance: *Can you give me a hand? I want to move that heavy chesterfield.* *v.* to give, using the hand or hands: *Please hand the mail to Aunt Gretchen.*
by hand using the hands instead of a machine: *The sweater was made by hand.*
change hands to move or pass from one person to another: *The store changed hands when Mr. Howard retired.*
hand down to pass along to another: *My grandmother's ring was handed down to my mother.*
hand in to give to a person in charge: *Hand in your reports to the teacher.*
hand out to give out: *Hand out the tests to all the pupils.*
hand over to give or return: *Hand over your books to the librarian.*
hands up **1.** a call for surrender: *'Hands up!' said the robber.* **2.** a request to raise an arm: *'If you know the answer,' the teacher said, 'put your hands up.'*
have your hands full to be as busy as a person can manage to be: *Tom has his hands full with his new job; he always gets home late at night.*
on hand available for use; in a person's possession: *I have enough food on hand to feed all of us.*
on the other hand but also; on the other side: *I would like to travel this summer; on the other hand, staying home would be nice, too.*
out of hand not in control: *Our dog gets out of hand when it smells its dinner; it starts to jump and bark.*

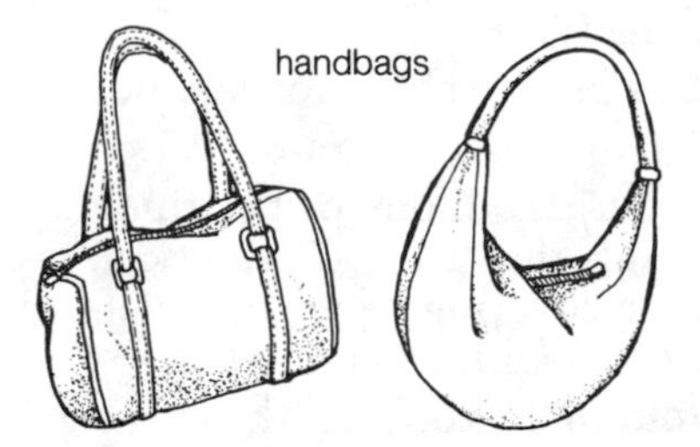

handbag (hand′ bag′) *n.* a woman's purse for holding money and small items.

handbook (hand′ bůk′) *n.* a small book with information about a certain subject: *a handbook on how to fill out an income-tax form.*

handcuffs (hand′ cufs) *n.pl.* a pair of connected metal rings that lock around the wrists: *Violent prisoners are usually placed in handcuffs.*

handful (hand′ fůl′) *n.* as much as the hand will hold. *pl.* **handfuls.**

handicap (han′ dē kap′) *n.* something that makes doing things harder: *Having little money can be a handicap to someone who likes to travel.*

handicapped (han′ dē kapt′) *adj.* having a handicap; disabled.

handicraft (hand′ i kraft′) *n.* **1.** the art or skill of making a certain article by hand, usually as a hobby. **2.** the article itself: *My favourite handicrafts are pottery and jewellery.*

handkerchief (hang′ kər chif) *n.* a cloth for wiping the nose or face. *pl.* **handkerchiefs.**

handle (handl) *n.* the part of a cup, pan, or tool by which it is held. *v.* **1.** to hold, touch, or move with the hands: *Handle the glasses carefully.* **2.** to control or manage: *How can you handle so much work when you're also moving to a new apartment?* **3.** to deal with; to have or do as part of a business: *Take the broken toaster to the repair shop that handles small appliances.* **handling. handled.**

handlebars (handl′ bärz′) *n.pl.* the part of a bicycle that the rider holds and uses for steering.

handshake (hand′ shāk′) *n.* the clasping of hands between two people as a sign of friendship, agreement, or greeting.

handsome (han′ səm) *adj.* **1.** good-looking: *a handsome man.* **2.** generous; large: *a handsome prize for winning a contest.*

handwriting (hand′ rīt′ing) *n.* writing done by hand, not printed or typed.

handy (han′ dē) *adj.* **1.** skilled with the hands: *Carmen is handy at repairs in the house.* **2.** useful to have nearby: *a handy tool; a handier one; the handiest tool in the workshop.*

hang (hang) *v.* **1.** to fasten something so that it may swing but does not fall: *Please hang the picture on that wall.* **hanging. hung** (hung). **2.** to put someone to death with a rope around his or her neck. **hanging. hanged.**
hang on to wait: *Hang on a minute; I'll be there as soon as I finish this telephone call.*
hang up 1. to place on a hanger or hook. **2.** to finish using a telephone.

hangar (hang′ ər) *n.* a building where aircraft are kept and repaired.

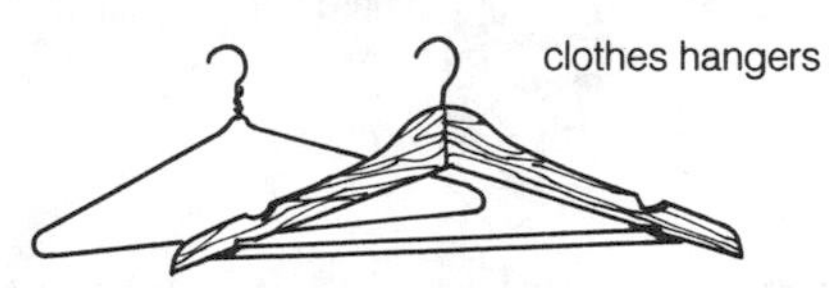
clothes hangers

hanger (hang′ ər) *n.* a wooden or wire frame for hanging clothes.

hang-up (hang′ up′) *n.* *(informal)* something that gets a person unusually worried or upset: *He has a hang-up about flying. He'll never take an airplane.*

happen (hap′ ən) *v.* to occur; to take place: *The accident happened last night.*

happily (hap′ i lē) *adv.* in a happy way: *The child went happily to school.*

happiness (hap′ i nəs) *n.* being pleased; pleasure: *Kim could not hide her happiness when she won the award.*

happy (hap′ ē) *adj.* pleased; cheerful; glad: *Jamie is happy; Sam is happier; and Kim is the happiest member of the family today.*

harass (har′ əs, hə ras′) *v.* to trouble with small, repeated attacks: *The big bully harassed the small boy.* **harassing. harassed.** he **harasses.**

harbour, harbor (här′ bər) *n.* a sheltered place for ships.

hard (härd) *adj.* **1.** firm; not soft: *a hard apple.* **2.** difficult: *a hard problem; hard work.* **3.** severe; violent: *a hard winter storm.* *adv.* with a real effort: *We tried hard to fix the machine.*
hard at work working with great effort: *We were hard at work when the lights went out.*

hard of hearing deaf or partly deaf.
hard up in need of: *I'm hard up for money this month.*

hard-boiled (hȧrd′ bȯild′) *adj.* boiled until cooked completely: *a hard-boiled egg.*

hard hat

hard hat (hȧrd′ hat′) **1.** a helmet of metal or plastic, worn for protection by construction workers and others. **2.** *(informal)* a construction worker.

hardly (hȧrd′ lē) *adv.* only just: *I can hardly reach it.*
hardly any very little or few: *There is hardly any food that I don't like.*
hardly ever seldom; almost never: *I hardly ever see my cousin John.*

hardware (hȧrd′ wer′) *n.* **1.** items used for fixing or constructing things, such as locks, chains, and tools. **2.** electric or mechanical equipment used with data processing, such as a computer.

hare (her) *n.* an animal with long ears and long back legs; it looks like a large rabbit.

harm (hȧrm) *v.* to hurt; to damage: *The early frost harmed the plants. The dog scared the child, but it did not harm her.*

harmful (hȧrm′ fəl) *adj.* causing harm; dangerous: *The berries on that tree are harmful. They can make you very ill if you eat them.*

harmonica (hȧr mon′ i kə) *n.* a small musical instrument, also called a mouth organ. The sound of a harmonica is made by blowing into it and by moving the lips and tongue. *pl.* **harmonicas.**

harmony (hȧr′ mə nē) *n.* **1.** a pleasing musical sound. **2.** a feeling of friendship, of agreeing on things: *There is perfect harmony between the two cousins.* *pl.* **harmonies.**

harness (hȧr′ nəs) *n.* the leather straps and other equipment used to hitch a horse or other animal to a cart or a plough. *pl.* **harnesses.** *v.* to control and use: *A windmill harnesses the power of the wind.* **harnessing. harnessed.** he **harnesses.**

harp (hȧrp) *n.* a large musical instrument played by plucking its strings.

harpoon (hȧr pün′) *n.* a spear with a rope fastened to it, fired at whales and other sea animals.

harrow (har′ ō) *n.* a large device with metal teeth or discs, used to break up ploughed land.

harsh (hȧrsh) *adj.* rough; unkind: *a cold, harsh winter; cruel, harsh punishment.*

harvest (hȧr′ vəst) *n.* the gathering of grain, fruit, and other crops at the end of the growing season. *v.* to gather these crops.

harvester (hȧr′ vəs tər) *n.* **1.** a person who harvests. **2.** a farm machine used to harvest.

has see **have.**

hasn't (haznt) short for **has not.**

hassle (hasl) *n.* *(informal)* a small and annoying struggle: *Taking three buses to work can be a hassle.*

haste (hāst) *n.* a great hurry: *He ran off in haste.*

hasty (hās′ tē) *adj.* quick; made or done in a hurry: *a hasty decision; a hastier one; the hastiest one of all.*

hat (hat) *n.* a shaped covering for the head.

hatch (hach) *n.* the opening in a ship's deck. *pl.* **hatches.** *v.* to bring baby birds or small fish out of eggs. **hatching. hatched.** it **hatches.**

hatchery (hach′ ərē) *n.* a place where the eggs of chicken or fish are kept until they develop into young. *pl.* **hatcheries.**

hatchet (hach′ ət) *n.* a small axe.

⊖**hate** (hāt) *n.* a very great feeling of dislike. *v.* to dislike very much; to detest: *I hate that song! Turn off the radio!* **hating. hated.**

hatred (hā′ trəd) *n.* strong dislike.

haul (hȯl) *v.* to drag; to pull with difficulty: *The horse hauled the logs along the ground.*

haunted (hȯn′ təd) *adj.* believed to be visited by ghosts: *a haunted house.*

have (hav) *v.* **1.** to own; to hold: *I have some money.* **2.** to cause something to happen or be done: *Have the store call me when my dress is ready.* **3.** to experience; to happen to someone or something: *Jill has trouble finding a new job. The children had fun at the swimming pool.* **4.** to give birth to: *The dog had a litter of six puppies.* **5.** to allow: *I won't have my garden paved with cement.* **having. had.** he **has** (haz).

have had it to have experienced all that a person wants to with someone or something: *I've had it with my boss. I quit!*

have to to be forced to; must: *I have to go home now.*

have to do with to be about: *This book has to do with computers.*

haven (hā′ vən) *n.* **1.** a sheltered harbour. **2.** any place of safety or shelter: *a haven of freedom.*

haven't (hav′ ənt) short for **have not.**

hawk (hȯk) *n.* a bird of prey with a hooked beak and long, curved claws.

hay (hā) *n.* grass cut and dried as food for animals.

hay fever (hā′ fē′ vər) an illness that is like a bad cold, caused by breathing the pollen in the air.

haystack (hā′ stak′) *n.* a large pile of hay placed outdoors.

⊖**hazard** (haz′ ərd) *n.* something that is dangerous or might cause harm: *That loose step is a hazard; someone might fall off it.*

haze (hāz) *n.* slight mist or smoke.

hazel (haz′ əl) *n.* **1.** a small tree with nuts that can be eaten. **2.** a greenish-brown colour. *adj.* having this colour.

hazy (hā′ zē) *adj.* misty; not clear: *a hazy sky; a hazier sky; the haziest sky I've ever seen.*

he (hē) *pron.* a man or boy: *He is my friend.* *pl.* **they** (t͟hā).

head (hed) *n.* **1.** the top part of the body; the part of the body that includes the brain, eyes, ears, nose, mouth, etc. **2.** the top or front of anything: *We are at the head of the line for the movies.* **3.** the chief leader: *the head of a country.* **4.** a single animal in a count of many animals: *The farmer bought sixty head of horses.* *v.* **1.** to lead: *He headed the Progressive Conservative Party.* **2.** to move in a certain direction: *The airplane headed east after it took off.*

go to a person's head **1.** to make conceited: *All the praise that Jeanne got really went to her head.* **2.** to make dizzy or unsteady: *If he drinks too much beer, it goes to his head very quickly.*

head for to go in the direction of: *We headed for home.*

head on with the front part first: *Rod ran his bicycle head on into the parked car.*

head over heels totally; completely: *I'm head over heels in love with you.*

in a person's head in a person's mind: *I have a lot of telephone numbers in my head.*
over a person's head beyond a person's understanding or ability: *Geometry has always been over Brad's head.*

headache (hed′ āk′) *n.* **1.** a pain in the head. **2.** an annoying problem: *Forgetting the keys was a headache for us.*

headlights

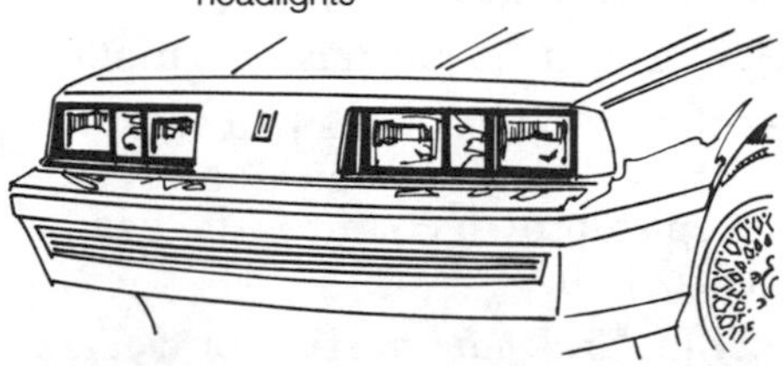

headlights (hed′ līts′) *n.pl.* The main front lights of a car, bus, truck, etc.

headline (hed′ līn′) *n.* the title of an article in a newspaper or magazine.

headphone (hed′ fōn′) *n.* a receiver for a telephone or radio, worn against the ear or ears.

headquarters (hed′ kwȯr′ tərz) *n.pl.* a main office: *police headquarters; the headquarters of a business.*

head start (hed′ stȧrt′) an advantage in time or distance that comes from having begun something early: *We got a head start on our science project by gathering our supplies last winter.*

heal (hēl) *v.* to make or become well again: *The cut healed in a week.*

health (helth) *n.* the general condition of the body and mind; how a person feels: *If you are well, you enjoy good health.*

healthy (hel′ thē) *adj.* in good health: *a healthy child; a healthier child; the healthiest child of all.*

heap (hēp) *n.* a pile: *a heap of papers.*

hear (hēr) *v.* **1.** to receive sounds through the ears. **2.** to receive information or news: *I heard that you went to Montreal last week.*
hearing. heard (hûrd).

hearing (hēr′ ing) *n.* **1.** one of the five senses; the ability to hear sounds. **2.** an opportunity to be listened to: *a hearing in a law court.*

hearse (hûrse) *n.* a car used in a funeral, in which the coffin is carried.

heart (hȧrt) *n.* **1.** the part of the body that pumps blood through the body. **2.** the centre: *Chris lives in the heart of the city.* **3.** a person's feelings. *a sad heart.* **4.** a playing card with one or more ♥ marks on it.
break a person's heart to cause someone great sadness: *Don't break my heart by marrying someone else!*
by heart from memory; able to say the words of a poem, a story, play, etc., without reading them from a book.
have the heart to have the courage: *I don't have the heart to tell her the bad news.*
heart-to-heart speaking seriously about something private: *a heart-to-heart conversation about his illness.*
take to heart to be greatly affected by: *Sam took his sister's scolding to heart; he's still feeling hurt.*
with all a person's heart sincerely; truly: *Doris thanked her hosts with all her heart.*

heart attack (hȧrt′ ə tak′) a sudden illness in which the heart stops working.

heartbreaking (hȧrt′ brāk ing) *adj.* causing great sorrow or grief: *The story of the sick child was heartbreaking.*

heat (hēt) *n.* warmth; hotness: *the heat from the sun; the heat from a* *fire.* *v.* to warm: *Please heat the potatoes.*

heated (hēt′ əd) *adj.* very angry or excited: *a heated argument.*

heater (hēt′ ər) *n.* a piece of equipment, such as a radiator, furnace, or stove, that produces heat.

heave (hēv) *v.* to lift up with a great effort: *We heaved the large box into the truck.* **heaving. heaved.**

heaven (hev′ ən) *n.* **1.** according to some religions, the place where good people go after they die. **2.** a place or state of great happiness.

heavenly (hev′ ən lē) *adj.* **1.** having to do with heaven or with the sky: *The stars are heavenly bodies.* **2.** very pleasant: *heavenly music.*

heavens (hev′ ənz) *n.pl.* the sky; the space that surrounds the earth: *the planets in the heavens.*

heavy (hev′ ē) *adj.* **1.** hard to lift: *a heavy box; a heavier one; the heaviest box of all.* **2.** more than usual: *heavy rain.*

hectare (hek′ ter, hek′ tȧr) *n.* a unit of measurement for area; **ha** is the symbol. 1 ha = 10 000 m^2.

he'd (hēd) short for **he had** or **he would.**

hedge (hej) *n.* bushes that grow close together and form a kind of fence.

heel (hēl) *n.* **1.** the back of the foot, under the ankle. **2.** the part of a shoe that is under a person's heel.

heifer (hef′ ər) *n.* a young cow that has not given birth to a calf.

height (hīt) *n.* how tall anyone or anything is: *Frank's height is 165 cm.*

heir (er) *n.* someone who will become the owner of another person's title, money, or property when that person dies: *The eldest princess is heir to the throne. William is the heir of Charles.*

held see **hold.**

helicopter

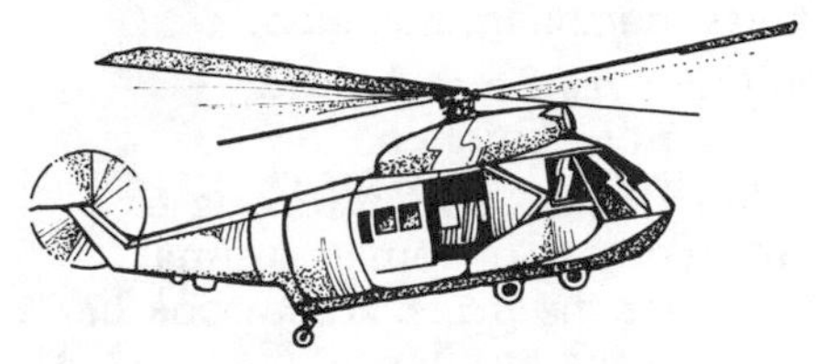

helicopter (hel′ i kop′ tər) *n.* an aircraft without wings. A helicopter is pulled by large propellers and can rise straight up from the ground.

hell (hel) *n.* according to some religions, a place of misery where wicked people go after they die.

he'll (hēl) short for **he will.**

hello (he lō′, hə lō′) *interj., n.* a greeting: *She said hello when I arrived.* *pl.* **hellos.**

helm (helm) *n.* the part of a ship or boat used for steering.

helmet (hel′ mət) *n.* a hard hat worn to protect the head.

help (help) *n.* **1.** aid; assistance: *These bags are heavy. Can you give me some help?* **2.** someone who or something that provides assistance: *Theo is a great help to me in the kitchen.* *v.* **1.** to assist; to share someone's work or troubles by doing something for him or her: *Mike helps with the shopping.* **2.** to stop from or avoid: *Randy couldn't help crying when he heard about the accident.*
help out to be useful in a time of need: *The neighbours helped us out when our home burned.*
help yourself to take what you want: *Help yourself to the salad.*

helpful (help′ fəl) *adj.* giving help: *Andrea is very helpful when there is work to be done.*

helping (help′ ing) *n.* a share; a portion: *Roger asked for a second helping of ice cream.*

hem (hen) *n.* the edge of a piece of cloth, turned over and stitched. *v.* to sew a hem: *She hemmed the dress.* **hemming. hemmed.**

hen (hen) *n.* a female bird, especially a chicken.

her (hûr) *pron., adj.* referring to a girl, woman, or female animal: *Give her the prize. Alice took her plate to the kitchen.*

⊖**herb** (hûrb, ûrb) *n.* a plant whose leaves, seeds, or stems are used in cooking or in making medicine.

herd (hûrd) *n.* a group of cattle or other large animals: *a herd of buffalo.*

here (hēr) *adv.* **1.** in or at this place: *Here I am.* **2.** to this place: *Come here!*

heritage (her′ i tij) *n.* something that a group of people have now because of what happened to their ancestors or what their ancestors did: *The right to vote in free elections is part of the Canadian heritage.*

hermit (hûr′ mit) *n.* a person who lives alone and stays away from other people.

hero (hēr′ ō) *n.* **1.** a man or boy who has done something very brave. **2.** the main man or boy in a story. *pl.* **heroes.**

heroic (hi rō′ ik) *adj.* brave; as it would be done by a hero or heroine: *a heroic deed.*

heroin (her′ ō in) *n.* a synthetic narcotic drug.

heroine (her′ ō in) *n.* **1.** a woman or girl who has done something very brave. **2.** the main woman or girl in a story.

heroism (her′ ō izm) *n.* great bravery.

heron (her′ ən) *n.* a large wading bird with a long beak, a long neck, and long legs.

herring (her′ ing) *n.* a small ocean fish used for food. *pl.* **herring.**

hers (hûrz) *pron.* belonging to her: *The prize is hers.*

herself (hûr self′) *pron.* she alone: *Tina built the cabin by herself.*

hertz (hûrts) *n.* a unit for measuring the frequency of vibrations and waves; **Hz** is the symbol. 1 Hz = 1 cycle per second. *pl.* **hertz.**

he's (hēz) short for **he is** or **he has.**

hesitate (hez′ i tāt′) *v.* to pause because of not being sure whether to do or say something: *He hesitated before jumping into the cold water.* **hesitating. hesitated.**

hesitation (hez′ i tā′ shən) *n.* a pause before doing something because of not being sure.

hey (hā) *interj.* *(informal)* a shout made to get the attention of others: *Hey! I'm over here!*

hi (hī) *interj.* *(informal)* a greeting; hello.

hibernate (hi′ bər nāt′) *v.* to sleep through the winter as bears and other animals do. **hibernating. hibernated.**

hiccup, hiccough (hik′ up) *n.* a short gasp, sometimes made when a person eats too much too quickly. *v.* to gasp in such a way. **hiccupping. hiccupped.**

hide (hīd) *n.* an animal's skin. *v.* **1.** to keep out of sight: *Let's hide in the other room and surprise him when he comes in.* **2.** to put out of sight: *Mrs. Granados hid the presents until her daughter's birthday.* **hiding. hid** (hid). I have **hidden** (hid′ ən).

high (hī) *adj.* **1.** tall; a long way up from the ground: *a high tower.* **2.** very great: *a high price.* *adv.* far above: *The bird flew high over the trees.*

high chair (hī′ cher′) a small chair with long legs and a tray, used by a baby when eating.

high-rise (hī′ rīz′) *n.* an apartment building with many storeys: *He* *lives on the eighth floor of a high-rise in Edmonton.*

high school (hī′ skül′) a secondary school for older boys and girls.

highway (hī′ wā′) *n.* a main road for vehicles. *pl.* **highways.**

hijack (hī′ jak′) *v.* to take control of a plane, truck, ship, etc., by threatening harm or damage to people or things on the vehicle.

hike (hīk) *n.* **1.** a long walk. **2.** an increase or raise: *a hike in the price of milk.* *v.* **1.** to go on a long walk. **2.** to increase or raise. **hiking. hiked.**

hilarious (hi ler′ i əs) *adj.* very, very funny: *a hilarious story.*

hill (hil) *n.* a raised part of the land, lower than a mountain.

him (him) *pron.* referring to a boy, man, or male animal: *Give him something to eat.* *pl.* **them** (t͟hem).

himself (him self′) *pron.* he alone: *George built the garage by himself.*

hind (hīnd) *adj.* rear or back: *the hind legs of a cow.*

hinder (hin′ dər) *v.* to block the way: *to hinder someone's chances for promotion.*

hinge (hinj) *n.* a joint on which a door or lid can move.

hint (hint) *n.* a clue; a helpful suggestion: *This book for carpenters has many good hints.* *v.* to provide a hint.

hip (hip) *n.* the part of the body that sticks out on each side below the waist.

hire (hīr) *v.* to arrange for someone to do work for pay: *The factory will be hiring ten more workers.* **hiring. hired.**

his (hiz) *pron., adj.* belonging to him: *This coat is his. George put his hat on the table.*

hiss (his) *n.* a sound like an 's'. *pl.* **hisses.** *v.* to make such a sound: *Geese and snakes hiss when angry.* **hissing. hissed.** it **hisses.**

historical (his tȯr′ i kəl) *adj.* about history: *a historical movie.*

history (his′ tə rē) *n.* the story of what happened in the past: *the history of Canada.* *pl.* **histories.**

hit (hit) *n.* **1.** a blow or stroke: *a hit on the head.* **2.** something popular: *The new song is a hit.* **3.** in baseball, a stroke by the batter that lets him or her get to at least first base. *v.* to strike; to knock: *Sonia hit the nail with the hammer.* **hitting. hit.**

hitch (hich) *v.* to fasten with a rope, hook, etc.: *to hitch a horse to a post.* **hitching. hitched.** he **hitches.**

hitchhike (hich′ hīk′) *v.* to travel somewhere by walking along a road and asking for free rides from vehicles that pass by. **hitchhiking. hitchhiked.**

hive (hīv) *n.* **1.** the home of bees. **2.** a large number of bees living together.

hives (hīvz) *n.pl.* a rash or inflammation caused by an allergy.

hoard (hȯrd) *v.* to store in a secret place: *The squirrels hoard nuts in the ground.*

hoarse (hȯrs) *adj.* sounding deep and husky: *a hoarse voice; a hoarser one; the hoarsest voice of all.*

hoax (hōks) *n.* a practical joke; a trick. *pl.* **hoaxes.**

hobby (hob′ ē) *n.* an activity that a person enjoys doing in his or her spare time: *Some hobbies are stamp collecting, bird watching, and reading.* *pl.* **hobbies.**

ice hockey

hockey (hok′ ē) *n.* **1.** a game played on ice by players wearing skates;

the players hit a puck with curved sticks to drive it across the goal. **2.** a field game played with curved sticks and a small ball.

hoe (hō) *n.* a long-handled tool for loosening the soil.

hog (hog) *n.* a pig that is full-grown.

hoist (hȯist) *v.* to lift up something by ropes, wires, etc.: *to hoist a flag.*

hold (hōld) *v.* **1.** to keep something with or in the hand: *He held the umbrella.* **2.** to keep something in a particular place: *She held the package on her lap.* **3.** to contain: *The bag holds flour.* **4.** to have: *to hold a meeting.* **holding. held** (held).
hold out to last: *Will our food hold out until next week?*
hold up **1.** to lift: *Will you please hold up your hand?* **2.** to cause delay: *I am late because I was held up by traffic on the highway.* **3.** to rob: *The bank was held up last week.*

hole (hōl) *n.* an opening or space in or through something solid: *a hole in a sock; a hole in a fence; a hole in the ground.*

holiday (hol′ i dā′) *n.* **1.** a special day when people remember an important event: *Thanksgiving is a holiday we celebrate in October.* **2.** a period of time away from work or school: *We drove through Quebec during our summer holiday.* *pl.* **holidays.**

hollow (hol′ ō) *n.* a hole; a pit. *adj.* not solid; empty; having a hole inside: *a hollow tube.*

holly (hol′ ē) *n.* a prickly evergreen shrub with red berries. *pl.* **hollies.**

holy (hō′ lē′) *adj.* sacred; having to do with God or religion: *a holy book; a holier book; the holiest one of all.*

home (hōm) *n.* **1.** the place where a person or animal lives. **2.** the place that a person comes from. **3.** a living place for people who cannot take care of themselves: *a home for the elderly.* **4.** in some games, such as baseball, the goal.

homemaker (hōm′ mak′ ər) *n.* a person who looks after a house or apartment and the people who live in it.

home run (hōm′ run′) in baseball, a hit that lets the batter score by moving to all the bases and back to home plate in one trip.

homesick (hōm′ sik′) *adj.* sad because of being away from home.

homework (hōm′ wûrk′) *n.* work done at home, especially schoolwork.

honest (on′ ist) *adj.* truthful and fair; not cheating, stealing, or lying.

honesty (on′ is tē) *n.* truthfulness.

honey (hun′ ē) *n.* **1.** a sweet, thick liquid made by bees. **2.** *(informal)* someone very dear. *pl.* **honeys.**

honeydew (hun′ i dyū′, hun′ i dū′) *n.* a large melon that has smooth, white skin and sweet, light green flesh.

honeymoon (hun′ i mūn′) *n.* the holiday taken by a newly married couple.

honk (hongk) *n.* the cry of a goose, or any sound like this. *v.* to make such a sound: *to honk a horn.*

honour, honor (on′ ər) *n.* **1.** respect; praise: *There was a parade in honour of the winning team.* **2.** a person's good reputation. **3. Honour**, a title of respect, for a judge and others: *"Your Honour", the lawyer said to the judge.* *v.* to treat with respect: *to honour your parents.*

honourable, honorable (on′ ə rəbl) *adj.* honest; truthful; fair: *Returning his wallet was the honourable thing to do.*

hood (hůd) *n.* **1.** a covering for the head and neck, sometimes fastened to a jacket. **2.** a covering over a car engine.

hoof (hůf, hūf) *n.* the horny foot of a horse, cow, sheep, goat, etc. *pl.* **hoofs**, or **hooves.**

hook (hůk) *n.* a bent and pointed piece of metal made to hold something: *a fish hook. v.* to catch or fasten with a hook.
hook up to connect the parts of a machine or a machine to a source of power: *to hook up a stereo system; to hook up a lamp and turn it on.*

hoop (hūp) *n.* a large ring made of wood, metal, plastic, etc.

hoot (hūt) *n.* the cry of an owl, or a similar sound. *v.* to make such a sound.

⊖**hop** (hop) *n.* **1.** a jump forward on one leg, or with both or all feet together. **2.** a plant whose flowers are used to flavour beer. *v.* to jump on one leg, or with two feet together. **hopping. hopped.**

hope (hōp) *n.* a wish or belief that something will happen the way a person wants: *Steve is full of hope that he will get a good job. v.* to wish that something will happen: *They hoped the weather would be nice on the weekend.* **hoping. hoped.**

hopeful (hōp′ fəl) *adj.* full of hope.

horizon (hə rī′ zən) *n.* the line where sea and sky, or earth and sky, seem to meet.

horizontal (hòr′ i zont′ əl) *adj.* lying flat or level with the ground: *A horizontal line goes from left to right. A vertical line goes from top to bottom.*

horn (hòrn) *n.* **1.** the hard, pointed growth on the head of cattle and some other animals. **2.** a musical wind instrument, usually made of brass: *A musical horn originally was made from the hollowed-out horn of an animal.* **3.** a warning signal: *a car horn.*

hornet (hòr′ nət) *n.* a large wasp that stings.

horrible (hòr′ əbl) *adj.* terrible; awful: *When you scrape a fingernail on the chalkboard, it makes a horrible noise.*

horrify (hòr′ i fī′) *v.* to upset or shock someone: *The terrible news horrified us.* **horrifying. horrified.** it **horrifies.**

horror (hòr′ ər) *n.* great fear; terror; fright: *My cousin is filled with horror at the sight of a snake.*

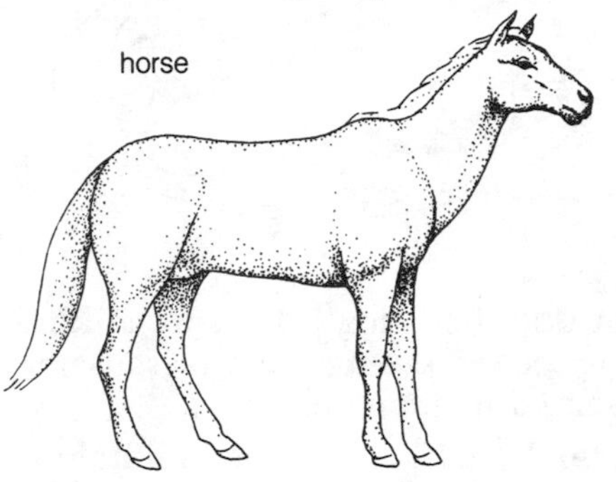

horse (hòrs) *n.* **1.** a large animal with hoofs and a mane, that is used for riding and for pulling wagons. **2.** a frame with legs, used to support something.

horseback (hòrs′ bak′) *adv.* on the back of a horse: *Do you ride horseback?*

horseshoe (hòrs′ shū′) *n.* a metal shoe nailed to the bottom of a horse's hoof.

hose (hōz) *n.* a long, thin, flexible tube used for carrying water or other liquids.

hospital (hos′ pi təl) *n.* a building where people who are ill or hurt are cared for by doctors and nurses.

host (hōst) *n.* a person who invites people somewhere and entertains them as guests.

hostess (hōs′ təs) *n.* a woman who invites people somewhere and entertains them as guests. *pl.* **hostesses.**

hostile (hos′ tīl, hos′ təl) *adj.* feeling or showing dislike; unfriendly: *a hostile remark.*

hot (hot) *adj.* **1.** full of heat: *a hot day; a hotter one; the hottest day of the summer.* **2.** having a burning taste: *a hot sauce.*

hot chocolate (hot′ chok′ ə lət) a hot drink made of cocoa powder and milk.

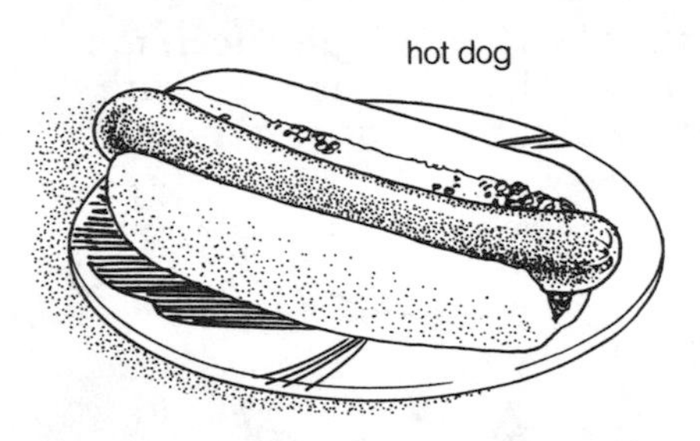
hot dog

hot dog (hot′ dog′) **1.** a special kind of cooked sausage. **2.** this sausage served in a long bun.

hotel (hō tel′) *n.* a large building where travellers pay money to stay and sleep.

hound (haůnd) *n.* a hunting dog. *v.* to annoy: *Stop hounding me!*

⊖**hour** (aůr) *n.* **1.** a length of time equal to sixty minutes; **h** is the symbol. **2.** the time for something: *My work hours are nine to five.*

hourly (oůr′ lē, aůr′ lē) *adv.* each hour: *Check on the patient hourly.*

house (haůs) *n.* **1.** a building where people live. **2.** a building used for a certain purpose: *a dog house.* **on the house** freely given by the owner: *The store served juice to everyone—on the house!*

house (haůz) *v.* to give a place to live: *We housed the campers in the barn.* **housing. housed.**

household (haůs′ hold′) *n.* the group of people living in a house. *adj.* having to do with the activites of those who live in a house: *Your weekly household job is shopping for groceries.*

House of Commons (haůs′ ov kom′ ənz) the elected government representatives of Canada who meet in Ottawa to make laws.

housewife (haůs′ wīf′) *n.* a woman who takes care of her family and the house they live in. *pl.* **housewives.**

housework (haůs′ wûrk′) *n.* cooking, cleaning, washing, and other jobs that people do in their homes.

housing (haůz′ ing) *n.* a group of places to live: *The housing by the lake is very crowded.*

how (haů) *adv.* **1.** in what way: *How did you do it?* **2.** to what amount: *How tall are you?*

however (haů ev′ ər) *conj.* and yet: *I fixed the clock; however, it stopped again.*

howl (haůl) *n.* a long cry: *the howl of a wolf or a dog.* *v.* to make such a cry.

huddle (hudl) *v.* to press close together: *The cows huddled under a tree.* **huddling. huddled.**

hug (hug) *n.* a close, tight hold with the arms. *v.* **1.** to clasp close in the arms: *The boy hugged his baby sister.* **2.** to keep close to: *The boat hugs the shore of the lake.* **hugging. hugged.**

huge (hyūj) *adj.* enormous; very, very big: *a huge rock.*

hull (hul) *n.* **1.** the frame or body of a ship. **2.** the outer part of a seed, nut, etc.

hum (hum) *v.* **1.** to make a buzzing noise like a bee. **2.** to make a musical sound without singing words: *Chris hummed as she worked.* **humming. hummed.**

human (hyū′ mən) *adj.* having to do with people, not animals or plants: *Men, women, and children are human beings.*

⊖**humane** (hyū mān′) *adj.* kind; good; gentle: *The Humane Society tries to see that animals are treated kindly.*

humble (humbl) *adj.* feeling not important; not proud: *Dale felt humble when he finished last in the race. a humble person; a humbler one; the humblest one of all.*

⊖**humid** (hyū′ mid) *adj.* moist; damp: *The weather is hot and humid, and we are all uncomfortable.*

humidity (hyū mid′ i tē) *n.* dampness in the air.

humiliate (hyū mil′ i āt′) *v.* to make someone feel ashamed: *She humiliated her parents when she was rude at the party.* **humiliating. humiliated.**

humorous (hyūm′ ə rəs) *adj.* funny; laughable: *Her humorous story made everyone smile.*

humour, humor (hyū′ mər) *n.* **1.** fun; joking: *Stefan has a good sense of humour. He can make anybody laugh.* **2.** a mood: *to be in bad humour.*

hump (hump) *n.* a large bulge or bump, usually on the back: *a camel's hump.*

hunch (hunch) *n.* a feeling that something will happen: *I have a hunch that there will be a letter from George. pl.* **hunches.** *v.* to bend or pull up into something like a hump: *Rita sat hunched in the corner, her knees near her chin.*

hundred (hun′ drəd) *n., adj.* ten times ten (100).

hundredth (hun′ drədth) *adj.* following ninety-ninth (100th).

hung see **hang.**

hunger (hung′ gər) *n.* the wish or need for something, especially food.

hungry (hung′ grē) *adj.* having a wish for something, especially food; needing food: *a hungry cat; a hungrier one; the hungriest cat on the street.*

hunt (hunt) *v.* **1.** to chase after something in order to catch it or kill it: *to hunt moose.* **2.** to search for: *Pierre hunted everywhere for his cap.*

hunter (hun′ tər) *n.* someone who hunts.

hurl (hûrl) *v.* to throw something with great strength.

hurrah (hə rȧ′) *interj.* a cheer; a shout of happiness: *Hurrah! The team just scored a goal!*

hurray (hə rā′) *interj.* hurrah.

hurricane (hûr′ i kān′) *n.* a storm with a very powerful wind and heavy rain.

hurry (hûr′ ē) *n.* a rush: *What is your hurry? We have lots of time. v.* to move fast: *Lee hurried to catch the bus.* **hurrying. hurried.** he **hurries.**

hurry up to move faster: *Hurry up! We're all waiting for you.*

hurt (hûrt) *v.* **1.** to cause harm, pain, or damage: *He hurt his back when he carried the table. Too much water may hurt the plant.* **2.** to cause grief or sadness: *She hurt his feelings by saying unkind things.* **3.** to feel pain or injury: *My head hurts.* **hurting. hurt.**

husband (huz′ bənd) *n.* a man to whom a woman is married.

hush (hush) *v.* to keep quiet. **hushing. hushed.** she **hushes.**

husk (husk) *n.* the dry covering on the outside of some fruits or vegetables, such as corn.

husky

husky (hus′ kē) *n.* a strong dog, used in very cold places for pulling sleds. *pl.* **huskies.** *adj.* **1.** sounding hoarse: *a husky voice; a huskier voice; the huskiest voice of all.* **2.** large and strong: *a husky person; a huskier person; the huskiest person of all.*

hut (hut) *n.* a small house or cabin, often made of wood.

hyacinth (hī′ ə sinth′) *n.* a plant that grows from a bulb; it has pink, blue, or white flowers.

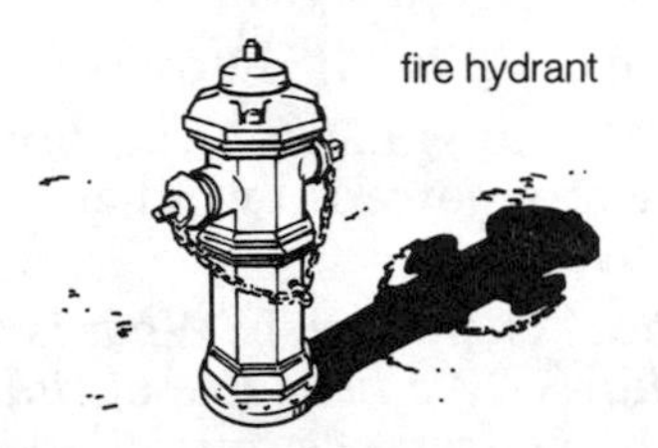
fire hydrant

hydrant (hī′ drənt) *n.* a wide pipe, usually in the street, to which fire hoses can be attached.

hydro (hī′ drō) short for **hydro-electric power.**

hydro-electric (hī′ drō i lek′ trik) *adj.* referring to electricity that is produced using energy from the movement of water.

hygiene (hī′ jēn) *n.* the rules and practice of keeping clean and healthy.

⊖**hymn** (him) *n.* a song of praise.

hyphen (hī′ fən) *n.* a short dash (-) used to separate a word at the end of a line, or to join two words: *A hyphen is found in the word 'twenty-one'.*

hypnotize (hip′ nə tīz′) *v.* to put a person into a sleep-like state. **hypnotizing. hypnotized.**

hysterical (his ter′ i kəl) *adj.* unable to stop laughing or crying, because of nervous excitement.

I

I (ī) *pron.* myself; me; the person who is talking or writing. *pl.* **we** (wē).

ice (īs) *n.* frozen water. *v.* **1.** to cover with ice: *The cold weather made the pond ice over.* **2.** to cover with icing: *to ice a cake.* **icing. iced.**

iceberg (īs′ bûrg′) *n.* a mountain of ice floating in the sea.

ice cream (īs′ krēm′) *n.* a flavoured cream, sweetened and frozen.

ice skate (īs′ skāt′) *n.* a boot with a metal blade that glides on the ice.

ice-skate (īs′ skāt′) *v.* to skate on ice. **ice-skating. ice-skated.**

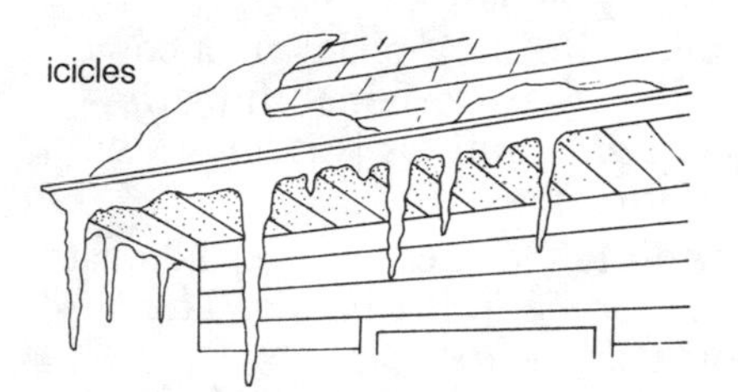

icicle (ī′ sikl) *n.* a pointed stick of hanging ice, formed by water that freezes as it drops.

icing (īs′ ing) *n.* a mixture of sugar, liquid, and flavours, used to cover cakes or cookies.

icy (ī′ sē) *adj.* **1.** covered with ice: *an icy sidewalk.* **2.** cold as ice: *an icy wind; an icier wind; the iciest wind of the winter.* **3.** very unfriendly: *an icy smile.*

I'd (īd) short for **I had** or **I would.**

idea (ī dē′ ə) *n.* a thought; a plan formed in the mind; a purpose: *Their idea is to build a larger garage. I have no idea what my cousin looks like; I haven't seen her in many years.*

ideal (ī dēl′) *adj.* perfect; exactly right: *ideal weather for sailing.*

identical (ī den′ ti kəl) *adj.* exactly the same: *identical twins.*

identification (ī den′ ti fi kā′ shən) *n.* **1.** a paper or card that shows that a person is who he or she claims to be: *A passport, a driver's licence, and a birth certificate are some forms of identification. Before he cashed the cheque, the clerk asked the man for identification.* **2.** the act of identifying.

identify (ī den′ ti fī′) *v.* to say or prove who someone is, what something is, or to whom something belongs: *Can you identify the woman sitting behind you?* **identifying. identified.** he **identifies.**

idiom (id′ i əm) *n.* a group of words whose meaning cannot be understood by defining each word separately. 'By heart', for example, does not mean 'near someone's heart'; it means 'from memory'.

idiot (id′ i ət) *n.* a stupid or foolish person.

idle (īdl) *adj.* lazy; not doing anything: *an idle person; an idler one; the idlest one of all.* *v.* to run slowly without transmitting power: *She left the car idling in the driveway.* **idling. idled.**

idol (ī′ dəl) *n.* **1.** a statue that is worshipped as a god. **2.** a hero or heroine; someone who is admired: *The famous doctor was his idol.*

if (if) *conj.* **1.** on condition that; supposing that: *I will go if you are going, too.* **2.** whether: *Let me know if you are going.*

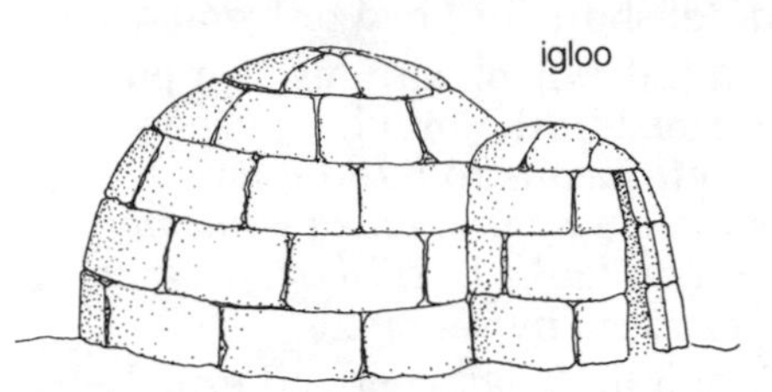

igloo (ig′ lū) *n.* a dome-shaped hut made of blocks of ice or hard snow: *Many Inuit build igloos to live in when they go hunting or fishing. pl.* **igloos.**

ignite (ig nīt′) *v.* to set fire to: *to ignite a match.* **igniting. ignited.**

ignition (ig nish′ ən) *n.* **1.** in a car or other vehicle, the device that starts the engine, or the place where the key is inserted. **2.** the setting on fire; combustion: *The ignition of a rocket is under remote control.*

ɵ**ignorant** (ig′ nə rənt) *adj.* knowing little or nothing.

ɵ**ignore** (ig nór′) *v.* to pretend not to see or hear; to refuse to notice: *He spoke to my sister and me, but he ignored my brother.* **ignoring. ignored.**

ill (il) *adj.* not well; sick: *I felt ill and went to bed.*

I'll (īl) short for **I will** or **I shall.**

illegal (i lē′ gəl) *adj.* against the law: *It is illegal to drive without a licence.*

illness (il′ nəs) *n.* sickness; poor health. *pl.* **illnesses.**

illusion (i lūz′ ən) *n.* **1.** something that is not real; a trick. **2.** a false idea or belief.

illustrate (il′ əs trāt′) *v.* **1.** to add pictures to: *to illustrate a story in a book.* **2.** to explain something by using pictures, diagrams, examples, etc.: *He used photographs to illustrate the lesson about Canada's mountains.* **illustrating. illustrated.**

illustration (il′ əs trā′ shən) *n.* **1.** a picture in a book. **2.** an example.

illustrator (il′ əs trā′ tər) *n.* the person who creates the pictures for a book.

im- a prefix meaning 'not': **impatient** means not patient; **imperfect** means not perfect.

I'm (īm) short for **I am.**

image (im′ ij) *n.* **1.** a copy: *She saw her image in the mirror.* **2.** what people think of someone or something: *The mayor worried about his image with the voters.*

imaginary (i maj′ i ner′ ē′) *adj.* not real; only thought of: *The child saw an imaginary camel in the clouds.*

imagination (i maj′ i nā′ shən) *n.* the ability to picture things in the mind: *If you don't know what to draw, use your imagination.*

imagine (i maj′ in) *v.* **1.** to picture a thing in the mind: *Can you imagine what Canada was like a hundred years ago?* **2.** to believe; to suppose: *I imagine that it will rain again tomorrow.* **imagining. imagined.**

imitate (im′ i tāt′) *v.* to copy; to do something the way someone else does: *Can you imitate my voice?* **imitating. imitated.**

imitation (im′ i tā′ shən) *n.* a copy; not the real or original thing: *Is that a diamond, or is it an imitation?*

immediately (i mē′ di ət lē) *adv.* at once: *Come immediately! The house is on fire!*

immense (i mens′) *adj.* huge; enormous: *an immense iceberg.*

immigrant (im′ i grənt) *n.* a person who comes into another country to live.

immigrate (im′ i grāt′) *v.* to come into another country to live. **immigrating. immigrated.**

immigration (im′ i grā′ shən) *n.* the coming into another country to live: *There has been much* *immigration to Canada throughout its history.*

immunize (im′ yə nīz′, im′ yū nīz′) *v.* to protect from disease: *The doctor gave Sara an injection to immunize her against measles.* **immunizing. immunized.**

impaired (im perd′) *adj.* weakened; less strong: *Malka needed eyeglasses because of her impaired vision.*

impatient (im pā′ shənt) *adj.* restless; finding it hard to wait: *Don't be so impatient! We'll be there in half an hour.*

imply (im plī′) *v.* to hint at without saying directly: *His tone implied that he was tired, though he said that he would work all day.* **implying. implied.** she **implies.**

import (im pȯrt′, im′ pȯrt) *v.* to bring something from one country to another: *Canada imports most of its oranges from the United States.*

importance (im pȯr′ təns) *n.* worth; value: *the importance of water is that it keeps most plants alive.*

⊖**important** (im pȯr′ tənt) *adj.* meaning a lot; having much value or responsibility: *important news; an important person.*

impose (im pōz′) *v.* to force or place on: *to impose a new tax.* **imposing. imposed.**

impossible (im pos′ əbl) *adj.* not able to happen or to be done: *It is impossible to change lead into gold.*

impress (im pres′) *v.* to have an influence on the mind or feelings: *Arthur tried to impress his date by sending flowers to her.* **impressing. impressed.** he **impresses.**

imprison (im priz′ ən) *v.* to put in prison.

improve (im prūv′) *v.* to make better; to become better: *They improved the farm by building a new barn. His health improved after he returned from the hospital.* **improving. improved.**

improvement (im prūv′ mənt) *n.* a change for the better: *The new chair is an improvement over the old one. She shows great improvement in her work.*

impulse (im′ puls) *n.* a sudden wish to do something: *When she leaned over the pool, I felt an impulse to pull her back.*

in (in) *prep.* **1.** inside: *in the bus.* **2.** at: *We live in the city.* **3.** during: *I can do this in a few minutes.* **4.** wearing: *dressed in red.*

in- a prefix meaning 'not': **incomplete** means not complete; **inexpensive** means not expensive.

incentive (in sen′ tiv) *n.* a reason to want to do something: *Offering employees an extra week's holiday is an incentive for them to work at our company.*

inch (inch) *n.* a measure of length, equal to about 2.5 cm. *pl.* **inches.**

incident (in′ si dənt′) *n.* something that happens; an event.

incidentally (in′ si dent′ lē, in′ si den′ təl ē) *adv.* by the way; words used to introduce a new subject: *Incidentally, have you seen my pen anywhere?*

incinerator (in sin′ ər ā′ tər) *n.* a place where unwanted things are destroyed by fire: *All the garbage from the building goes into the incinerator.*

inclined (īn klīnd′) *adj.* preferring one thing instead of another: *I'm inclined to eat beef rather than chicken.*

include (in klūd′) *v.* to count in; to put in: *Include the postal code on the envelope.* **including. included.**

income (in′ kum) *n.* the amount of money a person earns: *Her weekly income is two hundred dollars.*

income tax (in′ kum taks′) the part of the money a person earns that must be paid to the government. *pl.* **income taxes.**

incorporate (in kòr′ pə rāt′) *v.* **1.** to make into a corporation: *Mrs. Krachnik incorporated her business last year so that she would pay less tax.* **2.** to join together: *The show incorporated all the best songs from the last five years.* **incorporating. incorporated.**

increase (in′ krēs) *n.* growth in size or number: *a salary increase; a population increase.*

increase (in krēs′) *v.* to become bigger in size or number: *Increase your speed when you're on the highway. Decrease it when you get back to the city.* **increasing. increased.**

incredible (in kred′ əbl) *adj.* difficult to believe: *It's incredible that your hair has grown so quickly.*

incubate (ing′ kyū bāt′, ing′ kyə bāt′) *v.* to keep eggs warm so that they will hatch. **incubating. incubated.**

indeed (in dēd′) *adv.* certainly: *Yes, indeed, I believe you.*

indent (in dent′) *v.* to start a written or typed line farther from the margin than other lines: *Indent the first word of every paragraph.*

independence (in′ di pen′ dəns) *n.* freedom from the rule or control of another person or country.

independent (in′ di pen′ dənt) *adj.* **1.** not ruled by anyone else: *an independent nation.* **2.** not needing or wanting help from anyone else: *That baby won't let anyone help him. He's really independent.*

index (in′ deks) *n.* a list in alphabetical order, at the end of a book. An index lists the items in the book and the pages on which to find them. *pl.* **indexes**, or **indices** (in′ di sēz′).

index finger (in′ deks fing′ gər) the finger nearest to the thumb.

Indian (in′ di ən) *n.* **1.** a member of one of the groups of people that were living in North, Central, and South America before the first European explorers came. **2.** a person from India. *adj.* **1.** having to do with a North, Central, or South American Indian. **2.** belonging to or coming from India.

indicate (in′ di kāt′) *v.* to show; to point out: *Jack's car outside the house indicates that he is home from work.* **indicating. indicated.**

indifferent (in dif′ rənt, in dif′ ə rənt) *adj.* not having interest or concern: *I am indifferent about whether we go on a vacation this month or next month.*

indigestion (in′ di jes′ chən, in′ dī jes′ chən) *n.* a feeling of illness when the body doesn't digest food properly.

individual (in′ di vij′ ū əl) *n.* a single person or animal: *He is a kind individual.* *adj.* single; separate: *Every snowflake has an individual pattern.*

indoor (in′ dòr′) *adj.* done, played, or used inside: *Basketball is an indoor game.*

indoors (in′ dòrz′) *adv.* inside: *Douglas spent the morning indoors.*

industrious (in dus′ tri əs) *adj.* working a lot and very hard: *Alma is industrious in her new business.*

industry (in′ dəs trē) *n.* **1.** the kind of work or business in which large quantities are manufactured: *the automobile industry.* **2.** all forms of business and manufacturing: *There is little industry in our city.* *pl.* **industries.**

inevitable (in ev′ i təbl) *adj.* not something that could be avoided: *He told so many people the secret that it was inevitable I would find out too.*

inexpensive (in′ iks pen′ siv) *adj.* cheap; not expensive.

⊖**infant** (in′ fənt) *n.* a baby; a very young child.

⊖**infect** (in fekt′) *v.* to spread disease: *You have a bad cold, and if you go to work you may infect others.*

infection (in fek′ shən) *n.* a sickness caused by germs: *He cleaned the cut to avoid infection.*

⊖**inferior** (in fēr′ i ər) *adj.* low in quality or value: *an inferior painting.*

infield (in′ fēld′) *n.* **1.** the diamond-shaped part of a baseball field. **2.** the players in the field.

infinitive (in fin′ i tiv′) *n.* the form of a verb preceded by 'to'. 'To eat' is an example of an infinitive.

inflammable (in flam′ əbl) *adj.* catching fire easily: *Gasoline is highly inflammable.*

inflammation (in′ flə mā′ shən) *n.* a condition in which part of the body is swollen, painful, and often red: *an inflammation in a finger caused by a splinter.*

inflate (in flāt′) *v.* to make bigger by filling with a gas or liquid: *to inflate a car's tire with air.* **inflating. inflated.**

inflation (in flā′ shən) *n.* a sharp rise in prices and wages, with one trying to keep up with the other: *Inflation has made the dollar less valuable than it used to be.*

⊖**influence** (in′ flū əns) *n.* **1.** the power to get someone to form a certain opinion or to make a certain decision: *She used her influence to have the rules changed.* **2.** a person with this power: *She is a good influence on her younger brother.* *v.* to get someone to form a certain opinion or make a certain decision: *My father helped influence my sister to become a teacher.* **influencing. influenced.**

inform (in fȯrm′) *v.* to tell; to pass on information: *She informed her boss that she was leaving the job.*

⊖**information** (in′ fər mā′ shən) *n.* news; facts; knowledge: *The information about Niagara Falls will help us enjoy our trip there.*

ingredient (in grē′ di ənt) *n.* one of the things that is put in a mixture: *How many ingredients do you need for the cake?*

inhabit (in hab′ it) *v.* to live in a place: *People born in many countries now inhabit Canada.*

inhabitant (in hab′ i tənt) *n.* a person or animal that lives in a certain place: *the inhabitants of a village.*

inhale (in hāl′) *v.* to breathe in. **inhaling. inhaled.**

inherit (in her′ it) *v.* **1.** to receive money or property from someone who has died: *Marc inherited his uncle's gold watch.* **2.** to receive from your parents: *Helena inherited her mother's blue eyes.*

initial (i nish′ əl) *n.* the first letter of a name: *Claude Martin's initials are C.M.* *v.* to put initials on a piece of paper: *Please initial this change on your cheque.* **initialling. initialled.**

initiative (i nish′ i ə tiv, i nish′ ə tiv) *n.* **1.** the first step: *If we want to get the job started, someone must take the initiative.* **2.** the ability to start things: *Anita has great initiative.*

injection (in jek′ shən) *n.* the sticking of a hollow needle, filled with medicine, into the body to release the medicine: *The doctor gave Sam an injection to keep him from getting the measles.*

injure (in′ jər) *v.* to harm; to damage: *Lisa injured her knee when she fell.* **injuring. injured.**

injury (in′ jə rē) *n.* harm; damage: *How bad was her injury? pl.* **injuries.**

ink (ingk) *n.* coloured or black liquid used for writing.

inland (in′ lənd, in′ land) *adj.* away from the coast or border: *an inland town.*

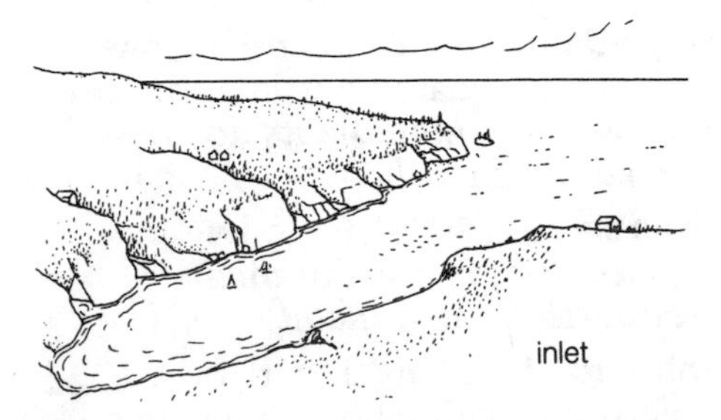
inlet

inlet (in′ let′, in′ lət) *n.* an arm of the sea; a narrow strip of water running into land or between islands.

inmate (in′ māt) *n.* a person who lives with others in an institution, especially a prison.

inn (in) *n.* a small hotel where travellers can get meals and a room.

inner (in′ ər) *adj.* inside: *the inner walls of a house.*

inning (in′ ing) *n.* in baseball, the period when each team has a time at bat: *There are nine innings in a baseball game.*

innocent (in′ ə sənt) *adj.* not guilty; blameless: *The jury found him innocent of the crime.*

Innuit see **Inuit.**

inquire (in kwīr′) *v.* to ask questions to find out information: *When we lost our dog, we inquired if anyone had seen it.* **inquiring. inquired.** (*also spelled* **enquire.**)

insane (in sān′) *adj.* mad; crazy.

insect (in′ sekt) *n.* a small creature such as an ant, bee, or fly. An insect has six legs and three parts to its body. Many insects have wings.

insecticide (in sek′ ti sīd′) *n.* a chemical substance that is used for killing insects.

insert (in sûrt′) *v.* to put something inside: *She inserted the coin into the vending machine, and a cup of coffee came out.*

inside (in′ sīd′) *n.* the inner side: *the inside of a shed.*
inside out with the inside part turned to the outside: *Thelma turned her bag inside out to search for her keys.*

inside (in′ sīd′) *adv.* within: *Let's go inside before it snows.*

insist (in sist′) *v.* to say firmly and strongly: *Michelle insisted that she was right.*

inspect (in spekt′) *v.* to examine very closely: *We inspected the car before beginning our trip.*

⊖**inspire** (in spīr′) *v.* to cause certain thoughts or feelings in people: *The song inspired the audience to cheer loudly.* **inspiring. inspired.**

install (in stol′) *v.* to put in place: *We installed new wiring when we moved to the old house.*

instalment, installment (in stol′ mənt) *n.* one part of a sum of owed money, paid at regular periods until the total amount is paid: *Robin is paying for her new motorcycle in ten instalments.*

⊖**instance** (in′ stəns) *n.* an example.
for instance for an example: *I enjoy all sorts of books; for instance, novels and biographies.*

instant (in′ stənt) *n.* a brief moment of time: *He stopped for an instant, then went on talking.*
adj. **1.** immediate: *The medicine gave instant relief.* **2.** able to be made quickly: *instant coffee.*

instantly (in′ stənt lē) *adv.* at once: *He turned on the radio, and instantly the house was filled with music.*

instead (in sted′) *adv.* in the place of someone, something, or some time: *I can't go to the gym today. I'll go tomorrow instead.*

instinct (in′ stingkt) *n.* a natural feeling or power that makes living creatures do things without being taught: *Squirrels climb trees by instinct.*

institution (in′ sti tyū′ shən, in′ sti tū′ shən) *n.* a group of people who help others in some way, or the buildings this group uses: *Schools, churches, hospitals, and charities are types of institutions.*

instruct (in strukt′) *v.* to teach; to show someone how to do something.

instructions (in struk′ shənz) *n. pl.* directions; an explanation of how to do things.

instructor (in struk′ tər) *n.* a teacher.

instrument (in′ strə mənt) *n.* **1.** a tool: *A thermometer is an instrument that measures temperature.* **2.** anything that makes music: *Violins and pianos are musical instruments.*

insulate (in′ sə lāt′) *v.* to stop from losing heat, electricity, etc., by covering or enclosing with special material: *Rubber will insulate an electric wire.* **insulating. insulated.**

insulation (in′ sə lā′ shən) *n.* material put in the roof and walls of a building to keep it warm: *Ever since we had more insulation put into our house, it has cost us less to keep it warm in winter.*

insult (in′ sult) *n.* a rude remark.

insult (in sult′) *v.* to make a rude remark.

insurance (in shūr′ əns) *n.* an agreement between a person and a company. The person makes small payments to the company on a regular basis. The company will then pay money if the person dies or if there is some sort of loss, injury, or damage: *When my car was stolen, I received three thousand dollars because I had insurance for it.*

insure (in shūr′) *v.* to make an arrangement with a company for money payment in case of death, injury, or loss of property. **insuring. insured.**

intellectual (in′ tə lek′ chū əl) *adj.* having to do with thinking, understanding, and reasoning: *Reading is a more intellectual activity than soccer.*

intelligence (in tel′ i jəns) *n.* the ability to learn and understand.

intelligent (in tel′ i jənt) *adj.* smart; showing the ability to learn and understand.

intend (in tend′) *v.* to mean to do something: *We intend to go skiing this weekend.*

intense (in tens′) *adj.* very powerful or great: *The intense storm caused the roof to blow off.*

intention (in ten′ shən) *n.* what a person plans or means to do.

intentional (in ten′ shən əl) *adj.* deliberate; on purpose, not by accident: *His breaking the window was intentional; I saw him aim the rock carefully.*

intercom (in′ tər kom′) *n.* a system within a building, ship, or plane that lets people hear voices in other areas.

intercourse (in′ tər kȯrs′) *n.* **1.** communication among people or groups of people. **2.** the act of having sex.

interest (in′ tə rest, in′ trəst) *n.* **1.** something a person enjoys doing or wants to learn more about: *Her main interests are hockey and reading.* **2.** money that is paid as a fee for borrowing a larger sum: *The bank pays us interest on our savings account. We pay interest on our loan.* **3.** a share in property, goods, etc.: *She has a quarter interest in the store.* *v.* to attract or hold attention: *This toy interests the child.*

interesting (in′ tə res′ ting, in′ trəs ting) *adj.* holding attention: *I find this book very interesting.*

interfere (in′ tər fēr′) *v.* to meddle; to get mixed up in: *Do not interfere with my work.* **interfering. interfered.**

interference (in′ tər fēr′ əns) *n.* **1.** the act of meddling: *Go away! I've had enough of your interference.* **2.** a disturbance in radio or television reception: *Whenever I turn on the vacuum cleaner, it causes interference on the television.*

interior (in tēr′ i ər) *n.* the inside: *The interior of the car is clean, but the exterior could use a wash.*

interjection (in′ tər jek′ shən) *n.* a word or phrase that shows strong feeling, such as anger, sadness, etc. Some examples of interjections are **hey** and **hurrah**.

⊖**intermission** (in′ tər mish′ ən) *n.* a rest in the middle of some activity: *an intermission during a concert.*

⊖**intern** (in′ tûrn′) *n.* a doctor who is working in a hospital to gain practical experience with patients.

internal (in tûr′ nəl) *adj.* dealing with the inside area: *an internal injury to a person; the internal politics of a country.*

international (in′ tər nash′ ən əl) *adj.* having to do with many nations: *The Olympic Games are an international sports event.*

⊖**interpret** (in tûr′ prət) *v.* to explain the meaning of something, often another language: *Can you interpret the words of that Spanish song?*

interpreter (in tûr′ prə tər) *n.* a person who can explain the meaning when someone is speaking or writing in another language.

interrupt (in′ tə rupt′) *v.* to break into what someone is saying or doing: *Don't interrupt me when I'm talking.*

intersect (in′ tər sekt′) *v.* to cross each other: *Where do the two streets intersect?*

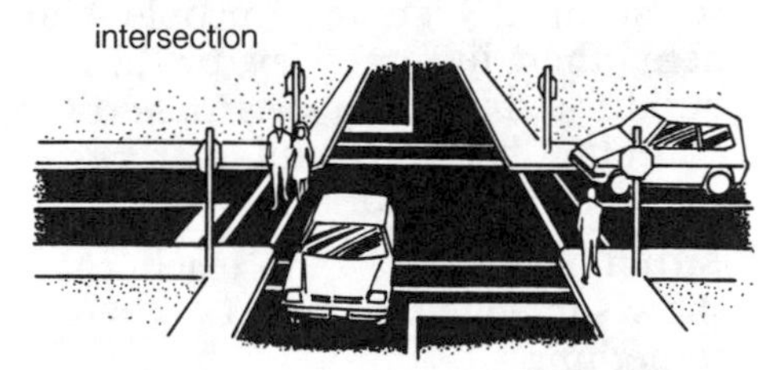

intersection (in′ tər sek′ shən) *n.* the place where two or more things, such as streets, cross: *Our supermarket is near a busy intersection.*

interview (in′ tər vyū′) *n.* a meeting with someone, in which questions are asked: *The interview with the soccer player is in today's newspaper. The interview for the job lasted an hour.* *v.* to meet with someone and ask questions: *Many people were interviewed for the job at the bank.*

intestine (in tes′ tin) *n.* a long tube in the body, where food is carried away from the stomach.

into (in′ tū) *prep.* **1.** to the inside of: *The children went into the stadium.* **2.** to the form of: *The snow changed into rain.* **3.** against: *to walk into a tree.*

intoxicate (in tok′ sə kāt′) *v.* to make drunk: *Too much beer will intoxicate me.* **intoxicating. intoxicated.**

ɵ**introduce** (in′ trə dyūs′, in′ trə dūs′) *v.* **1.** to say the names of people when they meet for the first time: *Please introduce your friend to me.* **2.** to make known for the first time: *He introduced me to the game of chess.* **introducing. introduced.**

ɵ**introduction** (in′ trə duk′ shən) *n.* **1.** a first meeting with a person or a subject: *As a child I received a letter from Australia. This was my introduction to stamp collecting.* **2.** the part of a book, near the beginning, which tells the reader something about the book.

Inuit, Innuit (in′ ū it′) *n.* a member of a people living in northern Canada, Alaska, and other arctic regions. *pl.* **Inuit**, or **Inuits.**

invade (in vād′) *v.* **1.** to enter another country, with an army, in order to attack it. **2.** to enter without permission: *Ants invaded the garden.* **invading. invaded.**

invalid (in′ və lid) *n.* someone who is very ill and cannot get around alone.

invalid (in val′ id) *adj.* having no value or power: *That parking permit is invalid; it expired last month.*

invasion (in vā′ zhən) *n.* the movement of large numbers of people or animals into a place.

invent (in vent′) *v.* to plan or make something for the very first time.

invention (in ven′ shən) *n.* a new thing that has been made or thought of.

inventor (in ven′ tər) *n.* someone who makes something that no one else has ever made.

inventory (in′ vən tòr′ ē) *n.* a list of items that a store has on hand for sale. *pl.* **inventories.**

invest (in vest′) *v.* to spend money on something, hoping that it will become more valuable: *They invested much money in their new business.*

investigate (in ves′ ti gāt′) *v.* to examine carefully in order to find out information: *The police are investigating the accident.* **investigating. investigated.**

ɵ**invisible** (in viz′ əbl) *adj.* not able to be viewed or seen: *The car had no headlights and was invisible in the darkness.*

invitation (in′ və tā′ shən) *n.* a request to come somewhere or to do something: *We received a written invitation to Aaron's party.*

invite (in vīt′) *v.* to ask someone to come to some place or to do something. **inviting. invited.**

invoice (in′ vòis) *n.* a list of items bought or of jobs done and the prices of those jobs: *The plumber wrote out an invoice for his work of replacing the pipes.*

involve (in volv′) *v.* to have something to do with: *What I have to say involves everyone here.* **involving. involved.**

iris (ī′ ris) *n.* **1.** the coloured part of the eye. **2.** a tall garden plant with thin leaves and a purple, white, or yellow flower. *pl.* **irises.**

Irish (ī′ rish) *adj.* belonging to or coming from Ireland.

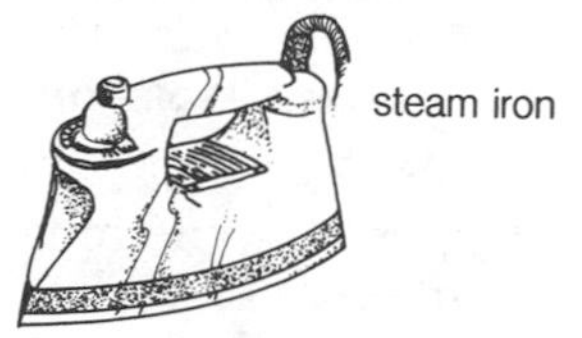

iron (ī′ ərn) *n.* **1.** a strong metal from which tools are made. **2.** something made of iron or a similar metal: *a steam iron.* *v.* to flatten with a hot piece of smooth iron, usually heated electrically: *to iron clothes.*

irregular (i reg′ yə lər) *adj.* **1.** not in the usual way: *an irregular route to work; irregular sleeping hours.* **2.** not smooth: *an irregular coastline.*

irresistible (ir′ i zis′ təbl) *adj.* very interesting; hard to turn away from: *The music on the radio is irresistible.*

irrigate (ir′ i gāt′) *v.* to bring water to land from a river or other source, using streams or pipes: *to irrigate a field.* **irrigating. irrigated.**

irritate (ir′ i tāt′) *v.* **1.** to make someone annoyed or angry: *He irritates his friends by always talking about himself.* **2.** to make part of the body sore: *The rough socks irritated Tim's feet.* **irritating. irritated.**

is (iz) *v.* a form of the verb (to) **be**; used with 'he' or 'she' or 'it', or with a person's name: *He is going to sleep. She is going to sleep. Jean is going to sleep. It is a nice day.*

-ish a suffix that means 'slightly', 'a little bit', or 'similar to': **greenish** means slightly green; **squarish** means shaped like a square.

island (ī′ lənd) *n.* a piece of land, smaller than a continent, with water all around it.

isn't (iznt) short for **is not.**

⊖**isolate** (ī′ sə lāt′) *v.* to keep away from others: *Sara had to be isolated from her family because she had a contagious disease.* **isolating. isolated.**

⊖**issue** (ish′ ū) *n.* **1.** something sent out: *a recent issue of the magazine.* **2.** a subject or problem to be talked over: *The issue of health was discussed in Parliament. He was issued a new licence.* **issuing. issued.**

it (it) *pron.* **1.** a thing or animal. **2.** something indefinite or not clearly stated: *It is going to rain today. pl.* **they** (t͟hā), **them** (t͟hem).

Italian (i tal′ yən) *n.* the language spoken in Italy. *adj.* belonging to or coming from Italy.

itch (ich) *n.* a feeling of tickling or soreness on the skin: *This rash is giving me an itch. pl.* **itches.** *v.* **1.** to produce such a feeling: *This shirt itches!* **2.** to have such a feeling: *My allergy sometimes makes me itch all over.* **itching. itched.** it **itches.**

item (ī′ təm) *n.* **1.** one thing on a list. **2.** an article in a newspaper or magazine.

it'll (itl) short for **it will.**

its (its) *adj.* the one belonging to it: *The cat drank its milk.*

it's (its) short for **it is.** *Note:* Do not confuse **its** and **it's**: *It's raining today. The dog lost its collar.*

itself (it self′) *pron.* its own self: *The dog stretched itself out on the rug.*

I've (īv) short for **I have.**

ivy (ī′ vē) *n.* a climbing plant, often having shiny green leaves. *pl.* **ivies.**

J

jab (jab) *v.* to stab; to poke: *The doctor jabbed the needle into my arm.* **jabbing. jabbed.**

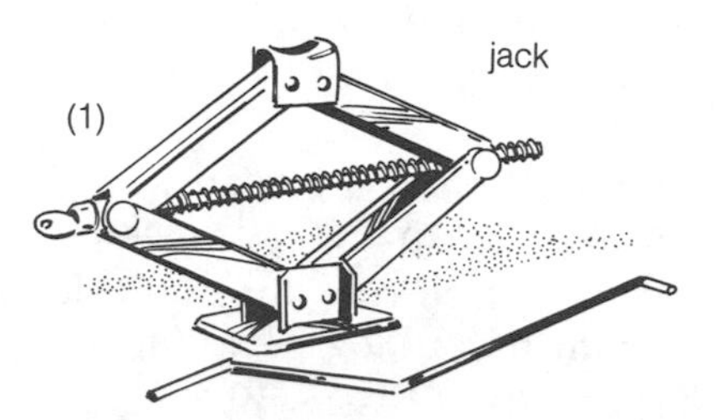

jack (jak) *n.* **1.** a tool used for lifting a car or some other heavy load. **2.** a playing card with the picture of a young man on it. **3.** an electric device into which a plug can be inserted: *Connect the telephone to the jack in the wall.*

jacket (jak′ ət) *n.* **1.** a short coat. **2.** a paper cover on a book; a cardboard cover on a record.

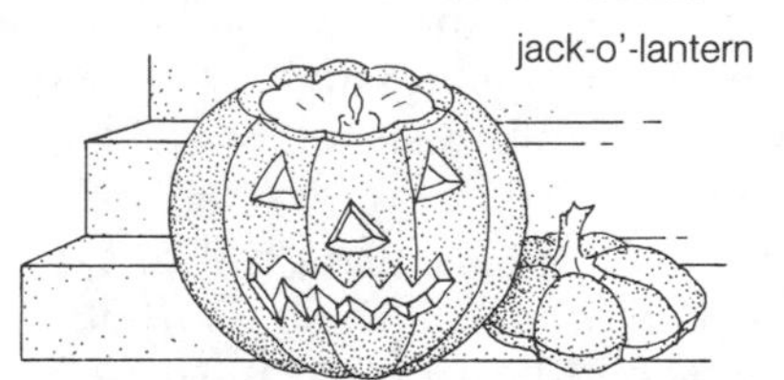

jack-o'-lantern (jak′ ə lan′ tərn) *n.* a pumpkin hollowed out and carved into a face for Halloween.

jackpot (jak′ pot′) *n.* the largest amount of money to be won in a lottery or a similar contest.

jagged (jag′ əd) *adj.* having rough, torn edges: *I cut my arm on a jagged piece of wood.*

jail (jāl) *n.* a prison; a building where criminals are locked up as punishment. *v.* to put or keep in prison.

jam (jam) *n.* **1.** fruit boiled with sugar until it is thick: *strawberry jam.* **2.** a tight crowd of people or vehicles: *a traffic jam.* *v.* **1.** to press together: *We're jammed in the crowded train.* **2.** to get stuck: *The window is jammed and won't open.* **3.** to push with force: *She jammed the brakes on when the cat ran in front of the car.* **jamming. jammed.**

janitor (jan′ i tər) *n.* the person who looks after and cleans a school or other building.

January (jan′ yü er′ ē) *n.* the first month of the year.

Japanese (jap′ ə nēz′) *n.* the language spoken in Japan. *adj.* belonging to or coming from Japan.

⊖**jar** (jȧr) *n.* a pot or a glass container. *v.* **1.** to shake: *The rough ride jarred the car's passengers.* **2.** to make an unpleasant sound; to have an unpleasant effect: *The loud whistle was jarring.* **jarring. jarred.**

jaw (jȯ) *n.* **1.** the upper and lower bones that form the frame of the mouth. The lower jaw is movable. **2.** one of two parts of a tool, such as a vise, that can close and hold an object tightly.

jay (jā) *n.* a kind of bird, such as a bluejay or a Canada jay, with a crest and bright feathers. *pl.* **jays.**

jaywalk (jā′ wȯk′) *v.* to cross a street without paying attention to traffic or without crossing at a proper place.

jazz (jaz) *n.* a lively kind of music with a strong rhythm.

jealous (jel′ əs) *adj.* **1.** unhappy because of wanting what another person has: *The child was jealous of his brother's new toy.* **2.** afraid of losing a loved one to somebody else.

jealousy (jel′ ə sē) *n.* a jealous feeling. *pl.* **jealousies.**

jeans (jēnz) *n.pl.* strong cotton trousers, usually blue.

jeep (jēp) *n.* a powerful car able to travel over rough ground.

jelly (jel′ ē) *n.* a soft, firm food that is usually made from fruit and sugar. *pl.* **jellies.**

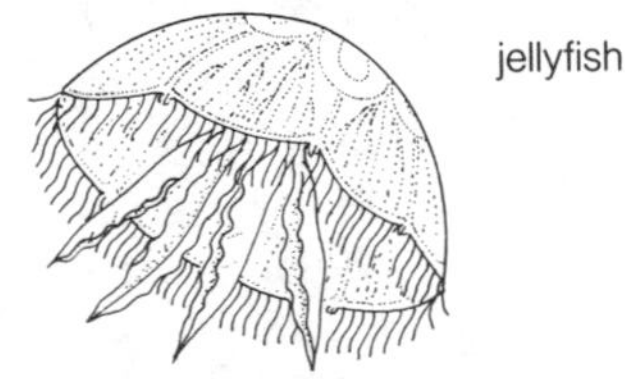

jellyfish

jellyfish (jel′ i fish′) *n.* a small sea animal that has a body like jelly. *pl.* **jellyfish.**

jerk (jûrk) *n.* a quick, sudden push or pull; a tug. *v.* to push or pull suddenly: *He jerked the newspaper out of my hand.*

jet (jet) *n.* **1.** a stream of liquid or gas, sent with force: *A fountain sends up a jet of water.* **2.** a type of airplane pushed forward by streams of hot gas.

jetty (jet′ ē) *n.* a wall built out into water where boats can tie up, or a structure built as protection against waves. *pl.* **jetties.**

jewel (jū′ əl) *n.* a gem; a valuable stone such as a diamond or ruby.

jeweller, jeweler (jū′ əl ər, jū′ lər) *n.* a person who sells or repairs jewels or jewellery.

jewellery, jewelry (jū′ əl rē, jūl′ rē) *n.* necklaces, rings, watches, and other ornaments.

jigsaw (jig′ sȧ) *n.* a kind of saw with a thin blade, used to cut curved lines and shapes.

jigsaw puzzle (jig′ sȧ puz′ əl) a picture cut into irregular pieces that have to be put together again.

jingle (jingl) *n.* a ringing sound, like that of a small bell: *the jingle of a set of keys on a chain.*

job (job) *n.* **1.** a task; a piece of work: *One of my son's jobs is to shovel the snow.* **2.** work done for pay: *My cousin has a job in a factory.*

jockey (jok′ ē) *n.* a person who rides horses in races. *pl.* **jockeys.**

jog (jog) *v.* **1.** to run along at a slow, constant pace: *I jogged to the bus stop this morning.* **2.** to shake lightly: *Jog your brother to wake him up.* **jogging. jogged.**

join (jȯin) *v.* **1.** to fasten; to put or come together: *to join two ropes.* **2.** to become part of a group of people: *to join a club; to join a company; to join a union.*

⊖**joint** (jȯint) *n.* a place where two parts meet: *The knuckle is a joint in the finger.*

joke (jōk) *n.* something said or done to make a person laugh. *v.* to say or do something as a joke. **joking. joked.**

⊖**jolly** (jol′ ē) *adj.* merry; full of fun; cheerful: *a jolly clown; a jollier one; the jolliest clown in the circus.*

jolt (jolt) *n.* a sudden bump or shake. *v.* to bump or shake suddenly: *The motorcycle jolted along the old road.*

jot (jot) *v.* (used with **down**) to make a quick note in writing: *Jot down the phone number before you forget it.* **jotting. jotted.**

journal (jûr′ nəl) *n.* **1.** a magazine or a newspaper. **2.** a diary; a small book in which to keep a record of what happens every day.

journalist (jûr′ nə list) *n.* someone whose job is to write articles for a newspaper or magazine.

⊖**journey** (jûr′ nē) *n.* a trip; travel from one place to another: *a journey across Canada.* *pl.* **journeys.**

joy (jȯi) *n.* a feeling of happiness and pleasure. *pl.* **joys.**

judge (juj) *n.* **1.** a person chosen to make decisions in a court of law: *A judge passes a sentence when someone is found guilty.* **2.** a person who decides the result of a contest, such as a sports event. **3.** a person with enough knowledge about something to have a reliable opinion about it: *a good judge of theatre; a bad judge of people's character.* *v.* to make a judgment. **judging. judged.**

judgment, judgement (juj′ mənt) *n.* an opinion or decision, often in a court of law.

judo (jū′ dō) *n.* a form of Japanese wrestling.

jug (jug) *n.* a container for liquids, usually having a handle.

juggle (jugl) *v.* to toss up several balls or other objects and keep them in the air at the same time. **juggling. juggled.**

juggler (jug′ lər) *n.* someone skilled at juggling.

juice (jūs) *n.* the liquid in fruits, vegetables, or meat: *orange juice; carrot juice.*

juicy (jūs′ ē) *adj.* full of juice: *a juicy grapefruit; a juicier one; the juiciest one of all.*

July (jū lī′) *n.* the seventh month of the year.

jumble (jumbl) *n.* a mixed-up mess: *A jumble of clothing is piled in the room.*

jump (jump) *n.* a leap from the ground: *a high jump.* *v.* to leap up, or to leap over something: *The price of gasoline jumped five cents a litre last week.*

jumper (jump′ ər) *n.* a dress without sleeves, usually worn over a blouse.

junction (jungk′ shən) *n.* a place where railway lines, roads, or rivers join or meet.

June (jūn) *n.* the sixth month of the year.

jungle (jungl) *n.* land in hot places that is thickly covered with trees and bushes.

junior (jūn′ yər) *n.* someone who is younger: *He is my junior by two years.* *adj.* **1.** referring to a boy or man with the same first name as his father: *This is Mr. Hal Jones Junior.* **2.** younger, or lower in rank: *The junior officer works with the senior officer.*

junk (jungk) *n.* **1.** worthless rubbish; things of no use or value. **2.** a Chinese sailing ship.

juror (jůr′ ər) *n.* a person who is a member of a jury.

jury (jůr′ ē) *n.* a group of people chosen to sit in a court of law to make a decision in a trial. *pl.* **juries.**

just (just) *adj.* fair: *The judge's decision was just; she awarded money to the accident victim.* *adv.* **1.** barely: *The baby was just able to reach the chair.* **2.** exactly: *The time is just one o'clock.* **3.** *(informal)* absolutely; certainly: *The price of coffee is just too much.*
just now very recently; a short while ago: *She left just now with her friend.*

justice (jus′ tis) *n.* fairness: *the justice of a decision from a jury.*

jut (jut) *v.* (used with **out**) to stick out: *The sharp rocks jut out into the sea.* **jutting. jutted.**

juvenile (jü′ və nīl′) *n.* a young person: *These books are enjoyed by juveniles and adults.*

juvenile (jü′ və nəl′) *adj.* having to do with young people: *the juvenile section of the clothing store.*

K

kangaroo (kang′ gə rū′) *n.* a large Australian animal with long, powerful hind legs and a long, thick tail. *pl.* **kangaroos.**

karate (kə ra′ ti) *n.* a Japanese form of unarmed self defence.

kayak (kī′ ak) *n.* a light, narrow, covered canoe, with an opening for one person, used by Inuit and others. Kayaks are also used in racing and other sports.

keen (kēn) *adj.* **1.** eager; enthusiastic: *a keen hockey player.* **2.** sharp: *a knife with a keen edge.*

keep (kēp) *v.* **1.** to continue to hold or do: *to keep a letter for years; to keep quiet; to keep warm.* **2.** not to go bad: *These eggs will keep in the refrigerator.* **3.** to stop; to prevent: *My work kept me from going to the movies.* **4.** to take care of: *to keep house.* **5.** to do what you say you will: *Julie kept her promise and wrote every week.* **keeping. kept** (kept).

keep on to continue: *George kept on working even though he was tired.*

keep up with to go at the same speed as: *I can't keep up with Irma; she works much faster than I do.*

kennel (ken′ əl) *n.* a shelter for dogs or cats.

kernel (kern′ əl) *n.* **1.** the inside part of a nut. **2.** a grain or seed: *a kernel of corn.*

kerosene (ker′ ȯ sēn) *n.* a thin, flammable oil often used as fuel in lamps or stoves.

ketchup (kech′ əp) *n.* a thick, red sauce used with meat, French fries, and other food. It is made with tomatoes, onions, and other ingredients.
(*also spelled* **catsup.**)

kettle (ketl) *n.* a metal container used for boiling liquid.

key (kē) *n.* **1.** a piece of metal shaped so that it will open a lock. **2.** one of the parts pressed down with the fingers on a piano, typewriter, etc. **3.** something that explains the symbols in a map, dictionary, etc. *pl.* **keys.** *adj.* very important; main: *a key scientific discovery.*

keyboard (kē′ bȯrd′) *n.* a group of keys in a typewriter, piano, etc.

kick (kik) *n.* a hit with the foot: *The player gave the ball a powerful kick.* *v.* to hit with the foot.

kick-off (kik′ of′) *n.* the start of a football game, in which the football is kicked by one team towards the other team's goal.

kid (kid) *n.* **1.** a young goat. **2.** *(informal)* a young child. *v.* to pretend; to joke: *Is it true, or are you kidding?* **kidding. kidded.**

kidnap (kid′ nap′) *v.* to take someone away against his or her will, demanding money or something else for returning him or her safely. **kidnapping. kidnapped.**

kidney (kid′ nē) *n.* one of two small organs in the body that separate waste matter and water from the blood. *pl.* **kidneys.**

kill (kil) *v.* to put to death; to cause someone or something to die.

kilo (kē′ lō, kil′ ō) short for **kilogram.** *pl.* **kilos.**

kilogram (kil′ ə gram′) *n.* a measure of mass; **kg** is the symbol. 1 kg = 1000 g.

kilometre (kil′ ə mē′ tər, ki lom′ ə tər) *n.* a measure of distance; **km** is the symbol. 1 km = 1000 m.

kilowatt (kil′ o wȧt′) *n.* a measure of electric power; **kW** is the symbol. 1 kW = 1000 W.

kilt

kilt (kilt) *n.* a traditional, pleated skirt, reaching the knees, often worn by men in Scotland and Ireland.

kin (kin) *n.* a person's relatives.
next of kin the closest relative who is living: *The application form asked for my next of kin.*

kind (kīnd) *n.* a type; a sort: *There are many kinds of animals in the zoo.* *adj.* helpful; friendly; nice to others.
kind of somewhat; not completely: *I'm kind of hungry, but I can wait until lunch for some food.*

kindergarten (kin′ dər gȧr′ tən) *n.* a school or grade for very young children.

kindness (kind′ nəs) *n.* helpfulness: *Helen thanked him for his kindness.* *pl.* **kindnesses.**

king (king) *n.* **1.** a man who, by inheritance, is ruler of a country. **2.** a playing card with a picture of a king on it. **3.** a piece in the game of chess or checkers.

kingdom (king′ dəm) *n.* a country ruled by a king or queen.

king-size (king′ sīz′) *adj.* much larger than usual: *a king-size chair.*

kiss (kis) *n.* a touch with the lips. *pl.* **kisses.** *v.* to touch someone with the lips as a greeting or show of affection.

kit (kit) *n.* **1.** a set of tools or materials needed to do a certain job: *a tool kit; a first-aid kit.* **2.** a group of parts meant to be put together to make something: *a kit for a model car.*

kitchen (kich′ ən) *n.* a room where food is prepared.

kites
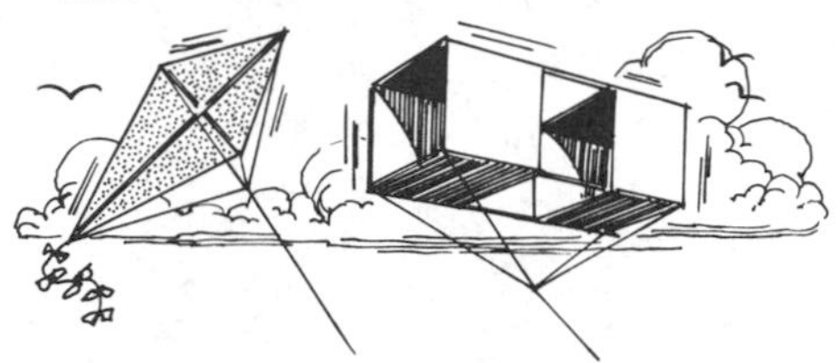

kite (kīt) *n.* a light wooden frame with paper, plastic, or cloth over it. A kite is attached to a long string and flown in the wind.

kitten (kit′ ən) *n.* a young cat.

knapsack (nap′ sak′) *n.* a bag made of leather or cloth. A knapsack is worn on the back. It may hold clothes, books, or supplies.

knead (nēd) *v.* to make a flour mixture into dough by pressing it with the hands.

knee (nē) *n.* the joint between the upper and lower part of the leg.

kneecap (nē′ cap′) *n.* the flat, moveable bone over the knee.

kneel (nēl) *v.* to go down on one or both knees. **kneeling. knelt** (nelt), or **kneeled.**

knew see **know.**

knife (nīf) *n.* **1.** a flat piece of metal, fastened in a handle, that is used for cutting or spreading. **2.** the sharp blade of some kinds of machines or tools. *pl.* **knives** (nīvz).

knight (nīt) *n.* a man with the title 'Sir'. A long time ago, a knight wore armour and fought for his king or queen.

knit (nit) *v.* **1.** to make wool or other yarn into cloth, using long needles or a machine. **2.** to grow together into one piece: *A broken bone will knit if it is held in place with a cast.* **knitting. knitted** or **knit.**

knob (nob) *n.* the round handle on a door, drawer, radio, television, etc.

knock (nok) *n.* **1.** a hard hit: *That falling book gave me a knock on the head.* **2.** a pounding or rattling sound in an engine. *v.* to hit something hard, often with the fist or knuckles: *to knock on a door.*
knock out to hit and make unconscious.
knock over to tip over; to cause to fall.

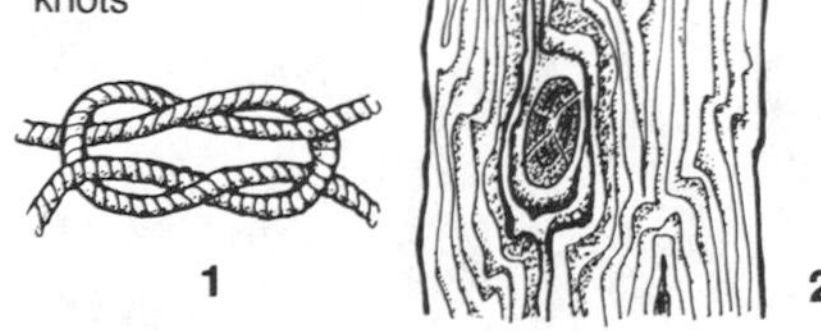

knot (not) *n.* **1.** a fastening made when pieces of rope, string, cord, etc., are tied together. **2.** the hard section of wood on a tree, where a branch grows out. **3.** a measure of the speed of ships.

know (nō) *v.* **1.** to understand because of learning or experience: *I know three languages. Do you know how to drive?* **2.** to recognize, to be familiar with: *I know Paul; we work at the same factory.* **knowing. knew** (nyū, nū). I have **known** (nōn).

knowledge (nol′ ij) *n.* understanding; having information: *He has a great knowledge of history.*

knuckle (nukl) *n.* a joint in a finger.

L

lab short for **laboratory.**

⊖**label** (lāb′ əl) *n.* a written or printed ticket attached to something and used to show what that thing is, who it belongs to, or where it is going. *v.* to attach a label to something. **labelling. labelled.**

laboratory (lab′ rə tôr′ ē, lab′ ə rə tôr′ ē) *n.* a place where scientific work is done or taught. *pl.* **laboratories.**

⊖**labour, labor** (lā′ bər) *n.* **1.** hard work: *The harvesting required many hours of labour.* **2.** working people, as a group: *The Premier is liked by labour.* **3.** the process of giving birth: *She was in labour for three hours.* *v.* to work hard: *He laboured at the letter, taking an hour to write it.*

Labrador (lab′ rə dôr′) *n.* the mainland area of the province of Newfoundland.

lace (lās) *n.* **1.** material made of thin threads that form a pattern. **2.** a cord or string used to hold something together: *a shoelace.*

lack (lak) *n.* a shortage: *The skinny animals suffered from a lack of food.* *v.* to be without something: *The plant died because it lacked water.*

lacquer (lak′ ər) *n.* a paint-like liquid that dries into a shiny coat when it is spread on wood, metal, etc.

lacrosse

lacrosse (lə krôs′) *n.* a game in which players use netted sticks for passing a rubber ball into the other team's goal.

lad (lad) *n.* a boy.

ladder (lad′ ər) *n.* a set of bars or rungs fastened between two long poles. *Ladders are used for climbing.*

ladle (lādl) *n.* a serving spoon with a long handle, used for carrying liquids.

lady (lā′ dē) *n.* **1.** any woman. **2.** a woman who is kind, helpful, and polite. *pl.* **ladies.**

ladybug (lā′ di bug′) *n.* a small beetle, red or orange with black spots.

lag (lag) *v.* to move slowly, in back of others: *He lagged far behind the other hikers.* **lagging. lagged.**

laid see **lay.**

lain see **lie.**

lake (lāk) *n.* a large body of water with land all around.

lamb (lam) *n.* a young sheep, or the meat of a young sheep.

lame (lām) *adj.* unable to walk normally, usually as a result of a physical disability: *a lame person; a lamer one; the lamest one of all.*

⊖**lamp** (lamp) *n.* a device that provides light by using electricity, gas, or oil.

⊖**land** (land) *n.* **1.** ground; soil: *the farmer's land.* **2.** the solid part of the earth's surface: *land and sea.* **3.** a country: *Finland is a northern land.* *v.* **1.** to reach earth from the sea or air: *The ship landed at Prince Rupert.* **2.** to arrive: *They landed at our house at midnight.*

landed immigrant (land′ əd im′ i grənt) a person who is permitted to settle in Canada and apply for citizenship after a certain amount of time.

landing (lan′ ding) *n.* **1.** a platform at the top of a stairway. **2.** an aircraft's coming down to earth, or a ship's coming back to land: *The plane made a safe landing.*

landlady (land′ lā′ dē) *n.* a woman who owns land, a house or other building, or an apartment, which she rents to someone else. *pl.* **landladies.**

landlord (land′ lȯrd′) *n.* a man who owns land, a house or other building, or an apartment, which he rents to someone else.

landmark (land′ märk′) *n.* something that stands out from the scenery and can be used as a guide.

landscape (land′ skāp′) *n.* **1.** a view of the land: *We drove out into the country and admired the landscape.* **2.** a painting of an area of land. *v.* to make an area more beautiful by changing the shape of the land or planting trees and flowers. **landscaping. landscaped.**

landslide (land′ slīd′) *n.* **1.** a fall of rocks and mud down a steep slope: *The landslide destroyed all the houses on the side of the hill.* **2.** in an election, a win by a great number of votes.

lane (lān) *n.* **1.** a path for vehicles travelling in one direction on a highway or other large road: *a lane for bicycles.* **2.** a narrow street or road.

⊖**language** (lang′ gwij) *n.* **1.** the words used when people speak or write: *We share ideas through language.* **2.** the speech used by the people of a country or group: *the Japanese language.*

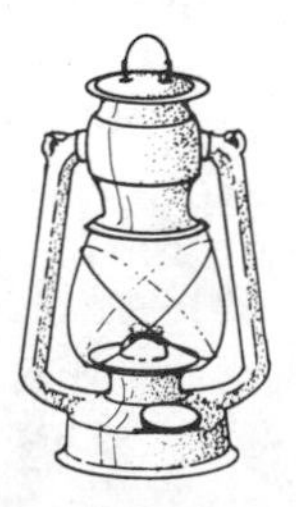

lantern

lantern (lan′ tərn) *n.* a metal and glass case with a light inside, often used when people go camping.

lap (lap) *n.* **1.** the top of the thighs when a person is sitting down: *The cat sat on my lap.* **2.** once around a track, or one length of a swimming pool: *The race was four laps around the field.*

lapel

lapel (lə pel′) *n.* the front section of a coat, folded back onto the coat: *He put a flower in his lapel.*

⊖**lard** (lärd) *n.* pig's fat used in cooking.

⊖**large** (lärj) *adj.* big; great in size: *a large car; a larger car; the largest car in the parking lot.*

largely (lärj′ lē) *adv.* mostly; mainly: *The work was largely finished by the time we arrived.*

larva (lär′ və) *n.* the early form of an insect: *A caterpillar is the larva of a butterfly. pl.* **larvae.**

laryngitis (lar′ in jī′ tis) *n.* an illness of the throat that makes talking difficult.

laser (lā′ zər) *n.* a device that makes a very straight and narrow beam of bright light: *The powerful laser burned a hole through a piece of metal.*

lash (lash) *n.* **1.** a stroke from a whip. **2.** a hair on an eyelid; an eyelash. *pl.* **lashes.**

lasso (la sū′) *n.* a long rope with a loop at the end, used for catching cattle and wild horses. *pl.* **lassos.** *v.* to catch with a rope.

last (last) *adj.* **1.** following all the others; coming at the end: *the last day of the month.* **2.** just before the present; the most recent: *I went to the movies last night. adv.* at the end; after everyone or everything else: *Henry arrived first*

and I arrived last. *v.* to continue; to serve: *The food must last us several days.*
at last finally; after waiting: *The food has arrived at last.*

latch (lach) *n.* a fastening for a door or gate: *The latch on the fence is broken.* *pl.* **latches.**

late (lāt) *adj.* **1.** coming after the usual or expected time: *The bus was late yesterday; it was later today; on Monday it was the latest it has ever been.* **2.** happening near the end: *I won't be finished until late afternoon.* *adv.* after the usual or expected time: *We stayed up late to watch a movie on television.*

lately (lāt′ lē) *adv.* a little while before; recently: *How have you been feeling lately?*

later (lā′ tər) *adv.* not now; in the future: *We'll be going to the movies later in the week.*

lathe (lāth) *n.* a machine that holds a piece of wood or metal and spins it quickly while it is cut into a certain shape: *The curved arms of that chair were cut on a lathe.*

lather (lath′ ər) *n.* a foam made from soap, shampoo, shaving cream, etc.

latitude (lat′ i tyūd′, lat′ i tūd′) *n.* the distance, measured in degrees, north or south of the equator: *Winnipeg, Manitoba, is at approximately fifty degrees north latitude.*

latter (lat′ ər) *adj.* the second of two things named: *I like both steak and chicken, but I prefer the latter.*

laugh (laf) *n.* a loud 'ha-ha' sound made when a person sees or hears something funny, or when a person is happy. *v.* to make such a sound, showing that something is funny or that a person is happy.

laughter (laf′ tər) *n.* the sound of laughing.

launch (lònch) *n.* a small motorboat. *pl.* **launches.** *v.* **1.** to send out into the air: *to launch a rocket.* **2.** to set afloat: *to launch a boat.* **launching. launched.** she **launches.**

laundromat (lòn′ drə mat′) *n.* a room with coin-operated washing machines and dryers.

laundry (lòn′ drē) *n.* **1.** clothes, sheets, and other cloth items to be washed. **2.** a place where clothes, sheets, etc., can be washed: *When I lived alone, I brought my clothes to the laundry.* *pl.* **laundries.**

lava (la′ və) *n.* hot melted rock coming from a volcano.

lavatory (lav′ ə tōr′ ē) *n.* a washroom or toilet. *pl.* **lavatories.**

law (lò) *n.* **1.** a rule or set of rules, made by a government. There are federal laws, provincial laws, and local laws: *It is against the law to steal. Don't break the law—drive safely.* **2.** the profession of being a lawyer: *Anne plans a career in law.*

lawn (lòn) *n.* an area of grass by a house, school, etc., usually well looked after.

lawn mower (lòn′ mō′ ər) a machine used for cutting the grass on a lawn.

lawyer (lò′ yər) *n.* someone who knows the law very well and can give people advice about it. A lawyer can represent people in court.

laxative (lak′ sə tiv) *n.* a medicine that makes it easier for a person to move the bowels.

lay (lā) *v.* **1.** to place something down: *Lay your head on the*

pillow. **2.** to drop an egg into a nest. **laying. laid** (lād).
lay off **1.** to let go or release from work for a temporary period. **2.** to stop; to bring to an end.

layer (lā′ ər) *n.* a thickness; a coating: *a layer of paint on a door.*

layoff (lā′ ȯf′) *n.* a period of time during which workers are sent away from their jobs: *The layoff at the factory has lasted for two weeks.*

lazy (lā′ zē) *adj.* not wanting to work or do much: *a lazy child; a lazier child; the laziest child of all.*

lead (led) *n.* **1.** a soft, heavy, grey metal that does not rust. **2.** in a pencil, the black material that leaves marks when a person writes.

lead (lēd) *v.* **1.** to go in front; to show the way: *She led us to her house.* **2.** to direct: *Mr. Nardi leads the singers.* **3.** to go in a certain direction: *The road leads to the lake.* **4.** in a race, to be in first place. **leading. led** (led).

leader (lēd′ ər) *n.* someone who leads.

leaf (lēf) *n.* one of the small, green, flat parts that grow on a plant or tree. *pl.* **leaves** (lēvz).

leaflet (lēf′ lət) *n.* a small sheet of writing, with information about a certain topic: *a leaflet announcing the opening of a new store.*

league (lēg) *n.* a group of teams that regularly play games against one another: *the Canadian Football League.*

leak (lēk) *n.* a small hole or crack through which gas or liquid comes in or escapes: *a leak in the boat.* *v.* for gas or liquid to come in or escape out of a small hole or crack.

lean (lēn) *adj.* **1.** thin: *a tall, lean man.* **2.** having little fat: *lean meat.* *v.* to rest or slant: *The ladder leans against a wall. The post leans to one side.*

leap (lēp) *n.* a jump over something: *He took a leap over the fence.* *v.* to spring upwards; to jump: *Gregory can leap over the fire hydrant.* **leaping. leaped**, or **leapt** (lept).

leap year (lēp′ yēr′) every fourth year, when February has twenty-nine days instead of twenty-eight.

learn (lûrn) *v.* **1.** to find out; to get to know new facts by study; to do new things by practice: *to learn math; to learn to cook; to learn about my friend's trip.* **2.** to memorize: *to learn a speech.* **learning. learned**, or **learnt** (lernt).

lease (lēs) *n.* an agreement that allows a person to use a house, apartment, land, etc., in return for paying rent to the owner. *v.* to pay money for the use of a house, apartment, land, etc.: *He leased the house from its owner for five hundred dollars a month.* **leasing. leased.**

leash (lēsh) *n.* a rope or strap for holding or tying a dog or other animal: *Whenever we take our dog for a walk he pulls on his leash.* *pl.* **leashes.**

least (lēst) *n.* the smallest amount: *I like football the least of all games. I like soccer the most.*
at least **1.** no less than: *The book will cost at least five dollars.* **2.** in any case: *Rita can't run fast, but at least she is trying her best in the race.*

leather (leth′ ər) *n.* an animal's skin, tanned and used to make shoes, gloves, etc.

leave (lēv) *n.* permission, such as to be away: *The soldier was on leave for a week.* *v.* **1.** to go away from: *She left her job when she returned to school.* **2.** to let something stay behind; to forget: *I left my gloves at home.* **3.** to give to another: *Just leave the cooking to me—I love preparing meals! I'm going out*

now; I'll leave the car keys for you. **leaving. left** (left).
leave out not to add or put in: *Jill left out the sugar when she made the cake.*

leaves plural of **leaf.**

ə**lecture** (lek′ chər) *n.* a talk that is meant to teach people: *Mrs. Williams gave an interesting lecture about the trees of Canada.* *v.* to give a talk to teach people: *The professor lectures at McGill University.* **lecturing. lectured.**

led see **lead.**

ledge (lej) *n.* a narrow shelf: *the window ledge.*

left (left) *adj.* in the direction opposite of right: *When you look at a map of Canada, Alberta is on the left side of Saskatchewan.*
v. see **leave.**

leftovers (left′ ō′ vərz) *n.pl.* the food that has not been eaten, after a meal is over: *After the meal, we put the leftovers in the refrigerator for tomorrow's dinner.*

leg (leg) *n.* **1.** one of the limbs on which people and animals stand or walk. **2.** anything like a leg: *a table leg.*
pull a person's leg to trick or fool: *You were pulling my leg when you said that I'd won!*

ə**legal** (lēg′ əl) *adj.* **1.** allowed by the law: *In Canada, the legal voting age is eighteen.* **2.** having to do with the law: *When we bought our house, we went to our lawyer for legal advice.*

legend (lej′ ənd) *n.* **1.** a story from the past that is probably not completely true. **2.** the words on a map, picture, etc., that help to explain it.

legible (lej′ ibl) *adj.* clear and easy to read: *A letter written on a typewriter is usually more legible than one written by hand.*

legislation (lej′ is lā′ shən) *n.* a law or laws: *the legislation on pollution control.*

legislature (lej′ is lā′ chər) *n.* a group of men and women who make laws: *Each province in Canada has a legislature.*

legitimate (lə jit′ i mit) *adj.* what is right, legal, or acceptable: *a legitimate reason for being late.*

leisure (lezh′ ər, lē′ zhər) *n.* the time when a person is free from work or other duties, and can do what he or she enjoys.

lemon (lem′ ən) *n.* a yellow citrus fruit with a sour taste.

ə**lemonade** (lem′ ən ād′) *n.* a drink made with lemon juice, water, and sugar.

lend (lend) *v.* to allow someone to have the use of something only for a time: *John lent me the book for two days. The bank lent me money to buy a new car.* **lending. lent** (lent).
lend a hand to give help: *Will you lend me a hand to move this desk?*

length (length) *n.* **1.** how long a thing is from end to end: *the length of a table.* **2.** how long a thing is from start to finish: *the length of a book; the length of a trip.*

lengthen (leng′ thən) *v.* to make longer: *He lengthened the pants.*

camera lens

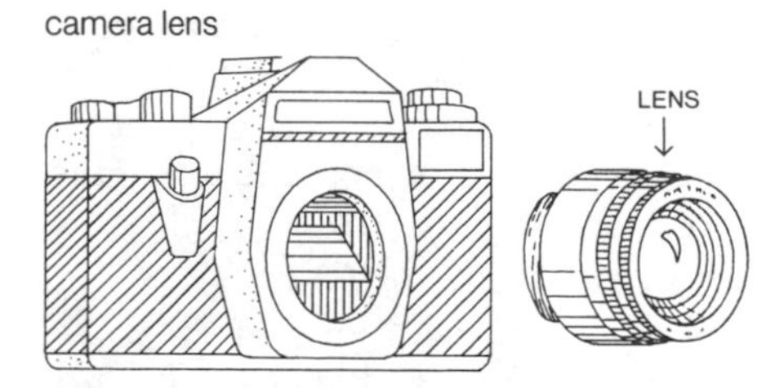

lens (lenz) *n.* a curved piece of glass used in eyeglasses, cameras, and telescopes. A lens may make something appear closer or farther away. *pl.* **lenses.**

lent see **lend.**

⊖**lentil** (len′ til) *n.* a small, round dried seed, like a pea, used for cooking.

leopard (lep′ ərd) *n.* a wild member of the cat family with black spots on its yellow coat. It lives in Africa and Asia.

leotard (lē′ ə tärd′) *n.* a tight, one-piece garment worn by dancers, gymnasts, and others.

less (les) *adj.* smaller; not as much: *Your hat costs less than mine.*

-less a suffix meaning 'without': **painless** means without pain; **toothless** means without a tooth.

lessen (les′ ən) *v.* to make less; to become less: *The thunder lessened as the storm moved away.*

lesson (les′ ən) *n.* something to be learned; time spent learning: *a music lesson.*

let (let) *v.* to permit; to allow to do or happen: *Her parents would not let her go there alone. Let the cat come in.* **letting. let.**
let down 1. to move to a lower position: *to let down a bucket from a roof.* **2.** to cause disappointment: *Don't let our team down; try as hard as you can in the race.*
let go 1. to set free. **2.** to fire; to dismiss from a job.
let off to excuse; to give little or no punishment: *The judge let him off with a small fine.*
let on to make known: *You didn't let on that you'd seen the movie.*
let out to make a piece of clothing bigger: *to let out a pair of pants.*
let up to stop or become less: *Has the snow let up yet?*

let's (lets) short for **let us.**

letter (let′ ər) *n.* **1.** one of the symbols of an alphabet: *A, B, and C are letters in many alphabets.* **2.** a written message put in an envelope and sent to someone.

letter carrier (let′ ər kar′ i ər) the person who delivers and picks up mail.

lettuce (let′ əs) *n.* a green vegetable with large leaves, eaten raw in salads.

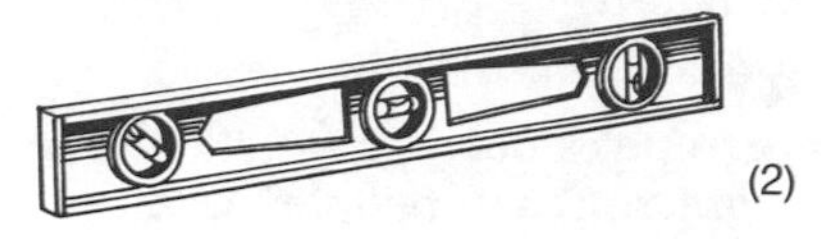

level (lev′ əl) *n.* **1.** a certain height or depth: *Our town is high above sea level.* **2.** a tool used to find out whether a surface is flat or not.
adj. smooth and flat: *level ground.*

lever (lev′ ər, lē′ vər) *n.* a bar or rod used for raising or lowering something, or for prying something open.

liable (lī′ əbl) *adj.* **1.** responsible according to law: *Devon was liable for the cost of repairs because he caused the accident.* **2.** likely; probably going to occur: *You're liable to catch a cold if you don't dress warmly.*

liar (lī′ ər) *n.* someone who tells lies.

liberal (lib′ ə rəl) *adj.* **1.** generous: *We were given liberal amounts of ice cream.* **2.** tolerant; able to understand that people can have different ideas and that things can change for the better.

Liberal Party (lib′ ə rəl pär′ tē) one of the main political parties of Canada.

liberty (lib′ ər tē) *n.* freedom; being able to do what you wish.
pl. **liberties.**

librarian (lī brer′ i ən) *n.* a person trained to work in a library.

⊖**library** (lī′ brer′ ē) *n.* a room or building where books are kept: *Books may be used in the library, or they may be borrowed.*
pl. **libraries.**

lice plural of **louse.**

⊖**licence, license** (lī′ səns) *n.* an official paper allowing a person to keep, use, or do something in return for payment: *a dog licence; a marriage licence.*

⊖**license, licence** (lī′ səns) *v.* to give official permission to do something: *An electrician is licensed to wire a house.* **licensing. licensed.**

lick (lik) *v.* **1.** to wet with the tongue: *to lick a stamp.* **2.** to eat by using the tongue: *to lick an ice cream cone.*

licorice (lik′ ə rish, lik′ ə ris) *n.* a black candy made from a plant root.

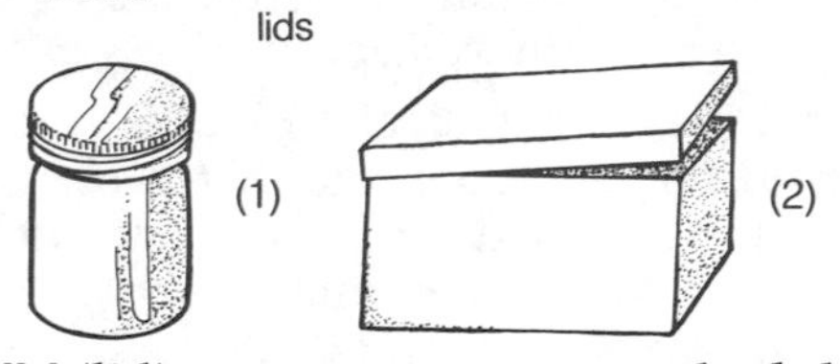

lid (lid) *n.* **1.** a cover; a cap: *the lid of a jar.* **2.** a movable flap: *the lid of a box; an eyelid.*

lie (lī) *n.* something a person says that he or she knows is not true. *v.* **1.** to tell a lie: *He lied when he said he was home yesterday.* **lying. lied. 2.** to rest stretched flat: *Lie down if you are tired.* **3.** to be in a certain place or position: *Toronto lies east of Winnipeg. The toy lay at the bottom of the pool until Tina removed it.* **lying. lay** (lā). I have **lain** (lān).

lieutenant (lef ten′ ənt, lū ten′ ənt) *n.* an officer in the armed forces.

Lieutenant-Governor (lef ten′ ent guv′ ər nər) the official head of a Canadian province, appointed by the Governor General.

life (līf) *n.* **1.** the state of being alive: *People, animals, and plants have life.* **2.** the time between birth and death or during which something works: *My grandmother had a long life. That battery has a life of one thousand hours.* **3.** a human being: *Several lives were lost in the fire. pl.* **lives** (līvz).

lifeboat (līf′ bōt′) *n.* a boat built for rescuing people in the water.

lifeguard (līf′ gärd′) *n.* a swimmer trained to save the lives of swimmers who may be drowning.

life insurance (līf′ in shůr′ əns) **1.** an amount of money paid regularly to an insurance company so that, when the person paying the money dies, the company will pay money to the person's family. **2.** the protection offered by a life insurance company.

lift (lift) *n.* **1.** a ride: *May I have a lift to school?* **2.** something that takes skiers to the top of a hill. *v.* to raise: *We lifted the heavy table.*

light (līt) *n.* brightness from something burning, such as the sun or a lamp. *adj.* **1.** not heavy: *as light as a feather.* **2.** not dark: *Joan is wearing a light green scarf. v.* **1.** to set fire to something. **2.** to brighten something. **lighting. lit** (lit).

light bulb (līt′ bulb′) a bulb that produces electric light.

lighter (līt′ ər) *n.* something that makes a flame: *a cigarette lighter.*

lighthouse (līt′ haůs′) *n.* a tower by a body of water. It has a powerful flashing light that guides ships around dangerous rocks.

lightning (līt′ ning) *n.* a flash of electricity in a thunderstorm.

likable, likeable (līk′ əbl) *adj.* pleasing; popular: *Pat is a likable person, always helpful and friendly.*

like (līk) *prep.* **1.** similar to; the same as: *The picture I drew looks like you.* **2.** in the mood for; wanting to: *I feel like eating soon.* **3.** probably going to happen: *It looks like rain.* *v.* **1.** to be fond of: *Wendy likes reading.* **2.** to want: *I'd like an apple.* **liking. liked.**

likely (līk′ lē) *adj.* probable; to be expected: *It is likely to snow today. a likely explanation; a likelier one; the likeliest one of all.*

likeness (līk′ nəs) *n.* a copy: *The photograph is a good likeness of you.* *pl.* **likenesses.**

lilac (lī′ lək) *n.* a garden shrub that has sweet-smelling white or purple flowers.

lily (lil′ ē) *n.* a tall garden flower that grows from a bulb and has large flowers, usually white. *pl.* **lilies.**

lima bean (lī′ mə bēn′) a flat bean, light green in colour, eaten as a vegetable.

limb (lim) *n.* **1.** an arm or a leg. **2.** a tree branch.

lime (līm) *n.* **1.** a green citrus fruit that looks like a small lemon. **2.** a white powder made by burning limestone or shells: *Lime is used to improve the soil.*

limestone (līm′ stōn′) *n.* a type of stone that contains calcium, the material also found in bones.

limit (lim′ it) *n.* the farthest point or edge: *I can spend ten dollars on the present. That is my limit.* *v.* to keep at a certain point or under a certain amount: *Try to limit the amount to five dollars.*

limp (limp) *n.* a lame step or walk: *He walked with a limp after his injury.* *adj.* not stiff; bending easily: *The vegetables went limp in the hot weather.* *v.* to walk with one leg moving less well than the other or others: *The dog limped for weeks until its broken leg healed.*

line (līn) *n.* **1.** a long, thin mark: *Connect the dots with a line.* **2.** a row: *a line of people waiting to go inside.* **3.** a cord, rope, or wire: *a clothes line.* **4.** a group of planes, buses, ships, etc., belonging to one company: *What bus line will you be using?* **5.** a short letter: *Drop your sister a line when you have time.* *v.* **1.** to mark with lines. **2.** to put a lining in a piece of clothing. **3.** to put on the inside of: *to line a box with coloured paper.* **lining. lined.**

line up to stand in line: *This movie is so popular that we will have to line up to buy tickets.*

linen (lin′ ən) *n.* **1.** cloth made from fibres of the flax plant. **2.** towels and sheets made from this cloth or from a similar material.

lingerie (lon′ jə rē, lã′ jə rē) *n.* women's underwear or nightgowns.

lining (līn′ ing) *n.* the thin inside covering in a suit, coat, or dress.

link (lingk) *n.* one of the rings in a chain.

linoleum (li nō′ li əm) *n.* a hard material used as a floor covering.

lion (lī′ ən) *n.* a strong wild animal of the cat family, living in Africa and Asia, that has a dark yellow coat.

lip (lip) *n.* **1.** one of the two pink, fleshy edges of the mouth. **2.** an edge of an opening: *a lip of a bottle.*

lipstick (lip′ stik′) *n.* a stick of make-up, used to colour the lips.

liquid (lik′ wid) *n.* water, or anything that can be poured like water.

⊖**liquor** (lik′ ər) *n.* a strong alcoholic drink.

list (list) *n.* a column or columns of names, numbers, words, etc.: *a shopping list.* *v.* to arrange names, numbers, words, etc. in such a column: *He listed the names and addresses of his friends.*

listen (lis′ ən) *v.* to try to hear; to pay attention when hearing: *We listened to the radio program.*

lit see **light.**

ɵ**literature** (lit′ ə rə chər) *n.* **1.** stories, poetry, and plays, especially those by good writers: *I enjoy reading Canadian literature.* **2.** any printed material: *Give me some literature on the new tape recorder.*

litre (lē′ tər) *n.* a liquid measure; **L** is the symbol. 1 L = 1000 ml.

litter (lit′ ər) *n.* **1.** a number of animals all born together: *a litter of pigs.* **2.** waste paper and other garbage left lying around. *v.* to leave such garbage around.

little (litl) *adj.* **1.** small: *The white mouse is little; the brown one is littler; and the grey one is the littlest in the cage.* **2.** not much: *I have little money; you have less; and he has the least of all.*
little by little gradually: *Little by little, Sara got better at hitting the ball.*

live (liv) *v.* **1.** to be alive; to have life: *My dog lived to be fifteen years old.* **2.** to dwell: *Fish live in the sea.* **3.** to eat or feed: *A person can't live on meat alone.* **4.** to keep life going: *I can live on a hundred dollars a week.* **living. lived.**

live (līv) *adj.* **1.** living; not dead: *A zoo keeps live animals.* **2.** having an electric current: *a live wire in a socket.* **3.** not an audio tape or videotape: *Bill listened to a live concert on the radio.*

livelihood (līv′ li hủd′) *n.* the way a person earns the money needed to provide food, shelter, and clothing: *He earns his livelihood as a mechanic.*

lively (līv′ lē) *adj.* full of quick movement: *a lively child; a livelier one; the liveliest child of all.*

liver (liv′ ər) *n.* an organ in the body that helps the body digest food.

lives plural of **life.**

livestock (līv′ stok′) *n.* animals that are raised to be sold and used for food.

living (liv′ ing) *n.* livelihood; the way a person earns money: *She teaches for a living.*

living room (liv′ ing rūm′) *n.* the main room in a home, where people can talk, play games, watch television, etc.: *A living room usually has a chesterfield and chairs.*

load (lōd) *n.* **1.** a pile of goods to be carried: *a load of hay on a wagon.* **2. loads** *(informal)* a great amount of: *We have loads of food for the picnic.* *v.* **1.** to place goods onto or into something: *We loaded the car with boxes. She loaded the camera with film.* **2.** to put a bullet into a gun.

loaf (lōf) *n.* a large lump of food baked into a certain shape: *a loaf of bread.* *pl.* **loaves** (lōvz). *v.* to be a little lazy: *I have work to do, but I feel like loafing.*

loan (lōn) *n.* something lent, usually money: *The loan from the bank helped us pay for the car.*

lobby (lob′ ē) *n.* a hall or waiting area in an office building or apartment house. *pl.* **lobbies.**

lobe (lōb) *n.* the fleshy lowest part of the ear.

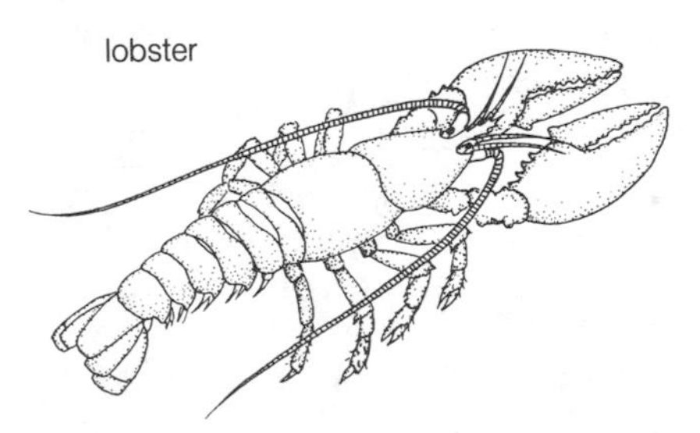

lobster (lob′ stər) *n.* a large shellfish with eight legs and two claws.

local (lo′ kəl) *adj.* nearby; close to a certain place: *Our local milk store is a block away.*

locate (lō′ kāt) *v.* **1.** to find the position of someone or something: *Can you locate the prairie provinces on this map?* **2.** to settle somewhere: *The company located the new factory in Halifax.* **locating. located.**

ɵ**location** (lō kā′ shən) *n.* a position or place: *The location of the school is a kilometre from my house.*

lock (lok) *n.* **1.** a fastening for a door or box, often needing a key to open it. **2.** a section of a canal, river, dam, etc., that allows ships to pass to a deeper or a shallower body of water. **3.** a curl of hair. *v.* **1.** to fasten something with a lock: *Don't forget to lock the front door!* **2.** to join or stick together: *When a car's brakes lock, the wheels will not turn.*

lockers

locker (lok′ ər) *n.* a small closet that can be locked.

locksmith (lok′ smith′) *n.* someone who makes or fixes locks, keys, etc.

locomotive (lō′ kə mō′ tiv) *n.* a railway engine.

ɵ**lodge** (loj) *n.* **1.** a house or an inn, usually in the country. **2.** a local branch of a club or other group. *v.* **1.** to pay rent to stay with someone for a time. **2.** to bring to a person in authority: *to lodge a complaint with a police officer.* **lodging. lodged.**

lodger (loj′ ər) *n.* a person who pays money to live in part of someone's home.

log (log) *n.* **1.** a thick, round piece of wood. **2.** a diary of a voyage: *A ship's captain keeps a daily log.*

logger (log′ ər) *n.* someone whose job is to cut down trees and take them to a sawmill.

logic (loj′ ik) *n.* a way of solving problems by using strict rules of thinking, and not by guessing or imagining.

lollipop (lol′ i pop′) *n.* a piece of hard candy on the end of a stick, eaten by licking or sucking.

lone (lōn) *adj.* by itself: *We looked at the lone star in the sky.*

lonely (lōn′ lē) *adj.* without companions; feeling sad because of being alone: *a lonely horse; a lonelier one; the loneliest horse on the farm.*

lonesome (lōn′ səm) *adj.* lonely.

long (long) *adj.* **1.** a large distance from end to end: *a long road.* **2.** taking much time: *a long wait for the doctor.* **3.** having a definite length: *How long is the desk?* *v.* (used with **for** or **to**) to want very much; to wish for: *It was very cold and we longed for summer to come; we longed for the warm weather.*
as long as if it happens that; since: *As long as you're going to the store, please buy me some milk.*
long ago a long time back: *She learned to ride horses long ago, when she was a child.*

longitude (lon′ ji tyūd′, lon′ ji tūd′) *n.* the distance, measured in degrees, east or west of Greenwich, England: *Moncton, New Brunswick is at approximately seventy degrees west longitude.*

look (lu̇k) *n.* a glance: *He gave me an angry look.* *v.* **1.** to watch; to see; to try to find: *Look at the mountains. Keep looking; I'm sure* *you'll find your glasses eventually.* **2.** to seem: *He looks unhappy. That cloud looks like an animal.* **3.** to face: *The house looks east.*

look after to take care of: *She looked after my plants when I was away.*

look down on (upon) to consider inferior: *Some people look down on others who are less educated.*

look for to search for: *He looked for his hat everywhere.*

look forward to to wait for with eagerness: *I look forward to my vacation.*

look into to investigate: *The police are looking into the affair.*

look out to be careful: *Look out! A car is coming.*

look over to examine: *Look over the papers before you sign them.*

look up to search for and find: *to look up a phone number.*

look up to to respect: *She looks up to her older brother.*

loom (lūm) *n.* a frame on which to weave threads into cloth.

⊖**loop** (lūp) *n.* a ring in a string, rope, etc. *v.* to make such a ring.

loose (lūs) *adj.* **1.** slack; not fastened or tight: *It is easy to untie the loose knot. loose clothing; looser clothing; the loosest clothing possible.* **2.** free: *The cat is loose in the office.*

loose-leaf (lūs′ lēf′) *adj.* having pages with holes so that the pages can be put into or taken out of a book.

loosen (lūs′ ən) *v.* to make loose.

lopsided (lop′ sīd′ əd) *adj.* uneven, with one side lower than the other.

Lord (lȯrd) *n.* God.

lose (lūz) *v.* **1.** to be without something that was once had: *I lost my hat on the bus. I want to lose weight.* **2.** not to win: *They lost by one point.* **3.** to be unable to find: *We lost our way in the city.* **losing. lost** (lost).

loss (los) *n.* something lost: *the loss of a game; the loss of a friendship. pl.* **losses.**

⊖**lot** (lot) *n.* **1.** a large number or amount: *He has a lot of friends. There are lots of flowers in the garden.* **2.** a piece of land: *There is an empty lot next to the house.*

lotion (lō′ shən) *n.* a cream put on the skin to heal, clean, or moisten it.

lottery (lot′ ə rē) *n.* a game of luck where people buy tickets with numbers on them in order to win a prize. *pl.* **lotteries.**

loud (laủd) *adj.* noisy; not quiet.

loudspeaker (laủd′ spēk′ ər) *n.* the part of a stereo, radio, or TV from which the sound comes.

lounge (laủnj) *n.* a sitting room with comfortable chairs. *v.* to sit in a comfortable, easy way. **lounging. lounged.**

louse (laủs) *n.* a small biting insect. *pl.* **lice.**

lousy (laủ′ zē) *adj. (informal)* worthless; not good: *This watch is lousy! You should return it to the store. a lousy idea; a lousier one; the lousiest idea of all.*

lovable (luv′ əbl) *adj.* worth loving; cute: *a lovable puppy.*

love (luv) *n.* **1.** a feeling of great liking or affection. **2.** in some games such as tennis, a score of nothing. *v.* to like very much; to care about very much. **loving. loved.**

lovely (luv′ lē) *adj.* beautiful; fine: *a lovely day; a lovelier one; the loveliest day of the month.*

low (lō) *n.* the gear setting of a machine that gives the machine the smallest speed and the most power: *Ada put the car into low and started to drive. adj.* not high: *a low hill; a low number; low prices; a low note in music.*

lower (lō′ ər) *adj.* less high: *Prices are lower in this store than in that* *one.* *v.* to make less high: *He lowered his voice when he told me the secret.*

loyal (lȯi′ əl) *adj.* faithful and true to family, friends, a country, etc.: *a loyal citizen.*

loyalty (lȯi′ əl tē) *n.* faithfulness: *The dog proved his loyalty when he barked for help.* *pl.* **loyalties.**

lubricate (lū′ brə kāt′) *v.* to put grease or oil on something, such as the parts of a machine, so that it will move without difficulty: *to lubricate the gears of a tractor.* **lubricating. lubricated.**

luck (luk) *n.* chance; good or bad fortune: *She has good luck when playing cards.*
in luck having good fortune: *You're in luck—I have an extra ticket for the concert.*

lucky (luk′ ē) *adj.* **1.** having good luck: *a lucky person.* **2.** bringing good luck: *a lucky number; a luckier number; the luckiest number of all.*

luggage (lug′ ij) *n.* a traveller's suitcases, bags, trunks, etc.

lukewarm (lūk′ wȯrm′) *adj.* not hot and not cold; slightly warm.

lullaby (lul′ ə bī′) *n.* a song to make a baby sleep. *pl.* **lullabies.**

lumber (lum′ bər) *n.* timber, logs, and boards cut and prepared for use.

lumberjack (lum′ bər jak′) *n.* a person who cuts down trees.

lump (lump) *n.* **1.** any small mass that has no definite shape: *a lump of clay.* **2.** a swelling or bump on or under the skin.

lunar (lū′ nər) *adj.* having to do with the moon: *a lunar eclipse.*

lunch (lunch) *n.* the noon meal. *pl.* **lunches.**

lung (lung) *n.* one of the two organs inside the chest that fill with air when a person or animal breathes in.

lure (lūr) *n.* bait: *a lure for fish.* *v.* to tempt; to attract: *The mouse was lured into the trap by the cheese.* **luring. lured.**

luxury (luk′ shə rē) *n.* something that is enjoyable, but isn't needed for life or health: *A fur coat is a luxury for most people.* *pl.* **luxuries.**

lye (lī) *n.* a strong chemical substance used in some detergents and soaps.

lying see **lie.**

lynx

lynx (lingks) *n.* a wild cat of North America and Europe; it has pointed ears, a short tail, and large paws. *pl.* **lynx**, or **lynxes.**

lyrics (lir′ iks) *n.pl.* the words of a song.

M

ma (mȧ) *n. (informal)* mother.

macaroni (mak′ ə rō′ nē) *n.* a food made of flour paste, often eaten with cheese or a tomato sauce.

machine (mə shēn′) *n.* a device, usually made of metal, that does a certain job: *a sewing machine; a washing machine.*

machinery (mə shēn′ ə rē) *n.* **1.** machines in general. **2.** the working parts of a machine.

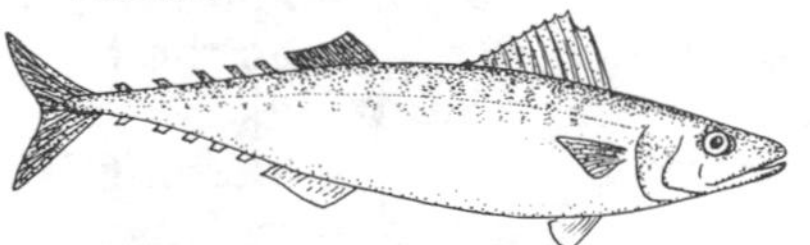
mackerel

mackerel (mak′ ər əl) *n.* a silvery fish, like tuna, that lives in ocean waters. *pl.* **mackerel.**

mad (mad) *adj.* **1.** not in a person's right mind; crazy. **2.** very angry: *a mad crowd; a madder crowd; the maddest crowd of all.* **3.** very excited or fond of: *He is mad about that new song.*
like mad very quickly; very hard: *She pedalled like mad on her bicycle to reach her mother.*

madam (mad′ əm) a polite or formal title for a woman: *May I help you, madam? Welcome to Ottawa, Madam Prime Minister.*

made see **make.**

magazine (mag′ ə zēn′, mag′ ə zēn′) *n.* a thin book with pictures and stories or articles, usually published weekly or monthly.

magic (maj′ ik) *n.* the use of clever tricks to make impossible things seem to happen.

magician (mə jish′ ən) *n.* a person who can do magic tricks.

magnet (mag′ nət) *n.* a piece of stone or a bar of iron or steel that has the power to pull pieces of iron or other metals towards it.

magnetic (mag net′ ik) *adj.* with the power of a magnet.

magnificent (mag nif′ i sənt) *adj.* wonderful; splendid; very grand: *a magnificent palace.*

magnify (mag′ ni fī′) *v.* to make something look larger: *A microscope is used to magnify objects.* **magnifying. magnified.** it **magnifies.**

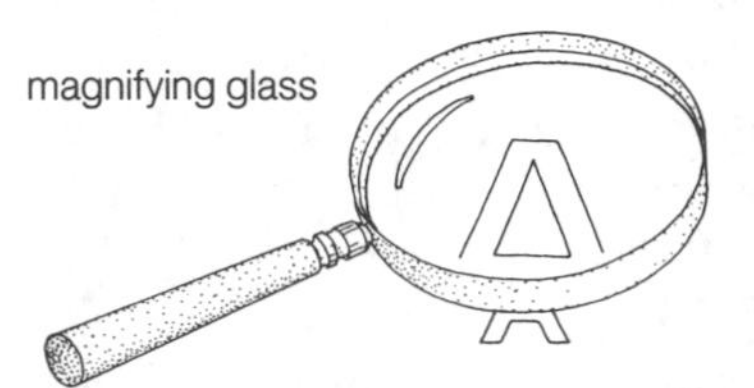

magnifying glass

magnifying glass (mag′ ni fī′ ing glas′) a lens that makes things look bigger than they really are. *pl.* **magnifying glasses.**

maid (mād) *n.* a female servant.

maiden name (mād′ ən nām′) the family name of a married woman before she was married.

mail (māl) *n.* letters, cards, packages, and anything else sent through the post office. *v.* to send letters, etc., through the post office.

mailbox (māl′ boks′) *n.* **1.** a container in which to put mail for the post office to send. **2.** a box in which mail is placed. *pl.* **mailboxes.**

mail carrier (māl′ kar′ i ər) the person who carries and delivers mail.

mailman (māl′ man′, māl′ mən) *n.* a mail carrier. *pl.* **mailmen.**

main (mān) *n.* a large cable or pipe for carrying water, gas, etc. *adj.* chief; most important; greatest in size: *a main road; the main post office in the city.*

mainland (mān′ land′, mān′ lənd) *n.* the major part of a continent or other land area.

⊖**maintain** (mān tān′) *v.* **1.** to keep something working; to look after something: *Our lawn mower is properly maintained.* **2.** to keep going at or doing something: *How do you maintain that speed?*

⊖**maintenance** (mān′ tə nəns) *n.* the work of keeping something operating properly: *This machine needs very little maintenance. Just keep it clean and oil it every three months.*

maize (māz) *n.* a kind of grain that grows on large ears; corn.

Majesty (maj′ əs tē) *n.* a title for a king or queen: *Your Majesty; His Majesty; Her Majesty. pl.* **Their Majesties.**

major (mā′ jər) *n.* an army officer, next in rank above a captain. *adj.* larger; more important: *The ball player moved from the minor league to the major league.*

majority (mə jȯr′ i tē) *n.* the greatest number in a group: *The majority of the class went to the play. pl.* **majorities.**

make (māk) *n.* brand; the kind of product that a certain company makes and sells: *What make of air conditioner does she have? v.* **1.** to build; to construct; to create: *She made shelves from the wood.* **2.** to prepare: *Please make coffee.* **3.** to earn: *How much money does he make at his job?* **4.** to add up to: *One and one make two.* **5.** to force: *Our dog makes me get up early to walk her.* **6.** to bring about; to cause something to be or happen: *His jokes make me laugh.* **7.** to get a position on: *to make the basketball team.* **making. made.**
make believe to pretend: *The children made believe that they were doctors and nurses.*
make it to be successful: *Yolande made it at the factory; now she's a supervisor.*
make out **1.** to manage; to do well: *How did he make out on his first day at school?* **2.** to see clearly: *Can you make out the name on the street sign?*
make sure to be sure: *Make sure you don't forget to eat lunch.*
make up **1.** to create in the mind: *The story is not true. I made it up.* **2.** to become friends again: *They made up a week after their fight.* **3.** to be the parts or sections of: *Two more people will make up a full class.*
make up a person's mind to make a decision: *Make up your mind. Are we going out or are we staying home?*

make-up (māk′ up′) *n.* **1.** powder, rouge, lipstick, etc., put on the face to make it more beautiful; cosmetics. **2.** the way something is composed or put together: *The make-up of the team is odd; there are two short people and three tall people.*

male (māl) *n.* **1.** a boy or a man. **2.** an animal that is, will be, or can be a father: *A bull is a male. A cow is a female.*

mall (mȯl) *n.* a shopping centre; a group of shops with a parking lot.

mallard (mal′ ərd) *n.* a kind of wild duck.

mallet (mal′ ət) *n.* a hammer that is made of rubber or wood.

malt (mȯlt) *n.* grain, usually barley, that is used to make beverages such as beer.

mama (mȧ′ mə) *n. (informal)* mother.

mammal (mam′ əl) *n.* a kind of animal that has warm blood and hair or fur. People, whales, dogs, and other animals are mammals. A female mammal can provide milk to feed her babies.

man (man) *n.* a grown-up male human being. *pl.* **men** (men).

manage (man′ ij) *v.* **1.** to take charge and look after; to be responsible for something: *to manage a store.* **2.** to be able to do something: *Can you manage to carry this package?* **managing. managed.**

manager (man′ ij ər) *n.* a person in charge of something: *The manager of the apartment building is away.*

mandatory (man′ də tȯr′ē) *adj.* required by the rules or by the law: *It is mandatory for all the construction workers to wear hard hats.*

mane (mān) *n.* the long hair on the neck of some animals such as horses and lions.

manhole (man′ hōl′) *n.* a hole through which a worker may enter a sewer or other underground area.

manicure (man′ i kyūr′) *n.* care of the fingernails, by cleaning, polishing, etc.: *She had a manicure when she went to have her hair cut.*

Manitoba (man′ i tō′ bə) *n.* the province between Saskatchewan on the west and Ontario on the east; its capital is Winnipeg. Short form: **Man.** A person living in or born in Manitoba is a **Manitoban.**

mankind (man′ kīnd′) *n.* all people; the human race.

man-made (man′ mād′) *adj.* created by human beings, not by nature; synthetic: *That valley is man-made; it was dug ten years ago.*

manner (man′ ər) *n.* the way something is done or occurs: *You said hello in a friendly manner.*

manners (man′ ərz) *n.pl.* how people act or behave towards others: *good manners, bad manners.*

mansion (man′ shən) *n.* a very large house, usually belonging to rich people.

manual (man′ yū əl) *n.* a guidebook: *Read the manual before you repair the bicycle.* *adj.* done by hand: *Chopping down trees is manual work.*

manufacture (man′ yə fak′ chər) *v.* to make something by machinery, usually in a factory. **manufacturing. manufactured.**

manure (mə nyūr′, mə nūr′) *n.* animal waste and straw put in the ground to make plants grow better.

many (men′ ē) *adj.* a great number: *Many Canadians live on farms; more live in towns; most Canadians live in cities.*

⊖**map** (map) *n.* **1.** a drawing of the earth's surface or of part of it, showing towns, roads, and rivers. **2.** any drawing that shows how to get somewhere.

maple (māpl) *n.* a tree having broad leaves and wood that is used to make furniture.

maple leaf (māpl′ lēf′) the leaf of the maple tree, chosen as an emblem of Canada (🍁). *pl.* **maple leaves.**

maple syrup (māpl′ sûr′ əp, mapl′ sir′ əp) a sweet, thick liquid made from the sap of a sugar maple tree.

marathon (mar′ ə thon) *n.* a long-distance running contest, usually about 42 km: *the Olympic Marathon.*

marble (mȧrbl) *n.* **1.** a hard stone used in making statues, buildings, floors, etc. **2.** a small glass ball used in a children's game. **3. marbles** the name of this game.

⊖**march** (mȧrch) *n.* **1.** a walk with regular steps, as done by soldiers. **2.** a piece of music people can march to. *pl.* **marches.** *v.* to walk in step with others, as soldiers do. **marching. marched.** he **marches.**

March (mȧrch) *n.* the third month of the year.

⊖**mare** (mār, mer) *n.* a female horse or donkey.

margarine (mȧrj′ ə rin, mȧrj′ ə rēn′) *n.* a spread made of oils and fats, used instead of butter.

margin (mȧr′ jin) *n.* space left at the top, bottom, and sides of written or printed pages.

marigold (mar′ i gōld′) *n.* a plant that has strong-smelling, dark yellow flowers.

marina (mə re′ nə) *n.* a place along the waterfront where boats may be docked. *pl.* **marinas.**

marine (mə rēn′) *adj.* having to do with ships or the ocean: *Coral is one form of marine life.*

maritime (mar′ i tīm′) *adj.* **1.** having to do with the ocean. **2.** on or near the ocean: *Halifax and Victoria are maritime cities.*

Maritime Provinces (mar′ i tīm′ prov′ ins əz) New Brunswick, Nova Scotia, and Prince Edward Island. These provinces are also called the **Maritimes.**

⊖**mark** (mȧrk) *n.* **1.** a scratch, stain, or cut: *The hot cup left a mark on the wooden table.* **2.** a score on a test; a grade on a report card: *a high mark on a test.* **3.** a written or printed symbol: *A comma is a punctuation mark.* *v.* **1.** to make a mark on something. **2.** to grade a test.

mark down to decrease the cost of: *The grocer marked down last week's fruit.*

mark off to separate one space from another: *Mark off the track that the runners will follow.*

mark up to increase the cost of: *The record store marked up the popular new album.*

market (mȧr′ kət) *n.* a place to buy and sell food or other goods.

marmalade (marm′ ə lād′) *n.* a kind of jam made with oranges, often spread on toast.

maroon (mə rūn′) *n.* a dark red colour. *adj.* having this colour.

marriage (mar′ ij) *n.* **1.** a wedding: *Their marriage took place last year.* **2.** living together as husband and wife: *a happy marriage.*

marrow (mar′ ō) *n.* the soft material in the centre of bones.

marry (mar′ ē) *v.* to become husband and wife. **marrying. married.** she **marries.**

marsh (mȧrsh) *n.* wet, swampy ground. *pl.* **marshes.**

marshmallow (mȧrsh′ mel′ ō, mȧrsh′ mal′ ō) *n.* a soft, sticky candy.

martyr (mȧr′ tər) *n.* a person who suffers or dies because he or she believes in something.

marvellous, marvelous (mȧr′ vəl əs, mȧrv′ ə ləs) *adj.* wonderful; astonishing: *The circus is a marvellous show.*

mascara (mas ka′ rə) *n.* a dark make-up that women wear on their eyelashes.

mascot (mas′ kot) *n.* an animal, person, or thing supposed to bring good luck.

masculine (mas′ kyə lin) *adj.* having to do with boys or men: *'He' is a masculine pronoun. 'She' is feminine.*

mash (mash) *n.* a mixture of bran and other grains that is fed to farm animals. *v.* to crush and mix to a soft mass: *to mash potatoes.* **mashing. mashed.** he **mashes.**

face mask

mask (mask) *n.* a covering over the face, worn as a disguise or a protection: *a Halloween mask; a hockey mask.*

mason (mā′ sən) *n.* a person whose job is building with brick, stone, etc.

mass (mas) *n.* **1.** a great lump or pile of something: *a mass of clay.* **2.** a large number of people gathered together. **3.** a measure of the quantity of matter in something: *a mass of one kilogram. pl.* **masses.**

massacre (mas′ ə kər) *n.* a bloody killing of a large number of people or animals. *v.* to kill in such a way. **massacring. massacred.**

mass media (mas′ mē′ di ə) the methods of communication that reach a large number of people, such as television, radio, and newspapers.

mast (mast) *n.* a tall pole, usually one that holds up sails on a ship.

master (mas′ tər) *n.* **1.** a person who has control over people, animals, or things: *Who is the dog's master?* **2.** a person with great skill: *He is a master at the game of chess. v.* to become a master of or at something.

⊖**mat** (mat) *n.* **1.** a small rug to wipe feet on: *a doormat.* **2.** a small piece of material used under dishes to protect a table: *a placemat.* **3.** a cushion used in gymnastics. **4.** a tangled mass. *v.* to become tangled: *The dog's hair is badly matted.* **matting. matted.**

match (mach) *n.* **1.** a small stick of wood or cardboard with a tip that flames up when struck. **2.** a game: *a tennis match. pl.* **matches.** *v.* to be the same or equal: *Your socks don't match. One is blue and the other is green.* **matching. matched.** it **matches.**

mate (māt) *n.* **1.** a companion; one of a pair: *Where is the mate to the glove?* **2.** a husband or wife; the male or female of a pair of birds or animals. **3.** an officer on a ship. *v.* to bring together as a pair. **mating. mated.**

⊖**material** (mə tēr′ i əl) *n.* **1.** what something is used for or made of: *Paper is a writing material. We used wood as the material for the table.* **2.** cloth: *I like the colour of the material of your coat.*

maternity (mat′ ər′ ni tē) *adj.* having to do with being a mother or a pregnant woman: *maternity clothes; maternity hospital.*

mathematics (math′ ə mat′ iks) *n.pl.* the study of numbers, shapes, and measurement, often called **math** for short.

⊖**matinée** (mat′ i nā′) *n.* an afternoon performance of a play, movie, concert, etc.

matter (mat′ ər) *n.* **1.** something of importance or concern: *His health is a matter for the whole family.* **2.** a problem: *You don't look happy. What's the matter?* **3.** what things are made of. **4.** an amount: *It's a matter of five days before we leave on vacation. v.* to be important: *Does it matter to you if we don't go away?*
as a matter of fact actually; in truth: *As a matter of fact, I came to see you.*
no matter regardless of: *Jan wanted to go to the movies, no matter what was playing.*

mattress (mat′ rəs) *n.* the thick, soft part of a bed. *pl.* **mattresses.**

⊖**mature** (mə chûr′, mə tyûr′) *adj.* **1.** fully grown; completely developed. **2.** sensible; able to make good decisions: *He is only twelve, but he is mature.*

maximum (mak′ si məm) *adj.* the most allowed or possible: *The maximum number of people allowed in the elevator is ten.*

may (mā) *v.* **1.** a verb used before another verb to mean 'to be allowed': *She may go if she wants to.* **2.** a verb used before another verb to mean 'to be possible': *She may be able to do it if she tries hard. I might go for a walk, but only if it's a sunny day.* **might** (mīt).

May (mā) *n.* the fifth month of the year.

maybe (mā′ bē) *adv.* perhaps: *I'm not sure; maybe it will snow this afternoon.*

mayonnaise (mā′ ə nāz′, mā′ ə nāz′) *n.* a sauce made from eggs, vinegar, oil, and salt.

mayor (mā′ ər) *n.* the head of a town, village, or city government.

maze (māz) *n.* a confusing series of paths or lines in which it is easy to get lost.

me (mē) *pron.* a form of the word **I**: *Leave me alone. pl.* **us.**

meadow (med′ ō) *n.* a field of grass or hay in the country.

meal (mēl) *n.* **1.** food eaten each day at a certain time. **2.** coarsely ground grain.

mean (mēn) *n.* average; being at the midway place: *The mean of 1, 2, 4, and 5 is 3. adj.* not kind; nasty: *a mean person; a mean dog; a mean thing to say. v.* **1.** to intend; to have a certain idea or plan: *We meant to visit our aunt, but we did not have time.* **2.** to be a sign of: *A red light means 'stop'.* **3.** to have a certain definition: *'Large' means 'big'.* **meaning. meant** (ment).

meaning (mēn′ ing) *n.* something that is meant: *the meaning of a word; the meaning of a book.*

means (mēnz) *n.pl.* **1.** the way of doing something: *She reached the roof by means of a ladder.*
2. money: *He hasn't the means to buy the car.*
by all means definitely; certainly: *By all means I'll come to your party.*
by no means definitely not: *By no means can you leave work early.*

meantime (mēn′ tīm′) *n.* the time between two events: *The train leaves in an hour; in the meantime I'll read the newspaper.*

meanwhile (mēn′ hwīl′, mēn′ wīl′) *adv.* **1.** during the time between two events: *The next game is on Tuesday. Meanwhile, we will have to practise very hard.* **2.** at the same time: *Tom, please cook dinner; meanwhile, I'll rest.*

measles (mē′ zəlz, mēzls) *n.* a catching disease that causes a rash and a fever.

measure (mezh′ ər) *n.* the size or amount of something: *a large measure of land; a small measure of sugar. v.* to find the size or amount of something: *to measure someone's height.* **measuring. measured.**

measurement (mezh′ ər mənt) *n.* size or amount: *The measurements of the room are eight by five metres.*

meat (mēt) *n.* **1.** animal flesh used as food: *My favourite meats are lamb and pork.* **2.** the edible part of some things: *the meat of a nut.*

⊖**mechanic** (mə kan′ ik) *n.* a person who is skilled in using and repairing machinery.

mechanical (mə kan′ i kəl) *adj.* having to do with a machine: *a mechanical problem at the factory.*

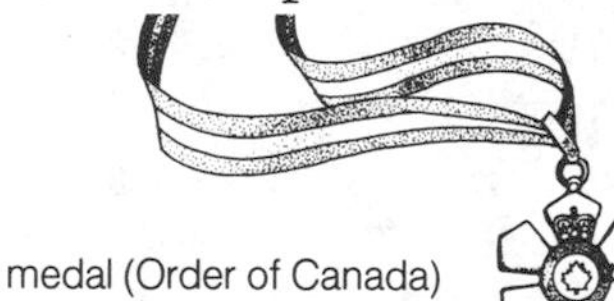

medal (Order of Canada)

medal (med′ əl) *n.* a flat piece of metal that is given as a prize or reward.

meddle (medl) *v.* to become involved with someone else's personal business without being wanted or asked: *Don't meddle in our conversation; read your book.* **meddling. meddled.**

media plural of **medium.**

mediate (mē′ di āt′) *v.* to settle an argument between two sides: *To end the strike, the judge mediated* *between the factory management and the workers.* **mediating. mediated.**

medical (med′ i kəl) *adj.* having to do with doctors and medicine: *Doctors are trained at medical school.*

⊖**medicine** (med′ i sən) **1.** a liquid, pill, or other substance taken for an illness or pain. **2.** the science of curing illness or injury.

⊖**medium** (mē′ di əm) *n.* **1.** a substance or element in which something lives: *Water is the medium of fish.* **2.** a means through which something is done: *Television is a medium for communicating with people.* *pl.* **media.** *adj.* being in the middle: *Medium height is between the shortest and the tallest.*

meet (mēt) *n.* a sports competition: *a swimming meet.* *v.* **1.** to join; to come together: *We'll meet at my house.* **2.** to be introduced to: *I met your sister yesterday.* **3.** to satisfy; to have enough for: *to meet the requirements for a job; to meet a loan payment.* **meeting. met** (met).

⊖**meeting** (mēt′ ing) *n.* a coming together of people to talk or listen to someone.

melody (mel′ ə dē) *n.* a tune that is easy to hum. *pl.* **melodies.**

melon (mel′ ən) *n.* a large, sweet, juicy fruit that grows on a vine: *A cantaloupe is a melon.*

melt (melt) *v.* to change from solid to liquid because of heat: *Snow and butter both melt under a hot sun.*

member (mem′ bər) *n.* someone who belongs to a club or group.

Member of Parliament (mem′ bər əv pår′ li mənt) the title given to each representative elected to the federal parliament; short form is **MP.**

Member of Provincial Parliament (mem′ bər əv prə vin′ shəl pår′ li mənt) the title given to each representative elected to the provincial legislature of Ontario; short form is **MPP.**

Member of the House of Assembly (mem′ bər əv t͟hə haůs′ əv ə sem′ blē) the title given to each representative elected to the provincial legislature of Newfoundland; short form is **MHA.**

Member of the Legislative Assembly (mem′ bər əv t͟hə lej′ is lā′ tiv ə sem′ blē) the title given to each representative elected to the provincial legislature of Alberta, British Columbia, Manitoba, New Brunswick, Nova Scotia, Prince Edward Island, Saskatchewan, the Northwest Territories, and the Yukon Territory; short form is **MLA.**

Member of the National Assembly (mem′ bər əv t͟hə nash′ ən əl ə sem′ blē) the title given to each representative elected to the provincial legislature of Quebec; short form is **MNA.**

memo (mem′ ō) *n.* a short note to remind yourself or others of something: *Karl left a memo on my desk about the office meeting.* *pl.* **memos.**

memorize (mem′ ə rīz′) *v.* to learn by heart: It took me a day to memorize my part in the play. **memorizing. memorized.**

memory (mem′ ə rē) *n.* **1.** the power of remembering things. **2.** something remembered: *a happy memory of home.* *pl.* **memories.**

men plural of **man.**

mend (mend) *v.* to fix something that is broken or torn.

menstruate (men′ strü āt′) *v.* to have a period (the monthly release of blood from a woman's uterus). **menstruating. menstruated.**

mental (men′ təl) *adj.* having to do with the mind.

mention (men′ shən) *v.* to make a remark about; to refer to: *I mentioned you in my letter.*

menu (men′ yū) *n.* a printed list of the foods that are served in a restaurant. *pl.* **menus.**

merchandise (mûr′ chən dīz′, mûr′ chən dīs′) *n.* goods that are bought and sold: *Our corner store sells different types of merchandise.*

merchant (mûr′ chənt) *n.* a person whose work is to buy and sell things: *a timber merchant.*

⊖**mercy** (mûr′ sē) *n.* kindness and pity shown to an unfortunate person or creature: *The children showed mercy towards the kitten and took it home.* *pl.* **mercies.**

merely (mēr′ lē) *adv.* simply; only: *I merely went shopping. Why were you concerned?*

merge (mûrj) *v.* to join together into one thing: *The two roads merged.* **merging. merged.**

merit (mer′ it) *n.* something worth praising: *Tom's plan to increase the farm's wheat production has great merit.*

merry (mer′ ē) *adj.* cheeful; happy; full of fun: *a merry laugh; a merrier laugh; the merriest laugh of all.*

merry-go-round (mer′ i gō raůnd′) *n.* an amusement that has toy animals on which people ride while the platform turns.

⊖**mess** (mes) *n.* a dirty or untidy group of things: *It took an hour to clear the mess from the table.* *pl.* **messes.** *v.* to make untidy: *to mess up a room.*

message (mes′ ij) *n.* spoken or written information sent from one person to another.

messenger (mes′ ən jər) *n.* someone who takes a message from one person to another.

messy (mes′ ē) *adj.* sloppy; not tidy: *a messy room; a messier one; the messiest room of all.*

met see **meet.**

metal (metl, met′ əl) *n.* a hard and shiny substance such as iron, steel, copper, lead, brass, or gold.

meteorology (mē′ ti ər ol′ ə jē) *n.* the science of weather and the atmosphere.

parking meters

meter (mē′ tər) *n.* a machine that measures amounts and times: *a parking meter.*

method (meth′ əd) *n.* a way of doing something: *Watch my method of sewing before you try to make the apron.*

metre (mē′ tər) *n.* a symbol of length; **m** is the symbol. 1 m = 100 cm.

metric system (met′ rik sis′ təm) a system of measurements based on the number ten.

⊖**metropolitan** (met′ rə pol′ ə tən) *adj.* having to do with a city and the area around it where people live: *More than a million people live in the metropolitan area.*

Mexican (mek′ sə kən) *adj.* belonging to or coming from Mexico.

MHA short for **Member of the House of Assembly.**

mice plural of **mouse.**

microphone

microphone (mī′ krə fōn′) *n.* an instrument for recording or carrying sounds, sometimes making them much louder.

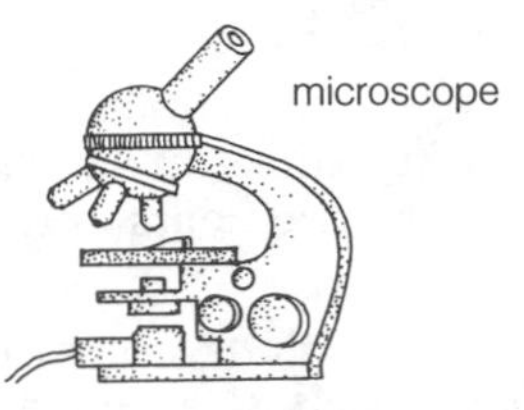

microscope (mī′ krə scōp′) *n.* a scientific instrument that makes tiny things look large:

microwave oven (mī′ kro wāv′ uv′ ən) a type of oven that cooks food very quickly.

mid- a prefix meaning 'middle'; **midday** means the middle of the day; **midnight** means halfway through the night.

middle (midl) *n.* the point that is halfway between two things: *I'll stand in the middle, between Paul and Bob.* *adj.* halfway between: *May I have the middle book?*

middle-aged (midl′ ajd′) *adj.* not yet an old person, but no longer young.

midget (mij′ it) *n.* someone or something that is much smaller than average size.

midnight (mid′ nīt′) *n.* twelve o'clock at night.

midst (midst) *n.* the middle: *When Dora arrived we were in the midst of our dinner.*

might (mīt) *n.* power; strength: *Use all your might to open the window.* *v.* see **may.**

migrate (mī′ grāt) *v.* to move to another place or country: *Some birds migrate to warmer lands in winter.* **migrating. migrated.**

mild (mīld) *adj.* **1.** gentle: *a mild breeze.* **2.** not strong: *Milk has a mild taste.* **3.** neither hot nor cold: *a mild day.*

mildew (mil′ dyū, mil′ dū) *n.* a type of fungus that grows on plants or on things left in a damp place: *Nobody had lived in the house for a long time, and the walls were covered with mildew.*

mile (mīl) *n.* a measure of distance on land equal to about 1610 m.

mileage (mīl′ ij) *n.* the number of miles that someone or something has travelled: *What is the mileage on the used car that you bought?*

military (mil′ i ter′ ē) *adj.* having to do with an army or war: *military equipment.*

milk (milk) *n.* the white liquid food that female mammals produce to feed their young: *We use cow's milk for drinking and cooking.* *v.* to get milk from an animal: *to milk a cow.*

milkshake (milk′ shāk′) *n.* a drink made of milk, flavoured syrup, and ice cream, shaken or mixed well.

Milky Way (mil′ kē wā′) a broad band of light, made up of stars, that stretches across the sky at night.

mill (mil) *n.* **1.** a machine used for grinding or crushing beans or seeds, such as coffee or grain. **2.** a building containing these machines. **3.** a factory where cloth or other goods are made. *v.* to grind: *to mill grain into flour.*

milligram (mil′ i gram′, mil′ ə gram′) *n.* a measure of mass; **mg** is the symbol. 1000 mg = 1 g.

millilitre (mil′ i lē′ tər, mil′ ə lē′ tər) *n.* a liquid measure; **mL** is the symbol. 1000 mL = 1 L.

millimetre (mil′ i mē′ tər, mil′ ə mē′ tər) *n.* a measure of length; **mm** is the symbol. 1000 mm = 1 m.

million (mil′ yən) *n., adj.* a thousand thousands (1 000 000).

millionaire (mil′ yə nār′, mil′ yə nār′) *n.* a very rich person who has at least a million dollars.

mince (mins) *v.* to cut into small pieces: *to mince beef.* **mincing. minced.**

mind (mīnd) *n.* the part of a person that thinks, remembers, understands, etc. *v.* **1.** to take care of: *I will mind the baby while you go shopping.* **2.** to feel bad about; to dislike: *Do you mind all the snow?* **3.** to follow another's orders: *Mind your mother; clean the kitchen before you leave.*
change a person's mind to change plans or opinions: *He always changes his mind about the movie he wants to see.*
keep in mind to remember; to pay attention to: *Keep in mind that we have to leave in an hour.*
make up a person's mind to come to a decision: *Make up your mind. What do you want to eat?*
on a person's mind in a person's thoughts: *You are on my mind whenever you are not with me.*

⊖**mine** (mīn) *n.* **1.** a deep tunnel in the earth from which gold, coal, nickel, diamonds, or other minerals are taken out. **2.** a bomb in the ground or the sea that explodes when something comes near it or touches it. *pron.* the one belonging to me: *This pen is mine. pl.* **ours.**

miner (mī′ nər) *n.* a person who works in a mine.

mineral (min′ ə rəl) *n.* anything dug out from the earth, such as coal, diamonds, or gold.

miniature (min′ i ə chər, min′ i chər) *adj.* very small; tiny: *The children put their miniature boats into the bathtub.*

minimum (min′ i məm) *adj.* the smallest allowed or possible: *The minimum wage is the lowest wage an employer is allowed to pay his or her workers.*

mining (mīn′ ing) *n.* the working of mines: *gold mining; coal mining; nickel mining.*

⊖**minister** (min′ is tər) *n.* **1.** a member of the clergy. **2. Minister** the head of a government department: *the Minister of Defence.*

mink (mingk) *n.* a small animal whose soft, thick fur is used to make expensive coats and other garments.

minnow (min′ ō) *n.* a very small freshwater fish often used for bait.

minor (mī′ nər) *n.* a person who, under law, is not considered an adult. *adj.* small or not important; not major: *The problem with the car is minor and won't take long to fix.*

minority (mə nôr′ i tē, mī nôr′ i tē) *n.* the smaller group: *Four of them wanted to ask for more money, and two didn't. Jane was in the minority. pl.* **minorities.**

mint (mint) *n.* **1.** a plant whose leaves are used as a flavouring for candy, toothpaste, etc. **2.** a place where coins are made.

minus (mī′ nəs) *adj.* less than, often less than zero: *The temperature overnight will go down to minus twenty. prep.* less. The symbol is –: *Twenty minus seven leaves thirteen. (20 – 7 = 13.)*

minute (min′ ət) *n.* **1.** sixty seconds of time; **min** is the symbol: *There are sixty minutes in one hour.*

minute (mī nyūt′, mī nūt′) *adj.* very tiny: *a minute speck of dust.*

miracle (mir′ əkl) *n.* a marvellous and unexpected happening: *It is a miracle that no ships were lost in the storm.*

mirror (mir′ ər) *n.* a glass, with shiny metal on the back, that reflects things.

mis- a prefix meaning 'bad', 'badly', or 'wrong': **misbehaving** means behaving badly; to **misspell** a word is to spell it the wrong way.

miscellaneous (mis′ ə lā′ nē əs) *adj.* mixed; not sorted into groups: *The child's coat pockets were filled with miscellaneous things: candy* *wrappers, strings, an old bus ticket, and a broken watch.*

mischief (mis′ chif) *n.* bad or silly behaviour that can annoy people.

mischievous (mis′ chi vəs) *adj.* full of mischief; naughty.

miser (mī′ zər) *n.* a greedy person who keeps money, trying not to spend any.

⊖**miserable** (miz′ ər əbl, miz′ rə bəl) *adj.* not happy; not well; not pleasant: *She feels miserable. It is a miserable, rainy day.*

misfortune (mis fôr′ chən) *n.* bad luck: *It was his misfortune to have lost his winning lottery ticket.*

misplace (mis plās′) *v.* to put in the wrong place: *I have misplaced my glasses. Will you help me find them?* **misplacing. misplaced.**

Miss (mis) a title put in front of the name of an unmarried woman or girl: *Miss Anne Jones.*

miss (mis) *v.* **1.** to fail to do something that one wants or tries to do; to fail to find, catch, reach, hit, see, hear, etc.: *to miss the bus; to miss the street sign; to miss the ball; to miss the class.* **2.** to feel lonely for someone or something: *I miss the place where I grew up and the people I knew there.* **missing. missed.** she **misses.**

missile (mis′ əl, mis′ īl) *n.* an object, usually a weapon, that can be thrown or fired through the air.

missing (mis′ ing) *adj.* not found; absent: *I looked everywhere for the missing books.*

mission (mish′ ən) *n.* **1.** a special job or task: *a rescue mission.* **2.** a group of people sent to do religious work, usually in another country.

misspell (mis spel′) *v.* to spell a word the wrong way.

mist (mist) *n.* a cloud of tiny drops of water in the air, making it hard to see what is ahead.

mistake (mis tāk′) *n.* something that is wrong; an error: *a mistake in adding. It was a mistake to take this busy highway.* *v.* to make an error: *It is sometimes easy to mistake plastic for glass.* **mistaking. mistook.** I am **mistaken.**

mistletoe (misl′ tō′) *n.* a climbing plant with white berries, used as a Christmas decoration.

misunderstand (mis′ un dər stand′) *v.* not to understand: *I misunderstood the directions and went north, not south.* **misunderstanding. misunderstood.**

mitt (mit) *n.* **1.** a baseball glove. **2.** a mitten.

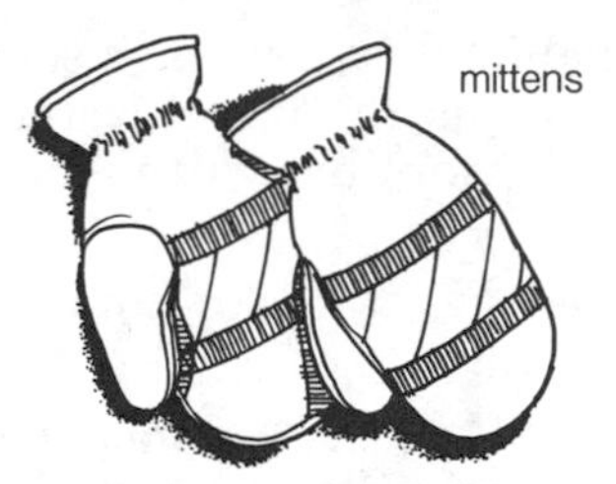
mittens

mitten (mit′ ən) *n.* a glove that covers four fingers together and the thumb separately.

mix (miks) *v.* to put different things together: *Pam mixed lettuce, cucumbers, and tomatoes.* **mixing. mixed.** she **mixes.**
mix up **1.** to shake up: *Mix up the paint.* **2.** to confuse; to mistake one thing for another: *I always mix up the names of the two brothers.*

mixer (mik′ sər) *n.* a machine for stirring or whipping substances: *a food mixer; a cement mixer.*

mixture (miks′ chər) *n.* something made of different things that have been combined: *That juice is a mixture of orange and grapefruit juices.*

MLA short for **Member of the Legislative Assembly.**

MNA short for **Member of the National Assembly.**

moan (mōn) *n.* a low groaning sound, often showing pain. *v.* to make such a sound.

mob (mob) *n.* an uncontrolled crowd of people. *v.* to crowd around in an uncontrolled way: *The people mobbed the famous singer.* **mobbing. mobbed.**

mobile (mō′ bīl, mōbl) *adj.* easily moved: *This chair has wheels, so it is very mobile.*

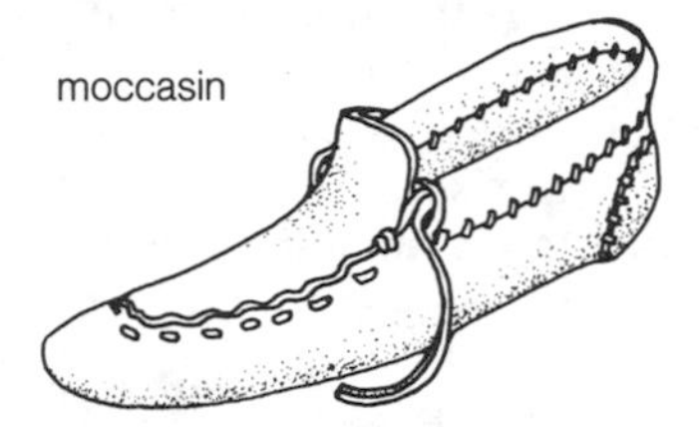

moccasin (mok′ ə sən) *n.* a shoe made completely of soft leather, originally worn by North American Indians.

mock (mok) *v.* to make fun of in an unkind way.

⊖**model** (mod′ əl) *n.* **1.** a small copy of something: *We saw a model of the house that was being built.* **2.** a person who poses for an artist or photographer, often to show off new clothes. **3.** a person who sets a good example: *He is a model of a good teacher.* **4.** a style or design: *the latest model of car.* *v.* **1.** to make a model. **2.** to pose for an artist or photographer, often to show off new clothes. **modelling. modelled.**

modern (mod′ ərn) *adj.* **1.** up-to-date; new: *The old factory was replaced with a modern one.* **2.** having to do with present times: *modern history.*

modest (mod′ ist) *adj.* **1.** not boasting: *She is very modest, never talking about all the prizes she has won.* **2.** enough, but not too much: *He earns a modest income.*

modify (mod′ i fī′) *v.* to change something, usually in a small way: *The carpenter was asked to modify the plans for the bookcase.* **modifying. modified.** she **modifies.**

module (mod′ yūl, moj′ ūl) *n.* a section of furniture, a building, a spaceship, etc., that can be separated from the whole.

moist (moist) *adj.* slightly wet; damp.

moisture (mois′ chər) *n.* dampness.

molar (mō′ lər) *n.* one of the large teeth at the back of the mouth, used for grinding food.

molasses (mə las′ iz) *n.* a thick, sweet, dark syrup, made from sugar cane.

mold see **mould.**

molding see **moulding.**

mole (mōl) *n.* **1.** a small, grey, furry animal that digs tunnels under the ground, leaving molehills on top. **2.** a small, dark spot on the skin.

molecule (mol′ ə kyūl′) *n.* the smallest chemical unit into which a substance can be divided.

molest (mə lest′) *v.* to bother and interfere with, sometimes causing injury.

mom (mom) *n.* *(informal)* mother.

moment (mō′ mənt) *n.* a very short amount of time: *I will answer the phone in a moment.*

monarch (mon′ ärk, mon′ ərk) *n.* a royal ruler such as a king, queen, or emperor. *pl.* **monarchs.**

Monday (mun′ dē) *n.* the second day of the week. *pl.* **Mondays.**

⊖**money** (mun′ ē) *n.* coins and paper notes used in buying and selling things. *pl.* **moneys.**
make money to receive money, often from working: *Andrea makes more money at her new job.*
money order a type of cheque that can be bought at a bank: *If you want to send money to someone by mail, it is a good idea to send it as a money order.*

monitor (mon′ i tər) *n.* **1.** a student chosen to help the teacher. **2.** a device that allows someone to watch certain activities carefully: *a* *monitor in a hospital room.* *v.* to get information by using a monitor or by listening or watching carefully.

monk (mungk) *n.* one of a group of religious men who have chosen to follow certain rules and to live together in a religious community known as a **monastery.**

monkey (mung′ kē) *n.* a furry mammal that lives in trees in many hot climates. It has long legs and arms, a long tail, and looks something like a person. *pl.* **monkeys.**

monkey wrench (mung′ kē rench′) a kind of wrench with an opening that can be adjusted to fit nuts and bolts of different sizes. *pl.* **monkey wrenches.**

monotonous (mə not′ ə nəs) *adj.* boring and never changing: *Her voice is so monotonous, it almost makes me fall asleep!*

monster (mon′ stər) *n.* **1.** a strange and frightening creature, either imaginary or real. **2.** a very cruel person.

month (munth) *n.* one of the twelve parts of the year: *January is the first month of the year.*

monthly (munth′ lē) *adv.* once a month: *The magazine comes out monthly.* *adj.* coming out or happening every month: *a monthly magazine.*

Montreal (mon′ trē ȯl′, mun′ trē ȯl) *n.* the largest city in the province of Quebec.

monument (mon′ yə mənt) *n.* a statue or building put up in memory of someone or some event.

mood (mūd) *n.* the way that someone feels at a certain time: *My brother is in a good mood today, smiling and laughing.*

moon (mūn) *n.* the large bright object that shines in the sky at night and revolves around the earth once in about thirty days.

moose (mūs) *n.* a large animal of the deer family that lives in the forests of Canada and the northern United States. The male moose has very large, flat antlers. *pl.* **moose.**

mop (mop) *n.* a sponge or pieces of cloth joined at the end of a long handle and used for cleaning. *v.* to clean with a mop. **mopping. mopped.**

moral (mȯr′ əl) *n.* **1.** a lesson to be learned, often from a story, about what is right and wrong, good and bad. **2. morals** beliefs about what is right or wrong. *adj.* having to do with what is right and wrong, good and bad.

morale (mə ral′) *n.* the way people feel about the job they have to do: *The morale at our office is good.*

more (mȯr) *adj.* extra; a bigger amount of: *May I have more cake?* *adv.* again: *Please read the story once more.*

more or less approximately; close to: *The trip will take us three hours, more or less.*

morning (mȯr′ ning) *n.* the first part of the day, ending at noon.

mortal (mȯr′ təl) *n.* a person. *adj.* **1.** not able to live forever: *All people are mortal.* **2.** causing death: *a mortal injury.*

mortar (mȯr′ tər) *n.* a mixture of water, lime, and sand, used to hold stones or bricks together.

mortgage (mȯr′ gij) *n.* an agreement in which someone agrees to lend another person money to buy property. If the money is not paid back on time, the lender (the **mortgagor**) can claim the property from the borrower (the **mortgagee**). *v.* to agree to such an arrangement; to offer property as security for a loan: *They mortgaged their home to get money for a new car.* **mortgaging. mortgaged.**

mosaic (mō zā′ ik) *n.* a picture made with bits of coloured glass, stone, or tile.

mosquito

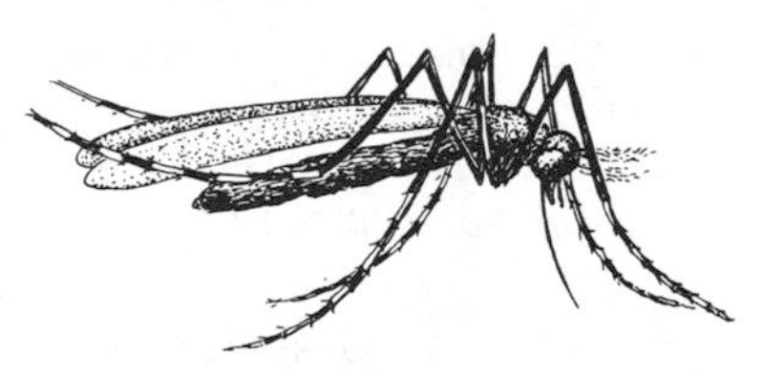

mosquito (məs kē′ tō) *n.* a small two-winged insect. The bite of the female causes itching, and some mosquitoes carry diseases. *pl.* **mosquitoes.**

⊖**moss** (mos) *n.* a small, smooth, green plant that grows on damp trees and stones. *pl.* **mosses.**

most (mōst) *adj.* the greatest number, amount, etc.: *Most dogs like bones. adv.* **1.** the greatest; the best: *Which sport do you like most? That is the most beautiful song I know.* **2.** very: *Inga is most anxious to come with us.*

motel (mō tel′) *n.* a hotel that is built near a main road and is often used by travellers with cars.

moth (moth) *n.* an insect that flies mostly at night and looks something like a butterfly. *pl.* **moths** (mo<u>th</u>z, moths).

mother (mu<u>th</u>′ ər) *n.* a female parent.

mother-in-law (mu<u>th</u>′ ər in lȯ′) *n.* the mother of a person's husband or wife. *pl.* **mothers-in-law.**

motion (mō′ shən) *n.* movement: *The whistle sounded, and the train went into motion.*

motion picture (mō′ shən pik′ chər) a series of pictures on a film, projected on a screen; a movie.

motivate (mō′ ti vāt′) *v.* to give someone a reason to do something: *Being fair to people can motivate them to work harder.* **motivating. motivated.**

motive (mō′ tiv) *n.* a reason for doing something: *Getting a better job was one of her motives for going back to school.*

motor (mō′ tər) *n.* an engine that gives other machines the power to move.

motorboat

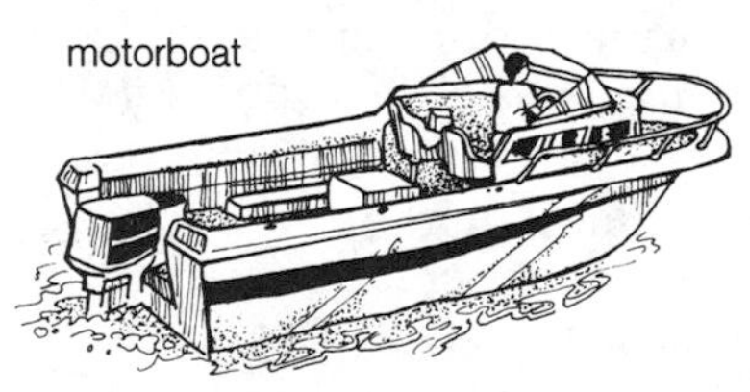

motorboat (mō′ tər bōt′) *n.* a boat propelled by a motor.

motorcycle

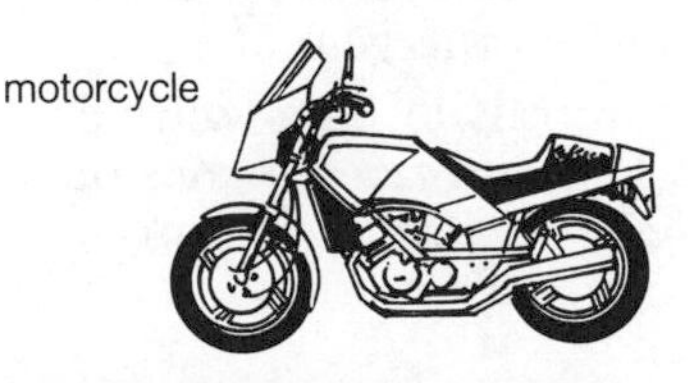

motorcycle (mō′ tər sīkl′) *n.* a two-wheeled vehicle powered by a motor.

motorist (mō′ tər ist) *n.* a person who drives an automobile.

mould, mold (mōld) *n.* **1.** a hollow container that gives its shape to what is put into it. **2.** a fuzzy or woolly growth, sometimes seen on old bread, cheese, or food. *v.* to make into a certain form.

moulding, molding (mōld′ ing) *n.* a piece of wood or plaster that is shaped around the edge of a doorway, window, etc.: *That moulding on the wall is very attractive.*

mound (maund) *n.* a large heap: *a mound of stones.*

mount (maunt) *n.* **1.** a hill or mountain. **2.** a horse for riding. *v.* **1.** to climb up: *to mount a horse.* **2.** to put in place: *to mount a diamond in a ring.*

mountain (maun′ tən) *n.* a very high hill or section of land.

mountainous (maun′ tən əs) *adj.* full of mountains: *Switzerland is a mountainous country.*

Mountie (maun′ tē) *n.* a member of the **Royal Canadian Mounted Police.**

mourn (mórn) *v.* to feel very sorry because someone or something has died or gone far away.

mouse (maus) *n.* a small, furry rodent with a pointed nose and a long tail. *pl.* **mice** (mīs).

moustache, mustache (mus′ tash, mə stash′) *n.* hair that grows above a man's top lip.

mouth (mauth) *n.* **1.** the opening in the face through which people and animals take food. **2.** any opening: *the mouth of a cave; the mouth of a river. pl.* **mouths** (mau<u>th</u>z).

mouthpiece (mauth′ pēs′) *n.* **1.** the part of a musical instrument that is placed against or in the mouth. **2.** the part of a telephone that is held near the mouth.

movable, moveable (mūv′ əbl) *adj.* able to be moved.

⊖**move** (mūv) *n.* **1.** in a game such as chess, a player's turn to go. **2.** a movement: *He did not make a move when we came in the room.* *v.* **1.** to go or to take from one place to another: *Elizabeth moved the chair to the kitchen.* **2.** to go to live somewhere else: *We are going to move next week.* **3.** to make someone feel an emotion: *That song always moves me.* **4.** to give motion to: *The wind moved the flag on the pole.* **moving. moved.**

move in to start to live or work in a new place: *There is an empty apartment in my building. Would you like to move in?*

movement (mūv′ mənt) *n.* **1.** a change from one place or position to another: *In recent years, there has been a movement of people from farms to cities.* **2.** a group of people who work towards a goal: *a movement to reduce pollution.* **3.** the working parts of a clock, watch, or other machine. **4.** a main part of a long piece of music.

mover (mūv′ ər) *n.* a person or company that moves people from one place to another.

movie (mū′ vē) *n.* a motion picture; a film.

mow (mō) *v.* to cut grass, hay, etc., with a lawn mower or other cutting machine. **mowing. mowed.** he has **mown**, or **mowed.**

MP short for **Member of Parliament.**

MPP short for **Member of Provincial Parliament.**

Mr. (mis′ tər) short for **Mister**, a title put in front of a man's name.

Mrs. (mis′ iz) short for **Mistress**, a title put in front of a married woman's name.

Ms (miz) a title put in front of a woman's name.

much (much) *adj.* large in amount, or degree: *much money, more money, the most money of all.* *adv.* very; to a large degree: *I am feeling much better.*

mucus (myū′ kəs) *n.* a wet, sticky substance that covers the inside of the mouth, throat, and other parts of the body.

mud (mud) *n.* soft, wet soil or dirt.

muddy (mud′ ē) *adj.* covered with mud: *a muddy road; a muddier road; the muddiest road of all.*

muffin (muf′ in) *n.* a small round cake for one person, often eaten with butter.

muffler (muf′ lər) *n.* **1.** something that helps to silence noises: *a muffler on a car.* **2.** a thick, woollen scarf.

mug (mug) *n.* a large drinking cup with a handle.

muggy (mug′ ē) *adj.* damp and warm: *a muggy day; a muggier day; the muggiest one of all.*

mukluks (muk′ luks) *n.pl.* **1.** high waterproof boots, often made of sealskin, worn by Inuit. **2.** any boots like these.

mule (myūl) *n.* a mammal that is half donkey and half horse.

multi- a prefix meaning 'several' or 'many': **multicultural** means having many cultures; **multilingual** means able to speak many languages.

multiple (mul′ tipl) *adj.* having more than one part: *He suffered a multiple fracture. His arm was broken in three places.*

multiplication (mul′ ti pli kā′ shən) *n.* multiplying one number by another.

multiply (mul′ ti plī′) *v.* to make a number several times larger: *When we multiply six by three, we get eighteen.* **multiplying. multiplied.** he **multiplies.**

mum (mum) *n.* *(informal)* mother.

mumble (mumbl) *v.* to speak low and not clearly. **mumbling. mumbled.**

mummy (mum′ ē) *n.* in ancient times, a dead body treated with chemicals and wrapped in cloths so that it would not decay: *Many mummies have been found in ancient Egyptian tombs.* *pl.* **mummies.**

mumps (mumps) *n.* a catching illness that makes the face and neck swell up so that it may be hard to swallow food and liquid.

munch (munch) *v.* to chew in a noisy way. **munching. munched.** he **munches.**

municipal (myū nis′ i pəl) *adj.* having to do with the government of a town or city: *In the last municipal election, the people voted for a new mayor.*

mural (myūr′ əl) *n.* a large, long painting, often done directly on a wall.

murder (mûr′ dər) *n.* the intentional and unlawful killing of a human being. *v.* to kill someone intentionally and unlawfully.

murmur (mûr′ mər) *n.* something said softly. *v.* to say something softly.

muscle (musl) *n.* one of the parts of the body that can be tightened or loosened, making the body move. Muscles are made up of strong fibres, and look like cords.

muscular (mus′ kyə lər, mus′ kyū lər) *adj.* having strong muscles: *a muscular body.*

museum (myū zē′ əm) *n.* a building in which interesting science or art objects are displayed for people to look at.

mush (mush) *n.* something soft and wet, like mud.

mushroom (mush′ rūm′) *n.* a fungus shaped like a small umbrella. Some mushrooms may be eaten, but others are poisonous. *v.* to grow quickly or appear suddenly: *Her business has mushroomed since she started to advertise in the newspaper.*

music (myū′ zik) *n.* **1.** a series of pleasant sounds or tones, made by singing or by playing an instrument. **2.** the written symbols of these sounds.

musical (myū′ zi kəl, myū′ zikl) *adj.* **1.** having to do with music. **2.** skilled in music.

musician (myū zish′ ən) *n.* someone who creates or plays music.

muskeg (mus′ keg) *n.* a large area of swamp or marsh, found in northern Canada.

muskrat

muskrat (musk′ rat′) *n.* a North American water animal that looks like a large rat and has brown fur.

muslin (muz′ lin) *n.* a kind of cotton cloth.

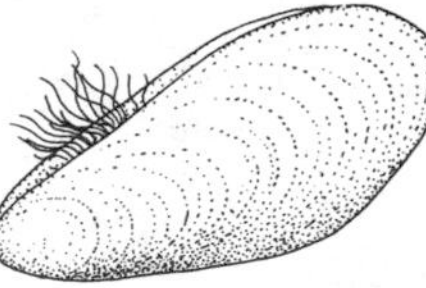
mussel

mussel (mus′ əl) *n.* a shellfish that can be eaten; it is something like a clam, with a narrow, black shell.

must (must) *v.* a verb used before another verb to mean 'to have to': *I must go out before the milk store closes.*

mustache see **moustache.**

mustard (mus′ tərd) *n.* a hot-tasting, yellow spice eaten with hot dogs and other foods.

mute (myūt) *adj.* not able to speak or make a sound.

mutter (mut′ ər) *v.* to speak or grumble in a soft voice.

mutual (myū′ chū əl) *adj.* shared, felt, or done by several people: *Our family has a mutual interest in golf.*

muzzle (muzl) *n.* **1.** the jaws and nose of an animal. **2.** leather straps put over an animal's mouth to keep it from biting. **3.** the open end of a gun barrel. *v.* to put a muzzle on an animal. **muzzling. muzzled.**

my (mī) *adj.* belonging to me: *This is my hat, not yours. pl.* **our.**

myself (mī self′) *pron.* I alone: *I cut myself. pl.* **ourselves.**

mysterious (mis tēr′ i əs) *adj.* not able to be explained; full of mystery: *mysterious footprints in the snow.*

mystery (mis′ tər ē) *n.* **1.** something very strange; something that is not explained: *It is a mystery how the bird got into the house.* **2.** a story about a crime. *pl.* **mysteries.**

myth (mith) *n.* a legend; a story that tells about heroes, heroines, and strange and magical things.

N

nag (nag) *v. (informal)* to keep on scolding and finding fault. **nagging. nagged.**

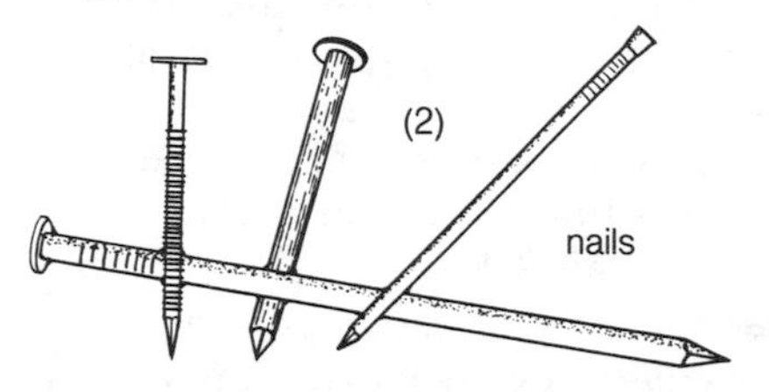

nail (nāl) *n.* **1.** the thin, hard covering at the end of fingers and toes. **2.** a small metal spike, pointed at one end and flat at the other. *v.* to hammer a nail into an object.

naive (naīv) *adj.* having very little experience; not wise: *You are naive to believe his promises.*

naked (nā′ kid) *adj.* bare; without clothes.

name (nām) *n.* what a person or thing is called. *v.* **1.** to give a name to a baby or pet. **2.** to state the name of someone or something: *The newspaper named Mr. Singh as the man who had saved the child's life.* **3.** to choose: *The mayor named Mr. Johnson as her assistant.* **naming. named.**
call names to insult someone by calling that person bad names.

namely (nām′ lē) *adv.* that is: *Only one person here finished the race—namely, Richard.*

⊖**nap** (nap) *n.* a brief sleep. *v.* to take a brief sleep. **napping. napped.**

napkin (nap′ kin) *n.* a piece of cloth or paper used at meals for wiping the hands and mouth.

narcissus (när sis′ əs) *n.* a sweet-smelling plant that grows from a bulb and has white or yellow flowers. *pl.* **narcissuses**, or **narcissi** (när sis′ ī).

narcotic (när kot′ ik) *n.* a drug that takes away pain and causes sleep. Narcotics are harmful and habit-forming if they are not used properly.

narrow (nar′ ō) *adj.* thin, not wide: *Drive carefully on the narrow bridge.*

nasty (nas′ tē) *adj.* unpleasant; miserable: *a nasty day; a nastier day; the nastiest day of all.*

nation (nā′ shən) *n.* **1.** the people of a particular land that has its own government. **2.** this land itself; a country.

national (nash′ ən əl) *adj.* belonging to a nation: *A national anthem is the special song of a nation.*

nationality (nash′ ə nal′ i tē) *n.* a large group of people sharing a language and culture. *pl.* **nationalities.**

⊖**native** (nā′ tiv) *n.* a person born in a certain country or place: *She is a native of Korea.* *adj.* **1.** born in a certain country or place: *Tom is a native Australian.* **2.** coming originally from a certain country or place: *The Canada goose is a native Canadian bird.* **3.** belonging to someone by birth: *Spanish is his native language.*

native people (nā′ tiv pēpl′) the first people ever to have lived in a place: *Indians and Inuit are the native peoples of Canada.*

natural (nach′ ə rəl) *adj.* **1.** found in nature; not man-made; not changed: *Wood is a natural material.* **2.** able to do things easily, without needing to be taught: *a natural dancer.*

naturalized (nach′ ə rəl īzd′) *adj.* given citizenship in a country other than the country in which a person has been born a citizen: *Malka is a naturalized Canadian citizen. She was born in Israel.*

naturally (nach′ ə rəl ē) *adv.* **1.** of course; certainly: *Naturally we will pay you for all the help you give us.* **2.** happening easily: *She is naturally good at swimming.*

⊖**nature** (nā′ chər) *n.* **1.** the outdoor world of plants and animals: *We go camping because we enjoy nature.* **2.** the special qualities of a person or thing: *It is Carla's nature to be kind.*

naughty (nȯ′ tē) *adj.* badly behaved; disobedient: *a naughty child; a naughtier child; the naughtiest child of all.*

nausea (nȯ′ zē ə, nȯ′ zhə) *n.* a feeling of sickness in the stomach.

nauseous (nȯ′ zi əs, nȯ′ zhəs) *adj.* feeling sick in the stomach: *He ate too much and became nauseous on the boat.*

naval (nav′ əl) *adj.* having to do with the navy: *a naval officer.*

navel (nav′ əl) *n.* the little round dent in the centre of the abdomen, where the umbilical cord was cut at birth.

navigate (nav′ i gāt′) *v.* to guide or plan the route for a ship or an aircraft. **navigating. navigated.**

navigator (nav′ i gā′ tər) *n.* someone who guides a ship or aircraft.

navy (nā′ vē) *n.* a country's warships and their crews. *pl.* **navies.**

NDP short for **New Democratic Party.**

near (nēr) *prep.* close to: *The hat is near the gloves.*

nearby (nēr′ bī′) *adv.* very close by: *They live nearby, and we visit them often.*

nearly (nēr′ lē) *adv.* almost: *It is nearly twelve o'clock.*

near-sighted (nēr′ sīt′ əd) *adj.* able to see things that are close, but not things that are far away.

neat (nēt) *adj.* clean and tidy: *a neat room; a neat person.*

necessary (nes′ ə ser′ ē) *adj.* needed; required; having to be done.

necessity (nə ses′ i tē) *n.* something necessary: *Food is a necessity, not a luxury. pl.* **necessities.**

neck (nek) *n.* **1.** the part of the body that joins the head to the shoulders. **2.** a narrow part like this: *the neck of a bottle.*
neck and neck even in a race: *The two runners were neck and neck at the finish line.*

necklace (nek′ ləs) *n.* a string of beads or jewels worn around the neck.

need (nēd) *n.* **1.** a desire for something: *Do you have a need for a new car?* **2.** a requirement or necessity: *There is no need to eat until lunch. v.* to require or want something: *I need a pen. We need food to live.*

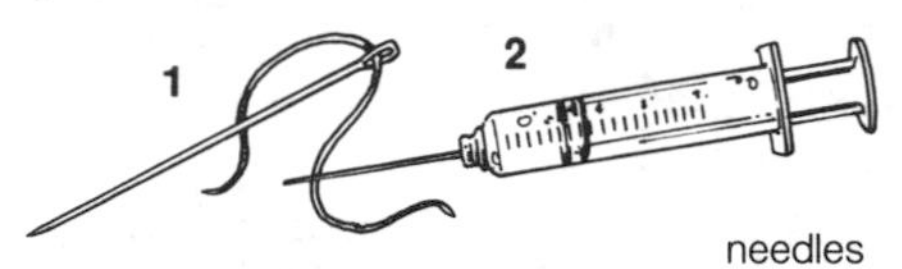

needles

needle (nēdl) *n.* **1.** a long, thin pointed piece of metal, with a hole or 'eye' at one end, used in sewing. **2.** an object having this general shape: *a knitting needle; a needle for a stereo; the needles of a pine tree; the needle a doctor uses to give injections.*

needn't (nēdnt) short for **need not**: *You needn't shout at me. I can hear you.*

needy (nē′ dē) *adj.* very poor: *a needy family; a needier one; the neediest one of all.*

negative (neg′ ə tiv) *n.* a photographic picture on film, in which the light areas and dark areas are changed around: *Photographic prints are made from negatives. adj.* **1.** meaning 'no' or 'not': *When they asked for a dog, they received a negative answer.*

2. not helpful or encouraging: *a negative attitude towards work.* **3.** not showing the presence of a disease: *Her flu test came back negative.*

neglect (ni glekt′) *v.* to give little attention to someone or something, or to fail to do something: *The plants will die if you neglect them.*

negotiate (ni gō′ shi āt′) *v.* to talk in order to reach an agreement: *The workers and the factory owners negotiated all night, but they could not agree on how much everyone should be paid.* **negotiating. negotiated.**

neighbour, neighbor (nā′ bər) *n.* someone who lives nearby.

neighbourhood, neighborhood (nā′ bər hủd) *n.* a small area of a city or town and the people who live there: *There are homes, apartment buildings, a few shops, and a school in our neighbourhood.*
in the neighbourhood of approximately; about: *The repairs will cost in the neighbourhood of two hundred dollars.*

neither (nē′ t͟hər, nī′ t͟hər) *conj.* not one or the other: *Neither Sally nor her brother is home.*
Note: **Neither** is followed by **nor**: *Neither Michael nor Paula is here.* **Either** is followed by **or**: *Either Bill or I will be there.*

nephew (nef′ yū) *n.* the son of a brother or sister: *My cousin Alan is my father's nephew.*

nerve (nûrv) *n.* **1.** one of the fibres in the body that carries feelings and messages to the brain.
2. *(informal)* courage; boldness: *He didn't have the nerve to say he didn't like her dress.*
get on a person's nerves to annoy or bother: *Sam's constant talking gets on my nerves.*

nervous (nûr′ vəs) *adj.* tense; easily excited or upset: *My nervous dog hides when someone rings the bell.*

nest (nest) *n.* a home of twigs, straw, grass, and other materials, made by birds or other creatures.

net (net) *n.* a woven material, usually of string or wire, with large or small spaces between the strings or wires. *adj.* remaining after subtracting certain expenses: *Net income is less than gross income.*

network (net′ wûrk′) *n.* **1.** a group of radio or television stations linked so that they can show the same programs at the same times: *The CBC and CTV are the largest television networks in Canada.* **2.** a group made up of many parts that communicate with one another: *a spy network; a computer network.* **3.** a system of many crossing lines: *a network of wires.*

neutral (nyū′ trəl, nū′ trəl) *n.* the position of a vehicle that is not in gear. *adj.* **1.** not helping either side in a war, argument, fight, etc. **2.** not having a strong colour or other quality: *A grey shirt can be worn with other colours because it is neutral.*

never (nev′ ər) *adv.* not at any time: *I have never flown in a plane.*
never mind don't worry; it does not matter.

new (nyū, nū) *adj.* **1.** not old: *a new shirt.* **2.** not seen or known before: *a new idea.*

newborn (nyū′ bỏrn′, nū′ bỏrn′) *adj.* recently born: *a newborn calf.*

New Brunswick (nyū′ brunz′ wik, nū′ brunz′ wik) the province between Quebec on the north, and Nova Scotia on the south; its capital is Fredericton. Short form: **N.B.** A person living in or born in New Brunswick is a **New Brunswicker.**

New Canadian (nyū′ kə nā′ di ən, nu′ kə nā′ di ən) **1.** a person who has recently come to Canada and plans to live here. **2.** a person who has recently become a Canadian citizen.

newcomer (nyū′ kum′ ər, nū′ kum′ ər) *n.* a person who has recently come to a country, town, etc.

New Democratic Party (nyū′ dem′ ə krat′ ik pȧr′ tē, nū′ dem′ ə krat′ ik pȧr′ tē) one of the main political parties of Canada.

Newfoundland (nyū′ fənd land′, nū′ fənd land′) *n.* the most eastern province of Canada. The island portion is bounded by the Atlantic Ocean on the east and the Gulf of St. Lawrence on the west; the mainland portion, **Labrador**, occupies the most eastern shore of Quebec; the capital of Newfoundland is St. John's. Short form: **Nfld.** A person living in or born in Newfoundland is a **Newfoundlander.**

news (nyūz, nūz) *n.* a report of events that happened recently: *We watch the news on television and read it in the newspaper.*

newscast (nyūz′ kast′, nūz′ kast′) *n.* a TV or radio program that presents the news.

newspaper (nyūz′ pā′ pər, nūz′ pā′ pər) *n.* a daily or weekly paper with news, stories, pictures, ads, etc.

newsstand (nyūz′ stand′, nūz′ stand′) *n.* a place that sells newspapers or magazines.

next (nekst) *adj.* **1.** the nearest: *I live in the next apartment.* **2.** the one after this: *I will phone you next week. adv.* in the nearest time or place: *What will you do next?* **next door** in the nearest room, apartment, building, etc.: *Olga's friends live next door to her.*

nibble (nibl) *v.* to eat something in small bites. **nibbling. nibbled.**

nice (nīs) *adj.* pleasant; good: *a nice day; a nice person; a nicer one; the nicest one of all.*

nick (nik) *n.* a small cut in the surface of something: *a nick in a table top.*

nickel (nik′ əl) *n.* **1.** a hard, silver-white metal. **2.** a five-cent coin in Canada and the United States.

nickname (nik′ nām′) *n.* a name used instead of a person's real name: *Barry was given the nickname 'Red' by his friends.*

niece (nēs) *n.* the daughter of a brother or sister: *My cousin Mary is my father's niece.*

night (nīt) *n.* the time when it is dark, between sunset and sunrise.

nightgown (nīt′ gaùn′) *n.* a loose dress worn to bed by women and girls.

nightly (nīt′ lē) *adv.* happening each night: *Erika runs nightly for exercise.*

nightmare (nīt′ mer′) *n.* a frightening dream.

nine (nīn) *n., adj.* one more than eight (9).

nineteen (nīn′ tēn′) *n., adj.* ten more than nine (19).

ninety (nīn′ tē) *n., adj.* ten times nine (90). *pl.* **nineties.**

ninth (nīnth) *adj.* following eighth (9th).

nipple (nipl) *n.* **1.** the small, round bump in the middle of each breast. **2.** the tip of a baby's bottle, which he or she sucks on.

no (nō) *adv.* the opposite of yes: *Can you swim? No.* *adj.* not any: *I have no brothers.*

nobody (nō′ budi, nō′ bod′ ē) *pron.* no one; not even one person: *Nobody is home.*

nod (nod) *v.* to bend the head up and down: *He nodded, showing that he agreed with what I said.* **nodding. nodded.**

noise (noiz) *n.* **1.** a loud and unpleasant sound: *the noise of the trucks.* **2.** any sound: *Do you hear a noise in the kitchen?*

noisy (noiz′ ē) *adj.* making a lot of noise: *a noisy truck; a noisier truck; the noisiest truck of all.*

nominate (nom′ i nāt′) *v.* to choose someone to be a candidate for a position in government, in a club, etc. **nominating. nominated.**

non- a prefix meaning 'no' or 'not': **nonsense** means something that makes no sense; a **non-stop** train does not stop along the way.

none (nun) *pron.* not one; not any: *None of my brothers is home.*

nonsense (non′ sens) *n.* action or talk that is silly and makes no sense.

noodles (nūdlz) *n.pl.* a food made of flour, water, and eggs, shaped in strips and boiled or fried.

noon (nūn) *n.* twelve o'clock in the daytime; the middle of the day.

no one (nō′ wun′) *pron.* nobody; no person: *No one wanted cake.*

noose (nūs) *n.* a loop of rope with a knot that tightens when the rope is pulled.

nor (nor) *conj.* and not; used after **neither**: *Neither my dog nor my cat likes to eat liver.*

normal (norml, nor′ məl) *adj.* ordinary; usual: *It is normal to be thirsty on a hot day.*

north (north) *n.* **1.** the direction to the left as a person faces the sunrise; opposite to south. **2. the North**, in Canada, the northern parts of provinces from Quebec to B.C.; the Northwest Territories; and the Yukon.

North American (north′ ə mer′ i kən) *n.* a person born in or living in Canada, Mexico, or the United States. *adj.* belonging to or coming from North America.

northern (nor′ thərn) *adj.* in or towards the north: *Canada is a northern country.*

North Pole (north′ pōl′) the most northern point of the earth; it is the north end of the axis of the earth.

Northwest Territories (north′ west ter′ i tō′ rēz) the territory in northern Canada, east of the Yukon Territory; its capital is Yellowknife. Short form: **N.W.T.**

nose (nōz) *n.* the part of the face that sticks out above the mouth. It has two nostrils or holes, through which people smell and breathe.
pay through the nose to pay too much for something.
under a person's nose easy to see; right in front of a person: *The hammer is right under your nose; it's on the table where you're sitting!*

nosey, nosy (nō′ zē) *adj.* overly curious; always wanting to know what others are doing: *a nosey person; a nosier one; the nosiest one of all.*

nostril (nos′ tril) *n.* one of the two openings in the nose.

not (not) *adv.* a word meaning 'no' or 'the opposite': *I will not be home. I do not like chocolate.*

notch (noch) *n.* a 'V'-shaped cut marked on an edge or surface of something. *pl.* **notches.** *v.* to make such a cut. **notching. notched.** he **notches.**

⊖**note** (nōt) *n.* **1.** a short letter: *She sent her friends a short note thanking them for the party.*

2. words written down to help a person remember something. **3.** a piece of paper money. **4.** a single musical sound, or a sign that stands for it. *v.* to notice closely; to pay attention to: *Note all the people in the picture.* **noting. noted.** **take note of** to pay attention to: *Take note of the hole in the road.*

notebook (nōt′ bůk′) *n.* a book with blank pages on which to write.

noted (nō′ təd) *adj.* famous: *a noted explorer.*

nothing (nuth′ ing) *n.* **1.** not anything: *She told me nothing.* **2.** in arithmetic, zero (0).

⊖**notice** (nō′ tis) *n.* **1.** a written or printed announcement or poster: *The notice says, 'Keep off the grass'.* **2.** a warning; an announcement in advance: *Two months' notice is required if you want to end this apartment lease.* *v.* to see: *Did you notice that I got my hair cut?* **noticing. noticed.**

notify (nō′ ti fī′) *v.* to let someone know; to send a note: *The dentist notified me about my appointment.* **notifying. notified.** he **notifies.**

notion (nō′ shən) *n.* an idea: *a strange notion.*

noun (naůn) *n.* a word giving the name of a person, place, quality, or thing: *'Alice', 'cat', 'honesty', 'football', and 'Canada' are some nouns.*

nourish (nûr′ ish) *v.* to give a living thing what it needs to grow strong and healthy: *Milk nourishes small children.* **nourishing. nourished.** it **nourishes.**

Nova Scotia (nō′ və skō′ shə) the province between New Brunswick on the north and the Atlantic Ocean on the south; its capital is Halifax. Short form: **N.S.** A person living in or born in Nova Scotia is a **Nova Scotian.**

⊖**novel** (nov′ əl) *n.* a long story, in a book form, usually about made-up people and events. *adj.* unusual, surprising or new: *Home computers were a novel idea in the 1960s.*

November (nō vem′ bər) *n.* the eleventh month of the year.

now (naů) *adv.* at present: *Please come now. The car is here.* **now and then** occasionally; once in a while: *Jim comes to visit now and then.*

nowhere (nō′ wer′, nō′ hwer′) *adv.* in no place; not anywhere: *My keys are nowhere to be found.*

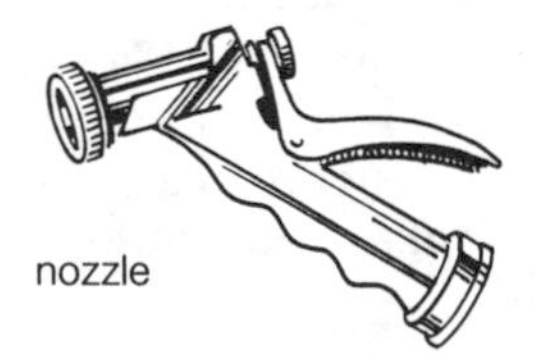
nozzle

nozzle (nozl) *n.* a tip on a pipe or hose that lets a person control the gas or liquid that flows out.

nuclear (nyū′ klē ər, nū′ klē ər) *adj.* having to do with atoms and the energy they release: *A nuclear reactor is a device that produces atomic energy.*

nude (nyūd, nūd) *adj.* naked; without clothes.

nudge (nuj) *v.* to push someone with an elbow to attract his or her attention. **nudging. nudged.**

nugget (nug′ ət) *n.* a rough lump of metal, usually gold.

⊖**nuisance** (nyū′ səns, nū′ səns) *n.* something that is annoying to people, or someone who bothers other people.

numb (num) *adj.* without any feeling: *My feet were numb with cold.*

⊖**number** (num′ bər) *n.* **1.** a word or symbol saying how many: **two, four, six, 2, 4,** and **6** are numbers. **2.** a particular set of numerals that identifies something: *a telephone number; a licence number.* **3.** a group: *A large number of people work here.* *v.* to count or to put a number to something: *Number the pages.*

numeral (nyū′ mər əl, nū′ mər əl) *n.* a written number: *4, IV, 21, 101, and twelve are all examples of numerals.*

numerator (nyū′ mər ā′ tər, nū′ mər ā′ tər) *n.* in a fraction, the number above the line: *In the fraction 3/8, 3 is the numerator.*

numerical (nyū mer′ i kəl, nū mer′ i kəl) *adj.* having to do with numbers: *1, 2, 3, 4, 5 are written in numerical order.*

numerous (nyū′ mər əs, nū′ mər əs) *adj.* very many: *Do you have time to answer my numerous questions?*

nun (nun) *n.* one of a group of religious women who have chosen to follow certain rules and live together in a religious community known as a **convent**.

nurse (nûrs) *n.* a person who looks after the sick, the old, and the very young. *v.* **1.** to care for these people. **2.** to give milk to a baby or small animal from a nipple. **nursing. nursed.**

nursery (nûr′ sər ē) *n.* **1.** a room or building for very young children. **2.** a place where young plants are looked after. *pl.* **nurseries.**

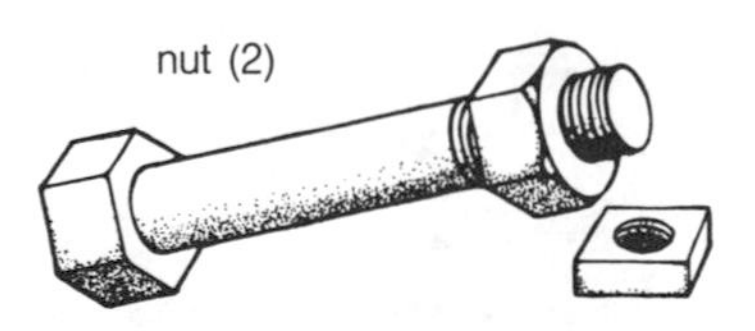

nut (nut) *n.* **1.** a dry fruit or seed with a hard shell: *A chestnut, a walnut, and a cashew are some kinds of nuts.* **2.** a small piece of metal with a hole in the centre: *A nut screws onto a bolt.* **3.** *(informal)* a person who does silly things.

nutritious (nyū trish′ əs, nū trish′ əs) *adj.* providing food that is needed for health: *This cereal is delicious and nutritious.*

nylon (nī′ lon) *n.* **1.** a strong substance made from chemicals and used to make thread, stockings, and other things. **2. nylons** women's stockings made of this material.

O

oak (ōk) *n.* a tree having nuts called **acorns**; its hard wood is made into furniture.

oar (ȯr) *n.* a long pole with a flat blade at one end, used for rowing a boat.

oath (ōth) *n.* a very serious promise to tell the truth or to do something: *The new mayor took an oath to do the best job he could.* *pl.* **oaths** (ōt͟hz).

oatmeal (ōt′ mēl′) *n.* crushed grains of oats, cooked to make cereal.

oats (ōts) *n.pl.* a grain, grown like wheat, used for cereal and as feed for animals.

obedient (ō bē′ di ənt) *adj.* willing to obey: *He is an obedient child, always doing what his parents ask.*

obey (ō bā′) *v.* to do what is asked: *She obeyed her parents and was home by ten o'clock. Obey the law and don't drive too fast.*

object (ob′ jəkt) *n.* **1.** a thing that can be seen and touched: *What is that object in your hand?* **2.** an aim; a goal: *David's object in life is to be a sailor like his father.*

object (əb jekt′) *v.* to disagree with; to complain against: *He objected to all the noise in the building.*

objection (əb jek′ shən) *n.* a complaint or argument against something; a disagreement: *I have no objections to your plans for the holiday.*

obligation (ob′ li gā′ shən) *n.* something that a person must do: *She has already been paid for her work, so she has an obligation to finish it.*

oblong (ob′ long′) *adj.* having a shape that is longer than it is wide: *Do you want a square envelope or an oblong one?*

observatory (ob zûr′ və tòr′ ē) *n.* a building where there are telescopes for studying the stars. *pl.* **observatories.**

observe (ob zûrv′) *v.* **1.** to watch carefully: *I observed every move he made.* **2.** to celebrate; to remember a special day: *We observed Thanksgiving by telling why we were thankful.* **3.** to follow; to obey: *Observe the rules of the game.* **observing. observed.**

obstacle (ob′ stəkl) *n.* something that is in the way, keeping a person from going forward.

obtain (ob tān′) *v.* to get something through effort: *He obtained the information by talking to five people.*

obvious (ob′ vi əs) *adj.* easy to see or understand. *It is obvious that David is taller than his brother.*

⊖**occasion** (o kā′ zhən) *n.* a particular event or time: *The picnic was a happy occasion.* **on occasion** once in a while: *Doris likes to go to the movies on occasion.*

⊖**occasional** (o kā′ zhən əl) *adj.* happening sometimes but not often: *There were occasional flashes of lightning.*

occupant (ok′ yə pənt) *n.* a person who lives in a certain place: *He has been the occupant of the old house for many years.*

occupation (ok′ yə pē′ shən) *n.* **1.** the work that someone does for a living; a job: *Farming is a farmer's occupation.* **2.** the act of occupying a place.

occupy (ok′ yə pī′) *v.* **1.** to fill in space; to live in: *My family occupies that apartment.* **2.** to fill in time: *Reading occupies much of her time in the evening.* **3.** to take possession and control of a place: *During the war, the soldiers occupied the city.* **occupying. occupied.** it **occupies.**

occur (ə kûr′) *v.* **1.** to take place; to happen or appear: *New Year's Day occurs on Monday this year.* **2.** to come to a person's thoughts: *It occurs to me that I must visit my friend.* **occurring. occurred.**

ocean (ō′ shən) *n.* **1.** the large area of salt water that covers a great part of the earth. **2.** one of the five sections into which this area is divided: *the Atlantic, Pacific, Indian, Arctic, and Antarctic Oceans.*

o'clock (ə klok′) short for 'of the clock' (according to the clock): *The time is ten o'clock.*

October (ok tō′ bər) *n.* the tenth month of the year.

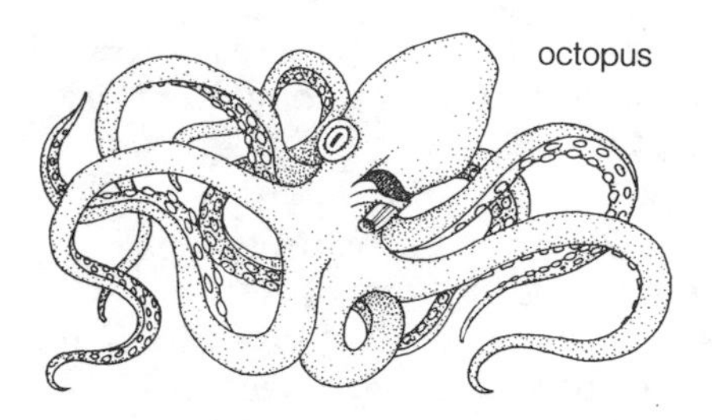

octopus (ok′ tə pəs) *n.* an animal that lives in the ocean; it has eight tentacles, with suckers on the end of each. *pl.* **octopuses** or **octopi** (ok′ tə pī).

odd (od) *adj.* **1.** not even in number; not able to be divided exactly by two: *Seven, nine, and eleven are odd numbers.* **2.** different; strange: *a very odd story.* **3.** occasional; not regular: *The student does odd jobs during the summer.*
odds and ends small things of different types, usually not valuable: *There are odds and ends in the bottom drawer.*

odour, odor (ō′ dər) *n.* a smell, usually an unpleasant one.

of (ov, uv, əv) *prep.* **1.** made from: *a piece of iron.* **2.** belonging to: *a member of the team.* **3.** holding: *a shaker of salt.* **4.** about: *I heard of the book in class.* **5.** called; that is: *the city of Halifax.*

off (of) *prep.* away from: *The book fell off the table.* *adj.* not happening: *The party is off.* *adv.* **1.** away: *Is he at work, or is he off today? The dog ran off.* **2.** the opposite of **on**: *Please take off your coat. Turn the light off before you leave.*
be off to leave: *It's late; we must be off soon.*
off and on once in a while; occasionally: *She lived at home off and on for a year.*

offence, offense (ə fens′, o′ fəns) *n.* **1.** a crime; a breaking of the rules: *Driving through a red light is a traffic offence.* **2.** an attacking team: *The hockey team has a strong offence.*

offend (ə fend′) *v.* to make someone angry or unhappy; to do something wrong: *His shouting offends many people.*

offensive (ə fen′ siv) *n.* an attack, usually in war or sports: *The team took the offensive.* *adj.* rude; unpleasant; causing hurt: *He apologized for the offensive remark.*

offer (of′ ər) *n.* **1.** a price suggested by a person who wants to buy something: *an offer of ten dollars.* **2.** a proposal: *an offer of marriage.* *v.* to present for someone to take or refuse: *She offered to help me with the work.*

⊖**office** (of′ is) *n.* **1.** a building or room where work is done: *a dentist's office.* **2.** an important position of responsibility: *the office of mayor.*

officer (of′ i sər) *n.* **1.** a member of the armed forces who has the responsibility to command others. **2.** a police officer. **3.** a person who has a job of responsibility in a company, government, or other organization.

official (ə fish′ əl) *n.* a person with certain important duties; an officer: *a bank official.* *adj.* genuine; approved; having authority: *English and French are the official languages of Canada.*

offshore (of′ shȯr′) *adj.* being away from the shore.

offspring (of′ spring′) *n.* children: *They were married for many years, but had no offspring.*

often (of′ ən, ȯf′ tən) *adv.* many times: *We often go swimming in the summer.*

oh (ō) *interj.* **1.** an expression used to express feelings such as happiness, surprise, or pain. **2.** an expression used when talking to someone before saying his or her name: *Oh, Paula, what are you doing on the weekend?*

oil (ȯil) *n.* **1.** a thick, greasy liquid that comes from animals and plants and is often used in cooking. **2.** a liquid or semi-solid mineral related to coal that is found in deposits under the ground. Also called **petroleum**. *v.* to grease something with oil.

ointment (ȯint′ mənt) *n.* a kind of medicine that is rubbed onto the skin.

okay, O.K. (ō′ kā′, ō′ kā′) *adj., adv.* all right; all correct: *Okay, I will go with you. Everything is okay.*

old (ōld) *adj.* **1.** having existed or lived for a long time: *an old tree.* **2.** having lived for a certain time: *The cat is six years old.*

old-fashioned (ōld′ fash′ ənd) *adj.* out-of-date; not modern: *The child put an old-fashioned dress on the doll.*

olive (ol′ iv) *n.* a small oily fruit, grown on an evergreen tree in warm places.

Olympic games (ō lim′ pik gāmz′) athletic contests in which athletes from different countries compete. Olympic games are held every four years.

Olympics short for **Olympic games.**

ombudsman (om′ bu̇dz mən) *n.* a government official who investigates people's complaints about the government. *pl.* **ombudsmen.**

omelette, omelet (om′ lət) *n.* a food made from eggs which have been whipped and fried: *a mushroom omelette; a cheese omelette.*

on (on) *prep.* **1.** on top of; touching: *The pencil is on the desk.* **2.** during: *I shopped on Monday.* **3.** in the state of: *The house is on fire.* **4.** about: *I read a book on the animals of Canada.* *adv.* **1.** farther: *Let us go on.* **2.** the opposite of **off**: *Please turn the light on.*
and so on and more of the same thing: *We brought apples, oranges, grapes, and so on.*

once (wuns) *adv.* **1.** one time: *I have worn these shoes only once.* **2.** in the past; a long time ago: *There was once a field where the house is now.* *conj.* as soon as: *Once you try to swim, you'll find that it is fun.*
at once **1.** now: *Do it at once!* **2.** at the same time: *They all answered at once.*
once in a while occasionally: *Ed visits his cousin once in a while.*

one (wun) *n.* the first whole number after zero (1). *adj.* **1.** a single: *There is one cup on the table.* **2.** some: *One day I will read that book.* *pron.* any person: *One never knows what may happen.*

one-way street (wun′ wā′ strēt′) a street with traffic going in one direction only.

onion (un′ yən) *n.* a round, strong-smelling bulb that is used as a vegetable.

only (ōn′ lē) *adj.* single: *an only child in a family.* *adv.* simply;

just: *I won only one game of chess.* *conj.* but: *I wanted to go, only I had a cold.*

Ontario (on terʹ i ō) *n.* the province between Manitoba on the west and Quebec on the east; its capital is Toronto. Short form: **Ont.** A person living in or born in Ontario is an **Ontarian.**

onto (onʹ tü) *prep.* to a position on: *He threw the ball onto the roof.*

ooze (üz) *v.* to leak or flow slowly: *Oil oozed through the crack.* **oozing. oozed.**

open (ōʹ pən) *adj.* **1.** not shut; able to let things in or out: *The door is open. The box is open.* **2.** wide and clear: *the open sky.* **3.** available: *The job of welder is open.* *v.* **1.** to unfasten, uncover, or unseal: *Please open the door. I opened the envelope.* **2.** to start or be ready to start: *The store opens at ten o'clock.*
open up **1.** to make or become unfastened or uncovered: *The trunk opened up when I dropped it.* **2.** to be less shy; to make your thoughts known: *He finally opened up and told me what was bothering him.*

opening (ōʹ pən ing) *n.* **1.** a gap; a space: *an opening in the fence.* **2.** a beginning: *the opening of the football season.*

opera (opʹ ə rə) *n.* a play set to music, with the performers singing their parts.

operate (opʹ ə rātʹ) *v.* **1.** to work; to run; to function: *Can you operate this machine? The car is not operating well.* **2.** to perform surgery on a sick or injured person: *Dr. Chang will operate on my knee.* **operating. operated.**

⊖**operation** (opʹ ə rāʹ shən) *n.* **1.** the way a machine works. **2.** the cutting open of the body in surgery.

⊖**operator** (opʹ ə rāʹ tər) *n.* a person who operates a machine: *a telephone operator.*

opinion (ə pinʹ yən) *n.* what a person thinks or believes about someone or something: *What is your opinion of the team?*

opponent (ə pōʹ nənt) *n.* a person who is against another in a fight, argument, game, etc.

⊖**opportunity** (opʹ ər tyüʹ ni tē, opʹ ər tüʹ ni tē) *n.* a chance to do something: *Tomorrow I will have an opportunity to ski.* *pl.* **opportunities.**

oppose (ə pōzʹ) *v.* to fight or argue against: *The people of the town opposed the closing of the swimming pool.* **opposing. opposed.**

opposite (opʹ ə zit) *n.* a person or thing that is completely different: *The opposite of 'up' is 'down'.* *adj.* completely different: *We are going in the opposite direction from you.* *prep.* across from: *The house is opposite the school.*

optician (op tishʹ ən) *n.* a person who makes or sells eyeglasses and contact lenses.

optimist (opʹ ti mist) *n.* a person who always sees the happy side of things and believes everything will turn out well: *Carlos is an optimist; even when everything is going wrong, he is smiling.*

optional (opʹ shən əl) *adj.* not required; left to a person's choice: *Attendance at the extra classes is optional. You don't have to go if you don't want to.*

optometrist (op tomʹ ə trist) *n.* a person who tests people's eyes to see if they need eyeglasses.

or (ôr) *conj.* a word used to show a choice: *You can have an apple or an orange, but not both.*

oral (ȯr′ əl) *adj.* **1.** spoken; not written: *an oral report.* **2.** having to do with the mouth.

orange (ȯr′ ənj, or′ ənj) *n.* **1.** a reddish-yellow citrus fruit. **2.** a reddish-yellow colour. *adj.* **1.** having the flavour of an orange: *orange sherbet.* **2.** having a reddish-yellow colour.

orbit (ȯr′ bit) *n.* the path that a satellite, planet, or other heavenly body takes as it moves around another thing in space: *The earth makes an orbit around the sun once a year.* *v.* to move in such a path.

orchard (ȯr′ chərd) *n.* a garden of fruit trees.

⊖**orchestra** (ȯr′ kəs trə) *n.* **1.** a group of musicians playing a variety of instruments. **2.** the main floor of a theatre. *pl.* **orchestras.**

orchid (ȯr′ kid) *n.* a plant that has three petals, usually white or purple, with the middle one sometimes shaped like a cup.

ordeal (ȯr dēl′) *n.* a painful or difficult experience: *It was an ordeal for them to hike through the forest during the storm.*

⊖**order** (ȯr′ dər) *n.* **1.** tidiness; neatness: *Ray keeps his books in order.* **2.** a command: *She gave her dog an order to lie down.* **3.** a request: *Please give the waiter your order for lunch.* **4.** the way one thing follows another: *The words in a dictionary are arranged in alphabetical order.* **5.** a portion of food: *Jenny asked for one order of pie to share with her friend.* *v.* to command or request: *He ordered the dog to sit.*
in order to for the purpose of: *In order to get on the team, Marika had to practise daily.*
out of order broken, not working: *I did not watch the program because the television was out of order.*

ordinary (ȯr′ di ner′ ē) *adj.* usual; not special: *Yesterday was an ordinary day. Nothing unusual happened.*

ore (ȯr) *n.* rock or earth containing metal.

organs (1)

⊖**organ** (ȯr′ gən) *n.* **1.** a large musical instrument with a piano keyboard and pipes, from which the sounds come. **2.** a part of an animal or plant that does a certain job: *The ear is the organ of hearing.*

⊖**organization** (ȯrg′ ə ni zā′ shən) *n.* **1.** a group of people who work together for a purpose: *He belongs to an organization for people who enjoy music.* **2.** the putting in order of something: *The organization of a big party takes a lot of work.*

organize (ȯr′ gən īz′) *v.* **1.** to plan and arrange something: *Cheryl organized her records.* **2.** to bring together for a certain purpose: *The workers were organized into a union.* **organizing. organized.**

origin (ȯr′ i jin) *n.* source; beginning: *Vietnam is her country of origin.*

⊖**original** (ə rij′ i nəl) *adj.* **1.** brand new; not copied: *This story is original. I made it up myself.* **2.** the first: *I am the original owner of the house.*

ornament (ȯr′ nə mənt) *n.* a small object that is used for decoration.

orphan (ȯr′ fən) *n.* a child whose parents are dead.

orthodontist (ȯr′ thə don′ tist) *n.* a kind of dentist whose work is straightening teeth.

other (u<u>th</u>′ ər) *adj.* **1.** different: *I have other things to do.* **2.** opposite: *She lives on the other side of the street.* **3.** left; remaining: *The first story is funny, but the other ones are sad. pron.* a different or remaining person or thing: *I took one glass and left the others.*
every other each second; not every: *Max exercises every other day.*

otherwise (u<u>th</u>′ ər wīz′) *adv.* in other ways: *He has a messy desk, but otherwise he is neat. conj.* if not: *Put on a sweater; otherwise, you will be cold.*

Ottawa (ot′ ə wȯ, ot′ ə wə) *n.* the capital city of Canada.

otter

otter (ot′ ər) *n.* a water animal that has shiny brown fur and eats fish.

ouch (aůch) *interj.* a sound that tells of sudden pain.

ought (ȯt, ot) *v.* a verb used before another verb to mean 'should' or 'have a duty': *You ought to visit your sick friend.*

ounce (aůns) *n.* a measure of mass or weight equal to about 28 g.

our (aůr) *adj.* belonging to us: *This is our car.*

ours (aůrz) *pron.* the one or ones belonging to us: *The house is ours.*

ourselves (aůr selvz′) *pron. pl.* we alone: *We shall do it ourselves.*

out (aůt) *adv.* **1.** away; outside; not in: *Father is out.* **2.** not burning: *The fire is out.* **3.** the opposite of **on**: *The lights are out next door.* **4.** being seen: *The flowers are out now that spring is here.*
out of **1.** without: *We are out of bread.* **2.** because of: *Anna helped me out of kindness.* **3.** from: *Drink the water out of this glass.* **4.** away from: *I am going out of town.*
out-of-date old-fashioned; not used now: *out-of-date equipment.*

out- a prefix meaning 'more than', 'better than', or 'outside of': to **outnumber** means to be greater or more in number; to **outfight** means to fight better than the other person; the **outfield** is outside the playing field in certain games.

outboard (aůt′ bȯrd′) *n.* a small motor, attached to the outside of the back of a boat.

outcome (aůt′ kum′) *n.* the final result: *What was the outcome of last night's hockey game?*

outdoor (aůt′ dȯr′) *adj.* in the open air: *outdoor games.*

outdoors (aůt′ dȯrz′) *adv.* in or into the open air: *They went outdoors to play soccer.*

outer (aůt′ ər) *adj.* on the outside: *Open the outer door, but leave the inner door closed.*

outer space (aůt′ ər spās′) space beyond the earth's atmosphere.

outfit (aůt′ fit) *n.* **1.** a set of clothes: *She wore her new outfit to the wedding.* **2.** a set of equipment: *The tire repair outfit has everything you need to fix a damaged bicycle tire.*

outgrow (aůt grō′) *v.* to grow too big or too old for something: *Children outgrow their clothes quickly.* **outgrowing. outgrew** (aůt grū′). she has **outgrown.**

outing (aůt′ ing) *n.* a short trip out: *The family went on an outing to the park.*

outlaw (aůt′ lȯ′) *n.* a criminal; a person who fights against the law. *v.* to make illegal: *The town outlawed firecrackers because of their danger.*

outlet (2)

outlet (aůt′ let′) *n.* **1.** a way out: *The lake has several outlets.* **2.** a place on a wall for putting in an electrical plug.

outline (aůt′ līn′) *n.* **1.** in drawing, a line showing the shape of an object. **2.** a list of the main ideas for a story, report, or plan.

outlook (aůt′ lůk′) *n.* **1.** the way a situation appears: *The outlook for the zoo was not good. Very few people were visiting, and it was losing money every month.* **2.** the way a person looks at things; an attitude: *He has a very cheerful outlook, seeing something good in almost every situation.*

outnumber (aůt′ num′ bər) *v.* to be more than: *At the zoo, the tigers outnumber the lions.*

outport (aůt′ pȯrt′) *n.* **1.** a small harbour. **2.** a small fishing village along the coast of Newfoundland.

output (aůt′ půt′) *n.* the amount of something that is produced: *the output of tires from a factory.*

outside (aůt′ sīd′, aůt′ sīd′) *n.* the outer part: *the outside of the building. adv.* outdoors: *The children went outside to play.*

outskirts (aůt′ skûrts′) *n.pl.* the outer edge of an area: *I live on the outskirts of town.*

outstanding (aůt′ stand′ ing) *adj.* **1.** very excellent: *I saw an outstanding movie.* **2.** not paid: *That bill is outstanding. You owe me a dollar.*

oval (ō′ vəl) *adj.* having the shape of an egg.

ovary (ō′ və rē′) *n.* the part of a female in which eggs are produced. *pl.* **ovaries.**

oven (uv′ ən) *n.* the inside space in a stove, used for baking, roasting, and heating.

over (ō′ vər) *adv.* **1.** finished: *The movie is over.* **2.** again: *Do the job over.* **3.** down: *He bent over to wipe his shoe.* **4.** up and out of: *The soup boiled over.* **5.** to the other side: *Turn the book over. prep.* **1.** above: *The bird flew over our heads.* **2.** more than: *The book cost over five dollars.* **3.** above and across: *Jump over the fence.* **4.** about: *They had an argument over money.*
all over everywhere (in): *We travelled all over Manitoba.*
over and over again and again: *They discussed the problem over and over.*

over- a prefix meaning 'extra' or 'over': **overtime** means extra time; **overshoes** are worn over regular shoes.

overall (ō′ vər ȯl) *adj.* complete; total: *The overall length of the book is two hundred pages, including the index.*

overalls (ō′ vər ȯlz′) *n.pl.* loose work trousers, often with a part covering the chest and straps that go over the shoulders.

overboard (ō′ vər bȯrd′) *adv.* over a ship's side and into the water: *The sailor fell overboard.*

overcast (ō′ vər kast′) *adj.* cloudy all over the sky: *The sky was grey and overcast. It looked as if it would rain.*

overcoat (ō′ vər kōt′) *n.* a coat worn outdoors, over other clothing.

overcome (ō′ vər kum′) *v.* to succeed in finding an answer to; to go beyond: *At last, he overcame his fear of speaking a new language.* **overcoming. overcame.** (ō′ vər kām′). he has **overcome.**

overdo (ō′ vər dü′) *v.* to do or try to do too much: *You'll be very tired if you overdo your exercises.* **overdoing. overdid.** she **overdoes** (ō′ vər duz′). she has **overdone** (ō′ vər dun′).

overdose (ō′ vər dōs′) *n.* too large an amount of a drug.

overdraw (ō′ vər drȯ′) *v.* to write cheques for more money than a person has in his or her bank account. **overdrawing. overdrew.** I have **overdrawn.**

overdue (ō′ vər dyü′, ō′ vər dü′) *adj.* behind time; late: *My library book is overdue and must be returned.*

overflow (ō′ vər flō′) *v.* to spill over; to flood: *Turn off the water! The tub is overflowing.* **overflowing. overflowed.**

overhaul (ō′ vər hȯl′) *v.* to examine closely and make any changes or repairs that are necessary: *to overhaul a tractor's engine.*

overhead (ō′ vər hed′) *n.* the expenses for running a business, such as rent, heating, or taxes. *adv.* high above: *Birds fly overhead.*

overhear (ō′ vər hēr′) *v.* to hear someone speaking, who does not know you are listening: *I overheard them talking about the secret plans.* **overhearing. overheard** (ō′ vər hûrd′).

overheat (ō′ vər hēt′) *v.* to become too hot: *If you forget to put water in a car, the engine will overheat.*

overjoyed (ō′ vər jȯid′) *adj.* more than happy: *I was overjoyed when I won the contest.*

overlap (ō′ vər lap′) *v.* to cover part of something and sometimes reach beyond it: *One piece of paper overlapped another.* **overlapping. overlapped.**

overload (ō′ vər lōd′) *v.* to put too heavy a load in or on something: *If you overload the car, it will be hard to drive up the hill.*

overlook (ō′ vər lůk′) *v.* not to think about, consider, or notice: *Hilda overlooked the 'closed' sign on the door and walked in.*

overnight (ō′ vər nīt′) *adj.* for or during one night: *an overnight train ride from Montreal to Toronto.*

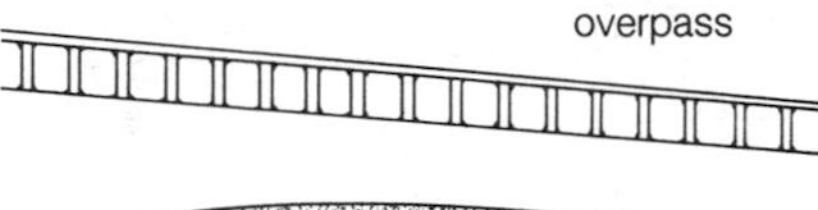

overpass (ō′ vər pas′) *n.* a road that is built high up so that it crosses over another road. *pl.* **overpasses.**

overseas (ō′ vər sēz′) *adv.* across the sea; in (to) another country: *My aunt lives overseas.*

overshoes (ō′ vər shüz′) *n.pl.* rubber or plastic shoes worn over ordinary shoes to keep them dry in the rain or snow.

overthrow (ō′ vər thrō′) *v.* to defeat; to force the people in charge to go: *The king was overthrown by the angry people.* **overthrowing. overthrew.** she has **overthrown.**

overtime (ō′ vər tīm′) *n.* **1.** extra time: *The game was tied, so they played overtime.* **2.** money paid for work done beyond the usual time.

overwhelming (ō′ vər wel′ ming, ō′ vər hwel′ ming) *adj.* enormous; too much to fight against: *The people gave their overwhelming support for the building of the new bridge.*

owe (ō) *v.* **1.** to have to pay; to be in debt: *I owe you a dollar.* **2.** to have to give: *He owes us an explanation for not coming home for dinner.* **owing. owed.**

owl (aůl) *n.* a bird with a large head, big eyes, and a sharp, hooked beak. Owls hunt at night.

own (ōn) *adj.* belonging to one person or group and nobody else: *This is my own boat.* *v.* to have; to possess: *Do you own that car?*

owner (ōn′ ər) *n.* a person who owns something.

oxygen (ok′ si jən) *n.* a gas that has no colour or smell, needed to keep animals and plants alive. Oxygen is part of the air we breathe.

oyster (ȯis′ tər) *n.* a round shellfish with a hard shell in two parts. Some kinds of oysters produce pearls, and others are eaten as food.

P

pa (pȧ) *n.* *(informal)* father.

pace (pās) *n.* the speed of moving: *A turtle moves at a slow pace.* *v.* to walk back and forth: *Father paced the room thinking about something.* **pacing. paced.**

Pacific (pə sif′ ik) *adj.* having to do with the Pacific Ocean: *Pacific salmon.*

Pacific Ocean the ocean extending from North America and South America to Asia and Australia.

⊖**pack** (pak) *n.* **1.** a bundle: *He carried a pack on his back.* **2.** a group of people, animals, or things: *a pack of wolves; a pack of cards.* *v.* **1.** to put into a bundle, or to put clothes into a case: *She packed for the trip.* **2.** to crowd into a room or other area: *There were many people packed into the elevator.*

package (pak′ ij) *n.* **1.** something wrapped in paper and closed with string or tape. **2.** a container with things inside: *a package of cereal.*

⊖**pad** (pad) *n.* **1.** sheets of paper for writing on, glued together on one edge. **2.** a cushion; a soft pillow. **3.** the launching area for rocket ships.

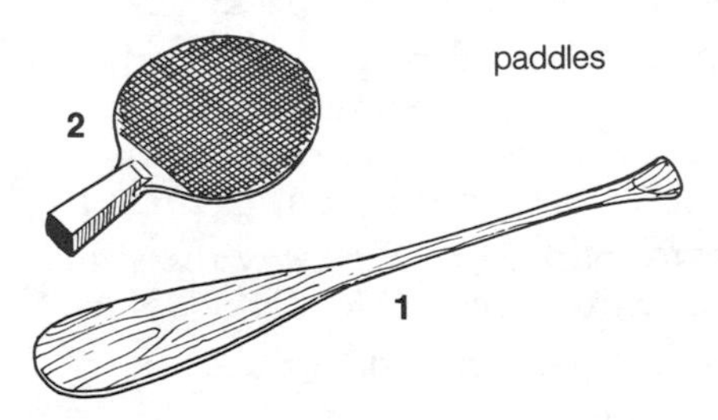

paddles

paddle (padl) *n.* **1.** a short oar used to move a canoe. **2.** a board used to hit the ball in the game of ping-pong. *v.* to move a canoe with a paddle. **paddling. paddled.**

page (pāj) *n.* **1.** one side of a sheet of paper. **2.** a person who does errands at a hotel, or who is a messenger at the House of Commons, the Senate, or the Legislative Assembly.

paid see **pay.**

pail

pail (pāl) *n.* a deep, round container with a handle; a bucket.

⊖**pain** (pān) *n.* an ache; the feeling of being hurt.

painful (pān′ fəl) *adj.* hurting; giving pain: *a painful injury.*

paint (pānt) *n.* a liquid to be brushed onto a surface for colour and protection. *v.* **1.** to cover with paint. **2.** to make a picture or a design with paint.

painting (pānt′ ing) *n.* a painted picture.

pair (per) *n.* two things of a kind that go together: *a pair of socks; a pair of gloves.*

pajamas see **pyjamas.**

pal (pal) *n.* a close friend.

palace (pal′ əs) *n.* the home of a king or other ruler, usually very large and beautiful.

pale (pāl) *adj.* weak in colour: *a pale colour; a paler colour; the palest colour of all. She has always had a pale complexion.*

⊖**palm** (pȧm) *n.* **1.** the inside of the hand. **2.** a type of tree, found in warm places, with fan-shaped leaves.

pamper (pam′ pər) *v.* to give someone whatever he or she wants; to be too kind.

pamphlet (pam′ flət) *n.* a thin booklet with a paper cover.

⊖**pan** (pan) *n.* a metal dish with a handle, used for cooking. *v.* to wash sand in a pan to separate the gold in it. **panning. panned.**

pancake (pan′ cāk′) *n.* a very thin, round cake of eggs, flour, and milk, mixed together and cooked in a pan: *Pancakes are usually served for breakfast, with butter and syrup.*

pane (pān) *n.* a sheet of glass in a window or door frame.

panel (pan′ əl) *n.* a part of something that is different in some way (higher, lower, thicker) from the surface around it: *We put wooden panels on the wall.* **2.** a board on which dials or instruments are fastened. **3.** a group of people taking part in a discussion or judging a contest.

panic (pan′ ik) *n.* sudden fear that makes people or animals want to run away. *v.* to have this kind of fear: *The horses panicked when they saw the fire.* **panicking. panicked.**

pansy (pan′ zē) *n.* a garden flower with flat, round, velvet-like blossoms. *pl.* **pansies.**

pant (pant) *v.* to gasp for breath: *After the race, everyone was panting.*

panties (pan′ təz) *n.pl.* **1.** a woman's underpants. **2.** a child's underpants.

pants (pants) *n.pl.* trousers.

panty hose (pan′ ti hōz′) sheer stockings, worn by women, that cover the feet, legs, and body up to the waist.

papa (pȧ′ pə) *n. (informal)* father.

paper (pā′ pər) *n.* a thin material used for writing, printing, wrapping things, etc.

paperback (pā′ pər bak′) *n.* a book with a soft cover.

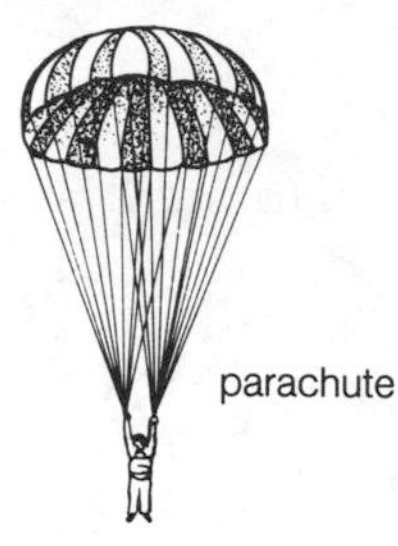

parachute (par′ ə shūt′) *n.* a large sheet of thin material that is shaped like an umbrella, with cords attached. A parachute is tied to someone's back so that he or she can jump out of an airplane and fall slowly to the ground.

parade (pə rād′) *n.* a march in honour of a special person or event.

paradise (par′ ə dīs′) *n.* heaven; a place of perfect happiness.

paragraph (par′ ə graf′) *n.* a few sentences on a page of writing: *A paragraph begins on a new line. The sentences in a paragraph are usually about the same subject.*

parallel (par′ ə lel) *adj.* going in the same direction and never meeting: *Railway lines are parallel.*

paralyse, paralyze (par′ ə līze′) *v.* to make part of the body unable to move or feel. **paralysing. paralysed.**

⊖**parcel** (pȧr′ səl) *n.* a package.

pardon (pȧr′ dən) *v.* **1.** to forgive; to free someone from punishment. **2.** to excuse: *Pardon me. I would like to get to the front of the bus.*

pare (pār) *v.* to cut away the skin of a fruit or vegetable. **paring. pared.**

⊖**parent** (per′ ənt) *n.* a father or mother.

parenthesis (pə ren′ thə sis) *n.* one of the curved lines () that are used to separate a special word or explanation from the rest of a sentence. The words 'the Rideau'

are in parentheses in the sentence, *A canal (the Rideau) flows through the City of Ottawa.*
pl. **parentheses** (pə ren′ thə sēz).

park (pärk) *n.* **1.** a piece of land with trees, benches, and play areas. **2.** a large piece of land protected by the government and used by campers, hikers, and others: *a provincial park; a national park.* *v.* to leave a car somewhere for a time.

parka (pär′ kə) *n.* a windproof jacket with a hood, made of fur or cloth and worn in cold places. *pl.* **parkas.**

parking lot (pär′ king lot′) a large area near a shopping centre, office building, apartment building, or other busy place where people leave their cars.

parkway (pärk′ wā′) *n.* a wide road or highway with trees and plants growing on the sides or in the centre. *pl.* **parkways.**

parliament (pär′ lə mənt) *n.* in certain countries, a group of people chosen to make laws: *The House of Commons and the Senate make up the Canadian Parliament.*

parlour, parlor (pär′ lər) *n.* **1.** a room in a house where visitors are entertained. **2.** a shop that offers a special service: *She had her hair cut at the beauty parlour.*

⊖**parole** (pə rōl′) *n.* an arrangement for letting a prisoner out of jail before the full sentence has been served. The **parolee** must obey certain rules during the period of his or her parole: *The thief was sentenced to ten years in prison, but behaved so well that he was released on parole after five years.*

parrot (par′ ət) *n.* a brightly coloured bird that lives in hot places, has a large curved beak, and can be taught to say words.

parsley (pärs′ lē) *n.* a plant with small leaves that are used to flavour foods.

⊖**part** (pärt) *n.* **1.** a piece; not the whole: *Chris and Jean ate part of the cake.* **2.** a person or character in a play, movie, television program, etc.: *The actress took the part of a famous writer.* **3.** one side in an argument: *I took Jason's part.* **4.** a line dividing the hair on the head. *v.* **1.** to separate: *to part your hair.* **2.** to leave: *After the meal, we decided to part.*

partial (pär′ shəl) *adj.* **1.** not complete: *His repairs to the car were a partial success. The engine started, but the car would not move.* **2.** liking one side more than the other: *We lost the game because the referee was partial to the other team.*

participate (pär tis′ i pāt′) *v.* to join in: *Everybody in the company participated in the yearly baseball game.* **participating. participated.**

participle (pär′ ti sipl) *n.* a form of a verb that helps another verb in a sentence.
Note: See **past participle** and **present participle.**

⊖**particular** (pär tik′ yə lər) *adj.* **1.** very careful; hard to please: *Kay is particular about keeping her desk clean.* **2.** special; having to do with a certain thing or person: *I like that particular car, but not the others.*

particularly (pär tik′ yə lər lē) *adv.* especially; most of all: *She likes all vegetables, particularly carrots.*

⊖**partition** (pȧr tish**′** ən) *n.* a small wall to divide an area in two parts: *A partition separated Linda's part of the room from her sister's part.*

partly (pȧrt**′** lē) *adv.* in part; not completely: *You are partly correct. A few facts are wrong.*

partner (pȧrt**′** nər) *n.* **1.** someone who shares a business. **2.** a husband or wife. **3.** someone dancing with another. **4.** someone playing on the same side in a game.

part of speech (pȧrt**′** uv spēch**′**) in grammar, the name given to a word that has a particular function, such as a verb, noun, adjective, or adverb.

partridge (pȧr**′** trij) *n.* a wild bird that has grey, white, and brown feathers.

part-time (pȧrt**′** tīm′, pȧrt′ tīm**′**) *adv.* working for only a few hours a day or a few days a week: *Bill goes to school during the day, and in the evenings he works part-time at the hospital.*

⊖**party** (pȧr**′** tē) *n.* **1.** a gathering for fun or celebration: *a birthday party.* **2.** a group of people with the same political ideas: *There are three major political parties in Canada.* **3.** a group of people doing something together: *A search party looked for the lost child.* *pl.* **parties.**

⊖**pass** (pas) *n.* **1.** a way or opening between mountains. **2.** a free ticket: *a pass for the movies.* **3.** the moving or throwing of a puck or ball between players. *pl.* **passes.** *v.* **1.** to go past: *We passed the slow car on the highway.* **2.** to hand something to someone: *Please pass the butter.* **3.** to complete a test successfully: *He passed the driving test.* **4.** to make into law: *Parliament passed the bill.* **passing. passed.** he **passes.**
Note: Do not confuse **passed** and **past**; **passed** is used only as a verb.

pass out 1. to hand out; to distribute: *The teacher passed out the papers to the class.* **2.** to faint: *When he won the money, he was so surprised that he nearly passed out.*

passage (pas**′** əj) *n.* **1.** the act of passing: *the passage of time.* **2.** a corridor or hallway. **3.** part of a piece of literature or music: *Certain passages of the symphony moved me deeply.*

passbook (pas**′** bu̇k′) *n.* a small book in which information about a person's bank account is shown.

passenger (pas**′** ən jər) *n.* a traveller in a ship, airplane, car, or some other vehicle, who is not the driver or a crew member.

passion (pash**′** ən) *n.* a strong feeling of love, hate, or excitement.

Passover (pas**′** ōv ər) *n.* a Jewish holiday in March or April, celebrating the Jewish people's freedom from slavery.

passport (pas**′** pȯrt′) *n.* special papers needed for passing from one country to another.

past (past) *n.* time that has gone by: *In the past, people travelled by horse.* *adj.* just ended: *It has rained a lot during the past month.* *prep.* beyond; passing by: *She drove past our house.*
Note: Do not confuse **past** and **passed**; **past** is never used as a verb.

pasta (pȧs**′** tə) *n.* spaghetti, macaroni, and similar foods made of flour and water and usually served with a sauce.

⊖**paste** (pāst) *n.* a thick mixture used for sticking things together. *v.* to use this mixture: *We pasted the paper on the wall.* **pasting. pasted.**

pasteurize (pas**′** ter iz′, pas**′** chər īz′) *v.* to heat milk enough to kill germs. **pasteurizing. pasteurized.**

past participle (past**′** pȧr**′** ti sipl) a form of a verb that is used with another verb to describe something that has already happened. In the sentences, 'The children have returned' and 'The dog had died', the words 'returned' and 'died' are past participles.

pastry (pās′ trē) *n.* **1.** a paste made of dough and used for the bottom, sides, and top of pies. **2.** sweet baked goods. *pl.* **pastries.**

pasture (pas′ chər) *n.* grassland for cattle or other animals to feed on.

pat (pat) *n.* a gentle tap: *a pat on the shoulder.* *v.* to tap gently with the hand: *Yvonne patted the friendly dog.* **patting. patted.**

patch (pach) *n.* **1.** a small piece of cloth that covers a hole: *I sewed a patch on my jeans.* **2.** a small area: *a vegetable patch.* *pl.* **patches.** *v.* to mend with a patch. **patching. patched.** she **patches.**

path (path) *n.* **1.** a trail or narrow way for walking, bicycling, etc.: *a path in the garden.* **2.** the route along which something moves: *the moon's path.* *pl.* **paths** (pat͟hz).

patience (pā′ shəns) *n.* the ability to wait a long time or work on a hard job without complaining.

patient (pā′ shənt) *n.* a person who is being treated by a doctor or dentist. *adj.* calm; waiting or working steadily without fuss: *Be patient! The bus will be here soon.*

patio (pat′ ē ō) *n.* a paved area attached to a house, used for sitting, eating, etc. *pl.* **patios.**

patriot (pā′ tri ət) *n.* a person who loves his or her country and supports it loyally.

patrol (pə trōl′) *n.* a small group of soldiers or police officers who are on guard. *v.* to walk about an area, guarding it. **patrolling. patrolled.**

pattern (pat′ ərn) *n.* **1.** a model to be copied: *a paper pattern for a dress.* **2.** a design: *a pattern of squares on a dress.*

patty (pat′ ē) *n.* a thin, round piece of food: *a meat patty; a salmon patty.* *pl.* **patties.**

pause (pȯs) *n.* a short stop: *They took a pause in their work.* *v.* to stop for a short time: *The runner paused for a drink.* **pausing. paused.**

⊖**pave** (pāv) *v.* to cover a street, driveway, etc., with a flat surface of tar or cement. **paving. paved.**

pavement (pāv′ mənt) *n.* a paved area.

paw (pȯ) *n.* the foot of a four-footed animal having nails or claws.

pawn (pȯn) *n.* in chess, one of the sixteen pieces of the lowest value. *v.* to leave an object at a pawn shop, getting money for it. The object can be taken back when the money is repaid, with interest.

pay (pā) *n.* the money received for work done: *After two weeks, he was given his pay.* *v.* **1.** to give money in return for goods, or for work done: *She paid for the coat.* **2.** to give something other than money: *Pay attention. I am saying something important.* **3.** to be good for a person in some way: *It pays to be honest.* **paying. paid.** he **pays.**
pay out to make payments to others: *That corporation pays out thousands of dollars every month.*

payment (pā′ mənt) *n.* money that is paid: *The payments on the car are made the first day of each month.*

pea (pē) *n.* a small, round green seed that grows in a pod and is used for food. *pl.* **peas.**

peace (pēs) *n.* **1.** a time of quiet. **2.** a time when there is no war.

peaceful (pēs′ fəl) *adj.* **1.** quiet and calm: *a peaceful day.* **2.** loving peace: *a peaceful nation.*

peach (pēch) *n.* a round, juicy fruit that has a velvet-like, yellow-orange skin and a large pit. *pl.* **peaches.**

peacock (pē′ kok′) *n.* a large male bird with beautiful green, blue, and gold tail feathers. The female does not have the same brilliant tail feathers.

peak (pēk) *n.* **1.** the highest point: *The peak of the mountain.* **2.** the front part of a cap.

peanut (pē′ nut′) *n.* a seed like a nut that grows in a yellow-brown shell: *One shell usually holds two peanuts.*

peanut butter (pē′ nut but′ ər) a spread made of ground-up peanuts.

pear (per) *n.* a green, yellow, or brown juicy fruit, round at the bottom and smaller near the stem end.

pearl (pûrl) *n.* a precious gem, usually white, found in some oyster and mussel shells.

⊖**peasant** (pez′ ənt) *n.* a farm worker in some countries.

pebble (pebl) *n.* a small, round stone.

pecan (pē kan′, pi kȧn′) *n.* a nut that grows in a thin, reddish shell and has a sweet taste.

peck (pek) *v.* to jab at food and pick it up with the beak: *a hen pecking at corn.*

peculiar (pi kyūl′ yər) *adj.* strange; different: *My cat is peculiar. It's scared of mice!*

pedal (ped′ əl) *n.* **1.** the part on which to place the foot in order to move a vehicle or other machine: *a bicycle pedal.* **2.** the part of a piano or organ on which to place the foot. *v.* to make a bicycle move by turning the pedals with the feet. **pedalling. pedalled.**

pedestrian (pə des′ tri ən) *n.* someone who travels on foot.

pediatrician (pē′ di ə trish′ ən) *n.* a doctor who looks after children.

peek (pēk) *n.* a quick look: *Take a peek at the baby.* *v.* to look at something quickly.

peel (pēl) *n.* the skin of a fruit or vegetable: *potato peel; orange peel.* *v.* to take off the outer skin of something: *Please peel the orange.*

peep (pēp) *n.* **1.** a quick look. **2.** a short, high sound made by a young bird or chicken. *v.* **1.** to look at something quickly. **2.** to make a sound like a peep.

peg (peg) *n.* a metal, wooden, or plastic pin, driven or fitted into something to fasten or support it: *a tent peg.*

pelt (pelt) *n.* the skin of an animal, usually with its fur. *v.* to throw or pound: *The rain pelted the roof.*

pen (pen) *n.* **1.** a tool used for writing with ink. **2.** an enclosed space in which animals are kept: *a pig pen.*

penalty (pen′ əl tē) *n.* a punishment for a crime or for breaking a rule. *pl.* **penalties.**

pencil (pens′ əl) *n.* a tool used for writing, made of wood with a stick of lead (graphite) in the centre.

pendulum (pen′ dyə ləm) a swinging weight that controls the action of a clock.

⊖**penetrate** (pen′ ə trāt′) *v.* **1.** to go into; to enter: *The bullet penetrated the body.* **2.** to see through: *The car lights could not penetrate the fog.* **penetrating. penetrated.**

penguin (peng′ gwin) *n.* a black and white sea bird that cannot fly, found near the South Pole.

penicillin (pen′ i sil′ in) *n.* a powerful medicine that destroys certain bacteria; it is used to treat many diseases.

peninsula (pə nin′ syə lə) *n.* a piece of land surrounded on three sides by water: *Nova Scotia is a peninsula. pl.* **peninsulas.**

penis (pē′ nis) *n.* the male sex organ. *pl.* **penises.**

penitentiary (pen′ i ten′ shə rē) *n.* a building where criminals are kept; a prison. *pl.* **penitentiaries.**

pennant (pen′ ənt) *n.* **1.** a flag or banner, often long and pointed, used as a signal or a decoration. **2.** a flag or trophy that is the emblem of an athletic or other championship: *a baseball pennant.*

penny (pen′ ē) *n.* a small copper coin worth one cent. *pl.* **pennies.**

⊖**pension** (pen′ shən) *n.* money paid regularly by a company or a government, to help support a person after he or she has stopped working.

penthouse (pent′ haůs) *n.* an apartment or condominium, usually the most expensive, at the highest level of a building.

people (pēpl) *n.* **1.** persons; men, women, boys, and girls. **2.** a nation: *The Canadian people come from many countries.*

pepper (pep′ ər) *n.* **1.** a hot-tasting spice that adds flavour to food. **2.** a green, yellow, or bright red vegetable, to be cooked or used in salads.

peppermint (pep′ ər mint′) *n.* a plant with a strong scent; its leaves are used to flavour some candies, medicines, and toothpastes.

per (pûr) *prep.* for each: *The speed limit here is sixty kilometres per hour (60 km/h).*

per cent, percent (pûr sent′) *n.* parts of a hundred: *Three per cent (3%) means 3 out of every 100.*

percentage (pûr sen′ tij) *n.* the part or portion of 100: *What percentage of Canadians is (are) over sixty-five?*

perch (pûrch) *n.* **1.** a fish that lives in rivers and lakes and is used for food. *pl.* **perch. 2.** a stick or a twig that a bird can rest on. *pl.* **perches.** *v.* to sit on or place on something: *We perched ourselves on the top of the hill.* **perching. perched.** it **perches.**

percussion instrument (pər kush′ ən in′ strə mənt) a musical instrument that is struck to produce a sound: *Xylophones, drums, and cymbals are some percussion instruments.*

perfect (pûr′ fikt) *adj.* without anything wrong; so good that it cannot be better: *A perfect score is 100%.*

perfect (pər fekt′) *v.* to make something so good that it cannot be any better: *The company spent years perfecting the design of the car.*

perform (pər fȯrm′) *v.* **1.** to do something in front of an audience: *to perform on the piano.* **2.** to do: *to perform a difficult job.*

performance (pər fȯr′ məns) *n.* **1.** an entertainment; a show for people: *We saw a performance by dancers.* **2.** the doing of an action: *The team's performance was excellent.*

performer (pər fȯr′ mər) *n.* an actor, actress, or other person who entertains by performing.

perfume (pûr′ fyūm) *n.* a liquid that has a pleasant smell.

perhaps (pər haps′) *adv.* it may be; possibly: *Sam is not at the party; perhaps he is sick.*

perimeter (pə rim′ ə tər) *n.* the outside edge of an area: *A fence goes around the perimeter of the park.*

period (pēr′ i əd) *n.* **1.** a length of time: *a period of thirty minutes; a period in a hockey game.* **2.** the dot (.) that marks the end of a sentence. **3.** the monthly flow of blood from a woman's uterus.

permafrost (pûr′ mə frost′) *n.* ground in very cold regions that is always frozen.

permanent (pûr′ ma nent) *adj.* always there; long-lasting: *The child has all her permanent teeth. Is your job permanent or temporary?*

⊖**permission** (pər mish′ ən) *n.* words that allow someone to do something: *We were given permission to go home early.*

permit (pûr′ mit) *n.* a written form that gives permission to do something: *We need a permit to fish here.*

permit (pər mit′) *v.* to allow; to let: *We are permitted to fish here.* **permitting. permitted.**

perogy, pirogy, pierogi (pə rog′ ē) *n.* a small pastry 'pocket' filled with meat, cheese, or vegetables. *pl.* **perogies.**

persecute (pûr′ sə kyūt′) *v.* to keep treating people in a cruel way, often because of their religious or political beliefs. **persecuting. persecuted.**

person (pûr′ sən) *n.* a human being.

personal (pûr′ sən əl) *adj.* private; a person's own: *You may not read this letter because it's personal.*

personality (pûr′ sə nal′ i tē) *n.* **1.** what makes one person act differently from another: *The personalities of the twins are different; he always smiles, and she is serious.* **2.** a well-known person: *a TV personality. pl.* **personalities.**

personnel (pûr′ sə nel′) *n.* employees; the people who work in a place: *When I applied for the job, I went to the company's personnel department.*

perspiration (pûr′ spə rā′ shən) *n.* wetness that is given off through the skin; sweat: *He wiped the perspiration from his forehead.*

perspire (pər spīr′) *v.* to give off perspiration; to sweat: *At the end of the race, all the runners were perspiring.* **perspiring. perspired.**

persuade (pər swād′) *v.* to talk to someone and get him or her to agree to something: *Although I was tired, he persuaded me to go shopping.* **persuading. persuaded.**

pessimist (pes′ i mist) *n.* a person who thinks things will turn out badly: *My brother is a pessimist. Whenever we take a trip, he thinks we will get lost.*

⊖**pest** (pest) *n.* a person or thing that causes trouble or is annoying.

pester (pes′ tər) *v.* to annoy or bother: *My brother sometimes pesters me when I'm trying to read.*

pet (pet) *n.* an animal friend that people keep at home and take care of. *v.* to pat gently: *to pet a dog.* **petting. petted.**

petal (pet′ əl) *n.* one of the coloured parts that grow from the middle of a flower.

petition (pə ti′ shun) *n.* a written request, usually signed by a large number of people: *We and our neighbours have signed a petition requesting traffic lights at our corner.*

petroleum (pə trō′ li əm) *n.* a thick black oil that is found underground. Petroleum can be made into gasoline, plastics, and many other things.

pew (pyū) *n.* a long wooden bench in a church.

⊖**pharmacy** (fär′ mə sē) *n.* a drug store; a store where medicines are sold. *pl.* **pharmacies.**

phase (fāz) *n.* a part of a slow change; a change that will not last: *He has been very sad recently, but I think it is just a phase he is going through.*

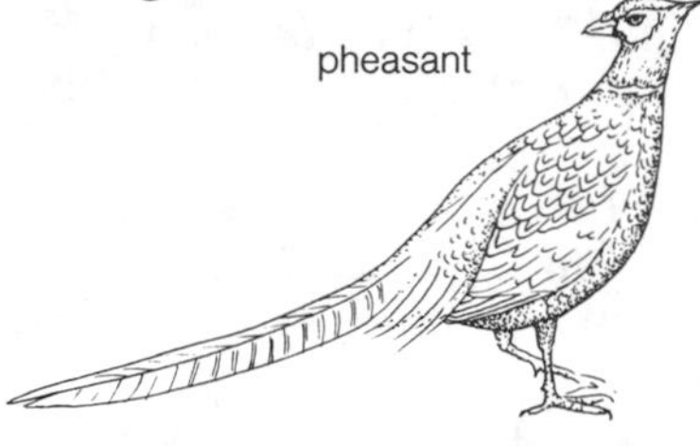
pheasant

pheasant (fez′ ənt) *n.* a wild bird with long, brightly coloured tail feathers.

phone (fōn) *n., v.* short for **telephone**: *There is a phone in the kitchen. I phoned you yesterday.* **phoning. phoned.**

phonograph (fōn′ ə graf′) *n.* a record player.

phony (fō′ nē) *adj.* fake; not real: *a phony dollar bill.*

photo (fō′ tō) short for **photograph.** *pl.* **photos.**

⊖**photograph** (fō′ tə graf′) *n.* a picture taken with a camera.

photographer (fə tog′ rə fər) *n.* a person who takes photographs.

⊖**phrase** (frāz) *n.* a group of words that are used together, usually as part of a sentence.

physical (fiz′ i kəl) *n.* a regular visit to the doctor, when he or she checks a person's health. *adj.* having to do with the body: *Physical exercise is the exercise of the body.*

physician (fə zish′ ən) *n.* a doctor; a person who treats sick and injured people.

physics (fiz′ iks) *n.* a science dealing with matter, energy, motion and force; it studies the way things move and the effects they have on one another.

pianist (pē′ ə nist) *n.* a person who plays the piano.

piano (pē an′ ō) *n.* a large musical instrument with black and white keys. When a piano key is pressed, a little hammer strikes a metal string, making a sound. *pl.* **pianos.**

pick (pik) *n.* a pointed tool used for breaking up hard ground. *v.* **1.** to gather, one by one: *to pick berries.* **2.** to choose: *Tony picked two library books.*
pick up **1.** to lift: *The box was too heavy to pick up.* **2.** to stop to give someone a ride: *We picked up Sam at his house.* **3.** to receive a radio or television station: *This radio can pick up thirty stations.* **4.** to buy: *We picked up some food at the store.* **5.** to improve: *His business is picking up.*

pickerel (pik′ ər əl) *n.* a large, thin fish that lives in lakes and rivers. *pl.* **pickerel.**

⊖**picket** (pik′ ət) *n.* **1.** a pointed piece of wood that is driven into the ground, often as part of a fence. **2.** a person who stands or marches in front of a store or business to protest something. *v.* to protest by standing or marching outside a store or business, trying to stop people from going in: *The workers felt they were not paid enough, so they picketed the factory.*

pickle (pikl) *n.* **1.** the salt water or vinegar in which certain foods are preserved. **2.** a cucumber preserved in pickle. *v.* to place vegetables or other foods in pickle to preserve them. **pickling. pickled.**

picnic (pik′ nik) *n.* a meal eaten outside, often away from home: *On Sunday, we went for a picnic in the park.* *v.* to go out and have a meal in the open air. **picnicking. picnicked.**

picture (pik′ chər) *n.* **1.** a drawing, painting, or photograph. **2.** a movie: *We saw a good picture last night.* **3.** a description in words: *The story gave us a good picture of life in England.* *v.* **1.** to draw or paint a picture. **2.** to imagine: *Close your eyes and picture yourself at the beach.* **picturing. pictured.**

pie (pī) *n.* fruit or other food baked in pastry: *apple pie; pumpkin pie; meat pie.*

⊖**piece** (pēs) *n.* **1.** a bit or part of something; not the whole thing: *a piece of cake.* **2.** one item among others: *a piece of mail; a chess piece.*

pier (pēr) *n.* a structure built from land out over water; it is used as a landing place for ships or as an area for entertainment.

pierce (pērs) *v.* to make a hole with something sharp: *Jane had her ears pierced.* **piercing. pierced.**

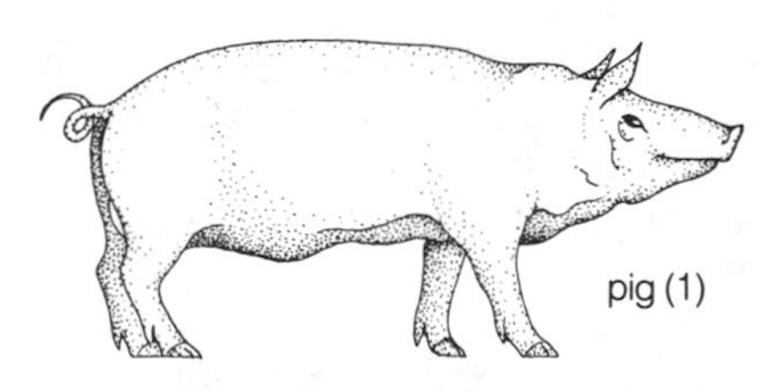

pig (1)

pig (pig) *n.* **1.** a farm animal, usually pink, with short legs, a curly tail, and a snout; its meat is called **pork**. **2.** *(informal)* a person who eats too much or is dirty.

pigeon (pij′ ən) *n.* a plump bird with soft grey feathers, often found near buildings in cities. Some pigeons are trained to carry messages.

pike (pīk) *n.* a long, thin fish that lives in lakes and rivers.

⊖**pile** (pīl) *n.* a lot of things on top of one another: *a pile of clothing; a wood pile.* *v.* to put things on top of one another; to put into a heap: *He piled up the magazines.* **piling. piled.**

pilgrim (pil′ grim) *n.* a person who travels to a holy place, often by walking there.

pill (pil) *n.* a hard bit of medicine to be swallowed.

pillar (pil′ ər) *n.* a large post that holds up part of a building.

pillow (pil′ ō) *n.* a cloth bag filled with soft material, for resting the head.

pilot (pī′ lət) *n.* **1.** the person who controls an airplane. **2.** the person who guides a ship into and out of a harbour.

pimple (pimpl) *n.* a small swelling on the skin, usually on the face.

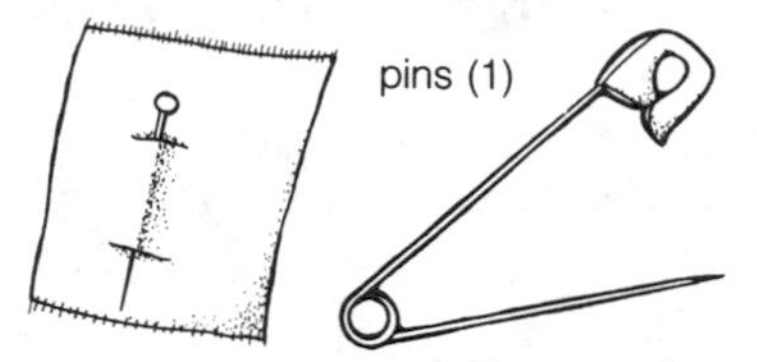

pins (1)

⊖**pin** (pin) *n.* **1.** a small, straight, pointed metal wire, used for fastening cloth, paper, etc. **2.** a piece of jewellery with a pin or clasp on the back. **3.** one of the pieces to be knocked down in the game of bowling. *v.* to fasten with a pin. **pinning. pinned.**

pinch (pinch) *n.* **1.** a squeeze with the thumb and finger. **2.** a small amount: *a pinch of salt.* *pl.* **pinches.** *v.* to squeeze between the thumb and a finger: *He pinched the baby's cheek.* **pinching. pinched.** he **pinches.**

pine (pīn) *n.* a tall evergreen tree with cones, and leaves that look like green needles.

pineapple (pīn′ apl′) *n.* a large, sweet fruit that grows in hot places; it has stiff, sharp leaves and sweet, yellow flesh.

ping-pong (ping′ pong′) *n.* table tennis; a game played on a marked table, in which the players use paddles to hit a plastic ball over a net.

pink (pingk) *n.* a very light red colour. *adj.* having this colour.

⊖**pint** (pīnt) *n.* a measure of capacity, equal to about 0.5 L.

pioneer (pī′ ə nēr′) *n.* **1.** one of the first people who settle in a new place, preparing the way for others to follow. **2.** someone who is the first to do something, preparing the way for others to follow: *a pioneer in computer studies.*

pipe (pīp) *n.* **1.** a long tube that carries gas, water, or other substances. **2.** a musical instrument shaped like a tube. **3.** a tube with a small bowl at one end in which tobacco is burned: *My uncle smokes a pipe.*

pipeline (pīp′ līn′) *n.* a line of pipes, sometimes very long, for carrying gas, oil, and other substances.

pirate (pī′ rət) *n.* someone who attacks and robs ships at sea.

pistol (pis′ təl) *n.* a small gun fired from one hand.

pit (pit) *n.* **1.** any deep hole in the ground. **2.** a hard seed or stone in a fruit: *a peach pit.*

pitch (pich) *n.* **1.** a throw of the baseball to the batter. **2.** the highness or lowness of a musical note. *pl.* **pitches.** *v.* **1.** to toss: *to pitch a ball.* **2.** to set up: *to pitch a tent.* **pitching. pitched.** he **pitches.**

pitcher (pich′ ər) *n.* **1.** a large jug used for liquids. **2.** the baseball player who tosses or pitches the ball.

pitchfork (pich′ fôrk′) *n.* a large fork used for lifting and tossing hay.

pity (pit′ ē) *n.* a feeling of sorrow for people who are ill or unhappy. *v.* to feel sorrow for: *Don't just pity the sick man; help him.* **pitying. pitied.** he **pities.**

pivot (piv′ ət) *n.* a pin or point on which a wheel or other object turns.

pizza (pēt′ sə) *n.* a flat dough covered with tomato sauce, cheese, and other foods, and baked in a very hot oven. *pl.* **pizzas.**

⊖**place** (plās) *n.* **1.** a position, spot, or location: *This is my place at the table. This is the place where I bought my coat. He finished the race in third place.* **2.** *(informal)* home: *Would you like to come to my place for lunch?*
in place of instead of: *I will go in place of my brother.*
take place to happen: *The wedding took place in the afternoon.* *v.* to put something in a certain location: *Ted placed the books on the shelf.*
placing. placed.

plaid (plad) *n.* **1.** a pattern of squares formed by stripes of different colours crossing one another. **2.** a cloth woven or printed with such a pattern.

plain (plān) *n.* a large area of flat or almost flat, treeless land: *the Saskatchewan plains.* *adj.* **1.** clear; easy to see or understand: *It is plain to see that you are not well.* **2.** simple; not fancy: *Do you want your cake plain or with ice cream?*

plan (plan) *n.* **1.** an outline or idea of something to be done: *We made plans for a holiday.* **2.** a drawing that shows the way a house, machine, etc. is arranged. *v.* to think about doing something and to make some arrangements: *to plan a picnic.* **planning. planned.**

⊖**plane** (plān) *n.* **1.** a carpenter's tool used for smoothing wood. **2.** a completely flat surface. **3.** short for **airplane.**

planet (plan′ ət) *n.* one of the heavenly bodies that orbit our sun. The nine planets are Mercury, Venus, Earth, Mars, Jupiter, Saturn, Uranus, Neptune, and Pluto.

planetarium (plan′ ə ter′ i əm) *n.* a building where there are displays of the stars and planets. *pl.* **planetariums**, or **planetaria.**

plank (plangk) *n.* a long, flat piece of wood.

plant (plant) *n.* **1.** any living thing that is not an animal: *a tomato plant; a house plant.* **2.** the buildings and equipment used in manufacturing something: *a steel plant.* *v.* to put in the ground to grow.

plaster (plas′ tər) *n.* a paste of sand, lime, and water that hardens when dry: *We put plaster in the holes in the wall.* *v.* to use this paste: *to plaster a wall.*

plastic (plas′ tik) *n.* a manufactured material that, when heated, can be moulded into any shape. *adj.* made of this material.

⊖**plate** (plāt) *n.* **1.** a dish, round and almost flat. **2.** a thin, flat piece of metal: *a licence plate.* **3.** in baseball, the home base.

plateau (pla tō′) *n.* an area of flat land located in the mountains or higher than sea level. *pl.* **plateaus.**

platform (plat′ fôrm) *n.* a raised floor or stage: *a railway platform.*

platter (plat′ ər) *n.* a large plate on which food is often served.

play (plā) *n.* **1.** a stage show: *We saw a famous play at the theatre.* **2.** an action in a game: *an excellent play at the end of the hockey game.* *pl.* **plays.** *v.* **1.** to take part in sports or games: *to play checkers; to play soccer.* **2.** to act in a play, movie, program, etc.: *Who plays the part of the prince?* **3.** to perform on a musical instrument: *to play the drums.* **playing. played.** she **plays.**

player (plā′ ər) *n.* a person who plays or performs: *a hockey player.*

playful (plā′ fəl) *adj.* full of fun: *a playful kitten.*

playground (plā′ ground′) *n.* a piece of land on which to play.

playoff (plā′ of′) *n.* **1.** an extra game played to break a tie. **2.** a series of games played to decide the championship.

plaza (pla′ zə, plä′ zə) *n.* **1.** a shopping centre. **2.** a public square in a city or town. *pl.* **plazas.**

plea (plē) *n.* **1.** a statement in a court of law in which the accused person claims to be guilty or not guilty. **2.** a request for something that a person wants very much: *a plea for help.* *pl.* **pleas.**

plead (plēd) *v.* **1.** for a person to say whether he or she is guilty or not guilty of a crime. **2.** to ask for something again and again: *He pleaded with me for the money.*

⊖**pleasant** (plez′ ənt) *adj.* **1.** giving pleasure: *We enjoyed a pleasant evening at our neighbour's house.* **2.** being kind and friendly: *a pleasant person.*

please (plēz) *v.* **1.** to give someone happiness: *We pleased her with our gift.* **2.** to choose: *You may leave whenever you please.* **3.** a polite word used when asking for something: *Please, may I come in the room?* **pleasing. pleased.**

pleasure (plezh′ ər) *n.* enjoyment; a feeling of being pleased: *She received much pleasure from the book.*

pledge (plej) *n.* a very serious promise: *a pledge to keep the city safe.* *v.* to make such a promise. **pledging. pledged.**

plenty (plen′ tē) *n.* a full supply; more than enough: *There is plenty of cake, so have another piece.*

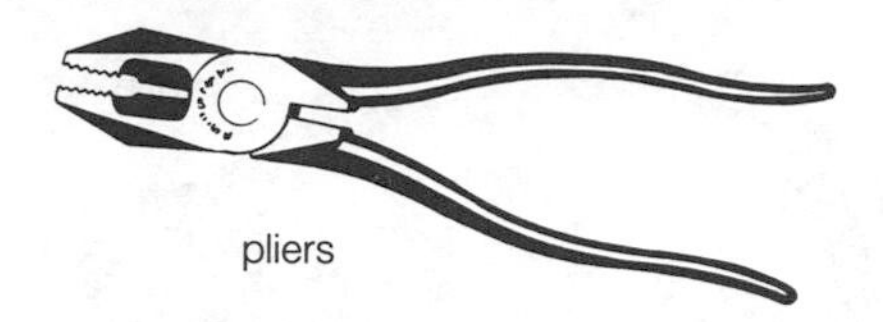

pliers (plī′ ərz) *n.pl.* a tool used for bending or cutting wire.

plot (plot) *n.* **1.** a small piece of ground: *a vegetable plot.* **2.** the things that happen in a book, play, or program: *an interesting plot.* **3.** a secret plan: *a plot to rob a bank.* *v.* to make secret plans. **plotting. plotted.**

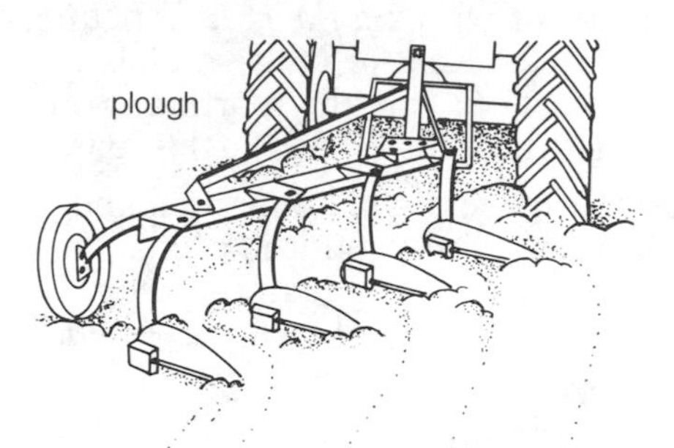

plough, plow (plau̇) *n.* **1.** a machine used for turning over the soil. **2.** a machine used for clearing away substances such as snow. *v.* **1.** to turn over the soil. **2.** to clear away snow.

pluck (pluk) *v.* **1.** to pull at: *to pluck the guitar strings.* **2.** to pull all the feathers off: *to pluck a hen.*

plug (plug) *n.* **1.** a piece of solid material that fills a hole: *a sink plug; a bathtub plug.* **2.** a piece of electrical equipment at the end of a cord, fitted into an outlet to make an electrical connection. *v.* to stop or fill up with a plug: *Why don't you plug that hole with cement?* **plugging. plugged.**
plug in to connect to an electrical outlet: *Plug in the toaster please, but don't unplug the radio!*

plum (plum) *n.* a soft, juicy fruit, purple, red, green, or yellow in colour.

plumber (plum′ ər) *n.* a person whose job is to work with the pipes and water systems of a building.

⊖**plume** (plūm) *n.* a bird's long and colourful feather.

plump (plump) *adj.* round and fat: *a plump chicken.*

plunge (plunj) *v.* to dive; to move suddenly into: *Henry plunged into the water.* **plunging. plunged.**

plural (plu̇r′ əl) *n.* more than one: 'boys', 'cherries', 'mice' are the plurals of 'boy', 'cherry', 'mouse'.

plus (plus) *prep.* added to: *three plus two equals five.* The symbol is +.

plywood (plī′ wu̇d′) *n.* a strong wood made by gluing together thin layers of wood.

p.m. The time from noon to midnight: *He went to bed at eleven p.m.*

pneumonia (nyū mōn′ yə, nū mōn′ yə) *n.* a disease that affects the lungs and makes breathing difficult.

poach (pōch) *v.* **1.** to cook an egg, without the shell, in boiling water. **2.** to hunt or fish on someone's land without permission. **poaching. poached.** he **poaches.**

pocket (pok′ ət) *n.* a small bag sewn into some clothes, for keeping things in.

pocketbook (pok′ ət bu̇k′) *n.* a small bag or case for holding money, papers, etc.; a purse.

pocket book (pok′ ət bu̇k′) *n.* a small book with a paper binding; a paperback.

pod (pod) *n.* the long part of some plants, such as beans or peas, that contains the seeds.

poem (pō′ im, pō′ əm) *n.* a piece of writing, often with lines that have a rhythm and a rhyme.

poet (pō′ it, pō′ ət) *n.* a person who writes poems.

poetry (pō′ i trē, pō′ ə trē) *n.* poems: *a book of poetry.*

⊖**point** (poi̇nt) *n.* **1.** a small mark or dot, such as the period at the end of a sentence. **2.** a sharp end: *the point of a blade.* **3.** the main idea or purpose: *What is the point of the story?* **4.** a certain place or position: *There are many points of interest in the province.* **5.** a score in a game: *We won by a point.* *v.* **1.** to show the direction of a place: *Point the way with your finger.* **2.** to aim: *to point a gun.* **3.** to indicate; to show: *She pointed out her house in the photograph.*

pointed (poi̇nt′ əd) *adj.* sharp; having a point.

poison (poi̇′ zən) *n.* a substance that could kill or injure a living creature. *v.* to harm or kill with such a substance.

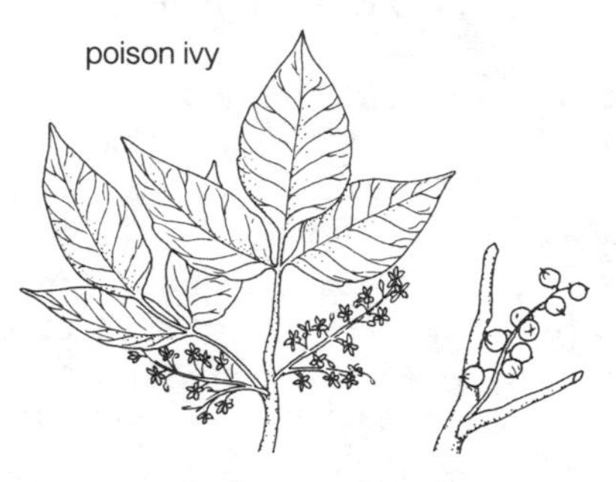
poison ivy

poison ivy (poi̇′ zən ī′ vē) a climbing plant that, when touched, causes a rash. Poison ivy has shiny three-parted leaves and white berries.

poisonous (poi̇′ zən əs) *adj.* full of poison: *A poisonous snake can pass venom into you with its bite.*

poke (pōk) *n.* a jab or light punch: *a poke in the ribs.* *v.* to jab or punch lightly. **poking. poked.**
poke fun at to tease; to joke about.

poker (pōk′ ər) *n.* **1.** a metal rod used for stirring a fire. **2.** a card game.

polar (pō′ lər) *adj.* having to do with the North or South Pole, or both.

polar bear

polar bear (pō′ lər ber′) a large white bear of the arctic regions.

pole (pōl) *n.* **1.** a long, thin, rounded piece of wood: *a flagpole; a fishing pole.* **2.** either of the two ends of a magnet. **3. Pole** the North or South Pole, the ends of the earth's axis.

⊖**police** (pə lēs′) *n.pl.* the men and women whose job it is to keep law and order. *v.* to guard or keep order: *to police the city.* **policing. policed.**

policeman (pə lēs′ mən) *n.* a member of the police.
pl. **policemen** (pə lēs′ men).

police officer (pə lēs′ of′ i sər) *n.* a member of the police; a police constable.

policewoman (pə lēs′ wu̇m′ ən) *n.* a member of the police.
pl. **policewomen** (pə lēs′ wim′ ən).

policy (pol′ i sē) *n.* **1.** a rule about the way something should be done: *It is the store's policy not to give refunds.* **2.** a written agreement between an insurance company and the person being insured.
pl. **policies.**

polio (pō′ li ō′) short for **poliomyelitis.**

poliomyelitis (pō′ li ō mī′ ə līt′ is) *n.* a serious illness, most common in children, that can cause the muscles to be paralysed.

Polish (pōl′ ish) *n.* the language spoken in Poland. *adj.* belonging to or coming from Poland.

polish (pol′ ish) *n.* a special wax, liquid, etc. rubbed on a surface to make it smooth and shiny. *v.* to make something smooth and shiny by rubbing it. **polishing. polished.** he **polishes.**

polite (pə līt′) *adj.* having good manners; courteous.

political (pə lit′ i kəl) *adj.* having to do with politics, politicians, or government: *There are several political parties in a democracy.*

politician (pol′ i tish′ ən) *n.* someone whose work is with politics: *Members of Parliament are politicians.*

politics (pol′ i tiks) *n.pl.* **1.** matters related to government or public office: *Our mayor has been in politics for many years.* **1.** opinions or beliefs about government: *Her politics are conservative; his are liberal.*

polka (pōl′ kə) *n.* a type of lively dance. *pl.* **polkas.**

poll (pōl) *n.* the collection of opinions from a large number of people to find out what they think about something: *The poll showed that most people wanted a new highway to be built.*

pollen (pol′ ən) *n.* a yellowish powder in the centre of flowers. Other flowers are made fertile when a bee or the wind moves pollen to them.

polls (pōlz) *n.pl.* the places where votes are taken.

pollute (pə lūt′) *v.* to make the air, land, or water impure or dirty: *The oil polluted the ocean.* **polluting. polluted.**

pollution (pə lū′ shən) *n.* the waste substances in the air, land, or water.

polyester (pol′ i es′ tər) *n.* a synthetic material, often used as material for clothing: *That shirt is polyester, not cotton.*

pond (pond) *n.* a small lake.

pony (pō′ nē) *n* a type of small horse or a small young horse. *pl.* **ponies.**

poodle (pūdl) *n.* a pet dog with thick and curly hair.

pool (pūl) *n.* **1.** a small pond, sometimes made for swimming in. **2.** a game, played on a long table, in which a player uses a stick to hit one ball against others, driving them into pockets. **3.** something shared by a group of people: *Each member of a car pool takes a turn driving the others.*

poor (pūr) *adj.* **1.** having very little money. **2.** not good: *poor work; poor weather.*

poorly (pūr′ lē) *adv.* not well: *The work is poorly done.*

pop (pop) *n.* **1.** a small bang. **2.** a fizzy drink. **3.** music that is popular at the present time. *v.* **1.** to make a small, sudden noise. **2.** to move about quickly: *to pop out of bed.* **popping. popped.**

popcorn (pop′ kȯrn′) *n.* corn kernels that burst open and puff out when heated.

Pope (pōp) *n.* the head of the Roman Catholic Church.

poplar (pop′ lər) *n.* a very tall, thin tree that has soft wood, wide leaves, and grows very quickly.

poppy (pop′ ē) *n.* a wild or garden plant with round, brightly coloured flowers, usually red. *pl.* **poppies.**

⊖**popular** (pop′ yə lər) *adj.* liked by many people: *a popular person; a popular song.*

population (pop′ yə lā′ shən) *n.* the number of people living in a certain place such as a city, province, or country: *In 1986, the population of Canada was about 26 000 000.*

porcelain (pȯr′ sə lən) *n.* a shiny, white, thin pottery used to make cups, plates, bowls, etc.

porch (pòrch) *n.* a covered area at the entrance to a house or other building. *pl.* **porches.**

porcupine (pòr′ kyə pīn′) *n.* a wild rodent that protects itself with the sharp needles or quills that cover its body.

pore (pòr) *n.* a very small opening in the skin.

⊖**pork** (pork) *n.* meat from a pig.

porridge (por′ ij) *n.* a breakfast food made by boiling oatmeal or other cereals in water.

⊖**port** (pòrt) *n.* **1.** a harbour or a town with a harbour. **2.** the left side of a ship as a person faces the front or bow.

⊖**portable** (pōr′ təbl) *adj.* light enough to be carried or moved easily: *a portable TV.*

portage (pòr tazh′) *n.* the carrying of canoes, boats, and goods over land from one body of water to another. *v.* to carry such items between bodies of water. **portaging. portaged.**

portion (pòr′ shən) *n.* a part: *Phil ate only a small portion of rice.*

portrait (pòr′ trət) *n.* a picture of someone, usually of the face.

portray (pòr trā′) *v.* to make something or someone look a certain way: *The newspapers portrayed him as a hero.* **2.** to act as a certain person in a play, movie, program, etc.: *In his new movie, the great actor portrays a king.* **portraying. portrayed.**

⊖**pose** (pōz) *n.* a position of the body: *Hold that pose until I take your picture! v.* to hold a position for a picture: *The family posed for the photograph.* **posing. posed.**

⊖**position** (pə zish′ ən) *n.* **1.** the place where someone or something is: *She changed the position of the desk.* **2.** a way of standing, sitting, lying down, etc.: *a comfortable position.* **3.** a job: *He has the position of accountant.*

⊖**positive** (poz′ i tiv) *adj.* **1.** completely sure: *I am positive that her birthday is in October.* **2.** meaning 'yes' or 'all right': *When we asked for a cat, we received a positive answer.*

possess (pə zes′) *v.* to have; to own: *to possess great wealth; to possess great knowledge.* **possessing. possessed.** he **possesses.**

possession (pə zesh′ ən) *n.* something that a person owns.

possessive (pə zes′ iv) *n.* **1.** a word that describes one thing's belonging to another. The pronouns 'hers', 'his', 'mine', 'yours', and 'ours' are possessives. *adj.* jealous; behaving as though other people may take something away: *She is very possessive about her cat, and won't let anyone else come near it.*

possibility (pos′ i bil′ i tē) *n.* a chance of happening: *There is a good possibility that it will snow today. pl.* **possibilities.**

possible (pos′ ibl) *adj.* able to happen or be done: *It is still possible for the team to win.*

⊖**post** (pōst) *n.* **1.** a strong pole of metal, wood, etc., set in a standing position to support something. **2.** the place where a soldier, guard, or police officer stands. *v.* **1.** to put something on a board or wall for people to see: *to post an announcement.* **2.** to send letters and packages by mail.

postage (pōs′ tij) *n.* the charge for sending a letter or package by mail.

postal code (pōs′ təl kōd′) numbers and letters of the alphabet that are written on a piece of mail to show the delivery area.

postcard (pōst′ kärd′) *n.* a card that can be mailed without an envelope: *Some postcards have a picture on one side.*

poster (pōs′ tər) *n.* a large notice or picture put up on a board or wall for people to see.

post office (pōst′ of′ is) a government office where mail is received and sorted, and where stamps are sold.

postpone (pōst pōn′) *v.* to delay until later: *We postponed our visit until next week.* **postponing. postponed.**

posture (pos′ chər) *n.* the way the body is held when sitting, standing, or walking: *My friend is trying to improve her posture. She walks with a book on top of her head.*

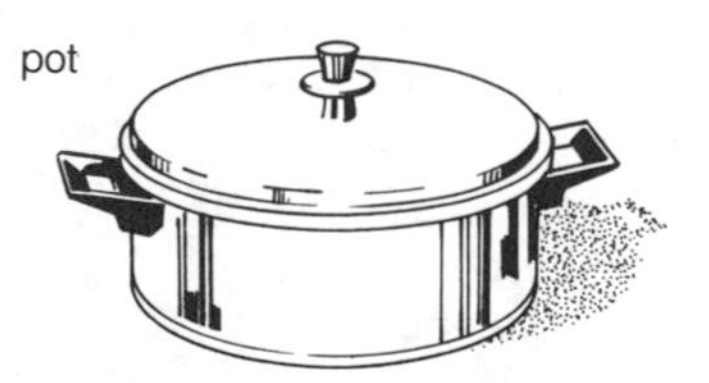

⊖**pot** (pot) *n.* a deep, rounded container: *The sauce is cooking in the pot.*

potato (pə tā′ tō) *n.* a vegetable with a brown skin; it grows underground, and can be baked, boiled, or fried. *pl.* **potatoes.**

potential (pə ten′ shəl) *n.* the things that a person or thing can do, but is not yet doing. *Lucy is not a champion swimmer yet, but her trainer thinks she has the potential to become one.*

pothole (pot′ hōl′) *n.* a hole in the surface of a road.

pottery (pot′ ə rē) *n.* bowls, cups, flowerpots, and other things made of baked clay.

⊖**pouch** (paůch) *n.* a small bag in which to hold things: *A kangaroo carries her young in a pouch.* *pl.* **pouches.**

poultry (pōl′ trē) *n.* chickens, turkeys, geese, and ducks, raised for their meat and often for eggs.

pound (paůnd) *n.* **1.** a measure of mass or weight, equal to about 0.5 kg. **2.** a unit of money used in Britain and some other countries. *v.* to hammer or beat heavily: *Don't pound on the door!*

pour (pȯr) *v.* **1.** to cause liquid or powder to flow: *Please pour me a glass of juice.* **2.** to rain heavily: *It poured yesterday.*

poverty (pov′ ər tē) *n.* being very poor: *Many people in the world live in a state of poverty.*

powder (paů′ dər) *n.* something crushed into fine bits or dust: *milk powder.*

power (paů′ ər) *n.* **1.** strength: *His muscles have great power.* **2.** force; energy: *The house is heated by electrical power.* **3.** a right to govern: *Which political party is in power in your province?* **4.** ability: *People have the power to think.* *v.* to make something work: *Gasoline powers this engine.*

powerful (paů′ ər fəl) *adj.* very strong: *a powerful wind; a powerful voice.*

practical (prak′ ti kəl) *adj.* **1.** able to be done or used efficiently: *a simple but practical plan; a practical table, with many drawers.* **2.** sensible; using ideas that come from practice or experience: *a practical person.*

practical joke (prak′ ti kəl jōk′) a trick played on one person by another, or others, for amusement: *I found sugar in the salt shaker at lunch! When my friends began to laugh, I realized it was a practical joke.*

practically (prak′ ti kə lē) *adv.* almost; nearly: *It is practically time for lunch.*

ⓔ**practice** (prak′ tis) *n.* **1.** something done many times, so that it can be done well: *Claude went to hockey practice.* **2.** a habit; something done regularly: *It is his practice to be kind.* **3.** a profession: *He has a law practice.*

ⓔ**practise, practice** (prak′ tis) *v.* to do something many times in order to do it better: *Sara practises the piano every day.* **practising. practised.**

prairie (prer′ ē) *n.* level or rolling land covered with grass but having few or no trees.

Prairie Provinces (prer′ ē prov′ in səz) Alberta, Saskatchewan, and Manitoba. The treeless area that stretches across these provinces is called the **Prairies**.

praise (prāz) *n.* words telling that someone or something is very good. *v.* to say such words: *Everyone praised her fine voice.* **praising. praised.**

pray (prā) *v.* to speak to God, a god, or gods.

prayer (prā′ ər, pre′ ər) *n.* words used in praying.

preach (prēch) *v.* **1.** to speak on a religious subject. **2.** to give advice, but sometimes to give too much. **preaching. preached.** he **preaches.**

precaution (pri kȯ′ shən) *n.* a thing that is done before something harmful or dangerous can happen: *She installed a fire alarm in the house as a precaution against fires.*

precede (pri sēd′) *v.* to go before something: *The number three precedes the number four.* **preceding. preceded.**

precious (presh′ əs) *adj.* very valuable: *Jewels are precious stones.*

precipitation (pri sip′ i tā′ shən) *n.* the amount of rain, snow, hail, sleet, etc., measured in centimetres of water.

precise (pri sīs′) *adj.* exact; accurate: *Scientists must be precise when they perform experiments.*

predict (pri dikt′) *v.* to say in advance that something will happen: *The weather office predicts rain.*

prediction (pri dik′ shən) *n.* an announcement in advance of something that may happen: *The prediction is for a warm day.*

preface (pref′ əs) *n.* a short message found at the beginning of some books.

prefer (pri fûr′) *v.* to like one thing more than another: *Jacques prefers apples to oranges.* **preferring. preferred.**

prefix (prē′ fiks) *n.* letters put at the beginning of a word to change its meaning. When you put the prefix 'dis' in front of the word 'appear', you get 'disappear'. *pl.* **prefixes.**

pregnancy (preg′ nən sē) *n.* the time of being pregnant. *pl.* **pregnancies.**

pregnant (preg′ nənt) *adj.* having one or more young developing inside the body.

prejudice (prej′ ə dis) *n.* an unfair belief that one person or thing is better or worse than another: *People show prejudice when they dislike others because they belong to a different religion.*

premature (prē′ mə chûr′, prē′ mə tyûr) *adj.* happening too early; happening before the right time: *A premature baby is born less than nine months after the beginning of pregnancy.*

premier (prem′ yər, prēm′ yər) *n.* the title of the head of certain governments; in Canada, the head of the government of a province.

preparation (prep′ ə rā′ shən) *n.* **1.** the act of getting ready: *There is much preparation needed for a party.* **2.** a mixture of different substances: *a preparation for cleaning wood.*

prepare (pri per′) *v.* **1.** to get ready: *We have to prepare for our visitors.* **2.** to make a special food or mixture: *The druggist prepared the medicine.* **preparing. prepared.**

preposition (prep′ ə zish′ ən) *n.* a word that begins a group of words that tell about a person, place, or thing. In the sentence, 'The ball went through the window and landed under the table', the prepositions are 'through' and 'under'.

prescribe (pri skrīb′) *v.* to order, usually to order as medicine. **prescribing. prescribed.**

prescription (pri skrip′ shən) *n.* a doctor's written order for medicine to be given to a patient.

present (prez′ ənt) *n.* **1.** a gift to someone. **2.** the time now, not the past. *adj.* attending, not absent: *How many people are present at the game?*

present (pri zent′) *v.* **1.** to give a prize or gift to someone: *The winner was presented with a gold medal.* **2.** to introduce oneself: *The new student presented herself to the teacher.*

present participle (prez′ ənt pär′ ti sipl) a form of a verb, ending with 'ing', used to show what is going on at the present time. In the sentence, 'Running through the woods, he fell', the word 'running' is a present participle.

preserve (pri zûrv′) *n.* an area where wild animals are protected. *v.* **1.** to keep something safe: *Sometimes the bodies of ancient animals are found preserved in ice.* **2.** to prepare pickles, jams, etc. for later use. **preserving. preserved.**

preserves (pri zûrvz′) *n.pl.* fruit boiled with sugar and stored for later use.

president (prez′ i dənt) *n.* **1.** the chief officer of a club, class, company, etc. **2.** the title of the head of certain governments: *the President of the United States.*

press (pres) *n.* **1.** a machine used for printing. **2.** a machine used for flattening things, such as clothing. **3.** newspapers and magazines, or the people who write for them: *The new mayor spoke to the press.* *pl.* **presses.** *v.* **1.** to push or squeeze: *Press the tape onto the paper. She pressed her way into the crowd.* **2.** to flatten clothes with an iron. **pressing. pressed.** he **presses.**

pressure (presh′ ər) *n.* **1.** a force or steady push against something: *The water pressure was too strong, and the hose burst.* **2.** trouble, worry, or stress from something: *the pressures of work.* *v.* to force someone to do something, such as make a decision: *He tried to pressure me into buying his car.*

prestige (pre stēzh′) *n.* the reputation that some rich, famous, or powerful people have: *He enjoys the prestige of being a famous judge.*

presume (pri zūm′) *v.* to suppose something is true: *I presumed she was your friend because she knew so much about you.* **presuming. presumed.**

⊖**pretend** (pri tend′) *v.* to claim that something is true, when it is not.

pretty (prit′ ē) *adj.* **1.** nice-looking; attractive; charming: *a pretty ring; a prettier one; the prettiest ring in the store.* **2.** quite; more than a little: *It is pretty windy, so wear a scarf.*

pretzel (pret′ səl) *n.* a hard, salted, and usually twisted cracker.

⊖**prevent** (pri vent′) *v.* to stop something from happening, or to stop someone from doing something: *She held onto her little brother to prevent him from falling.*

previous (prē′ vi əs) *adj.* earlier; the one before: *We went by bus on Tuesday, but walked the previous day.*

prey (prā) *n.* an animal or animals hunted by another for food: *Mice are the prey of cats.*

price (prīs) *n.* the cost of something.

priceless (prīs′ ləs) *adj.* beyond any price; so valuable that it cannot be bought: *The paintings in the museum are priceless.*

prick (prik) *n.* a small scratch or stab. *v.* to stab with a sharp point: *The thorn pricked me.*

pride (prīd) *n.* **1.** a feeling of pleasure from doing something well: *She takes pride in her work.* **2.** a high opinion of oneself: *His pride keeps him from saying that he is wrong.*

pried, pries see **pry.**

priest (prēst) *n.* a minister in certain religions, trained to perform religious services.

primary (prīm′ ə rē, pri′ mer ē) *adj.* first in time or importance: *The first grades in school are called the primary grades.*

⊖**prime** (prīm) *adj.* first in importance.

prime minister (prīm′ min′ i stər) the chief officer of some countries, including Canada.

prince (prins) *n.* **1.** the son of a king or queen. **2.** the title given to certain noblemen.

Prince Edward Island (prins′ ed′ wərd ī′ lənd) the province in the Gulf of St. Lawrence, east of New Brunswick and north of Nova Scotia; its capital is Charlottetown. Short form: **P.E.I.** A person living in or born in Prince Edward Island is a **Prince Edward Islander.**

princess (prin′ ses) *n.* **1.** the daughter of a king or queen. **2.** the wife of a prince. *pl.* **princesses.**

principal (prin′ si pəl) *n.* the head of a school. *adj.* highest in importance or interest: *The Parliament Buildings are the principal interests of Ottawa.*

principle (prin′ sipl) *n.* an important general rule or belief: *a principle of science; the principle of democracy; the principle of honesty.*

print (print) *n.* **1.** printed letters, not script. **2.** a mark made by pressing: *a footprint in the snow.* **3.** a photograph, or a picture that has been printed. *v.* **1.** to mark words or pictures onto something, using a printing machine. **2.** to write, using separate letters.

priority (prī ȯr′ i tē) *n.* the importance of doing something compared with the importance of other things that must be done: *This job has a high priority. You must finish it before you start anything else.* *pl.* **priorities.**

prison (priz′ ən) *n.* a jail; a building where criminals are kept.

prisoner (priz′ ən ər) *n.* a person kept in prison or captured in war.

⊖**private** (prī′ vət) *n.* a soldier in the army who is not an officer. *adj.* not to be shared with others: *This is a private letter, so don't read it.*

privilege (priv′ i lij) *n.* a special favour given only to some people.

prize (prīz) *n.* a reward for doing well or winning a contest.

pro (prō) *n.* **1.** *(informal)* short for **professional**; an athlete who plays for money: *He was an amateur football player last year; now he is a pro.* **2.** *(informal)* a person who knows a lot about something: *When it comes to chess, he is a real pro.*

pro- a prefix meaning 'in favour of' or 'on the side of': *If a person supports Mrs. Lee in the election, then he or she is 'pro-Lee'.*

probable (prob′ ə bl) *adj.* likely to happen or to be true.

probably (prob′ ə blē) *adv.* very likely: *It will probably rain, so take an umbrella.*

probation (prō bā′ shən) *n.* a testing period to see if a person will be able to do a job properly: *People who are new at a job are often put on probation for the first few weeks or months.*

problem (prob′ ləm) *n.* a puzzle or question that is not easy to answer.

procedure (prə sē′ jər) *n.* the correct, regular way something is done: *He explained the procedure for changing oil in the car.*

proceed (prō′ sēd′, prə sēd′) *v.* to continue; to move forward: *It was cloudy, but we proceeded to go to the beach.*

⊖**process** (prō′ ses, pros′ es) *n.* a method of making or doing something, involving several procedures: *a process for making glass. We are in the process of building a new barn. v.* to treat in a special way: *We process fruits to make them into jams. pl.* **processes.**

procession (prə sesh′ ən) *n.* a large number of people marching or riding on some special occasion.

produce (prə dyūs′) *v.* to make, create, or bring out: *The factory produces chairs. The cow produces milk. The farm produces vegetables.* **producing. produced.**

produce (prod′ yūs) *n.* vegetables and fruit sold in food stores.

product (prod′ əkt) *n.* something that is produced: *Milk is a dairy product.*

production (prə duk′ shən) *n.* manufacture: *The production of cars is an important industry.*

⊖**profession** (prə fesh′ ən) *n.* a job requiring special learning, such as that of a doctor, lawyer, accountant, or engineer.

⊖**professional** (prə fesh′ ən əl) *adj.* **1.** doing as a job what others do for fun: *a professional musician.* **2.** having to do with a job that requires special learning: *Law is a professional career.*

⊖**professor** (prə fes′ ər) *n.* a university teacher having a high rank.

profile (prō′ fīl) *n.* a side view, usually of a person's face.

profit (prof′ it) *n.* the money made by selling something for more than the price paid for it.

⊖**program, programme** (prō′ gram) *n.* **1.** a written outline of the things to be seen or heard at a concert, play, game, etc. **2.** a performance: *a television program.* **3.** the subjects or classes offered at a school or university: *a program of studies.* **4.** a set of computer instructions: *a BASIC program.*

progress (prō′ gres, pro′ gres) *n.* a forward movement or improvement: *He is making progress in swimming.*

progress (prō gres′, prə gres′) *v.* to move forward, go ahead, or show improvement: *Our plans for the trip are progressing.*

progressive (prō gres′ iv) *adj.* being in favour of changes that will bring improvement: *He has many progressive ideas, always thinking of ways to make things better.*

Progressive Conservative Party (prō gres′ iv kən sûr′ və tiv′ pär′ tē) one of the main political parties of Canada.

prohibit (prō hib′ it) *v.* to forbid or prevent: *The notice says, 'Bicycling Prohibited'.*

project (prō′ jekt, proj′ ekt) *n.* something that is planned: *The mayor discussed the project to build houses near the river.*

project (prə jekt′) *v.* **1.** to 'throw' forward: *The teacher projected pictures onto a screen. Prem projected his voice from the stage.* **2.** to extend forward: *The roof projects over the walls.*

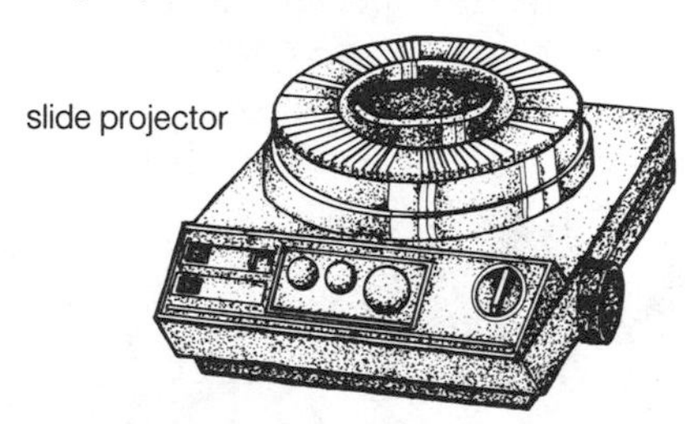
slide projector

projector (prə jek′ tər) *n.* a machine used to 'throw' pictures onto a screen.

promise (prom′ is) *n.* words saying that something will be done for sure: *I made a promise to walk the dog.* *v.* to say such words: *Bill promised to return my book.* **promising. promised.**

promote (prə mōt′) *v.* **1.** to give a higher position to: *The vice-president was promoted to president.* **2.** to help in the growth or change of something: *Too much sugar promotes tooth decay.* **promoting. promoted.**

⊖**promotion** (prə mō′ shən) *n.* a better job; a higher position: *She received more pay along with her promotion.*

prompt (prompt) *adj.* quick; done at once: *Ralph received a prompt reply to his letter.*

prong (prong) *n.* one of the pointed ends on a fork.

pronoun (prō′ naůn) *n.* a word used instead of a noun, such as 'I', 'you', 'who', 'what', and 'this'. In the sentence, 'Bill said he would ride the bicycle' the word 'he' is a pronoun.

pronounce (prə naůns′) *v.* **1.** to say the sound of a word: *The word 'photo' is pronounced 'fō′ tō'.* **2.** to say that something will be: *The couple was pronounced husband and wife.* **pronouncing. pronounced.**

pronunciation (prə nun′ si ā′ shən) *n.* the way to say a word: *The pronunciation of 'phone' is 'fōn'.*

proof (prūf) *n.* something that shows beyond doubt that a thing is true: *The footprints in the mud are proof that someone came here.*

-proof a suffix meaning 'giving protection against': **waterproof** means not letting water pass through; **bullet-proof** means safe from bullets.

proofread (prūf′ rēd′) *v.* to read something carefully and make sure that it contains no mistakes. **proofreading. proofread** (prōf′ red).

prop (prop) *n.* a support: *The sagging plant needs a prop.* *v.* to support with a prop: *Prop up the plant with a stick.* **propping. propped.**

propel (prə pel′) *v.* to push forward. **propelling. propelled.**

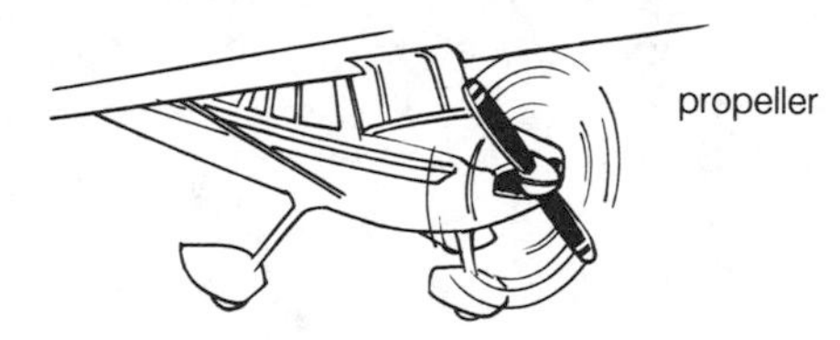
propeller

propeller (prə pel′ ər) *n.* a device with blades that turn at high speeds, pushing forward a ship or plane.

⊖**proper** (prop′ ər) *adj.* right; correct; suitable: *This is the proper way to saw wood.*

proper noun (prop′ ər naůn′) a word that begins with a capital letter and is the name of a certain person, place, or thing. 'Jack', 'Lethbridge', and 'July' are some proper nouns.

property (prop′ ər tē) *n.* anything that is owned, especially a building or land: *This property is for sale.* *pl.* **properties.**

prophet (prof′ ət) *n.* **1.** a person who tells about things that will happen in the future. **2.** a person who believes he or she has received a message from God to be told to others.

proportion (prə pōr′ shən) *n.* the amount of one part compared to another: *A large proportion of Canada's population lives in cities.*

⊖**propose** (prə pōz′) *v.* **1.** to suggest something: *Claude proposed that we take a trip.* **2.** to make an offer of marriage. **proposing. proposed.**

proprietor (prō prī′ ə tər) *n.* the owner of a business.

prosecute (pros′ ə kyūt′) *v.* to bring someone to trial before a court of law. **prosecuting. prosecuted.**

protect (prə tekt′) *v.* to defend from harm; to keep safe: *The dogs protected my house. The boots protect my shoes from the snow.*

protection (prə tek′ shən) *n.* someone or something that protects: *An umbrella gives protection from the rain.*

protein (prō′ tēn) *n.* a substance that the body needs which is found in many foods: *Eggs, meat, and cheese are some foods that contain protein.*

protest (prō′ test) *n.* a complaint about something: *a protest against an increase in rent.*

protest (prə test′) *v.* to object; to complain: *The neighbours protested against the smoke from the factory.*

Protestant (prot′ əs tənt) *n.* a member of a Christian but not Roman Catholic or Eastern Orthodox church.

proud (praůd) *adj.* **1.** pleased at having done something well: *Sergio had done well in school, and his parents were proud of him.* **2.** conceited; having too high an opinion of oneself: *He is too proud to be seen with his poor friends.*

prove (prūv) *v.* to show for certain that something is correct: *Can you prove that this wallet is yours?* **proving. proved.** he has **proved** or **proven.**

proverb (prov′ ərb) *n.* a well-known old saying; words that give advice: 'Better safe than sorry' is a proverb.

provide (prə vīd′) *v.* to supply what is needed: *The teacher provided pencils and paper for the test.* **providing. provided.**

provided (prə vīd′ əd) *conj.* if; on condition that: *We'll go skiing, provided there is enough snow.*

province (prov′ ins) *n.* one of the large divisions of some countries, such as Canada: *I was born in the province of Manitoba.*

provincial (prə vin′ shəl) *adj.* having to do with provinces or a province: *a provincial law.*

prowl (praůl) *v.* to move about silently, often looking for something to eat or steal: *The thief prowled about the house.*

prowler (praůl′ ər) *n.* a person who prowls about; a thief.

⊖**prune** (prūn) *n.* a dried plum. *v.* to cut short the unwanted branches of a tree or bush. **pruning. pruned.**

pry (prī) *v.* **1.** to look with curiosity: *My cat is prying in the closet.* **2.** to raise or move with force: *Can you pry the lid off the paint can?* **prying. pried.** he **pries.**

P.S. short for **postscript**: *When you want to add a message at the end of a letter, you first write, 'P.S.'*

psalm (säm) *n.* a religious song or poem.

psychiatrist (sī kī′ ə trist, si kī′ ə trist) *n.* a type of doctor who treats mental illness.

psychologist (sī kol′ ə jist) *n.* a person whose job is to study the way people think. Some psychologists treat mental illness.

puberty (pyū′ bər tē) *n.* the age at which children become physically mature.

public (pub′ lik) *n.* the people; everyone: *The beach is open to the public. adj.* open to or belonging to everyone: *a public park.*

public school (pub′ lik skūl′) a free school, from kindergarten through Grade 12 or 13, that is supported by the taxes people pay.

publication (pub′ li kā′ shən) *n.* **1.** a printed book, magazine, newspaper, etc., made available to people. **2.** the act of letting people know something by printing it in a book, magazine, or newspaper: *the publication of a weekly magazine.*

publish (pub′ lish) *v.* to bring out a book, newspaper, or magazine for sale. **publishing. published.** she **publishes.**

puck (puk) *n.* a hard rubber disc used to score a goal in hockey.

pudding (pu̇d′ ing) *n.* a soft, thick, sweet dessert: *chocolate pudding.*

puddle (pudl) *n.* a small pool of water.

puff (puf) *n.* a quick blow of breath, smoke, or wind. *v.* **1.** to blow out smoke, steam, or air. **2.** to become larger: *He breathed in, and his chest puffed out.*

⊖**pull** (pu̇l) *n.* the act of moving something towards oneself: *Give the door handle a strong pull.* *v.* **1.** to move something towards oneself: *Pull the door open.* **2.** to drag along: *The horse pulled the wagon.* **3.** *(informal)* to do; to make happen: *Stop pulling tricks!*

pulley (pu̇l′ ē) *n.* a wheel that has a groove around the outside part. A pulley is attached to a rope and is used to lift heavy things. *pl.* **pulleys.**

pullover (pu̇l′ ō′ vər) *n.* a warm piece of clothing worn on the top half of the body; it is put on by pulling it over the head.

pulp (pulp) *n.* **1.** the soft part of a fruit or vegetable. **2.** soft, ground-up wood, mixed with chemicals to make paper.

pulse (puls) *n.* the regular beat of the arteries, caused by the pumping of the heart; it can be felt on the wrist and elsewhere on the body: *The doctor measured the man's pulse to find out how fast his heart was beating.*

pump (pump) *n.* a machine that forces liquid or gases into or out of things: *a bicycle pump. v.* to work such a machine.

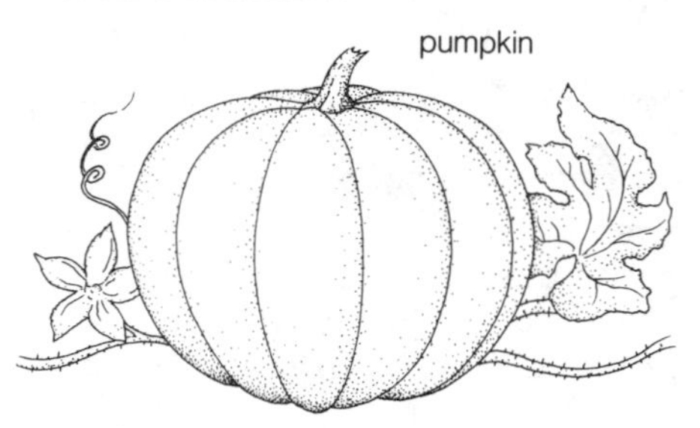
pumpkin

pumpkin (pump′ kin) *n.* a large, round, orange fruit, with a pulp used in pies and for animal feed.

punch (punch) *n.* **1.** a tool used for making holes. **2.** a quick hit with the fist. **3.** a drink made from a mixture of liquids such as fruit juices. *pl.* **punches.** *v.* **1.** to stamp holes in with a punch. **2.** to hit with the fist. **punching. punched.** she **punches.**

punctual (pungk′ chū əl, pungk′ tyū əl) *adj.* not late; doing things at the right time: *She is punctual. She always arrives at work on time.*

punctuation (pungk′ chū ā′ shən, pungk′ tyū ā′ shən) *n.* the use of periods, commas, and other marks: *Punctuation helps to make the meaning of a written sentence clear.*

punctuation marks marks used in writing to help make the meaning clear: *Some punctuation marks are commas, periods, and question marks.*

puncture (pungk′ chər) *n.* a small hole caused by something sharp: *I cannot ride the bicycle. There is a puncture in the tire.* *v.* to make a hole with something sharp: *The sharp rocks punctured the side of the small boat.* **puncturing. punctured.**

punish (pun′ ish) *v.* to make someone suffer for a wrong he or she has done. **punishing. punished.** he **punishes.**

punishment (pun′ ish mənt) *n.* the penalty a person must suffer for doing something wrong: *The punishment for stealing was a year in jail.*

pup (pup) *n.* a young dog.

pupil (pyū′ pəl) *n.* **1.** someone who is being taught by a teacher. **2.** the opening in the centre of the eye, through which light passes.

puppet (pup′ ət) *n.* a doll that can be moved and made to perform, usually on a stage.

puppy (pup′ ē) *n.* a young dog. *pl.* **puppies.**

purchase (pûr′ chəs) *n.* something that is bought: *We made a few purchases before going home.* *v.* to buy: *I purchased a scarf before the winter.* **purchasing. purchased.**

pure (pyūr) *adj.* clean and fresh; not mixed with other things: *pure wool; pure water; pure gold.*

purple (pûrpl) *n.* a colour made by mixing blue and red. *adj.* having this colour.

purpose (pûr′ pəs) *n.* **1.** the reason for doing something: *The purpose of my visit is to see my friends.* **2.** the use that something has: *What is the purpose of that part of the machine?*

on purpose as planned or intended, not by mistake or by accident: *The bad child spilled the milk on purpose.*

purr (pûr) *n.* the sound that a happy cat makes. *v.* to make such a sound.

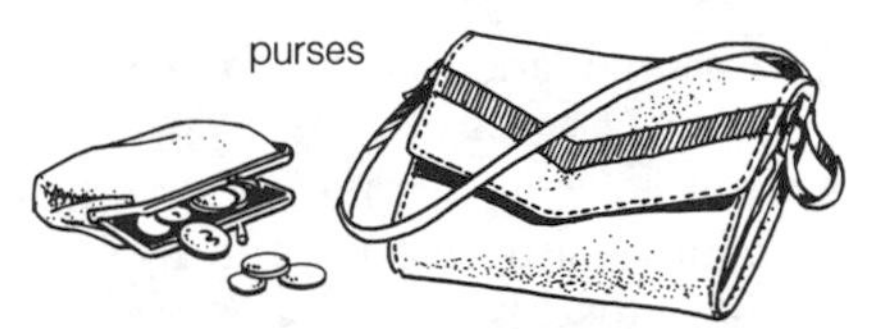

purse (pûrs) *n.* a small bag in which money, keys, and other things are kept.

pursue (pûr sū′) *v.* **1.** to chase after; to follow in order to catch: *The police pursued the speeding car.* **2.** to continue to work at: *She pursued a career in law.* **pursuing. pursued.**

push (pu̇sh) *n.* a shove away from oneself; the opposite of **pull.** *pl.* **pushes.** *v.* to press or move something away from oneself: *The drawer is not closed. Push it a little harder.* **pushing. pushed.** he **pushes.**

pussycat (pu̇s′ i kat′, pu̇s′ ē kat′) *n. (informal)* a cat.

put (pu̇t) *v.* to place something somewhere: *Put the plate on the table. Put your shoes on.* **putting. put.**

put off to delay till later: *We put off our visit until our uncle felt better.*

put out **1.** to stop something from burning: *Put out that fire!* **2.** to annoy; to trouble: *Will it put you out if I stay till tomorrow?*

put up with to accept something, even though there may be a problem: *Our neighbours are noisy, but we put up with them.*

putty (put′ ē) *n.* a soft, greyish mixture used for holding glass in a window frame and for filling in cracks.

puzzle (puzl) *n.* a question that is hard to answer, or a problem that is fun and challenging to solve: *a jigsaw puzzle; a crossword puzzle.* *v.* to confuse; to make someone think about something: *His illness puzzled the doctors.* **puzzling. puzzled.**

pyjamas (pə jȧm′ əs, pə jam′ əs) *n.pl.* a set of clothes to sleep in.

pyramid (pir′ ə mid′) *n.* a structure that has a square base and four sides shaped like triangles: *The points of the sides of a pyramid meet at the top.*

Q

quaint (kwānt) *adj.* old-fashioned in an odd or interesting way: *a quaint dress for the child's doll.*

quake (kwāk) *v.* to shake; to tremble: *The bridge quaked as the heavy trucks moved along.* **quaking. quaked.**

qualifications (kwȯl′ i fi kā′ shənz) *n.pl.* experience and education that help make a person right for a job: *She explained her qualifications when she applied for the job.*

⊖**qualify** (kwȯl′ i fī′) *v.* to have the ability, training, or skills needed to get into certain schools, get certain jobs, join certain teams, etc. **qualifying. qualified.** he **qualifies.**

⊖**quality** (kwȯl′ i tē) *n.* **1.** how good a thing is: *This fruit is of fine quality.* **2.** something special that makes a person, animal, or thing what it is: *One of the qualities of fur is softness. pl.* **qualities.**

quantity (kwȯn′ ti tē) *n.* a group or number: *I have a large quantity of records. pl.* **quantities.**

quarrel (kwȯr′ əl) *v.* to disagree and argue, often using angry words. **quarrelling. quarrelled.**

quarry (kwȯr′ ē) *n.* a place where stone for buildings is dug or cut. *pl.* **quarries.**

⊖**quart** (kwȯrt) *n.* a measure of liquid, equal to a little more than 1 L.

⊖**quarter** (kwȯr′ tər) *n.* **1.** one of four equal parts: *Divide the paper into quarters.* **2.** a 25-cent coin of Canada and the United States.

quarterback (kwȯr′ tər bak′) *n.* the football player who calls the signals for the team.

quartz (kwȯrtz) *n.* a hard mineral: *Some types of quartz are clear, and other types have brilliant colours.*

quay (kē) *n.* a place, often built of stone, where ships load and unload. *pl.* **quays.**

Quebec (kwe bek′, ki bek′) *n.* the province between Ontario on the west, Labrador and New Brunswick on the east; its capital is Quebec City. Short form: **Que.** or **P.Q.** A person born in or living in Quebec is a **Quebecker** or **Québécois** (kā bek wȧ′).

queen (kwēn) *n.* **1.** a woman who is ruler of a country, or a king's wife. **2.** a playing card with a picture of a queen on it. **3.** a piece in the game of chess. **4.** a female bee or ant that lays eggs.

queer (kwēr) *adj.* strange; unusual; odd.

quench (kwench) *v.* to put an end to: *I need another drink to quench my thirst.* **quenching. quenched.** it **quenches.**

question (kwes′ chən) *n.* something asked: *"Why is the sky blue?" is a question that many children ask.* *v.* to ask in order to get information: *The lawyer questioned the witness.*

question mark (kwes′ chen mȧrk′) the punctuation mark (?) put at the end of a sentence that asks a question.

quick (kwik) *adj.* fast; speedy; done in a short time: *a quick way home; a quick dinner.*

quicksand (kwik′ sand′) *n.* loose; wet sand into which a person can sink.

quiet (kwī′ ət) *adj.* noiseless; peaceful; calm: *a quiet child; a quiet room.*

⊖**quill** (kwil) *n.* **1.** a large, stiff feather. **2.** one of the stiff, sharp hairs on a porcupine.

quilt (kwilt) *n.* a thick bed covering made of two pieces of cloth filled with soft material.

quit (kwit) *v.* to leave; to give up: *My brother quit his job and returned to school.* **quitting. quit.**

quite (kwīt) *adv.* **1.** completely: *I felt quite alone when my friend moved away.* **2.** very: *It was quite cold.* **3.** really: *This is quite a surprise!*

quiver (kwiv′ ər) *n.* a case for arrows. *v.* to shake; to tremble: *The dog quivered with fear during the storm.*

quiz (kwiz) *n.* a short test. *pl.* **quizzes.** *v.* to give such a test. **quizzing. quizzed.** she **quizzes.**

quota (kwō′ tə) *n.* a stated number; a limit on an amount: *There is a quota of fifty on the number of students allowed in this class.* *pl.* **quotas.**

quotation (kwō tā′ shən) *n.* a repeating of the exact words that someone has said or written.

quotation marks (kwō tā′ shən märks) the punctuation marks (" ") put at the beginning and at the end of a quotation.

quote (kwōt) *v.* **1.** to repeat someone's exact words: *The newspaper quoted part of the Prime Minister's speech.* **2.** to state the amount or the estimated amount of something: *Can you please quote a price for fixing the roof?* **quoting. quoted.**

R

rabbi (rab′ ī) *n.* a Jewish religious leader. *pl.* **rabbis.**

rabbit (rab′ it) *n.* a small, furry animal with long ears; it lives in holes which it digs in the ground.

rabies (rā′ bēz) *n.* a very serious disease that dogs, bats, foxes, and other mammals can get. People can catch rabies if bitten by an animal that has this disease.

raccoon

raccoon (ra kūn′) *n.* a small, greyish-brown mammal with dark patches around its eyes; its bushy tail has rings of dark fur.

⊖**race** (rās) *n.* **1.** a contest to see who can go the fastest: *a fifty-metre race; a car race; a horse race.* **2.** a group of people having some features in common: *the human race; the European race.* *v.* **1.** to compete in a contest of speed. **2.** to move very fast: *Al raced to the bus stop.* **racing. raced.**

racism (rās′ izm) *n.* prejudice or discrimination; the belief that some races are better than others: *That book contains many examples of racism; the author shows a clear bias.*

rack (rak) *n.* a frame on which to hang things: *a towel rack.*

⊖**racket** (rak′ ət) *n.* **1.** a loud noise: *Don't make such a racket! The baby is sleeping.* **2.** a handle and frame with a net of strings, used to strike a ball in tennis, squash, and other games.
(*also spelled* **racquet.**)

radar (rā′ dår) *n.* a system that uses radio waves to locate distant objects and identify their speed and size.

radiation (rā′ di ā′ shən) *n.* rays of heat or energy: *Uranium gives off dangerous radiation.*

radiator (rā′ di ā′ tər) *n.* **1.** a heating device used for warming the air in a room. **2.** a device in a car that is filled with water to keep the engine cool.

radio (rā′ di ō′) *n.* **1.** a system for sending out and receiving words and other sounds across long distances. **2.** a machine for sending or receiving such sounds. *pl.* **radios.** *v.* to send a message by radio: *We radioed the ship for help.* **radioing. radioed.** she **radios.**

radioactive (rā′ di ō ak′ tiv) *adj.* producing radiation: *Uranium is a radioactive element.*

radish (rad′ ish) *n.* a small, red-skinned vegetable used in salads. *pl.* **radishes.**

radius (rā′ di əs) *n.* a straight line going from the centre of a circle or sphere to the circumference or surface. *pl.* **radii** (rā′ di ī), or **radiuses.**

⊖**raffle** (rafl) *n.* a contest in which people buy tickets, and those holding the winning tickets receive prizes.

raft (raft) *n.* logs or planks tied together to make a kind of flat boat.

rafter (raf′ tər) *n.* one of the sloping beams that supports a roof.

rag (rag) *n.* a small piece of cloth, usually used for cleaning.

⊖**rage** (rāj) *n.* great anger: *He left the room in a rage.*

raid (rād) *n.* a sudden attack: *an enemy raid.* *v.* to attack suddenly.

rail (rāl) *n.* **1.** a long, narrow bar usually made of metal or wood; it can be used for protection or for supporting things. **2.** railway: *Do you like to travel by rail?*

railing (rāl′ ing) *n.* a fence made of a rail or rails: *Hold onto the railing when you go down the staircase.*

railroad (rāl′ rōd′) *n.* a railway.

railway (rāl′ wā′) *n.* **1.** a track of steel rails on which trains run. **2.** tracks, stations, trains, and the people who manage them. *pl.* **railways.**

rain (rān) *n.* water falling in drops from the clouds. *v.* **1.** to fall in drops of water. **2.** to fall or drop like rain.

rainbow (rān′ bō′) *n.* an arch of colours in the sky, caused by the sun shining through rain or mist.

raincoat (rān′ kōt′) *n.* a waterproof coat.

rainy (rā′ nē) *adj.* having much rain: *a rainy day; a rainier day; the rainiest day of the year.*

raise (rāz) *n.* an increase in something, usually money: *After working for a year, he received a raise in pay.* *v.* **1.** to lift up or make higher: *to raise a window; to raise your voice.* **2.** to grow: *to raise corn; to raise cattle.* **3.** to collect: *to raise money for a new hospital.* **raising. raised.**

⊖**raisin** (rā′ zin) *n.* a small dried grape, used in cakes, cookies, cereals, etc.

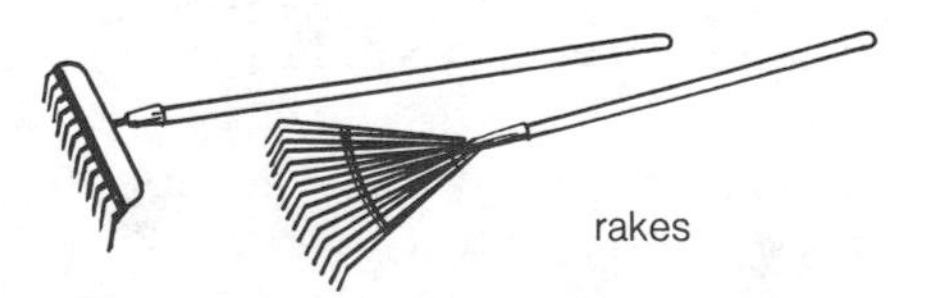

rakes

rake (rāk) *n.* a garden tool that has a row of spikes attached to one end of a long handle. *v.* to move with a rake: *Rake the leaves. Rake the hay.* **raking. raked.**

rally (ral′ ē) *n.* a large meeting for a certain purpose: *a political rally to support a candidate.* *pl.* **rallies.** *v.* to meet together; to bring together: *The candidate rallied his supporters.* **rallying. rallied.** he **rallies.**

⊖**ram** (ram) *n.* a male sheep. *v.* **1.** to crash against: *In the chase, one car rammed another.* **2.** to force into place: *He rammed the post into the ground.* **ramming. rammed.**

ramble (rambl) *v.* **1.** to wander about; to go for a long walk: *We rambled through the forest.* **2.** to talk or write in a way that confuses people: *Don't ramble on. Talk about one thing at a time.* **rambling. rambled.**

ramp (ramp) *n.* a short, sloping road connecting different levels: *a highway ramp.*

ran see **run.**

ranch (ranch) *n.* a very large farm on which cattle, horses, or sheep are raised. *pl.* **ranches.**

random (ran′ dəm) *adj.* not planned; not able to be predicted: *The results of the poll were based on a random sample of adults.*

rang see **ring.**

⊖**range** (ranj) *n.* **1.** a connected row of mountains. **2.** a large, open area of land where cattle, sheep, or horses roam. **3.** a stove with burners and an oven. **4.** the way things can be different or can vary between limits: *Between morning and night, there can be a wide range of temperatures.* **5.** an area where people can practise shooting guns; an area where missiles are tested. **6.** the distance at which a person can be seen or heard: *Come closer. You're not in hearing range.* *v.* **1.** to roam; to wander: *The cattle ranged over the hills.* **2.** to vary between certain limits: *The prices range from a quarter to a dollar.* **ranging. ranged.**

⊖**ranger** (rān′ jər) *n.* a person whose job is to look after a large area of forest.

rank (rangk) *n.* a position; a level: *He held the rank of captain in the army.*

ransom (ran′ səm) *n.* money paid for the return of someone who has been taken prisoner or kidnapped.

rap (rap) *n.* a quick, light tap: *a rap on the door.* *v.* to tap quickly. **rapping. rapped.**

⊖**rape** (rāp) *n.* a crime in which one person forces another to have sex. *v.* to commit this crime. **raping. raped.**

rapid (rap′ id) *adj.* very fast: *a rapid train; a rapid worker.*

rapids (rap′ idz) *n.pl.* a part of a river where the water is shallow and moves very fast, often over rocks.

rare (rer, rār) *adj.* **1.** not happening often; not often found or seen: *That old coin is valuable because it is so rare.* **2.** not cooked very much: *a rare steak, a rarer one; the rarest one of all.*

rascal (ras′ kəl) *n.* a mischievous, naughty person.

rash (rash) *n.* small red spots on the skin, caused by illness or an inflammation. *pl.* **rashes.**

rasp (rasp) *n.* **1.** a harsh, grating sound; the sound of a file moving against wood. **2.** a tool with rough, sharp 'teeth', used for smoothing wood or metal.

raspberry (raz′ ber′ ē) *n.* a small, red, juicy fruit that grows on bushes. *pl.* **raspberries.**

rat (rat) *n.* **1.** a long-tailed, gnawing rodent that looks like a large mouse. **2.** *(informal)* a nasty person.

rate (rāt) *n.* **1.** speed: *a rate of sixty kilometres per hour.* **2.** a price or charge for something: *What is the mechanic's hourly rate?* *v.* to consider how good or bad something is: *How do you rate the new movie?* **rating. rated.**

rather (rat͟h′ ər) *adv.* **1.** more gladly: *Mark would rather eat meat than fish.* **2.** more than a little bit: *I felt rather cold standing outside.*

ratio (rā′ shi ō′) *n.* the relationship between the amount of one thing and the amount of another: *The ratio of men to women was two to one. There were ten men for every five women.* *pl.* **ratios.**

ration (rash′ ən) *n.* an amount that is allowed: *Each hiker had a daily ration of food.* *v.* to allow only certain amounts of something: *During a war, food and supplies are often rationed.*

rational (rash′ ən əl) *adj.* **1.** sensible; having a reason: *There must be a rational explanation for this mystery.* **2.** able to think clearly: *Everybody thought the man was mad, but when we talked to him he seemed quite rational.*

rationalize (rash′ ən əl īz′) *v.* to make up false reasons for doing something or thinking something: *He rationalizes his fear of driving by saying that it is healthier to walk.* **rationalizing. rationalized.**

rattle (ratl) *n.* **1.** the sound made by shaking a lot of hard things together. **2.** a baby's toy that makes this sound. *v.* to make such a sound: *The cans rattled in the bag.* **rattling. rattled.**

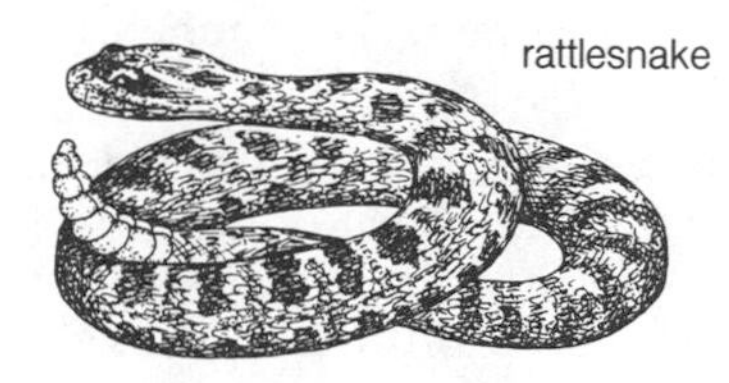
rattlesnake

rattlesnake (ratl′ snāk′) *n.* a poisonous snake that makes a rattling sound with its tail.

rave (rāv) *v.* to talk excitedly; to be very pleased about: *Everyone raved about the cake that he made.* **raving. raved.**

⊖**ravine** (rə vēn′) *n.* a long, deep, narrow valley.

raw (rȯ) *adj.* **1.** not cooked: *raw meat.* **2.** not manufactured, treated, etc.: *Raw sugar is refined to make white sugar.* **3.** damp and cold: *a raw day.*

ray (rā) *n.* **1.** a thin beam of light: *a ray of sunshine through the clouds.* **2.** a small amount: *There was only a ray of hope that the sick man would get well. pl.* **rays.**

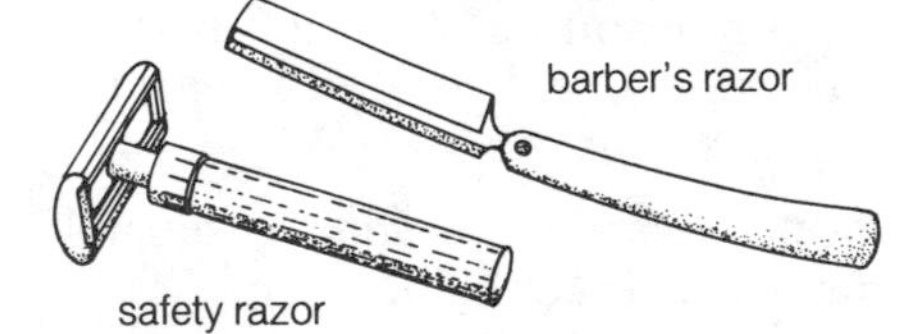

razor (rā′ zər) *n.* a sharp cutting instrument used for shaving off hair.

RCMP short for **Royal Canadian Mounted Police.**

re- 1. a prefix meaning 'again': to **reopen** means to open again. **2.** a prefix meaning 'back': to **repay** means to pay back.

reach (rēch) *v.* **1.** to stretch out and touch or get: *Can you reach the book on the top shelf? He reached across the table for the butter.* **2.** to arrive at: *They reached the city in the morning.* **3.** to contact; to get in touch with someone: *You can reach me by telephone.* **reaching. reached.** she **reaches.**

react (rē akt′) *v.* **1.** to respond; to do something because of something that has already been done: *How would you react if I told you that you had won a million dollars?* **2.** to change as a result of being mixed with another substance: *Hydrogen reacts with oxygen to form water.*

reaction (rē ak′ shən) *n.* **1.** a response; the result of something that has been done: *As she told me the news, she watched to see my reaction.* **2.** a change in a substance: *In a nuclear reaction, much heat is produced as one metal is changed into another.*

read (rēd) *v.* to look at words and understand their meaning. **reading. read** (red).

reader (rēd′ ər) *n.* **1.** a book that helps to teach reading. **2.** a person who reads.

ready (red′ ē) *adj.* prepared: *I will be ready to go in five minutes.*

real (rēl) *adj.* **1.** true; not imaginary: *a real person, not a ghost.* **2.** not artificial or made-up: *These are real plants.*

real estate (rēl′ əs tāt′) land and the buildings, trees, etc. on it.

realize (rē′ ə līz′) *v.* to understand clearly: *I didn't realize that your car was so large.* **realizing. realized.**

really (rē′ ə lē) *adv.* truly: *I really mean what I say!*

rear (rēr) *n.* the back part: *the rear of the train. v.* **1.** to take care of and support: *They reared three children.* **2.** for a horse or other animal, to rise on the back legs.

⊖**reason** (rē′ zən) *n.* **1.** an explanation; a cause for something happening: *The reason I am happy is that you are here.* **2.** the ability to think, which human beings have. *v.* **1.** to think: *People can reason, but other animals cannot.* **2.** to use arguments to persuade someone: *I tried to reason with them to stop fighting.*

reasonable (rē′ zən abl) *adj.* **1.** sensible; not foolish: *a reasonable person.* **2.** fair; not expensive: *a reasonable price.*

rebate (rē′ bāt′) *n.* the return of part of the money paid; a partial refund: *a rent rebate; a tax rebate.*

rebel (rebl, reb′ əl) *n.* a person who fights against the people in charge and refuses to obey their orders.

rebel (ri bel′) *v.* to refuse to follow orders; to be a rebel. **rebelling. rebelled.**

rebellion (ri bel′ yən) *n.* a fight against a person's own government or against any authority.

recall (ri kȯl′, rē kȯl′) *v.* **1.** to call someone or something back: *The automobile company recalled a thousand cars because the brakes did not work properly.* **2.** to remember: *I cannot recall his name.*

receipt (ri sēt′) *n.* a note stating that a person has paid for something.

receive (ri sēv′) *v.* to take what is given: *Dan received many presents.* **receiving. received.**

receiver (ri sēv′ ər) *n.* **1.** the part of a telephone that is put to the ear. **2.** a person or thing that receives.

recent (rē′ sənt) *adj.* made or having happened a short time before: *a recent visit.*

⊖**reception** (ri sep′ shən) *n.* the way people react to something they have heard: *She was pleased by the audience's reception to her speech.* **2.** a party to welcome people: *A wedding reception is a party to welcome the guests at a wedding.* **3.** the quality of a radio or television signal: *The reception on the TV last night was bad because of the storm.*

recess (rē′ ses) *n.* **1.** a short rest period. **2.** a space in a wall that is set back. *pl.* **recesses.**

recession (ri sesh′ ən) *n.* a period of time when people have less money to spend because there is not as much business happening as usual: *He found it hard to find a job during the recession.*

recipe (res′ i pē′) *n.* directions on how to make something to eat or drink.

recital (ri sīt′ əl) *n.* a public performance, often by pupils: *a dance recital.*

recite (ri sīt′) *v.* to tell a story or a poem from memory. **reciting. recited.**

reckless (rek′ ləs) *adj.* being careless and risking danger: *Reckless driving causes many accidents.*

recline (ri klīn′) *v.* to lie back: *I reclined on the couch.* **reclining. reclined.**

recognize (rek′ əg nīz′) *v.* **1.** to remember; to know again: *I didn't recognize him because he grew a beard.* **2.** to admit that something is real: *Not everyone recognized the king as the leader.* **recognizing. recognized.**

recommend (rek′ ə mend′) *v.* **1.** to speak in favour of someone or something: *I can recommend her for the job. She is an excellent worker.* **2.** to suggest: *I recommend that you try another store.*

reconditioned (rē′ kən dish′ ənd) *adj.* repaired and made to work well: *We could not afford a new car, so we bought a reconditioned used car.*

record (rek′ ərd) *n.* **1.** a written account or diary: *When we have a meeting, we keep a record of everything that is said.* **2.** a performance that is the best yet: *He holds the record for running.* **3.** a flat disc, to be played on a stereo or record player.

record (ri kȯrd′) *v.* **1.** to write down events: *He recorded the amount of money he spent.* **2.** to put sounds on a tape or record: *Music is recorded in a special room.*

recorder (ri kôr′ dər) *n.* **1.** a wind instrument made of wood or plastic. **2.** a person whose job is taking notes. **3.** a machine that records sounds on a tape.

recover (ri kuv′ ər) *v.* **1.** to get better after an illness. **2.** to get something back: *We recovered the stolen car within a week.* **3.** to put new material on a chair, chesterfield, etc.

recovery (ri kuv′ ə rē) *n.* **1.** getting well after illness: *We wish you a quick recovery.* **2.** getting back something that was lost, stolen, or sent away: *the recovery of a lost dog. pl.* **recoveries.**

recreation (rek′ rē ā′ shən) *n.* games, hobbies, and other enjoyable things done for amusement.

recruit (ri krūt′) *n.* a new member of the army, navy, police force, or other group. *v.* to encourage a person to join such a group.

rectangle (rek′ tangl) *n.* a figure that has four sides and four right angles: *Oblongs and squares are rectangles.*

rectum (rek′ təm) *n.* the lowest end of the intestine, through which solid waste passes.

recycle (rē sīkl′) *v.* to put into use again: *Don't throw away the cans. They can be recycled.* **recycling. recycled.**

red (red) *n.* the colour of blood. *adj.* having such a colour: *a red tie; a redder one; the reddest tie of all.*

redeem (ri dēm′) *v.* **1.** to exchange something for money: *This coupon can be redeemed for cash.* **2.** to make up for: *The boring film was redeemed only by the beautiful scenery.*

reduce (ri dūs′) *v.* to make something smaller, cheaper, slower, etc.: *The price of yesterday's bread is reduced. The driver reduced his speed.* **reducing. reduced.**

reduction (ri duk′ shən) *n.* **1.** the act of reducing: *There was a reduction on the price of that dress.* **2.** the amount that something is being reduced: *a thirty per cent reduction.* **3.** a smaller copy of a photograph, picture, etc.

reed (rēd) *n.* **1.** a tall grass that grows at the edge of water. **2.** a thin piece of wood, metal, etc., used in the mouthpieces of some musical instruments. When air is blown into the mouthpiece, the reed vibrates, producing sounds.

reef (rēf) *n.* a line of rocks, sand, coral, etc., that lies just below or above the surface of the sea.

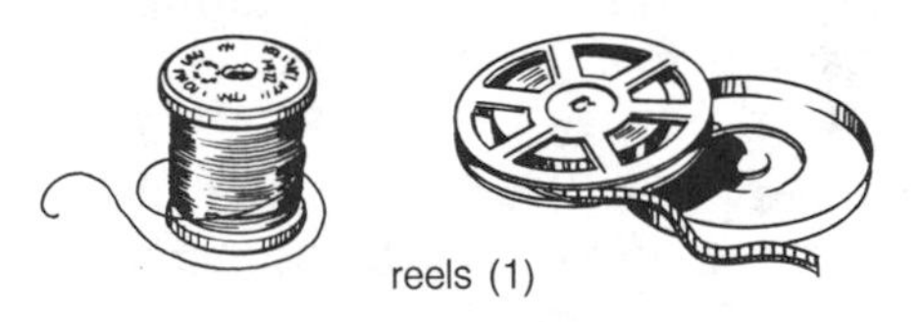

reels (1)

reel (rēl) *n.* **1.** a spool-like frame used for winding thread, film, fishing line, etc. **2.** a lively dance.

re-elect (rē′ i lekt′) *v.* to elect again.

re-entry (rē′ en′ trē) *n.* the return of a spacecraft to the earth's atmosphere. *pl.* **re-entries.**

refer (ri fûr′) *v.* to send or direct for information or help: *The librarian referred me to the dictionary. The doctor referred me to another doctor.* **2.** to look at for information: *She referred to her notebook.* **3.** to mention; to speak about: *He referred to Ottawa as the world's coldest capital city.* **referring. referred.**

referee (ref′ ə rē′) *n.* someone who sees that the rules of a game or contest are obeyed.

reference (ref′ ər əns) *n.* **1.** something used for information: *A dictionary is a book of reference.* **2.** a statement about a person's ability: *When he left his* *job he asked for a letter of reference.* **3.** a mention of something: *In the report, he made reference to the people who helped him.*

referendum (ref′ ə ren′ dəm) *n.* a special vote by all the people of a country or an area to decide something important. *pl.* **referendums**, or **referenda.**

refine (ri fīn′) *v.* to make something more pure; to improve something: *to refine impure water into pure water.* **refining. refined.**

refined (ri fīnd′) *adj.* **1.** knowing how to behave properly: *She is very refined. She always knows the right thing to say to people.* **2.** made pure: *refined sugar.*

reflect (ri flekt′) *v.* **1.** to give back a picture or light, as water or a mirror does. **2.** to think seriously about something: *Henrietta reflected on what had happened during the past year.*

reflection (ri flek′ shən) *n.* **1.** a picture or light, reflected from a shiny surface. **2.** serious thinking about something. **3.** one thing that shows or represents another: *The beautiful cabinet is a reflection of her skill as a carpenter.*

reform (ri fȯrm′) *n.* improvement or correction. *v.* to make something better; to improve or correct: *The criminal reformed his behaviour, and now he spends his time helping other people.*

refreshments (ri fresh′ mənts) *n.pl.* things to eat or drink: *There will be refreshments at the party.*

refrigerate (ri frij′ ə rāt′) *v.* to keep cool; to put inside a refrigerator: *Please refrigerate the bacon as soon as you get home.* **refrigerating. refrigerated.**

refrigerator (ri frij′ ə rā′ tər) *n.* a machine that keeps stored food cold.

refuge (ref′ yūj) *n.* shelter: *It was storming, and we took refuge in a shelter.*

refugee (ref′ yu jē, ref′ yū jē′) *n.* someone who has fled from one place to another to find safety or protection.

refund (rē′ fund) *n.* money paid back: *The pen did not work, so I asked for a refund.*

refund (ri fund′) *v.* to pay back money: *The store manager refunded my money because the radio did not work.*

refuse (ref′ yūz) *n.* garbage: *The refuse was thrown into a large green bag.*

refuse (ri fyūz′) *v.* to say 'no'; not to do what is asked: *The child refused to eat her lunch.* **refusing. refused.**

⊖**regard** (ri gȧrd′) *n.* respect; admiration: *I have a great regard for Tom.* *v.* to think of: *I regard Tom highly.*

regardless (ri gȧrd′ ləs) *adv.* ignoring something; in spite of: *He walked into the old house, regardless of the danger.*

regards (ri gȧrdz′) *n.pl.* best wishes: *Give my regards to your cousin when you visit her.*

⊖**regime** (rə zhēm′) *n.* a system of government: *There was a revolution in the country, and the old regime was changed.*

Regina (ri jīn′ ə) *n.* the capital city of Saskatchewan.

region (rē′ jən) *n.* a large area of land: *the northern region of the province; the northern region of the country; a region of mountains.*

register (rej′ i stər) *n.* **1.** a machine that keeps a record of certain items: *a cash register.* **2.** a written list of names and other information: *The hotel register is at the front desk.* *v.* to sign in: *We* *registered at the hotel desk before going to our room.*

regret (ri gret′) *v.* to be sorry about something: *I regretted hurting the other player in the game.* **regretting. regretted.**

regular (reg′ yə lər) *adj.* **1.** usual; normal: *My regular way of getting there is to take a bus.* **2.** steady; happening again and again at the same time: *the regular ticking of the clock.*

regulation (reg′ yə lā′ shən) *n.* a rule: *It is against traffic regulations to drive through a red light.*

rehearsal (ri hûr′ səl) *n.* a practice to get ready for a performance: *The actors had many rehearsals before the play opened.*

rehearse (ri hûrs′) *v.* to practise something, such as a play, in order to prepare for a performance. **rehearsing. rehearsed.**

reign (rān) *n.* the period of time that a king or queen rules: *The reign lasted ten years.* *v.* to rule, as king or queen: *The queen reigned for many years.*

reindeer (rān′ dēr′) *n.* a large deer that has antlers and lives in northern regions. *pl.* **reindeer.**

reinforce (rē′ in fôrs′) *v.* to make something stronger: *These wire coat hangers are reinforced with cardboard so that they will not bend.* **reinforcing. reinforced.**

⊖**reins** (rānz) *n.pl.* leather straps attached to a horse's bridle: *The rider held the reins to guide her horse.*

reject (rē′ jekt) *n.* something that is not wanted: *The reason these shoes are so cheap is that they are factory rejects.*

reject (ri jekt′) *v.* to treat something as worthless: *He rejected everything I had to say. She rejected our plans.* **2.** to refuse to accept: *They rejected him for the army because his health was poor.*

rejoice (ri jȯis′) *v.* to show how very pleased or happy someone is: *We rejoiced when we heard the lost children were found.* **rejoicing. rejoiced.**

relate (ri lāt′) *v.* to tell; to describe: *The traveller related his adventures to the children.* **relating. related.**

related (ri lāt′ əd) *adj.* connected; belonging to the same family: *How are you related to him?*

relationship (ri lā′ shən ship′) *n.* **1.** what two or more things or people have to do with each other: *What is your relationship to that man? Is he your father?* **2.** the way that people behave towards each other: *They have a good relationship. They are always kind to each other.*

relative (rel′ ə tiv) *n.* a person who belongs to the same family as someone else: *I have lots of relatives: two brothers, two sisters, my parents, four uncles, five aunts, and twelve cousins.*

relax (ri laks′) *v.* to take a rest and do something for pleasure: *After work, he relaxes by reading the newspaper.* **relaxing. relaxed.** she **relaxes.**

relaxation (rē′ lak sā′ shən, ri lak sā′ shən) *n.* something done for enjoyment: *Swimming is my favourite form of relaxation.*

relay (rē′ lā′) *v.* to take and pass along: *The messenger relayed the information.*

release (ri lēs′) *v.* **1.** to let go: *Release your hold on the rope.* **2.** to set free: *Release the prisoner.* **releasing. released.**

relevant (rel′ ə vənt) *adj.* having something to do with what is being talked about or thought about: *What you have said about dirty water is very relevant to our talk on pollution.*

reliable (ri lī′ əbl) *adj.* able to be trusted: *He is a reliable person. I know he will keep his promise.*

⊖**relief** (ri lēf′) *n.* freedom from worry, trouble, or pain: *It was a relief to hear that nobody was hurt in the accident.*

relieve (ri lēv′) *v.* **1.** to end worry or pain: *The medicine relieved his headache.* **2.** to take over a duty from someone: *The day nurse relieved the night nurse at seven o'clock.* **relieving. relieved.**

religion (ri lij′ ən) *n.* the belief in God, or in a god or gods.

religious (ri lij′ əs) *adj.* having to do with religion: *a religious service.*

relish (rel′ ish) *n.* a kind of pickle of chopped vegetables or fruits, served with hamburgers and other foods. *pl.* **relishes.**

reluctant (ri luk′ tənt) *adj.* not wanting to do something; unwilling: *Jane's doctor was reluctant to let her leave the hospital so soon after her illness.*

rely (ri lī′) *v.* (used with **on**) to depend on, to trust: *We rely on you to show us the way.* **relying. relied.** she **relies.**

remain (ri mān′) *v.* **1.** to stay behind or in the same place: *After the party we remained at his house.* **2.** to be left over: *All that remains is one piece of cake.* **3.** to stay: *They remained friends for many years.*

remainder (ri mān′ dər) *n.* **1.** what is left over: *the remainder of the cake.* **2.** in arithmetic, the number left over when a number cannot be divided evenly.

⊖**remark** (ri mȧrk′) *n.* a short statement: *Joan made a nice remark about my new shirt.* *v.* to say a few words: *Kenneth remarked that he felt tired.*

remarkable (ri mȧrk′ əbl) *adj.* surprising; special; worth talking about: *His memory is remarkable. He doesn't forget anything.*

remedial (ri mē′ di əl) *adj.* making a situation better: *The teacher put my brother in a remedial math class to help him improve his math.*

remedy (rem′ ə dē) *n.* something that makes an illness or other situation better; a cure: *What is a good remedy for a cold?* *pl.* **remedies.**

remember (ri mem′ bər) *v.* **1.** to bring back to mind: *Although I read the book years ago, I remember it well.* **2.** to keep in mind: *Remember to take a pen to school.*

Remembrance Day (ri mem′ brəns dā′) *n.* November 11, the day we honour the people who died in the First and Second World Wars.

remind (ri mīnd′) *v.* to help someone remember: *I reminded them about the picnic.*

reminder (ri mīn′ dər) *n.* a few words or a note to someone, to help him or her to remember.

remote (ri mōt′) *adj.* far off; distant: *a remote area far away from any town; a remoter area; the remotest one of all.*

remote control (ri mōt′ kən trōl′) the control of a TV or other machine from a distance, usually by radio signals.

remove (ri müv′) *v.* to take away: *Please remove the papers from the table.* **removing. removed.**

renew (ri nyü′, ri nü′) *v.* to borrow or get for another period of time: *to renew a book; to renew a driver's licence.*

renovate (ren′ ə vāt′) *v.* to make something old seem new again: *It took us a year to renovate the old house.* **renovating. renovated.**

⊖**rent** (rent) *n.* money paid for the use of an apartment, house, or something else a person does not own. *v.* **1.** to pay for the use of something: *to rent an apartment from someone.* **2.** to charge rent for allowing someone to use something: *We rent a room to a student.*

repair (ri per′) *v.* to fix something that is broken or torn.

repay (rē pā′) *v.* to return money to someone who has lent it. **repaying. repaid.**

repeat (ri pēt′) *v.* to say or do something again: *I repeated the directions to make sure he understood them.*

⊖**repetition** (rep′ ə tish′ ən) *n.* the saying of a thing or the doing of a thing more than once.

replace (ri plās′) *v.* **1.** to take the place of: *Otto will replace Paul as captain of the team.* **2.** to put back: *He replaced the book on the shelf.* **replacing. replaced.**

reply (ri plī′) *n.* an answer: *Denis sent a reply to the invitation.* *pl.* **replies.** *v.* to answer: *He replied to the letter the same day he received it.* **replying. replied.** she **replies.**

report (ri pȯrt′) *n.* a written or spoken description or statement of something: *The student wrote a report about the country he was born in.* *v.* to give a report about something: *He reported the fire to the fire department.*

report card (ri pȯrt′ kard′) a written statement that describes or judges a student's school work at the end of a certain period.

reporter (ri pȯr′ tər) *n.* someone who collects news for a newspaper, magazine, or radio or TV show.

represent (rep′ ri zent′) *v.* **1.** to stand for; to mean: *The symbol of a maple leaf represents Canada.* **2.** to act for or speak for: *Your Member of Parliament represents your community in Ottawa.*

representative (rep′ ri zen′ tə tiv) *n.* a person chosen to act or speak for others.

reproduce (rē′ prə dyüs′, rē′ prə düs′) *v.* **1.** to make a copy: *This tape recorder reproduces my voice perfectly.* **2.** to produce young: *Rabbits reproduce very quickly.* **reproducing. reproduced.**

reproduction (rē′ prə duk′ shən) *n.* **1.** a copy: *This painting is not real. It is only a reproduction.* **2.** the making of young: *The reproduction of plants involves seeds.*

reptile (rep′ tīl′) *n.* a cold-blooded animal that creeps or crawls: *Snakes, turtles, and crocodiles are some reptiles.*

republic (ri pub′ lik) *n.* a nation that is headed by a president: *The United States is a republic.*

reputation (rep′ yə tā′ shən) *n.* what people think and say of someone or something: *He has a reputation for being an honest person. This kind of car does not have a good reputation.*

request (ri kwest′) *v.* to ask for something in a polite way: *She requested permission to leave early.*

require (ri kwīr′) *v.* to need: *How many stamps does this letter require?* **requiring. required.**

requirement (ri kwīr′ mənt) *n.* something that is needed: *One of the requirements for the job is a knowledge of English and French.*

rescue (res′ kyū) *n.* the saving from danger or harm: *The cat was in the tree, and my friend came to its rescue. v.* to save from danger or harm: *The firefighter rescued three people from the burning house.* **rescuing. rescued.**

research (rē′ sûrch) *n.* work that is done to find out something: *After a day's research in the library, I found the information I wanted. pl.* **researches.**

resemblance (ri zem′ bləns) *n.* a similar appearance: *There is a great resemblance between my brother and me.*

resemble (rē zembl′) *v.* to look similar to: *Ellen resembles her sister, and sometimes people call her by the wrong name.* **resembling. resembled.**

reservation (rez′ ər vā′ shən) *n.* an arrangement made ahead of time: *We made a reservation for dinner at the restaurant.*

reserve (ri zûrv′) *n.* land set aside for a special purpose: *an Indian reserve. v.* to arrange for something to be kept available: *Before we began our holiday, we reserved a room at the motel.* **reserving. reserved.**

reservoir (rez′ ər vwår′) *n.* a large tank or pond where water is collected and stored for later use.

residence (rez′ i dəns) *n.* the place where a person lives.

residential (rez′ i den′ shəl) *adj.* to do with where people have their homes: *This is a residential area. There are no factories or office buildings here, only houses and apartment buildings.*

resign (ri zīn′) *v.* to give up a job or position: *He resigned from his job because he was moving.*

resist (ri zist′) *v.* to fight or struggle against: *The robber resisted the police officer.*

resolution (rez′ ə lū′ shən) *n.* a decision to do something: *She has made a resolution to stop smoking.*

⊖**resort** (ri zȯrt′) *n.* a holiday place. *v.* (used with **to**) to use or turn to, when nothing else helps: *The countries could not live peacefully, and finally they resorted to war.*

resource (ri sȯrs′, rə zȯrs′) *n.* **1.** a supply of something that will meet a need: *Canada has many natural resources, including minerals, fish, and lumber.* **2.** a person or thing that is used for help or information.

respect (ri spekt′) *n.* a good opinion of someone or something: *I have great respect for doctors. v.* to admire; to have a good opinion of someone or something: *I respect your ideas.*

respiration (res′ pə rā′ shən) *n.* breathing: *Artificial respiration means making a person breathe again by forcing air into and out of the lungs.*

respond (ri spond′) *v.* **1.** to answer with words: *She responded to the question.* **2.** to answer with an action: *The sick boy responded well to the medicine.*

response (ri spons′) *n.* **1.** a reply: *I asked who was there, but heard no response.* **2.** a result of something that has been done: *The doctors were pleased with her response to the medicine.*

responsible (rē spon′ səbl) *adj.* **1.** being in charge: *Ms. Woods is responsible for locking the doors of the office.* **2.** being the main cause: *Who was responsible for the accident?* **3.** able to be trusted: *He's a responsible worker. You can trust him with the money.*

⊖**rest** (rest) *n.* **1.** a time of quiet and, sometimes, sleep: *Get some rest before you take the trip.* **2.** what is left; the people who are left: *Have the rest of the salad. Jim went to work, and the rest of us stayed home.* **3.** in music, a period of silence. *v.* **1.** to stop working; to relax or have a nap. **2.** to support: *Rest your head on the pillow.*

restaurant (res′ tər änt) *n.* a place where people can buy and eat a meal.

restless (rest′ ləs) *adj.* not able to be still and quiet: *The movie was very long, and my little brother became restless.*

restore (ri stôr′) *v.* to bring something back to the way it was before: *The workers are restoring the old town hall.* **restoring. restored.**

restrain (ri strān′) *v.* to hold back, to keep in control: *She restrained her dog from chasing the cat.*

restrict (ri strikt′) *v.* to keep under control or within certain limits: *My parents restricted my brother to making two phone calls a night.*

result (ri zult′) *n.* **1.** the final score or sum: *The result of adding five and four is nine.* **2.** something that happens because of something else: *Her broken arm was the result of a bad fall.* *v.* to end; to come to a conclusion.
result in to have as an outcome: *The soccer game resulted in a tie.*
result from to have as a cause: *An accident may result from driving a car too fast.*

resume (ri zyūm′, ri zūm′) *v.* to continue after stopping for a time: *I must go to bed now. We can resume our conversation in the morning.* **resuming. resumed.**

⊖**résumé** (rez′ ū mā′) *n.* a list of the jobs and education a person has had: *Employers often look at a résumé when they are deciding whether to hire someone.*

retail (rē′ tāl) *adj.* to do with being sold in a store: *The retail price of something is the amount that it is sold for in a store.*

retain (ri tān′) *v.* to keep; to hold: *When I bought the lamp, I mailed the guarantee and retained my receipt.*

retire (ri tīr′) *v.* **1.** to give up work, usually because of reaching a certain age: *He retired from his job at sixty-five.* **2.** to go to bed. **retiring. retired.**

retrieve (ri trēv′) *v.* to get back or to find again: *My brother jumped in the lake to retrieve my lost ring.* **retrieving. retrieved.**

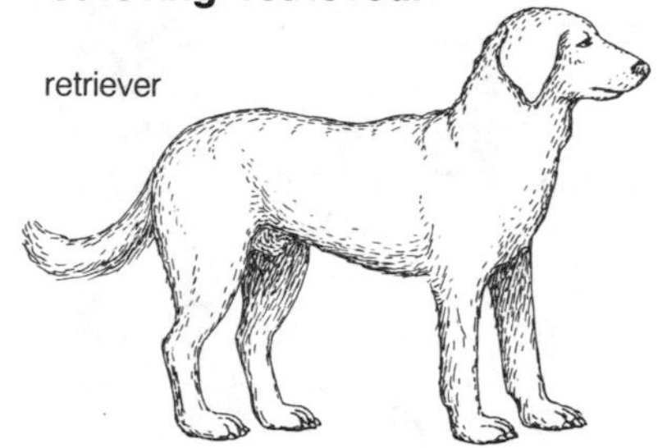
retriever

retriever (ri trēv′ ər) *n.* a dog that can be trained to retrieve things.

return (ri tûrn′) *n.* **1.** the giving back of something: *The library asked for the return of the overdue book.* **2.** a statement of official information: *an income tax return; election returns.* *v.* **1.** to come or go back: *to return home.* **2.** to give back: *He returned the book to the library.*

⊖**reunion** (rē yūn′ yən) *n.* a coming together again of a group of people: *Our family has a reunion each year.*

reveal (ri vēl′) *v.* to make known: *Don't reveal my secret!*

revenge (ri venj′) *n.* something done to harm a person because of harm done by that person.

revenue (rev′ ə nyū′, rev′ ə nū′) *n.* money that is received: *The government gets most of its revenue from taxes.*

⊖**reverence** (rev′ ə rəns) *n.* great respect, especially for holy things.

Reverend (rev′ ə rənd) *n.* a title given to certain members of the clergy.

reverse (ri vûrs′) *n.* **1.** the opposite: *He did the reverse of what I said. I told him to turn left, and he went right.* **2.** the position of gears that makes a car move back instead of forward. *v.* to go or turn in the opposite way. **reversing. reversed.**

⊖**review** (ri vyū′) *n.* **1.** a written or spoken account of a book, play, film, etc.: *The book received a good review.* **2.** a going over or checking of something: *He gave his answers a careful review before giving the test to the teacher.* *v.* **1.** to give a written or spoken account: *She reviews movies for the newspaper.* **2.** to go over something and check it.

revise (ri vīz′) *v.* to correct mistakes and make improvements: *I revised the letter several times, until it was right.* **revising. revised.**

revive (ri vīv′) *v.* to bring someone back to life or to being conscious: *They revived the drowning man by giving him artificial respiration.* **reviving. revived.**

revolt (ri vōlt′) *n.* a refusal to obey orders; a rebellion. *v.* to rebel.

revolution (rev′ ə lū′ shən) *n.* **1.** a complete changing of government and laws in a country: *There is often much force used when a revolution occurs.* **2.** a circular movement around a central point: *the revolution of the moon around the earth.*

revolve (ri volv′) *v.* to turn around and around in a circular path: *The earth revolves around the sun.* **revolving. revolved.**

revolver (ri vol′ vər) *n.* a hand gun that can be fired several times without having to be loaded again.

reward (ri wȯrd′) *n.* money or a prize given for something done. *v.* to give a reward: *We rewarded the man who found our lost dog.*

rheumatism (rū′ mə tiz′ əm) *n.* a disease in which the joints and muscles are stiff and painful.

rhubarb (rū′ bȧrb) *n.* a plant with reddish, sour-tasting stalks that can be cooked and eaten.

rhyme (rīm) *n.* a word having the same last sound as another: 'cat' is a rhyme for 'bat'; 'able' is a rhyme for 'table'. *v.* to sound alike in the last part: 'boy' rhymes with 'toy'. **rhyming. rhymed.**

rhythm (ri<u>th</u>′ əm) *n.* a regular beat or flow of sounds or movements: *the rhythm of a poem, dance, or song.*

rib (rib) *n.* one of the bones that curve around the chest, protecting the lungs.

ribbon (rib′ ən) *n.* a narrow strip of cloth such as silk, velvet, or satin: *a hair ribbon.*

rice (rīs) *n.* a cereal grass that grows in warm, wet regions and is used for food.

rich (rich) *adj.* **1.** having much wealth: *a rich person.* **2.** having much sugar, fat, or flavouring: *rich food.* **3.** having much value: *rich soil.*

rid (rid) *v.* to get free of something that is not wanted: *to rid the garden of weeds.* **ridding. rid**, or **ridded.**

riddle (ridl) *n.* a puzzling question such as: *What goes up when the rain falls down? (An umbrella.)*

⊖**ride** (rīd) *n.* **1.** a trip in a car or other vehicle, or on an animal's back. **2.** an amusement, such as a roller coaster, merry-go-round, etc. *v.* to travel in a vehicle or on an animal's back. **riding. rode** (rōd). I have **ridden** (rid′ ən).

ridge (rij) *n.* the long and narrow top part of something, such as a roof that slopes.

ridiculous (ri dik′ yə ləs) *adj.* very silly or foolish: *a ridiculous story.*

riding (rīd′ ing) *n.* an area in Canada represented by a Member of Parliament or a Member of the Legislative Assembly.

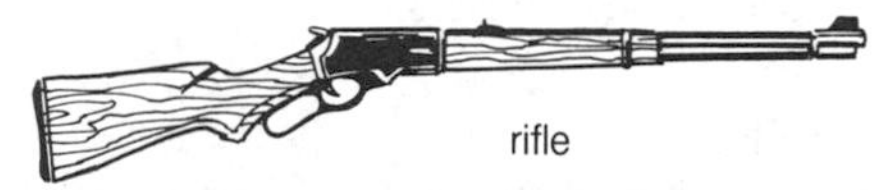
rifle

rifle (rīfl) *n.* a long gun that is fired from the shoulder.

right (rīt) *n.* **1.** what is good; the opposite of wrong. **2.** a claim; what is fair: *I have a right to the money. I worked for it. adj.* **1.** in the direction opposite of left: *When you look at a map of Canada, Alberta is on the right side of British Columbia.* **2.** true; correct: *Your answers are right.*

right angle (rīt′ angl′) an angle of ninety degrees: *The corners of a square are right angles.*

rigid (rig′ id) *adj.* **1.** hard to bend: *a rigid steel bar.* **2.** strict; never changing: *I tried to explain the need for the new rules, but the coach's ideas are very rigid.*

rim (rim) *n.* the outer edge of a cup, bowl, wheel, etc.

rind (rīnd) *n.* a thick peel: *Oranges, watermelons, and lemons have rinds.*

ring (ring) *n.* **1.** a circle: *The children formed a ring.* **2.** a metal band to wear on the finger: *a gold ring.* **3.** the sound of a bell: *I hear a ring at the door.* **4.** an area roped off for the performance of a sport: *a boxing ring; a wrestling ring. v.* to sound a bell, or to make a sound like that of a bell. **ringing. rang** (rang). I have **rung** (rung).

rink (ringk) *n.* **1.** a sheet of ice used by hockey players and other skaters. **2.** a sheet of ice used in the game of curling. **3.** a smooth floor used for roller-skating.

rinse (rins) *v.* to use clean water to wash away soap or dirt. **rinsing. rinsed.**

riot (rī′ ət) *n.* **1.** a violent and noisy disturbance caused by a group of people. **2.** *(informal)* something or someone who is very funny: *My friend is a riot. She always makes me laugh.*

rip (rip) *n.* a torn place: *a rip in your pants. v.* to tear roughly and quickly: *to rip your pants; to rip open an envelope.* **ripping. ripped.**

ripe (rīp) *adj.* ready to be eaten: *A ripe peach; a riper apple; the ripest fruit of all.*

ripple (ripl) *n.* a tiny wave on smooth water.

rise (rīs) *v.* **1.** to get up: *Donna rises very early each morning.* **2.** to move up: *The sun rises in the east.* **3.** to slope up: *The road rises from the village.* **rising. rose** (rōz). it has **risen** (riz′ ən).

risk (risk) *n.* a chance of harm or of losing something: *Mike took a risk by petting the unfriendly dog. v.* to take such a chance: *Firefighters sometimes risk their lives.*

⊖**risky** (ris′ kē) *adj.* full of risk: *a risky move; a riskier one; the riskiest move of all.*

rival (rī′ vəl) *n.* a person or group competing with another: *Those teams are rivals for the championship.*

river (riv′ ər) *n.* a large stream of water that flows into an ocean, bay, or lake, or into another river.

rivet (riv′ ət) *n.* a metal pin that passes through holes and is used to fasten pieces of metal together.

road (rōd) *n.* a long, narrow path on which vehicles travel; a street or highway.

roam (rōm) *v.* to wander; to travel about without a purpose: *The deer roamed through the forest.*

roar (rȯr) *n.* a deep sound made by a lion, heavy traffic, the waves of the sea, etc. *v.* to make such a sound.

roast (rōst) *n.* **1.** a large piece of meat that has been cooked, or is to be cooked. **2.** an outdoor meal where food is cooked over an open fire: *a wiener roast. v.* to cook in an oven or over a fire: *to roast meat.*

rob (rob) *v.* to steal; to take something that belongs to another person by using force: *to rob a bank.* **robbing. robbed.**

robber (rob′ ər) *n.* a thief.

robbery (rob′ ə rē) *n.* stealing; taking something that belongs to another person by using force: *a bank robbery. pl.* **robberies.**

robe (rōb) *n.* a long, loose outer garment.

robin (rob′ in) *n.* a small bird with a reddish breast.

robot (rō′ bot′) *n.* a machine that can do some human jobs.

rock (rok) *n.* **1.** the stone forming the earth's surface, or a piece of this hard material. **2.** a kind of popular music with a strong rhythm. *v.* to move gently back and forth: *to rock in a rocking chair.*

rocket (rok′ ət) *n.* **1.** a long, tube-shaped machine that is pushed high into the air or space by burning gases. Rockets may be used to put a space capsule into orbit, or to fire explosives at an enemy. **2.** a firework that goes high in the air when lit.

Rockies (rok′ ēz) short for **Rocky Mountains.**

rocky (rok′ ē) *adj.* bumpy, or being full of rocks: *a rocky road; a rockier road; the rockiest road in the county.*

Rocky Mountains (rok′ ē maůn′ tənz) a mountain range that extends through western Canada and the western United States.

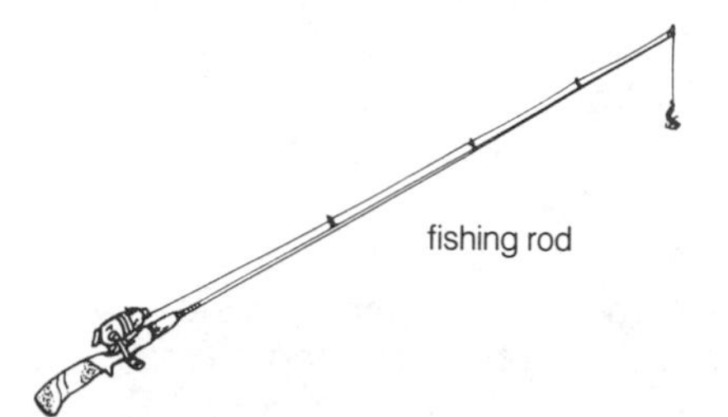
fishing rod

rod (rod) *n.* a long, thin piece of wood, metal, plastic, etc.: *a fishing rod.*

rode see **ride.**

rodent (rō′ dənt) *n.* any of a group of animals that have sharp front teeth used in gnawing: *Rats, mice, rabbits, squirrels, and beavers are some rodents.*

rodeo (rō′ di ō, rō dā′ ō) *n.* a contest of skill in riding horses, roping cattle, etc.: *The Calgary Stampede is the world's biggest rodeo. pl.* **rodeos.**

role (rōl) *n.* a part played by an actor or actress: *In the play, I have the role of the king.*

roll (rōl) *n.* **1.** something flat that is rolled up: *a roll of toilet paper.* **2.** a small loaf of bread, enough for one sandwich. *v.* **1.** to turn over and over: *The ball rolled down the stairs.* **2.** to wrap around itself: *to roll up a carpet.* **3.** to sway from side to side: *The ship rolled in the rough sea.*

roller (rō′ lər) *n.* a cylinder that can roll, and may be used to shape something: *hair rollers.*

roller coaster (rō′ lər kōst′ ər) a railway ride at an amusement park or fair.

roller skates

roller skate (rō′ lər skāt′) a skate that has four small wheels on the bottom for skating on a flat surface.

roller-skate (rō′ lər skāt′) *v.* to skate on roller skates. **roller-skating. roller-skated.**

Roman Catholic (rō′ mən kath′ ə lik) *n.* a person who belongs to the Christian church that has the Pope as its head.

romance (rō mans′, rō′ mans) *n.* **1.** a love story. **2.** love: *a movie about romance.*

romantic (rō man′ tik) *adj.* having to do with love: *a romantic song.*

roof (rūf, rủf) *n.* **1.** the outside top covering of a building or vehicle. **2.** the top of the inside of the mouth. *pl.* **roofs**, or **rooves** (rūvz).

rookie (rủk′ ē) *n.* a person who is new to a group and has no experience.

room (rūm, rủm) *n.* **1.** one of the inside spaces of a building: *a bathroom, a bedroom.* **2.** space: *There is plenty of room on the bus.*

roommate (rūm′ māt′, rủm′ māt′) *n.* a person, usually not a relative, with whom another person shares a room or apartment.

roomy (rūm′ ē, rủm′ ē) *adj.* full of room or space: *a roomy tent; a roomier tent; the roomiest tent of all.*

rooster (rūs′ tər) *n.* a male chicken.

root (rūt) *n.* **1.** the part of a plant that grows into the soil. **2.** a word from which other words are made: 'hair' is the root of 'hairy'.

rope (rōp) *n.* a strong thick cord. *v.* **1.** to tie with a rope: *We roped the packages together.* **2.** to catch with a lasso or rope: *The cowgirl roped the calf.* **roping. roped.**

rosary (rō′ zər ē) *n.* a set of beads used by Roman Catholics for counting prayers. *pl.* **rosaries.**

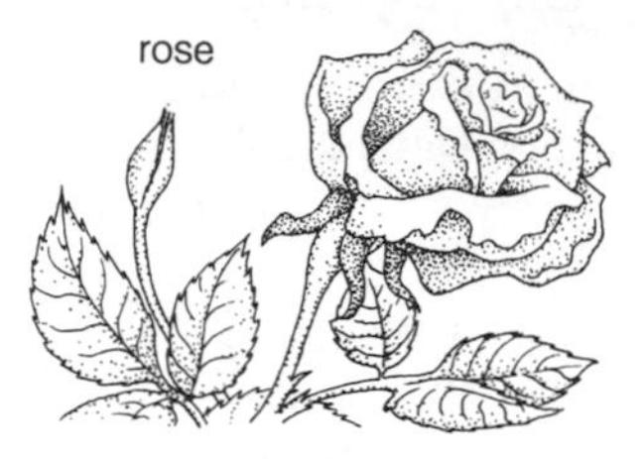
rose

rose (rōz) *n.* a sweet-smelling flower that grows on a thorny bush. *v.* see **rise.**

Rosh Hashona, Rosh Hashana (rōsh′ hə shon′ ə) the Jewish New Year, celebrated in September or October.

rot (rot) *v.* to go bad; to decay. **rotting. rotted.**

rotate (rō′ tāt) *v.* **1.** to turn around in circles: *The earth rotates on its axis.* **2.** to take turns: *We rotate our crops. This year we planted beets where the beans were last year.* **rotating. rotated.**

rotation (rō tā′ shən) *n.* the moving around in a circle: *the rotation of a bicycle wheel.*

rotten (rot′ ən) *adj.* going bad or gone bad: *rotten eggs; rotten apples.*

⊖**rouge** (rūzh) *n.* red make-up used to colour the cheeks.

rough (ruf) *adj.* **1.** not smooth: *rough ground.* **2.** stormy: *a rough sea.*

roughly (ruf′ lē) *adv.* **1.** in an unkind or careless way: *Don't treat your dog so roughly!* **2.** approximately; not exactly: *There are roughly two hundred people on the plane.*

round (raủnd) *n.* **1.** a period in a sport such as boxing. **2.** one shot of a gun. **3. rounds** a regular route from one place to another: *Every* *night, the nurse made the rounds of the rooms. adj.* **1.** in the shape of a circle: *a round ring.* **2.** in the shape of a sphere: *a round apple. v.* to make a turn: *I rounded the corner.*

round trip (raůnd′ trip′) the journey to a place and back again.

⊖**route** (rūt, raůt) *n.* **1.** a way of getting to a place: *There are many traffic lights on this route.* **2.** the area that a salesperson has: *a newspaper route.*

routine (rū tēn′) *n.* the usual way of doing things: *My daily routine begins when the cat wakes me up. adj.* regular; ordinary; usual: *Shopping is a routine job that must be done.*

row (rō) *n.* a line of people or things: *a row of chairs. v.* to make a boat move by using oars.

rowboat (rō′ bōt′) *n.* a small boat that is moved with oars.

royal (ròi′ əl) *adj.* having to do with kings or queens or their families: *a royal palace.*

Royal Canadian Mounted Police

Royal Canadian Mounted Police (ròi′ əl kə nā′ di ən maůnt′ əd pə lēs′) the federal police force of Canada: *In all provinces except Quebec and Ontario, the RCMP also act as provincial police.*

royalty (ròi′ əl tē) *n.* a royal person or royal persons.

R.R. short for **rural route**: *My address is R.R.3, Peterborough, Ontario.*

rub (rub) *v.* to move one thing against another; to wipe: *He rubbed the dirt off his jacket.* **rubbing. rubbed.**

rubber (rub′ ər) *n.* **1.** a springy, elastic material used to make tires, tubing, and other things. **2.** a soft piece of this substance used for wiping out pencil marks; an eraser. **3.** a low overshoe made of rubber.

rubber band (rub′ ər band′) a narrow band of rubber or elastic, used for holding things together.

rubbish (rub′ ish) *n.* garbage.

ruby (rū′ bē) *n.* a clear, deep red jewel. *pl.* **rubies.**

rudder (rud′ ər) *n.* a flat, movable piece of wood or metal, attached to the back of a ship or aircraft and used for steering.

⊖**rude** (rūd) *adj.* bad-mannered; not polite: *a rude person; a rude remark; a ruder comment; the rudest behaviour of all.*

rug (rug) *n.* a thick fabric used for covering a floor.

rugged (rug′ əd) *adj.* having a rough and strong appearance: *rugged mountains.*

ruin (rū′ in) *n.* an old building that has fallen to pieces or is falling down: *Ruins of many ancient buildings are found in Greece and Italy. v.* to spoil; to make useless: *The heavy frost ruined the fruit crop.*

rule (rūl) *n.* a direction that tells what ought to be done: *Follow the rules of the game. v.* **1.** to control or govern: *to rule a country.* **2.** to use a ruler: *to rule a straight line.* **ruling. ruled.**

ruler (rū′ lər) *n.* **1.** a person who controls or governs. **2.** a strip of marked wood, plastic, or metal, used for drawing lines or for measuring.

rumble (rumbl) *n.* a deep, rolling sound: *the rumble of thunder.*

v. to make such a sound: *The train rumbled in the distance.* **rumbling. rumbled.**

⊖**rumour, rumor** (rü′ mər) *n.* a story or information, which may not be true, repeated from one person to another.

run (run) *n.* **1.** a quick movement on the feet: *I go for a run each morning.* **2.** a trip made regularly: *This is the first run of the train.* **3.** a period of time during which something continues to happen: *a run of hot weather.* **4.** a slope for skiers. **5.** a scoring point in baseball. **6.** a long tear in a stocking. **7.** an enclosed area for a dog, chickens, etc. *v.* **1.** to move quickly on the feet: *He ran down the stairs. She ran down the street.* **2.** to travel regularly: *The train runs twice a day.* **3.** to compete in a race or in an election: *Mrs. Kahn is running for mayor.* **4.** to continue to appear during a period of time: *The movie ran for two weeks.* **5.** to be in charge of: *Ms. Grimaldi runs a gas station.* **6.** to go or move from place to place: *The road runs from one village to the other.* **7.** to work, flow, move, etc.: *The engine is running. Are you running water for the bath?* **8.** for a colour to spread: *Wash the sweater in cold water so it won't run.* **running. ran** (ran). I have **run.**
run across to find by chance: *I ran across these boots while I was looking for shoes.*
run into 1. to meet by chance: *On my way to work I ran into my cousin.* **2.** to hit or crash into: *He almost ran into the glass wall.*
run out of to have none left: *Please go to the store. We ran out of bread.*
run over to knock someone or something down with a vehicle: *He called for an ambulance when he saw that the man had been run over.*

runaway (run′ ə wā′) *n.* a person or animal that runs away. *pl.* **runaways.**

rung (rung) *n.* one of the steps of a ladder. *v.* see **ring.**

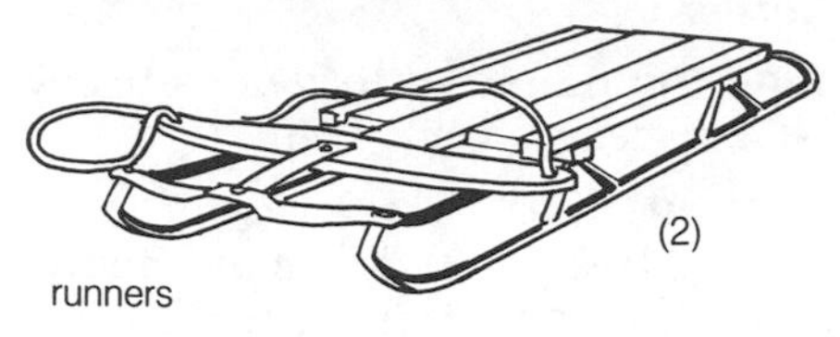

runners

runner (run′ ər) *n.* **1.** a person who runs. **2.** one of the sharp, thin blades on which a skate or sled moves over ice or snow.

runner-up (run′ ər up′) *n.* the one who finishes in second or third place in a race or contest. *pl.* **runners-up.**

runway (run′ wā′) *n.* a wide and long concrete path for airplanes to start from and land on. *pl.* **runways.**

rupture (rup′ chər) *v.* to break open; to burst: *A water pipe has ruptured, and water is pouring through the ceiling.* **rupturing. ruptured.**

rural (rür′ əl) *adj.* having to do with the country, not with the city: *Most of the children in the school come from rural areas.*

rush (rush) *n.* a sudden movement: *She's always in a rush; a rush of wind.* *pl.* **rushes.** *v.* to hurry about; to move fast: *She rushed to work.* **rushing. rushed.** she **rushes.**

Russian (rush′ ən) *n.* the language spoken in Russia. *adj.* having to do with Russia.

rust (rust) *n.* a reddish-brown coating that forms on iron and some other metals when they are exposed to water or damp air. *v.* to become coated with rust.

rustle (rusl) *n.* a soft, crackling sound: *the rustle of leaves in the wind.* *v.* to make this sound. **rustling. rustled.**

rusty (rus′ tē) *adj.* covered with rust: *a rusty car; a rustier car; the rustiest car in the garage.*

ɵ**rut** (rut) *n.* a deep track made by a wheel.
in a rut leading a dull life, with no changes happening: *He was in a rut until he decided to learn a new skill.*

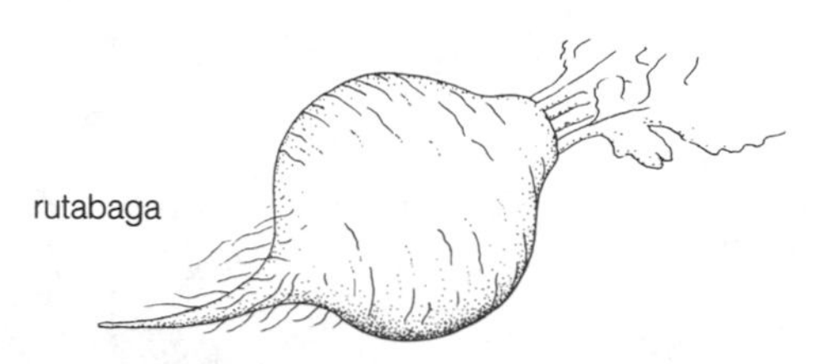
rutabaga

rutabaga (rū′ tə bā′ gə) *n.* a kind of turnip; a large root vegetable that has thick skin and white-yellow flesh. *pl.* **rutabagas.**

rye (rī) *n.* a grain, grown like wheat, used for making flour and as feed for animals.

S

sabbath (sab′ ath) *n.* a day of the week that some people use for rest and worship: *Sunday is the sabbath for most Christians. Saturday is the sabbath for Jews.*

⊖**sac** (sak) *n.* a bag-like part in a plant or in the body of an animal.

sack (sak) *n.* a large bag made of strong material.

sacred (sā′ krid) *adj.* holy; having to do with God or a god: *a sacred temple; sacred music.*

sacrifice (sak′ ri fīs′) *n.* 1. a gift to a god. **2.** something that a person gives up for the sake of others: *It was a sacrifice to send money to his sick relatives.*

sad (sad) *adj.* not happy: *sad news; sadder news; the saddest news of all.*

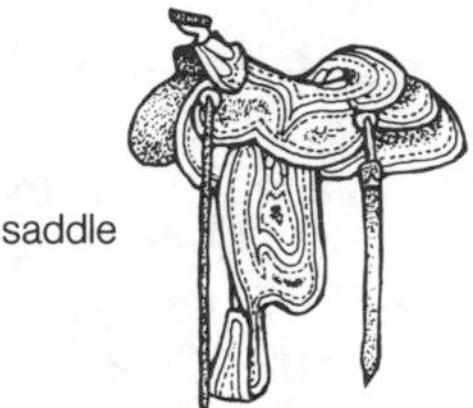
saddle

saddle (sadl) *n.* a seat for the rider of a horse. *v.* to put a saddle on a horse. **saddling. saddled.**

safe (sāf) *n.* a strong metal box in which valuable things are locked. *adj.* **1.** free from danger or harm: *I feel safe now that I'm off the thin ice.* **2.** careful: *My sister is a safe driver; I am a safer driver; our mother is the safest one of all.*

safety (sāf′ tē) *n.* **1.** freedom from harm or danger. **2.** the state of being safe: *The workers wore hard hats for their safety.*

safety belt (sāf′ tē belt′) a seat belt.

sag (sag) *v.* to bend low in the middle: *The old mattress sags.* **sagging. sagged.**

said see **say.**

sail (sāl) *n.* a sheet of canvas or other material that is attached to a ship: *A sail catches the wind and makes the ship move.* *v.* to travel over the water: *We went sailing in Ron's boat.*

sailboats

sailboat (sāl′ bōt′) *n.* a small boat moved by the wind blowing against its sails.

sailor (sā′ lor) *n.* a member of a ship's crew.

saint (sānt) *n.* a man or woman who has lived a very holy life.

Saint John (sānt′ jon′) the largest city in the province of New Brunswick.

St. John's (sānt′ jonz′) the capital city of the province of Newfoundland.

sake (sāk) *n.* a cause; benefit: *She didn't want to drive to the lake, but she did it for the sake of her family.*

salad (sal′ ad) *n.* a mixture of raw or cold cooked vegetables, sometimes with cold meat, fish or eggs: *Salad is often served with a dressing.*

salami (sə lȧ′ mē) *n.* a spicy kind of sausage.

salary (sal′ ə rē) *n.* regular payment of money for work done. *pl.* **salaries.**

sale (sāl) *n.* **1.** the selling of something: *Our car is for sale.* **2.** the selling of goods at prices lower than usual: *Coats are on sale at the department store.*

salesperson (sālz′ pûr′ sən) *n.* a person whose job it is to sell things.

sales tax (sālz′ taks) a tax on the price of an article. *pl.* **sales taxes.**

saliva (sə lī′ və) *n.* the liquid in the mouth that helps people chew and digest food.

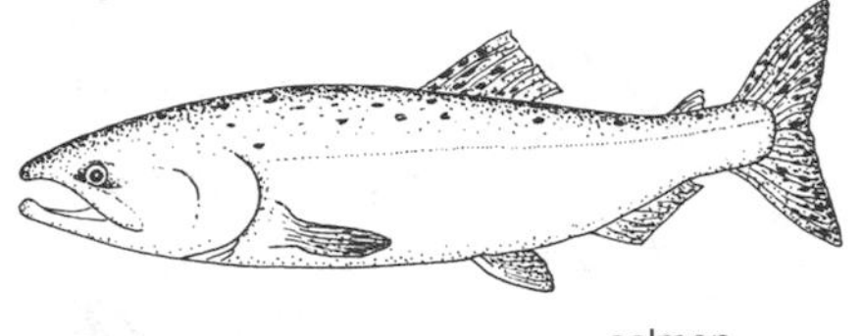

salmon

salmon (sam′ ən) *n.* a large fish with pink flesh, used for food. Salmon live in the sea but lay their eggs in fresh water. *pl.* **salmon.**

salon (sə lȯn′) *n.* a place where women receive haircuts or cosmetic treatments: *a beauty salon.*

salt (sȯlt) *n.* a white substance, found in the earth and in sea water, which is used to flavour and preserve food.

salt shaker (sȯlt′ shāk′ ər) a small container used to sprinkle salt on food.

⊖**salute** (sə lūt′) *n.* to greet or honour someone in a polite or formal way. **saluting. saluted.**

same (sām) *adj.* **1.** exactly like another: *I have the same shirt as you do.* **2.** exactly alike; not another: *That is the same dog I saw yesterday.*

sample (sampl) *n.* a small part of something that shows what the rest is like: *The store gave us a free sample of a new soap, so we could see if we liked it.* *v.* to take as a sample: *She sampled the stew, then added salt.* **sampling. sampled.**

sand (sand) *n.* tiny grains of earth or rock found on beaches and in deserts. *v.* to rub a surface with sandpaper.

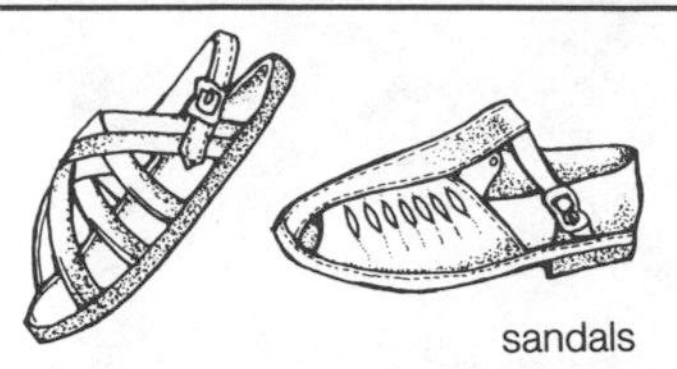

sandals

sandal (san′ dəl) *n.* a light, open shoe fastened to the foot by straps.

sand dune (sand′ dyūn′, sand′ dūn′) a mound of sand on a desert or by the ocean.

sandpaper (sand′ pā′ pər) *n.* a heavy paper that has a coating of sand for smoothing and cleaning wood and other surfaces.

sandwich (sand′ wich) *n.* two slices of bread with meat, cheese, peanut butter, fish, jam, or some other food in between. *pl.* **sandwiches.**

sandy (san′ dē) *adj.* **1.** having a light brown or beige colour. **2.** filled with sand: *a sandy beach; a sandier beach; the sandiest beach on the lake.*

sane (sān) *adj.* **1.** not mad: *Was he sane or insane when he committed the crime?* **2.** sensible; showing good judgment and good sense: *a sane decision; a saner one; the sanest one of all.*

sang see **sing.**

sanitary (san′ i ter′ ē) *adj.* completely free from dirt and disease.

sanitation (san′ i tā′ shən) *n.* the protection of good health by keeping living conditions clean.

sank see **sink.**

Santa Claus (san′ tə klȯz′) the jolly old man said to give out presents on Christmas Eve.

sap (sap) *n.* the liquid inside plants and trees that carries their water and food.

sarcastic (sȧr kas′ tik) *adj.* meaning the opposite of what is said, often unkindly: *a sarcastic remark; sarcastic humour.*

sardine (sȧr dēn′) *n.* a small, silvery fish sold for food, usually in cans.

sari (sȧr′ ē) *n.* a piece of clothing worn by women and girls of India and some other countries in Asia. *pl.* **saris.**

sash (sash) *n.* **1.** a wide ribbon worn around the waist or over the shoulder. **2.** the frame in a window or door that holds the glass. *pl.* **sashes.**

Saskatchewan (sas kach′ ə wȧn′, sas kach′ i wȧn′) *n.* the province between Alberta on the west and Manitoba on the east; its capital is Regina. Short form: **Sask.** A person living in or born in Saskatchewan is a **Saskatchewanian.**

sat see **sit.**

satellite (sat′ ə līt′) *n.* **1.** a smaller heavenly body moving around a larger one: *The moon is a satellite of the earth.* **2.** a spaceship moving regularly around the earth. **3.** a country controlled by or dependent on another.

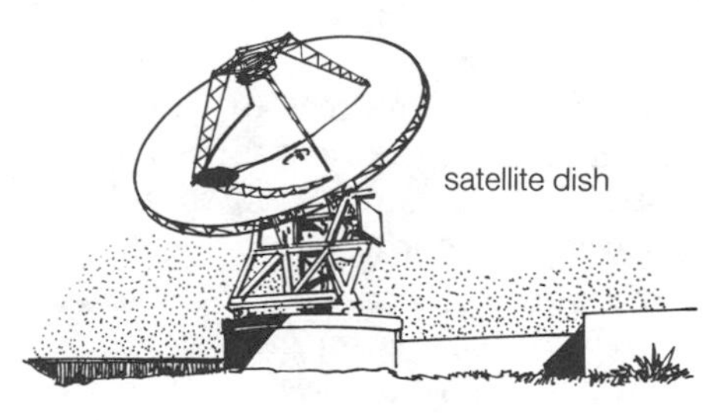
satellite dish

satellite dish (sat′ ə līt dish′) a saucer-shaped device used to receive television signals from a satellite.

satin (sat′ in) *n.* a smooth, very shiny kind of cloth.

satisfaction (sat′ is fak′ shən) *n.* pleasure; enjoyment: *Doing her job so well gives Teresa great satisfaction.*

satisfactory (sat′ is fak′ ta rē) *adj.* good enough to please: *satisfactory work.*

satisfy (sat′ is fī′) *v.* **1.** to please; to give what is wanted or needed: *The soup satisfied him.* **2.** to convince: *Her letter satisfied me that the family was well.* **satisfying. satisfied.** it **satisfies.**

Saturday (sat′ ər dā′) *n.* the seventh day of the week. *pl.* **Saturdays.**

⊖**sauce** (sȧs) *n.* a thick liquid mixture served with or on food to make it taste better: *tomato sauce.*

saucer (sȧs′ ər) *n.* a small, round dish for a cup to rest on.

sauerkraut (saůr′ kraůt′) *n.* a food made from chopped cabbage that has been mixed with salt and left for a long time.

sauna (sȯna) *n.* a place to have a steam bath, where water is poured over very hot rocks. *pl.* **saunas.**

sausage (sȯ′ sij) *n.* chopped meat that is mixed with spices and stuffed into a thin tube.

⊖**savage** (sav′ ij) *adj.* wild and fierce: *a savage bull.*

save (sāv) *v.* **1.** to rescue; to free from danger or harm: *The man at the beach saved the child from drowning.* **2.** to keep something for later use: *I'm saving some money for her birthday present.* **3.** to avoid using up money, time, strength, etc.: *I save gas with the new car. You can save time if you drive on the highway.* **4.** to keep safe; to hold: *Please save my place in line while I make a phone call.* **saving. saved.**

savings (sā′ vingz) *n.pl.* money that has been saved: *My savings are in the bank.*

saw (sȯ) *n.* a tool with a row of sharp teeth on a thin blade, used for cutting wood, metal, etc. *v.* **1.** see **see. 2.** to cut with a saw. **sawing. sawed.** I have **sawed**, or **sawn.**

sawdust (sȯ′ dust′) *n.* powdered wood from sawing.

sawmill (sȯ′ mil′) *n.* a place where logs are cut into lumber.

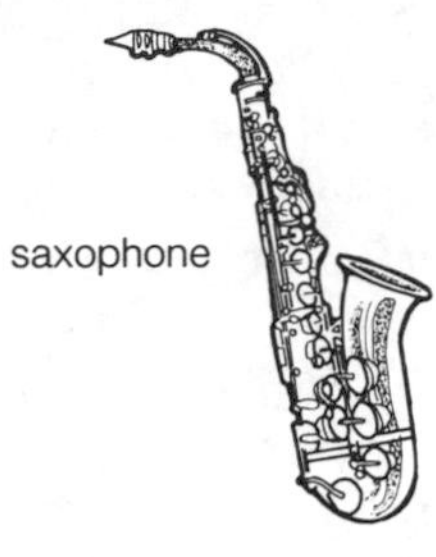

saxophone (sak′ sə fōn′) *n.* a metal musical instrument that is curved, has many keys, and is played by blowing into the mouthpiece.

say (sā) *v.* **1.** to speak words: *He said he was home yesterday. I didn't hear you; what did you say?* **2.** to state in words: *What does the newspaper say about the weather?* **saying. said** (sed). she **says** (sez).

scab (skab) *n.* **1.** a crust that forms over a wound. **2.** *(informal)* a worker who refuses to go on strike, or who takes the job of a worker who is striking.

scaffold (skaf′ əld) *n.* a platform that is used to hold window washers and other people while they work on a building: *Ropes and pulleys are used to move a scaffold up and down the side of a building.*

scald (skȯld) *v.* to burn with very hot liquid or steam.

scale (skāl) *n.* **1.** machine used for weighing people or things, showing how heavy they are. **2.** a line divided into equal spaces and used for measuring. **3.** the size of a model compared with the actual size: *On this map, the scale is one centimetre equals fifty kilometres.* **4.** one of many thin flakes on the skin of a fish or reptile. **5.** a regular series of musical notes. *v.* to climb something steep: *She scaled the wall quickly.* **scaling. scaled.**

scallop (skal′ əp) *n.* a shellfish used for food, enclosed by two round shells that have wavy edges.

scalp (skalp) *n.* the skin and hair on top of the head.

scar (skȧr) *n.* a mark left on the skin after a cut or a burn has healed. **scarring. scarred.**

scarce (skers) *adj.* difficult to get; rare: *Some fresh fruit is scarce during the winter. In a desert, plants are scarce, animals are scarcer, and water is scarcest of all.*

scarcely (skers′ lē) *adv.* hardly; only just: *We had scarcely started to eat when the telephone rang. I am very tired and have scarcely enough energy to take the dog for a walk.*

scare (sker) *n.* a frightening experience: *The fire in the building gave me a scare.* *v.* to frighten: *The child was scared of the loud thunder.* **scaring. scared.**

scarecrow (sker′ crō′) *n.* a figure dressed like a person; it is set up in a field to frighten birds from a farmer's crops.

scarf (skȧrf) *n.* a piece of cloth worn around the neck or head, usually for warmth. *pl.* **scarves** (skȧrvz) or **scarfs.**

scary (sker′ ē) *adj.* causing a scare: *a scary movie; a scarier one; the scariest one of all.*

scatter (skat′ ər) *v.* to throw, fall, or move in all directions: *to scatter seeds on a field.*

⊖**scene** (sēn) *n.* **1.** a view: *a pretty scene by the river.* **2.** a part of an act in a play: *The actors practised the second scene.* **3.** a place where something happened: *This is the scene of the fire.*

scenery (sēn′ ə rē) *n.* **1.** what is seen outside: *We enjoyed the scenery on our drive to Saint John.* **2.** a painted cloth or board, at the back of a stage, showing where a play takes place. *pl.* **sceneries.**

scent (sent) *n.* **1.** a pleasant smell: *I like the scent of roses.* **2.** an animal's trail: *The dog followed the scent of the fox.*

schedule (sked′ yül, shed′ yül) *n.* a list of events, usually shown with times: *a train schedule shows when the trains arrive and depart.* *v.* to plan; to put into a schedule: *The plane is scheduled to arrive in an hour.* **scheduling. scheduled.**

⊖**scheme** (skēm) *n.* **1.** a plan to do something, often secretly and often something bad: *a scheme to make money dishonestly.* **2.** an arrangement of something: *the colour scheme of a room.*

scholar (skol′ ər) *n.* a person who studies and has much knowledge.

scholarship (skol′ ər ship) *n.* money given students to help them pay for their education.

school (skül) *n.* **1.** a place where people are taught. **2.** a large group of fish swimming together.

schooner (skü′ nər) *n.* a sailing ship that has two or more masts on it.

science (sī′ əns) *n.* **1.** knowledge that comes from experimenting, studying facts, and observing how things work together. **2.** a subject for which this kind of knowledge is needed: *The science of biology is about the study of life.*

⊖**scientific** (sī′ ən tif′ ik) *adj.* having to do with science: *a scientific discovery.*

scientist (sī′ ən tist) *n.* someone who studies a science.

scissors

scissors (siz′ ərz) *n.pl.* a cutting tool that has two blades joined by a screw in the middle.

scold (skōld) *v.* to speak to someone in an angry way.

scoop (sküp) *n.* **1.** a little shovel, for lifting flour, sugar, etc. **2.** a special rounded spoon for serving ice cream. *v.* to lift up with a scoop.

scope (skōp) *n.* **1.** the range or limits of what someone or something can do: *This math problem is beyond the child's scope.* **2.** a device for finding things or looking at things more closely: *The submarine captain looked through the scope and saw a ship ahead.*

scorch (skȯrch) *v.* to burn slightly: *I scorched my shirt with the iron.* **scorching. scorched.** it **scorches.**

score (skȯr) *n.* the number of points, goals, etc. made in a game: *The score was two to one.* *v.* to make a point, goal, etc. in a game: *Rosa scored three goals.* **scoring. scored.**

scorn (skȯrn) *n.* a feeling of dislike or of no respect: *He stole money from his friends, and they treated him with scorn.*

scorpion (skȯr′ pi ən) *n.* an animal that looks like a spider with a long tail and can give a poisonous sting.

Scots (skots) *adj.* Scottish.

Scottish (skot′ ish) *adj.* belonging to or coming from Scotland.

scour (skaůr) *v.* **1.** to scrub; to rub hard: *to scour a dirty sink.* **2.** to search everywhere: *They scoured the hills for the lost child.*

Scout (skaůt) *n.* a person who is a member of the Boy Scouts.

scout (skaůt) *n.* someone sent ahead to gather information. *v.* to go ahead to gather information.

scramble (skrambl) *v.* **1.** to mix together: *To scramble eggs, stir together the white and yellow parts as you cook them in butter.* **2.** to climb or crawl using hands and knees: *The children scrambled up a hill.* **scrambling. scrambled.**

scrap (skrap) *n.* **1.** a small piece: *a scrap of paper.* **2.** worn or used articles, such as cars, that can be sold for the value of their metal or other materials.

scrapbook (skrap′ bůk′) *n.* a large book for keeping newspaper items, photographs, and other flat things.

scrape (skrāp) *n.* a mark made from something being scratched or rubbed. *v.* **1.** to scratch or rub: *I scraped my knee when I fell.* **2.** to rub smooth with something hard or sharp: *Andrea scraped the mud off her shoes.* **scraping. scraped.**

scratch (skrach) *n.* a mark left by something sharp: *The cat's claw made a scratch on my arm.* *pl.* **scratches.** *v.* **1.** to make a mark with something sharp: *The cat scratched her.* **2.** to rub the part of the skin that itches. **scratching. scratched.** he **scratches.**

scream (skrēm) *n.* a high, loud cry: *We heard screams for help from the burning building.* *v.* to make such a sound: *to scream with pain, fear, anger, laughter, etc.*

screech (skrēch) *n.* a high, loud noise: *the screech of brakes as the car stopped suddenly.* *pl.* **screeches.** *v.* to make such a noise: *Turn off the record. The singer is screeching.* **screeching. screeched.** he **screeches.**

screen (skrēn) *n.* **1.** wire mesh in a frame: *A screen is put on a window to let in air, but to keep out bugs.* **2.** any frame that is covered to hide, protect, or divide. **3.** the surface on which television pictures or movies are seen.

screw (skrū) *n.* a kind of nail with a spiral groove twisting around it. *v.* to fix in place by using a twisting movement: *to screw a cap on a bottle.*

screwdriver (skrū′ drī′ vər) *n.* a tool used for turning screws into place.

scribble (skribl) *n.* to write or draw in a quick and careless way. **scribbling. scribbled.**

script (skript) *n.* **1.** writing in which the letters are joined together, as in *script*. **2.** the written words of a play, movie, or television or radio program.

scrub (skrub) *v.* to clean by rubbing hard: *I scrubbed my hands. I scrubbed the floor.* **scrubbing. scrubbed.**

sculptor (skulp′ tər) *n.* someone who makes statues or shapes from wood, clay, stone, metal, etc.

sculpture (skulp′ chər) *n.* **1.** the art of making statues or shapes from wood, clay, stone, metal, etc.: *He studies sculpture at art school.* **2.** a statue or shape made by a sculptor.

scythe (sīth) *n.* a long handle with a large curved blade at the end, used for cutting grass and crops.

sea (sē) *n.* **1.** the great body of salt water that covers almost three-fourths of the earth's surface. **2.** any large body of salt water: *the Labrador Sea; the Mediterranean Sea, the Philippine Sea.* *pl.* **seas.**

sea gull, seagull (sē′ gul′) a grey and white bird that lives near a large body of water and eats fish.

seal (sēl) *n.* **1.** a large animal that lives in and by the sea and has flippers for swimming. **2.** a special mark or design, attached to or pressed into a paper, to show that it is official, approved, authorized, etc.: *a seal on the diploma.* *v.* to fasten or close tightly, often by using something sticky: *Kay sealed the envelope.*

sea lion (sē′ lī′ ən) a large seal that lives off the Pacific coast of North America.

seam (sēm) *n.* a line where two edges are joined together: *a seam in the cloth.*

search (sûrch) *n.* a looking for someone or something: *the search for the lost child. pl.* **searches.** *v.* to try to find by looking carefully: *Nina searched the house for her keys.* **searching. searched.** she **searches.**

searchlight (sûrch′ līt′) *n.* a special light that gives off a powerful beam: *Lighthouses and airport control towers use searchlights.*

sea shell, seashell (sē′ shel′) the shell of a sea animal, such as an oyster, clam, or mussel.

seashore (sē′ shȯr′) *n.* land along the edge of the sea.

season (sē′ zən) *n.* **1.** one of the four parts of the year: spring, summer, autumn, winter. **2.** a special time for something: *the football season. v.* to add salt, pepper, or other flavours to food.

seasonal (sē′ zən əl) *adj.* having to do with the different times of year: *Sales of ice cream are seasonal. Many people buy ice cream in summer when it is hot, but fewer people buy it in the winter.*

seat (sēt) *n.* **1.** something to sit on; a chair, bench, etc. **2.** membership in Parliament or another important group: *She has had her seat in the House of Commons for six years. v.* **1.** to give someone a seat: *The smaller children were seated in the front row.* **2.** to have seats for: *Our arena seats a thousand people.*

seat belt, seatbelt (sēt′ belt′) a strong belt that holds a person in the seat of a vehicle or airplane in case of a bump or crash. Also called a **safety belt.**

seaway (sē′ wā′) *n.* a passage to the sea: *the St. Lawrence Seaway.*

seaweed (sē′ wēd′) *n.* a plant that grows in the ocean.

second (sek′ ənd) *n.* a very small measure of time; **s** is the symbol: *There are 60 seconds in a minute. adj.* next after the first: *He took the second newspaper from the pile.*

secondary school (sek′ ən der′ ē skūl′) a school attended after elementary school or junior high school.

second-hand (sek′ ənd hand′) *adj.* used or owned before by someone else: *There are many things to check when buying a second-hand car.*

second-rate (sek′ ənd rāt′) *adj.* of low quality; not the best: *He is a second-rate actor and should not be the star of the new television show.*

secret (sē′ krət) *n.* some news that is known only by one, two, or a few people: *David shared the secret with his brother. adj.* known to only one, two, or a few people: *a secret place for keeping money.*

secretary (sek′ rə ter′ ē) *n.* someone who writes letters and keeps records for another person, a business, or an organization. *pl.* **secretaries.**

section (sek′ shən) *n.* a part of anything: *A section of the roof is leaking. I read a large section of the book.*

secure (si kyūr′) *adj.* **1.** safe: *My money is secure in the bank.* **2.** firmly fastened: *Tie the box with a secure knot.*

security (si kyūr′ i tē) *n.* **1.** freedom from danger, harm, worry, etc.: *Our home is a place of security.* **2.** something valuable that is owned by a person who borrows money. He or she promises to give the lender this item if the money is not repaid: *She borrowed six hundred dollars, using her car as security.* *pl.* **securities.**

see (sē) *v.* **1.** to receive a picture of something through the eyes: *Can you see a boat?* **2.** to understand: *I see what you mean.* **3.** to visit: *I saw the dentist about my bad tooth.* **seeing. saw** (sȯ). I have **seen.**

seed (sēd) *n.* the tiny grain of a plant from which new plants can grow.

seedling (sēd′ ling) *n.* a young tree or plant grown from a seed.

seeing-eye dog (sē′ ing ī′ dog′) a dog trained to guide a blind person.

seek (sēk) *v.* **1.** to search for: *to seek a new job.* **seeking. sought** (sȯt).

seem (sēm) *v.* to look as if something is true: *The baby seems to be asleep.*

seen see **see.**

segment (seg′ mənt) *n.* a module or section: *a segment of a TV show; a segment of an orange.*

seize (sēz) *v.* to grasp; to take hold of: *Lou seized the rope and pulled in the boat.* **seizing. seized.**

seldom (sel′ dəm) *adv.* rarely; not often: *Michael seldom hears from his brother in Australia.*

select (si lekt′) *v.* to choose carefully: *Lisa selected two good apples from the basket.*

selection (si lek′ shən) *n.* **1.** a collection: *There is a good selection of books in the library.* **2.** a thing chosen: *This book is my selection.*

⊖**self** (self) *n.* a person's own feelings, thoughts, wishes, etc.: *He has a strong sense of self; nobody can make him do what he doesn't want to do.* *pl.* **selves.**

self- a prefix meaning 'by, to, or with oneself or itself': **self-confident** means confident in oneself; **self-defence** means the protection of oneself.

selfish (sel′ fish) *adj.* thinking and caring only about oneself, not about other people: *The selfish child took both pieces of cake, although her brother wanted one.*

sell (sel) *v.* **1.** to hand over something in return for money: *He sold the clock for twenty dollars.* **2.** to offer for money: *This store sells toys.* **selling. sold** (sōld).

semester (sə mes′ tər) *n.* half of a university or college year: *The first semester starts in September, and Chris will be taking classes in science and literature.*

semi- a prefix meaning 'half': a **semicircle** means half a circle.

semi-annual (semi′ i an′ yū əl) *adj.* happening every half-year: *This magazine is semi-annual; it comes out once in January and once in July.*

semicircle (semi′ i sûrkl′) *n.* half a circle: *The seats were arranged in a semicircle in front of the stage.*

semicolon (semi′ i cō′ lən) *n.* a punctuation mark made from a dot with a comma beneath it (;). It is used to combine two sentences into one, as in this example: *They kept running; they just didn't know when to stop.*

semi-finals (sem′ i fīn′ əlz) *n.pl.* the series of games that comes before the finals.

Senate (sen′ ət) *n.* one of the two Houses of the Canadian Parliament. Members of the Senate are appointed by the Governor General; members of the House of Commons are elected by citizens.

Senator (sen′ ə tər) *n.* a member of the Senate.

send (send) *v.* to make something or someone go from one place to another: *to send a letter; to send the child to bed.* **sending. sent.**

senior (sēn′ yər) *n.* someone who is older: *I am his senior by a year.* *adj.* older, more experienced, or having higher rank: *The senior mechanic receives more pay than the junior mechanic.*

seniority (sen yȯr′ i tē) *n.* a person's greater importance because of the number of years he or she has been working in one place: *People are promoted according to seniority in this company. Those who have been with the company longest are promoted first.* *pl.* **seniorities.**

sensation (sen sā′ shən) *n.* **1.** a feeling: *I had a sensation of cold when I walked into the room.* **2.** great excitement: *The team caused a sensation by winning the gold medal.*

sensational (sen sā′ shən əl) *adj.* causing great excitement or other strong feelings: *a sensational soccer game.*

sense (sens) *n.* **1.** one of the five ways people get to know the world: *The five senses are sight, hearing, touch, smell, and taste.* **2.** a special kind of understanding or feeling: *I have a sense that he is in trouble. You have a good sense of humour.* **3.** good judgment: *He does not have the sense to stay away from trouble.* **4.** meaning: *Can you explain the sense of the paragraph?* *v.* to feel something; to be aware: *I sense that you are angry.* **sensing. sensed.**

⊖**sensible** (sen′ sibl) *adj.* full of good sense: *It is sensible to count your change after buying something.*

⊖**sensitive** (sen′ si tiv) *adj.* **1.** easily affected; able to feel something quickly or sharply: *My eyes are sensitive to bright light.* **2.** easily upset: *He is very sensitive when you talk about his car.*

sensitivity (sen′ si tiv′ i tē) *n.* an understanding of how people feel: *The nurse showed great sensitivity when talking to the family of the sick child.* *pl.* **sensitivities.**

sent see **send.**

⊖**sentence** (sen′ təns) *n.* **1.** a number of words that make a complete statement or thought. **2.** a punishment given in a court of law: *The thief was given a sentence of two years in prison.* *v.* to punish someone with a sentence. **sentencing. sentenced.**

sentimental (sen′ ti men′ təl) *adj.* showing emotions about a person, a thing, or a memory: *He becomes very sentimental when he thinks about his childhood.*

separate (sep′ ə rət) *adj.* not together; apart: *Keep these pins separate from the others.*

separate (sep′ ə rāt′) *v.* to divide; to set apart: *We separated the ripe apples from the unripe ones.* **separating. separated.**

September (sep tem′ bər) *n.* the ninth month of the year.

septic tank (sep′ tik tank′) a large underwater container where dirty water and waste are made cleaner.

sequel (sē′ kwəl) *n.* a play, movie, novel etc., that follows another and is usually based upon it: *The movie Airplane II* is a sequel to *Airplane*.

sequence (sē′ kwəns) *n.* a number of things happening one after the other: *Monday, Tuesday, and Wednesday follow each other in sequence.*

sergeant (sar′ jənt) *n.* **1.** an officer of the police force. **2.** a soldier who is next in rank above a corporal.

serial number (sēr′ i əl num′ bər) a number printed on a machine or other object, used for identification: *Write down the serial number of the television as soon as you bring it home.*

series (si′ rēz) *n.* similar things coming one after another: *Some television series continue for several years. pl.* **series.**

serious (sēr′ i əs) *adj.* **1.** important and needing attention: *Pollution is a serious problem.* **2.** dangerous: *a serious sickness.* **3.** not joking or fooling: *I am serious. We must fix the car now.*

sermon (sûr′ mən) *n.* a public talk on religion or religious subjects.

serpent (sûr′ pənt) *n.* a snake.

servant (sûr′ vənt) *n.* someone who is paid to work in someone else's home.

serve (sûrv) *n.* in tennis and other games, the putting into play of the ball: *It's your serve. v.* **1.** to work for someone or something: *A police officer serves the people.* **2.** to give out food to others: *She served lunch.* **3.** to have a certain use: *The box can serve as a table.* **4.** to spend time in prison: *They served three years.* **5.** in some games, to put a ball into play. **serving. served.**

service (sûr′ vis) *n.* **1.** a helpful act: *She did a service by taking me to the doctor.* **2.** a business or activity that helps others: *mail service; bus service.* **3.** a religious meeting or ceremony. *v.* to fix or make ready: *The mechanic serviced our car.* **servicing. serviced.**

service station (sûr′ vis stā′ shən) a place that sells gasoline, oil, and other things for cars.

⊖**serviette** (sûr′ vi et′) *n.* a piece of paper or cloth used to clean the hands and mouth while eating.

serving (sûrv′ ing) *n.* a helping of food.

session (sesh′ ən) *n.* a meeting of people for some purpose; often a meeting of people who work in a court or a government.

set (set) *n.* **1.** a group of things that go together: *a set of dishes; a set of instructions.* **2.** a television or radio receiver. **3.** in mathematics, a group of numbers between two braces: *{1, 2, 3, 4} is a set of numbers. v.* **1.** to put things in place: *Please set the table for breakfast.* **2.** to go down: *When does the sun set tonight?* **3.** to fix; to adjust: *Jody set her hair after she washed it. The time is wrong, so please set the clock.* **4.** to become hard or firm: *The cement has not set.* **5.** to move: *He set aside the fork to make room for the plate.* **setting. set.**

set an example to show other people how to behave: *His parents set a good example by being kind and honest.*

set out to begin a trip: *We will set out for Winnipeg tomorrow.*

set up to prepare; to assemble: *We set up our tent in the campground.*

setback (set′ bak) *n.* a halt in progress; an event that stops forward movement: *Her broken leg was a setback to her running career.*

settle (setl) *v.* **1.** to get comfortable and stay in a place: *He settled in his chair and went to sleep.* **2.** to decide or agree on something. *We settled the argument and everyone was pleased* **3.** to make a new home: *People from many countries have settled in Canada.* **settling. settled.**

settlement (setl′ mənt) *n.* **1.** the settling of people in a new place. **2.** a payment: *the settlement of a bill.* **3.** an agreement that ends an argument: *After shouting at each other for an hour, they finally reached a settlement.*

seven (sev′ ən) *n., adj.* one more than six (7).

seventeen (sev′ ən tēn′) *n., adj.* ten more than seven (17).

seventh (sev′ ənth) *adj.* following sixth (7th).

seventy (sev′ ən tē) *n., adj.* ten times seven (70). *pl.* **seventies.**

several (sev′ ə rəl) *adj.* not many, but more than two or three.

severe (sə vēr′) *adj.* harsh; serious: *It was a severe winter. I have a severe cold.*

sew (sō) *v.* to stitch with a needle and thread. **sewing. sewed.** I have **sewn** or **sewed.**

sewage (sū′ ij) *n.* waste material that is carried off by sewers and drains.

sewer (sū′ ər) *n.* an underground drain pipe that carries away waste from buildings.

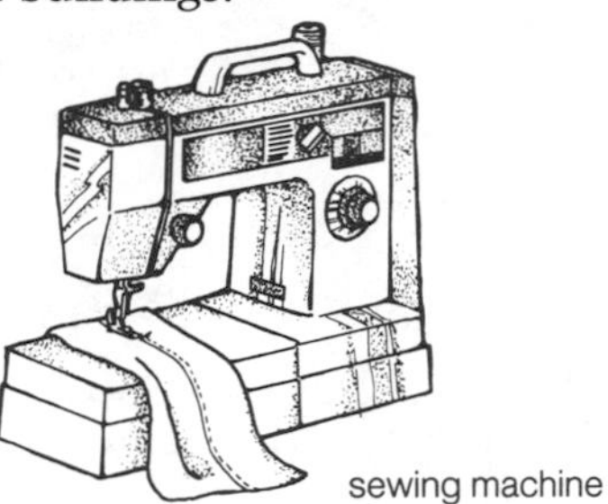
sewing machine

sewing machine (sō′ ing mə shēn′) a machine for sewing things.

sewn see **sew.**

sex (seks) *n.* **1.** either of the two groups, female or male, that people and animals can be divided into. *pl.* **sexes. 2.** the condition of being either female or male. **3.** sexual activity: *We did not like the amount of sex and violence in the movie.*

sexual (sek′ shū əl, seks′ yu əl) *adj.* having to do with sex, or involving the sexes.

shack (shak) *n.* a roughly built wooden hut.

shade (shād) *n.* **1.** a place hidden from the sun: *We sat in the shade, under the tree.* **2.** something that blocks out strong light: *He pulled the window shade over the window.* **3.** the strength of a colour: *a deep shade of blue.*

shadow

shadow (shad′ ō) *n.* a patch of darkness caused by something standing in the way of a light.

shaft (shaft) *n.* **1.** a long handle, as on a rake or an arrow. **2.** a deep space, inside a building or leading down into a mine. **3.** a beam of light.

shaggy (shag′ ē) *adj.* having long, thick, rough hair: *a shaggy dog; a shaggier dog; the shaggiest dog of all.*

shake (shāk) *v.* **1.** to move from side to side or up and down: *We shook the tree to make the apples fall.* **2.** to tremble: *I am shaking with cold.* **shaking. shook** (shůk). I have **shaken.**

shall (shal) *v.* a verb placed before another verb, to say what the person or people speaking are going to do: *I shall read. We shall play.*

shallow (shal′ ō) *adj.* not deep: *a shallow lake.*

shame (shām) *n.* **1.** a feeling of being unhappy, caused by doing something dishonest, foolish, unkind, etc.: *She felt shame for having been rude to her grandmother.* **2.** an unfortunate situation: *It's a shame that you are too ill to come to the party.*

shampoo (sham pū′) *n.* a liquid soap for washing hair, rugs, etc. *pl.* **shampoos.** *v.* to wash hair, a rug, etc.

shape (shāp) *n.* **1.** the outline or form of anything: *The shape of the moon changes through the month.*

2. condition or appearance: *The swimmer stays in good shape by exercising every day.* *v.* to form or make: *She shaped the clay into a beautiful statue.* **shaping. shaped.**

share (sher) *n.* a part of something: *We each had to do a share of the work.* *v.* **1.** to divide something and give part to oneself and part to others: *I shared the dessert with my friends.* **2.** to use together: *The boys shared a bedroom.* **sharing. shared.**

shark

shark shärk) *n.* a large, grey ocean fish that has many sharp teeth; it eats other fish and can be dangerous to people.

sharp (shärp) *adj.* **1.** having an edge or point that can easily make a cut: *a sharp knife; sharp scissors.* **2.** having a pointed end: *a sharp pencil.* **3.** having a sudden change in direction: *a sharp bend in the road.* **4.** being quick to understand or notice something: *sharp eyes.* **5.** having a bitter taste, as a lemon does.

sharpen (shär′ pən) *v.* to make sharp: *to sharpen a pencil.*

shatter (shat′ ər) *v.* to break suddenly into small pieces: *The stone shattered the glass.*

shave (shāv) *n.* the cutting off of hair with a razor: *a shave every morning* *v.* **1.** to cut off hair with a razor. **2.** to slice off very thin strips from wood or another surface. **shaving. shaved.**
close shave a narrow escape: *The pilot had a close shave when the plane lost an engine.*

shawl (shôl) *n.* a piece of cloth worn around the shoulders or wrapped around a baby.

she (shē) *pron.* a girl, woman, or female animal. *pl.* **they** (thā).

shear (shēr) *v.* to cut with large scissors. **shearing. sheared.** I have **shorn** (shôrn), or **sheared.**

shears (shērz) *n.pl.* a cutting tool for trimming hedges or shearing sheep.

shed (shed) *n.* a hut for storing tools or materials: *a garden shed.* *v.* to let fall: *Many trees shed their leaves in autumn.* **shedding. shed.**

she'd (shēd) short for **she had** or **she would.**

sheep

sheep (shēp) *n.* a farm animal that is raised for its wool, meat, and skin. *pl.* **sheep.**

sheer (shēr) *adj.* **1.** very thin; allowing a person to see partly through: *sheer curtains.* **2.** steep: *There is a sheer drop from the edge of the cliff.*

sheet (shēt) *n.* **1.** a large piece of thin cloth that is put on a bed. **2.** a large, thin piece of anything: *a sheet of paper.*

shelf (shelf) *n.* **1.** a board on a wall or in a closet for putting things on. **2.** anything shaped like a shelf: *a shelf of sand in the sea.* *pl.* **shelves** (shelvz).

shell (shel) *n.* **1.** a thin, hard covering that protects: *Eggs, nuts, beetles, and many sea animals have shells.* **2.** a large bullet that explodes when it hits something.

v. **1.** to take out of a shell: *We shelled the nuts.* **2.** to fire explosives.

she'll (shēl) short for **she will.**

shellac (shə lak′) *n.* a kind of varnish.

shellfish (shel′ fish′) *n.* a water animal that has a shell: *Oysters, crabs, and lobsters are some shellfish. pl.* **shellfish.**

shelter (shel′ tər) *n.* a place that gives protection or cover: *In some cities, there are bus shelters to protect people who are waiting in the rain, snow. v.* to protect; to cover: *The doorway sheltered us from the wind.*

shelves plural of **shelf.**

shepherd (shep′ ərd) *n.* a man who looks after sheep.

sherbet (shûr′ bit, shûr′ bət) *n.* a frozen dessert made of fruit juice and other ingredients.

she's (shēz) short for **she is** or **she has.**

shield (shēld) *n.* **1.** a large piece of armour once carried by soldiers. **2.** anything that protects: *An umbrella is a shield against the rain. v.* to protect.

shift (shift) *n.* **1.** movement or change: *a shift in the wind.* **2.** a group of workers, or the time that they work: *She is on the night shift at the hospital. v.* to move; to change the position of something: *The driver shifted gears when she reached the highway.*

shin (shin) *n.* the front of the leg between the knee and the ankle.

shine (shīn) *n.* a brightness: *Wax gave the car a brilliant shine. v.* **1.** to give out light: *The light shone in my eyes.* **shining. shone** (shon). **2.** to polish: *Greg shined his shoes.* **shining. shined.**

shingle (shingl) *n.* a thin piece of wood or other material used to cover a roof.

shiny (shī′ nē) *adj.* bright; glittering: *a shiny floor; a shinier floor; the shiniest floor in the house.*

ship (ship) *n.* a large boat. *v.* to send by ship, bus, train, or plane: *We shipped the presents to my brother in Japan.* **shipping. shipped.**

shipment (ship′ mənt) *n.* goods or materials sent to one place all at once.

shipwreck (ship′ rek′) *n.* a ship that is damaged and sinks at sea.

shirt (shûrt) *n.* a piece of clothing for the upper part of the body, usually worn by men and boys.

shiver (shiv′ ər) *v.* to shake with fear or cold: *We shivered in the cold house.*

shock (shok) *n.* **1.** the feeling that comes from a sudden and strong blow, crash, explosion, etc.: *We felt the shocks caused by the earthquake.* **2.** a sharp feeling caused by electricity: *Martin felt a shock when he touched the wire.* **3.** a feeling in the mind that can happen suddenly when a person experiences something very sad, frightening, etc. *v.* to cause such feelings: *We were shocked to learn that he had died.*

shoe (shū) *n.* **1.** an outer covering for the foot, often made of leather. **2.** a bent piece of iron nailed to a horse's hoof to protect it.

shoelace (shū′ lās) *n.* a string that fastens a shoe.

shone see **shine.**

shook see **shake.**

shoot (shūt) *n.* a new or young plant. *v.* **1.** to fire a bullet, shell, or arrow. **2.** to kill with a bullet, arrow, etc.: *to shoot a moose.* **3.** to move fast: *to shoot a puck towards the goal.* **4.** to make a movie: *The film was shot in Alberta.* **shooting. shot** (shot).

shop (shop) *n.* a building where things are sold or repaired. *v.* to buy from stores. **shopping. shopped.**

shoplift (shop′ lift′) *v.* to steal things that are for sale in a store.

shopping centre (shop′ ing sen′ tər) a place away from the street, where there are many stores together.

shore (shȯr) *n.* land at the edge of an ocean, lake, or large river.

shorn see **shear.**

short (shȯrt) *adj.* not measuring much in height, length, or time.

shortage (shȯr′ tij) *n.* a situation where there is not enough of something: *There is a shortage of coffee in the stores; most places have sold out of it.*

shortbread (shȯrt′ bred′) *n.* a thick biscuit made with flour, butter, and sugar.

short-circuit (shȯrt′ sûr′ kit) *n.* a direct flow of electric current, such as between two bare wires or when electrical connections get wet, that usually results in a melted fuse: *Be careful when you use the hair dryer! If it falls in the water, there will be a short-circuit!*

short cut (shȯrt′ kut′) a quicker way to go somewhere or do something: *We took a short cut home and arrived before everybody else.*

shorten (shȯrt′ ən) *v.* to make shorter: *I shortened the dress.*

shortening (shȯrt′ ən ing) *n.* a fat, like vegetable oil or lard, used in cooking to make pastry crisp.

shorthand (shȯrt′ hand′) *n.* a way of writing quickly, using symbols to represent speech instead of correct spelling.

shortly (shȯrt′ lē) *adv.* soon; in a little while: *The game will begin shortly.*

⊖**shorts** (shȯrts) *n.pl.* **1.** short pants worn above or just below the knees. **2.** men's or boys' underpants.

short-wave (shȯrt′ wāv′) *n.* a type of radio wave that is used to send messages around the world.

shot (shot) *n.* **1.** the firing of a gun: *I heard a loud shot.* **2.** a person who fires a gun: *He is a good shot.* **3.** a tiny ball of metal fired from a gun. **4.** an injection of medicine: *a measles shot.* **5.** the sending off of a spaceship: *a moon shot.* **6.** an aimed throw or stroke in some games: *We took a practice shot before the basketball game began.* *v.* see **shoot.**

should (shu̇d) *v.* a verb placed before another verb to mean 'ought to': *I should be doing my work, but I'm not.*

shoulder (shōl′ dər) *n.* the part of the body between the neck and the arm.

shouldn't (shu̇d′ ənt) short for **should not.**

shout (shau̇t) *n.* a loud call or cry: *a shout of joy; a shout for help.* *v.* to call out in a loud voice: *Don't shout! I can hear you.*

shove (shuv) *n.* a hard push. *v.* to push hard: *We shoved the boxes to the side when we cleaned the garage.* **shoving. shoved.**

shovel

shovel (shuv′ əl) *n.* a tool with a wide scoop, used to dig and move earth, snow, etc. *v.* to use a shovel. **shovelling. shovelled.**

show (shō) *n.* **1.** a performance or program seen in a theatre or on television, or heard on the radio. **2.** a special display or program: *a horse show; a flower show.* *v.* **1.** to let someone see something: *Lena showed us a picture of her family.* **2.** to explain, usually by actions: *She showed me how to*

change a tire. **3.** to indicate; to point out: *Can you show me the way to Main Street?* **showing. showed.** I have **shown.**
show off to brag; to display an ability or a possession to others: *Don't show off; everyone knows you can speak four languages.*
show up to appear; to come into view: *I arrived at the restaurant on time, but my boy friend didn't show up until eight thirty.*

shower (shaů′ ər) *n.* **1.** a gentle fall of rain. **2.** a washing of the body while standing under a spray of water. **3.** a party where gifts are brought in honour of someone: *a baby shower.*

shown see **show.**

show-off (shō′ of′) *n.* a person who often tries to show people how clever, good, etc. he or she is at something.

shrank see **shrink.**

shred (shred) *n.* a tiny strip or scrap of something: *The dog tore the material to shreds.* *v.* to cut or tear into strips: *to shred papers; to shred cabbage.* **shredding. shredded** or **shred.**

shrew (shrū) *n.* a small mouse-like animal that feeds on insects.

shrewd (shrūd) *adj.* having good judgment; wise.

shriek (shrēk) *n.* a very high shout. *v.* to give a very high shout: *to shriek with laughter; to shriek with pain.*

shrill (shril) *adj.* very high and loud: *the shrill cry of the birds.*

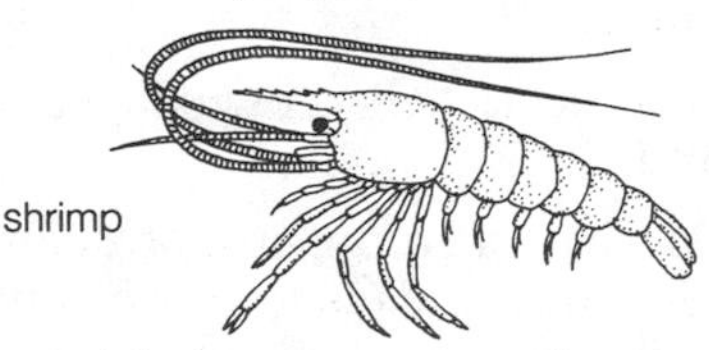
shrimp

shrimp (shrimp) *n.* a small, grey, long-tailed shellfish that turns pink when cooked. *pl.* **shrimp.**

shrine (shrīn) *n.* a place that is holy to certain people.

shrink (shringk) *v.* to become smaller: *Some kinds of cloth shrink in hot water.* **shrinking. shrank** (shrangk). it has **shrunk** (shrungk).

shrivel (shriv′ əl) *v.* to become very dry and curl up like a dead leaf: *The plants shrivelled in the dry weather.* **shrivelling. shrivelled.**

shrub (shrub) *n.* a bush with many branches on it, most of them coming from near the bottom of the plant.

shrug (shrug) *v.* to move the shoulders in a way that means 'I don't know' or 'I don't care'. **shrugging. shrugged.**

shrunk see **shrink.**

shudder (shud′ ər) *v.* to shake suddenly with fear or cold.

shuffle (shufl) *v.* **1.** to mix up playing cards before dealing. **2.** to walk without lifting the feet. **shuffling. shuffled.**

shut (shut) *v.* to close: *to shut a door; to shut your eyes.* **shutting. shut.**

shutdown (shut′ daůn′) *n.* the stopping of work; the closing down of a factory, mine, or other place for a time.

shut-in (shut′ in′) *n.* a person who is unable to leave his or her home because of age, illness, or injury.

shut-out (shut′ aůt′) *n.* a win against a team that scores no points.

shutter (shut′ ər) *n.* **1.** a movable wooden cover for a window. **2.** the part of a camera that opens and closes between the lens and the film.

shuttle (shutl) *n.* a method of transport from one place to another, with few or no stops on the way: *a space shuttle; a shuttle bus; a shuttle to an airport.*

shy (shī) *adj.* finding it difficult to speak to or to meet people; bashful: *a shy person; a shyer (shier) one; the shyest (shiest) one of all.*

sick (sik) *adj.* **1.** ill; not well. **2.** *(informal)* tired or bored: *I'm sick of listening to that song!*

side (sīd) *n.* **1.** one of the surfaces or lines that form the outside or limits of a thing: *the sides of a box; the four sides of a square.* **2.** either of the two surfaces of a thin, flat object such as a paper, cloth, or door. **3.** a place away from a central point or line: *the north side of the city; the far side of the building.* **4.** the left part or the right part of a person: *I have a pain in my side.* **5.** one of the groups playing, fighting, or arguing against another: *Which side do you play for?* **6.** an opinion: *We heard all sides of the argument.* **7.** a slope of a mountain or hill. *adj.* at, on, or by one side, not the front or the back: *the side door of the house.*

sidewalk (sīd′ wòk′) *n.* a place to walk at the side of a street: *Sidewalks are usually paved.*

sideways (sīd′ wāz′) *adv.* to one side: *Don't look backwards or forwards. Look sideways.*

⊖**siege** (sēj) *n.* a time when an enemy surrounds a place and stops help or food from getting in.

sieve

sieve (siv) *n.* a fine metal or plastic net that lets only liquids and small pieces pass through: *Shaking flour through a sieve removes the lumps.*

sift (sift) *v.* to use a sieve to separate fine powders from lumps or stones.

sigh (sī) *n.* a heavy breathing out that shows a person is tired, bored, or unhappy. *v.* to breathe out in this way.

sight (sīt) *n.* **1.** one of the five senses; the ability to see: *Jonathan has very good sight.* **2.** something that is seen: *The sunset was a wonderful sight.*

sign (sīn) *n.* **1.** something, such as a mark or a movement, that has a special meaning: *Signs in arithmetic include* +, −, ×, ÷. *He moved his hand as a sign for me to come closer.* **2.** a board, poster, etc. that advertises something or gives directions or other information: *The sign on the highway says, 'Regina, 100 km'.* *v.* for a person to write his or her name: *She signed her name at the bottom of the letter.*

signal (sig′ nəl) *n.* a message sent by movement, sound, or light: *A red traffic signal means that drivers should stop.* *v.* to give such a message: *She signalled for the bus to stop by moving her arms.* **signalling. signalled.**

signature (sig′ nə chər) *n.* the way a person writes his or her name.

significant (sig nif′ i kənt) *adj.* important; worth remembering: *The discovery of oil in Alberta was a significant event in the history of Canada.*

Sikh (sēk) *n.* a person who is a member of a religious group based in India.

silence (sī′ ləns) *n.* the absence of sound.

silent (sī′ lənt) *adj.* not making any sound.

silk (silk) *n.* a shiny, smooth cloth made from threads that are spun by silkworms.

sill (sil) *n.* a ledge below a window or door.

silly (sil′ ē) *adj.* foolish: *a silly idea; a sillier one; the silliest one of all.*

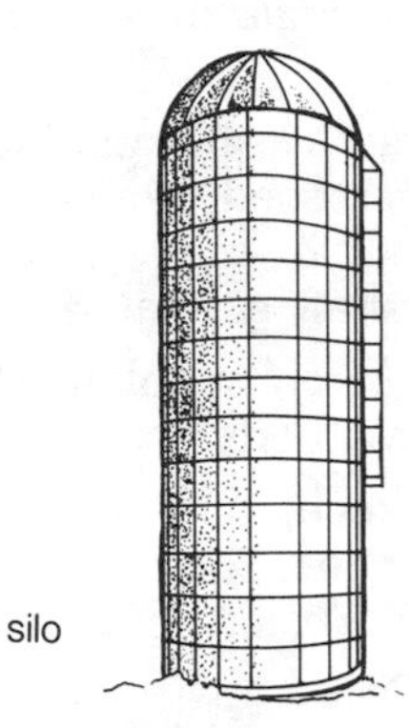
silo

silo (sī′ lō) *n.* a tall tower, usually round, that is used to store farm crops and food for livestock. *pl.* **silos.**

silver (sil′ vər) *n.* **1.** a precious, white metal that can be polished brightly. **2.** the colour of silver. *adj.* having this colour.

silverware (sil′ vər wār′) *n.* articles, especially cutlery, made from silver or a similar metal.

similar (sim′ i lər) *adj.* very much the same: *My dress is similar to yours. The only difference is that mine has buttons, not a zipper.*

similarity (sim′ i lar′ i tē) *n.* resemblance; looking very much the same: *There is a similarity between the two hats.* *pl.* **similarities.**

simmer (sim′ ər) *v.* to cook at a heat that is just less than boiling.

simple (simpl) *adj.* **1.** easy to understand; not difficult: *simple questions on a test.* **2.** plain; not fancy or complicated: *a simple pattern; a simple machine; a simpler one; the simplest one of all.*

simplify (sim′ pli fī′) *v.* to make something easier: *This calculator will simplify your math homework.* **simplifying. simplified.** it **simplifies.**

simply (sim′ plē) *adv.* **1.** in a simple way: *The teacher spoke simply so that everyone would understand.* **2.** really; truly: *I feel simply wonderful today.*

simultaneously (sī′ məl tā′ ni əs lē) *adv.* at the same time: *The two meetings are held simultaneously. Which one will you attend?*

sin (sin) *n.* a deed that is wrong or bad, and can be against the laws of a religion. *v.* to do such a deed. **sinning. sinned.**

since (sins) *adv.* from that time until now: *I have been away since Monday.* *conj.* because: *Since you ask, I will tell you the story.*

sincere (sin sēr′) *adj.* honest; meaning what is said: *He is sincere when he makes a promise.*

sing (sing) *v.* to make music with the voice, usually using words. **singing. sang** (sang). I have **sung** (sung).

⊖**singe** (sinj) *v.* to burn slightly: *He singed his hair.* **singeing. singed.**

singer (sing′ ər) *n.* a person who sings.

single (sing′ ər) *adj.* **1.** one only: *A single apple was left in the bag.* **2.** unmarried: *a single man.* **3.** for one only: *a single bed.* *v.* (used with **out**) to pick from others: *He singled out the grey hat as the one he wanted.* **singling. singled.**

singular (sing′ gyə lər) *adj.* referring to one only: 'dog' is a singular noun; 'dogs' is a plural noun.

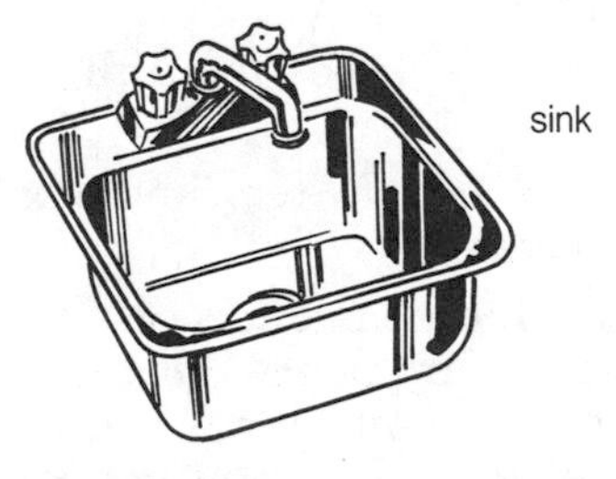
sink

sink (singk) *n.* a basin with faucets that is used for washing. *v.* to go to or towards the bottom of water, mud, etc.: *The ship is sinking.* **sinking. sank** (sangk). it has **sunk** (sungk).

sip (sip) *n.* a small drink: *Robin had a sip of water.* *v.* to drink in small amounts. **sipping. sipped.**

sir (sûr) **1.** a title given to a knight by a king or queen. **2.** mister; a polite title used when speaking to a man: *Do you know the correct time, sir?*

siren (sī′ rən) *n.* a machine that makes a loud screaming noise to warn people about something: *an ambulance siren.*

sister (sis′ tər) *n.* a girl or woman who has the same parents as another person.

sit (sit) *v.* **1.** to rest on the lower part of the body: *to sit on a chair; to sit on the ground.* **2.** to meet, as Members of Parliament do. **sitting. sat** (sat).

site (sīt) *n.* the place where something was built or will be built; a location.

sitter (sit′ ər) *n.* a babysitter.

situation (sit yū ā′ shən, sich′ ū ā′ shən) *n.* a group of things that are happening: *The situation at work is improving. There are more people to help, and we will receive more pay.*

six (siks) *n., adj.* one more than five (6). *pl.* **sixes.**

sixteen (siks tēn′) *n., adj.* ten more than six (16).

sixth (siksth) *adj.* following fifth (6th).

sixty (siks′ tē) *n., adj.* ten times six (60). *pl.* **sixties.**

size (sīz) *n.* **1.** the largeness or smallness of something: *What is the size of the room? What is the size of the class?* **2.** a measurement used for clothes and shoes: *What size shoes do you wear?*

sizzle (sizl) *v.* to make a hissing sound because of heat: *The sausages sizzle in the pan.* **sizzling. sizzled.**

skate (skāt) *n.* a metal blade that can be fastened to a boot or shoe. *v.* to glide or move along on skates. **skating. skated.**

skeleton (skel′ ət ən) *n.* the set of bones in a body.

sketch (skech) *n.* a quick drawing. *pl.* **sketches.** *v.* to make a quick drawing. **sketching. sketched.** she **sketches.**

skis

ski (skē) *n.* one of two long strips of wood, metal, or plastic that curve up at the front and are attached to a boot: *Skis are used for downhill skiing, cross-country skiing, or waterskiing.* *pl.* **skis.** *v.* to travel on skis: *We skied down the hill.* **skiing** (skē′ ing). **skied** (skēd). she **skis** (skēz).

skid (skid) *n.* a sudden sideways slide on something slippery or very smooth. *v.* to slide sideways on a wet or icy surface: *The car skidded on the icy highway.* **skidding. skidded.**

skier (skē′ ər) *n.* a person who skis.

skill (skil) *n.* the ability to do something well that comes from study or practice: *Martin shows skill in painting pictures of people.*

skim (skim) *v.* **1.** to remove something that is floating on the top of a liquid. **2.** to read very quickly, looking for the main ideas. **3.** to glide over a surface, hardly touching it: *The boat skimmed across the pond.* **skimming. skimmed.**

skim milk (skim′ milk′) milk from which the cream has been removed.

skin (skin) *n.* **1.** the outer covering of the body of a person or animal. **2.** the outer covering of certain fruits or vegetables: *the skin of a banana.* *v.* to remove the skin of an animal. **skinning. skinned.**

skin diver (skin′ dīv′ ər) a person who swims under water for long periods of time, wearing a face mask and flippers and sometimes using special equipment for breathing.

skinny (skin′ ē) *adj.* very thin: *a skinny child; a skinnier child; the skinniest child of all.*

skip (skip) *v.* **1.** to jump lightly from one leg to the other, often over a rope, as children sometimes do. **2.** to leave out parts, or to pass from one part to another: *I skipped two of the questions on the test. He skipped three pages of the book.* **skipping. skipped.**

skirt (skûrt) *n.* a garment, worn by women and girls, that hangs down from the waist below a blouse.

skull (skul) *n.* the bony part of the head which protects the brain.

skunk

skunk (skungk) *n.* a furry black animal with white stripes and a bushy tail; it can spray a bad-smelling liquid when it is frightened.

sky (skī) *n.* the space above the earth where the sun, moon, stars, and clouds can be seen. *pl.* **skies.**

Toronto skyline

skyline (skī′ līn′) *n.* the outline of buildings against the sky: *As we drove towards Toronto, we saw the city's skyline.*

skyscraper (skī′ skrāp′ ər) *n.* a building that is very tall.

slab (slab) *n.* a flat, thick piece: *a slab of stone; a slab of meat.*

slack (slak) *adj.* **1.** not tight; hanging loose: *a slack rope.* **2.** slow: *His business is slack.*

slacks (slaks) *n.pl.* loose-fitting long pants.

slam (slam) *v.* to shut or put down with much force and noise: *Don't slam the car door! He slammed the telephone down.* **slamming. slammed.**

slang (slang) *n.* a very informal word or expression that is often used in conversation, but isn't used in proper writing.

slant (slant) *n.* a tilt: *Please make the mirror straight. It's hanging at a slant.* *v.* to tilt or slope; to lean in a direction that is not straight up and down.

slap (slap) *n.* a hit, usually with an open hand. *v.* to hit with the open hand. **slapping. slapped.**

slash (slash) *n.* a long cut made with sweeping strokes. *pl.* **slashes.** *v.* to make such a cut. **slashing. slashed.** he **slashes.**

slaughter (slò′ tər) *n.* **1.** the killing of animals for food. **2.** the cruel killing of many people. *v.* **1.** to kill animals for food. **2.** to kill cruelly and in great numbers.

slave (slāv) *n.* a person who is owned by another person. *v.* to work very hard and with little rest. **slaving. slaved.**

sled (sled) *n.* a wooden frame on metal runners, used to carry people or things over snow. *v.* to ride on a sled. **sledding. sledded.**

sleep (slēp) *n.* the state of resting unconsciously that happens naturally for people and animals. *v.* to rest in an unconscious state. **sleeping. slept** (slept).

sleepy (slē′ pē) *adj.* tired; wanting to sleep: *a sleepy baby; a sleepier baby; the sleepiest baby of all.*

sleet (slēt) *n.* a mixture of falling rain and fine snow.

sleeve (slēv) *n.* the part of a garment that covers the arm.

sleigh (slā) *n.* a sled.

slender (slen′ dər) *adj.* **1.** thin or narrow: *a slender branch on a tree.* **2.** not large; not enough: *She has only a slender chance of winning the tennis game.*

slept see **sleep.**

slice (slīs) *n.* a thin, flat piece cut from something: *a slice of bacon; a slice of bread.* *v.* to cut off a slice; to cut into slices: *Chris sliced the cheese.* **slicing. sliced.**

slid see **slide.**

slide (slīd) *n.* **1.** a smooth surface on which to slip down smoothly: *a slide for children to play on.* **2.** a small, thin piece of glass or plastic: *Objects are put on a slide and looked at through a microscope.* **3.** a transparent picture or photograph that is projected onto a screen. **4.** rocks, ice, mud, snow, etc., falling from above in large amounts. *v.* to move smoothly along a surface: *The children slid along the ice.* **sliding. slid** (slid).

slight (slīt) *adj.* not very big or important: *Helen has a slight cold.*

slim (slim) *adj.* slender; thin: *a slim chance; a slim person; a slimmer one; the slimmest one of all.*

slime (slīm) *n.* soft, sticky mud or something like it.

sling (sling) *n.* **1.** a loop of cloth hanging from the neck, which will hold steady an injured arm. **2.** a rope or strap for holding steady something being moved, lifted, or lowered.

⊖**slip** (slip) *n.* **1.** a loose garment worn under a dress or skirt. **2.** a small piece of paper: *I wrote down your address on a slip of paper.* **3.** a quick fall or slide. *v.* **1.** to slide suddenly: *He slipped on the ice and almost fell.* **2.** to move quietly: *Jo slipped into her seat.* **slipping. slipped.**

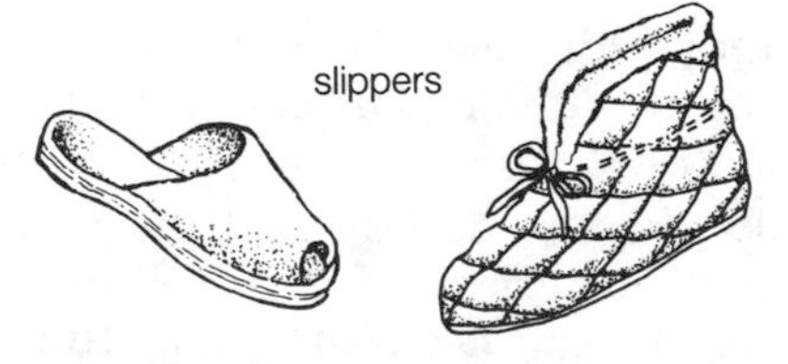

slipper (slip′ ər) *n.* a soft shoe worn indoors.

slippery (slip′ ə rē) *adj.* having a surface that is hard to hold onto or walk on: *slippery soap; a slippery road; a slipperier one; the slipperiest one of all.*

slit (slit) *n.* a long cut or narrow opening. *v.* to make such a cut: *to slit open an envelope.* **slitting. slit.**

sliver (sliv′ ər) *n.* a small, thin, sharp piece of wood, metal, glass, etc.: *I carefully removed the sliver of wood from my thumb.*

slogan (slō′ gən) *n.* a word, or words, that are easy to remember, used by a group or business to describe itself.

slope (slōp) *n.* a line or a piece of land that is on a slant: *a ski slope.* *v.* to slant or tilt; to be higher at one end than at the other. **sloping. sloped.**

sloppy (slop′ ē) *adj.* **1.** wet and muddy: *sloppy weather.* **2.** messy and careless: *a sloppy pile of clothes; a sloppy worker; a sloppier one; the sloppiest one of all.*

slot (slot) *n.* a straight, narrow opening: *a slot for putting in a coin; a slot for putting in an envelope.*

slouch (slaủch) *v.* to walk, stand, or sit with the shoulders drooping. **slouching. slouched.** he **slouches.**

slough (slū) *n.* a pond of water formed in the spring by rain or melting snow.

slow (slō) *adj.* taking a long time; moving at less than normal speed: *a slow train.* *v.* to go or move at a slower speed: *The car slowed down as it came to the red light.*

slug (slug) *n.* **1.** a kind of snail with no shell. **2.** a small piece of lead or other metal that is fired from a gun. *v. (informal)* to hit hard with the fist or a baseball bat. **slugging. slugged.**

sluice (slūs) *n.* an artificial channel of water with a gate at the upper end. The gate can be opened or closed to control the flow of water of a pond, river, lake, etc.

slum (slum) *n.* a poor and crowded part of some cities.

slump (slump) *n.* a time when there is much unemployment and business is slow. *v.* to fall or drop suddenly or heavily: *The sick child slumped to the ground. The sale of toys slumped in January.*

slush (slush) *n.* snow that is partly melted and has become messy.

sly (slī) *adj.* clever at doing things in a secret way: *a sly person; a slyer (slier) one; the slyest (sliest) one of all.*

smack (smak) *n.* **1.** a hard hit with the open hand. **2.** a loud noise made by the lips. *v.* **1.** to hit hard with the open hand. **2.** to make a loud noise with the lips.

small (smȯl) *adj.* **1.** little; not large in size: *He drives a small car. We live in a small town.* **2.** not large in amount: *We paid a small price.* **3.** not important: *I have a small problem with the furnace.*

smart (smȧrt) *adj.* **1.** quick to understand: *He is a smart boy.* **2.** neat and well-dressed: *The boys look smart in their new suits.* *v.* to feel a stinging pain: *My eyes smart when I am near smoke.*

smash (smash) *v.* to break into pieces, often noisily: *The ball smashed the window.* **smashing. smashed.** he **smashes.**

smear (smēr) *v.* **1.** to spread a wet or greasy substance on something, sometimes in a messy way: *to smear butter on bread.* **2.** to stain with something wet or greasy: *She smeared paint on her coat.*

smell (smel) *n.* **1.** a scent: *the smell of burning wood.* **2.** one of the five senses: *Some animals have an excellent sense of smell.* *v.* **1.** to give off a scent: *The flowers smell sweet.* **2.** to give off a bad scent: *The garbage smells.* **3.** to be aware of something by using the nose: *Do you smell the cookies baking?*

smelt (smelt) *n.* a small, silvery fish found in lakes and rivers and used for food. *pl.* **smelt**, or **smelts.** *v.* to melt ore in order to separate the metal in it.

smelter (smel′ tər) *n.* a place where certain rocks are heated so that the metal they contain is released.

smile (smīl) *n.* a turning up of the corners of the mouth to show pleasure. *v.* to make a smile. **smiling. smiled.**

smoke (smōk) *n.* a cloud of vapour and gas given off by something burning. *v.* **1.** to give off smoke: *The fireplace is smoking.* **2.** to draw in and breathe out smoke from tobacco: *He smokes a pipe.* **3.** to preserve and flavour food by using smoke. **smoking. smoked.**

smooth (smūth) *adj.* even and flat, not rough or bumpy: *a smooth table top.* *v.* to make even and flat: *Tony smoothed the wooden bowl with sandpaper.*

smother (smuth′ ər) *v.* **1.** to stop someone breathing by covering the mouth and nose. **2.** to cover all over: *Dave smothered his hamburger with ketchup.*

smoulder, smolder (smōl′ dər) *v.* to burn slowly without a flame but with a lot of smoke.

smuggle (smugl) *v.* to take goods into or out of a country secretly, against the law. **smuggling. smuggled.**

snack (snak) *n.* a small amount of food or a light meal that is easy to prepare.

snail (snāl) *n.* a small, slow-moving creature with a shell on its back.

snake (snāk) *n.* a long, thin, smooth reptile that has no legs and glides along on its body. Snakes usually feed on other animals, and many have a poisonous bite.

snap (snap) *n.* **1.** a sudden sharp sound or break: *He gave the twig a snap.* **2.** a metal fastener for clothes. *v.* **1.** to make a sudden sound: *He snapped his fingers.* **2.** to break suddenly: *The branch snapped.* **3.** to speak in a sudden, angry way: *I'm sorry I snapped when you arrived late.* **4.** to take a photograph: *to snap a picture.* **snapping. snapped.**

snapshot (snap′ shot′) *n.* a photograph.

snare (snār) *n.* a trap used for catching birds or small animals. *v.* to trap. **snaring. snared.**

snatch (snach) *v.* to grab; to take hold of suddenly: *The dog snatched the cookie from my hand.* **snatching. snatched.** he **snatches.**

sneak (snēk) *v.* to move in a sly way, trying not to be seen or be heard.

sneakers (snēk′ ərz) *n.pl.* running shoes.

sneeze (snēz) *n.* a loud noise made when air rushes out of the nose. *v.* to make such a noise: *The pepper made me sneeze.* **sneezing. sneezed.**

sniff (snif) *v.* to breathe air in quickly through the nose: *to sniff the flowers.*

snip (snip) *v.* to cut with short, quick strokes, using scissors or another cutting tool. **snipping. snipped.**

⊖**snob** (snob) *n.* a person who believes that he or she is better than others because of being richer, smarter, from a more important family, etc.

snore (snȯr) *v.* to breathe noisily while asleep. **snoring. snored.**

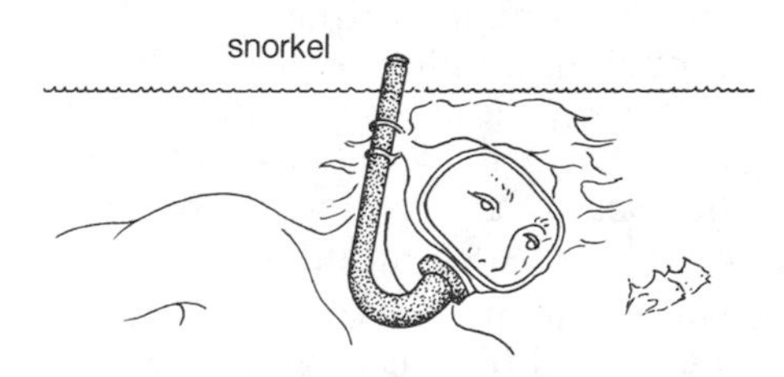

snorkel (snȯr′ kəl) *n.* a tube for someone to breathe through while swimming just beneath the surface of the water.

snout (snaůt) *n.* the part of an animal's head that sticks out and includes the jaws and the nose: *a pig's snout.*

snow (snō) *n.* soft white flakes that fall towards the ground, formed by the freezing of water vapour in the air. *v.* to fall in flakes of snow: *It will snow tomorrow.*

snowball (snō′ bȯl′) *n.* a ball made of tightly packed snow.

snowflake (snō′ flāk′) *n.* one piece of snow.

snowmobile (snō′ mə bēl′) *n.* a vehicle with a motor, driven over the snow.

snowplough, snowplow (snō′ plaů′) *n.* a heavy vehicle for clearing snow from roads.

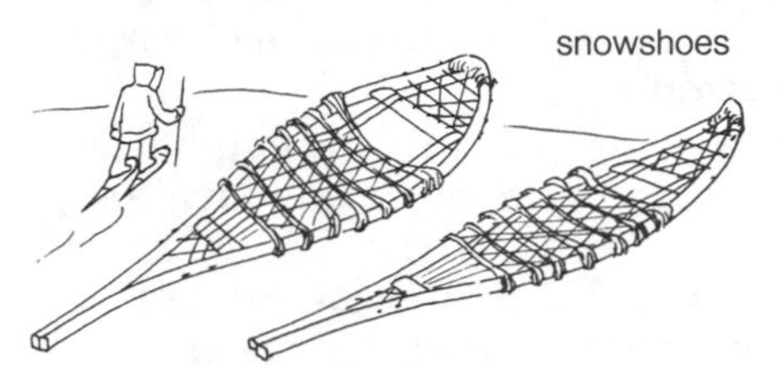

snowshoes (snō′ shüz′) *n.pl.* shoes, shaped like tennis rackets, strapped to the boots and used for walking over deep snow.

snowy (snō′ ē) *adj.* having to do with or covered with snow: *a snowy day; a snowier day; the snowiest day of the winter.*

so (sō) *adv.* **1.** to such a degree or amount: *Don't talk so loudly!* **2.** very: *I am so glad you are here.* **3.** also: *Are you going to the game? So am I.* **4.** approximately: *It took a week or so for the letter to arrive.* **5.** true; correct: *Is it raining? I think so. conj.* therefore; as a result: *We missed the bus, so we had to walk.*

soak (sōk) *v.* **1.** to wet something completely: *The rain soaked us.* **2.** to stay wet for a long time: *to soak the bread in milk; to soak in the bathtub.*

soap (sōp) *n.* a mixture of fat and other substances, used with water for washing and cleaning.

soar (sȯr) *v.* to rise high in the sky: *The plane soared towards the clouds and disappeared.*

sob (sob) *v.* to cry, taking short breaths. **sobbing. sobbed.**

sober (sō′ bər) *adj.* **1.** not under the influence of alcohol. **2.** serious: *He is very sober and hardly ever laughs or smiles.*

soccer (sok′ ər) *n.* a type of football game played by two teams of eleven players, in which the ball may not be touched by the hands or arms, except by the goalkeeper.

sociable (sō′ shəbl) *adj.* friendly; liking to be with and to meet people.

social (sō′ shəl) *adj.* having to do with people and how they live together in groups: *Social studies include history and geography.*

socialize (sō′ shə līz′) *v.* to mix with other people: *Harry enjoys socializing, and he goes to many parties.* **socializing. socialized.**

society (sə sī′ ə tē) *n.* **1.** human beings living together: *Cures for diseases can benefit society.* **2.** people who join together because they have the same interest: *Matthew belongs to the Ottawa hiking society. pl.* **societies.**

sock (sok) *n.* a cloth covering for the foot and the lower part of the leg.

socket (sok′ ət) *n.* a hollow part into which something fits: *a socket for a light bulb.*

sod (sod) *n.* a layer of earth with grass and roots growing in it.

soda (sō′ də) *n.* **1.** a soft drink made with soda water, flavoured syrup, and sometimes, ice cream. **2.** a powder used in baking products and cleaning agents. *pl.* **sodas.**

soda water (sō′ də wo′ tər) water filled with a special gas to make it bubbly.

sofa (sō′ fə) *n.* a long, soft seat with arms and a back, for two or more people to sit on. *pl.* **sofas.**

soft (soft) *adj.* **1.** not hard or stiff: *a soft seat.* **2.** gentle; quiet: *a soft voice.* **3.** smooth; not rough: *soft skin.*

soft drink (soft′ dringk′) a beverage that does not contain alcohol and is usually sweet and made with soda water.

softly (soft′ lē) *adv.* in a soft way: *Walk softly! The baby is sleeping.*

software (sȯft′ wãr′) *n.* a general name given to a set, or sets, of instructions that makes a computer serve a certain purpose.

soggy (sog′ ē) *adj.* damp, soft, and messy: *soggy ground; soggier ground; the soggiest ground of all.*

soil (sȯil) *n.* ground in which plants grow. *v.* to make something dirty: *He soiled his pants when he fell.*

solar (sō′ lər) *adj.* having to do with the sun.

solar system (sō′ lər sis′ təm) the sun and all the planets and other heavenly bodies that orbit around it.

⊖**sold** see **sell.**

solder (sod′ ər) *n.* a soft metal that can be melted and used to join things together: *Electrical parts are often joined together with solder.* *v.* to join together using solder: *He soldered a new wire inside the radio.*

soldier (sōl′ jər) *n.* someone who belongs to an army.

sole (sōl) *n.* **1.** the bottom part of a foot, sock, or shoe. *pl.* **soles.** **2.** a kind of flat fish that lives in the ocean and is used for food. *pl.* **sole.** *adj.* single; being the only one or only ones: *She is the sole survivor of the plane crash.*

solemn (sol′ əm) *adj.* very serious; dignified: *A funeral is a solemn occasion.*

solicitor (sə lis′ ə tər) *n.* a lawyer.

solid (sol′ id) *adj.* firm right through; not hollow or liquid: *a bar of solid iron.*

solitary (sol′ i ter′ ē) *adj.* single: *Not a solitary person lived on the island.*

solo (sō′ lō) *n.* a piece of music to be played or sung by one person. *pl.* **solos.** *adj.* played or done by one person: *a solo performance.*

solution (sə lü′ shən) *n.* **1.** the answer to a problem, puzzle, or mystery. **2.** a mixture made of a solid or gas dissolved in a liquid.

solve (solv) *v.* to find the answer to a problem, puzzle, or mystery: *The detective solved the crime.* **solving. solved.**

some (sum) *adj.* **1.** a certain but not an exact number or amount: *We picked some berries. We ate some cake.* **2.** being unrecognized or unknown: *Some salesperson phoned us today.* **3.** one or another: *We will find some way out of the park.* *adv.* about: *Some thirty people were at the party.*

somebody (sum′ bud′ ē, sum′ bod′ ē) *pron.* some person: *Will somebody help me?*

somehow (sum′ haů′) *adv.* in a way not yet known: *We shall finish the job somehow.*

someone (sum′ wun′) *pron.* some person: *Someone phoned, but he did not tell me his name.*

something (sum′ thing′) *pron.* a thing not known: *Something flew into my eye. Can you see it?*

sometimes (sum′ tīmz′) *adv.* once in a while; now and then: *I sometimes like to have ice cream after dinner.*

somewhat (sum′ hwot′, sum′ wot′) *adv.* a little; slightly; rather: *You look somewhat pale today.*

somewhere (sum′ hwer′, sum′ wer′) *adv.* in, at, or to a place not known: *She lives somewhere in Alberta, but I don't know the name of the town.*

⊖**son** (sun) *n.* a male child: *My grandparents have two sons. My parents have one son.*

song (song) *n.* **1.** words that are sung. **2.** the musical sounds of a bird.

son-in-law (sun′ in lȯ′) *n.* the husband of a person's daughter. *pl.* **sons-in-law.**

soon (sūn) *adv.* in a very short while: *Mark ran and was soon at school.*

soot (sut) *n.* black dust formed by burning.

soothe (sûth) *v.* to make someone feel calmer, or more comfortable: *The hot bath will soothe your sore muscles.* **soothing. soothed.**

sophisticated (sə fis′ ti kāt′ əd) *adj.* **1.** smart and knowing much about how to behave correctly: *She is a very sophisticated woman. She reads books written in Latin, and is an expert on tasting wine.* **2.** very complicated: *A computer is a sophisticated device.*

sore (sȯr) *n.* a painful place on the body where the skin is hurt: *Vic put a bandage on the sore on his knee.* *adj.* painful; tender: *a sore throat; a sorer throat; the sorest throat of all.*

sorrow (sor′ ō, sȯr′ ō) *n.* sadness; unhappiness: *We expressed our feelings of sorrow to our friend whose father had died.*

sorry (sor′ ē, sȯr′ ē) *adj.* feeling unhappy or sad about something: *a sorry person; a sorrier one; the sorriest one of all. I am sorry that you cannot come to the party.*

⊖**sort** (sȯrt) *n.* a kind: *There are all sorts of flowers in the garden.* *v.* to put things in groups of the same kind: *She sorted her bills, receipts, and cheques.*

sought see **seek.**

soul (sōl) *n.* the part of a person that is thought to be separate from the body: *Many people believe that the soul goes on living after the body dies.*

sound (saůnd) *n.* **1.** a noise: *I can hear the sound of the drums.* **2.** a narrow passage of water that joins two seas or that is between the mainland and an island. *adj.* **1.** deep: *a sound sleep.* **2.** wise; making sense: *a sound idea.* *v.* **1.** to make sound: *The music sounds lovely.* **2.** to seem, when heard: *Your plans for the trip sound interesting.*

soundproof (saůnd′ prūf′) *adj.* able to keep sound out.

soup (sūp) *n.* a liquid food usually made with pieces of vegetables, meat, or fish boiled in water.

sour (saůr) *adj.* having the kind of sharp taste that lemons and vinegar have: *sour fruit.*

source (sȯrs) *n.* the place where something has come from; the beginning of something: *the source of a river; a good source of information.*

south (saůth) *n.* the direction to the left as a person faces the setting sun; opposite to north.

South American (saůth′ ə mer′ i kən) *n.* a person born in or living in South America. *adj.* having to do with the continent of South America.

southern (suth′ ərn) *adj.* in the direction of the south: *Niagara Falls is in southern Ontario.*

South Pole (saůth′ pōl′) the most southern point of the earth; it is the south end of the axis of the earth.

⊖**souvenir** (sü′ və nėr′) *n.* something kept as a reminder of a certain time, place, person, etc.

sow (saů) *n.* a female pig.

sow (sō) *v.* to plant seeds in the ground. **sowing. sowed.** he has **sown** (sōn).

space (spās) *n.* **1.** the distance between things: *a space of two metres.* **2.** a place that is empty: *a space where you can sit.* **3.** all the places beyond the earth's atmosphere: *The astronauts travelled in space.*

spacecraft (spās′ kraft′) *n.* a vehicle that can carry astronauts beyond the earth's atmosphere.

spaceship (spās′ ship′) *n.* a spacecraft.

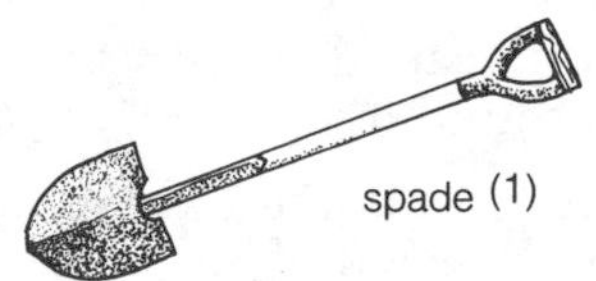
spade (1)

spade (spād) *n.* **1.** a garden tool used for digging; it has a long handle and a flat blade. **2.** a playing card with one or more ♠ marks on it.

spaghetti (spə get′ ē) *n.* a food made of flour and water shaped into little strings, often served with a sauce.

span (span) *n.* **1.** the space between two supports of a bridge or other structure. **2.** the length of anything: *The life span of most dogs is more than ten years.*

spaniel

spaniel (span′ yəl) *n.* a dog with long hair, large drooping ears, and short legs.

spank (spangk) *v.* to slap on the backside as a punishment.

spanking (spangk′ ing) *n.* a slap or slaps on the backside, given as a punishment.

spare (sper) *adj.* left over; not being used: *After we painted the fence, we had some spare paint.* *v.* to give or lend something: *Can you spare some matches?* **sparing. spared.**

sparerib (sper′ rib′) *n.* a piece of an animal's rib with some meat attached to it.

spark (spårk) *n.* **1.** a speck of something burning: *Sparks rose from the fire.* **2.** a tiny electric flash.

sparkle (spårkl) *n.* a gleam; a bright, flashing shine: *He had a sparkle in his eyes.* *v.* to shine with bright flashes: *The jewels sparkled in the light.* **sparkling. sparkled.**

spark plug (spårk′ plug′) the part of a car's engine that makes a spark of electricity; this ignites the gasoline and makes the engine run.

sparrow (spar′ ō) *n.* a common bird that is small and has brownish feathers.

spat see **spit.**

spatter (spat′ ər) *v.* to splash with liquid or mud.

spatula (spach′ yü lə) *n.* a flat kitchen tool used for scraping or spreading: *Hans flipped the eggs with a spatula.* *pl.* **spatulas.**

spawn (spȯn) *n.* the eggs of fish, frogs, newts, and other water animals. *v.* to produce these eggs.

speak (spēk) *v.* to talk; to use the voice to make words: *Don't speak so quickly. Agnes spoke to us about her trip. Will speaks four languages.* **speaking. spoke** (spōk). I have **spoken** (spōk′ ən).

⊖**speaker** (spēk′ ər) *n.* **1.** the person who is talking. **2.** a device used for making sounds louder: *the speakers of a stereo.*

spear (spēr) *n.* a weapon with a long handle and a sharp point.

special (spesh′ əl) *adj.* different; not the usual kind: *You need a special needle if you are sewing leather.*

special delivery (spesh′ əl di liv′ ər ē) a method of delivering a letter or package sent through the mail very quickly, at extra cost. *pl.* **special deliveries.**

specialty (spesh′ əl tē) *n.* something a person is very good at doing: *Try some cake. It's the cook's specialty.* *pl.* **specialties.**

species (spē′ sēz, spē′ shēz) *n.* a group of living things that are of the same general kind and can breed together: *There are many species of animals in the world.* *pl.* **species.**

specify (spes′ i fī′) *v.* to say exactly: *You said that you need a tool for cutting. Would you please specify which tool?* **specifying. specified.**

speck (spek) *n.* a tiny bit; a small spot: *Sima had a speck of dirt in her eye.*

spectacle (spek′ təkl) *n.* an unusual sight or show: *The parade was a colourful spectacle.*

spectator (spek′ tā tər) *n.* a person who watches a game, parade, or other event.

sped see **speed.**

speech (spēch) *n.* **1.** the power of speaking. **2.** a special talk given to some people: *The Prime Minister's speech to the country was about the economy.* *pl.* **speeches.**

speed (spēd) *n.* how quickly something moves or happens: *The car went at a slow speed.* *v.* to move quickly: *The car sped down the road.* **speeding. sped** (sped) or **speeded.**

speedometer (spid om′ ə tər) *n.* an instrument that shows the speed of a vehicle.

spell (spel) *v.* to write or say letters in correct order to make a word.

spend (spend) *v.* **1.** to pay money: *Kate spent two dollars for the present.* **2.** to use time: *Philip spent the weekend at his sister's home.* **spending. spent.**

sperm (spûrm) *n.* one or many male cells of reproduction.

sphere (sfēr) *n.* any object shaped like a ball.

spice (spīs) *n.* part of a plant used to flavour food: *Ginger, nutmeg, and cinnamon are some spices.* *v.* to add spice to food: *Mark spiced the pizza with pepper.* **spicing. spiced.**

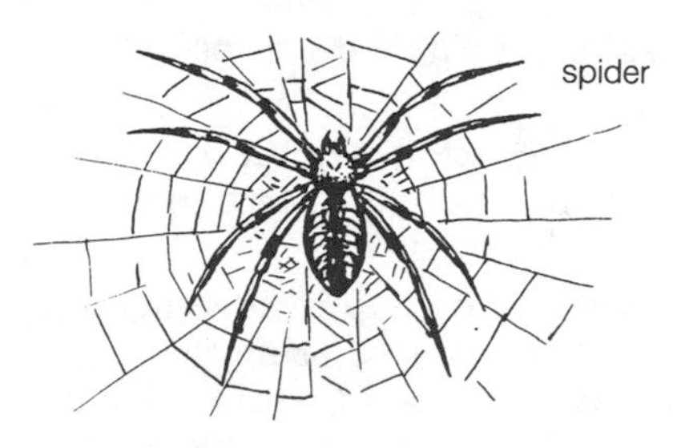

spider (spī′ dər) *n.* a small creature with eight long legs and no wings: *Many types of spiders spin webs to catch flying insects.*

spied, spies see **spy.**

spike (spīk) *n.* a very large, sharp nail.

spill (spil) *v.* to let a liquid overflow or pour out, without meaning for it to happen. *I spilled some milk on the table.* **spilling. spilled**, or **spilt.**

spin (spin) *v.* **1.** to turn around quickly, as wheels do. **2.** to make threads by twisting cotton, wool, or other materials. **spinning. spun** (spun).

spinach (spin′ ich) *n.* a dark green, leafy vegetable.

spine (spīn) *n.* **1.** a long set of little bones that fit together down the middle of the back. **2.** a sharp point that grows on a plant or animal.

spiral (spī′ rəl) *n.* a curve that continues to wind around: *a spiral on a screw.*

spirit (spir′ it) *n.* **1.** a person's soul. **2.** a ghost. **3.** an angel.

spit (spit) *v.* to shoot something out of the mouth: *Bill spat out an orange pit.* **spitting. spat** (spat).

spite (spīt) *n.* a wish to hurt someone by cruel behaviour.
in spite of despite: *We went for a walk in spite of the bad weather.*

splash (splash) *n.* the noise made when something heavy or someone falls into water. *pl.* **splashes.** *v.* to throw liquid about: *The girls in the lake splashed each other.* **splashing. splashed.** she **splashes.**

splendid (splen′ did) *adj.* magnificent; wonderful; excellent: *splendid weather; a splendid holiday.*

splice (splīs) *v.* to join together two ends of rope by twisting the threads, or to join together two end pieces of film or tape. **splicing. spliced.**

splint (splint) *n.* a piece of wood or other stiff material that is tied to an arm, leg, etc., to hold a broken bone in place.

splinter (splin′ tər) *n.* a thin, sharp piece of wood, metal, etc.: *Toni had a splinter in her thumb.*

split (split) *n.* a crack; a long, thin break: *a split in the board.* *v.* to crack or break into pieces. **splitting. split.**

spoil (spȯil) *v.* **1.** to make something less good or less useful: *The car problems spoiled our trip.* **2.** to become less good or less useful: *The fish was spoiled, and we had to throw it away.* **3.** to give someone more than may be good for him or her: *to spoil children by giving them all they ask for.*

spoke (spōk) *n.* one of the rods that connect the centre of a wheel to the outside edge. *v.* see **speak.**

sponge (spunj) *n.* **1.** a soft pad, full of holes, that soaks up liquid and is used to clean things. **2.** an ocean animal whose skeleton soaks up liquids.

sponsor (spon′ sər) *n.* **1.** a person who is responsible for another person: *When Louise came to Canada, her uncle was her sponsor.* **2.** a person or company that pays for some event: *The cat food company is the sponsor of my favourite television program.* *v.* to act as a sponsor.

spontaneous (spon tān′ i əs, spon tā′ nē əs) *adj.* done without planning; not forced: *We made a spontaneous decision to drive to the mountains.*

spool (spūl) *n.* a small cylinder on which to wind wire, thread, film, fishing line, etc.

spoon (spūn) *n.* an eating utensil with a small, shallow bowl at the end of a handle.

sport (spȯrt) *n.* any game that requires physical activity, and in which people often compete with one another: *Some sports are football, hockey, soccer, and bowling.*

⊖**spot** (spot) *n.* **1.** a small mark: *There is a spot on my coat.* **2.** a special place: *This is the spot where I fell.* *v.* to see; to notice: *Ben spotted an owl in the tree.* **spotting. spotted.**

spouse (spaůs) *n.* a husband or wife: *A man's spouse is his wife; a woman's spouse is her husband.*

spout (spaůt) *n.* the narrow part of a container through which a liquid pours out: *the spout of a kettle.*

sprain (sprān) *v.* to twist a joint of the body so that it becomes painful: *Doris sprained her ankle when she fell.*

sprang see **spring.**

sprawl (spról) *v.* to sit or lie with arms and legs spread out: *Jack sprawled across the couch.*

spray (sprā) *n.* liquid flying or blowing in tiny drops. *pl.* **sprays.** *v.* to scatter fine drops of liquid.

spread (spred) *n.* a covering for a surface: *a woollen spread for the bed.* *v.* **1.** to open out: *The eagle spread its wings.* **2.** to cover a surface: *to spread butter on toast.* **3.** to extend over a large area: *Fire spread through the house. The disease spread through the town.* **spreading. spread.**

spring (spring) *n.* **1.** the season after winter. **2.** a place where water flows out of the ground. **3.** a metal spiral that goes back into shape after it has been pressed or stretched: *a bedspring.* *v.* to jump up suddenly: *I sprang out of bed when the alarm rang.* **springing. sprang** (sprang). it has **sprung** (sprung).

sprinkle (springkl) *v.* to scatter in tiny bits or drops. **sprinkling. sprinkled.**

sprint (sprint) *v.* to run very quickly for a short distance.

sprout (spraůt) *n.* young growth on a plant; a shoot. *v.* for a plant to begin to grow from a seed.

spruce (sprūs) *n.* a tall evergreen tree with cones, and leaves that look like green needles.

sprung see **spring.**

spun see **spin.**

spur (spûr) *n.* a spiked wheel on a rider's boot, sometimes used to make the horse go faster.

spy (spī) *n.* someone who tries secretly to find out things about a person or another country. *pl.* **spies.** *v.* **1.** to watch secretly. **2.** to see suddenly: *The dog spied a rabbit in the field.* **spying. spied** (spīd). he **spies.**

squad (skwod) *n.* a small number of soldiers or other people working together.

square (skwer) *n.* **1.** a flat shape with four equal sides and four equal angles. **2.** a four-sided open space in a city or town. *adj.* having the shape of a square.

square root (skwer′ rūt′) the number which, when multiplied by itself, gives a certain second number. The first number is called the square root of the second number. The square root of 9 is 3, because 3 × 3 = 9. The symbol for square root is $\sqrt{}$)

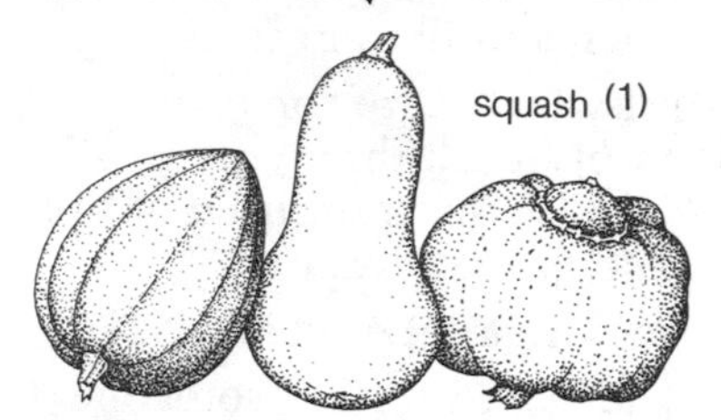

squash (skwosh) *n.* **1.** any of many vegetables that grow along the ground on vines, in different shapes, colours, and sizes: *Zucchini is a summer squash.* *pl.* **squash.** **2.** a game like tennis, played in a four-walled court by two or four people who hit a small rubber ball with rackets. *v.* to squeeze or crush: *I stepped on the orange and squashed it.* **squashing. squashed.** he **squashes.**

squat (skwot) *v.* to sit on the floor or the ground with legs bent in front of the body. **squatting. squatted.**

squeak (skwēk) *n.* a short, high sound; the sound made by a mouse, or by a door that needs to be oiled. *v.* to make this sound.

squeeze (skwēz) *v.* **1.** to press something tightly: *to squeeze juice from a lemon; to squeeze toothpaste from a tube.* **2.** to push together: *We all squeezed into the car.* **squeezing. squeezed.**

squid (skwid) *n.* a sea creature that has ten long arms at the end of its long, thin body and is used for food. *pl.* **squid.**

squint (skwint) *v.* to look with half-closed eyes: *The sun shining on the snow made me squint.*

squirrel

squirrel (skwûr′ əl) *n.* a small rodent that has a long, fluffy tail, eats nuts, and lives in trees.

squirt (skwûrt) *v.* to force a thin stream of liquid through a small opening: *Water is squirted out of the hole in the pipe.*

St. short for **street** or **saint.**

stab (stab) *v.* to wound someone with a knife or other pointed object. **stabbing. stabbed.**

stable (stābl) *n.* a building in which horses are kept. *adj.* not likely to be changed or moved; steady: *a stable government; a stabler one; the stablest one of all.*

stack (stak) *n.* a large pile: *a stack of bricks; a haystack. v.* to pile up: *We stacked the boxes outside.*

stadium (stā′ di əm) *n.* a large building for sports with rows of seats all around. *pl.* **stadiums**, or **stadia.**

staff (staf) *n.* **1.** a stick or pole: *the staff of a flag.* **2.** a group of people working together in an organization such as a school, hospital, library, or business.

⊖**stage** (stāj) *n.* **1.** a raised platform in a theatre. **2.** the particular period someone has reached in doing something: *the different stages of a person's life. v.* to present, arrange, or organize: *to stage a play.* **staging. staged.**

stagger (stag′ ər) *v.* to walk in an unsteady way: *The man felt dizzy and staggered home.*

stain (stān) *n.* **1.** a spot that has marked something. **2.** a substance used to change the colour of wood or some other materials. *v.* **1.** to mark or soil: *I stained my pants with grease.* **2.** to change the colour of wood or some other materials.

staircase

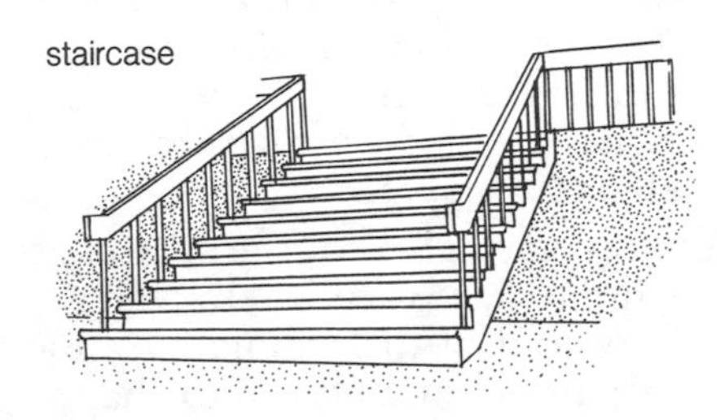

staircase (ster′ kās′) *n.* a set of steps with a handrail.

stairs (sterz) *n.pl.* a set of steps leading from one floor of a building to another.

stake (stāk) *n.* a thick post, pointed at one end and hammered into the ground.

stale (stāl) *adj.* old; not fresh: *stale bread; staler bread; the stalest bread of all.*

stalk (stók) *n.* a stem of a flower or plant. *v.* to hunt quietly, keeping out of sight.

stall (stól) *n.* **1.** a place for a cow or horse to stand in a barn or stable. **2.** a place for displaying things at a market or fair. *v.* to stop going because there isn't enough power: *The car stalls on very cold mornings.*

stallion (stal′ yən) *n.* a male horse.

⊖**stamp** (stamp) *n.* a small piece of printed paper, sticky on one side, to be put on letters and packages that are being mailed in order to pay the postage. *v.* **1.** to stick a stamp on a letter or package. **2.** to bang the foot on the ground.

stampede (stam pēd′) *n.* **1.** a sudden rush of confused people or animals. **2.** a rodeo, often with other amusements: *The Calgary Stampede is held every summer.* *v.* to rush madly in confusion: *The buffalo stampeded when they heard the shot.* **stampeding. stampeded.**

⊖**stand** (stand) *n.* **1.** an opinion about something: *What is your stand on the question of the lowering of the voting age?* **2.** a place where something is or should be: *We waited for the taxi at the taxi stand.* *v.* **1.** to be on the feet, not sitting or lying down: *He stood near the door. I stood up and gave the old man my seat.* **2.** to accept; to bear: *I can't stand the pain in my tooth.* **3.** to be in an upright position: *After the fire, only the barn still stands.* **4.** (used with **for**) to mean: *B.C. stands for British Columbia.* **standing. stood** (stůd).
stand behind to guarantee; to back up; to support: *This company stands behind all its products.*
stand by **1.** to help: *She stood by her brother when he was in trouble.* **2.** to wait nearby; to be ready to help: *The police stood by in case they were needed.*
stand in to serve as a substitute for someone: *When Paolo did not arrive at the game, Bruno stood in for him.*

standard (stan′ dərd) *n.* **1.** a car that does not change gears automatically. **2.** an example with which other things are compared: *The metre is a standard of measure. Her work is usually of a very high standard.* *adj.* **1.** basic; ordinary; usual: *As you can see, this is just a standard radio.* **2.** agreed upon; accepted: **The Canadian Encyclopedia** *is a standard work of reference.*

standard time (stan′ dərd tīm′) a system of keeping the time of day the same over large areas of the world: *Standard time in Edmonton is one hour ahead of standard time in Vancouver. When it is 11 o'clock in Edmonton, it is 10 o'clock in Vancouver.*

Stanley Cup

Stanley Cup (stan′ li cup′) the trophy given to the winners of the National Hockey League championships.

staple (stāpl) *n.* **1.** a metal wire with two points used to hold papers together. **2.** a food that is eaten very often: *Wheat is a staple in many parts of the world.* *v.* to fasten papers together using staples. **stapling. stapled.**

⊖**star** (stȧr) *n.* **1.** a heavenly body that looks like a speck of light at night. **2.** an outstanding or very famous actor, actress, singer, sports player, etc. **3.** a performer with a large part in a play, movie, or program. *v.* to have a large part in a play, movie, or program: *My favourite actor is starring in a new movie.* **starring. starred.**

starboard (stȧr′ bȯrd′, stȧr′ bərd) *n.* the right side of a ship looking forward towards the bow.

starch (stȧrch) *n.* **1.** a powder or liquid used to make clothes stiff. **2.** a white substance that is found in potatoes, rice, bread, and other foods. *pl.* **starches.**

stare (ster) *n.* a long and steady look. *v.* to watch someone or something for a long time with a steady look: *He stared at the moon for five minutes.* **staring. stared.**

starfish (stärʹ fishʹ) *n.* a small sea ceature that has a flat body shaped like a star. *pl.* **starfish.**

start (stärt) *n.* **1.** a beginning: *The boats in the race were off to a good start.* **2.** a sudden movement of surprise: *He stood up with a start when he heard the loud music.* *v.* to begin: *He started to write a letter but did not finish it. What time does the movie start?*

startle (stärtl) *v.* to make someone feel surprised or frightened: *Your voice startled me because I thought I was alone.* **startling. startled.**

starve (stärv) *v.* **1.** to be very ill or die because there is not enough food to eat. **2.** to want food very much: *I'm starving! When are we eating?* **starving. starved.**

state (stāt) *n.* **1.** the condition of someone or something: *What is the state of your health? The room is in a messy state.* **2.** one of the parts of certain countries: *There are fifty states in the United States of America.* *v.* to say clearly in written or spoken words: *All the rules are stated in the book.* **stating. stated.**

statement (stātʹ mənt) *n.* information that is stated: *A monthly bank statement states the amount of money in a person's bank account.*

static (statʹ ik) *n.* electricity in the air that causes a crackling sound on radios and TV sets.

station (stāʹ shən) *n.* **1.** a stopping place along a route: *a railway station; a bus station.* **2.** a building or place that provides a certain service: *a gas station; a police station.* **3.** a building from which radio or television programs are broadcast. **4.** the organization that makes such broadcasts.

stationary (stāʹ shən erʹ ē) *adj.* not moving; staying in one place: *a stationary machine.*

stationery (stāʹ shən erʹ ē) *n.* writing materials such as paper and envelopes.

station wagon

station wagon (stāʹ shən wagʹ ən) a long car with a door at the back and folding seats. It can be used to carry people as well as large objects.

statistics (stə tisʹ tiks) *n.pl.* facts that are collected and arranged to provide information about large numbers of people or things: *According to the statistics, most people in Canada do not smoke.*

statue (stachʹ ū) *n.* a figure of a person or animal that is made of clay, stone, metal, or some other solid material.

status (staʹ təs, statʹ əs) *n.* **1.** a person's position according to the law or another authority: *His marital status is 'single'.* **2.** the condition of something: *The nurse gave the doctor a report on the sick man's status.* **3.** a person's importance: *Because of his status, the president of the company has the best parking space.* *pl.* **statuses.**

stay (stā) *v.* **1.** to remain in the same place: *Father stayed at home while the family went shopping.* **2.** to continue to be: *We stayed friends after Anna moved to the city.* **3.** to live somewhere for a short time: *We stayed at my cousin's home when we visited Toronto.*

steady (sted′ ē) *adj.* **1.** firm in position; not shaking or moving: *The ladder is steady.* **2.** regular; not changing: *a steady fall of rain; a steady job; a steadier one; the steadiest job of all.*

steak (stāk) *n.* **1.** a thick slice of meat or fish for cooking. **2.** a thick slice of beef.

steal (stēl) *v.* to take something without permission; to rob. **stealing. stole** (stōl). I have **stolen** (stōl′ ən).

steam (stēm) *n.* water in the form of gas or vapour, produced by boiling. *v.* **1.** to give off steam. **2.** to loosen or cook with steam.

steel (stēl) *n.* a strong metal, made from iron mixed with other substances.

steep (stēp) *adj.* having a sharp slope: *a steep hill.*

steeple (stēpl) *n.* the top of a church tower.

steer (stēr) *n.* a young bull whose testicles have been removed. *v.* to guide: *to steer a ship; to steer a car.*

steering wheel (stēr′ ing hwēl′, stēr′ ing wēl′) the wheel on the inside of a car, used by the driver to control the car's direction.

stem (stem) *n.* the main stalk of a plant that holds up a leaf, flower, or fruit.

stencil (sten′ sil) *n.* a thin sheet of material in which letters and shapes are cut out.

step (step) *n.* **1.** a movement made by putting the foot down in a new place: *She took ten steps forward.* **2.** the part of a staircase on which the foot is put down. *v.* to make a movement with the feet: *Val stepped forward when the teacher called her name.* **stepping. stepped.**

stepfather (step′ fa′ t͟hər) *n.* a man who is not a person's father but is married to the mother.

stepmother (step′ mut͟h′ ər) *n.* a woman who is not a person's mother but is married to the father.

stereo (ster′ i ō) *n.* a record player that gives different sounds out of two or more speakers. *pl.* **stereos.**

sterile (ster′ īl, ster′ əl) *adj.* **1.** free from germs: *a sterile room in a hospital.* **2.** not able to produce young.

sterilize (ster′ i līz′) *v.* to make sterile: *to sterilize a baby's bottle.* **sterilizing. sterilized.**

stern (stûrn) *n.* the back part of a ship. *adj.* strict or harsh: *The children were given a stern warning not to lie again.*

stew (styū, stū) *n.* meat and vegetables cooked slowly together in a liquid.

steward (styū′ ərd, stū′ ərd) *n.* a person in charge of food and other services on an airplane, train, or ship.

stick (stik) *n.* **1.** a thin piece of wood: *We need some sticks to start the fire.* **2.** an object shaped like a stick: *a stick of chalk.* **3.** a shaped piece of wood: *a hockey stick.* *v.* **1.** to fasten or be fastened with glue, paste, etc. *Hannah stuck the label on the envelope.* **2.** to remain in a place and not be able to move: *The window is stuck. Can you help me open it?* **3.** to push a pointed object into something: *He stuck his finger into the cake.* **sticking. stuck** (stuk).

stiff (stif) *adj.* not possible or not easy to bend: *Cartons are made of stiff material. My knees are stiff today.*

still (stil) *adj.* quiet and with no movement: *a still pond.* *adv.* now as before: *He is still in bed.*

stimulate (stim′ yū lāt′) *v.* to make someone feel more lively or more like doing something: *The cold air stimulates me. It makes me want to work.* **stimulating. stimulated.**

sting (sting) *n.* a prick or stab made in the skin by an insect: *a bee sting.* *v.* **1.** for an insect or thorn to prick the skin: *Tricia was stung by a wasp.* **2.** to hurt like a sting: *The smoke made my eyes sting.* **stinging. stung** (stung).

stingy (stin′ jē) *adj.* not willing to spend money or share something: *a stingy person; a stingier one; the stingiest one of all.*

stink (stingk) *n.* a bad smell. *v.* to smell awful: *That old soup really stinks!* **stinking. stank** (stangk) or **stunk** (stungk).

stir (stûr) *v.* **1.** to mix soft or liquid things by moving them around with a spoon or a similar object: *Chris stirred sugar into his tea.* **2.** to start to move: *The bird flew away when the child stirred.* **stirring. stirred.**

stirrups (stûr′ əps, stir′ əps) *n.pl.* the loops that hang from the saddle of a horse to support the rider's feet.

stitch (stich) *n.* **1.** in sewing and knitting, a loop of thread made with a needle. **2.** thread used by doctors to hold skin together after an operation or an injury. *pl.* **stitches.** *v.* to join with stitches. **stitching. stitched.** he **stitches.**

⊖**stock** (stok) *n.* **1.** a supply of things kept for sale to customers or for use in the future: *The furniture store has a large stock of tables.* **2.** broth from cooked meat, fish, or vegetables. *v.* to keep a supply: *We stocked our cottage with firewood.*

stock exchange (stok′ iks chānj′) a place where certificates of ownership can be bought and sold.

stocking (stok′ ing) *n.* a long, close-fitting cover for the leg and foot.

stock market (stok′ mȧr′ kət) **1.** the buying and selling of shares in companies. **2.** a stock exchange.

stole (stōl) *n.* a wide scarf worn by women around the shoulders. *v.* see **steal.**

stolen see **steal.**

stomach (stum′ ək) *n.* the organ inside the body that stores food and partly digests it before passing it on to the intestines. *pl.* **stomachs.**

stone (stōn) *n.* **1.** the hard substance that rock is made of. **2.** a piece of rock: *I have a stone in my shoe.* **3.** a jewel: *a precious stone.* **4.** the hard seed of some fruits: *a peach stone.*

stood see **stand.**

stool

stool (stūl) *n.* a small seat with no back or arms.

stoop (stūp) *v.* to bend the body forward and down: *Owen stooped to pick up the coin.*

⊖**stop** (stop) *n.* **1.** a place where people wait to get on a bus, train, etc. **2.** the act of not moving: *The car came to a stop when the traffic light changed to red.* *v.* **1.** to keep from moving, going, continuing, etc.: *The referee stopped the game.* **2.** to end; to no longer go, move, etc.: *Denise stopped reading. The clock stopped.* **stopping. stopped.**

stop light (stop′ līt′) a traffic light.

storage (stȯr′ ij) *n.* a place for keeping something that is not being used: *We use the basement for the storage of our old furniture.*

⊖**store** (stȯr) *n.* a shop; a place that sells things: *a furniture store; a grocery store.* *v.* to put away for use in the future: *The squirrels stored nuts for the winter.* **storing. stored.**

storey, story (stȯr′ rē) *n.* a whole floor of a building, with all its rooms. *pl.* **storeys**, or **stories.**

stork (stȯrk) *n.* a large bird, usually white, with a long beak, a long neck, and long legs.

storm (stȯrm) *n.* bad weather with heavy rain or snow, strong winds, and sometimes thunder.

storm window (stȯrm′ win′ dō) an extra outside window that can be opened or closed over an ordinary window.

story (stȯr′ ē) *n.* **1.** words that tell about something that someone has imagined: *a story about ghosts.* **2.** words that tell about something that has really happened: *This book tells the story of Canada since 1900.* *pl.* **stories.**

stove (stōv) *n.* a large object, made of heavy metal, that provides heat for cooking or warmth.

straight (strāt′) *adj.* not bent, curved, crooked, or curly: *The road is straight. My hair is straight.* *adv.* **1.** in a way that is not bent, curved, or crooked: *My back hurts and I cannot stand up straight.* **2.** immediately; directly: *Ronald went straight to work in the morning.*

straighten (strāt′ ən) *v.* **1.** to take the bends and curves out of something; to make something straight. **2.** to make something tidy: *I straightened up my desk so that I could find everything more easily.*

strain (strān) *n.* an injury caused by too much effort. *v.* to stretch, pull, push, or try too much: *Louise strained her back when she lifted the typewriter.*

strainer (strān′ ər) *n.* a kitchen tool used to take the lumps out of a liquid.

strait (strāt) *n.* a narrow body of water connecting two larger bodies of water: *The Strait of Georgia runs between Vancouver Island and the mainland.*

strand (strand) *n.* one of many threads or wires twisted together to make a rope or cable. *v.* to leave in a helpless way: *The sailors were stranded on a lonely island.*

strange (strānj) *adj.* **1.** unusual: *I like the chair, although it has a strange shape. a strange idea; a stranger one; the strangest idea of all.* **2.** not seen or known until now: *A strange cat came to our house.*

⊖**stranger** (strān′ jər) *n.* someone not seen or known until now: *A stranger asked me the way to Main Street.*

strangle (strangl) *v.* to choke; to kill by squeezing the throat. **strangling. strangled.**

strap (strap) *n.* a strip of leather or cloth, used for attaching things. *v.* to attach with a strap: *Ray strapped his books to his bike.* **strapping. strapped.**

strategy (strat′ ə jē) *n.* a plan for getting a certain result: *The football players' strategy surprised the other team.* *pl.* **strategies.**

straw (strȯ) *n.* **1.** the dried stems of corn, wheat, rye, or other cereals. **2.** a thin tube used for sucking up a liquid.

strawberry

strawberry (strȯ′ ber′ ē) *n.* the soft and juicy red fruit of a plant that grows close to the ground. *pl.* **strawberries.**

stray (strā) *n.* a lost child or animal. *pl.* **strays.** *adj.* lost: *We found a stray animal in the park.* *v.* to wander about and get lost: *Tina's dog strayed from home.*

streak (strēk) *n.* a long, narrow stripe. *v.* to move quickly: *The plane streaked across the sky.*

stream (strēm) *n.* **1.** a small river. **2.** a movement of things or people: *a steady stream of cars.* *v.* to flow or move steadily: *People streamed out of the stadium.*

street (strēt) *n.* a road with buildings on each side.

streetcar

streetcar (strēt′ kȧr′) *n.* a vehicle found in many cities, that can carry many passengers. Streetcars are powered by electricity and run on rails.

strength (strength) *n.* the quality of being strong: *Although she is small, she has the strength to carry the heavy load.*

strengthen (streng′ thən) *v.* to make something more strong: *All the exercise Don has been doing has strengthened the muscles in his arms.*

stress (stres) *n.* pressure; strain: *The old bridge almost collapsed under the stress of the trucks. He is under stress at work because there is so much to do by the end of the week.* *v.* to give importance to something: *We stress the first syllable when we say the word 'birthday'.*

stretch (strech) *v.* **1.** to make something longer or wider by pulling it: *Chan stretched the piece of elastic.* **2.** to reach out with the arms or legs: *Daisy stretched her arms, then got out of bed.* **stretching. stretched.** she **stretches.**

stretcher (strech′ ər) *n.* a frame of poles and material for carrying a sick or wounded person.

strict (strikt) *adj.* following a rule very carefully: *John's parents are strict about the time he must be home each night.*

strike (strīk) *n.* **1.** a stopping of work, usually for better conditions or more money: *The factory workers went on strike for higher pay.* **2.** a pitch in baseball that counts against the batter. **3.** the finding of a large amount of oil or minerals. *v.* **1.** to hit with a lot of force: *Don't strike the dog.* **2.** to rub: *to strike a match.* **3.** to find suddenly: *to strike oil.* **4.** to stop work; usually for better conditions or more money. *The workers are striking.* **striking. struck** (struk).

string (string) *n.* **1.** a thin cord for tying things together. **2.** a long line of things: *a string of beads.* **3.** a cord or wire on a musical instrument. *v.* to put something on a string; to put a string on something: *The jeweller strung the pearls. The musician strung her guitar.* **stringing. strung** (strung).

stringed instrument (stringd′ in′ strə mənt) a musical instrument that has strings and is played with a bow or with the fingers: *Some stringed instruments are the violin, harp, and cello.*

strip (strip) *n.* a long, narrow piece: *a strip of cloth.* *v.* **1.** to take off: *to strip wallpaper from a wall.* **2.** for a person to remove all his or her clothing. **stripping. stripped.**

stripe (strīp) *n.* a long, narrow band of colour: *stripes of red and white paint.*

strive (strīv) *v.* to try very hard: *She is striving to become the fastest runner in the province.* **striving. strived**, or **strove** (strōv). he has **striven** (striv′ ən).

stroke (strōk) *n.* **1.** a hard hit: *a stroke of an axe.* **2.** a swimming movement: *Patsy swims the breast stroke well.* **3.** a mark made by one movement of a pen, crayon, brush, etc. **4.** a sudden illness in the brain that can paralyse part of the body. *v.* to rub something often, in a gentle way: *Alberto stroked his dog.* **stroking. stroked.**

stroll (strōl) *n.* a slow, quiet walk for pleasure. *v.* to walk slowly for pleasure: *We strolled along the beach with our friends.*

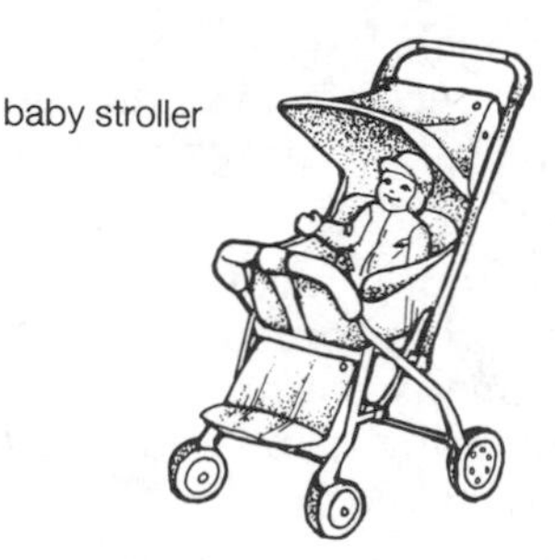
baby stroller

stroller (strōl′ ər) *n.* a small chair with wheels in which a baby or small child can be pushed around.

strong (strong) *adj.* **1.** powerful; having strength, force, energy, etc.: *I'll carry the boxes because my arms are strong. Tim is a strong man. The car is shaking because of the strong wind.* **2.** firm and solid: *The box broke because it was not strong.* **3.** having a great effect on the senses: *He has a strong voice. Please add milk because the coffee is strong.*

strove see **strive.**

struck see **strike.**

structure (struk′ chər) *n.* **1.** the way in which something is built or put together: *The structure of the bridge is simple but strong.* **2.** anything that is built or put together: *Towers, bridges, and houses and other buildings are some structures.*

struggle (strugl) *n.* **1.** a great fight. **2.** a great effort. *v.* **1.** to fight with much force: *The soldiers struggled against the enemy.* **2.** to make a great effort: *Pete struggled with the math problem.* **struggling. struggled.**

strung see **string.**

stub (stub) *n.* a short piece that is left: *the stub of an old pencil.* *v.* to bang a toe into something. **stubbing. stubbed.**

stubborn (stub′ ərn) *adj.* not giving in or changing easily: *The stubborn child refused to eat her soup.*

stucco (stuk′ ō) *n.* a layer of plaster with a rough pattern. *pl.* **stuccos**, or **stuccoes.**

stuck see **stick.**

student (styū′ dənt, stū′ dənt) *n.* someone who is learning things, usually at school.

studio (styū′ di ō′, stū′ di ō′) *n.* **1.** a room where an artist or photographer works. **2.** a room or building where movies, radio or television programs, or records are made. *pl.* **studios.**

studious (styū′ di əs, stū′ di əs) *adj.* doing a lot of reading and learning: *Lillian is a very studious girl, and she receives high marks in school.*

study (stud′ ē) *n.* **1.** the gathering of information or knowledge. **2.** in a house, the room where a person studies or reads. *v.* **1.** to try to learn: *Jennifer is studying for the history test.* **2.** to look at carefully: *We studied the map but could not find Highway 20 on it.* **studying. studied.** she **studies.**

stuff (stuf) *n.* **1.** material that a thing is made of: *Is the coat made of wool or of other stuff?* **2.** a thing or things, often useless: *There is a lot of old stuff in the basement.* *v.* to pack something until it is very full: *to stuff a drawer with socks.*

stuffing (stuf′ ing) *n.* **1.** padding in a pillow or cushion. **2.** a filling to be stuffed into a chicken, turkey, or other food before cooking it.

stumble (stumbl) *v.* to trip over something and nearly fall. **stumbling. stumbled.**

stump (stump) *n.* the part of a tree left in the ground after the trunk has been cut down. *v. (informal)* to puzzle completely: *The students and the teacher were stumped by the question.*

stun (stun) *v.* **1.** to knock unconscious, or nearly so. **2.** to give someone shocking or very surprising news: *We were stunned to hear that our cousin had died. Joanna was stunned to hear that she had won the prize.* **stunning. stunned.**

stung see **sting.**

stunk see **stink.**

stunt (stunt) *n.* an act that shows skill and attracts attention: *the stunts at a circus. The actor performed a dangerous stunt for the movie.* *v.* to stop someone or something from growing: *Lack of water stunted the growth of these plants.*

stupid (styū′ pid, stū′ pid) *adj.* **1.** silly: *a stupid joke.* **2.** slow to understand: *a stupid dog.*

sturdy (stûr′ dī) *adj.* strong and healthy: *a sturdy tree; a sturdier one; the sturdiest tree in the yard.*

sty (stī) *n.* **1.** a place where pigs are kept. **2.** a sore on the edge of an eyelid. *pl.* **sties.**

style (stīl) *n.* **1.** a way of doing something: *I don't like his style of skating; he moves too slowly.* **2.** the present way of dressing: *Are short dresses in style?*

sub- a prefix meaning 'under': **sub-zero** means that the temperature is below zero. A **subway** is an underground way.

subdivision (sub′ di vizh′ ən) *n.* an area of land that has been split into many parts on which houses have been built or will be built.

⊖**subject** (sub′ jekt) *n.* **1.** what something is about: *The subject of this book is airplanes.* **2.** a school course: *I am taking six subjects in school.* **3.** a person who will obey another person: *a subject of the Queen.* *adj.* likely to be affected by something: *He is subject to hay fever in the summer.*

subject (səb jekt′) *v.* to make something receive: *Your dog has been subjected to rough treatment.*

sublet (sub′ let′) *v.* **1.** to rent a property from someone who is renting it from someone else. **2.** to rent a property to someone which you are renting from someone else. **subletting. sublet.**

submarine (sub′ mə rēn′) *n.* a ship that can travel under water.

submerge (səb mûrj′) *v.* to go beneath the surface of a liquid: *The children submerged their boats in the tub.* **submerging. submerged.**

submit (səb mit′) *v.* to give in; to surrender: *Wanda submitted her report to her employer.* **submitting. submitted.**

subscription (səb skrip′ shən) *n.* a promise to take and pay for something, such as a number of issues of a magazine.

substance (sub′ stəns) *n.* **1.** what a thing is made of: *Wood is a substance used in many objects.* **2.** the most important part; the main idea: *What is the substance of this newspaper article?*

substitute (sub′ sti tyūt′, sub′ sti tūt′) *n.* someone or something used instead of another: *The company hired a substitute when the secretary left for her holidays.* *v.* to put someone or something in place of another: *If you don't have sugar, you can substitute honey when baking this cake.* **substituting. substituted.**

subtract (səb trakt′) *v.* to take away: *Subtract 5 from 7, and 2 is left.*

subtraction (səb trak′ shən) *n.* the taking away of one number from another.

suburb (sub′ ərb) *n.* an area of houses very close to a city.

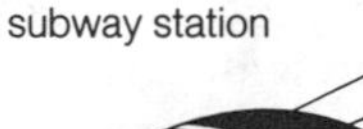

subway station

subway (sub′ wā′) *n.* **1.** an underground passage. **2.** an electric railway that travels underground in many large cities. *pl.* **subways.**

ə**succeed** (sək sēd′) *v.* **1.** to happen the way someone wants something to happen: *Jerry succeeded in winning the race.* **2.** to follow and take the place of somebody: *When Carl retired, Simone succeeded him as president of the company.*

success (sək ses′) *n.* **1.** the result or goal that was tried for: *After three days, I had success in finding a job.* **2.** a person or thing that succeeds in what is tried: *The concert was a great success.* *pl.* **successes.**

successful (sək ses′ fəl) *adj.* succeeding; getting the results that were tried for: *a successful singer; a successful song.*

successive (sek ses′ iv) *adj.* following in order; coming one after the other: *four successive days of rain.*

such (such) *adj.* **1.** so much, so large, so great, etc.: *It is such a good movie, I will see it again.* **2.** of the same kind; similar to: *I like sweet food, such as cake, pie, and ice cream.*

suck (suk) *v.* **1.** to draw liquid into the mouth, using the lips and tongue: *to suck lemonade through a straw.* **2.** to roll something in the mouth, but not chew it: *to suck a candy.*

sucker (suk′ ər) *n.* **1.** something that can stick to things by suction: *the suckers on an octopus.* **2.** *(informal)* a person who can be cheated or tricked very easily. **3.** a lollipop.

sudden (sud′ ən) *adj.* happening quickly; unexpected: *a sudden illness; a sudden storm.*

suds (sudz) *n.pl.* the bubbles that appear when soap is mixed with water.

sue (sū) *v.* to take a person or company to a court of law because of an accident, unfair treatment, etc.: *The hockey player sued the team for firing him.* **suing. sued.**

suede (swād) *n.* a soft leather that looks and feels like velvet: *suede gloves; a suede jacket.*

suffer (suf′ ər) *v.* **1.** to feel pain or sorrow: *Tom is suffering from a cold.* **2.** to become less good: *Her work suffered because she was ill.*

sufficient (sə fish′ ənt) *adj.* enough; all that is needed: *Do you have sufficient time to finish the job? Do you have sufficient money for the present?*

suffix (suf′ iks) *n.* letters put at the end of a word to change its meaning or form another word. When you put the suffix 'proof' at the end of the word 'water', you get 'waterproof'. *pl.* **suffixes.**

suffocate (suf′ ə kāt′) *v.* **1.** to choke; to die or be very uncomfortable because there is not enough air to breathe. **suffocating. suffocated.**

sugar (shůg′ ər) *n.* a sweet substance, used in cooking and put in drinks, that comes from sugar cane or the juice of sugar beets.

suggest (səg jest′, sə jest′) *v.* to offer an idea or a plan to other people: *Lucy suggested that we go fishing on Saturday.*

suggestion (səg jes′ chən, sə jes′ chən) *n.* an idea or plan that is suggested.

suicide (sū′ i sīd′) *n.* the killing of oneself: *He committed suicide by jumping from a tall building.*

⊖**suit** (sūt) *n.* **1.** a set of clothes made of the same material and worn together. **2.** any of the four types of playing cards: *clubs, diamonds, hearts, and spades.* *v.* to be right for: *Because you are short, a long coat may not suit you.*

suitable (sūt′ əbl) *adj.* good for doing something; right: *Those heavy boots are not suitable for wearing in this hot weather.*

suitcase (sūt′ kās′) *n.* a flat case with a handle for carrying clothes.

sum (sum) *n.* the total amount when numbers are added: *The sum of 3, 5, and 9 is 17.*

summarize (sum′ ə rīz′) *v.* to say in a few words what something is about. **summarizing. summarized.**

summary (sum′ ə rē) *n.* a short description giving the main points. *pl.* **summaries.**

summer (sum′ ər) *n.* the season after spring.

summit (sum′ it) *n.* **1.** the top; the peak of a mountain. **2.** a high-level meeting, usually of government representatives, dealing with political or economic matters.

summons (sum′ ənz) *n.* a request for a person to be somewhere: *He received a summons to be a witness in court.* *pl.* **summonses.**

sun (sun) *n.* the very bright and hot star that is seen during the day. The earth and the other planets revolve around the sun, which provides heat and light.

sunburn (sun′ bûrn′) *n.* the burning of the skin caused by strong rays from the sun.

sundae (sun′ dā) *n.* ice cream served with a candy sauce, nuts, cherries, and whipped cream.

Sunday (sun′ dā) *n.* the first day of the week. *pl.* **Sundays.**

sunflower

sunflower (sun′ flau̇′ ər) *n.* a large yellow flower that grows on a tall plant.

sung see **sing.**

sunglasses (sun′ glas′ əz) *n.pl.* dark glasses that people wear to keep the sun out of their eyes: *People often wear sunglasses on bright and sunny days.*

sunk see **sink.**

sunny (sun′ ē) *adj.* lit up with sunshine: *a sunny day; a sunnier day; the sunniest day of the summer.*

sunrise (sun′ rīz′) *n.* the time when the sun comes up.

sunset (sun′ set′) *n.* the time when the sun goes down.

sunshine (sun′ shīn′) *n.* the light of the sun when it is shining.

super- a prefix meaning 'more' or 'greater'. A **supermarket** carries more goods than other markets or stores.

superb (sū pûrb′) *adj.* excellent; splendid; wonderful: *Janet is a superb singer. This cake is superb.*

superintendent (sū′ pər in ten′ dənt) *n.* a person who supervises or directs the work done in a school, apartment building, or other organization.

⊖**superior** (sə pēr′ i ər) *adj.* **1.** better than: *These apples are superior to those.* **2.** higher in rank: *A general is superior to a captain.*

supermarket (sū′ pər mär′ kət) *n.* a very large store where people shop for food and other goods, serving themselves and paying when they are ready to leave.

superstition (sū′ pər stish′ ən) *n.* a belief that comes from a fear of unknown things and a trust in magic; it has nothing to do with facts: *It is a superstition that Friday the thirteenth is an unlucky day.*

supervise (sū′ pər vīz′) *v.* to make sure that people work correctly. **supervising. supervised.**

supervision (sū′ pər vizh′ ən) *n.* the act of watching or managing people to make sure they do their work correctly.

supervisor (sū′ pər vī′ zər) *n.* a person who is in charge of the work of others: *He gave his supervisor a weekly report.*

supper (sup′ ər) *n.* the last meal of the day, eaten in the evening.

supplement (sup′ li mənt) *n.* a thing that is added to make something complete. *v.* to add to a thing, making it more complete.

supply (sə plī′) *n.* things kept ready to be used or sold: *The market has a large supply of plums.* *pl.* **supplies.** *v.* to provide; to give what is needed or wanted: *The butcher supplies us with good meat.* **supplying. supplied.** he **supplies.**

⊖**support** (sə pòrt′) *n.* **1.** a thing or things that hold up another object: *We need more support for the table, or else it will fall.* **2.** money provided to help someone live. **3.** help; encouragement: *After the death of their father, the children gave each other great support.* *v.* **1.** to hold up: *This desk can't support the typewriter.* **2.** to provide money so someone can live: *Mr. and Mrs. Lee support two children and Mr. Lee's father.* **3.** to give help and encouragement: *We support our local hockey team.*

⊖**suppose** (sə pōz′) *v.* **1.** to imagine: to pretend: *Let us suppose that we don't know each other.* **2.** to think something is likely to happen: *Jacques is always late, and I suppose he will be late tonight.* **supposing. supposed.**

sure (shūr) *adj.* certain; reliable: *John is sure that Helena's birthday is May 19th. a sure method; a surer one; the surest one of all.*

surf (sûrf) *n.* waves breaking on the seashore.

surface (sûr′ fəs) *n.* the outside part of anything, or the top part of a liquid.

surfing

surfing (sûrf′ ing) *n.* the sport of riding to shore on a wave.

surgeon (sûr′ jən) *n.* a doctor who does operations.

surgery (sûrj′ ərē) *n.* the treatment of illness and injury by operations on the body.

surname (sûr′ nām′) *n.* a person's last name: *Mark Smith's surname is Smith.*

surprise (sər prīz′) *n.* **1.** a feeling caused when something happens that is not expected. **2.** the thing that causes this feeling: *The present from her family was a surprise. v.* to do something that someone does not expect: *The children surprised their parents by cooking dinner.* **surprising. surprised.**

surrender (sə ren′ dər) *v.* to give up; to yield, often to an enemy.

surround (sə raůnd′) *v.* to be all around: *Trees surround the house.*

survey (sûr′ vā) *n.* **1.** the job of measuring the shape and size of an area of land. **2.** a collection of information that shows what people think: *The survey showed that most people in our city like to eat potatoes. pl.* **surveys.**

survive (sər vīv′) *v.* to remain alive after the death of another person, or following a dangerous situation: *He survived his wife by four years. Two people survived the plane crash.* **surviving. survived.**

survivor (sər vī′ vər) *n.* a person who survives.

suspect (sus′ pekt) *n.* someone who is thought to be guilty but has not been proven guilty: *The police arrested a suspect in the robbery.*

suspect (sə spekt′) *v.* to think something may be true, although there is no proof: *I suspect the rain will continue all day.*

suspend (sə spend′) *v.* **1.** to hang something so that it can swing. **2.** to stop someone from doing something or going somewhere for a period of time: *to be suspended from school.* **3.** to cancel a privilege for a period of time: *A judge may suspend the licence of drivers who drive while drunk.*

suspense (sə spens′) *n.* the feeling of being uncertain and worried that something may happen: *I was kept in suspense until I came to the last page of the exciting book.*

suspicion (sə spish′ ən) *n.* a feeling that something is so: *I have a suspicion that he took the jacket, but I cannot prove it.*

suspicious (sə spish′ əs) *adj.* feeling that something is wrong; not trusting: *My neighbour is suspicious of people she doesn't know well.*

swallow (swol′ ō) *v.* to pass food and liquids down the throat and into the stomach.

swam see **swim.**

swamp (swomp) *n.* an area of soft, very wet ground. *v.* **1.** to flood with water: *Water swamped the boat.* **2.** (used with **with**) to receive too much of something: *We are swamped with work and need more people to help.*

swan (swon) *n.* a very large, graceful water bird, usually white, that has a long neck.

swarm (swȯrm) *n.* **1.** a large group of insects: *a swarm of bees.* **2.** a large group of people or animals.

sway (swā) *v.* to swing from side to side: *The trees swayed in the wind.*

swear (swer) *v.* **1.** to make a promise or take an oath: *In the courtroom, the witness swore to* *tell the truth.* **2.** to use curse words. **swearing. swore** (swôr). I have **sworn** (swôrn).

sweat (swet) *n.* perspiration; the moisture that can come from the skin when a person is very hot or ill. *v.* to give off this moisture.

sweater (swet′ ər) *n.* a knitted piece of clothing worn over or in place of a shirt or blouse.

sweep (swēp) *v.* to clean the floor or ground with a brush or broom. **sweeping. swept** (swept).

sweet (swēt) *adj.* **1.** tasting like sugar: *a sweet drink.* **2.** pleasant to smell: *a sweet flower.* **3.** pleasant to hear: *a sweet voice.* **4.** pleasant and kind: *a sweet person.*

sweet potato (swēt′ pə tā′ tō) a yellow-orange root vegetable with a slightly sugary taste. *pl.* **sweet potatoes.**

swell (swel) *v.* to keep growing bigger: *The river swelled during the flood.* **swelling. swelled.** it has **swollen** (swōl′ ən), or **swelled.**

swept see **sweep.**

swerve (swûrv) *v.* to change direction quickly: *Bob swerved on his bicycle to avoid the cat.* **swerving. swerved.**

swift (swift) *adj.* fast: *a swift automobile; a swift reply to the letter.*

swim (swim) *v.* to move through water using arms and legs, or the fins and tail. **swimming. swam** (swam). I have **swum** (swum).

swindle (swindl) *v.* to cheat someone out of money or property. **swindling. swindled.**

swine (swīn) *n.* a pig. *pl.* **swine.**

swing (swing) *n.* a seat hanging on ropes or chains that moves backwards and forwards. *v.* **1.** to move backwards and forwards or from side to side: *The children were swinging on a rope.* **2.** to move or turn in a curve: *to swing a baseball bat.* **swinging. swung** (swung).

switches

(2)

switch (swich) *n.* a small knob or button used to turn something on or off: *a switch for the light.* *pl.* **switches.** *v.* **1.** to exchange or replace one thing with another: *We switched from oil to gas for heating the house.* **2.** to turn on or off with an electrical switch. **switching. switched.** he **switches.**

swollen see **swell.**

sword (sôrd) *n.* a weapon with a long steel blade set in a handle.

swore, sworn see **swear.**

swum see **swim.**

swung see **swing.**

syllable (sil′ əbl) *n.* a separate sound in a word: 'Canada' has three syllables; 'winter' has two syllables; 'go' has one syllable.

symbol (sim′ bəl) *n.* something that represents something else. A symbol can be a mark, sign, letter, or picture: *The symbol '+' means 'add'. The lion is a symbol of courage.*

⊖**sympathetic** (sim′ pə thet′ ik) *adj.* **1.** feeling sorry for someone who is sad: *He was very sympathetic when he heard that my grandfather had died.* **2.** understanding someone's feelings: *The lawyer was sympathetic to our problem and said that she would try to help us.*

⊖**sympathy** (sim′ pə thē) *n.* a feeling of being sorry for someone who is ill, sad, or in trouble. *pl.* **sympathies.**

⊖**symphony** (sim′ fə nē) *n.* **1.** a long piece of music written for an orchestra. **2.** a large orchestra: *The Toronto Symphony has made many records. pl.* **symphonies.**

symptom (simp′ təm) *n.* a sign of an illness, or of something being wrong: *One of the symptoms of measles is a red rash.*

synagogue (sin′ ə gog′) *n.* a building for Jewish worship and teaching.

synonym (sin′ ə nim′) *n.* a word that means the same as another word. 'Ill' is a synonym for 'sick'.

synthetic (sin thet′ ik) *adj.* made by people, not made by nature: *Nylon and other plastics are synthetic materials.*

syrup (sûr′ əp, sir′ əp) *n.* a thick, sweet, sticky liquid: *Would you like syrup on your pancakes?*

system (sis′ təm) *n.* **1.** an arrangement of things that form a whole: *the highway system; the railway system.* **2.** a plan or method; a way of doing things: *What system does the library use to arrange books?*

T

tab (tab) *n.* a small flap or loop that is attached to something.

table (tābl) *n.* **1.** a piece of furniture with a flat top and legs. **2.** a list of numbers or information: *A table of contents lists the chapters in a book.*

tablespoon (tābl′ spūn′) *n.* a large spoon used to serve food at the table and to measure ingredients.

ɵ**tablet** (tab′ lət) *n.* a small flat piece of certain things such as medicine or soap.

table tennis

table tennis (tābl′ ten′ is) a game like tennis, played on a table with paddles and a plastic ball. Another name for table tennis is ping-pong.

tack (tak) *n.* a short, sharp nail with a flat head. *v.* **1.** to fasten with tacks. **2.** to sew pieces of cloth together with a long, quick stitch. **3.** to change the course of a ship.

tackle (takl) *n.* the things needed for some sports or jobs: *fishing tackle.* *v.* **1.** to try to do something hard. **2.** in football, to bring an opponent down. **tackling. tackled.**

tact (takt) *n.* knowing what to do and say without making people angry or upset: *She showed tact when she told her boss that he was wrong.*

tag (tag) *n.* a label: *The price tag on the dress showed that it was on sale.*

ɵ**tail** (tāl) *n.* **1.** the movable back end of an animal, fish, or bird. **2.** something that has the shape of a tail, or is in the position of a tail, such as the back end of an airplane. **3.** the side of a coin that does not show the head. *v.* *(informal)* to follow closely behind: *The police tailed the speeding car.*

tailor (tā′ lər) *n.* a person who makes or alters outer clothes.

take (tāk) *v.* **1.** to get hold of and carry: *Take your umbrella. Someone took my wallet.* **2.** to use: *I take a bus to go to work. I'm going to take a bath.* **3.** to do or make: *He took a driving test. Please take my photograph. Let's take a walk.* **4.** to receive; to accept: *Take your medicine at night. Take my advice and go to the doctor. Do you take sugar with your tea?* **5.** to require: *It took three people to carry the load.* **6.** to remove: *He took an apple from the bowl.* **taking. took** (tůk). I have **taken.**

take after to be like: *The child takes after her father; he is always smiling and so is she.*

take in **1.** to receive; to accept; to make: *The new store took in $500.00 on the first day.* **2.** to alter a piece of clothing by making it smaller: *My new pants were too big, but I had them taken in.* **3.** to trick or fool someone: *Don't be taken in by false advertising.*

take off **1.** to remove something: *I took off my coat when I came home.* **2.** to begin a flight: *The plane took off an hour late.*

take on **1.** to accept a new job, responsibility, etc.: *The company took on an important building project.* **2.** to employ: *The company took on a new secretary.*

take one's time not to rush: *The movie starts in an hour, so take your time walking there.*

take over to do something in place of someone else: *I took over as head nurse when Lee quit.*

take part in to participate in: *Our three children took part in the parade.*
take place to happen: *When does the party take place? Where does it take place?*
take turns to do something with other people, one person at a time: *We took turns shovelling the snow.*
take up **1.** to start to do: *At the age of ninety, Mrs. Collins took up swimming.* **2.** to occupy time or space: *The program took up an hour of my time.* **3.** to shorten: *She took up the dress by one centimetre.*

take-home pay (tāk′ hōm pā′) the earnings that remain after taxes, pension, insurance, etc., have been deducted from a person's pay.

take-off (tāk′ of′) *n.* the moment when a plane leaves the ground: *We had to keep our seatbelts on for several minutes after take-off.*

take-out restaurant (tāk′ au̇t res′ to rənt) a restaurant where food is taken to be eaten outside or at home.

tale (tāl) *n.* a story, true or made-up.

talent (tal′ ənt) *n.* a natural ability to do something well: *Carmella has a talent for singing.*

talk (tok, tȯk) *n.* a speech; something said: *Mr. Santini gave all the workers a talk about safety on the job.* *v.* to speak; to put ideas or information into spoken words: *My brother loves to talk. The teacher talked about Canada's provinces.*

talkative (tok′ ə tiv, tȯk′ ə tiv) *adj.* fond of talking.

tall (tȯl) *adj.* higher than usual: *a tall man; a tall tower.*

tame (tām) *adj.* not wild; trained to be obedient: *Some of the circus animals look wild, but they really are tame. a tame animal; a tamer one; the tamest one of all.* *v.* to train a wild animal or bird to be friendly or obedient.

tamper (tam′ pər) *v.* (used with **with**) to interfere with something; to make changes without having permission: *Somebody tampered with the radio and now it does not work.*

tan (tan) *n.* a light brown colour. *adj.* having such a colour. *v.* **1.** to make animal hides into leather by soaking them in an acid solution. **2.** to become tan from the sun. **tanning. tanned.**

tangerine (tan′ jə rēn′) *n.* a small, juicy orange with a loose skin that peels easily.

tangle (tangl) *v.* to twist together in knots or in a confused way: *The child tangled the thread, and it took me a long time to untangle it.* **tangling. tangled.**

⊖**tank** (tangk) *n.* **1.** a large container that holds liquid or gas. **2.** a large, powerful vehicle with guns attached to it, used by armies.

tanker (tangk′ ər) *n.* a ship, truck, or airplane with large tanks for carrying oil or other liquid.

tantrum (tan′ trəm) *n.* a fit of anger: *The child had a tantrum and threw her toys at the wall.*

tap (tap) *n.* a device for allowing liquid to come out of a pipe; a faucet. *v.* **1.** to knock lightly: *She tapped her fingers on the table.* **2.** to make a hole in something so that liquid can get out: *The farmer tapped the sugar maple tree and collected the sap.* **tapping. tapped.**

⊖**tape** (tāp) *n.* **1.** a long, narrow strip of cloth, plastic, or other material, used for fastening, tying, or repairing things. Some tape has one side that is sticky. **2.** a magnetic strip of plastic, used for recording sounds. *v.* **1.** to fasten with tape. **2.** to record sounds on tape. **taping. taped.**

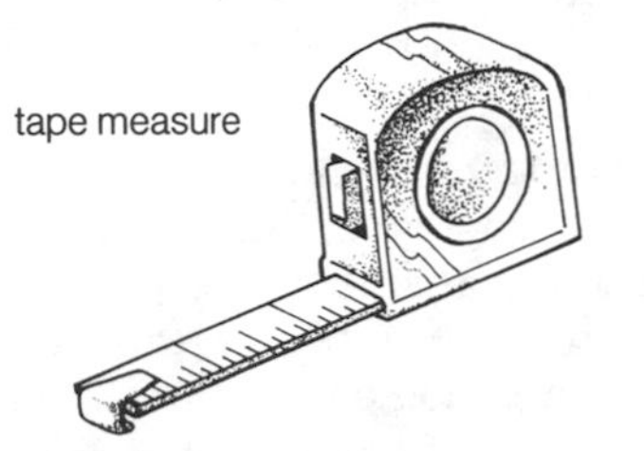

tape measure (tāp′ mezh′ ər) a long, narrow strip of cloth, plastic, or metal, marked in centimetres or inches, used for measuring.

tape recorder (tāp′ rə kȯr′ dər) a machine that records sounds on magnetic tape, which can be played back later.

tar (tȧr) *n.* a thick, black, sticky substance, which comes from wood or coal, used to cover roads. *v.* to cover with tar. **tarring. tarred.**

target (tȧr′ gət) *n.* **1.** an object to be aimed at in shooting practice, or an object or place to be aimed at with missiles. **2.** a person or thing that is criticized: *The politician's expensive car is a target for complaints.* **3.** a goal to be achieved: *The company's target is to sell four more machines this month.*

⊖**tariff** (tar′ if) *n.* money that must be paid to government when certain things are brought into or out of the country: *The tariffs on foreign cars often make them much more expensive than cars built in Canada.*

tarnish (tȧr′ nish) *v.* to lose a shine and become dull, as some metals do. **tarnishing. tarnished.** it **tarnishes.**

⊖**tart** (tȧrt) *n.* a small pie of fruit, custard, or some other filling. *adj.* having a sharp or sour taste: *a tart green apple.*

task (task) *n.* a job to be done: *The children share the task of milking the cows.*

tassel (tas′ əl) *n.* a group of threads tied together at one end and left hanging at the other: *a tassel on the end of a scarf.*

taste (tāst) *n.* **1.** one of the five senses; it allows different flavours to be identified. **2.** the flavour of food or drink: *a sweet taste; a sour taste; a bitter taste.* **3.** a small amount of food or drink: *The cook had a taste of the fish before she served it.* **4.** a personal liking for something: *We have the same taste in music.* **5.** a special feeling for things that are beautiful, fine, good, etc.: *She shows good taste in choosing her clothes.* *v.* **1.** to have a certain flavour: *Rabbit tastes a bit like chicken.* **2.** to eat or drink a little of something to try its flavour: *Taste the spinach and tell me if you like it.* **tasting. tasted.**

tasty (tās′ tē) *adj.* having a good flavour: *a tasty dessert; a tastier one; the tastiest one of all.*

tattoo (ta tü′) *n.* a coloured picture put on the skin with needles and dyes. *pl.* **tattoos.**

taught see **teach.**

tavern (tav′ ərn) *n.* a place where people go to buy and drink beer, wine, and other alcoholic beverages.

⊖**tax** (taks) *n.* money that is paid to a government to help pay for the costs of roads, education, etc. *pl.* **taxes.**

taxi (tak′ sē) *n.* a car and driver that is hired, usually for short distances. *pl.* **taxis.** *v.* for an airplane to move slowly on the ground or on water. **taxiing. taxied.** it **taxis.**

tea (tē) *n.* a drink made by pouring boiling water over dried leaves of the tea plant: *Tea leaves come from China, India, Sri Lanka, and other countries. pl.* **teas.**

teach (tēch) *v.* to show people how to do things; to give lessons; to help people learn. **teaching. taught** (tȯt). she **teaches.**

teacher (tēch′ ər) *n.* someone who teaches, usually in a school.

team (tēm) *n.* **1.** a group of people playing or working together, often in a game: *a football team.* **2.** a group of animals working together: *a team of horses pulling a wagon.*

teamwork (tēm′ wûrk′) *n.* people doing a job together: *It took teamwork to pull the truck out of the ditch.*

teapot

teapot (tē′ pot′) *n.* a pot with a handle and spout, in which tea is made.

tear (tēr) *n.* a drop of salty water from the eye.

tear (ter) *v.* **1.** to pull something in pieces or apart: *He tore the cloth into rags.* **2.** to come apart or to pieces when pulled: *That paper tears easily.* **tearing. tore** (tōr). I have **torn** (tōrn).

tease (tēz) *v.* to bother or make fun of in a playful way: *Don't tease the dog. He may bite you.* **teasing. teased.**

teaspoon (tē′ spün′) *n.* a small spoon used for eating, measuring, and stirring.

technical (tek′ ni kəl) *adj.* having to do with a special skill, usually one that involves science or complicated machines: *According to the technical information, these machine parts should be oiled every fifty hours.*

technician (tek nish′ ən) *n.* a person who has been trained in certain skills: *The technician quickly repaired the computer.*

technique (tek nēk′) *n.* a certain method of doing something: *The artist's technique is to use very bright colours.*

technology (tek nol′ ə jē) *n.* knowledge of scientific or mechanical skills: *Many jobs today involve computer technology. pl.* **technologies.**

teenager (tēn′ āj′ ər) *n.* a person who is between thirteen and nineteen years of age.

teens (tēnz) *n.pl.* the age between thirteen and nineteen.

teeth plural of **tooth.**

teethe (tēth) *v.* to have teeth growing for the first time. *Most babies cry a great deal when they are teething.* **teething. teethed.**

telecast (tel′ ə kast′) *n.* a television program.

telegram (tel′ ə gram′) *n.* a message sent by a telegraph.

telegraph (tel′ ə graf′) *n.* a system used for sending messages over a long distance. A telegraph message is sent by code, along electric wires.

telephone (tel′ ə fōn′) *n.* a device or system for sending voices from a distance, over electric wires or by radio waves. *v.* to call someone by dialling a telephone. **telephoning. telephoned.**

telescope

telescope (tel′ ə skōp′) *n.* a tube with glass lenses that make distant things look larger and nearer.

television, TV (tel′ ə vizh′ ən) *n.* **1.** a system for sending pictures by radio waves. **2.** the device on which such pictures are seen.

tell (tel) *v.* **1.** to say; to give information by talking: *Ed told us about his new job.* **2.** to give information in other ways: *The book tells us everything about fishing.* **3.** (used with **from**) to know the difference between: *Can you tell one twin from the other?* **telling. told** (tōld).

teller (tel′ ər) *n.* a person whose job in a bank is to give out, take in, and count money: *I gave a cheque to one of the tellers, and he gave me a twenty-dollar bill.*

temper (tem′ pər) *n.* **1.** the mood someone is in: *a bad temper; a good temper.* **2.** a mood of anger: *My sister has quite a temper when she is unhappy.*
lose one's temper to be very angry: *When I dropped the parcel the third time, I finally lost my temper.*

temperature (tem′ pə rə chər, tem′ pra chər) *n.* a measure of how hot or cold something is.

⊖**temple** (templ) *n.* **1.** a building for prayer and worship. **2.** one of the two sides of the forehead, just above the cheeks.

temporary (tem′ pə rer′ ē) *adj.* for a short time only; not for always: *The problem is temporary. It will soon be solved.*

tempt (tempt) *v.* to try to make someone do something, usually something that is foolish or wrong: *He was tempted to tell the secret, but he stayed quiet.*

ten (ten) *n., adj.* one more than nine (10).

tenant (ten′ ənt) *n.* a person or group that pays money to live in an apartment or building that belongs to someone else.

tend (tend) *v.* **1.** to look after: *A gardener tends plants.* **2.** to often be a certain way: *Be polite to him. He tends to get angry very easily.*

tendency (ten′ dən sē) *n.* likeliness to be a certain way or to do something in a certain way: *My car has a tendency to break down on the highway. pl.* **tendencies.**

tender (ten′ dər) *adj.* **1.** soft; not tough: *tender meat.* **2.** gentle; loving: *a tender smile; a tender hug; a tender word.*

tennis (ten′ is) *n.* a game in which two or four players use rackets to hit a hollow ball over a net.

tense (tens) *n.* the form of a verb that shows when the action happens: 'loved' is the past tense of 'love'. *adj.* uncomfortable; not relaxed: *He looked very tense as he waited in the hospital. a tense moment; a tenser one; the tensest one of all. v.* to pull something tight: *He tensed his arms and showed us his muscles.* **tensing. tensed.**

tension (ten′ shən) *n.* **1.** the state of being stretched tight: *The spring stretched under the tension.* **2.** an uncomfortable feeling: *The scenes in the movie where the zebra was being hunted by the lion were moments of great tension.*

tent

tent (tent) *n.* a canvas or nylon shelter, held up by poles and attached to the ground by ropes and pegs.

tentacle (ten′ təkl) *n.* a long limb, especially on an octopus, used for moving and feeling.

tenth (tenth) *adj.* following ninth (10th).

⊖**term** (tûrm) *n.* **1.** a certain period of time: *a school term; the mayor's term in office.* **2.** part of a contract or agreement: *A term in our lease says we can't have pets.* **3.** a word or words with a special meaning: *The lawyer used many legal terms.*

⊖**terminal** (tûr′ mi nəl) *n.* the building in which a railway, bus, or airplane trip starts or ends.

terminate (tûr′ mi nāt′) *v.* to stop; to end: *The temporary job terminates on Friday.* **terminating. terminated.**

terminology (tûr′ mi nol′ ə jē) *n.* the special words used in a subject: *The lawyer used so much legal terminology that we could hardly understand him.* *pl.* **terminologies.**

termite (tûr′ mīt) *n.* a small, ant-like insect that lives in large groups and eats wood.

⊖**terrible** (ter′ əbl) *adj.* awful; causing terror: *a terrible accident.*

terrier (ter′ i ər) *n.* one of several kinds of small, clever dogs.

terrific (tə rif′ ik) *adj.* very good; very great: *a terrific hockey game; a terrific problem.*

terrify (ter′ i fī′) *v.* to cause great fear: *The large, angry dog terrified the small child.* **terrifying. terrified.** it **terrifies.**

territory (ter′ i tȯr′ ē) *n.* any large area of land: *We were in familiar territory when we reached the city.* **2.** in Canada, an area that has its own legislature but is not a province. **3.** an area visited by a salesperson. *pl.* **territories.**

terror (ter′ ər) *n.* great fear; panic.

terrorist (ter′ ər ist) *n.* a person who tries to make people afraid so that the government will do what he or she wants.

test (test) *n.* an examination: *The class had a test in math.* *v.* **1.** to find out how much someone knows: *The teacher tested the class in spelling.* **2.** to try out: *The driver tested his brakes.*

testicle (tes′ tikl) *n.* one of the two male sex glands.

testify (tes′ ti fī′) *v.* to tell the truth very seriously: *She was a witness to the crime, and had to testify in court.* **testifying. testified.** he **testifies.**

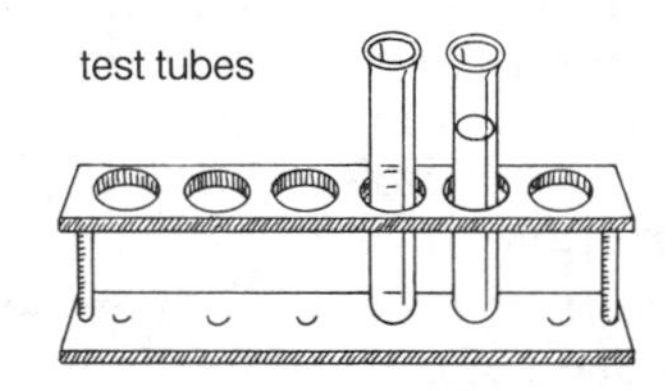

test tube (test′ tyūb′, test′ tūb′) a small glass container, closed at one end, often used to mix chemicals in.

tetanus (tet′ ən əs) *n.* a serious sickness which causes muscles to become stiff.

⊖**text** (tekst) *n.* **1.** the main part of reading material in a book: *The book has one hundred pages of text and twenty pages of pictures.* **2.** short for **textbook.**

textbook (tekst′ bu̇k′) *n.* a book used for study by school students: *a science textbook.*

textile (teks′ tīl, teks′ til) *n.* cloth, or something that can be made into cloth: *Nylon, wool, and cotton are some textiles.*

texture (teks′ chər) *n.* the feel of something; the smooth or rough quality that a surface has: *Toast and sandpaper have a rough texture.*

than (t͟han) *conj.* compared with: *She is older than I am.* *Note:* Do not confuse **than** and **then**; **than** is used to compare things.

thank (thangk) *v.* for a person to show gratitude and appreciation for a present, a kind deed, etc.

thankful (thangk′ fəl) *adj.* grateful; pleased: *They were thankful to be home again.*

thanks (thangks) *n.pl.* a way of saying thank you.

Thanksgiving Day (thangks′ giv′ ing dā′) a holiday on which to give thanks for all that we have; in Canada, it is celebrated on the second Monday in October.

that (that) *adj.* **1.** the person or thing being talked about or shown: *That ring belonged to my grandmother.* **2.** the person or thing being further away: *Look at that tree behind the house, not at this one. pl.* **those** (thōz). *pron.* **1.** the person or thing being talked about or shown: *That is an old ring.* **2.** the person or thing being further away: *That is a maple tree, and this is an apple tree. pl.* **those. 3.** which, who, whom: *I like trees that have many leaves. conj.* a word used to join two parts of a sentence: *I am happy that my grandmother gave me her ring.*

that's (thats) short for **that is.**

thaw (thȯ) *n.* the melting of ice and snow in mild weather: *the spring thaw. v.* to melt: *The ice thawed in the sun.*

the (thə) *art.* 'a certain one' or 'certain ones': *The boys are in the school.*

⊖**theatre, theater** (thi′ ə tər) *n.* a building where plays are acted or movies are shown.

theft (theft) *n.* the act of stealing; the crime of stealing: *They were arrested for the theft of the car.*

their (ther) *adj.* belonging to them: *their coats.*

theirs (therz) *pron.* the one or ones belonging to them: *The house is theirs.*

them (them) *pron.* those persons, animals, or things: *I like them.*

theme (thēm) *n.* the subject of a book, article, report, speech, etc.

themselves (them selvz′) *pron.* them alone: *The children cooked dinner by themselves.*

then (then) *adv.* **1.** at some time: *We went shopping, and then we came home.* **2.** therefore; for that reason: *If you have enough money, then you can go to the movies. Note:* Do not confuse **then** with **than; then** is never used for comparing things.

theory (thē′ ə rē, thi′ ər ē) *n.* an idea to explain something: *None of us could offer any theories on why he had run away. pl.* **theories.**

therapy (ther′ ə pē) *n.* treatment for an illness or an injury: *The doctor said that she was tired, and that rest would be the best therapy for her. pl.* **therapies.**

there (ther) *adv.* in that place; to that place; at that place: *They went there last summer. Put the book there, not here.*

therefore (ther′ fȯr′) *adv.* for that reason; because of that: *He felt ill, and therefore he went to bed.*

there's (therz) short for **there is.**

thermal (thûr′ məl) *adj.* having to do with heat: *I wear thermal underwear to keep me warm in the winter.*

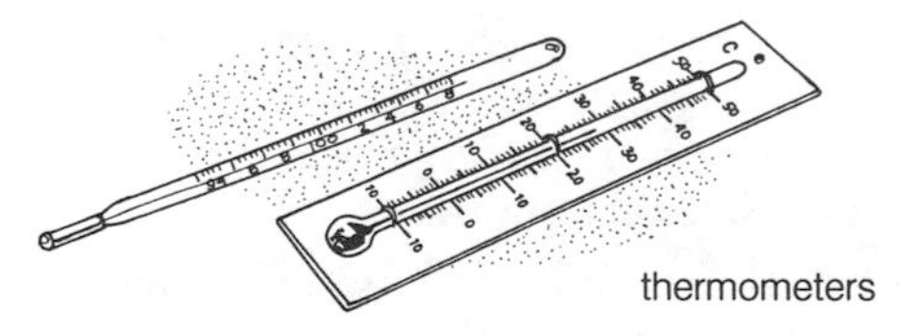

thermometers

thermometer (thər mom′ ə tər) *n.* an instrument that measures temperature in degrees.

thermostat (thûr′ mə stat) *n.* a device that can control the temperature in a room or building.

thesaurus (thi sȯr′ əs) *n.* a book that lists groups of words that have the same or similar meanings. *pl.* **thesauri** (thi sȯr′ ī) or **thesauruses.**

these plural of **this.**

they plural of **he, she,** or **it.**

they're (t̲h̲er) short for **they are.**

thick (thik) *adj.* **1.** having much distance from one surface to the opposite one: *a thick slice of bread; thick wool.* **2.** not watery: *thick soup.* **3.** hard to see through: *thick fog.*

thief (thēf) *n.* someone who steals. *pl.* **thieves.** (thēvz).

thigh (thī) *n.* the part of a person's leg between the knee and hip.

thimble (thimbl) *n.* a metal or plastic cap, worn to protect the end of the finger when sewing.

thin (thin) *adj.* **1.** having little distance from one surface to the opposite one: *a thin person; a thin board; a thinner board; the thinnest board of all.* **2.** watery: *thin soup.*

thing (thing) *n.* any object that can be seen or touched but is not alive: *A book is a good thing to take on a trip. What are those things on the table?* **2.** something that can be done, thought, or felt: *Reading is a good thing to do on a trip. Friendship is a wonderful thing.*

think (thingk) *v.* **1.** to use the mind: *I was thinking about what he said.* **2.** to have an opinion; to believe: *I think Sam is telling the truth.* **thinking. thought** (thȯt).

third (thûrd) *adj.* following second (3rd).

thirst (thûrst) *n.* a need or wish for something to drink.

thirsty (thûrs′ tē) *adj.* wanting something to drink: *a thirsty baby; a thirstier one; the thirstiest baby of all.*

thirteen (thûr tēn′) *n., adj.* ten more than three (13).

thirteenth (thûr tēnth′) *adj.* following twelfth (13th).

thirty (thûr′ tē) *n., adj.* ten times three (30). *pl.* **thirties.**

this (t̲h̲is) *adj.* **1.** the person or thing being talked about or shown: *This coat is mine.* **2.** the person or thing being closer: *I like this picture, not the one on the other wall.* *pl.* **these** (t̲h̲ēz). *pron.* **1.** the person or thing being talked about or shown: *This is a new hat, and I'm wearing it already.* **2.** the person or thing being closer: *This dish is the one I will use.* *pl.* **these.**

thistle

thistle (thisl) *n.* a prickly plant with purple flowers.

thorn (thȯrn) *n.* **1.** a sharp point on a plant. **2.** a plant, bush, or tree that has such sharp points.

thorough (thûr′ ō) *adj.* **1.** complete: *The doctor told my brother that he needed a thorough rest.* **2.** careful and well-done: *The mechanic gave the car a thorough check.*

those plural of **that.**

though (t̲h̲ō) *conj.* in spite of the fact that: *We went to the game, though it was going to rain.*

thought (thȯt) *n.* **1.** the act or process of thinking: *We gave much thought to the problem before trying to fix the machine.* **2.** an idea, plan, belief, etc.: *Tara had a good thought about where to go this evening.* *v.* see **think.**

thoughtful (thȯt′ fəl) *adj.* **1.** thinking deeply: *Tom was very thoughtful after talking to his teacher.* **2.** kind to others; giving attention to the feelings of others: *You were thoughtful to send me a birthday card.*

thoughtless (thȯt′ ləs) *adj.* careless; not thinking about other people or things.

thousand (thau̇′ zənd) *n., adj.* ten times one hundred (1000).

thread (thred) *n.* **1.** a thin string of cotton, silk, or other material used in sewing. **2.** the groove that winds around a screw. *v.* to put thread in a needle.

threat (thret) *n.* **1.** a warning that harm or punishment may be coming: *When the robbers made a threat on his life, he gave them the money.* **2.** danger; a sign that something bad may happen: *a threat of a hail storm.*

threaten (thret′ ən) *v.* **1.** to make threats against. **2.** to warn of danger: *The clouds threaten a storm.*

three (thrē) *n., adj.* one more than two (3).

threw see **throw.**

thrifty (thrif′ tē) *adj.* careful about the way money is saved and spent: *thrifty shoppers; thriftier ones; the thriftiest shoppers of all.*

thrill (thril) *n.* a sudden feeling of joy or excitement: *the thrill of skiing down the mountain.* *v.* to give an excited feeling.

throat (thrōt) *n.* the front of the neck, or the inside passage of the neck.

throne (thrōn) *n.* a chair on which a king or queen sits during certain ceremonies.

through (thrū) *prep.* **1.** from the beginning to the end of: *We drove through the village. I read through the book.* **2.** into: *We looked through the window when nobody answered.* *adv.* **1.** from one side to the other: *Carol opened the door, and we walked through.* **2.** as a result of: *We completed the job through much hard work.*
adj. finished: *Are you through with my pencil?*

throughout (thrū au̇t′) *prep.* all over; everywhere: *There is a noise throughout the house.*

throw (thrō) *v.* **1.** to pitch or toss something through the air: *Kay threw the football to her friend.* **2.** to cause to fall: *The frightened horse threw its rider.* **throwing. threw** (thrū). I have **thrown** (thrōn). **throw away** to dispose of; to get rid of: *Lee threw away the newspaper when he finished reading it.*

thrust (thrust) *v.* to push hard and quickly: *The farmer thrust the fork into the hay.* **thrusting. thrust.**

thumb (thum) *n.* the short, thick finger that is separate from the other fingers.

thunder (thun′ dər) *n.* the loud noise that follows lightning in a storm. *v.* to make a loud, booming sound: *The planes thundered.*

Thursday (thûrz′ dā) *n.* the fifth day of the week. *pl.* **Thursdays.**

tick (tik) *n.* **1.** the sound that a clock makes. **2.** a little mark (✓) put next to a number, name, etc., to show that it is correct. *v.* **1.** to keep on making little sounds: *A clock ticks.* **2.** to make a tick mark: *The teacher ticked the answers that were right.*

⊖**ticket** (tik′ ət) *n.* **1.** a small piece of paper or a card that gives a person certain rights: *José bought two tickets for the movie.* **2.** a paper that orders someone to pay a fine or come to court: *a traffic ticket.* **3.** a label showing the price of something.

tickle (tikl) *v.* to touch lightly to make someone giggle and laugh. **tickling. tickled.**

tidal wave (tī′ dəl wāv′) a powerful and dangerous ocean wave caused by an underground earthquake, hurricane, or strong winds.

tide (tīd) *n.* the regular rise and fall of the ocean that happens twice each day.

tidy (tī′ dē) *adj.* neat, with everything in its correct place: *a tidy desk; a tidier one; the tidiest desk in the room.*

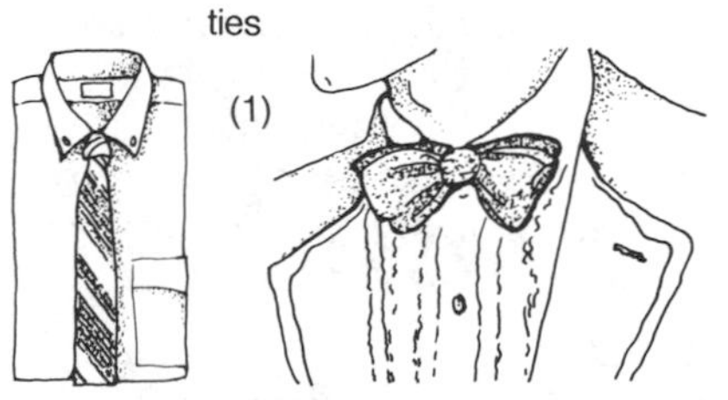

tie (tī) *n.* **1.** a strip of cloth worn around the neck and fastened in front with a knot. **2.** an equal score in a game, contest, or election. **3.** a string, rope, etc., that joins two or more things. *v.* **1.** to join two or more things with a string, rope, etc.: *We tied the box with a ribbon.* **2.** to be even in a game: *The two teams tied, with a score of one goal each.* **tying. tied.** she **ties.**
tie up 1. to fasten with string or rope: *She tied up her shoelaces.* **2.** to make very busy doing something, with no time to do anything else: *I can't help you now. I'm tied up with my work.*

tie-up (tī′ up) *n.* a problem that slows things down: *The delivery will be late because there has been a tie-up at the factory.*

tiger (tī′ gər) *n.* a wild animal of the cat family that has black stripes on its yellow fur; it lives in India and other parts of Asia.

tight (tīt) *adj.* **1.** fitting very closely: *a tight shoe.* **2.** firmly joined or stretched: *a tight knot.*

tighten (tīt′ ən) *v.* to make tight: *Please tighten the string around the box.*

tightrope (tīt′ rōp′) *n.* a rope, stretched out high above the ground, that acrobats perform on.

tile (tīl) *n.* a flat piece of plastic, baked clay, or other material used to cover walls, floors, roofs, or ceilings.

till (til) *n.* a drawer or box where money is kept in a store or bank. *prep.* up to the time of: *Wait here till I come back.* *v.* to prepare land for planting.

tilt (tilt) *v.* to lean or to make something lean: *If you tilt the table, the apples will roll off.*

⊖**timber** (tim′ bər) *n.* **1.** large trees in a forest. **2.** trees used in building.

timber wolf (tim′ bər wu̇lf′) a large, grey wolf that lives in forests in Canada and the northern United States. *pl.* **timber wolves** (tim′ bər wu̇lvz).

⊖**time** (tīm) *n.* **1.** a moment shown on the clock: *What is the time?* **2.** a certain period; a space in our lives measured in years, months, days, hours, minutes, or seconds: *It is a long time since I saw Joan.* **3.** a regular beat in music.
in time with enough time: *The police arrived in time to catch the burglar.*
on time at the correct time: *I arrived on time, but my friend was late.*
time off days or hours missed at work or school.
time out a stop or rest in some activity or sport: *The captain of the losing team called 'time out' in order to speak to the coach.*

times (tīmz) *prep.* multiplied by: *Three times five equals fifteen.*

timetable (tīm′ tābl′) *n.* a schedule that shows the times trains, buses, planes, etc., arrive and leave.

timid (tim′ id) *adj.* shy; nervous; easily scared.

tin (tin) *n.* **1.** a soft, silver-coloured metal that does not rust easily. **2.** a can; a metal container: *a sardine tin; a cake tin.*

tinsel (tin′ səl) *n.* thin strips of shiny material, usually used to decorate Christmas trees.

tint (tint) *n.* a pale shade of a colour: *The wall is painted white with a blue tint.*

tiny (tī′ nē) *adj.* very small: *a tiny mouse; a tinier mouse; the tiniest mouse in the cage.*

tip (tip) *n.* **1.** a pointed end: *a finger tip.* **2.** extra money given for a service: *We paid for the meal and left a tip for the waiter.* **3.** a piece of helpful information: *The book gave us good tips for planting vegetables.* *v.* **1.** to tilt or turn: *The baby tipped over the glass of milk.* **2.** to give extra money for a service: *We tipped the waitress.* **tipping. tipped.**

tiptoe (tip′ tō′) *v.* to walk quietly on the tip of the toes: *Joel tiptoed past the sleeping puppy.* **tiptoeing. tiptoed.** she **tiptoes.**

⊖**tire** (tīr) *n.* a tube of rubber, containing air, that fits around the wheel of a car, bicycle, or other vehicle.

tired (tīrd) *adj.* wanting to rest or sleep.

⊖**tissue** (tish′ ū) *n.* **1.** a group of cells in a plant or animal that have a certain use: *muscle tissue.* **2.** paper that is very light and soft: *He bought a box of tissues because he had a cold. We need toilet tissue for the bathroom.*

title (tītl) *n.* **1.** the name of a book, movie, song, etc. **2.** a word before a name to show a person's rank or importance: *'Doctor', 'Sir', and 'Professor' are some titles.*

to (tū) *prep.* **1.** in the direction of: *Let's drive to the park.* **2.** as far as: *We went to the river.* **3.** until: *We were away from Friday to Monday.* **4.** before: *It is ten minutes to three.* **to and fro** backwards and forwards.

toad (tōd) *n.* an animal that lives on land and in water; it looks like a frog, but has rougher skin.

toadstool (tōd′ stūl′) *n.* a poisonous mushroom.

⊖**toast** (tōst) *n.* bread that is made crisp and brown by heating it. *v.* **1.** to make bread crisp and brown with heat. **2.** to have a drink in honour of someone or a special occasion: *We toasted the bride and groom at their wedding.*

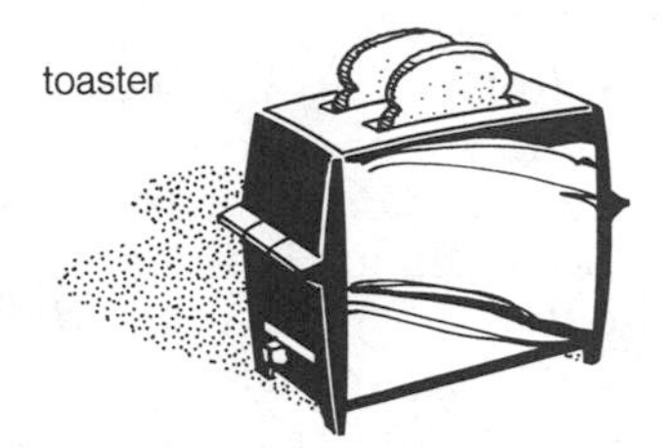
toaster

toaster (tōs′ tər) *n.* an electrical device that toasts bread.

tobacco (tə bak′ ō) *n.* a plant whose leaves are dried and used for smoking in pipes, cigars, or cigarettes. *pl.* **tobaccos.**

toboggan

toboggan (tə bog′ ən) *n.* a light, flat sled without runners.

today (tə dā′) *n.* this present day: *Today is Thanksgiving.* *adv.* on this day: *My cousin arrived today.*

toddler (tod′ lər) *n.* a small child just learning to walk.

toe (tō) *n.* one of the five parts at the front of each foot.

together (tə geth′ ər) *adv.* with each other; in one group: *together for a swim.*

toil (toil) *n.* hard work. *v.* to do hard work: *They toiled in the fields all day.*

⊖**toilet** (toi′ lət) *n.* **1.** a bowl containing water, used for flushing away body wastes. **2.** a bathroom.

token (tō′ kən) *n.* **1.** a special coin used instead of money: *Tokens are often used in buses, streetcars, and subways.* **2.** something small that stands for something much larger: *He gave his friend chocolates as a token of his love.*

told see **tell.**

tolerant (tol′ ə rənt) *adj.* not becoming angry at something that may be annoying; able to put up with something: *He is very tolerant of the two noisy children who live in the next apartment.*

tolerate (tol′ ər āt′) *v.* to not get angry at something; to put up with something: *I don't know how you can tolerate this noisy office.* **tolerating. tolerated.**

toll (tōl) *n.* a tax paid for the right to use something: *We paid a toll to cross the bridge.* *v.* for bells to ring slowly.

tomatoes

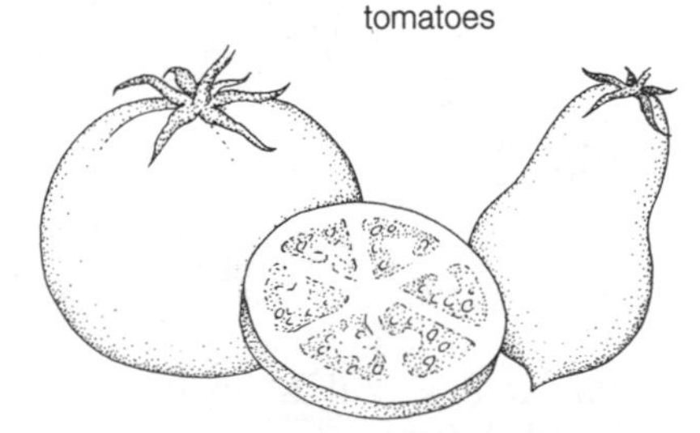

tomato (tə mā′ tō, tə mȧ′ tō) *n.* a plant with round, juicy, red fruit, that is used in salads, sauces, etc. *pl.* **tomatoes.**

tomb (tūm) *n.* a grave or building for the burial of the dead.

tombstone (tūm′ stōn′) *n.* a stone over a grave.

tomorrow (tə mor′ ō, tə mȯr′ ō) *n.* the day after today: *Tomorrow will be Tuesday.* *adv.* on the next day: *My cousin will go home tomorrow.*

tone (tōn) *n.* **1.** the quality of the sound of a voice or a sound of music: *a low tone; an angry tone.* **2.** a shade of a colour: *a light tone of blue; a dark tone of green.*

tongue (tung) *n.* **1.** the soft, fleshy part of the mouth used for licking and tasting. **2.** the language of a certain country.

tonight (tə nīt′) *n.* this night coming: *Tonight is a holiday.* *adv.* on this night: *My favourite television program is seen tonight.*

tonne (tun) *n.* a unit for measuring mass; **t** is the symbol. 1 t = 1000 kg.

tonsils (ton′ səlz) *n.pl.* two oval pieces of flesh at the back of the mouth.

too (tū) *adv.* **1.** also, as well: *I am going out, and Frank is coming too.* **2.** more than what is needed or wanted: *I had too much to eat! The pants are too long for you.*

took see **take.**

tool (tūl) *n.* any hand-held instrument that helps a person do work: *Hammers, saws, and axes are some tools.*

tooth (tūth) *n.* **1.** one of the bony parts attached to the jaws and set in the gums of the mouth, used for chewing and biting. **2.** a prong or pointed edge on a saw, wheel, or gear. *pl.* **teeth** (tēth).

toothache (tūth′ āk′) *n.* a pain in a tooth.

toothbrush (tūth′ brush′) *n.* a small brush on a long handle, used to clean teeth. *pl.* **toothbrushes.**

toothpaste (tūth′ pāst′) *n.* a paste put on a toothbrush for cleaning the teeth.

toothpick (tūth′ pik′) *n.* a small, narrow piece of plastic or wood, used to remove pieces of food from between the teeth.

top (top) *n.* **1.** the highest point: *the top of a hill.* **2.** the upper side: *the top of a box.* **3.** a toy which can be made to spin.

topic (top′ ik) *n.* what something is about: *The topic of his report is 'safe driving'.*

toque see **tuque.**

torch (tȯrch) *n.* **1.** a stick that burns at one end and can be carried by the other end. **2.** something that is like a torch: *a blowtorch shoots out a hot flame. pl.* **torches.**

tore, torn see **tear.**

torn (tȯrn) *adj.* ripped; having a tear: *The material is torn and should be repaired.*

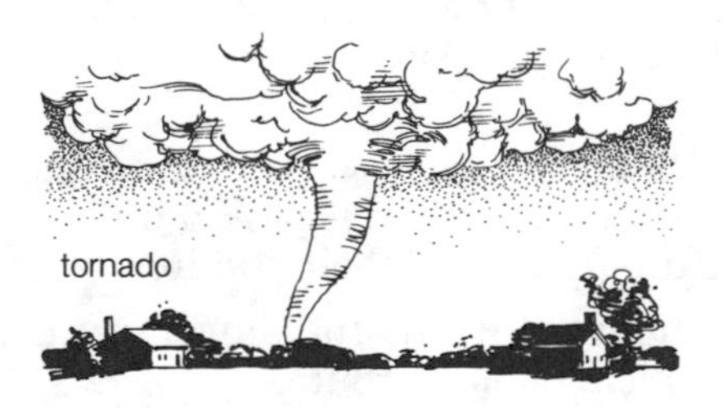

tornado (tȯr nā′ dō) *n.* a violent storm, with dark winds that whirl around at a high speed. *pl.* **tornadoes.**

Toronto (tə ron′ tō) *n.* the largest city in Canada and the capital city of Ontario.

tortoise (tȯr′ təs) *n.* a large turtle that lives on land.

torture (tȯr′ chər) *v.* to cause great pain to someone, often to make him or her tell a secret or confess. **torturing. tortured.**

toss (tos) *v.* **1.** to throw something into the air: *Diana tossed the ball to Nina.* **2.** to roll about: *Karl could not sleep and he tossed in bed.* **tossing. tossed.** she **tosses.**

toss-up (tos′ up′) *n.* something that might or might not happen: *It's a toss-up whether it will rain on Saturday.*

total (tō′ təl) *n.* the whole amount when two or more numbers are added: *The total of 3 plus 5 plus 2 is 10.*

touch (tuch) *n.* one of the five senses; feeling. *pl.* **touches.** *v.* **1.** to feel with the fingers or some other part of the body. **2.** to be against: *The back of the chair touches the wall.* **touching. touched.** he **touches.**

in touch communicating through letters or telephone calls: *We don't see each other often, but we try to stay in touch.*

out of touch not able to understand; not aware: *My grandparents are out of touch with the world of computers.*

touch up to make small improvements: *The paint on the wall is nice, but it needs to be touched up.*

touchdown (tuch′ daůn′) *n.* in football, a score made by getting the ball across the other team's goal line.

tough (tuf) *adj.* **1.** not easily broken or bent: *a tough piece of rubber.* **2.** hard to chew: *tough meat.* **3.** hard; difficult: *a tough problem in arithmetic.*

⊖**tour** (tūr) *n.* a trip; usually one led by a guide. *v.* to travel about from place to place: *Our family will tour the Rockies next summer.*

tourist (tūr′ ist, tûr′ ist) *n.* a person on holiday who travels about to see different places and things.

tournament (tūr′ nə mənt, tûr′ nə mənt) *n.* a series of matches in a game or sport, often involving many players or teams from different places.

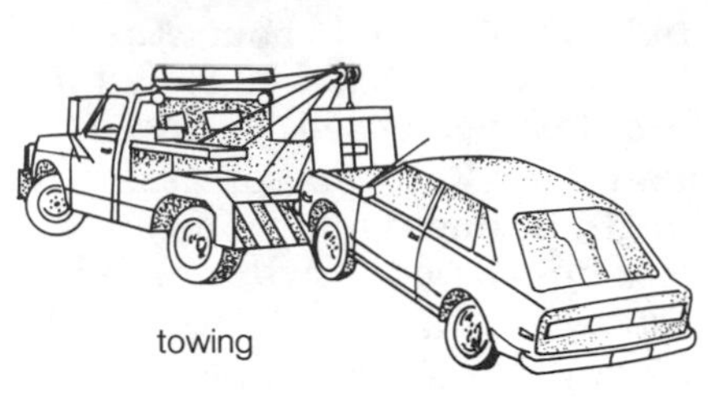
towing

tow (tō) *v.* to pull or drag something with a rope: *The car broke down, and a truck towed it away.*

towards, toward (tə wȯrdz′, tə wȯrd′) *prep.* in the direction of: *They walked towards the village.*

towel (tau̇l) *n.* a cloth or paper that is used for drying or wiping something wet.

tower (tau̇′ ər) *n.* a tall and narrow building or part of a building. *v.* to stand much higher than others: *The tall pine trees tower over the smaller trees.*

town (tau̇n) *n.* an area with houses, factories, stores, etc., usually larger than a village and smaller than a city.

township (tau̇n′ ship′) *n.* a part of a county that has certain powers of government.

toxic (tok′ sik) *adj.* containing a substance that could kill or injure a living creature: *Chlorine is a toxic gas.*

toy (tȯi) *n.* something to play with. *pl.* **toys.** *v.* to play with; to amuse oneself: *He toyed with his ring.*

⊖**trace** (trās) *n.* a very small amount: *There is a trace of grease on the glass.* *v.* **1.** to copy a picture by placing transparent paper on top of it and drawing over the lines. **2.** to find out about someone or something, using clues: *We asked the post office to trace the lost parcel.* **tracing. traced.**

track (trak) *n.* **1.** the set of metal rails a train travels along. **2.** marks on the ground left by something moving: *the tracks of the squirrel.* **3.** the course followed by runners in a race.

tractor

tractor (trak′ tər) *n.* a machine with wheels and a powerful engine that is used on farms for pulling a plough or heavy loads.

trade (trād) *n.* **1.** the business of buying and selling: *There is much trade between Canada and other countries.* **2.** a job needing the use of tools: *Ed is a carpenter by trade.* *v.* to exchange one thing for something else. **trading. traded.**
trade in to use something as partial payment for a newer model: *She traded in her old car for a new one.*

tradition (trə dish′ ən) *n.* something done over and over, passed on from parents to their children.

⊖**traffic** (traf′ ik) *n.* the movement of vehicles along a route.

traffic light (traf′ ik līt′) a light, or set of lights of different colours, used to direct traffic.

⊖**tragedy** (traj′ ə dē) *n.* **1.** a very sad happening: *The young man's death was a tragedy for his family.* **2.** a story, play, movie, etc., with a sad ending. *pl.* **tragedies.**

tragic (traj′ ik) *adj.* very sad: *a tragic accident.*

trail (trāl) *n.* **1.** marks on the ground showing which way some animal or person has gone. **2.** a path made across rough country. *v.* to follow behind: *Our team trailed by one point. The dog trailed the rabbit.*

trailer (trāl′ ər) *n.* a vehicle that can be pulled along by another vehicle. One kind of trailer is for people to live in. Another kind is used to carry goods.

train (trān) *n.* railway cars connected together. *v.* to practise for something: *Lisa is training to be a ballet dancer.*

trainee (trān ē′) *n.* a person who is learning a job: *After a year as a trainee, she will be given a job managing an office.*

trainer (trān′ ər) *n.* someone who teaches or prepares a person for some exercise or sport.

traitor (trā′ tər) *n.* someone who works against his or her friends or country.

tramp (tramp) *n.* a person who has no home or job and travels from place to place. *v.* **1.** to walk heavily. **2.** to go for a trip on foot; to hike.

trample (trampl) *v.* to walk heavily all over something. **trampling. trampled.**

trampoline (tram′ pə lēn′) *n.* a piece of canvas held to a frame by strong springs, on which a person can bounce, do exercises, etc.

tranquillizer, tranquilizer (trang′ kwil ī′ zər) *n.* a drug that makes people or animals relax or sleep.

transfer (trans′ fər, tranz′ fər) *n.* a ticket that lets a person go from one vehicle to another without having to pay the full fare again. *v.* to move something or somebody to another place: *The insurance company transferred two employees to an office in another city.* **transferring. transferred.**

transistor (tranz is′ tər) *n.* a very small device that controls the amount of electric current being used in some radios, televisions, calculators, watches, etc.

transit (tran′ sit, tran′ zit) *n.* the act of carrying things or people from one place to another: *The package was lost in transit.*

translate (trans′ lāt, tranz′ lāt) *v.* to put into another language: *He translated the Chinese story into English.* **translating. translated.**

⊖**translation** (trans lā′ shən, tranz lā′ shən) *n.* **1.** something that has been translated: *This story is an English translation of a Chinese story.* **2.** the act of translating: *The translation of the story is hard to do.*

transmit (trans mit′, tranz mit′) *v.* **1.** to pass from one person to another: *Some diseases can be transmitted by coughing.* **2.** to send a radio or television signal: *Marconi transmitted the first radio message across the Atlantic Ocean.* **transmitting. transmitted.**

transparent (trans per′ ənt) *adj.* clear; able to be seen through: *Glass is transparent.*

transplant (trans′ plant) *n.* the removal of a living thing from one place and the placing of it somewhere else.

transplant (trans plant′) *v.* to remove a living thing from one place and put it somewhere else: *The trees were transplanted into our garden from the forest.*

transport (trans′ pȯrt) *n.* **1.** the moving of people or goods from one place to another. **2.** a large plane or ship used for carrying materials.

⊖**transport** (trans pȯrt′) *v.* to move people or goods from one place to another.

transportation (trans′ pər tā′ shən) *n.* the act of moving people or goods from one place to another.

⊖**trap** (trap) *n.* something made for catching birds or animals: *The mouse was caught in the trap.* *v.* to catch with a trap. **trapping. trapped.**

trapeze (trə pēz′) *n.* a swinging bar held by two ropes, used by acrobats and gymnasts.

trapper (trap′ ər) *n.* someone who makes a living by trapping wild animals for their fur.

trash (trash) *n.* garbage; anything worthless or useless.

travel (trav′ əl) *v.* to make a trip. **travelling. travelled.**

traveller, traveler (trav′ ə lər) *n.* someone who travels.

trawl (trȯl) *n.* a net dragged along the bottom of the ocean. *v.* to fish with such a net.

trawler

trawler (trȯl′ ər) *n.* a ship used in fishing with a trawl net.

tray (trā) *n.* a flat board of wood, plastic, metal, etc., used for carrying food, cups, dishes, and other objects. *pl.* **trays.**

treasure (trezh′ ər) *n.* something very valuable; great riches: *treasure buried at the bottom of the sea.* *v.* to value very highly: *We treasure our friendship.* **treasuring. treasured.**

treasurer (trezh′ ər ər) *n.* the person who looks after the money of a business or club.

treasury (trezh′ ə rē) *n.* a place where the money of a government, club, etc. is kept. *pl.* **treasuries.**

treat (trēt) *n.* a special pleasure: *The trip to the beach was a treat for the children.* *v.* **1.** to give someone a special pleasure: *We treated ourselves to a boat trip.* **2.** to behave towards someone in a certain way: *He treated his grandparents with respect.* **3.** to give careful attention to something: *The doctor treated the injury immediately.* **4.** to pay for someone else: *John treated me to the meal.*

treatment (trēt′ mənt) *n.* **1.** a way of behaving towards someone or dealing with something: *We spoke to the neighbour about his unkind treatment of his dog.* **2.** a medical or special care: *What is the doctor's treatment for your cold?*

treaty (trē′ tē) *n.* a formal agreement made between two countries, usually about peace or commerce. *pl.* **treaties.**

tree (trē) *n.* a large plant with a wood trunk and branches.

tremble (trembl) *v.* to shake or shiver with fear, excitement, or cold. **trembling. trembled.**

tremendous (tri men′ dəs) *adj.* huge; unusually large: *a tremendous whale; a tremendous cheer from a crowd.*

trench (trench) *n.* a long, narrow, deep ditch dug in the ground. *pl.* **trenches.**

⊖**trespass** (tres′ pas, tres′ pəs) *v.* to go on someone's property without permission. **trespassing. trespassed.** he **trespasses.**

trespasser (tres′ pas ər, tres′ pəs ər) *n.* someone who goes onto private property without permission.

tri- a prefix meaning three: a **triangle** is a figure with three sides; a **tricycle** is a cycle with three wheels.

trial (trī′ əl) *n.* **1.** the hearing of a case before a judge in a court of law. **2.** a testing of something to see how it works: *the trial of a new piece of machinery.*

triangle (trī′ angl) *n.* **1.** a space or area enclosed by three straight lines whose ends meet. **2.** a musical instrument made from a steel rod bent in this shape.

triangular (trī ang′ gyū lər) *adj.* having the shape of a triangle.

tribe (trīb) *n.* a group of people who share certain customs, religious beliefs, etc., and have the same leader.

trick (trik) *n.* a clever act; a quick action that fools people: *a magic trick.* *v.* to fool or cheat: *He tricked me into paying too much.*

trickle (trikl) *n.* a small flow of something: *Only a trickle of water came out of the tap.* *v.* to flow in drops or a small quantity: *A few people trickled into the room.* **trickling. trickled.**

tricycle (trī′ sikl) *n.* a small vehicle with three wheels and two pedals, usually used by children.

tried, tries see **try.**

trigger (trig′ ər) *n.* the small lever on a gun or pistol that is pulled to make it fire. *v.* to set off; to begin: *The shot triggered the race.*

trim (trim) *adj.* in good condition: *The athlete was told to stay trim.* *v.* to make something neat by clipping it: *to trim a hedge; to trim hair.* **trimming. trimmed.**

trip (trip) *n.* a journey: *a trip to the zoo.* *v.* to stumble; to strike the foot against something and fall or start to fall: *He tripped on the banana peel that was on the floor.* **tripping. tripped.**

triple (tripl) *adj.* three times as much: *The cat is triple the size of the kitten.* *v.* to multiply by three: *When you triple the number two, you get six.* **tripling. tripled.**

triplet (trip′ lət) *n.* any one of three children born at the same time to the same mother.

triumph (trī′ umf) *n.* a great victory or success: *a triumph in battle.*

trivial (triv′ i əl) *adj.* not important: *One of your complaints is important, but the others are really trivial.*

⊖**trombone** (trom′ bōn, trom bōn′) *n.* a brass musical instrument with a sliding tube pushed in and out when played.

troop (trūp) *n.* a body of soldiers or a group of other people.

trophy (trō′ fē) *n.* a cup, plaque, or other object given to the winner of a contest. *pl.* **trophies.**

tropical (trop′ i kəl) *adj.* having to do with the warmest parts of the world.

trot (trot) *n.* a light, gentle run. *v.* to run gently: *The horse trotted to the fence.* **trotting. trotted.**

⊖**trouble** (trubl) *n.* anything that bothers or disturbs; a difficult situation: *The trouble with the house is that it is too old. The child will be in trouble with his parents if he is late.* *v.* to bother, disturb, or worry: *He is troubled by a bad cold.* **troubling. troubled.**

trough (trof) *n.* a long, narrow, open box that holds water or food for animals.

trousers (traů′ zərz) *n.pl.* a pair of long pants.

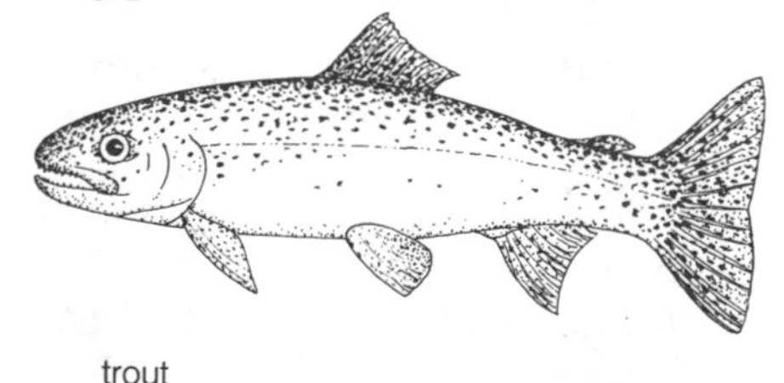

trout

trout (traůt) *n.* a fish that lives in fresh water and is used for food. *pl.* **trout.**

truce (trūs) *n.* a pause in a battle or disagreement: *During the truce, both sides tried to make peace.*

truck (truk) *n.* a large motor vehicle that carrries heavy loads. *v.* to carry heavy loads in a truck: *The cans of vegetables were trucked across the province.*

true (trū) *adj.* **1.** correct, exactly right: *a true story; a truer one; the truest story of all.* **2.** loyal; honest; to be relied on: *Frank is a true friend.*

truly (trū′ lē) *adv.* really; honestly: *I am truly sorry that you are not well.*

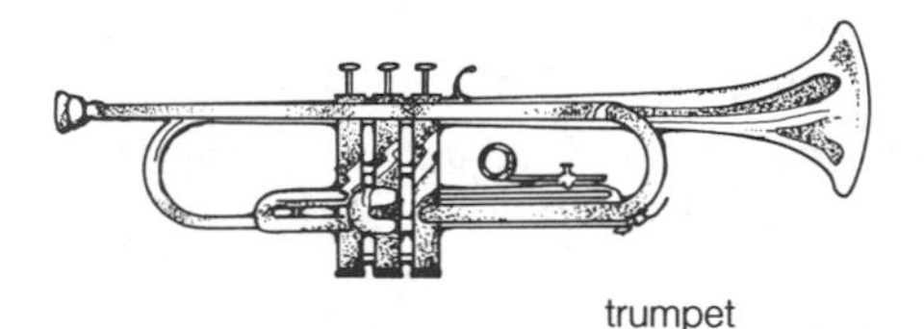

trumpet

trumpet (trum′ pət) *n.* a brass musical instrument with a curving tube that widens at one end.

trunk (trungk) *n.* **1.** the main part of a tree. **2.** the main part of a person's body; the part without the limbs or the head. **3.** a big box or chest, used for storing or carrying personal belongings. **4.** the part of an automobile that holds luggage, a spare tire, groceries and other goods. **5.** the nose of an elephant.

trunks (trungks) *n.pl.* men's or boy's short pants worn for swimming or other sports.

trust (trust) *n.* a belief that someone or something is good, honest, correct, etc.: *I have trust in our mayor.* *v.* to believe that someone is honest, loyal, capable, etc.: *I don't trust him with my money.*

truth (trūth) *n.* what is true; what really happened: *Are you telling the truth about the fight?*

truthful (trūth′ fəl) *adj.* speaking the truth.

try (trī) *n.* an attempt: *Although Sam did not win the race, he made a good try.* *pl.* **tries.** *v.* **1.** to attempt; to aim at doing something: *The child tried to climb the tree.* **2.** to examine facts in a court of law: *He was tried for the crime, and the jury found him not guilty.* **trying. tried.** she **tries.**
try on to wear something, usually in a store, to see how it looks and if it fits: *Try on the shoes to be sure they are comfortable.*
try out to use or test something to see if it works well: *He tried out the bicycle before he bought it.*

T-shirt (tē′ shûrt′) *n.* a light shirt with short sleeves and no collar.

tub (tub) *n.* a large container for holding water.

tuba (tyū′ bə, tū′ bə) *n.* a large, brass musical instrument that produces very low sounds. *pl.* **tubas.**

⊖**tube** (tyūb, tūb) *n.* **1.** a long, hollow pipe; a container of metal, rubber, glass, etc., used for carrying liquids or gases. **2.** a soft container used for holding toothpaste or other products that can be squeezed out.

tuck (tuk) *n.* a fold in cloth. *v.* to fold up or to wrap up: *Father tucked the baby into her bed.*

Tuesday (tyūz′ dā, tūz′ dā) *n.* the third day of the week. *pl.* **Tuesdays.**

tug (tug) *n.* **1.** a strong, quick pull. **2.** short for **tugboat.** *v.* to pull at something: *The children tugged at their mother's arm.* **tugging. tugged.**

tugboat (tug′ bōt′) *n.* a small, powerful boat used for pulling or pushing ships in and out of a harbour.

tulip (tyū′ lip, tū′ lip) *n.* a brightly coloured flower that grows from a bulb and is shaped like a cup.

tumble (tumbl) *v.* to fall in an awkward way. **tumbling. tumbled.**

tumbler (tum′ blər) *n.* **1.** a drinking glass. **2.** an acrobat.

tumour, tumor (tyū′ mər, tū′ mər) *n.* a growth, in some part of the body, that is not normal and may be harmful.

tuna (tyū′ nə, tū′ nə) *n.* a large ocean fish that is caught for food. *pl.* **tunas**, or **tuna.**

tundra (tun′ drə) *n.* one of the very large areas of flat, treeless land in the Arctic.

tune (tyūn, tūn) *n.* a set of musical notes that form a melody.

tunnel (tun′ əl) *n.* an underground passage for trains, automobiles, etc.: *a railway tunnel under the river.* *v.* to dig a tunnel: *The workers tunnelled through the mountain.* **tunnelling. tunnelled.**

tuques

tuque (tūk) *n.* a heavy stocking cap, usually made of wool. (*also spelled* **toque.**)

turban (tûr′ bən) *n.* a long cloth wound about a cap or around the head to cover the hair.

turbulence (tûr′ byů ləns) *n.* moving about with great force: *the turbulence of a hurricane.*

turf (tûrf) *n.* soil with short grass growing on it.

turkey

turkey (tûr′ kē) *n.* a large bird that has red-brown feathers and is raised for food. *pl.* **turkeys.**

turn (tûrn) *n.* **1.** a movement in a circle or in part of a circle: *a turn of the wheel.* **2.** a change of direction: *Make a right turn at the traffic light.* **3.** a time for something: *It is my turn to wash the dishes.* *v.* **1.** to make something go around: *She turned the handle.* **2.** to change direction: *Turn right.* **3.** to change into something else: *The snow turned to slush.*

turn away **1.** to look in the opposite direction: *Please turn away while I change my clothes.* **2.** to refuse to accept; to exclude: *There was no more room in the store; the owner had to turn away many customers.*

turn off to stop something from working: *Turn off the radio! Turn off the lights!*

turn on to make something work: *Turn on the television.*

turn up to arrive; to come into view or sight: *We didn't invite Jeanne to the party, but she turned up anyway.*

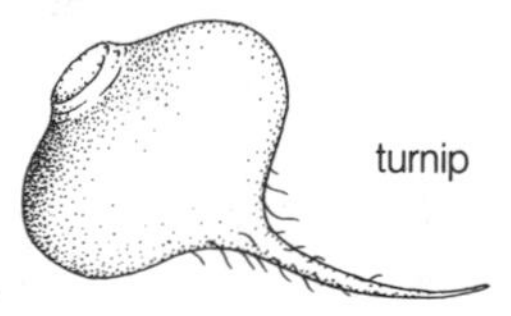

turnip

turnip (tûr′ nip) *n.* a plant with a large, round, white or yellow root that is used as a vegetable.

turnstile (tûrn′ stīl′) *n.* a type of gate that has arms which turn in one direction only; it allows people into or out of a place, one at a time.

turntable (tûrn′ tābl′) *n.* the part of a stereo that plays records.

turpentine (tûr′ pən tīn′) *n.* an oil from pine trees, used to make paints and varnishes thinner.

turquoise (tûr′ koiz) *n.* **1.** a precious stone with a green-blue colour. **2.** a greenish-blue colour. *adj.* having such a colour.

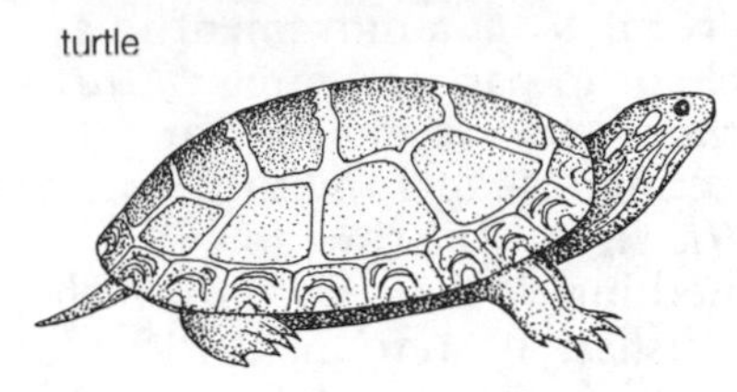
turtle

turtle (tûrtl) *n.* a reptile that lives on land or in water; it has a hard shell, and moves very slowly.

tusk (tusk) *n.* a very long pointed tooth that sticks out from the mouth of an elephant, walrus, etc.

⊖**tutor** (tyū′ tər, tū′ tər) *n.* a teacher who gives private lessons to one student or a small group of students.

TV short for **television.**

twelfth (twelfth) *adj.* following eleventh (12th).

twelve (twelv) *n., adj.* one more than eleven (12).

twenty (twen′ tē) *n., adj.* ten times two (20). *pl.* **twenties.**

twice (twīs) *adv.* two times: *Sydney went to the store twice.*

twig (twig) *n.* a small branch on a tree or bush.

twilight (twī′ līt′) *n.* the period of hazy light just before sunrise or just after sunset.

twin (twin) *n.* either one of two children born at the same time to the same mother.

twine (twīn) *n.* a thick string.

twinkle (twingkl) *n.* to shine with a quick, flashing light: *The stars twinkle in the sky.* **twinkling. twinkled.**

twist (twist) *n.* a curve or bend: *Be careful of the twist in the road.* *v.* **1.** to wind one thread, string, etc., around another. **2.** to curve; to turn: *The road twisted around the mountain.* **3.** to bend something and change its shape: *Alan twisted the wire into a ring.*

two (tū) *n., adj.* one added to one (2). *pl.* **twos.**

tying see **tie.**

⊖**type** (tīp) *n.* **1.** a kind; one of a group of things that share certain qualities: *A maple is a type of tree.* **2.** printed letters: *The type in this book is easy to read.* *v.* to write with a typewriter. **typing. typed.**

typewriter (tīp′ rīt′ ər) *n.* a machine that prints letters, numbers, etc., on paper when the keys are pressed.

typhoon (tī fūn′) *n.* a powerful storm, much like a hurricane, that happens in the regions of the Western Pacific Ocean and the China Sea.

typical (tip′ i kəl) *adj.* usual; like most others: *The weather today is typical for this time of the year.*

typist (tī′ pist) *n.* someone whose job is to type letters, reports, etc.

U

udder (ud′ ər) *n.* the bag-like part of a cow or goat where the milk is made and stored.

UFO short for **unidentified flying object.**

ugly (ug′ lē) *adj.* not pretty or nice to look at: *an ugly picture; an uglier one; the ugliest picture on the wall.*

Ukrainian (yū krān′ yən) *n.* the language spoken in the Ukraine. *adj.* belonging to or coming from the Ukraine.

ukulele (yū′ kə lā′ lē) *n.* a small guitar with four strings, played in Hawaii and other places. (*also spelled* **ukelele.**)

ulcer (ul′ sər) *n.* an open sore that is not a wound and may appear on the skin or inside the body.

umbilical cord (um bil′ ikəl kord′) *n.* the narrow tube that connects a baby to its mother inside the womb.

umbrella

⊖**umbrella** (um brel′ ə) *n.* a thin steel frame covered with material to give protection from the rain or sun. *pl.* **umbrellas.**

⊖**umpire** (um′ pīr) *n.* a person who sees that the rules of a game are followed: *a baseball umpire; a tennis umpire.*

un- a prefix meaning 'not' or 'the opposite of': **unable** means not able; **unfold** means to open out.

unable (un ābl′) *adj.* not able: *Alex was unable to go to work because he was ill.*

unanimous (yū nan′ i məs) *adj.* agreed to by everyone: *The decision was unanimous. Everyone on the team wanted Ram to be captain.*

unavoidable (un′ ə vȯid′ əbl) *adj.* not able to be avoided or prevented: *Her coming late was unavoidable because there was an accident on the highway.*

unbelievable (un′ bi lēv′ əbl) *adj.* impossible or very hard to believe: *an unbelievable story.*

uncertain (un sûr′ tən) *adj.* not certain: *David was uncertain about which way to go.*

uncle (ungkl) *n.* the brother of one's father or mother; the husband of one's aunt.

uncomfortable (un kum′ fər təbl) *adj.* not comfortable: *an uncomfortable chair; an uncomfortable position.*

unconscious (un kon′ shəs) *adj.* not conscious; stunned and not able to see or feel anything.

uncover (un kuv′ ər) *v.* **1.** to take the cover or wrapping off: *Zandra uncovered the package.* **2.** to make known; to find: *to uncover a secret plan.*

undecided (un′ di sīd′ əd) *adj.* not certain; not having reached a decision: *We were undecided about what to do. Magda wanted to stay home, Ralph wanted to go to the hockey game, and I wanted to go to the movies.*

under (un′ dər) *prep.* below; less than; beneath: *under the sea; under two dollars.*

under- a prefix meaning 'below', 'less than', or 'beneath': **underwater** means beneath the water; to **undercharge** means to charge less than the correct price.

underarm (un′ dər ȧrm′) *n.* the hollow place under a person's arm, at the shoulder; the armpit.

underground (un′ dər graůnd′) *adj.* under the ground: *an underground road.*

undergrowth (un′ dər grōth′) *n.* small plants and bushes growing close to the ground.

underline (un′ dər līn′) *n.* a line drawn under some writing, often to show that something is important. *v.* to draw a line under some writing. **underlining. underlined.**

underneath (un′ dər nēth′) *prep.* directly under: *Your key is underneath the wallet.*

underpants (un′ dər pants′) *n.pl.* shorts worn under a person's regular clothing, next to the skin.

understand (un′ dər stand′) *v.* **1.** to know the meaning of: *I understand three languages. I don't understand how this machine works.* **2.** to know; to have been told: *I understand that your cousin is my friend.* **understanding. understood** (un′ dər stůd′).

undertaker (un′ dər tak′ ər) *n.* a person whose job is to arrange funerals.

underwater (un′ dər wȯt′ ər) *adj.* found or used below the surface of the water: *underwater plants; underwater diving equipment. adv.* below the surface of the water: *to swim underwater.*

underwear (un′ dər wer′) *n.* clothes worn under a person's outer clothes.

undo (un dū′) *v.* to loosen, open, or unfasten something: *Jimmy undid the buttons of his coat.* **undoing. undid** (un did′). he has **undone** (un dun′). he **undoes** (un duz′).

undress (un dres′) *v.* to take off clothes. **undressing. undressed.** he **undresses.**

unemployed (un′ im plȯid′) *adj.* out of work; without a job.

unemployment (un′ im plȯi′ mənt) *n.* the condition of being unemployed.

uneven (un ē′ vən) *adj.* not even, flat, or smooth: *an uneven board.*

unexpected (un′ ik spek′ təd) *adj.* not expected; coming as a surprise: *an unexpected present.*

unfair (un fer′) *adj.* not fair; not right.

unfasten (un fas′ ən) *v.* to open something that has been fastened: *to unfasten a seat belt.*

unforgettable (un′ fər get′ əbl) *adj.* impossible to forget: *The trip to the Rocky Mountains was unforgettable.*

unfortunate (un for′ chən ət) *adj.* not lucky; having bad luck.

unfriendly (un frend′ lē) *adj.* not friendly: *an unfriendly person; an unfriendlier one; the unfriendliest one of all.*

ungrateful (un grāt′ fəl) *adj.* not grateful; not thankful.

unhappy (un hap′ ē) *adj.* not happy; not pleased: *an unhappy child; an unhappier one; the unhappiest child of all.*

unhealthy (un hel′ thē) *adj.* **1.** not in good health: *an unhealthy person; an unhealthier one; the unhealthiest one of all.* **2.** not good for the health: *Some climates are unhealthy.*

unidentified (un′ ī den′ ti fīd) *adj.* not recognized; unknown; strange.

uniform (yū′ ni fȯrm′) *n.* special clothes worn to show that people belong to the same group. *adj.* all the same; identical: *The walls are painted a uniform colour.*

unimportant (un′ im pȯr′ tənt) *adj.* not important.

⊖**union** (yūn′ yən) *n.* **1.** a joining together: *Marriage is a union of a husband and wife.* **2.** a group of workers in the same occupation who have joined together to make sure that they are all treated fairly by the people who employ them.

unique (yū nēk′) *adj.* the only one of its kind; rare or unusual: *The Mona Lisa is a unique painting.*

unit (yū′ nit) *n.* **1.** one person or one complete thing or group that is part of a larger group. **2.** an amount used in measurement: *The metre is a unit of length.*

unite (yū nīt′) *v.* to join together: *The players united to form a team.* **uniting. united.**

United States of America (yū nīt′ əd stāts′ əv ə mer′ i kə) the country that forms the southern border of Canada and includes Alaska.

unity (yū′ ni tē) *n.* the condition or feeling of being joined with others to form a whole: *There is unity among the hospital staff. All do their best to help the patients.* *pl.* **unities.**

universe (yū′ ni vûrs′) *n.* everything that exists, including the earth, the other planets, the stars, the sun, and outer space.

university (yū′ ni vûr′ si tē) *n.* a place for higher education, usually made up of different colleges, which awards degrees to graduates. *pl.* **universities.**

unkind (un kīnd′) *adj.* not kind; cruel.

unknown (un nōn′) *adj.* not known; strange.

unlawful (unlȯ′ fəl) *adj.* illegal; not allowed by law.

unless (un les′) *conj.* except if: *I shall not go unless the weather is good.*

unlike (un līk′) *prep.* different from; not similar to: *Unlike most of my family, I like vegetables.*

unlikely (un līk′ lē) *adj.* probably not going to happen: *It is unlikely that Fran will be late.*

unload (un lōd′) *v.* **1.** to remove a load from a ship or a truck or other vehicle. **2.** to take the shells from a gun, pistol, etc.

unlock (un lok′) *v.* to open a lock by using a key or a combination number.

unlucky (un luk′ ē) *adj.* not lucky; having bad luck or causing bad luck: *an unlucky man; an unlucky day; an unluckier one; the unluckiest one of all.*

unnecessary (un nes′ ə ser′ ē) *adj.* not necessary; not needed.

unpack (un pak′) *v.* to empty from a bag, suitcase, or other container the things that have been packed into it.

unpleasant (un plez′ ənt) *adj.* not pleasant or nice: *The soup has an unpleasant smell. What did you put in it?*

unplug (un plug′) *v.* **1.** to take away material that blocks or is in the way: *I'm glad the plumber unplugged our sink; now the drain will work better.* **2.** to stop the flow of electricity by removing the connection: *Please unplug the lamp; I want to replace the socket.* **unplugging. unplugged.**

unsafe (un sāf′) *adj.* not safe: *It is unsafe to drive at night without lights. Some parts of the city are unsafe at night.*

unskilled (un skild′) *adj.* not having or requiring certain skills or experience: *The new factory is hiring unskilled workers.*

untie (un tī′) *v.* to undo something that has been tied. **untying. untied.**

until (un til′) *conj.* up to the time when: *Stay here until ten o'clock.*

unusual (un yū′ zhū əl) *adj.* not usual; strange: *It is unusual for Jean to be late.*

unwrap (un rap′) *v.* to take the wrapping off: *to unwrap a package.* **unwrapping. unwrapped.**

up (up) *prep.* **1.** from a lower to a higher place: *We walked up the hill.* **2.** towards the source: *We sailed up the river.* **3.** to a place further along: *The school is up the street. adj., adv.* **1.** to a higher place or level: *The price of bread is up.* **2.** to or in a straight position: *Stand up!* **3.** out of bed: *It is time to get up.* **4.** at an end: *The game is up.*
up to **1.** close to: *He walked up to his teacher.* **2.** as many as: *Up to six people can stand in the elevator.* **3.** depending on: *Are you having a party? It's up to my parents.* **4.** busy with: *The children are up to mischief.*

upholstery (up hōl′ stər ē) *n.* the stuffing and coverings of a piece of furniture: *Our couch has holes in it; it needs new upholstery.*

upon (ə pon′) *prep.* on or on top of: *She stood upon a chair to reach the shelf.*

upper (up′ ər) *adj.* higher or top: *He bit his upper lip.*

upright (up′ rīt′) *adj.* standing or being straight up and down: *They bought an upright piano small enough to fit into their living room.*

upset (up set′) *v.* **1.** to knock over: *I upset the plant when I was cleaning.* **2.** to make very sad: *The bad news upset us.* **3.** to make ill: *I ate too much cake, and it upset my stomach.* **upsetting. upset.**

upstairs (up sterz′) *adv.* up to or on a higher floor.

upstream (up strēm′) *adv.* against the current of a river.

up-to-date (up′ tə dāt′) *adj.* modern; in the latest style or having the most recent information: *The map is not up-to-date because it does not show the new highway.*

upwards, upward (up′ wərdz, up′ wərd) *adv.* towards a higher place or level.

urban (ûr′ bən) *adj.* having to do with cities and towns: *We prefer living in urban areas. They prefer rural areas.*

urge (ûrj) *n.* a sudden strong wish to do something: *Tai had an urge to go swimming. v.* to try hard to get someone to do something; to persuade: *We urged her to go to the doctor.* **urging. urged.**

urgent (ûr′ jənt) *adj.* needing attention at once; very important: *We received an urgent message for help.*

urinate (yūr′ i nāt′) *v.* to pass urine out of the body. **urinating. urinated.**

urine (yūr′ in) *n.* the waste liquid passed out of the body by the kidneys.

us (us) *pron.* me and others: *Please help us.*

use (yūs) *n.* **1.** the act of using: *You may have the use of the car when I am away.* **2.** a function; a purpose; the way something is used: *What is the use of that tool? A knife has many uses.*

⊖**use** (yūz) *v.* to put to a purpose: *Use the umbrella for protection against the rain.* **using. used.**
use up to finish: *We used up all the tomatoes to make the salad.*
used to **1.** familiar with through regular contact or habit: *I'm used to getting up early each morning.* **2.** indicating a former habit: *He used to smoke, but he quit this habit a year ago.*

⊖**used** (yūzd) *adj.* not new: *a used car.*

useful (yūs′ fəl) *adj.* helpful: *a useful idea; a useful tool.*

useless (yūs′ ləs) *adj.* not helpful; worth nothing: *An umbrella with holes is useless.*

usher (ush′ ər) *n.* someone who shows people their seats in a theatre, stadium, or other place.

usual (yū′ zhū əl) *adj.* as generally happens; regular; common: *Six o'clock is our usual time for dinner.*

usually (yū′ zhū əl ē) *adv.* most of the time: *I usually have bread with dinner.*

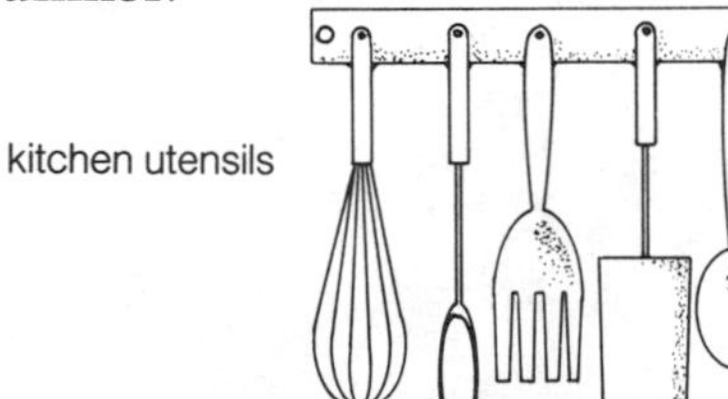
kitchen utensils

utensil (yū ten′ sil) *n.* a piece of equipment, usually one used in the kitchen: *Pots, spoons, and measuring cups are some cooking utensils.*

uterus (yū′ tə rəs) *n.* the womb; the organ of female mammals where the embryo and fetus develop before birth. *pl.* **uteri** (yū′ tə rī).

V

vacant (vā′ kənt) *adj.* empty; not in use; not occupied: *a vacant house.*

vacation (və kā′ shən) *n.* a holiday: *They left for their summer vacation.*

vaccinate (vak′ si nāt′) *v.* to inject someone with a vaccine. **vaccinating. vaccinated.**

vaccination (vak′ si nā′ shən) *n.* an injection of vaccine into the body.

vaccine (vak sēn′) *n.* a preparation that is injected into the body, to protect people against polio, measles, and other diseases.

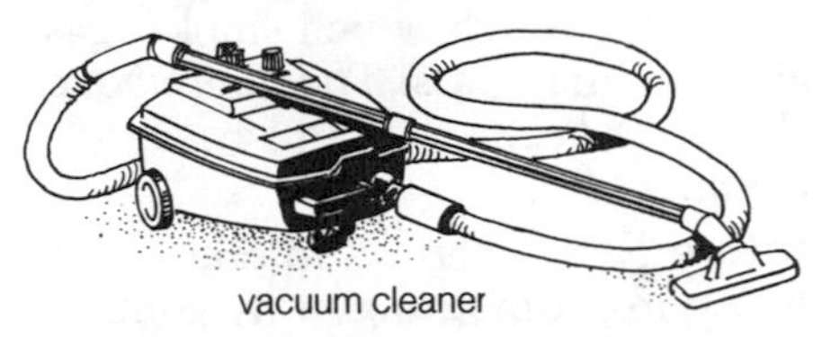

vacuum cleaner

vacuum (vak′ yū əm, vak′ yum) *n.* **1.** an empty space with no air in it. **2.** a vacuum cleaner. *v.* to clean with a vacuum cleaner.

vacuum cleaner (vak′ yū əm klēn′ ər, vak′ yum klēn′ ər) a machine that uses suction to clean carpets, floors, curtains, etc.

vagina (və jī′ nə) *n.* the passage in a woman that leads out from the uterus. *pl.* **vaginas.**

vague (vāg) *adj.* uncertain; not clear: *I have only a vague idea about where we are. Your idea is even vaguer. He doesn't have the vaguest notion.*

vain (vān) *adj.* **1.** proud; having too high an opinion of oneself: *He is a vain man, always admiring himself in the mirror.* **2.** useless; not having the desired result: *a vain attempt to win the race.*
in vain without the desired result: *They tried in vain to win the game.*

valid (val′ id) *adj.* **1.** legal; official: *My passport is valid for one more year.* **2.** truthful; based on facts; acceptable: *Do you have a valid excuse for not taking the test?*

valley (val′ ē) *n.* an area of low land between hills or mountains, often with a river running through it. *pl.* **valleys.**

valuable (val′ yū əbl) *adj.* having great value; worth much money: *a valuable ring.*

value (val′ yū) *n.* **1.** the amount of money something could be sold for: *What is the value of your ring?* **2.** the worth or importance of something: *Friendship has great value.* *v.* to believe that something is important: *We value our good health.* **valuing. valued.**

valve (valv) *n.* a part in a pipe that controls the flow of liquid, air, or gas.

van

van (van) *n.* a covered truck for carrying goods.

Vancouver (van kū′ vər) *n.* the largest city in the province of British Columbia.

Vancouver Island (van kū′ vər ī′ land) a large island just off the west coast of British Columbia.

vandal (van′ dəl) *n.* someone who destroys property just for pleasure.

vane (vān) *n.* a flat or curved metal blade: *A weather vane is attached to a high object, and shows the direction of the wind.*

vanilla (və nil′ ə) *n.* a flavouring used in candy, cake, ice cream, etc. It comes from the vanilla bean, which grows in hot climates.

vanish (van′ ish) *v.* to disappear suddenly; to go out of sight: *The magician made the scarf vanish.* **vanishing. vanished.** it **vanishes.**

vapour, vapor (vā′ pər) *n.* liquid in the form of gas, as seen in steam, fog, mist, etc.

variety (və rī′ ə tē) *n.* **1.** a number of different things: *a variety of books in the library.* **2.** change; different things to be done: *Does your job have variety, or do you do the same work all day? pl.* **varieties.**

various (vər′ i əs, var′ i əs) *adj.* several, and different from one another: *I like various kinds of books.*

varnish (var′ nish) *n.* a liquid applied to wood or other surfaces; it provides a hard and shiny covering when it dries. *pl.* **varnishes.**

vary (ver′ ē, var′ ē) *v.* to make different; to change: *During March, the temperature always varies.* **varying. varied.** it **varies.**

vase (vāz, våz) *n.* a jar or other container for holding flowers.

vast (vast) *adj.* very large in size or amount: *a vast number of people filled the stadium.*

vat (vat) *n.* a large container for liquids.

vault (vȯlt) *n.* a safe room, found in banks and other places, used to store money or other valuable things. *v.* to leap over something, using a pole or the hands: *Richard vaulted the low fence.*

veal (vēl) *n.* the meat from a young calf.

vegetable (vej′ təbl, vej′ ə təbl) *n.* a plant or part of a plant used for food.

vehicle (vē′ ikl) *n.* something built to be driven by an engine or pulled by an animal, and to carry people or things over land: *A car is a motor vehicle.*

veil (vāl) *n.* a thin piece of cloth worn to protect or hide the face from the sun, insects, etc.

vein (vān) *n.* one of the thin, long tubes in the body that carry blood to the heart after the blood has been pumped through the body.

velvet (vel′ vət) *n.* a kind of cloth that is very soft and very smooth on one side.

vending machine (vend′ ing mə shēn′) a machine that stores cold drinks, hot drinks, candy, or other things, and releases them when a coin or coins are put into a slot.

venom (ven′ əm) *n.* the poison of some snakes and spiders.

⊖**vent** (vent) *n.* an opening in a wall or floor through which smoke, gas, air, etc., may pass: *The vent above the stove keeps the kitchen air clean.*

venture (ven′ chər) *v.* to take a risk by saying something or by going somewhere: *He ventured into the forest alone.* **venturing. ventured.**

Venus (vē′ nəs) *n.* **1.** in ancient times, the Roman goddess of love. **2.** one of the planets.

verandah, veranda (və ran′ də) *n.* an outdoor platform with a roof, joined to a house. *pl.* **verandahs, verandas.**

verb (vûrb) *n.* an action word; a word in a sentence that says what someone or something is doing: 'go, dream, move, fall,' and 'open' can all be used as verbs.

verdict (vûr′ dikt) *n.* the decision of a jury at the end of a trial: *The jury came to a verdict of guilty.*

⊖**verse** (vûrs) *n.* **1.** poetry: *A poet writes verse.* **2.** a group of lines in a poem.

version (vûr′ zhən) *n.* one person's telling or description of something: *Three people saw the same accident. Each one had a different version of what happened.*

vertical (vûr′ ti kəl) *adj.* straight up and down; in an upright position: *A tower is built in a vertical position. A vertical line is drawn from top to bottom; a horizontal line is drawn from left to right.*

very (ver′ ē) *adv.* extremely: *a very good singer; a very bad dancer; a very tall man; a very nice child; to be very happy.*

vessel (ves′ əl) *n.* a ship or large boat.

⊖**vest** (vest) *n.* a sleeveless piece of clothing worn over a shirt and often under a jacket.

vet (vet) short for **veterinarian**, a doctor who treats animals.

veteran (vet′ ər ən, vet′ rən) *n.* **1.** a person who has been a member of the armed forces. **2.** anyone who has been working at something for a long time.

via (vī′ ə, vē′ ə) *prep.* by way of: *We travelled from Regina to Edmonton via Saskatoon.*

vibrate (vī′ brāt) *v.* to tremble or shake: *The table vibrated from the loud music in the room.* **vibrating. vibrated.**

vibration (vī brā′ shən) *n.* a trembling or shaking feeling.

vicious (vish′ əs) *adj.* wicked or evil; very mean: *a vicious criminal.*

victim (vik′ tim) *n.* someone who has been killed, hurt, or robbed.

Victoria (vik tôr′ i ə) *n.* the capital city of the province of British Columbia.

victory (vik′ tə rē) *n.* a win in a battle, game, or contest. *pl.* **victories.**

videotape (vid′ ē ō tāp′) *n.* a special tape used for recording pictures.

view (vyū) *n.* **1.** everything that can be seen from one place: *a view of the ocean.* **2.** an opinion: *Robert and his sister have different views on politics.* *v.* to see or look at; to watch: *We viewed the slides of Inez's trip.*

⊖**vigour, vigor** (vig′ ər) *n.* strength; energy: *My old dog is still full of vigour.*

village (vil′ ij) *n.* a small group of houses and stores which form a community that is smaller than a town.

⊖**villain** (vil′ ən) *n.* a wicked person: *The villain in the story scared the young children.*

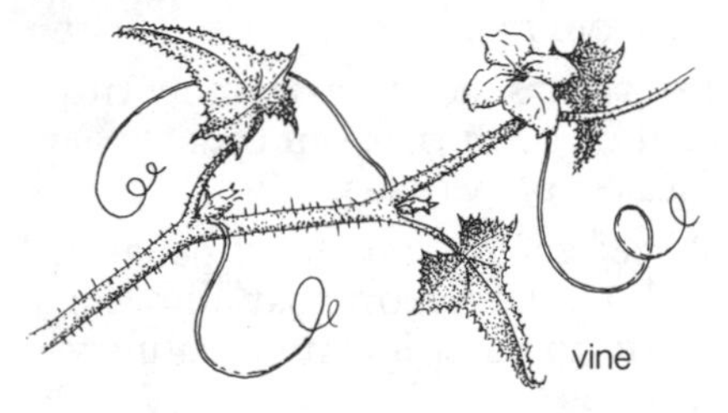
vine

vine (vīn) *n.* a climbing plant: *Grapes, cucumbers, and melons are vines.*

vinegar (vin′ ə gər) *n.* a sour liquid used to flavour or preserve food.

vineyard (vin′ yərd) *n.* a large piece of land where grapes for wine are grown.

vinyl (vī′ nil) *n.* a plastic used for making records, floor polishes, covers for automobile seats, etc.

viola (vī ō′ lə) *n.* a musical instrument similar to a violin, but much larger and with a deeper tone. *pl.* **violas.**

violence (vī′ ə ləns) *n.* great force, often causing harm to people or property.

violent (vī′ ə lənt) *adj.* very rough and causing harm to people or property: *a violent storm; a violent crime.*

violet (vī′ ə lət) *n.* a small plant with blue, purple, yellow, or white flowers.

violin (vī′ ə lin′) *n.* a wooden musical instrument with four strings, played with a bow.

violinist (vī′ ə lin′ ist) *n.* a violin player.

virgin (vûr′ jin) *n.* a person who has never experienced sexual intercourse. *adj.* pure; clean: *This is virgin soil. It has never been farmed.*

virtue (vûr′ tyū) *n.* **1.** a good quality; an advantage: *Good habits are a great virtue. Your new design has many virtues.* **2.** good character: *She is always honest; she is a woman of virtue.*

virus (vī′ rəs) *n.* an extremely tiny form of germ that can cause disease. *pl.* **viruses.**

visa (vē′ zə) *n.* an official paper or mark on a passport that allows a person to enter a certain country. *pl.* **visas.**

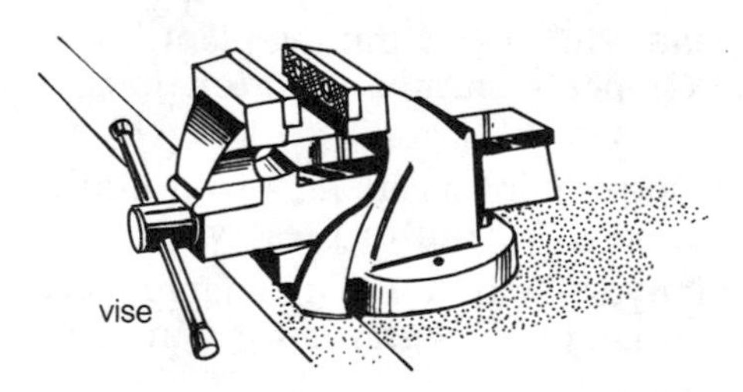

vise (vīs) *n.* a tool that is used to hold a piece of wood, metal, etc., in place while it is being worked on.

⊖**visible** (viz′ əbl) *adj.* able to be seen: *Is the moon visible tonight?*

vision (vizh′ ən) *n.* **1.** the sense of sight; the ability to see: *Eyeglasses improve a person's vision.* **2.** a picture in the mind.

visit (viz′ it) *n.* a short time spent at some place, such as a person's home. *v.* to go to see someone or something: *We visited the zoo.*

visitor (viz′ i tər) *n.* someone who visits; a guest.

visual (vizh′ ū əl) *adj.* having to do with sight or seeing: *The eyes are visual organs.*

vitamin (vī′ tə min) *n.* one of many substances that are needed for good health: *Citrus fruit is a good source of vitamin C.*

vocabulary (vō kab′ yū ler′ ē) *n.* all the words that a person knows: *Ed has a large vocabulary.* *pl.* **vocabularies.**

vocation (vō kā′ shən) *n.* the type of work that a person decides he or she should or can do: *I am interested in a vocation that involves languages.*

voice (vȯis) *n.* the sound of speaking or singing.

void (vȯid) *adj.* not valid; not effective: *He made a mistake on his cheque, so he wrote the word 'void' on it. Now, nobody can cash it.*

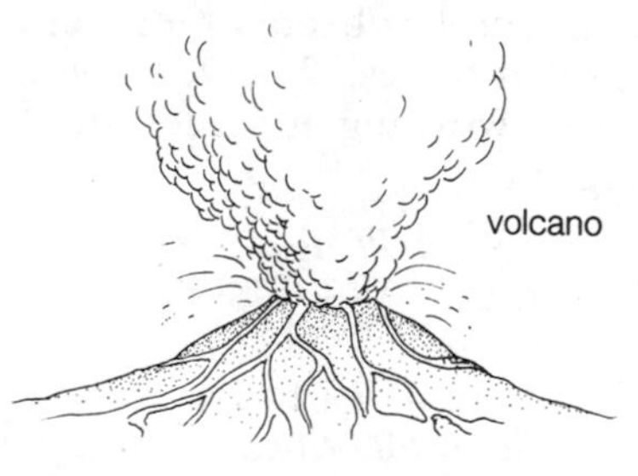

volcano (vol kā′ nō) *n.* an opening in the surface of the earth through which melted rock, hot ashes, and flames pour out. *pl.* **volcanoes.**

volleyball (vol′ i bȯl′) *n.* **1.** a game in which two teams, on either side of a net, hit a large ball from side to side over the net. **2.** the ball used in this game.

volt (vōlt) *n.* a unit that measures the force of an electric current.

volume (vol′ yūm) *n.* **1.** a book, or one of a set of books or magazines: *Some dictionaries are in two volumes.* **2.** loudness: *Please lower the volume of the radio.* **3.** the amount of space something fills: *What is the volume of the box?* **4.** a large amount: *a volume of traffic on the road.*

volunteer (vol′ ən tēr′) *n.* someone who offers to do some work without having to, or without pay. *v.* to offer to do something as a volunteer: *He volunteered to work on the holiday.*

vomit (vom′ it) *n.* the substance brought up from the stomach when a person is sick. *v.* to bring up material from the stomach.

vote (vōt) *n.* a person's choice made in an election: *She won the election by five votes.* *v.* to say or write a choice in an election. **voting. voted.**

vow (vaủ) *n.* a sincere promise: *The bride and groom exchanged vows.* *v.* to make a vow.

vowel (vaủ′ əl) *n.* any of the five letters a, e, i, o, u.

voyage (vȯi′ ij) *n.* a long trip, usually by water or through space.

vulture (vul′ chər) *n.* a large bird, similar to a hawk, that has a bald head and eats dead animals.

W

waddle (wodl) *n.* a swaying kind of walk. *v.* to walk in such a way, as a duck does. **waddling. waddled.**

wade (wād) *v.* to walk through shallow water. **wading. waded.**

wafer (wā′ fər) *n.* a thin, crisp cookie.

waffle (wofl) *n.* a thin, crisp cake that has a pattern of squares on each side: *Waffles are often eaten with syrup at breakfast.*

wag (wag) *v.* to move quickly from side to side: *The dog wagged its tail.* **wagging. wagged.**

wage (wāj) *n.* money employees get for doing work.

wagon (wag′ ən) *n.* **1.** a vehicle with four wheels, usually one pulled by horses. **2.** a small cart for children to pull.

wail (wāl) *n.* a long cry that shows pain or sadness. *v.* to make such a cry.

waist (wāst) *n.* the part of a person's body between the ribs and hips.

wait (wāt) *n.* the act of staying in a place until something happens or someone arrives: *We had a long wait for a bus.* *v.* to stay in a place until something happens or someone arrives: *We waited in the rain for Mary.*

waiter (wāt′ ər) *n.* a man who is paid to serve meals in a restaurant.

waitress (wāt′rəs) *n.* a woman who is paid to serve meals in a restaurant. *pl.* **waitresses.**

wake (wāk) *n.* the staying up all night with a dead body before the burial. *v.* (often used with **up**) **1.** to stop someone from sleeping longer: *The baby woke her parents up when she began to cry.* **2.** to stop sleeping: *I wake up at six o'clock each morning.* **waking. woke** (wōk), or **waked.** I have **woken** (wōk′ ən).

walk (wȯk) *n.* a trip on foot: *Let's take a walk in the park.* *v.* to go on foot: *They walked to the store.*

walkout (wȯk′ aůt′) *n.* a strike by workers: *The walkout at the factory lasted for two weeks.*

wall (wȯl) *n.* a structure built to form the side of a building or room.

wallet (wol′ ət) *n.* a flat, folding case, usually made of leather, for holding paper money, cards, and pictures.

wallpaper (wȯl′ pā′ pər) *n.* paper, often with designs, that is used to cover and decorate the walls of a room.

walnut (wol′ nut′, wȯl′ nut′) *n.* **1.** a hard, round nut with a rough shell. **2.** the tree that produces this nut.

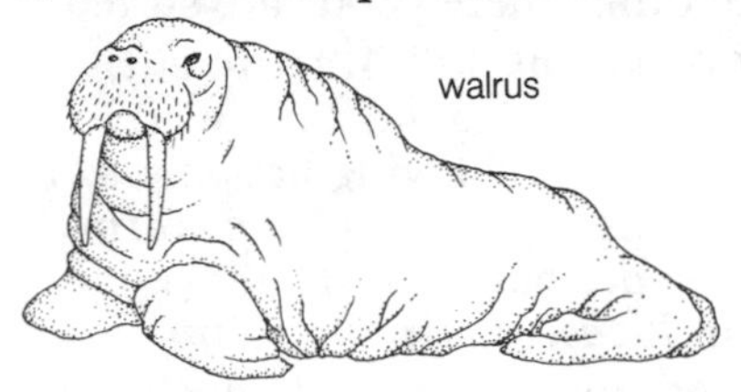

walrus (wol′ rəs, wȯl′ rəs) *n.* a large sea mammal of the arctic region that has flippers and two long tusks. *pl.* **walruses.**

waltz (wȯltz) *n.* a graceful dance with a gliding motion. *pl.* **waltzes.** *v.* to dance a waltz. **waltzing. waltzed.** she **waltzes.**

wander (won′ dər) *v.* **1.** to move from one place to another, not having any real purpose: *We wandered through the shopping centre, looking at windows.* **2.** to go off the correct path: *The child wandered off the road and got lost.*

want (wont) *v.* to wish to have or do something: *She wants a pair of skates. He wants to learn to skate.*

war (wȯr) *n.* **1.** a long fight with weapons and soldiers, usually between countries. **2.** any long fight.

ward (wȯrd) *n.* **1.** a large bedroom for patients in a hospital. **2.** a division or part of a city or town. **3.** a young person left in the care of an older person known as a guardian.

warden (wȯr′ dən) *n.* **1.** a person in charge of a prison. **2.** a person who guards or protects something, such as areas of parkland.

wardrobe (wȯrd′ rōb′) *n.* **1.** the clothes that one person owns: *My sister has a large wardrobe.* **2.** a closet for clothes.

-ware a suffix that is used to mean a category or group: **silverware** means items made of silver; **dinnerware** means the materials needed to serve and eat food.

warehouse (wer′ haůs′) *n.* a large building where goods are stored.

warm (wȯrm) *adj.* **1.** fairly hot, between hot and cold: *a warm climate.* **2.** showing happiness: *The winning team received a warm welcome home.* *v.* to make fairly hot: *Please warm the soup.*

warmth (wȯrmth) *n.* the feeling of being warm.

warn (wȯrn) *v.* to tell someone about possible danger or trouble: *Michel warned Guy to stay off the thin ice.*

warning (wȯrn′ ing) *n.* something told or heard, telling of possible danger: *The sailors listened carefully to the storm warning.*

warp (wȯrp) *v.* to bend or twist out of shape: *The heat warped the wood.*

warrant (wȯr′ ənt) *n.* an official paper that gives an officer authority to arrest a person or search a place.

warranty (wȯr′ ən tē) *n.* a written promise to fix or replace something if anything goes wrong with it before a certain time: *Our new radio has a five-year warranty.* *pl.* **warranties.**

wart (wȯrt) *n.* a small, hard lump that grows on the skin.

wary (we′ rē) *adj.* careful; cautious; watching for danger: *a wary person; a warier one; the wariest one of all.*

was (wuz, woz) *v.* a form of the verb **to be**; used with 'I', 'he', 'she', or 'it', or with a name or other noun: *I was going to sleep. He was away. She was on holiday. It was raining.*

wash (wȯsh) *n.* the act of cleaning: *The car needs a wash.* *v.* to clean with soap and water. **washing. washed.** he **washes.**

washer (wȯsh′ ər) *n.* **1.** a person or machine that washes. **2.** a flat metal or rubber ring placed between a nut and bolt, often to stop leaks.

washing machine (wȯsh′ ing mə shēn′) a machine for washing clothes, sheets, towels, etc.

washroom (wȯsh′ rūm′) *n.* a room that has a toilet and sink: *Is there a washroom in the restaurant?*

wasn't (wuz′ ənt, woz′ ənt) short for **was not.**

wasp

wasp (wosp) *n.* a stinging insect that has a narrow waist and black and yellow stripes.

waste (wāst) *n.* **1.** a poor use of something: *The class was a waste of time because the teacher never arrived.* **2.** garbage; something that can be thrown away. *v.* to use carelessly; to spend more money, or use more time or material than is needed: *If you buy too much food, you may waste some of it.* **wasting. wasted.**

watch (wȯch) *n.* a small clock, usually worn on the wrist. *pl.* **watches.** *v.* to look at: *I watched television for an hour last night.* **watching. watched.** she **watches.**

water (wȯ′ tər) *n.* the liquid that falls as rain. *v.* to put water on: *to water the plants.*

waterfall (wȯ′ tər fȯl′) *n.* a stream of water falling from a high place.

watermelon (wȯ′ tər mel′ ən) *n.* a large melon that has a sweet, pink pulp, many seeds, and a thick, green rind.

waterproof (wȯ′ tər prūf′) *adj.* not letting water through: *a waterproof coat.*

water ski (wȯ′ tər skē′) one of a pair of skis used for gliding along water. *pl.* **water skis.**

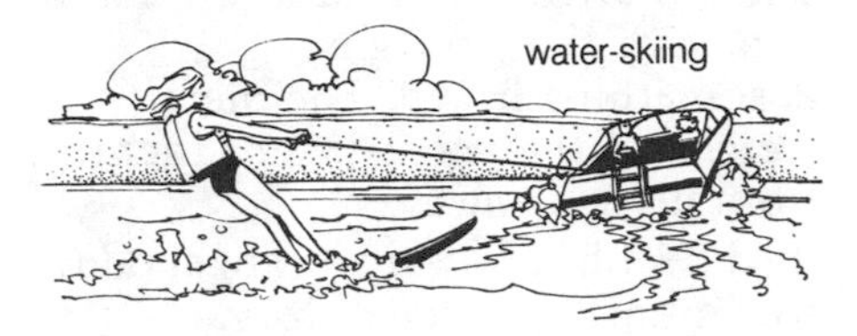

water-ski (wȯ′ tər skē′) *v.* to glide along water on water skis while holding a rope that is attached to a motorboat. **water-skiing. water-skied.** she **water-skis.**

watertight (wȯ′ tər tīt′) *adj.* waterproof.

watt (wot) *n.* a unit of electric power: *This light bulb is too bright. It should be 60 watts, not 100 watts.*

wave (wāv) *n.* **1.** a rippling movement: *an ocean wave.* **2.** a movement of the hand and arm meaning hello or good-bye. *v.* to move the hand and arm as a way of saying hello or good-bye. **waving. waved.**

wavy (wā′ vē) *adj.* looking like waves: *wavy lines; wavy hair; wavier hair; the waviest hair of all.*

wax (waks) *n.* **1.** a solid substance made by bees. It is used to make candles and other things. **2.** any substance that resembles this: *furniture wax. pl.* **waxes.** *v.* to put wax onto something; to polish: *to wax furniture; to wax the floor.* **waxing. waxed.** he **waxes.**

way (wā) *n.* **1.** a road; a direction: *Which way are you going?* **2.** a plan for doing something; a method: *This is the way to use the computer.* **3.** distance: *Edmonton is a long way from Halifax.* *pl.* **ways.**
by the way on the same subject; as well; in addition: *By the way, have you heard the news about Chantal? I'm going to visit Paul tonight. By the way, did you know he got married last week?*

we (wē) *pron.* the word used to refer to yourself and one or more other people: *We are going to visit our friends.*

weak (wēk) *adj.* not strong; *a weak animal; weak tea.*

wealth (welth) *n.* a large amount of money and possessions.

wealthy (wel′ thē) *adj.* having wealth: *a wealthy person; a wealthier one; the wealthiest person in the world.*

weapon (wep′ ən) *n.* anything used for fighting or hunting: *Swords, spears, and guns are some weapons.*

wear (wer) *v.* **1.** to be dressed in something; to have clothing on part of the body: *Marie wore her new coat. Remember to wear your gloves.* **2.** to become weak or damaged from much use: *The arms of the old chair are worn.* **wearing. wore** (wȯr). I have **worn** (wȯrn).
wear out 1. to become useless after being worn for some time: *The pants are worn out at the knees.* **2.** to make or become very tired: *A long run can wear me out.*

weary (wēr′ ē) *adj.* very tired: *a weary person; a wearier one; the weariest one of all.*

weasel (wē′ zəl) *n.* a small, thin animal that has red-brown fur and feeds on smaller animals such as birds and mice.

weather (weth′ ər) *n.* what it is like outside: *Weather is usually wet or dry, hot or cold, sunny or cloudy, windy or calm.*
Note: Do not confuse **weather** with **whether**; **whether** means 'if'.

weatherproof (weth′ ər prūf′) *adj.* protecting against snow, rain, cold, or wind.

weave (wēv) *v.* to make cloth by putting threads over and under one another. **weaving. wove** (wōv). I have **woven** (wōv′ ən).

weaver (wē′ vər) *n.* a person who does weaving.

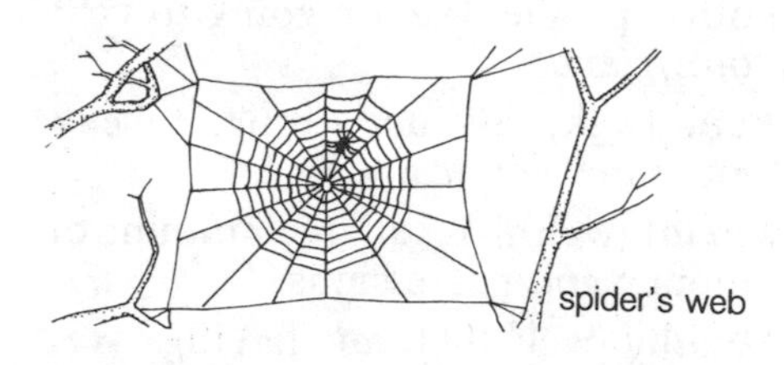
spider's web

web (web) *n.* **1.** a net of sticky threads spun by a spider to catch flying insects. **2.** the skin between the toes of some water birds and animals, such as ducks, geese, and otters.

wed (wed) *v.* to marry. **wedding. wedded**, or **wed.**

we'd (wēd) short for **we had** or **we would.**

wedding (wed′ ing) *n.* the time when a man and woman become husband and wife.

wedge (wej) *n.* a v-shaped piece of wood or metal, very thin at one end and wider at the other.

Wednesday (wenz′ dā) *n.* the fourth day of the week. *pl.* **Wednesdays.**

weed (wēd) *n.* any useless wild plant. *v.* to remove the weeds from an area: *Jack weeded the garden.*

week (wēk) *n.* a period of seven successive days.

weekday (wēk′ dā′) *n.* any day of the week except Saturday and Sunday. *pl.* **weekdays.**

weekend (wēk′ end′) *n.* Saturday and Sunday, or the period of time between Friday evening and Monday morning.

weekly (wēk′ lē) *adv.* once a week: *The magazine comes out weekly.* *adj.* coming out or happening every week.

weep (wēp) *v.* to cry; to sob. **weeping. wept** (wept).

weigh (wā) *v.* to find how heavy a person or thing is by using a scale.

weight (wāt) *n.* **1.** the amount that a person or thing weighs.
2. something heavy: *The metal weight on the papers keeps them from blowing away.*

weird (wērd) *adj.* very strange; odd: *weird noises; a weird story.*

welcome (wel′ kəm) *n.* a friendly greeting: *We gave our visitors a happy welcome.* *v.* to receive someone in a friendly way: *We welcomed our friends at the bus station.* **welcoming. welcomed.**
you're welcome a statement made to a person who has said, 'thank you'.

weld (weld) *v.* to join pieces of metal to each other after they have been heated.

welfare (wel′ fer′) *n.* **1.** health and happiness: *We have not heard from our cousin for a long time, and are concerned about her welfare.* **2.** a government agency that provides money and other help to people in need.

well (wel) *n.* a deep hole made in the ground to get out the water, oil, or gas at the bottom.

adj. healthy; not ill: *I feel very well.* *adv.* in the right way: *You did the job well.*

we'll (wēl) short for **we will** or **we shall.**

well-to-do (wel′ tə dū′) *adj.* having more money than most people do: *They are a well-to-do family. They live in a very large house and have three cars.*

went see **go.**

wept see **weep.**

were (wûr) *v.* a form of the verb **to be**; used with 'you', 'they', and 'we', or with names or other nouns: *You were going to sleep. They were skating. We were away.*

we're (wēr) short for **we are.**

west (west) *n.* the direction of sunset, opposite to east.

western (west′ ərn) *adj.* in the direction of the west: *Vancouver is in western British Columbia.*

West Indies (west′ in′ dēz) islands in the Atlantic Ocean between South America and Florida.

wet (wet) *adj.* full of a liquid or covered with a liquid: *a wet towel; a wetter one; the wettest towel of all.* *v.* to make wet: *Please wet the cloth and wipe off the car.* **wetting. wetted**, or **wet.**

we've (wēv) short for **we have.**

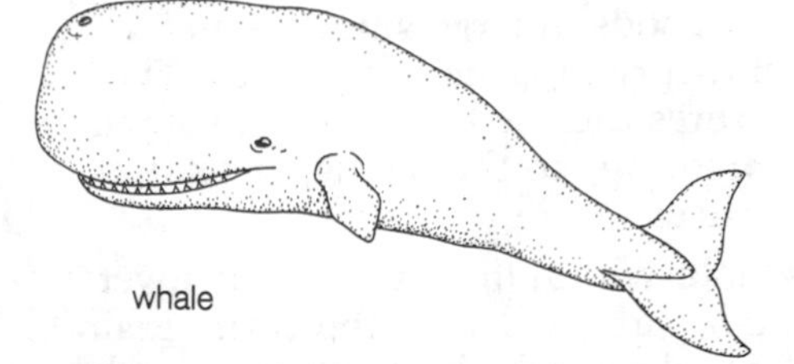
whale

whale (wāl, hwāl) *n.* a very large ocean animal that has a body like a fish but is really a mammal.

wharf (wȯrf, hwȯrf) *n.* a landing place for ships, where they can load and unload. *pl.* **wharves.**

what (wut, wot, hwot) *adj.* which: *What time is it?* *pron.* that which: *He doesn't know what is in the jar.*

whatever (wut ev′ ər, wot ev′ ər, hwot ev′ ər) *pron.* anything at all: *I will do whatever I can to help you.*

what's (wuts, wots, hwots) short for **what is** or **what has.**

wheat (wēt, hwēt) *n.* **1.** a plant that looks like tall grass; its grains are ground to make flour. **2.** the grains of this plant.

wheel (wēl, hwēl) *n.* a circular object of wood, plastic, or metal that can keep turning on an axle: *Trains and cars move on wheels.* *v.* to push on wheels: *They wheeled the baby carriage through the park.*

wheelbarrow (wēl′ bar′ ō, hwēl′ bar′ ō) *n.* a small cart with two handles and one wheel, used to move small loads.

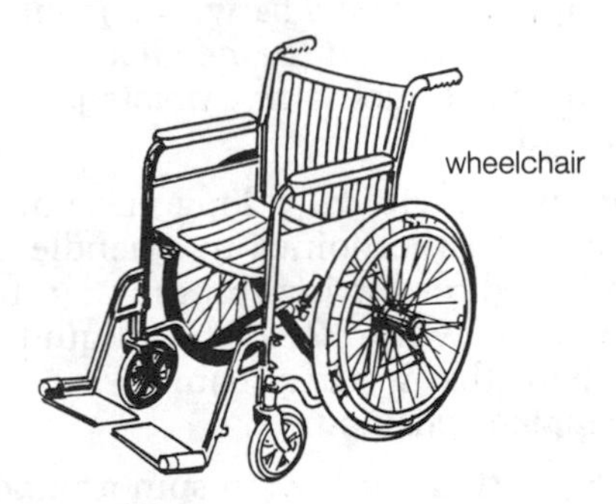
wheelchair

wheelchair (wēl′ cher′, hwēl′ cher′) *n.* a chair on wheels for the use of people who can't walk.

when (wen, hwen) *adv.* at what time: *When did the game begin?* *conj.* at the time: *We arrived when everything was over.*

whenever (wen ev′ ər, hwen ev′ ər) *conj.* at any time: *We will go whenever you are ready.*

where (wer, hwer) *adv.* **1.** at what place: *Where are my keys?* **2.** in the place that: *We will stop where we can rest.*

wherever (wer ev′ ər, hwer ev′ ər) *adv.* in any place: *I will go wherever you want to go.*

whether (we<u>th</u>′ ər, hwe<u>th</u>′ ər) *conj.* if: *Carole did not know whether she could go.* *Note:* Do not confuse **whether** with **weather**; **weather** means 'what it is like outside'.

which (wich, hwich) *adj.* what person or thing: *Which coat is yours? pron.* a word showing the one being talked about: *His coat, which is brown, is in the closet.*

while (wīl, hwīl) *n.* a space of time: *Mark slept for a short while. conj.* during the time that: *I watched television while dinner was cooking.*

whimper (wim′ pər, hwim′ pər) *n.* a soft, sad cry. *v.* to make such a cry.

whine (wīn, hwīn) *n.* a long, complaining cry: *The whine from our dog bothered the neighbours. v.* to make such a cry. **whining. whined.**

whip (wip, hwip) *n.* a long piece of rope or leather joined to a handle and used for hitting things. *v.* **1.** to hit with a whip. **2.** to stir a liquid so hard that it has a foam. **whipping. whipped.**

whirl (wûrl, hwûrl) *v.* to spin around quickly.

whiskers (wis′ kərz, hwis′ kərz) *n.pl.* **1.** the stiff hair at each side of the mouth of cats and some other animals. **2.** the hair that grows on the sides of a man's face.

whisky, whiskey (wis′ kē, hwis′ kē) *n.* an alcoholic drink made from grains such as rye, corn, and barley. *pl.* **whiskies**, or **whiskeys.**

whisper (wis′ pər, hwis′ pər) *n.* a sound made softly. *v.* to speak very softly: *Nadia whispered because the baby was sleeping.*

whistle (wisl, hwisl) *n.* **1.** a high, sharp sound made by pushing air through the lips or teeth. **2.** a small pipe that makes such a sound. *v.* to make a high, sharp sound by pushing air through the lips or teeth or by using a whistle. **whistling. whistled.**

white (wīt, hwīt) *n.* **1.** the colour of fresh snow. **2.** the substance of an egg around the yolk. *adj.* having the colour of fresh snow: *white linen; whiter linen; the whitest linen of all.*

white-out (wīt′ aůt′, hwīt′ aůt′) *n.* a period of sudden snow and wind that makes it very difficult or impossible to see what is ahead: *The car hit the truck in front during the white-out.*

whittle (witl, hwitl) *v.* **1.** to cut chips from wood with a knife. **2.** to carve wood with a knife. **whittling. whittled.**

who (hū) *pron.* **1.** which person or persons: *Who left the message?* **2.** the person or persons that: *The boy who is talking is my brother.*

whoever (hū ev′ ər) *pron.* anyone who: *Whoever has a watch, please tell me the time.*

whole (hōl) *adj.* complete, entire: *I spent the whole day shopping. Jacques read the whole book.*

wholesale (hōl′ sāl′) *n.* the selling of goods in large amounts and at low prices, usually to stores. The stores then sell the goods in smaller amounts, to the public, at retail prices.

whole-wheat (hōl′ wēt′, hōl′ hwēt′) *adj.* prepared with the entire grain of wheat, which has been ground: *whole-wheat flour; whole-wheat bread.*

whom (hūm) *pron.* which person or persons; used after 'to', 'for', 'from', 'with', or 'by': *To whom did you tell the secret?*

who's (hūz) short for **who is** or **who has.**

whose (hūz) *pron.* belonging to what person: *I know whose hat this is.*

why (wī, hwī) *adv.* for what reason: *Why did you telephone me?*

wick (wik) *n.* the string that burns in a candle or oil lamp.

wicked (wik′ əd) *adj.* very bad; evil: *a wicked person; a wicked deed.*

wide (wīd) *adj.* **1.** measuring a long way from one side to the other; broad: *a wide street.* **2.** having a certain width: *The table is a metre long. How wide is it? a wide road; a wider one; the widest road of all.* *adv.* completely: *The window was wide open.*

widen (wīd′ ən) *v.* to make or become wider: *Workers widened the tunnel. The road widens here.*

widow (wid′ ō) *n.* a woman whose husband has died and who has not married again.

widower (wid′ ō ər) *n.* a man whose wife has died and who has not married again.

width (width) *n.* how wide something is; the distance of something from side to side.

wiener (wē′ nər) *n.* a reddish sausage, usually made of beef and pork.

wife (wīf) *n.* a woman to whom a man is married. *pl.* **wives** (wīvz).

wig (wig) *n.* false hair worn on the head, often over someone's own hair.

wiggle (wigl) *v.* to move with short, quick movements from side to side. **wiggling. wiggled.**

wild (wīld) *adj.* **1.** not controlled by people; not tame: *A lion is a wild animal.* **2.** growing naturally, without the care of people: *wild strawberries.*

wildcat (wīld′ kat′) *n.* a cougar, lynx, ocelot, or other medium-sized wild animal related to the common cat.

wilderness (wil′ dər nəs) *n.* an open place where no people live.

wildlife (wīld′ līf′) *n.* a group of wild animals and birds that live in an area.

will (wil) *n.* **1.** the power of the mind to choose to do something: *The sick man has a strong will to live.* **2.** a legal statement saying who is to have a person's money and things when he or she is dead. *v.* a verb used with another verb to say what is going to happen in the future: *I will go. She will play. They will work. I would help you if I could. Do you think she would let us use the car if we asked politely?* **would** (wůd).

willing (wil′ ing) *adj.* glad and ready to do what is wanted: *I am willing to help you finish your work.*

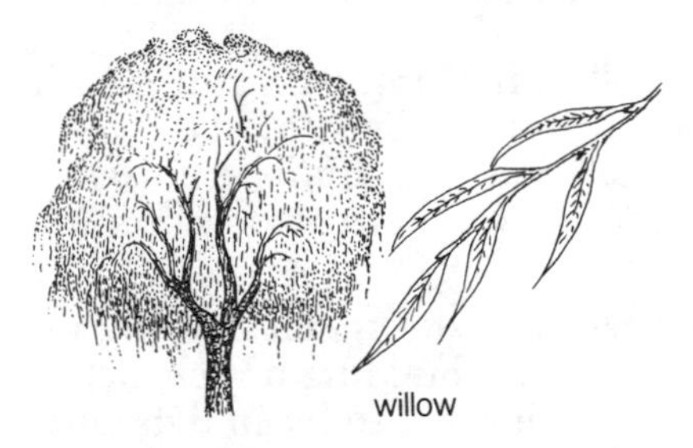
willow

willow (wil′ ō) *n.* a tree that has long, narrow leaves and thin branches that bend easily.

wilt (wilt) *v.* to droop, to wither: *The plant is wilting because nobody watered it.*

win (win) *n.* a victory over someone else in a game, fight, argument, etc. *v.* **1.** to be first in a game, fight, argument, etc.: *We won two games and lost three.* **2.** to gain something by luck: *I have never won a lottery.* **3.** to gain something by effort: *Helen won an award at school.* **winning. won** (wun).

wind (wind) *n.* air moving past quickly.

wind (wīnd) *v.* **1.** to twist around or wrap around: *The river winds through the town. Richard wound the string around a stick.* **2.** to tighten the spring of a watch. **winding. wound** (wau̇nd).

windbreak (wind′ brāk′) *n.* a row of trees or hedges, or a fence or other structure, which serves as a shelter from the force of the wind.

windbreaker (wind′ brāk′ ər) *n.* a short sports jacket worn outdoors that helps protect a person from the wind.

windmill (wind′ mil′) *n.* a mill with sails or vanes turned by the force of the wind: *Windmills are used to pump water and to grind grain into flour.*

window (win′ dō) *n.* an opening in the side of a building or vehicle, filled with glass, to let in light and air.

windshield (wind′ shēld) *n.* the glass or plastic screen of an automobile, motorcycle, etc., that protects a driver from wind and rain.

wine (wīn) *n.* an alcoholic drink made from the juice of grapes or other fruit.

wing (wing) *n.* **1.** one of the parts of a bird, bat, or insect used for flying. **2.** a flat stretch of metal on either side of an airplane that helps to keep it in the air. **3.** a building attached to a larger main building.

wink (wingk) *n.* a quick closing and opening of an eyelid. *v.* to close and open an eyelid quickly: *He winked at the child to show that he was not really angry.*

winner (win′ ər) *n.* a team or person who wins something.

Winnipeg (win′ i peg′) *n.* the capital city of Manitoba.

winter (win′ tər) *n.* the season after autumn.

wipe (wīp) *v.* to rub something with a cloth to make it clean or dry. **wiping. wiped.**

wire (wīr) *n.* a metal thread. *v.* to put in wires for electricity: *The electrician wired the new house.* **wiring. wired.**

wisdom (wiz′ dəm) *n.* knowledge of what is right and good: *He did not finish school, but he has great wisdom.*

wise (wīz) *adj.* showing or having good judgment: *It is wise to stay in bed if you are not well. I learned many things from my wise aunt. I am not very wise; my mother is wiser; my uncle is the wisest in the family.*

wish (wish) *n.* a want or desire; a hope that something will happen: *My wish has come true—I have finally graduated.* *pl.* **wishes.** *v.* to have such a feeling: *I wish it would stop raining!* **wishing. wished.** he **wishes.**

witch (wich) *n.* a woman in children's stories who is thought to have magic powers, usually evil ones. *pl.* **witches.**

with (with) *prep.* **1.** in the company of: *He lives with his brother.* **2.** having: *My cousin is the man with the umbrella.* **3.** because of: *Neil shouted with happiness.* **4.** using: *Sam kicked the ball with his foot.* **5.** employed by: *Guido has been with the company for two years.* **6.** against: *She had an argument with her sister.*

withdraw (with drȯ′) *v.* to take back; to remove: *He said he would help, but then he withdrew his offer. I withdrew money from the bank.* **withdrawing. withdrew** (with drü′). I have **withdrawn.**

wither (wiṯẖ′ ər) *v.* to become dry and smaller. *The plant withered in the hot sun.*

within (with in′) *prep.* inside; not beyond: *Is the high shelf within your reach, or do you need a ladder?*

without (with aůt′, wiṯẖ aůt′) *prep.* not having: *Plants cannot live without water.*

witness (wit′ nəs) *n.* someone who saw something happen: *The lawyer asked the witness to tell about the car accident that she saw.* *pl.* **witnesses.** *v.* to see something happen. **witnessing. witnessed.** he **witnesses.**

wives plural of **wife.**

wizard (wiz′ ərd) *n.* a man in children's stories who is thought to have magic powers.

woke, woken see **wake.**

wolf

wolf (wůlf) *n.* a wild animal of the dog family, usually grey, that often hunts in packs. *pl.* **wolves** (wůlvz).

wolverine (wůl′ və rēn′) *n.* a dark brown North American mammal that looks like a large weasel.

woman (wům′ ən) *n.* a mature female human being. *pl.* **women** (wim′ in).

womb (wüm) *n.* the uterus; the organ of a woman or other female mammal, inside which the young develop.

women plural of **woman.**

won see **win.**

wonder (wun′ dər) *n.* **1.** a surprising or unusual thing: *Niagara Falls is one of the world's great wonders.* **2.** a feeling of amazement: *We watched in wonder as the magician did his tricks.* *v.* to want to know: *I wonder where Michel is.*

wonderful (wun′ dər fəl) *adj.* amazing; excellent: *The waterfall is a wonderful sight. You look wonderful today. I feel wonderful, too.*

won't (wōnt) short for **will not.**

wood (wůd) *n.* the hard part of a tree, under the bark: *The table is made of wood.*

woodchuck (wůd′ chuk′) *n.* another name for a groundhog.

wooden (wůd′ ən) *adj.* made of wood: *a wooden chair.*

woodpecker (wůd′ pek′ ər) *n.* a bird that has a long, pointed bill used for tapping on trees to get at the insects under the bark.

woods (wůdz) *n.pl.* a forest; a large number of trees growing together.

wool (wůl) *n.* **1.** the thick hair of sheep and some other animals. **2.** the thread made from this hair.

woollen, woolen (wůl′ ən) *adj.* made of wool.

word (wûrd) *n.* **1.** letters in a group that mean something when spoken, written, or read. **2.** a promise: *I give you my word that I will finish the job.* **3.** news or information: *Have you had any word from your friend since he moved?*

wore see **wear.**

work (wûrk) *n.* **1.** a person's job: *Betty leaves for work at seven in* *the morning.* **2.** an activity of the body or the mind: *Writing the report is hard work. Chopping down the trees is hard work, too.* **3.** something that has been done or made by someone: *Mike's picture is a beautiful work of art.* *v.* **1.** to do something for pay: *I work in a restaurant.* **2.** to do or make something through an effort of the body or the mind: *He worked for an hour trying to fix the sink.* **3.** to run or operate properly: *The television is not working. This radio does't work.*

worker (wûrk′ ər) *n.* someone who works.

working order (wûrk′ ing or′ dər) able to be used; functioning properly.

workshop (wûrk′ shop′) *n.* a place where things are made or repaired by hand or by machine.

world (wûrld) *n.* **1.** the earth and all the people, animals, and plants that live on it: *My aunt has travelled all over the world.* **2.** the people on the earth: *The new medicine will help the world.* **3.** another planet in space: *I think there is life on other worlds.*

worm (wûrm) *n.* a crawling animal that has a soft body, no legs, and looks like a very small snake.

worn see **wear.**

worry (wû′ rē) *n.* a troubled feeling: *His greatest worry is about his parents' health.* *pl.* **worries.** *v.* to feel upset or troubled; to be anxious: *The child's parents were worried when he did not come home for dinner.* **worrying. worried.** he **worries.**

worse (wûrs) *adj.* more than bad: *Tom's cold is bad. Rob's is worse.*

worship (wûr′ ship) *n.* prayers and respect given to God or a god. *v.* to show love for God or a god. **worshipping. worshipped.**

worst (wûrst) *adj.* the most bad: *I am a bad soccer player; he is worse; my cousin is worst of all.*

worth (wûrth) *adj.* **1.** having a value of: *The ring is worth one hundred dollars.* **2.** good or important enough for: *The book is worth reading.*

worthwhile (wûrth′ wīl′) *adj.* worth doing; good enough to spend time or money on: *Swimming is a worthwhile exercise.*

would see **will.**

wouldn't (wůd′ ənt) short for **would not.**

wound (wūnd) *n.* an injury such as a cut. *v.* to hurt or injure: *Two soldiers were wounded in the battle.*

wound see **wind.**

wove, woven see **weave.**

wrap (rap) *v.* to put paper or cloth all around something: *Victor wrapped his friend's birthday present.* **wrapping. wrapped.**

wrapping (rap′ ing) *n.* a piece of paper or some other material placed around something: *The wrapping on the gift is too pretty to remove!*

wreath (rēth) *n.* a large ring of flowers, branches, etc., twisted together.

wreck (rek) *n.* anything destroyed, such as a ship on rocks or a crashed airplane. *v.* to destroy or badly damage: *He wrecked the car, but nobody was hurt.*

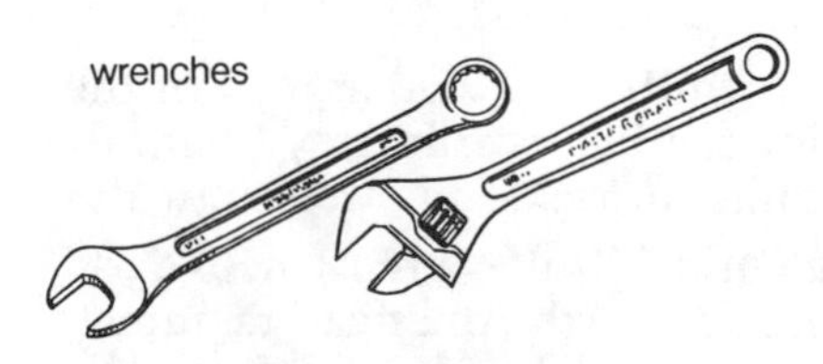
wrenches

wrench (rench) *n.* a tool that is used to twist nuts on and off bolts. *pl.* **wrenches.** *v.* to twist or pull: *I* *wrenched a muscle in my arm.* **wrenching. wrenched.** it **wrenches.**

wrestle (resl) *v.* to struggle with someone and try to force him or her to the ground. **wrestling. wrestled.**

wrestling (res′ ling) *n.* a sport in which two people struggle hand to hand.

wriggle (rigl) *v.* to twist and turn: *The child tried to wriggle through the hole in the fence.* **wriggling. wriggled.**

wring (ring) *v.* to twist and squeeze: *After Dave washed the table, he wrung out the wet cloth.* **wringing. wrung** (rung).

wrinkle (ringkl) *n.* a crease or fold on the surface of something such as cloth or the skin. *v.* to make creased: *The new shirt became wrinkled in the bag.* **wrinkling. wrinkled.**

wrist (rist) *n.* the joint between the hand and arm.

write (rīt) *n.* **1.** to put words or signs on something such as paper so that people can read them. **2.** to be an author; to write a story or poem, or an article for a magazine or newspaper: *My sister earns her living by writing.* **writing. wrote** (rōt). I have **written** (rit′ ən).

writer (rīt′ ər) *n.* a person who writes, usually as a job.

writing (rīt′ ing) *n.* the act of making letters and words with pen, pencil, chalk, etc.

written see **write.**

wrong (rong) *adj.* **1.** bad; not good: *It is wrong to lie.* **2.** incorrect; not true: *Two answers are right and two are wrong.* **3.** not operating or working correctly: *What is wrong with your car?*

wrote see **write.**

Xmas short for **Christmas.**

X-rays (eks′ rāz′) *n.pl.* special rays that are used to see or photograph what is inside the body or other solids.

xylophone (zī′ lə fōn′) *n.* a musical instrument made of wooden or metal bars that are hit with a small hammer.

Y

yacht (yot) *n.* a sailing ship used for pleasure trips or racing.

yak (yak) *n.* a long-haired animal, related to buffalo, that lives in Asia.

yam (yam) *n.* a kind of sweet potato.

yard (yȧrd) *n.* **1.** an area of ground next to or around a home or other building, often planted with grass. **2.** a unit of length, equal to a little less than one metre.

yarn (yȧrn) *n.* thick thread used in sewing, weaving, or knitting.

yawn (yȯn) *v.* to take a deep breath with the mouth wide open, because of being tired or bored.

year (yēr) *n.* a measure of time lasting 365 days (366 days in a leap year), 52 weeks, or 12 months.

yearly (yēr′ lē) *adv.* once a year: *He sees the dentist yearly.* *adj.* coming out or happening every year: *We take our yearly holiday each July.*

yeast (yēst) *n.* a living substance used in making bread rise, and in making beer and other alcoholic beverages.

yell (yel) *n.* a loud shout. *v.* to shout very loudly.

yellow (yel′ ō) *n.* the colour of a lemon, grapefruit, or dandelion. *adj.* having such a colour.

yes (yes) *adv.* the opposite of no.

yesterday (yes′ tər dā′) *n.* the day just past; the day before today: *Yesterday was Sunday.* *pl.* **yesterdays.** *adv.* on the day before today: *My cousin telephoned me yesterday.*

yet (yet) *adv.* **1.** up to now: *I have not read the book yet.* **2.** at some time that is coming: *He may arrive yet.* *conj.* but: *Helen ran for the train, yet she missed it.*

yield (yēld) *v.* **1.** to give way to someone or something; to surrender: *The car yielded, allowing the truck to pass first.* **2.** to produce: *The orchard yields much fruit.*

yogurt, yoghurt (yō′ gərt) *n.* a thick, creamy food made from milk.

yoke (yōk) *n.* a wooden frame placed over the necks of two work animals, joining them together.

yolk (yōk) *n.* the yellow substance of an egg.

Yom Kippur (yom kip′ ər) a Jewish holy day, observed in September or October.

you (yü) *pron.* the person or people being spoken to or written to.

you'd (yüd) short for **you had** or **you would.**

you'll (yül) short for **you will.**

young (yung) *n.* the baby or babies of a person or animal: *The bird looked for worms for her young.* *adj.* being in the early part of life; not middle-aged or old.

youngster (yung′ stər) *n.* a young boy or girl.

your (yür) *adj.* belonging to you: *Is this your hat?*

you're (yür) short for **you are.**

yours (yürz) *pron.* the one belonging to you: *Is this hat yours?*

yourself (yür self′) *pron.* you alone: *Can you see yourself in the mirror? Can you do all the work by yourself?* *pl.* **yourselves.**

youth (yüth) *n.* **1.** the time between being a child and being an adult: *In his youth, my father played soccer.* **2.** a young person. *pl.* **youths** (yü<u>th</u>z).

you've (yüv) short for **you have.**

Yukon (yü′ kon) *n.* a territory in northwestern Canada; its capital is Whitehorse. Short form: **Y.T.**

yule (yül) *n.* Christmas, or the Christmas season.

Z

zebra (zē′ brə) *n.* a wild horse-like animal that lives in parts of Africa and has black stripes on a white body. *pl.* **zebras.**

zero (zēr′ ō) *n.* nothing; the figure 0. *pl.* **zeros.**

zigzag (zig′ zag′) *adj.* formed of short, sharp turns from one side to the other. A zigzag looks like /\/\/\/\/\/\/\/\/\/\/\/\/\/\

⊖**zinc** (zingk) *n.* a grey-white metal that is used in making medicines, paints, and other things.

zip (zip) *v.* to close with a zipper. **zipping. zipped.**

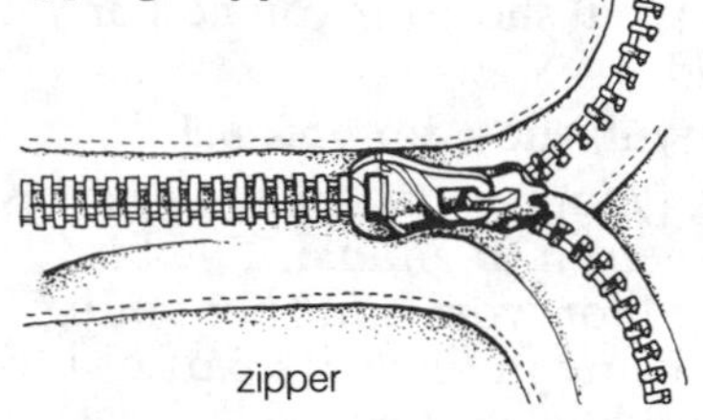
zipper

zipper (zip′ ər) *n.* a device with a sliding tab, for joining together two edges of material.

zone (zōn) *n.* a special area: *a no-parking zone; a school zone.*

zoo (zū) *n.* a place where wild animals are kept in special areas and cages so that people may look at them. *pl.* **zoos.**

zoom (zūm) *v.* to move or climb suddenly: *The airplane zoomed into the sky, and was gone.*

zucchini (zū kē′ nē) *n.* a type of summer squash that looks like a cucumber and has dark green skin. *pl.* **zucchini** or **zucchinis.**

Planets of the Solar System

Planet	*Distance from the Sun (millions of kilometres)* *minimum*	*maximum*
Mercury	46 021	69 848
Venus	107 522	108 991
Earth	147 162	152 167
Mars	206 748	249 339
Jupiter	741 235	815 989
Saturn	142 302	1 508 785
Uranus	2 734 733	2 992 892
Neptune	4 442 289	4 540 939
Pluto	4 435 918	7 324 545

Continents of the Earth

	Area (millions of km²)	*Percentage of Earth's population*
Asia	44 045	59.7
Africa	30 284	10.9
North America	24 267	8.3
South America	17 829	5.5
Europe	10 408	15.1
Australia	7 685	0.3
Antarctica	13 214	—

Provinces and Territories of Canada

Provinces (West to East)	*Capital*	*Date of Joining Confederation*
British Columbia (B.C.)	Victoria	1871
Alberta (Alta.)	Edmonton	1905
Saskatchewan (Sask.)	Regina	1905
Manitoba (Man.)	Winnipeg	1870
Ontario (Ont.)	Toronto	1867
Quebec (Que., P.Q.)	Quebec	1867
New Brunswick (N.B.)	Fredericton	1867
Nova Scotia (N.S.)	Halifax	1867
Prince Edward Island (P.E.I.)	Charlottetown	1867
Newfoundland (Nfld.)	Saint John's	1949
Territories		
Northwest Territories (N.W.T.)	Yellowknife	
Yukon (Y.T.)	Whitehorse	

Prime Ministers of Canada

	Time in Office
Sir John Alexander Macdonald	1867–1873
	1878–1891
Alexander Mackenzie	1873–1878
Sir John Joseph Caldwell Abbott	1891–1892
Sir John Sparrow	1892–1894
David Thompson	1894
Sir Mackenzie Bowell	1894–1896
Sir Charles Tupper	1896
Sir Wilfrid Laurier	1896–1911
Sir Robert Laird Borden	1911–1920
Arthur Meighen	1920–1921
	1926
William Lyon Mackenzie King	1921–1926
	1926–1930
	1935–1948
Richard Bedford Bennett	1930–1935
Louis Saint-Laurent	1948–1957
John George Diefenbaker	1957–1963
Lester Bowles Pearson	1963–1968
Pierre Elliott Trudeau	1968–1979
	1980–1984
Charles Joseph Clark	1979–1980
John Napier Turner	1984
Martin Brian Mulroney	1984–

Government of Canada

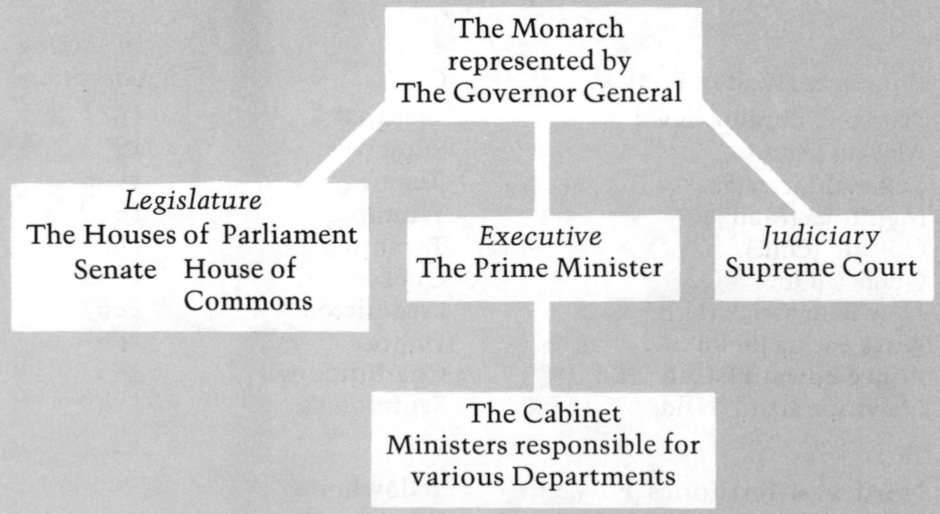

The Monarch
represented by
The Governor General

Legislature
The Houses of Parliament
Senate House of Commons

Executive
The Prime Minister

Judiciary
Supreme Court

The Cabinet
Ministers responsible for
various Departments

Major Canadian Cities

City	*Population (1985)*
Toronto (Ont.)	3 202 400
Montreal (Que.)	2 878 200
Vancouver (B.C.)	1 348 600
Ottawa/Hull (Ont./Que.)	769 900
Edmonton (Alta.)	683 600
Calgary (Alta.)	625 600
Winnipeg (Man.)	612 100
Quebec (Que.)	593 500
Hamilton (Ont.)	559 700
St. Catharines (Ont.)	309 400
Kitchener (Ont.)	303 400
London (Ont.)	292 700
Halifax (N.S.)	290 600
Windsor (Ont.)	249 800
Victoria (B.C.)	245 100
Regina (Sask.)	174 800
Oshawa (Ont.)	172 800
Saskatoon (Sask.)	170 100
St. John's (Nfld.)	160 700
Sudbury (Ont.)	147 600
Chicoutimi/Jonquière (Que.)	139 400
Thunder Bay (Ont.)	123 500
Saint John (N.B.)	116 800
Trois-Rivières (Que.)	114 300

Metric Symbols

Symbol	*Meaning*	*Symbol*	*Meaning*
a	year	L	litre
cm	centimetre	m	metre
cm^2	square centimetre	m^2	square metre
cm^3	cubic centimetre	m^3	cubic metre
d	day	mg	milligram
g	gram	min	minute
h	hour	mL	millilitre
ha	hectare	s	second
kg	kilogram	t	tonne
km	kilometre	°C	degree(s) Celsius
km^2	square kilometre		

Days and Months

Days of the Week	*Months of the Year*	
Sunday (Sun.)	January (Jan.)	31 days
Monday (Mon.)	February (Feb.)	28 (29 in a leap year)
Tuesday (Tues.)	March (Mar.)	31
Wednesday (Wed.)	April (Apr.)	30
Thursday (Thurs.)	May	31
Friday (Fri.)	June (Jun.)	30
Saturday (Sat.)	July (Jul.)	31
	August (Aug.)	31
	September (Sept.)	30
	October (Oct.)	31
	November (Nov.)	30
	December (Dec.)	31

Punctuation Marks

Name	*Mark*	*Example*
apostrophe	'	I'm going to buy my friend's bicycle.
comma	,	Red, blue, green, and yellow are my favourite colours.
colon	:	The letter began like this: "Dear Sir:".
dash	—	I like only one kind of cake—chocolate.
exclamation mark	!	Stop! You are in danger!
hyphen	-	The one-room school had thirty-five students.
period	.	Mr. Gendron is 1.8 m tall.
question mark	?	What did you say?
quotation marks (quotes)	" "	When Alexander Graham Bell spoke on the first telephone, he did not say "hello"; he said: "Mr. Watson, come here. I want you."
semicolon	;	We would like to stay; however, we must go.

Numbers

Numeral	*Cardinal*	*Ordinal*
1	one	first
2	two	second
3	three	third
4	four	fourth
5	five	fifth
6	six	sixth
7	seven	seventh
8	eight	eighth
9	nine	ninth
10	ten	tenth
11	eleven	eleventh
12	twelve	twelfth
13	thirteen	thirteenth
14	fourteen	fourteenth
15	fifteen	fifteenth
16	sixteen	sixteenth
17	seventeen	seventeenth
18	eighteen	eighteenth
19	nineteen	nineteenth
20	twenty	twentieth
21	twenty-one	twenty-first
30	thirty	thirtieth
40	forty	fortieth
50	fifty	fiftieth
60	sixty	sixtieth
70	seventy	seventieth
80	eighty	eightieth
90	ninety	ninetieth
100	one hundred	hundredth
200	two hundred	two hundredth
1000	one thousand	thousandth
1 000 000	million	millionth
1 000 000 000	billion	billionth
1 000 000 000 000	trillion	trillionth

Irregular Verbs

		have, has	
arise	arose		arisen
awake	awoke, awaked		awaked, awoken
be	was		been
bear	bore		borne
beat	beat		beaten
become	became		become
begin	began		begun
bend	bent		bent
bind	bound		bound
bite	bit		bitten
bleed	bled		bled
blow	blew		blown
break	broke		broken
bring	brought		brought
build	built		built
burn	burned, burnt		burned, burnt
burst	burst		burst
buy	bought		bought
catch	caught		caught
choose	chose		chosen
cling	clung		clung
come	came		come
cost	cost		cost
creep	crept		crept
cut	cut		cut
deal	dealt		dealt
dig	dug		dug
dive	dived, dove		dived
do	did		done
draw	drew		drawn
drink	drank		drunk
drive	drove		driven
eat	ate		eaten
fall	fell		fallen
feed	fed		fed
feel	felt		felt
fight	fought		fought
find	found		found
fling	flung		flung
fly	flew		flown
forget	forgot		forgotten
forgive	forgave		forgiven
freeze	froze		frozen
get	got		got, gotten
give	gave		given

go	went	*have, has* gone
grind	ground	ground
grow	grew	grown
hang	hung (hanged)	hung (hanged)
have	had	had
hear	heard	heard
hide	hid	hidden, hid
hit	hit	hit
hold	held	held
hurt	hurt	hurt
keep	kept	kept
kneel	knelt	knelt
knit	knit	knit
know	knew	known
lay	laid	laid
lead	led	led
lean	leaned, leant	leaned, leant
leap	leapt	leapt
learn	learned, learnt	learned, learnt
leave	left	left
lend	lent	lent
let	let	let
lie	lay	lain
light	lit, lighted	lit, lighted
lose	lost	lost
make	made	made
mean	meant	meant
meet	met	met
mistake	mistook	mistaken
mow	mowed	mown, mowed
pay	paid	paid
put	put	put
read	read	read
ride	rode	ridden
ring	rang	rung
rise	rose	risen
run	ran	run
saw	sawed	sawn, sawed
say	said	said
see	saw	seen
sell	sold	sold
send	sent	sent
shake	shook	shaken
shoot	shot	shot
show	showed	shown
shred	shredded	shredded
shrink	shrank	shrunk

shut	shut	*have, has* shut
sing	sang	sung
sink	sank	sunk
sit	sat	sat
sleep	slept	slept
slide	slid	slid, slidden
sling	slung	slung
slink	slunk	slunk
smell	smelled, smelt	smelled, smelt
speak	spoke	spoken
spell	spelled, spelt	spelled, spelt
spend	spent	spent
spill	spilled, spilt	spilled, spilt
spin	spun, span	spun
spit	spat	spat
split	split	split
spoil	spoiled, spoilt	spoiled, spoilt
spread	spread	spread
spring	sprang	sprung
stand	stood	stood
steal	stole	stolen
stick	stuck	stuck
sting	stung	stung
stink	stank	stunk
strike	struck	struck, stricken
swear	swore	sworn
sweat	sweated, sweat	sweated, sweat
sweep	swept	swept
swell	swelled	swollen
swim	swam	swum
swing	swung	swung
take	took	taken
teach	taught	taught
tear	tore	torn
tell	told	told
think	thought	thought
throw	threw	thrown
understand	understood	understood
undo	undid	undone
upset	upset	upset
wear	wore	worn
weave	wove	woven
weep	wept	wept
win	won	won
wind	wound	wound
wring	wrung	wrung
write	wrote	written

Common Abbreviations

A	ampere
A.C.	alternating current
adj.	adjective
adv.	adverb
a.m.	*ante meridiem* (before noon)
anon.	anonymous
approx.	approximately
apt.	apartment
av., ave.	avenue
B.A.	Bachelor of Arts
blvd., boul.	boulevard
B.Sc.	Bachelor of Science
C	Celsius, centigrade
C.A.	chartered accountant
cal.	calorie
Cdn.	Canadian
cert.	certificate
cf	compare
chap.	chapter
c/o	care of
C.O.D.	cash on delivery
conj.	conjunction
cont.	continued
co-op	co-operative
CPP	Canada Pension Plan
cres.	crescent
C.V.	curriculum vitae (résumé)
3-D	three-dimensional
D.C.	direct current
Dept.	department
Dip.	diploma
DJ	disk jockey
Dr.	Doctor
e.g.	*exempli gratia* (for example)
esp.	especially
est.	established, estimated
et al.	and (the) others
etc.	et cetera (and so on)
fig.	figure
G.P.	general practitioner
H.P.	horsepower
H.Q.	headquarters
H.R.H.	Her/His Royal Highness
i.e.	*id est* (that is)

incl.	including
Inst.	Institute
interj.	interjection
I.O.U.	I owe you
I.Q.	intelligence quotient
J.P.	Justice of the Peace
Jr.	junior
kilo	kilogram
K.O.	knockout
Lib.	Liberal, liberation
log	logarithm
M.	Monsieur
M.A.	Master of Arts
max.	maximum
M.C.	Master of Ceremonies
M.D.	Doctor of Medicine
min.	minimum
misc.	miscellaneous
Mlle	Mademoiselle
Mme	Madame
Mt.	Mount, mountain
n.	noun
N.B.	*nota bene* (note well)
NDP	New Democratic Party
No	number
O.A.P.	old age pensioner
p.	page
PC	Progressive Conservative, police constable
Ph.D.	Doctor of Philosophy
pl.	plural
p.m.	*post meridiem* (after noon)
P.M.	Prime Minister
P.O.	Post Office
pop.	population
poss.	possessive, possible
pp.	past participle, pages
P.R.	public relations
prep.	preposition
pres.	present, president
prof.	professor
pron.	pronoun
P.S.	postscript
P.T.O.	please turn over
Q.C.	Queen's Counsel
Q.P.P.	Quebec Pension Plan
R.S.V.P.	*répondez s'il vous plaît* (please reply)

sec.	second
sing.	singular
Sr.	senior
St.	Saint, street
tel.	telephone
temp.	temperature, temporary
T.V.	television
UFO	unidentified flying object
U.N.	United Nations
v.	verb
VIP	very important person
vs.	versus
Xmas	Christmas

Pronunciation Key

a	apple, cat
ā	ape, cake
ȧ	arm, car
aủ	owl, brow
b	bat, cab
ch	chocolate, watch
d	dog, head
e	elbow, head
ē	eagle, feet
f	foot, photograph
g	goat, log
h	hat, behind, who
i	bit, tip
ī	tie, try, buy, eye
j	jaw, gem
k	cat, seek, tuque
l	lip, ball
m	man, dome
n	nose, pan
ng	ring, singer
o	off, top
ō	oats, toe, blow, go
ȯ	door, corn
ȯi	oil, boy
p	pan, cap
r	ring, car
s	sun, chess, cent
sh	shoe, dish, nation
t	toe, mat
th	birthday, earth
t͟h	that, mother
u	umbrella, judge
ủ	cookie, bull
ū	boot, two, true
ûr	earth, fur
v	van, oven
w	wind, woman
y	year, young
yū	you, view
z	zoo, rose
zh	treasure, rouge
ə	father, above, upon
ks	extra, box
gz	exam
hw	whisker
kw	quick

PRIMARY (HEAVY) STRESS: **′**

SECONDARY (LIGHT) STRESS: ′